# The Uttaratantra of Maitreya

Containing
Introduction, E. H. Johnson's Sanskrit Text and
E. Obermiller's English Translation

## By the Same Author

(1) ***Amalā Prajñā : Aspects of Buddhist Studies***
(Co-edited with N. H. Samtani, 1989)

(2) ***Essays on Time in Buddhism*** (Edited)

(3) ***Time in Indian Philosophy*** (Edited)

(4) ***The Buddhist Philosophy of Time***

Bibliotheca Indo-Buddhica Series No. - 79

# *The*
# *Uttaratantra of Maitreya*

**Containing**
**Introduction, E. H. Johnson's Sanskrit Text and**
**E. Obermiller's English Translation**

*Introduction & Edited by*

**H.S. PRASAD**
MA (BHU), PhD (ANU)
*Department of Philosophy*
*University of Delhi*

**Sri Satguru Publications**
A Division of
**Indian Books Centre**
Delhi

*Published by*
**© Sri Satguru Publications**
Indological and Oriental Publishers
A Division of
**Indian Books Centre**
40/5, Shakti Nagar,
Delhi - 110007
India

First Edition, Delhi, 1991
Reprinted, Delhi, 1997

ISBN—81-7030-263-3

Published by Sunil Gupta for Sri Satguru Publications a division of Indian Books Centre, 40/5, Shakti Nagar, Delhi - 110 007, India and printed at Mudran Bharti, Delhi - 110 009

**To My Revered Teacher**

**Shri Gorakh Rao**

*Lecturer*

Janta Inter College

Ramkola, Deoria, U.P. (India)

# CONTENTS


Acknowledgements ... ... ... ... xiii

## Part - I

**Introduction**
(by H.S. Prasad) ... ... 1

1. The Development of the Gotra Theory ... ... 2
2. The Mahāyāna Spiritual Discipline ... ... ... 5
3. Gotra : The Foundation of Mahāyāna, and its Types ... ... ... 9
4. The Characteristics of the Gotra ... ... ... 12
5. The Gotra-based Classification of the Sentient Beings ... ... ... ... 16
6. Notes ... ... ... 19
7. Bibliography ... ... ... ... 46

## Part - II

**Sanskrit Text**
The Ratnagotravibhāga Mahāyānottaratantraśāstra
(edited by E.H. Johnson)

1. Introductory Note (by T. Chowdhury) ... ... 53
2. Foreword (by E.H. Johnson) ... ... ... 57
3. Abbreviations ... ... ... ... ... 67
4. Corrections ... ... ... ... ... 68
5. Chapter I : Tathāgatagarbhādhikāra ... ... 69
6. Chapter II : Bodhyādhikāra ... 147
7. Chapter III : Guṇādhikāra ... ... ... ... 159

8. Chapter IV : Tathāgatakṛtyakriyādhikāra ... ... 166

9. Chapter V : Anuśaṃsādhikāra ... ... ... 183

10. Index of Metres ... ... ... ... ... 188

11. Index of Authorities ... ... ... ... 189

12. Index of Technical Terms ... ... ... 190

13. Index of Rare Words and Uses ... ... ... 197

## Part - III

**Corrections and Emendations**
to the Sanskrit Text of the Ratnagotravibhāga
(by J. Takasaki) ... ... 203

## Part - IV

**English Translation**
The Sublime Science of the Great Vehicle to Salvation
Being a Manual of Buddhist Monism
The Work of Ārya Maitreya with a Commentary by Āryāsaṅga
(by E. Obermiller)

**Introduction**

I. The 5 Treatises of Maitreya and their Subject-matter ... 211

II. The Authorship of the Treatises of Maitreya ... ... 222

III. The Different Theories regarding the Fundamental Element or Germ of Enlightenment ... ... ... 226

a) The Term Gotra and its Interpretation in Hīnayāna. 227

b) The Yogācāra Theories Concerning Dhātu or Gotra 229

IV. The Standpoint of the Mādhyamikas. The Teaching of the Element of Buddhahood according to the Uttaratantra ... ... ... 234

**The Sublime Science of the Great Vehicle to Salvation**

I. The Contents of the Work . . . . . . . . . . . . 241

The Explanation of the Verse by Āryāsaṅga . . . . . . 242

The 7 Subjects according to
the Dhāraṇīśvara-rāja-paripṛcchā . . . . . . . . . 245

The Germ of Buddhahood and the Other 3 Subjects
according to the Dhāraṇīśvara-rāja-paripṛcchā . . . 249

The Connexion between the 7 Subjects . . . . . . 252

The Jewel of the Buddha . . . . . . . . . . . . 253

Āryāsaṅga on the Jewel of the Buddha . . . . . . 255

Reference to the Jñāna-āloka-alamkāra-sūtra . . . . . . 257

The Jewel of the Doctrine . . . . . . . . . . . . 261

Reference to Scripture Concerning Extinction . . . . . . 263

The Path as the Cause of Extinction . . . . . . 265

The Jewel of the Congregation . . . . . . . . . 267

The Saint's Knowledge of the Absolute Truth . . . 268

The Empirical Knowledge of the Saints 270

The Perception of the Saints is
Introspective Knowledge . . . . . . . . . . . . 271

The Hīnayānistic Congregation is not
Worthy of Being Worshipped . . . . . . . . . . . 272

The 3 Jewels in their Character of a Refuge . . . 273

The Motives for the Establishment of the 3 Refuges from
the Empirical Standpoint as Explained by Āryāsaṅga . . . 273

The Doctrine and the Congregation are not
Refuges in the Ultimate Sense . . . . . . . . . 274

The Buddha is the Unique Absolute Refuge . . . . . . 276

The Meaning of "The 3 Jewels" ... ... ... 277
The Germ, Enlightenment, the Attributes and the Acts of the Buddha in their Inconceivable Nature ... 278
The Parable of the Cloth of Silk ... ... 281
The Acts of the Buddha in their Inconceivable Character 283
The Germ and the 3 other Subjects as a Causes and Conditions of Buddhahood 285
The Germ of the Absolute 286
Analysis of the Germ from 10 Points of View ... 287
The Essence of the Germ (1) and the Causes of its Purification (2) ... ... ... ... 288
The Impediments and the Causes of Purification ... 289
The Result of Purification (3) and the Functions of the Germ (4) ... ... ... 294
Concordance between the 4 Absolute Properties and the 4 Causes of Purification ... ... 297
The Impediments to the Attainment of the 4 Absolute Properties ... ... ... 299
Reference to Scripture ... ... ... ... 302
The Motives of the 4 Absolute Properties ... ... 302
The Functions of the Germ of the Buddha (4) ... 305
The Annihilation of the Germ is to be Understood in a Conventional Sense ... ... ... 307
The Relations of Germ to the Factors and the Result of Purification (5) ... ... ... 308
Reference to Scripture ... ... ... ... 311
The Manifestations of the Germ (6) ... ... 311
The Different States of the Germ (7) ... ... 313

Reference to Scripture Concerning the 3 Different States of the Germ . . . 314

The All-Pervading Character of the Germs (8). . . . . . 314

Reference to Scripture Concerning the All-pervading Character . . . 315

The Germ in its Unalterable Character (9) . . . 315

The Germ of the Buddha with the Saints (Partly Pure and Partly Impure) ... ... . . . 322

The Parable of the Householder ... ... . . . 325

The Partly Pure and Partly Impure State of the Bodhisattva as Compared with the Ordinary Being and the Buddha . . . ... . . . 330

The Absolute in the State of Perfect Purification . . . 333

The Essence of Buddhahood in its Indivisible Character ... ... ... . . . 335

The Parable of the Painters . . . ... ... . . . 338

The 9 Examples Illustrating the Essence of Buddhahood in the Living Beings . . . ... . . . 342

The Varieties of the Defiling Elements Illustrated by the 9 Examples ... . . . 351

The Concordance between the Examples Illustrating the Obscurations and the Points Expressed by them . . . 354

Reference to the Mahāparinirvāṇa-sūtra ... . . . 363

The True Conception of Relativity and Non-substantiality ... ... ... ... . . . 364

Controversy ... ... ... ... . . . 367

II. Enlightenment and the Absolute free from Defilement ... ... ... . . . 370

Summary ... ... ... ... . . . 372

The Functions of Enlightenment ... ... . . . 376

The Body of Absolute Existence ... ... 381

The Body Obliss ... ... ... ... ... 383

The 12 Acts of the Buddha as a mere Manifestation of His Apparitional Body ... ... 384

The Eternal Character of the 3 Bodies ... ... 385

The Inconceivable Character of Buddhahood ... ... 386

III. The Properties of the Buddha ... ... 388

Summary ... ... ... ... ... 389

The 10 powers ... ... ... ... ... 389

The 4 Forms of Intrepidity ... ... ... 390

The 18 Exclusive Properties ... ... 391

The Body of Bliss ... ... ... ... ... 393

The 32 Characterstics of the Super-man ... ... 393

IV. The Acts of the Buddha ... ... ... ... 397

The 9 Examples Illustrating the Acts of the Buddha ... 399

The Points of Dissimilarity between the Examples and the Manifestations of the Buddha ... 417

V. The Merits of Founding one's Belief in the Doctrine of the Essence of Buddhahood ... ... 419

Conclusion ... ... ... ... ... 425

Technical Terms ... ... ... ... ... 427

Works, Authors, and Schools ... ... ... 434

# Acknowledgements

I am greatly indebted to my *ādi guru* Shri Gorakh Rao for constantly inspiring me to study philosophy as a spiritual discipline. I dedicate this Volume to him as a token of my respect and gratitude.

My sincerest thanks are due to Professor P.N. Ojha, Honorary General Secretary, and Shri Gopi Raman Choudhary, Registrar, both of the Bihar Research Society, Patna, for their kind permission to reprint the Sanskrit text of the *Ratnagotravibhāga* (the *Uttaratantra*).

I am also thankful to Messrs. Naresh Gupta and Sunil Gupta of *Indian Books Centre* for the idea to bring out this Volume.

**H.S. Prasad**

# PART - I

# INTRODUCTION

*By*

**H. S. Prasad**

# Introduction

*H.S. Prasad*

The *Uttaratantra* is one of the five works[1] attributed to Maitreya. It is an abbreviated name of the *Ratnagotravibhāga Mahāyānottaratantraśāstra* (as E.H. Johnson[2] has given the title of the text). It is also called the *Ratnagotravibhāga*[3] or the *Mahāyānottaratantraśāstra* (as referred to in its Tibetan translation). The first part of the title, *Ratnagotravibhāga,* speaks of the spiritual character of its subject-matter as it deals with the cosmic principle of the essence (*gotra = tathāgatagarbha*)[4] of the *triratna* (Buddha, Dharma and Saṅgha to which the entire Buddhism is assimilated).[5] Realising ontological non-differentiation in sentient beings, it professes the common metaphysical substance in all of them, their equal status, their universal good and universal Buddhahood. In this sense, it represents the superior or even the supermost (*uttara*) of all the paths of Ultimate Freedom (*nirvāṇa*). Hence it is called by the name of *Uttaratantra,* which is perhaps the most popular name of the text. This is the reason why I have retained this title for the present Volume.

Two manuscripts of the Sanskrit text of the *Uttaratantra*[6] were discovered by Rahula Sankrityayana[7] in Tibet after E. Obermiller had translated the same with its commentary by Asaṅga into English from its Tibetan version.[8] The two differ from each other in many respects. Zuiryu Nakamura[9] has further published a study of the text based on comparison and contrast between the Sanskrit original and its Chinese translations. Jikido Takasaki's[10] study of the *Uttaratantra*[11] excels all other studies of this text. It includes a critical Introduction, a synopsis of the text, an English translation from the original Sanskrit text in comparison with its Tibetan and Chinese versions, critical notes, appendixes and indexes. Herein I have tried to present a philosophical interpretation of the *gotra (= tathāgatagarbha)* theory substantiating my thesis on the basis of these materials as well as other Buddhist texts.

The *Uttaratantra* is a text with Mādhyamika leanings. The Mādhyamika and the Yogācāra drastically differ from each other while preparing the philosophical backgrounds for their spiritual disciplines, the former by rejecting all the mutually conflicting philosophic views (*sarvadṛṣṭiśūnyatā*, a linguistic analysis) and the latter by culminating the analysis of illusory experiences. Once the grounds are prepared, both go hand in hand. Their views vary in this course at some points, but these variations are just like those which are seen within a system without forsaking its philosophic thrust and direction. Since the preparatory role of the *Uttaratantra* is the same as that of the Mādhyamika, it is said to be written from the Mādhyamika point of view. On the whole, it is truly a Mahāyāna text.[12]

The English translation of the *Uttaratantra* and Asaṅga's commentary on it from Tibetan by E. Obermiller together with his penetrating Introduction, detailed subtitles of the contents, numerous notes with equivalent Sanskrit terms and the two indices of (i) Sanskrit-Tibetan technical terms and (ii) Works, Authors and Schools, is one of the great contributions in the Buddhist studies. In his Introduction, he writes:

> In the translation the greatest care has been bestowed on a faithful rendering of all technical terms of which the work is full. This has been made in accordance with the method adopted by Prof. Stcherbatsky. Not a single term is left without translation, but in order to facilitate control, the original term (Sanskrit and Tibetan) is always given in the note.[13]

The importance of the *Uttaratantra* lies in the fact that it discusses those notions of Buddhism whose prior understanding is essential to understand the Mahāyāna, especially the Mādhyamika, spiritual discipline. The most important of them is the notion of *gotra*, which has a history of its development. Its allied notions are *āśraya*, *prāpti*, *bīja*, *vāsanā*, *dharmatā*, *tathatā*, *tathāgatadharma*, *tathāgatagarbha*, etc.

## The Development of the Gotra Theory

As we know, the Buddhist presupposition - *sarvam anityam* - and its logical culmination in the doctrine of momentariness or instantaneousness rule out the possibility of causal continuity and the very substratum of the events, thus leading to the futility, absurdity and hollowness of any spiritual discipline whether individual or social. To get rid of this paradoxical predicament different Buddhist schools suggested different remedies.

**Prāpti Theory :** To overcome these difficulties arising from the logical implications of momentariness, the Sarvāstivādins or the Vaibhāṣikas postulated a new metaphysical category *(viz. dravya)* of 'possession'*(prāpti)*, which as a matter of fact is a relation between the possessor and what is possessed, and its opposite, *aprāpti*, a negative relation, i.e. the denial of relation between the two. The Sarvāstivādins or the Vaibhāṣikas are typical realists who substantialize everything as a *dharma*. That is why they call *'prāpti'* and *'aprāpti'* substances *(dravya-dharma)*.[14]

Like any other realists, the Vaibhāṣikas seem to have been guided by the linguistic expressions of facts and the logic of natural language or structure of subject-predicate-relation type of language. They, like other Buddhists, are in search of personal identity of the stream of consciousness *(citta-saṃtāna)* which is said to have acquired certain *dharmas (=prāpti)* and abandoned certain other *dharmas (=aprāpti)*.[15] For example, during the course of the training of spiritual discipline, *prāpti* acts as a force in bringing and associating the wholesome *dharmas (kuśaladharma)* with the person and *aprāpti* simultaneously acts as a force in preventing the unwholesome *dharmas (akuśaladharma)* from coming into existence. All this requires a conscious substratum *(āśraya)*[16] which on the basis of his *kuśala* or *akuśala* acts determines his 'lineage' *(gotra)* or nature. This makes *nirvāṇa* possible for an aspirant. The momentariness of a *dharma* applies only to its ever-changing states *(avasthā)*, not to its underlying substance which is its substratum.[17] If momentariness is applied universally, i.e. without restriction, the talk of spiritual training, rising to a higher level of consciousness, the difference between a layman *(pṛthagjana)* and an enlightened man *(bodhisattva)*, and cultivating and promoting social virtues would be meaningless.

Thus the Vaibhāṣikas postulated two foreign elements – *prāpti* and *aprāpti* - to explain the possibility of spiritual discipline leading to the Ultimate Freedom *(nirvāṇa)*. But the *prāpti theory* is rejected by the Sautrāntikas, because by the same logic *prāpti* and *aprāpti* would require further such elements, which may bring them into relation ship with the person on the one hand, and the acquired element on the other, and so *ad infinitum.*[18]

**Bīja Theory**: The ingenious Sautrāntikas introduced a new idea derived from the notion of 'stream of consciousness' itself to solve the above difficulties. They formulated the *theory of 'seed'* or *'germ' (bīja)* which replaced the *prāpti theory* and later on became the basis for the development of the Mahāyāna tradition. Instead of arbitrarily postulating a new element in order to get out of the paradox, the Sautrāntikas conceived of the substratum *(āśraya)*[19] which is the locus of momentary changes in the stream of consciousness. Each moment, according to this theory, represents a new state *(anyathātva)*[20] of the substratum, which itself remains essentially unchanged. This is to admit the personal identity of a stream of consciousness. The same is the case with the *dharmas* other than consciousness. The *bīja theory* simply sees the potentiality *(śakti)*[21] in each *dharma* which manifests itself in many forms. The term *'bīja'* can be rendered as 'the essence of psycho-physical organism' (*nāma-rūpa*)[22], 'biological gene', 'embryo', 'matrix', 'seed', 'germ' and so on according to the context. In the Abhidharma texts, it is called the complex of the five *skandhas.*[23]

By introducing the *bīja theory,* the Sautrāntika aims at solving the puzzles of the continuity of the agent in the *karma-phala* process, acquiring knowledge, memory, apperception, final release, etc. It is the harbinger of the *ālayavijñāna* in the Yogācāra. This has been discussed in detail by L. Schmithausen in his latest book: *Ālayavijñāna* (On the origin and the early development of a central concept of Yogācāra philosophy).[24]

The controversy between the Vaibhāṣikas and the Sautrāntikas on the *prāpti theory*[25] is found in *AK* (with *AKB* and *AKV*) and *AD* (with *ADV*). The *prāpti-aprāpti theory* of the Vaibhāsikas is first criticised on the ground, as we have seen, that it leads to infinite regress. Secondly, there is no need of conceiving *prāpti* as an external element to mediate, for example, between *karma* and retribution. *Karma* is always volitional,[26] i.e. mind-generated and of two kinds: (1) bad volition *(akuśalacitta),*[27] viz. covetousness *(abhidhyā,*[28] rooted in *lobha*[29]), malevolence *(vyāpāda*[30], rooted in *dveṣa,)*[31] and holding erroneous, unethical and unjust view (*mithyādṛṣṭi*[32] rooted in *moha)*[33], and (2) good volition *(kuśalacitta)*[34], viz. non-covetousness *(anabhidhyā)*[35], non-malevolence *(avyāpāda)*[36] and viewing the reality as it is *(samyagdṛṣṭi)*[37] rooted in *alobha*[38], *adveṣa*[39] and *amoha*[40] respectively. These volitions nourish and impregnate a person's stream-consciousness determining its future evolution which is nothing but its transition from one state to another *(anyathātva)*[41]. The volitional act of a person stirs the latent germ *(bīja)* of its corresponding nature in him. It habituates his attitude accordingly. All this determines his response to a situation in which he is placed. Take for example, a social situation in which he, alongwith others, needs a particular thing, say a piece of cloth. The evil volition, if it dominates in him, will pursue his private good; whereas, on the contrary, his good volition will pursue the good of others. The seed of both evil *(akuśala)* and good *(kuśala)* volitions are present in a person. The good or bad nature of the personality of a man is carved out by cultivating and developing good and evil volitions respectively. All this happens in the person himself.[42] This means that a person has the potentiality *(śakti)* of rising to a higher level of consciousness. This theory gives rise to the *gotra theory* of the Mahāyāna Buddhism, particularly the Yogācāra school.

## The Mahāyāna Spiritual Discipline

The emergence and development of Mahāyāna Buddhism was a revolutionary and radical departure from private good to public good and from *pratyekabuddhayāna* to *ekayāna* or *mahāyāna*. In India, a philosophical school always tries to fulfill the religious and spiritual aspirations of common man. It preaches to lead a way of life based on a view of life derived from the correct understanding of the facts (*yathābhūtajñāna*). The two schools of Mahāyāna, the Mādhyamika and the Yogācāra, although aim at the essential unity of sentient beings, set their spiritual paths on two different but not opposite philosophical backgrounds. In the end they seem to merge with each other on central issues like human values, moral virtues and social emotions ignoring the minor differences between them.

Takasaki[43] thinks that the spiritual discipline based on the *tathāgatagarbha* theory is an entirely new and later development of Mahāyāna Buddhism. While discussing the position of the *Ratnagotravibhāga (Uttaratantra)* in Mahāyāna Buddhism[44], he erroneously maintains that this text aims at the criticism of the *prajñāpāramitā*. He takes modification of the *Prajñāpāramitā* doctrines as their criticism or even rejection by the *tathāgatagartha* theory. I am of the view that the *śūnyatā theory* is complementary to the *tathāgatagarbha theory*. Without the former, whether it is *sarvadṛṣṭiśūnyatā* of the Mādhyamika or the *bāhyārtha- śūnyatā* of the Yogācāra-Vijñānavāda, the latter will be impossible to establish. *Śūnyatā* does not negate *astitva* of the *gotra* or the *tathāgatagarbha.*

The Mādhyamika spiritual discipline is an outgrowth of its *śūnyatā* theory, the logical implications of which establish a kind of Absolutism, or Universalism. The development of *śūnyatā* theory is made possible by the critical analysis of the logic of natural language which is taken to be cognitive and referential. Its own language is non-cognitive and non-referential. Some discussion here on the *śūnyatā* theory will not be out of place.

Philosophy in India, generally, is considered as consisting in the interpretation of experiences in order to search for the underlying principle so that we may guide our life. The process is thus: When a person is struck by an experience, say an illusory cognition of a snake in place of a rope and its subsequent sublation, he is stimulated to reflective inquiry which generates knowledge of the underlying principle because of which he had such an experience. The resultant knowledge is another experience which is of the second order, reflective and intellectual, the former being of the first order. All the Indian philosophical systems start their reflective inquiry with the first order experiences of one type or the other, but the Mādhyamika does so with the second order experiences, i.e. the reflective experiences of the other schools. He is struck by the conflicting nature of these experiences. He exhibits the voidness of such reflective inquiries on this ground and thus develops the concept of *śūnyatā.*

According to some Mādhyamikas, *śūnyatā* is an end in itself. But other Mādhyamikas are not happy with this negative approach to philosophy as found in the *Madhyamaka-kārikā* and the *Vigrahavyāvartanī* of Nāgārjuna. They feel that this negative attitude has neglected religious and ethical ideals,. which are necessarily required to generate a view of life or a world-view and the corresponding way of life. To serve a practical purpose, *śūnyatā* and the religious and ethical ideals should be blended together. So they adopt the concept of *śūnyatā* and reconcile it with the path of liberation *(vimukti-mārga) en route* to universal compassion *(karuṇā)*. They have thus revived those religious and ethical ideals which were earlier ignored by the Mādhyamikas or which were meant for selfish purposes in the early schools of Buddhism.

The Mādhyamika, like Śāntideva, thinks that a way of life must imply a view of life, a world-view, a view of reality, and thus a metaphysic. He treats philosophical speculation without an ethic and a religion as purposeless enterprise. That's why he puts maximum emphasis on spiritual discipline, practice of virtues *(śīla)* and concentration of mind *(samādhi)*, because only these will give us an insight into the nature of reality.[45] Such insight is technically called *yathābhūta-jñāna* (Pali, *yathābhūta-ñāṇa)*.

For the Mādhyamika, philosophy should not be only speculative in nature, it must have ethical and practical bearings also on our life which are born of deep philosophical insight of *śūnyatā*. *Śūnyatā* is a reflective awareness of philosophical speculation *(dṛṣṭi)* about reality *(tattva)*. It also shows the essential dependence of things *(niḥsvabhāvatā)*.[46] The two, *śūnyatā* and *niḥsvabhāvatā*, are thus not different from each other. It is in this sense that the doctrine of dependent origination *(pratītya-samutpāda)* is identified with *śūnyatā*.[47] *Pratītyasamutpāda* as a causal law regulates the things conditioned by *kleśa* and *karma* in the three time-epochs — past, present and future.[48] But otherwise it shows the essential voidness of things.

*Śūnyatā* is the nature of things and so it is not different from them *(na śūnyatā bhāvād vyatiriktā)*.[49] When voidness of all things or views is shown, the philosophical speculation *(kalpanā)* ceases to be. In this situation there is neither any gain nor any loss on the part of the things.[50] But on the part of the person, his attachment with the things and the philosophic views *(dṛṣṭi)*, and his subsequent suffering are eliminated. In this sense, *śūnyatā* is called the destroyer of all kinds of suffering *(duḥkha śamani).*[51] Thus, the realisation of *śūnyatā* transforms the whole personality of a man.

The realisation of *śūnyatā* is nothing but *prajñā* which arises from the insight of the voidness of phenomenal things and all philosophical speculations. Śāntideva particularly insists upon the perfection of wisdom *(prajñāpāramitā)* which seems to dominate the entire Mādhyamika thinking whether metaphysical, epistemological, religious or ethical. The other *pāramitās (dāna, śīla, kṣānti, vīrya* and *dhyāna)* are considered to be ancillary to or preparatory for the development of the *prajñāpāramitā (prajñā-pradhānā dānādayo guṇā ucyate)*[52].

When one achieves the state of *prajñā,* his knowledge about reality is non-dual *(advaya-jñāna)* and non-conceptual *(nirvikalpaka).* He sees the reality as free from the framework of *catuṣkoti* – the four alternative but exhaustive ways of propounding philosophic views *(catuṣkoṭivinirmukta).* The two of them, ens *(sat)* and non-ens *(asat),* affirmation and negation are the primary ones. The third alternative is formed by taking these two together *(ubhayasaṃkīrṇātma)* and the fourth by denying the two together *(ubhayapratiṣedha)*[53].

The Yogācāra philosophy is the culmination of the epistemological analysis of illusory cognition. It resurrected philosophy from its all-out onslaught by the Mādhyamika *sarvadṛṣṭiśūnyatā* by pointing out that everything can be denied, but that, i.e. subjectivity, by which everything is denied cannot be denied. This element of subjectivity is pure-consciousness *(vijñaptimātratā),* which is the ultimate reality. At empirical level it appears as subject and object. Its nature is such that it projects itself into many forms.[54] In this way it differs from the Mādhyamika in establishing Absolutism.

The Yogācāra and the Vijñānavāda are two branches of the same school. The Yogācāra is so named because its emphasis is on the experiences of deep meditation *(dhyāna).* In order to maintain the causal continuity between the past, present and future moments, the Yogācārins, following the Sautrāntika theory of *bīja,* postulated the store-consciousness *(ālayavijñāna)* as the substratum of all transformations, evolutions or revolutions *(āśraya-parāvṛtti).*[55] The

Vijñānavādins, the followers of Diṅnāga, postulated the six internal bases of consciousness *(ṣaḍāyatana)*[56] instead of *ālayavijñāna.* But both accept the same underlying principle or force *(gotra)* which causes transformations in the substratum.

The most revolutionary development in the history of Buddhism is the emergence of the Mahāyāna tradition in which is maintained the identification of phenomena *(saṃsāra)* with the Absolute *(nirvāṇa)*, leading to the changes in the meaning of the word 'Buddha' from human being *(Sākyamuni Buddha)* to the metaphysical principle of all sentient beings *(dharmakāya)*[57], and even as cosmic principle of everything, sentient as well as non-sentient. In *Encyclopedia* of *Buddhism*[58], G.P. Malalasekera succinctly describes this development as follows:

> Thus, by Buddha was meant at first a great teacher. Then he was treated as a super-man and raised to the level of a super-human, transcendental being. The next step of development was to regard Buddha as a 'Principle', the Ultimate Reality (i.e., *Dharma-kāya*). Then it was believed that the Buddha, the Ultimate Reality, is not something external that has to be achieved or attained, but a potential ability, called Buddha-nature, that has to be awakened (i.e., to be realised). And this Buddha-nature is inherent not only in human beings but also in every specific being and in every concrete matter.

In the Yogācāra, the *ālayavijñāna* was further interpreted as the *tathāgatagarbha,* "the fundamental element of the Absolute as existing in every living being."[59]

## Gotra : The Foundation of Mahāyāna, and its Types

The main concern of the *Uttaratantra* is to discuss and elaborate the concept of *gotra* which is the basis and source of various Mahāyāna notions, such as *dhātu*[60], *dharmadhātu*[61], *buddhatā*[62], *tathāgatagarbha*[63], *tathatā*[64], *dharmatā*[65], *nihsvabhāvatā*[66], *śūnyatā,*[67], *pudgalanairātmya*[68], *samatā*[69], *trikāya*[70] and *ekayāna*[71]. The word *'gotra'* is variously translated as family, clan, spiritual lineage, germ, seed, class, category, mine and matrix.

The etymology of *'gotra'* is quite interesting. D. Seyfort Ruegg has explored its etymology:

> Concerning the hermeneutic etymology *(nirukta)*, because the good qualities are realized - produced - from it, it is *gotra*. Again, because they *go (gam-)* sentient beings are *go-*; and because of protecting them *(tra-)* it is *go-tra-*. Again (according to the *Śuddhimatī*), here *gam-* (the root of *go-* ) is used in the sense of being present; for example, the *ākāśa* is universally present, and accordingly *go-* meaning 'to go, be present' [is] the supported factor *(ādheyadharma)*. And because of protection, holding unshakeably (indestructibly), one speaks of a *go-tra*, viz. (what is termed) support.[72]

In the Yogācāra-Vijñānavāda, the *gotra* is something different from the *ālayavijñāna* or *ṣaḍāyatana* or *tathāgatagarbha*, whereas in the Mādhyamika it is the very essence *(tathatā, dharmatā)* of the Ultimate Reality, uniform *(ekarasa, samarasa)*, eternal *(nitya)*, immutable *(asaṃskṛta)*, Absolute *(dharmadhātu)*, the metaphysical principle of Absolute *(svabhāvakāya, dharmakāya)*, of spiritual nature *(cittasvabhāva)* and total essence of all *dharmas*.[73] When a person is impregnated with ignorance *(avidyāvāsanā)*[74] or lacks the knowledge of the nature of reality (*yathābhūtajñāna*), his volitional acts *(karma)* cause him suffering. His personality is then supposed, as we see in the Abhidharma, to be constituted of 5 *skandhas*, 12 *āyatanas*, or 18 *dhātus*. In this case, the *gotra* is said to be concealed by the adventitious but impure factors *(āgantukamala)*. Their *śūnyatā* theory is meant to remove such unwanted factors. The *śūnyatā-dṛṣṭi* is one of the first requirements to cultivate and develop the enlightened mind *(bodhicitta)* which helps an individual to rise to a higher level of consciousness so that he may treat all human beings at *par (sama)*. When these conditioning factors are removed, the *gotra* becomes unconditioned *(asaṃskṛta)*. As a matter of fact, the *gotra* is uniform in nature and essence *(ekarasa)* like space. This non-qualificative *(nirviśeṣa)* aspect of the *gotra* engulfs the multivalued or plurality of the Ābhidharmika *dharmas* and thus becomes one-valued *(ekarasa)* and eternal reality, the single ontological foundation of epistemic maniness.[75]

Since the *gotra* is the locus of all appearances or *dṛṣṭi*-constructions, in the secondary sense it is called the substratum *(āśraya, ālambana)*, and motivating and productive cause *(hetu, upādānakāraṇa)*. It is the support of all kinds of spiritual and meditative practices *(pratipatti)*.[76] In the primary sense, its nature or essence is identical with the Absolute *(dharmadhātu)*.[77] The *gotra* is thus one and ubiquitous *(sāmānyavartin)*. The apparent differentiations *(bheda)* in the non-differentiated *(abheda)* nature of the *gotra* is due to the level of understanding of the person who is short of attaining perfection in the realization of the true nature of reality. These differentiations need for their appearances a non-differentiated locus and that is *gotra*.[78] Ruegg has discussed the *gotra* "under the rubrics of (i) proof of its existence, (ii) nature, (iii) varieties, (iv) inferential mark, (v) good qualities, (vi) disadvantages, and (vii) the hermeneutic etymology."[79]

Since the *gotra* is of spiritual nature, its manifestation is noticed in the form of good qualities *(kuśaladharma)*, such as spiritual attitudes, universal compassion, friendliness and enlightenment in individuals. These are the marks for the existence of the *gotra*. It gives rise to thirteen-fold comprehensions *(adhigama)*[80] and twenty-two stages of thought-production *(cittotpāda)*.[81] As to the varieties of the *gotra*, it is originally unique and identical in nature with the essence of the Absolute *(dharmadhātu)*. This form of the *gotra* is called *prakṛtisthagotra*[82]. "The *prakṛtistha-gotra*, whose nature is *dharmadhātu* and which is acquired in virtue of *dharmatā*, is evidently assimilated to *śūnyatā*. This assimilation is of importance for the theory of the *tathāgatagarbha* also since the latter has been connected with this *gotra*."[83] The origin of the *prakṛtistha-gotra* is atemporal *(anādikālagata)* and to be realised in the background of the *sarvadṛṣṭiśūnyatā* theory. It is equated with *dharmatā*, the essence of all *dharmas*.[84]

When looked at from lower level of consciousness or defiled mind, the *gotra* appears as differentiated. This kind of the *gotra* is called developed *(samudānīta, paripuṣṭa, abhisaṃskṛta)*. The *prakṛtistha-gotra*, because of being the locus of all metamorphoses, is called the cause *(kāraṇa)* of the *samudānīta-gotra*, which is its effect *(phala)*. The talk of the *gotra* in other forms than its original state, when it is quiescent, one, and said to be the metaphysical or cosmic principle of the universe *(dharmakāya*, the cosmic body of the Buddha), is to talk of the *gotra* at its manifested or developed or resultant level when it is called *samudānīta*. This means that any discussion of the notions of *tathatā, tathāgata, buddhagotra, tathāgatagarbha, sambhogakāya, nirmāṇakāya*, etc. are at this level. In short, the *prakṛtistha-gotra* is the essence of the *samudānīta-gotra*.[85]

## The Characteristics of the Gotra

The *Uttaratantra* discusses the *gotra* from the following ten points of view[86]:

(1) Essence *(svabhāva*, of the *dharmakāya, dharmatā* and the *sarvasattvadhātu)*. This is the original state of the *gotra*. It is essentially efficacious *(prabhāva)*, unalterable *(ananyathātva)* and loving *(snigdha)*. Its specific characteristics *(svalakṣana)* resemble the characteristics of the wish-fulfilling gem *(cintāmaṇi)*, space *(nabha)* and water *(vāri)*. It fulfills the desires of the aspirants (in attaining, for example, Final Freedom) just as the wish-fulfilling gem fulfills the desires of a man. It is like all-pervasive space in magnitude which encompasses everything and is in itself indivisible and unalterable. Being of spiritual or consciousness nature *(cittaprakṛti)* it possesses universal compassion and is loving and soothing like water. Its general characteristic *(sāmānyalakṣaṇa)* is its absolute purity in essence *(prakṛtipariśuddhi)* which underlies the specific characteristics.[87]

(2) Cause *(hetu)*: It is the cause of one's adherence *(adhimukti = adhimokṣa)*[88] to the Mahāyāna doctrines *(dharma)*, Supreme Wisdom *(adhiprajñā)*, profound meditation *(samādhi)* and universal compassion *(karuṇā)*. They in turn remove the defilements *(āvaraṇa)*, such as aversion to the Mahāyāna doctrines *(dharmapratigha)*, adherence to the self theory *(ātmadarśana)*, tendency of being afraid of phenomenal sufferings *(saṃsāraduḥkhabhirutva)* and attitude of indifference to the welfare of fellow beings *(sattvārtha-nirapeksatā)*.[89] These are the factors which prevent one from realizing the true nature of the *gotra*. In the secondary sense, the *gotra* is considered to be the cause *(upādānakāraṇa)* of the plurality of the *dharmas* whose nomenclatures are sheer metaphorical.

(3) Effect *(phala):* On the removal of the above defilements, the *gotra* is understood from the resultant realisation of the Absolute with its four transcendental and perfect characteristics: universal good *(śubha-pāramitā)*, blissful experience *(sukha-pāramitā)*, identification of all *dharmas (ātmapāramitā)*, and atemporality *(nitya-pāramitā)*. These properties are the antidotes of the four erroneous views *(viparyāsa)*, viz., mistaking the impermanent things *(anitya)* as permanent *(nitya)*, experience of pleasure *(sukha)* in the worldly life which is full of suffering *(duḥkha)*, looking for personal Ego *(ātma)* in impersonal *(anātma) dharmas*, and taking something as good *(śubha)* which is ultimately evil *(aśubha)*. The realisation of the four characteristics of the Absolute gives rise to the four kinds of correct understanding *(aviparyāsa)* of impermanence, suffering, impersonality and evil character of phenomenal things.[90]

(4) Function *(karma)*: The function of the inherent *gotra* in an individual is that it arouses detachment from the evil-loaded phenomena and then creates will-power *(chanda)*[91] in him so that he can make resolutions *(praṇidhi)*[92] to achieve the quiescent state *(nirvāṇa)*.[93] On the other hand, if there were no *gotra (=buddhadhātu)* in an individual, there would be no frustration with the worldly suffering, no aspiration *(icchā)*[94] for Final Release, no request *(prārthanā)*[95] for it and no resolve for attaining it[96]. Thus, this absolutely pure essence of the Buddha *(buddhadhātu = viśuddhigotra)*, which is ever present even in those sentient beings who are heretics, discharges its efficacy in two ways: first, its preparatory function is to create awareness in the sentient beings about the evil nature of the phenomena and secondly, it motivates and activates them to achieve Ultimate Freedom from these evils.[97]

(5) Relation *(yoga*, of the *gotra* with *hetu* and *phala)*: The *gotra* is causally connected with those factors (viz. *adhimukti, samādhi, prajñā* and *karuṇā)* which (i) remove the impediments concealing the cosmic principle *(dharmakāyaviśuddhihetu)*, (ii) give rise to the Buddha-Wisdom *(buddhajñānasamudāgama-hetu)*, and (iii) cause manifestation of universal compassion of the *tathāgata (tathāgata-mahākaruṇāvṛttihetu)*. Of these

three, the first is demonstrated in one's determined and concentrated adherence to the Mahāyāna doctrines; the second, in one's focal attention on the perfect wisdom and deep meditation; and the third, in one's tunning up his mind and body to act spontaneously but consciously where universal compassion of the Bodhisattvas has to be manifested.[98]

The relation of the *gotra* with *phala* is shown by the simile of a flame *(dīpa)*. The *gotra* resembles the flame. Its effect, Supreme Knowledge *(abhijñā)*, resembles the light of the flame. Just as the light of the flame destroys the darkness, so does the Supreme Knowledge destroy the defiling forces, such as volitional acts *(karma)* and passions *(kleśa)*.[99] In this way, the *gotra* is related to its effects.

(6) The manifestation (*vṛtti*, of the *gotra*): The *gotra* manifests itself in varying degrees as the case may be . In the case of a layman, who is under the impact of erroneous views mentioned above, it becomes impossible for him to know the nature of the Truth *(=atattvadarśī)*, because his *gotra* is completely concealed. In the case of a spiritually superior person *(āryapudgala)*, who knows the Truth *(tattvadarśī)* and who has discarded these erroneous views, the *gotra* is partly manifested and partly concealed as he still has to attain the Highest Wisdom. Finally, in the case of the perfectly Enlightened *Tathāgata*, who is completely free from all defilements, the *gotra* is manifested the maximum, the next step of which is the *dharmakāya* of the Buddha. All this shows that the *gotra (=tathāgatadhātu)*, which is the absolutely pure essence of all *dharmas* and conception-free *(nirvikalpa, niṣprapañca)*, is present in all sorts of sentient beings.[100]

(7) State *(avasthā*, of the *gotra)*: The different states of the *gotra* are considered in accordance with its manifestations in various ways.In its defiled *(aśuddha)* state as found in a layman, it is called the essence of the sentient beings. In its partly-defiled-partly-undefiled *(aśuddhaśuddha)* state as found in the bodhisattvas, it is called the essence of the Bodhisattva. And in its absolutely pure *(suviśuddha)* state as found in the *Tathāgata*[101], it is called the Absolute.[102]

(8) All-pervasive *(sarvatrānugata)* character of the *gotra*: From the manifestations and different states of the *gotra*, its all-pervasive character is implied. The Mādhyamika *śūnyatā* doctrine and the subsequent elimination of the plurality of *dharmas* clear the ground for the establishment of Monism or Absolutism, the natural corollary of which is pantheism.[103]

(9) Unmodifiable essence *(avikāritva)* of the *gotra*[104]: From the preceding discussion it is now clear that the *gotra* possesses the unmodifiable essential character in the Mādhyamika pantheism. This is not perceived in ordinary way because of its transcendental *(saukṣmya)* nature. Transcendental in the sense that the knowledge of the real nature of the *gotra* is beyond our physical sense-organs which can perceive only the superficial aspect of it. The above characteristics of the *gotra* can be realised only through the Perfect Wisdom *(prajñā)* backed by the *śūnyatā* doctrine.

(10) Unitary character *(asambheda)* of the *gotra*: Essentially unalterable and ubiquitous character of the *gotra* proves its unitary character. In this sense, the *gotra* is identified with the cosmic principle of the Buddha *(dharmakāya)* which is the Ultimate Truth *(āryasatya)* and the state of *nirvāṇa*. From this it follows that the Ultimate Freedom *(nirvāṇa)* is nothing other than the realisation of this Truth and this state is the state of the Buddhahood *(buddhatva)*[105]. It is in this epistemic sense that ontologically *nirvāṇa* and *saṃsāra* are identical. This is one of the most revolutionary theses of the Mādhyamikas in the light of which only can we appreciate the social relevance of their spiritual discipline.

The *Uttaratantra* gives four synonyms of the Buddhahood: (i) Since it is unitary in character it is *dharmakāya*, (ii) since the *gotra* has turned it into the Absolute, it is *tathāgata*, (iii) since it is identical with the Ultimate Truth and free from delusions, it is called *paramārthasatya*, and (iv) since it is free from epistemic and linguistic errors of the plurality of the *dharmas*, it is a state of tranquillity *(nirvāṇa)*[106]

## The Gotra-based Classification of the Sentient Beings

The varieties of the *gotra* can be determined from the degrees of its manifestation. In the Buddhist scriptures we find that this fact is the basis for the classification or categorisation of sentient beings[107], namely *śrāvakagotraka*[108], *pratyekabuddhagotraka*[109], *bodhisattvagotraka*[110], *aniyatagotraka*[111], and *agotraka*[112]. The Mādhyamika will say that in each category the *gotra* is essentially and potentially present. Its manifestation in different degrees is based on certain conditions. They profess the doctrine of universal Buddhahood, at least in the potential form. The Yogācāra also admits that all sentient beings are capable of becoming *tathāgata*[113], i.e. they are potential Buddhas. But there is at least one text in the Yogācāra literature, viz. the *saṃdhinirmocanasūtra* which goes against this theory. It maintains that the *śrāvakayāna*, etc. can never be incorporated in the *tathāgatagotra* and the *ekayāna* or *mahāyāna* respectively. Obermiller translates the relevent passage as : "There are individuals who belong to the Śrāvaka lineage and whose aim is solely the attainment of quiescence . . . Although all the Buddhas taken together may apply their energy, it is impossible to secure for the said individuals the Essence of Supreme Enlightenment."[114] This single exception makes Ruegg think unjustly that the Yogācāra "does not admit the doctrine of universal buddhahood implied by the usual interpretation of the *ekayāna* theory."[115] The contention of this passage is certainly incompatible with the *tathāgatagarbha* theory of the Mādhyamika-Yogācāra spiritual discipline. The general approach of Mahāyāna is: Those belonging to the three Orders – *śrāvakayāna*, *pratyekabuddhayāna* and *tathāgata( = bodhisattva)yāna* are said to belong to the three lineages *śrāvakagotra*, *pratyekabuddhagotra* and *tathāgata(= bodhisattva)gotra*, and follow the three spiritual paths[116] — *prayogamārga*, *bhāvanāmārga* and *darśanamārga* — respectively. For Total or Ultimate Freedom the first two have to incorporate themselves into the third, i.e. the Mahāyana or Ekayāna doctrines.

The *Laṅkāvatārasūtra*, a prominent Yogācāra text, mentions apart from the above three, two more categories of sentient beings: (i) *aniyatagotraka* and (ii) *agotraka*. The former are those whose spiritual lineage is not yet determined. They may join anyone of the three lineages according to their convenience or choice or opportunity.[117] Obermiller discusses the distinction between determined (*niyata*) and undetermined *(aniyata)* lineages in a different way depending on whether the aspirant has overcome one or both the obscurations — *kleśāvaraṇa*[118] and *jñeyāvaraṇa*[119]. Such aspirants who, he writes, have entered the lineage of the Mahāyāna, are said to be of two kinds:

> 1) the Boddhisattva who from the outset belongs to the Mahāyānistic lineage, and 2) the Arhat (Śrāvaka or Pratyekabuddha) who has subsequently entered the Mahāyānistic Path. The former has to remove simultaneously both Obscurations. The latter in his turn has fully extirpated all the passions, &c., i.e. the Obscuration of Moral Defilement. Therefore he has to remove only the Obscuration of Ignorance, viz. the realistic views regarding the separate elements.[120]

The last category of the persons is that in which an individual is either reluctant in entering anyone of the three lineages; in other words, he is simply not interested in attaining *nirvāṇa (aparinirvāṇa-gotraka)*[121], or he simply does not possess any *gotra (= agotraka).* The latter possibility is ruled out in the theory of the *tathāgatagarbha*[122]. I disagree with Ruegg in his contention that "this allusion of a cut-off *gotra* refers simply to the difficulty of attaining liberation"[123]. Any aspirant belonging to anyone of the three categories does have difficulty because of rigorous training in getting perfection in that spiritual order, but he is not considered lacking *gotra (=agotra). Agotra* should be understood in the former sense in which concerned persons are called *icchantikas*[124], those who act according to their desire *(icchā).* They are of two kinds: (i) Those who do not believe in or desire to follow the Mahāyāna spiritual discipline, order and values. They find maximum pleasure in the worldly things and thus give no value to *nirvāṇa.* They have forsaken every root of good deed *(sarvakuśala-mūlotsarga)*[125]. Such persons never enter the path of Enlightenment and never attain Ultimate Freedom *(atyantāparinirvāṇa-dharmaka)*[126], and (ii) the second category of the *icchantikas* is that of the bodhisattvas whose altruistic impulse forbids them from entering the state of tranquillity *(nirvāṇa).* They deliberately do so in order to help their fellow beings achieve the bliss of *nirvāṇa*. They continue to do so till each one of them is finally liberat ed. In the very beginning of their boddhisattva career they resolve to liberate every sentient being from the worldly suffering without forsaking their virtuous paths. Although a bodhisattva has in principle fulfilled all the requirements and has realised the Ultimate Truth, he does not wish that his altruistic activity should stagnate by his entering the eternally blissful but passive state of *nirvāṇa*.

The first type of the *icchantikas*, who have forsaken their roots of merit, regain the same in association with the bodhisattvas, because the essence of the *tathāgata* is still present in them. Knowing this fact, the bodhisattvas, in the hope that even such non-believers will one day be inducted into the Mahāyāna spiritual discipline, keep working for their liberation suspending indefinitely their own Ultimate Freedom, a state of Ultimate Tranquillity *(parinirvāṇa)*[127].

The *gotra* theory or the *tathāgatagarbha* theory has its close interrelation with the concepts of *ekayāna (mahāyāna)*, *niḥsvabhāvatā*, *śūnyatā*, *nairātmya*, *dharmatā*, *tathatā*, *triratna*, and *triyāna*. This is clear from the above discussion. The detailed treatment of these concepts is not within the purview of this *Introduction*.

The *Uttaratantra*, in all fairness, is a Mahāyāna text with its leanings toward the Mādhyamika. But with regard to the spiritual discipline, both the Mādhyamika and the Yogācāra are in agreement. The difference between them lies in their initial methods of approach to the Absolute Reality, the former through the analysis of the logic of natural language (i.e. linguistic analysis), and the latter through the analysis of the experience of illusory cases (i.e. epistemological analysis). But both maintain that (1) the Ultimate Reality is of spiritual nature *(cittasvabhāva, cittaprakṛti)* and one *(advaya)*, (2) Perfect Wisdom and *Nirvāṇa* are identical *(ekarasa*, literally, of the same taste [in experience]), and (3) all sentient beings are equal *(sama)* and potential Buddhas.

## Notes

(1) According to the Tibetan sources, the five works of Maitreya are: *Mahāyānasūtrālaṃkāra, Madhyāntavibhāga, Abhisamayālaṃkāra, Dharmadharmatāvibhāga* and *Uttaratantra.* But according to the Chinese sources, his works are: *Yogācārabhūmi, Yogavibhāga* (now lost), *Mahāyānasūtrālaṃkāra, Madhyāntavibhāga* and *Vajracchedikavyākhyā.* In the Chinese sources, the *Uttaratantra* is attributed to Sāramati (350-450 A.D.). Hajime Nakamura (pp.261-62, fn.59) thinks that E.H. Johnson, following H. Ui and Yoshifumi Uyeda, erroneously attributed it to Sthiramati.

(2) See Johnson (1950).

(3) "*Ratnagotravibhāga.* The word *'vibhāga'* is the correct Skt. form of Pali *'vibhaṅga'* which means 'explanation', 'commentary'. In BHS, however, the form *'vibhaṅga'* is more often used as in cases of *Madhyāntavibhāga, Dharmadharmatāvibhāga* and so on. In these cases, *'vibhaṅga'* is taken in the sense of 'distinction between two'. But here, the meaning 'analysis' seems more suitable, because the word *'ratnagotra'* indicates *'dhātu'* or *'tathāgatagarbha'*, and not *'ratna & gotra'*. Cf. *gotraṃ ratnatrayasya* [*RGV*, I.24a]." - Takasaki, p.141, fn.1.

(4) Ruegg (1976, p.351) remarks: "...there can be no question of the *ratnagotra* of *RGV* 1.23-4 being simply a synonym of *tathāgatagarbha*, for the *tathāgatagarbha* = *samalā tathatā* is only one of four components of the *ratnagotra.* The only *gotra* identifiable with the *tathāgatagarbha* is then the *prakṛtistha-gotra*, or perhaps more loosely the double *gotra* of the second part of ch. 1 of the *RGV*". Again, in fn.73, he observes: "cf. *RGV* 1.149 and 1.86. This identification, however, would not be accepted by a commentator who holds the *tathāgatagarbha* to be the Fruit (*...phala*) when the *gotra* is, according to *RGV* 1.27, the cause on to which the name of the Fruit is metonymously transferred (cf. *RGVV* 1.149-52)."

(5) A long passage from Takasaki (pp.21-22) is here noteworthy: "Then, what is *'ratnagotra'* ? This word is interpreted by the commentator as *'gotraṃ ratnatrayasya'* (v.I, 24), the Germ of the

3 jewels, and explained in the *śloka* (v. I, 23) as *'viṣayaḥ paramārthadarśināṃ śubharatnasargako yataḥ'*, the sphere of those who have the highest perception from which the pure 3 jewels rise. Here, *'gotra'* means something original, while *'ratnatraya'*, its result. The word *'gotra'* is one of the special terms difficult to be conveyed by any other language, but the basic line of interpretation for this word among the Buddhist literatures is *'gotra'* = *'dhātu'* = *'hetu'*, or *'gotra'* = *'bīja'*, and hence it may be translated into English by 'element', 'cause', 'source', 'origin', 'basis', 'ground', 'essence', or 'nature'. In India, however, by a common use, this word means 'family', 'clan' or 'lineage', and analogically, it is used in the sense of 'germ', 'mine', or 'matrix'. Actually, in the word *'gotra'*, all of these senses are included, and besides *'dhātu'*, *'hetu'* and *'bīja'*, as synonyms of *'gotra'* with the range of senses, we can get various words such as *'pada'*, *'āśraya'*, *'mūla'*, *'sthāna'* (for 'basis' or 'ground'); *'nidāna'* (for 'cause'); *'svabhāva'*, *'prakṛti'*, *'dharma'* (for 'nature'); *'sāra'* (for 'essence'); *'nidhi'*, *'nidhāna'*, *'ākāra'* (for 'mine'), *'yoni'*, *'garbha'* (for 'matrix'); *'vaṃśa'* (for 'lineage'); *'parigraha'* (for 'family') etc. On the other hand, *'ratna'* or *'ratnatraya'* is a name for the Absolute when it is regarded as the *'śaraṇa'* (refuge), or the object of worship. *Par excellence*, it is the *'buddharatna'*, and the other two, i.e. the *'dharmaratna'* and *'saṅgharatna'* are merely the 'natural outflow' (*dharmatāniṣyanda*) of the former (p.7). In this sense, *'ratnatraya'* is synonymous with *'buddha'*, *'tathāgata'*, or *'jina'*. And combining these terms of both sides, we can get those terms like *'tathāgatagarbha'*, *'buddhagarbha'*, *'jinagarbha'*; *'tathāgata-dhātu'*, *'buddhadhātu'*; *'tathāgatagotra'*, *'buddhagotra'*, etc. as synonyms of *'ratnagotra'*. Thus we know the word *'ratnagotra'* used in the title indicates what is called *'tathāgatagarbha'* and this text is a treatise on the *Tathāgatagarbha* theory."

(6) The Sanskrit text was first published in part by H.W. Bailey and E.H. Johnson in the *Bulletin of the School of Oriental Studies* (London Institute), Vol.8, Part I, 1935, pp.77-89. (See Hajime Nakamura, p.261, fn.59). It was later published in full by E.H. Johnson (1950) under the title: *The Ratnagotravibhāga Mahāyānottaratantraśāstra*.

(7) "About the Mss., see *JBORS*, XXI, p.31 (III. Ṣalu monastery, vol. XI-5, No.43) and XXIII, p.34 (VII. Ṣalu monastery, vol. XIII-5, No.242)." – Taka saki, p.5, fn.1.

(8) See Obermiller (1931) being reprinted herewith.

(9) See Zuiryu Nakamura (1961).

(10) See Jikido Takasaki (1966).

(11) Being reprinted herewith fron Johnson's edition.

(12) Also see Takasaki (1966), pp.37-38 on this issue.

(13) Obermiller (1931), p.110.

(14) Cf. *AK*, II.36 together with *AKB* and *AKV*.

(15) *Ibid*. Also see Jaini (1959), p.238.

(16) Usually *āśraya* means: a complex of five *skandhas (nāmarūpa, pañca-skandha)* in the Sautrāntika, *ālayavijñāna* in the Yogācāra, *ṣaḍāyatana* in the Vijñānavāda, and *tathāgatagarbha* or *gotra* in the Mādhyamika. Schmithausen (1987, pp.625-26) has discussed different connotations of *āśraya*, viz. *āśraya* (lit. substratum) = basis of personal existence (*ātmabhava*) = *nāmarūpa (pañcaskandha)* = *citta-caitta-saṃtāna* = *ṣaḍāyatana* = corporeal basis of existence/ body, etc. Cf. *AKB* on *AK*, III.41. The term *āśraya* is frequently found in combination with *parāvṛtti* or *parivṛtti*. Cf. *Madhyāntavibhāgaśāstra*, p.65.23: *āśrayaparāvṛttir bodhiḥ, āśrayo nirmalatathatā; Mahāyānasūtrālamkāra*, XIX.54.

A.K. Chatterjee (1975, pp.160-61) writes: "Āśrayaparāvṛtti is the disappearance of the unreal object, and the realisation of Tathatā; and this is freedom (mokṣa). Impelled by the Transcendental Illusion of the idea of objectivity, it goes on projecting the forms of the so-called empirical objects, giving rise to various pravṛtti-vijñānas which, in their own turn, replenish it further. The Ālaya is thus the support (āśraya) of the entire phenomenal world. A vicious circle is started from which there is no escape. The Ālaya creates an 'other' to consciousness and the 'other' makes it create still further forms. Consciousness loses its equanimity and forgets its essential nature. This is saṃsāra. But when the unreality of the object is realised, there is nothing to govern the forward movement of the Ālaya. Consciousness is no longer diversified into the moments of empirical forms. "Realising everything to be imaginary, the Bodhisattva ceases to imagine anything at all; this is Bodhi or Enlightenment". Consciousness gets rid of the subject-object duality and rests again in itself. This is nirvāṇa which is also supreme bliss (sukha). It is identical with the Tathāgata."

Sthiramati's commentary on the following *Triṃśikā-kārikās* is so relevant here that I am quoting it extensively:

On *kā*.19: *anādikāliko dhātuḥ sarvadharmasamāśrayaḥ/*

*tasmin sati gatiḥ sarvā nirvāṇādhigamo 'pi vā //*

*...saṃsāranivṛttir api ālayavijñāne asati na yujyate. saṃsārasya hi karma kleśāś ca kāraṇaṃ tayoś ca kleśāḥ pradhānam. tathā hi kleśādhipatyatvāt karma punar bhavākṣepasamarthaṃ bhavati nānyathā. tathā ākṣiptapunarbhavam api karmakleśādhipatyād eva punar bhavo bhavati nānyathā. evaṃ ca kleśā eva saṃsārapravṛtteḥ pradhānatvān mūlam. atas teṣu prahīṇeṣu saṃsāro vinivartate nānyathā. na cālayavijñānam antareṇa tat prahāṇaṃ yujyate. kathaṃ punar na yujyate. sammukhībhūto vā kleśaḥ prahīyate. bījāvastho vā. tatra sammukhībhūtaḥ prahīyata iti. aniṣṭir eveyam. tatra prahāṇamārgasthāyināṃ vā bījāvastho 'pi naiva prahīyate. na hi pratipakṣāt tadānīṃ kiṃ cid anyad abhyupagamyate. yatra kleśabījaṃ vyavasthitaṃ tat pratipakṣeṇa prahīyate. atha pratipakṣacitta eva kleśabījānuśakta iṣyate. na hi tat kleśabījānuśaktam eva tat pratipakṣo bhavitum arhati. na cāprahīṇakleśabījānāṃ saṃsāranivṛttiḥ sambhavati. tasmād avaśyam ālayavijñānaṃ tad anyavijñānasahabhūmiḥ kleśopakleśair bhavyate svabījapuṣṭyādānata ity abhyupeyam. ye punaś cittata eva saṃtatipariṇāmaviśeṣād yathābalaṃ vāsanāvṛttilābhe sati kleśopakleśāḥ pravartante teṣāṃ cālayavijñānavyavasthitaṃ bījaṃ tat sahabhuvā kleśapratipakṣamārgeṇāpanīyate. tasmiṅś cāpanīte na punas tenāśrayeṇa kleśānām utpattir iti sopadhiśeṣo nirvāṇadhātuḥ prāpyate. pūrvakarmākṣiptajanmanirodhe ca tato 'nyajanmāpratisaṃdhānān nirupadhiśeṣo nirvāṇadhātuḥ. na hi karma vidyamānam api kleśeṣu prahīṇeṣu sahakārikāraṇābhāvāt punar bhavam abhinirvartayituṃ samartham. evam ālayavijñāne sati saṃsārapravṛttir nivṛttiś ca. nānyathety avaśyaṃ cakṣurādivijñānavyatiriktam ālayavijñānam. tad eva ca sarvadharmabījānugataṃ na cakṣurādivijñānam ity abhyupagantavyam. vistaravicāras tu pañcaskandha-*

*kopanibandhād veditavyaḥ.* (A.K. Chatterjee, 1971, pp.61.1-2, 61.23-62.7)

On *kārikās* 29 & 30: *...āśrayasya parāvṛttir iti. āśrayo 'tra sarvabījakaṃ ālayavijñānam. tasya parāvṛttir yā dauṣṭhulya-vipākadvayavāsanābhāvena nivṛttau satyāṃ karmaṇyatādharma-kāyādvayajñānabhāvena parāvṛttiḥ. sā punar āśrayaparāvṛttiḥ kasya prahāṇāt prāpyate. ata āha. dvidhā dauṣṭhulyahānitaḥ dvidheti kleśāvaraṇadauṣṭhulyaṃ jñeyāvaraṇadauṣṭhulyaṃ ca. dauṣṭhulyam āśrayasyākarmaṇyatā. tat punaḥ kleśajñeyāvaraṇayor bījam. sā punar āśrayaparāvṛttiḥ śrāvakādigatadauṣṭhulyahānitaś ca prāpyate. yad āha. vimuktikāya iti. bodhisattvagatadauṣṭhulya-hānitaś ca prāpyate. yad āha. dharmākhyo 'pi mahāmuner iti dvidhā āvaraṇabhedena sottarā niruttarā ca āśrayaparāvṛttir uktā. atra gāthā —*

*jñeyam ādānavijñānaṃ dvayāvaraṇalakṣaṇam /*
*sarvabījaṃ kleśabījaṃ bandhas tatra dvayor dvayoḥ //*

*iti. śrāvakabodhisattvayoḥ. ādyasya kleśabījam itarasya dvayā-varaṇabījaṃ tad udghātāt sarvajñatāvāptir bhavatīti. sa evānāsravo dhātur iti sa evāśrayaparāvṛttirūpaḥ. anāsravo dhātur ity ucyate. nirdauṣṭhulyatvāt sa tv āsravavigata ity anāsravaḥ. āryadharma-hetutvād dhātuh. hetv artho hy atra dhātuśabdaḥ. acintyas tarkagocaratvāt. pratyātmavedyatvāt. dṛṣṭāntābhāvāc ca. kuśalo viśuddhālambanatvāt kṣematvāt anāsravadharmamayatvāc ca. dhruvo nityatvāt. akṣayatayā. sukho nityatvād eva yad nityaṃ tad duḥkham ayaṃ ca nitya iti. asmāt sukhaḥ. kleśāvaraṇaprahāṇāt śrāvakāṇāṃ vimuktikāyaḥ. sa evāśrayaparāvṛttilakṣaṇo dharmākhyo 'py ucyate. mahāmuner bhūmipāramitādibhāvanayā kleśajñeyāvaraṇa-prahāṇāt. āśrayaparāvṛttisamudāgamāt. mahāmuner dharmakāya ity ucyate. saṃsāraparityāgāt yad anupasaṃkleśatvāt sarvadharma-vidhutvalābhataś ca dharmakāya ity ucyate. mahāmuner iti paramamauneyayogāt buddho bhagavān mahāmunir iti. (Ibid.,* p.69.3.23)

Jikido Takasaki (pp.40-45) discusses this issue on the basis of the *Mahāyānasūtrālaṃkāra* IX. To quote his conclusion (p.43) where he briefly mentions a variety in usage of the term *āśraya*:

1. *āśraya* (in pl.) = *cakṣurvijñāna*, etc.
2. *āśraya* = *bīja* = *ālayavijñāna* (whose *parāvṛtti*, i.e. *anyathāpti* is *buddhatva*), and

3. *āśraya = āśrayaparāvṛtti = tathāgatānāṃ parivṛtti = sarvatragāśraya = amalāśraya = anāsravadhātu = dharmakāya = buddhatva = āryagotra = svadhātu.*

(17) Cf. *AK*, V, 25-26 and *AKB, AKV* thereon for the views of the four Sarvāstivādins and their Sautrāntika polemic.

(18) See Padmanabh S. Jaini, pp. 238-239. The Sautrāntika defines *prāpti* as *bhāvāntara* (AKB, p.212.7). Vide *AKB* and *AKV* on *AK*, II.36.

(19) Cf. *AKB* on *AK*, II.36 and III.41.

(20) Cf. *AKB*, p.217.5: *ko'yaṃ pariṇāmo nāma. saṃtater anyathātvam.*

(21) Cf. *AKB*, p.217.3-4: *kiṃ punar idaṃ bījaṃ nāma. yan nāmarūpaṃ phalotpatau samarthaṃ sākṣāt pāramparyeṇa vā; saṃtati-pariṇāmaviśeṣāt.*

For Saṃghabhadra's criticism of *bīja-śakti*, cf. *AKV*, p.218. 16-23: *sa eva ca śaktiviśeṣalakṣaṇaṃ bījabhāvaṃ ācāryeṇa vyavasthāpitāṃ dūṣayati. kim ayaṃ śaktiviśeṣaś cittād arthāntaram. utānarthāntaram. kiṃ cātaḥ. arthāntaraṃ cet, prāptir astīti, saṃjñāmātre tu vivādaḥ. anarthāntaraṃ cet. nanv akuśalaṃ kuśalasya bījam abhyupagataṃ bhavati, akuśalasya ca kuśalam. ko hi nāmauṣṇy asya tejeso 'narthāntaratve satyauṣṇyam eva dāhakamadhyavasyen na tejaḥ. kuśalabījaṃ hy akuśale cetasya-vyākṛte vā vartate. evam akuśalabījaṃ kuśale cetasyavyākṛte vā vartate. tathaiva cāvyākṛtabījam api kuśale cākuśale ca vartate. sāśravabījaṃ cānāsrave, anāsravabhījaṃ ca sāsrave cetasi vartate — iti sāṃkaryadoṣaḥ prasajyata iti.*

For the Sautrāntika reply, cf. *ibid.*, pp.218.24- 219.32: *atra vayaṃ brumaḥ. anarthāntarabhāve sāṃkaryadoṣo bhavet. tat tu bījaṃ na cittād arthāntaraṃ vaktavyam, nāpy anarthāntaram; upādāyaprajñaptirūpatvāt. athāpy anarthāntarabhāvaḥ. tathāpy adoṣaḥ. kuśalena hi cittenotpannena svajātīye 'nyajātīye vā svasaṃtānacitte bījam ādhīyeta. tataḥ kāraṇaviśeṣāt kāryaviśeṣa iti viśiṣṭam. tena tac cittam utpadyeta. tad viśiṣṭaṃ cittaṃ kuśalabījakāryakriyāyāṃ samartham utpadyeta. evam akuśalenāpi svajātīye 'nyajātīye vā svasaṃtānacitte bītam ādhīyeta. tac ca tena viśiṣṭam akuśalabījakāryakriyāyāṃ samartham utpadyeta. evam avyākṛtenāpi cittena svajātīye anyajātīye vā svasaṃtānacitte bījam ādhīyeta. tac cāpi tena viśiṣṭam avyākṛtakāryakriyāyāṃ samartham utpadyeta. sāsraveṇāpy anāsrave citte bījam ādhīyeta. anāsraveṇāpi sāsrave. ity evam anyonyabījādhāyakam anyonyajanakaṃ ca cittaṃ cittāntarād utpadyamānam anyonyavāsyavāsakatvena pravartate. na ca kuśale nākuśale citte śaktiviśeṣa āhita iti tad akuśalaṃ kuśalatām āpadyate. kuśalaṃ vā tad akuśalatām. śaktiviśeṣamātratvāt. śaktibījaṃ vāsanety eko 'yam arthaḥ evam akuśalādivāsanāpi vaktavyā. yāvat sāsraveṇānāsrave śaktiviśeṣādhane 'pi, anāsraveṇāpi sāsrave śaktiviśeṣādhāne. na tat sāsravam anāsravaṃ sampadyate, anāsravaṃ vā sāsravam iti. bhavatāṃ api vaibhāṣikānām idaṃ cintyate. yadā sāsravacittasamantaram anāsravam anāsravacittasamantaram vā sāsravacittam utpadyate. tadā kiṃ pūrvakaḥ sāsravakalāpo 'nāsravakalāpo vā śaktimān samanatarapratyayādibhāvenottarakalāpotpatau. utāśaktimān. kiṃ cātaḥ. yady aśktimān, samanantarapratyayādibhāvo 'py asya hīyeta. atha śaktimān, sā śaktiḥ kiṃ sāsrave cetasi sāsrava, āhosvidanāsravā. tac citaṃ sāsravasyānāsrava sya ca cittāntarasya samanantarapratyayādibhāvaṃ kurvat kiṃ yayaiva śaktyā sāsravasya samanan tarapratyayādibhāvaṃ kuryāt tayaivānāsravasya. yadi ca tayaiva, kathaṃ śaktikāryasāṃkaryaṃ na bhavet. athānyayā śaktyā sāsravasya, anyayānāsravasya samanantarapratyayādibhāvaṃ kuryāt. katham anayor ekatra śaktyos tasmāc cittād ananyayor bhinnarūpatā bhinnakāryatā ca yujyate. yujyate cet. asmākam api cittād ananyāsāṃ śaktīnāṃ tatrāvasthānaṃ kāryabhedaś ca bhaviṣyati. evam anāsravasyāpi cittasya sāsravānāsravacittasamananantarapratyayādibhāvena sambhavataḥ. tathaiva śaktyor bhinnarūpatā kāryabhedaś ca vaktavyaḥ. tena yad uktam. nanv akuśalaṃ kuśalasya bījam abhyupgataṃ bhavatītyādi, tad ayuktam. na hi kuśalāhitena śaktiviśeṣeṇa viśiṣṭaṃ samartham akuśalam akuśalabījakāryaṃ karoti. kiṃ tarhi. kuśalabījakāryam eva karoti. svāhitena tu śaktiviśeṣeṇa tad akuśalaṃ svabījakāryaṃ karoti. tat katham idam ucyate. kuśalasyākuśalaṃ na bhavatīti. brūyas tvam. akuśalacitte tat kuśalabījam āhitaṃ kim akuśalaṃ na bhavatīti. na bhavanto bījārthaṃ jānate. kuśalena cittena nirudhyamānena tathā śaktiviśiṣṭam akuśalam cittaṃ janyeta. yathā tac cittaṃ svotpattiyogyaṃ bhaviṣyati sākṣāt pāramparyeṇa veti śaktiviśeṣa eva bījam. na bījaṃ nāma kiñcid asti. prajñaptisattvāt. ata eva prāpty aprāptī prajñaptisatyāv ucyete. dravyasatyāv eva tu vaibhāṣikā varṇayanti.*

Also see *AD*, 199 and *ADV* thereon; *Encyclopedia of Buddhism*, Vol. III, pp. 105-108; *AKV*, p. 990.22: *bījaṃ sāmarthyaṃ cetaso gotram.*

(22) Cf. *AKB*, p. 217. 3-4: *kiṃ punar idaṃ bījaṃ nāma. yan nāmarūpaṃ phalotpattau samarthaṃ sākṣāt pāramparyeṇa vā. saṃtatipariṇāmaviśeṣāt.*

(23) Cf. *AKV*, p. 217.15-17: *kiṃ punar idaṃ bījaṃ nāmeti dravyāsaṃkayā pṛcchati. yan nāmarūpaṃ phalotpattau samartham. yat pañcaskandhātmakaṃ rūpaṃ phalotpattisamartham. sākṣāt anantaram. pāramparyeṇa dūrataḥ.*

(24) L. Schmithausen (1987).

(25) Cf. *AK*, II. 35-36, *AKB* and *AKV* thereon; *AD*, 129-134 and *ADV* thereon.

(26) Cf. *AKV*, (on *AK*, IV. 65), p. 674.16-675.16: *sañcetanīyasūtre vacanād iti. "sañcetanīyaṃ karma kṛtvopacitya narakesūpapadyate. kathaṃ ca bhikṣavaḥ sañcetanīyaṃ karma kṛtaṃ bhavaty upacitam. iha bhikṣava ekatyaḥ sañcitya trividhaṃ kāyena karma karoty upacinoti, caturvidhaṃ vācā, trividhaṃ manasā" iti vistareṇoktvāha — "kathaṃ bhikṣavas trividhaṃ manasā sañcetanīyaṃ karma kṛtaṃ bhavaty upacitam. yathāpīhaikatyo 'bhidhyālur bhavati vyāpannacitto yāvan mithyādṛṣṭiḥ. khalu bhikṣava ihaikatyo bhavati viparītadarśī " iti vistaraḥ. na cānyad abhidhyādivyatiriktaṃ tatra manaskarmoktam iti abhidhyādaya eva manaskarmeti. dārṣṭāntikāḥ sautrāntikaviśeṣā ity arthaḥ.*

*evaṃ tu sati karmakleśayor aikyaṃ syād iti. abhidhyāvyāpādamithyādṛṣṭayaḥ kleśāḥ, ta eva karmeti tad aikyaṃ syāt. naitad asti. kaścit kleśo 'pi karma syād iti. "cetanā karma cetayitvā ca" iti vacanāt. yady evaṃ sañcetanīyaṃ sūtraṃ kathaṃ nīyate. ity āha - sūtre tv iti vistaraḥ. sūtre tu cetanāyās tanmukhenābhidhyādimukhena pravṛttes tair abhidhyādibhis tāṃ cetanāṃ darśayati. "abhidhyāluḥ khalu bhikṣavo bhavati" iti vistareṇa. anyathā "cetanāmataṃ bhikṣavaḥ karma vadāmi cetayitvā ca" ity etad virudhyate. karmakleśayoś caikye abhidharmavirodhaḥ syāt.*

(27) "Unlike healthy attitudes [*kuśalacitta*] which are rooted in detached love and knowledge, unhealthy attitudes

[*akuśalacitta*] are incompatible with spiritual development, because their structural pattern is infected by various effective instabilities such as cupidity (*lobha*), antipathy (*dveṣa*, Pali *dosa*), and delusion-bewilderment *(moha)*" – Guenther, p.88. Cf. *AKB* on *AK*, V. 20c and *Ibid.*, on *AK*, IV. 65: *akarmasvabhāvam apy asti trividhaṃ manoduścaritaṃ cetanārthāntarabhūtam — abhidhyā, vyāpādaḥ, mithyādṛṣṭiś ca.*

(28) Cf. *AK*, IV. 77d and *AKB* thereon:

*.... abhidhyā tu parasvaviṣamaspṛhā //*

*'aho bata yat pareṣāṃ tan mama syāt' iti parasv ebhyo yā viṣameṇānyāyena spṛhā svikāraṇecchā balād vā copāyād vā sā 'bhidhyā karmapathaḥ. sarvaiva kāmāvacarī tṛṣṇā abhidhyety apare. tathā nivaraṇādhikāre kāmacchandam adhikṛtyoktaṃ sūtre — "so 'bhidhyāṃ loke prahāya" ity evam ādi. yady api sarvābhidhyā na tu sarvā karmapathaḥ; audārikaduścarita-saṃgrahādity apare. mā bhūccakravartināṃ uttarakaurvāṇāṃ cābhidhyā karmapatha iti.*

*Arthaviniścayasūtra*, p. 38-6-8: *tatrābhidhyā katamā. para-dravyasvīkāraṇecchā abhidhyā. "yānyasya dravyāṇi tāni mama syu"r iti. iyam ucyate 'bhidhyā; Aṭṭhasālinī*, III. 545 (p. 20 25-11); *Encyclopedia of Buddhism*, Vol. I, pp. 90-92, on *abhijjhā*.

(29) "Cupidity *(lobha)* makes the individual chase after the sensuous and sensual objects which he believes will satisfy his craving, but to the same extent that he obtains the desired objects, his craving also increases so that he is driven relentlessly from one object to the other, to let it go almost the same moment he grasped it. His attachment to the objects of worldliness are compared with fresh meat put into a heated vessel, a separation of the two not being possible, or since there is no check on his craving, no sense of renunciation, attachment spreads like an oil-ointment, all over the body. Craving, like a stream that increases continuously with its progress and turbulently rushes down to the ocean, carries the individual along with it into the abyss of low existence *(apāya)*". - Guenther, pp. 90-91. Also cf. *Aṭṭhasālinī*, III.544 (pp. 201.27- 202.4)

(30) Cf. *AK*, IV.78a and *AKB* there on: *vyāpādaḥ sattvavidveṣaḥ, sattveṣu vidveṣo vyāpādaḥ parapīḍākārapravṛttaḥ;*

*Arthaviniścayasūtra*, p. 38.9-11: *tatra vyāpādaḥ parajīvitavyaparopaṇāvacchedanapī- ḍādicintanam. ayam ucyate vyāpādaḥ.*

(31) *Pāli dosa*. "When unhealthy attitudes are grounded in antipathy *(dosa)*, the general mood is one of sullenness *(domanassa)* and one is easily shocked at everything, because one sees everywhere something offensive, distasteful, and contrary to one's principles (which after all are not much worth) *(patigha)*; therefore one constantly selects the unpleasant side of life. In their overt forms such attitudes are marked by hatred and malevolence. A person whose attitude is grounded in antipathy poisons the whole atmosphere with his maliciousness and at the same time undermines his own position. Wherever and whenever he finds a chance he rouses enmity. This malevolence also finds its expression in the venomous remarks he is apt to make at any moment. His words lack courtesy and smoothness, and his speech is abrupt, for "at the moment of anger there is no coherent speech". Worst of all such a person is unable to find contentedness." - Guenther, p.92.

(32) Cf. *AK*, IV.78c and *AKB* thereon: *mithyādṛṣṭiḥ, . . . / / śubhe cāśubhe ca karmaṇi yā nāstīti dṛṣṭiḥ sā mithyādṛṣṭiḥ. tad yathā — "nāsti dattam, nāstīṣṭam, nāsti hutam, nāsti sucaritam, nāsti duścaritam ity evam ādi yāvan na santi loke 'rhantaḥ" iti. saiṣā sākalyena karmaphalāryāpavādikā mithyādṛṣṭir bhavati.*

(33) Cf. *AKB*, p. 191-8: *moho nāmāvidyā, ajñānam asamprakhyānam.*

(34) *Kuśalacitta* is *kuśalamūla*. "That which lends itself to and assists articulation is known as 'healthy roots' *(kuśalamūla)*, because any function or any event which is assisted by it, is strong and healthy, "just as trees which have firm roots are strong and well grounded". These 'roots' which support and nourish a man's attitude are non-cupidity, non-antipathy, and non-delusion. This negative expression does not mean mere absence of cupidity, antipathy, and delusion, but attempts to convey the meaning of something absolutely positive, which in the final analysis is beyond affirmation and negation." — Guenther, p. 79. Cf. *AKB*, p. 674.13: *iṣṭaṃ kuśalaṃ kāyavāṅgamanaskarma - anabhidhyā 'vyāpāda samyagdṛṣṭayaś ca.*

(35) Pali *anabhijjhā*. "The absence of covetousness *(anabhijjhā)* together with good-will *(avyāpāda)*, right attention *(sammāsati)* and right concentration *(sammāsamādhi)* are called collectively the four bases of the Dhamma *(cattāri dhammapadāni...)*... In this context, *dhamma* should be taken to stand for moral righteousness rather than doctrine, for the factors constituting it are the opposites of the evil roots of greed *(lobha)*, hate *(dosa)* and delusion *(moha)*." -*Encyclopedia of Buddhism*, Vol. I, p. 92.

(36) "AVYĀPĀDA, the absence of malevolence which is both a latent tendency *(anusaya)* and a hindrance *(nīvaraṇa)*. The mere absence of ill-will, however, does not do full justice to the acquired meaning of this type of 'hatelessness', which is loving kindness *(mettā)*. As such, it is one of the three kinds of good thought *(kusala-vitakka)*, of good intention *(kusala-saṅkappa)* and of good disposition *(kusala-dhātu)*, namely, the thought, intention, perception and disposition of renunciation *(nekkhamma)*, of good-will *(avyāpāda)* and of harmlessness *(avihiṃsā)*.

"It is, moreover, one of the four characteristics of the Buddha's teaching *(cattāri dhammapadāni...)* which are reckoned as ancient, of long standing, as traditional, primeval, pure and unadulterated now as then, not confounded nor despised by discerning *samaṇas* and *brāhmaṇas*, namely, the absence of coveting *(anabhijjhā)*, the absence of ill-will *(avyāpāda)*, right mindfullness *(sammā-sati)* and right concentration *(sammāsamādhi)*...

"Frequently, the absence of ill-will *(avyāpāda)* is met in its synonyms, the absence of hate *(adosa)* and loving kindness *(mettā)*, although subtle differences may be observed. The absence of hate *(abosa)* is a root of good *(kulsala-mūla)* and has, therefore, more general characteristics and applications with a distinctly positive meaning of loving kindness *(mettā)*. It is due to this root that ill-feeling *(vyāpāda)* is absent, and good-will finds a place in the tenfold wholesome course of action *(kusala-kamma-patha)*, among the final triad, the absence of lust *(anabhijjhā)*, of ill-will *(avyāpāda)* and of wrong views, i.e., right views *(sammā-diṭṭhi)*, representing wholesome mental activity". — *Encyclopedia of Buddhism*, Vol. II, p. 467.

(37) Cf. *Arthaviniścayasūtra*, p.35.4-8: *tatra bhikṣavaḥ samyagdṛṣṭiḥ katamā. asty ayaṃ lokaḥ. asti paralokaḥ. asti mātā. asti pitā. asti dattam. asti hutam. asti iṣṭāniṣṭasukṛtaduṣkṛtānāṃ karmaṇāṃ phalavipākaḥ. santi loke samyaggatāḥ, samyak- pratipannā iti. iyaṃ bhikṣavaḥ samyagdṛṣṭiḥ. tad viparītā mithyādṛṣṭiḥ*. Also See Guenther, pp. 69-74.

(38) "Non-cupidity *(alobha)* has the characteristic of not being desirous for an object and not being attached to it, to the same extent that water will not cling to the leaves of a lotus flower. Its function is not caring for possession, to the extent that a man who has renounced worldliness does not care for the acquisition of possession. Its basis is the fact that it does not remain stuck, just as a man who has fallen into a dirty pit does not allow wallow in the dirt. It is the effective remedy against avarice and hence is the foundation and help of liberality." - Guenther, p.79. Cf. *Aṭṭhasālinī*, III. 241 (pp. 104.22 ff.).

(39) "Non-antipathy *(adveṣa*, Pāli *adosa)* has as its characteristic non-churlishness and non-obstructiveness and is like a helpful friend. Its function is to remove ill-will and worries and hence is soothing like sandal paste. Its basis is gentleness and pleasantness, and therefore is likened to the splendour of the full moom. It is a potent remedy against bad manners and unethical behaviour and a solid foundation of ethics and manners." - Guenther, p.81. Cf. *Aṭṭhasālinī, ibid.*

(40) "Non-delusion non-bewilderment *(amoha)* is essentially identical with analytical appreciative understanding...It is a sustaining power for the development of all that is healthy and therefore indispensable for the actual practice of all that leads to the goal of liberation."-Guenther, p.82. Cf. *Aṭṭhasālinī, ibid.*

(41) Cf. *AKB*, p.217.5: *ko 'yaṃ pariṇāmo nāma. saṃtater anyathātvam.*

(42) Compare and contrast *svasaṃtānapatita* of the Vaibhāṣikas (*AK*, II. 36c) and *saṃtater anyathātva* of the Sautrāntikas *(AKB*, p.217.5 on the same *kārikā*).

(43) Takasaki, pp. 32-33.

(44) *Ibid.*, pp. 54-61.

(45) Cf. *Bodhicaryāvatāra*, IX. 1a: *imaṃ parikaraṃ sarvaṃ prajñārthaṃ hi munir jagau.*

(46) Cf. *Bodhicaryāvatāra-pañjikā*, p.198.14-16: *na ca śūnyatā bhāvād vyatiriktā, bhāvasyaiva tat svabhāvatvāt. anyathā śūnyatāyā bhāvād vyatireke dharmāṇām niḥsvabhāvatā na syāt. niḥsvabhāvatā tat svabhāva iti prasādhitaṃ prāk.*

(47) Cf. *yaḥ pratītyasamutpādaḥ śūnyatā saiva te matā/ bhāvaḥ svatantro nāstīti siṃhanādas tavātulaḥ//* quoted in *ibid.*, p. 198. 24-25.

(48) Cf. *yathākṣepaṃ kramād vṛddhaḥ saṃtānaḥ kleśakarmabhiḥ/ paralokaṃ punar yātīty anādi bhavacakram// sa pratītyasamutpādo dvādaśāṅgas trikāṇḍakaḥ/* quoted in *ibid.*, p. 187. 6-8.

(49) Cf. *supra*, fns. 46 and 47.

(50) Cf. *Bodhicaryāvatāra*, IX. 152: *evaṃ śūnyeṣu dharmeṣu kiṃ labdhaṃ kiṃ hṛtaṃ bhavet/ satkṛtaḥ paribhūto vā kena kaḥ sambhaviṣyati//*

(51) Cf. *ibid.*, 56b: *śūnyatā duḥkhaśamanī tataḥ jāyate bhayam//*

(52) *Bodhicaryāvatāra-pañjikā*, p. 168.15.

(53) Cf. *ibid.*, p. 173.27-28: *na ca bhāvābhāvayor uktakrameṇa asatve pratipādite tad ubhayasaṃkirṇātmatā sambhavati ubhayapratiṣedhasvabhāvatā vā, bhāvavikalpasyaiva sakalavikalpanibandhanatvāt. tasmin nirākṛte sarva eva amī ekaprahāreṇa nirastā bhavantīti.* Also cf. p.174.11- 12: *na sann āsanna sad asan na cāpy anubhayātmakam/ catuṣkoṭivinirmuktaṃ tattvaṃ mādhyamikā viduḥ //*; *RGV*, I.10-12 and Asaṅga's commentary thereon.

(54) See H. S. Prasad (1989) and A.K. Chatterjee (1975).

(55) See *supra*, fn. 16.

(56) Obermiller (1931), pp. 99, 101, 102.

(57) "As the Dharmakāya, Buddha fully realised his identity with the Absolute (dharmatā, śūnyatā) and unity (samatā) with all beings. It is the oneness with the Absolute that enables Buddha to intuit the Truth, which it is his sacred function to reveal to phenomenal beings. This is the fountain-source of his implicit strength which he concretises in the finite sphere." - T.R.V. Murti, p. 284.

"The Sanskrit name for the cosmical Body is dharmakāya. The word Kāya is derived from the verb-root *ci-* to collect, accumulate. (The Cosmical Body) is thus regarded as the accumulation, the aggregate of all the elements, uninfluenced (by defiling agencies). The *Satyadvaya-vibhaṅga* accordingly says: The cosmical Body is thus called, being the aggregate of all the elements. The substratum of all the unthinkable virtues, and the essence of all things, the nature of which agrees with logic."- Buston's *History of Buddhism*, Vol. I, pp.128-9 (quoted in Murti, p.285, fn.4).

(58) Vol. III, p.372.

(59) Obermiller (1931), p.95. Also cf. *Laṅkāvatārasūtra*, pp.90.28-91.10: .....*yadi hi mahāmate ālayavijñānasaṃśabditas tathāgatagarbho 'tra na syād iti asati mahāmate tathāgatagarbhe ālayavijñānasaṃśabdite na pravṛttir na nivṛttiḥ syāt. bhavati ca mahāmate pravṛttir nivṛttiś ca bālaryāṇām. svapratyātmāryagatidṛṣṭadharmasukhavihāreṇa ca viharanti yogino 'nikṣiptadhurā duṣprativedhaś ca. mahāmate ayaṃ tathāgatagarbhālayavijñānagocaraḥ sarvaśrāvakapratyekabuddhatīrthyavitarkadarśanānāṃ prakṛtipariśuddho 'pi san aśuddha ivāgantukleśopakliṣṭatayā teṣām ābhāti na tu tathāgatānām. tathāgatānāṃ punar mahāmate karatalāmalakavat pratyakṣagocaro bhavati. etad eva mahāmate mayā śrīmālāṃ devīm adhikṛtya deśanāpāṭhe anyāṃś ca sūkṣmanipuṇaviśuddhabuddhīn bodhisattvānadhiṣṭhāya tathāgatagarbha ālayavijñānasaṃśabditaḥ saptabhir vijñānaiḥ saha pravṛtty abhiniviṣṭānāṃ śrāvakāṇāṃ dharmanairātmyapradarśanārthaṃ śrīmālāṃ devīm adhiṣṭhāya tathāgataviṣayo deśito na śrāvakapratyekabuddhānyatīrthakaratarkaviṣayo 'nyatra mahāmate tathāgataviṣaya eva tathāgatagarbha ālayavijñānaviṣayas tvat sadṛśānāṃ ca sūkṣmanipuṇamatibuddhiprabhedakānāṃ bodhisattvānāṃ mahāsattvānām arthapratiśaraṇānāṃ no tu yathārutadeśanāpāṭhābhiniviṣṭānāṃ sarvānyatīrthyaśrāvakapratyekabuddhānām. tasmāt tarhi mahāmate tvayā anyaiś ca bodhisattvair mahāsattvaiḥ sarvatathāgataviṣaye 'smins tathāgatagarbhālayavijñānaparijñāne yogaḥ karaṇiyaḥ. na śrutamātrasantuṣṭair bhavitavyam.*

On *tathāgatagarbha* and *ālayavijñāna*, see Alex Wayman (1990) pp. 52- 55.

(60) Cf. The eighteen phenomenal elements of existence in the

Abhidharma. In Mahāyāna, they lack independent ontological status. Their existence is epistemic only but their appearances are grounded in the ultimate essence *(gotra)*.

(61) The underlying substance and root cause of the *dharmas*; identified with the Absolute. Its "Other synonyms are 'non-duality' 'the realm of non- discrimination', 'non-production', 'the true nature of Dharma', 'inexpressible', 'the unconditioned', 'the unimpeded' *(sishprapañca)*, 'the actual fact' *(tattva)*, 'that which really is' *(yathābhūta)*, 'the truth' *(satya)*, 'the true reality' *(yathābhūta)*, 'Nirvāṇa', 'cessation', 'Buddhahood', and also 'wisdom', 'enlightenment', 'the cognition which one must realize within oneself', the Dharmabody, the Buddha, etc."—Conze, p.226.

Cf. *RGV*, p.10.4: *dharmadhātum iti svadharmatāprakṛtinirviśiṣṭatathāgatagarbham;*

*Madhyāntavibhāgaśāstra*, pp.38.21- 39.2: *tathatā bhūtakoṭiś cā 'nimittaṃ paramārthatā / dharmadhātuś ca paryāyāḥ śūnyatāyāḥ samāsataḥ //15//*

*iti....tad yathā - advayatā, avikalpadhātu, dharmatā, anabhilapyatā, anirodhaḥ, asaṃskṛtaṃ nirvāṇadi;* p.39.9: *āryadharmahetutvāt dharmadhātuḥ;* p. 141.11- 14: ......*dharmadhātau tridhā punaḥ //15b// aśuddhā 'śuddhaśuddā ca viśuddhā ca yathā 'rhataḥ /16a/*

*tatrā 'śuddhā 'vasthā hetv avasthām upādaya yāvat prayogāt; aśuddhaśuddhā 'vasthā śaikṣāṇām; viśuddhā 'vasthā 'śaikṣāṇām;*

p. 165.7.18: *dharmadhātuvinirmukto yasmāt dharmo na vidyate //19b// sāmānyalakṣaṇantasmāt sa ca tatrā 'viparyayaḥ /20a/ na hi dharmanairātmyena vinā kaścid dharmo vidyate. tasmād dharmadhātuḥ sarvadharmāṇāṃ sāmānyam lakṣaṇam iti yad evaṃ jñānam ayaṃ sāmānyalakṣaṇe 'viparyāsaḥ.*

*viparyastamanaskārā 'vihāniparihāṇitaḥ //20b//*

*tad aśuddhir viśuddhiś ca sa ca tatrā 'viparyayaḥ /21a/ viparyastamanaskārā 'prahāṇantasya dharmadhātor aviśuddhiḥ, tat prahāṇaṃ viśuddhir iti yad evaṃ jñānam ayam aviśuddhau viśuddhau cā 'viparyāso yathākramam.*

*dharmadhātor viśuddhatvāt prakṛtyā vyomavat punaḥ //21b//*

*dvasyāgantukatvaṃ hi sa ca tatrā 'viparyayaḥ* /22a/ *dharmadhātoḥ punar ākāśavat prakṛtiviśuddhatvād dvayam apy etad āgantukam - aviśuddhir viśuddhiś ca paścād iti yad evaṃ jñānam ayam āgantukatve 'viparyāsaḥ.*

(62) Its synonyms are *buddhatva, buddhabhāva, buddhasvabhāva,* etc. "When impermanence *(anityatā)* is overcome, the immutable state of *Buddhatā* results. Thus to the Buddhists the true state of reality is the state without any specific nature *(mādhyamika).* When this view is negatively expressed it indicates the true negation, the void *(śūnya).* But, positively it is called *Buddhatā, Dharmadhātu, Dharmakāya, Buddhasvabhāva, Tathāgatagarbha, Tathatā,* etc. As void *(śūnya)* it is not nothingness but the unconditioned. This state of Buddha-nature, unlimited in time and in space, is attainable by man, is the great message of Buddhism to the suffering humanity". - *Encyclopedia of Buddhism,* Vol.III, p.442. For the eight qualities of *buddhatva* see *RGV,* I.4-8 and *vṛtti* thereon.

Cf. *Laṅkāvatārasūtra,* p.57.22-29: *punar api mahāmatir āha — deśayatu me bhagavān buddhānāṃ bhagavatāṃ kathaṃ bhagavān buddhānāṃ buddhatā bhavati. bhagavān āha — dharmapudgalanairātmyāvabodhān mahāmate āvaraṇadvayaparijñānāvabodhāc ca cyutidvayādhigamāt kleśadvayaprahāṇāc ca mahāmate buddhānāṃ bhagavatāṃ buddhatā bhavati. eteṣām eva mahāmate dharmāṇām adhigamāc chrāvakapratyekabuddhasambuddhatā bhavati. ata etasmān mahāmate ekayānaṃ deśayāmi.*

*tatredam ucyate — nairātmyasya dvayaṃ kleśas tathaivāvaraṇadvayam/ acintyapariṇāminyāś cyuter lābhāt tathāgatah//*

(63) Here are some of the significant passages on *tathāgatagarbha* from Takasaki :

P. 22: The *tathāgatagarbha* is in a concrete way, a name for *'sattvadhātu',* the multitude of the living beings. This *'sattvadhātu',* or *'sattvarāśi'* (in other words, *sarvasattvāḥ, sarva-dehinaḥ,* all living beings) is, according to the text, called *'tathāgatagarbhaḥ',* those who have the Matrix of the *Tathāgata,* just because 1) the Wisdom of the Buddha penetrates it, 2) it is by nature identical with purity, i.e. the Absolute, and 3) it is the *'gotra',* through which the result, i.e. *'ratnatraya'* or, *par excellence,* the Tathāgata makes its appearance. [*RGV,* I.27]

P. 25, fn.44: The word *tathāgatagarbha* is interpreted in the *Ratnagotravibhāga* in three ways, namely: 1) *tathāgatasya ime garbhāḥ sarvasattvāḥ*. [p.70.17]; 2) *tathāgatas tathataiṣāṃ garbhaḥ sarvasattvānām* [p.71.11]; and 3) *tathāgatadhātur eṣāṃ garbhaḥ sarvasattvānām* [p.72. 8-9]. They correspond to *dharmakāya, tathatā* and *tathāgatagotra*, respectively.

P. 286, fn. 140: *tathāgatasya ime garbhāḥ sarvasattvāḥ*. This is the first way of interpreting the term *tathāgatagarbha*, regarding this Bahuvrīhi compound as consisting of two words whose interrelation is the dependent determinitive (Tatpuruṣa). Here, '*garbha*' means 'interior' and hence the compound has the sense of 'one who is within the Tathāgata'. This meaning comes from the idea of '*antargama* of *buddhajñāna*', i.e. the penetration of the Absolute into everything from inside and this signifies the all-pervadingness of the Absolute.

P. 287, fn.151: *tathāgatas tathatā eṣāṃ garbhaḥ sarvasattvānām*. This is the second interpretation of the term *tathāgatagarbha*, in which the two words *tathāgata* and *garbha* are related appositionally to each other, i.e. *garbha* being *tathāgata*. Here the word *garbha* means 'essence', i.e. *tathatā* which is represented by *tathāgata*. Because of this identification with *tathatā*, *tathāgatagarbha* is called '*samalā tathatā*'. The difference, if there is any, between *tathāgata* and *tathāgatagarbha* is merely in their appearance, the former being '*śuddhim āgatā tathatā*', i.e. '*nirmalā tathatā* and the latter being '*samalā tathatā*. From this point, *tathāgatagarbha* is a special name for *tathatā* when it is hidden by (or covered with) *kleśas*.

P. 290, fn.170: *tathāgatadhātur eṣāṃ garbhaḥ sarvasattvānām*. This is the third interpretation of the term *tathāgatagarbha*, '*garbha*' here means inner essence *(dhātu)*, being the cause *(hetu)* from which the *Tathāgata* is arisen. This stands for the original sense of the term *tathāgatagarbha*.

Also see *Mahāyānasūtrālaṃkāra*, IX.37, and the commentary on it: *sarveṣām aviśiṣṭāpi tathatā śuddhim āgatā/ tathāgatatvaṃ tasmāc ca tad garbhāḥ sarvadehinaḥ// sarveṣāṃ nirviśiṣṭā tathatā tad viśuddhisvabhāvaś ca tathāgataḥ ataḥ sarve sattvās tathāgatagarbhā ity ucyate*; Ruegg (1977), pp. 287, 288 and fns. 23 and 32, and Wayman (1990).

(64) *Tathatā* is actually the non- qualificative mode of expressing the Absolute. But from transcendental and empirical points of view it is called pure *(nirmalā)* and impure *(samalā)* respectively. Cf. *RGV*, p.21.8-10: *tatra samalā tathatā yo dhātur avinirmuktakleśakośas tathāgatagarbha ity ucyate. nirmalā tathatā sa eva buddhabhūmāv āśrayaparivṛttilakṣaṇo yas tathāgata-dharmakāya ity ucyate;* I.28a: *sambuddhakāyaspharaṇāt tatha-tāvyatibhedataḥ;* p.27.7-8: *tathatāyām ananyathābhāvasva-bhāvatāṃ svalakṣaṇam ārabhyākāśasādharmyaṃ veditavyam;* and p.71.7-8: *yac cittam aparyantakleśaduḥkhadharmānugatam api prakṛtiprabhāsvaratayā vikārānudāhṛterataḥ kalyāṇasuvarṇavad ananyathābhāvārthena tathatety ucyate.*

*Laṅkāvatārasūtra*, 93.8.9: *yan nāmanimittayor atya-ntānupalabdhitā buddhipralayād anyonyānanubhūtapari-kalpitatvād eṣāṃ dharmāṇāṃ sā tathateti* ; *Madhyāntavibhāgaśāstra*, p.39.15-16: *ananyathā 'rthena tathateti avikārārthenety arthaḥ. tad eva pradarśanārtham āha nityaṃ tathaiveti kṛtvā nityaṃ sarvadā 'saṃskṛtatvān na vikriyata ity arthaḥ.*

(65) *Dharmatā* is used mainly for the underlying essence or principle of all *dharmas*. "There is a reality *(dharmatā)* that endures, it is the realm beyond the ken of discriminatiton *(vikalpa)*; it is the mind itself but free from the entanglements of speculation and imagination; it reveals itself through our empirical consciousness when our empirical consciousness goes beyond itself, that is, when it transcends dualism. *Dharmatā* or reality, then is no other than the supreme wisdom *āryajñāna* realised inwardly by and in oneself *(pratyātmā- dhigama)*. When this realisation comes to one, no proofs are now needed for the doctrine of "Mind-only" - Suzuki, pp. 275-76.

Cf. *Madhyāntavibhāgaśāstra*, p.106.1-9: *trividhaṃ rūpam. katham. parikalpitaṃ rūpaṃ vikalpitaṃ rūpaṃ dharmatārūpaṃ ca...dharmatārūpaṃ yo rūpasya pariniṣpannaḥ svabhāva iti. tad vikalpitarūpaparikalpitarūpavigatātmikā śūnyatā*. Also cf. *RGVV*, p.59. 11ff.

(66) Cf. *Madhyamakakārikāvṛtti (Prasannapadā)*, p.193.5-6: *śūnyāḥ sarvadharmā niḥsvabhāvayogena. nirnimittāḥ sarvadharmā nirnimittatām upādāya. apraṇihitāḥ sarvadharmā apraṇidhāna-yogena. prakṛtiprabhāsvarāḥ sarvadharmāḥ prajñāpāramitāpari-*

*śuddhyā*; also see *Madhyamakakārikā*, XV: *Svabhāvaparīkṣā* and *Vṛtti* on it.

(67) Here *śūnyatā* means *sarvadṛṣṭiśūnyatā* as well as *bāhyārtha-śūnyatā*. For classic studies, see T.R.V Murti and A.K. Chatterjee (1975).

(68) The Mahāyāna schools maintain *pudgala nairātmya* as well as *dharmanairātmya*. "The Mahāyāna systems... speak of the *pudgalanairātmya* — the denial of substance — as intended to pave the way for Absolutism. *Śūnyatā* is the unreality of the elements as well *(dharma-nairātmya)*". — Murti, p.50.

Cf. *Madhyāntavibhāgaśāstra*, p. 165.7-10: *dharmadhātuvinirmukto yasmāt dharmo na vidyate //19b// sāmānyalakṣaṇantasmāt sa ca tatrā 'viparyayaḥ /20a/ na hi dharmanairātmyena vinā kaścid dharmo vidyate. tasmād dharmadhātuḥ sarvadharmāṇāṃ sāmānyaṃ lakṣaṇam iti yad evaṃ jñānam ayam sāmānyalakṣaṇe 'viparyāsaḥ.*

*Laṅkāvatārasūtra*, p.57. 22-29: *punar api mahāmatir āha — deśayatu me bhagavān buddhāṇāṃ bhagavatāṃ kathaṃ bhagavān buddhāṇāṃ buddhatā bhavati. bhagavān āha — dharmapudgalanairātmyāvabodhān mahāmate āvaraṇadvayaparijñānāvabodhāc ca cyutidvayādhigamāt kleśadvayaprahāṇāc ca mahāmate buddhāṇāṃ bhagavatāṃ buddhatā bhavati. eteṣām eva mahāmate dharmāṇām adhigamāc chrāvakapratyekabuddhasambuddhatā bhavati. ata etasmān mahāmate ekayānaṃ deśayāmi. tatredam ucyate —*

*nairātmyasya dvayaṃ kleśās tathaivāvaraṇadvayam/*
*acintyapariṇāminyāś cyuter lābhāt tathāgataḥ//*

*Viṃśatikā, kā.* 10: *tathā pudgalanairātmyapraveśo hy anyathā punaḥ/ deśanā dharmanairātmyapraveśaḥ kalpitātmanā//* and commentary thereon.

(69) Cf. *yatra na kecit saṃskārās tad asaṃskṛtam /*
*yad asaṃskṛtaṃ tad āryāṇāṃ gotram /*
*samam tad gotram ākāśasamatayā /*
*nirviśeṣaṃ tad gotraṃ dharmaikarasatayā /*
*nityaṃ tad gotraṃ sadā dharmatathatayā /*

—Vimuktisena's *Vṛtti*, quoted in Ruegg (1977), n. 124.

See Conze (1967), pp. 228-31. The concept of *'samatā'* is derived from the cosmic principle immanent in all beings. The whole *tathāgatagarbha* theory, as found in the *Uttaratantra* (the *Ratnagotravibhāga)* and the *Śrīmālāsiṃhanāda-sūtra* (Alex Wayman, 1990), shows this pantheistic state of the Absolute. This realisation, says Asaṅga, is the source of social emotions, such as compassion toward fellow beings. He also discusses the process of change in one's attitude to work for the welfare of humanity.

Cf. *Mahāyānasūtrālaṃkāra,* XIV, 30, 31, 37-41 and the commentary thereon:

*dharmadhātoś ca samatāṃ pratividhya punas tadā /*

*sarvasattveṣu labhate sadātmasamacittatām //30//*

*nirātmatayāṃ duḥkhārthe kṛtye niḥpratikarmaṇi/*

*sattveṣu samacitto 'sau yathānye 'pi jinātmajāḥ //31//*

*dharmanairātmyena ca dharmasamatāṃ pratividhya sarvasattveṣu sadā ātmasamacittatāṃ pratilabhate. pañcavidhayā samatayā. nairātmyasamatayā duḥkhasamatayā svaparasaṃtāneṣu nairātmya-duḥkhatayor aviśeṣāt. kṛtyasamatayā svaparaduḥkhaprahāṇakāmatā-sāmānyāt. niṣpratikārasamatayā. ātman iva parataḥ pratikārāna-bhinandanāt. tad anyabodhisattvasamatayā ca yathā tair abhisamitaṃ tathābhisamayāt.*

(70) "The dual nature of Buddha, as one with the Absolute (Śūnya) and at once actively pursuing the welfare of beings, supplies the philosophical basis for the theological conception of the Trikāya of Buddha. The three bodies or aspects of Buddha are:

(1) The Dharma Kāya - The Cosmical body in his essential nature; it is one with the Absolute;

(2) Sambhogakāya - The body of bliss; and the

(3) Nirmāṇakāya - Assumed body.

As the Dharmakāya, Buddha fully realises his identity with the Absolute (dharmatā, śūnyatā) and unity (samatā) with all beings. It is the oneness with the Absolute that enables Buddha to intuit the Truth, which it is his sacred function to reveal to phenomenal beings. This is the fountain-source of his implicit strength which he concretises in the finite sphere. The Sambhoga Kāya is the concrete manifestation to himself (svasambhoga) and to the elect (parasambhoga) the power and splendour of god-head. In furtherance of the great resolve to succour all beings, Buddha incarnates himself from time to time in forms best calculated to achieve this end (nirmāṇakāya)." — Murti, pp.284-85.

Cf. *Mahāyānasūtrālaṃkāra*, pp. 47.3- 48.15:.....*trividhaḥ kāyo buddhānām. svābhāviko dharmakāya āśrayaparāvṛttilakṣaṇaḥ. sāmbhogiko yena parṣan maṇḍalaṣu dharmasambhogaṃ karoti. nairmāṇiko nirmāṇena sattvārthaṃ karoti.... tatra sāmbhogikaḥ sarvalokadhātuṣu parṣan maṇḍalabuddhakṣetranāmaśarīra-dharmasaṃyogakriyābhir bhinnaḥ.... svābhāvikaḥ sarvabuddhā-nāṃ samo nirviśiṣṭatayā. sūkṣmo durjñānatayā. tena sāmbhogikena kāyena sambaddhaḥ sambhoga vibhutve ca hetur yatheṣṭaṃ bhogadarśanāya.....nairmāṇikas tu kāyo buddhānām aprameyaprabhedaṃ buddhanirmāṇaṃ sāmbhogikaḥ svārtha-sampattilakṣaṇaḥ. nairamāṇikaḥ parārthasampattilakṣaṇaḥ. evaṃ dvayārthasampattir yathākramam dvayoḥ pratiṣṭhitā sāmbhogike ca kāye nairmāṇike ca* . . . .

(71) *Mahāyāna* and *ekayāna* are used synonymously. "But we must remember that the Ekayāna has really nothing to do with the number of Yānas though *eka* means "one"; *eka* in this case rather means "oneness", and Ekayāna is the designation of the doctrine teaching the transcendental oneness of things, by which all beings inclusive of the Hīnayānists and Mahāyānists are saved from bondage of existence". — Suzuki, p.359.

Therefore, *'ekayāna'* should not be taken in literal sense. The concept of *ekayāna* ensues from the highest Wisdom in which one identifies himself with the Absolute. The *Laṅkāvatārasūtra*, III. 1-2, emphasizes this point:

*na me yānaṃ mahāyānaṃ na ghoso na ca akṣarā /*
*na satyā na vimokṣā vai na nirābhāsagocaram //1//*
*kiṃ tu yānaṃ mahāyānaṃ samādhivaśavartitā /*
*kāyo manomayaś citro vaśitāpuṣpamaṇḍitaḥ //2//*

The talk of different *yānas* is only for those who are at lower level of consciousness. At highest level such differentiation is simply not needed:

*triyānam ekayānam ca ayānaṃ ca vadāmy aham /*
*bālānāṃ mandabuddhinām āryānāṃ ca viviktatām //129//*
*dvāraṃ hi paramārthasya vijñaptir dvayavarjitā /*

*yānatrayavyavasthānaṃ nirābhāse sthite kutaḥ //130// -Ibid.*, II.129-130.

The *ekayāna* theory is a corollary of the *tathāgatagarbha* theory. Also see Arnold Kunst (1977), and the *Saddharmapuṇḍarīkasūtra*, pp. 54. 20-56.2.

(72) Ruegg (1977), p. 301.

(73) Obermiller (1931), p. 105. fn. 3: *sarvadharmāṇāṃ kāyaḥ, sarvajagatas tathāgata-anatikramāt;* Also cf. *Mahāyānasūtrālaṃkāra*, IX.15:

*yathāmbaraṃ sarvagataṃ sadāmataṃ tathaiva tat sarvagataṃ sadāmatam / yathāmbaraṃ rūpagaṇeṣu sarvagaṃ tathaiva tat sattvagaṇeṣu sarvagam //*

(74) "Vāsanā is to be understood as the motive force governing the evolutionary process" (*iṣyate vāsanāvidbhiḥ śaktirūpā hi vāsanā)* —A. K. Chatterjee (1975), p. 88; also see pp. 140- 42 on the nature of *avidyā*.

(75) See *supra*, n. 60.

(76) *Mahāyānasūtrālaṃkāra*, chapters V and XIII are exclusively on *pratipatti*.

(77) See Ruegg (1977), n. 49: *ādhāraḥ pratipatteś ca dharmadhātusvabāvakaḥ.*

(78) See *Ibid.*, n. 50 : *ādheyadharmabhedāt tu tad bhedaḥ parigīyate*, and n. 42: *dharmadhātor asambhedād gotrabhedo na yujyate.*

(79) *Ibid.*, p. 290.

(80) Cf. *Ibid.*, n. 61: "*saṃvṛtyā punaḥ pratipattidharmasyāvasthāntarabhedena dharmadhātusvabhāva eva buddhadharmādhāro bodhisattvas trayodaśavidho gotram iti nirdiśyatė* — Ārya Vimuktisena, *Vṛtti*, p. 77: And on the *dharmadhātu* as the cause of comprehension of the *āryadharmas* see *yadi dharmadhātor evāryadharmādhigamāya hetutvāt tadātmako bodhisattvaḥ prakṛtistham anuttarabuddhadharmāṇāṃ gotraṃ dharmatāsaṃjñakam....*"; also see *Ibid.*, pp. 292-93.

(81) See Ruegg (1977), p. 293. *Mahāyānasūtrālaṃkāra*, chapter IV, is exclusively on *cittotpāda*.

(82) See Ruegg (1977), n. 84: *prakṛtistham anuttarabuddhadharmāṇāṃ gotraṃ dharmatāsaṃjñakam.*

(83) Ruegg (1977), n. 129.

(84) Cf. *Abhisamayālaṃkāra-āloka: anādi-kāla-āyātadharmatā-pratilabdham.* (Quoted in Obermiller, 1931, p. 103, fn.1)

(85) Cf. *RGV*, I.149-52; also I. 27, 28, 140, 144.

(86) Cf. *Ibid.*, I.29.

(87) Cf. *Ibid.*, I.31 and *Vṛtti* thereon.

(88) Cf. *Abhidharmasamuccaya*, p. 6.5-6: *adhimokṣaḥ katamaḥ. niścite vastuni yathāniścayaṃ dhāraṇā. asaṃhāryatākarmakaḥ;* Sthiramati on *Triṃśikā*, 10: *adhimokṣo niścite vastuni tathaivāvadhāraṇam. niścitagrahaṇam aniścitapratiṣedhārtham. yuktita āptopadeśato vā yad vastu asaṃdigdhaṃ tan niścitaṃ yenaivākāreṇa tan niścitm anityaduḥkhādyakāreṇa tenaivākāreṇa tasya vastunaś cetasyābhiniveśam evam etan nānyathety avadhāraṇam adhimokṣaḥ; AKB*, p. 187.5- 6: *adhimokṣo 'dhimuktiḥ samādhiś cittasyaikāgratā*

(89) Cf. *RGV*, I. 32.

(90) Cf. *Ibid.*, I.35a and *Vṛtti* on it (p. 30.11-18).

(91) Cf. *Abhidharmasamuccaya*, p.6.4: *cchandaḥ katmaḥ. īpsite vastuni tat tad upasaṃhatā kartṛkāmatā.*

(92) Cf. *RGVV*, p.36.6-7: *praṇidhir yābhilaṣitārthe cetanā cittābhisaṃskāraḥ.*

(93) Cf. *RGV*, I. 35b.

(94) Cf. *RGVV*, p. 36.5: *icchābhilaṣitārthaprāptāv asaṃkocaḥ.*

(95) Cf. *Ibid.*, p. 36.6: *prārthanābhilasitārthaprāptyupāyaparimārgaṇā.*

(96) Cf. *RGV*, I.40.

(97) Cf. *Ibid.*, I.41.

(98) Cf. *RGVV*, pp. 37.16-38.3.

(99) Cf. *RGV*, I. 44 with *Vṛtti.*

(100) *Ibid.*, I. 45-46.

(101) "The word is here taken in the sense of *tathatāṃ gata iti tathāgataḥ* "He who has coalesced with the Absolute"."—Obermiller (1931), p. 183, fn. 4.

(102) Cf. *RGV*, I. 47.

(103) Cf. *Ibid.*, I. 49-50 with *Vṛtti.*

(104) Cf. *Ibid.*, I.51-64.

(105) *Ibid.*, I.84.

(106) *Ibid.*, I. 85-86 with *Vṛtti.*

(107) Cf. *Laṅkāvatārasūtra*, p. 27. 18-20: *punar aparaṃ mahāmate pañcābhisamayogotrāṇi. katamāni pañca. yad uta śrāvakayānābhisamayagotraṃ pratyekabuddhayānābhisamayagotraṃ tathāgatayānābhisamayagotram aniyataikataragotram agotraṃ ca pañcamam.*

(108) Cf. *Ibid.*, p.27.20-30: *kathaṃ punar mahāmate śrāvakayānābhisamayagotraṃ pratyetavyaṃ. yaḥ skandhadhātvāyatanasvasāmānyalakṣaṇaparijñānādhigame deśyamāne romāñcitatanur bhavati. lakṣaṇaparicayajñāne cāsya buddhiḥ praskandati, na pafityasamutpādavinirbhāgalakṣaṇaparicaye. idaṃ mahāmate śrāvakayānābhisamayagotram. yaḥ śrāvakayānābhisamayaṃ dṛṣṭvā ṣaṭpañcabhyāṃ bhūmau paryutthānakleśaprahiṇo vāsanākleśaprahiṇo 'cintyācyutigataḥ samyaksiṃhanādaṃ nadati – kṣīṇā me jātiḥ, uṣitaṃ brahmacaryam, ity evam ādi nigadya pudgalanairātmyaparicayādyāvannirvāṇabuddhir bhavati.*

*anye punar mahāmate ātmasattvajīvapoṣapuruṣapudgalasattvāvabodhān nirvāṇam anveṣante. anye punar mahāmate kāraṇādhīnān sarvadharmān dṛṣṭvā nirvāṇagatibuddhayo bhavati. dharmanairātmyadarśanābhāvān nāsti mokṣo mahāmate. eṣā mahāmate śrāvakayānābhisamayagotrakasyāniryāṇaniryāṇabuddhiḥ. atra te mahāmate kudṛṣṭivyāvṛtty arthaṃ yogaḥ karaṇīyaḥ.*

(109) Cf. *Ibid.*, p. 28.1-5: *tatra mahāmate pratyekabuddhayānābhisamayagotrakaḥ, yaḥ pratyekābhisamaye deśyamāne aśrudṛṣṭaromāñcitatanur bhavati. asaṃsargapartyayād bhāvābhiniveśabahuvividhasvakāyavaicitryarddhivyastayamakaprātihāryadarśane nirdiśyamāne 'nunīyate, sa pratyekabuddhayānābhisamayagotraka iti viditvā pratyekabuddhayānābhisamayānurūpā kathā karaṇīyā. etan mahāmate pratyekabuddhayānābhisamayagotrakasya lakṣaṇam.*

(110) Cf. *Ibid.*, p.28.6-10: *tatra mahāmate tathāgatayānābhisamayagotraṃ trividham — yad uta svabhāvaniḥsvabhāvadharmābhisamayagotram, adhigamasvapratyātmāryābhisamayagotram, bāhyabuddhakṣetraudāryābhisamayagotraṃ ca. yadā punar mahāmate trayāṇām apy eṣām anyatame deśyamāne svacittadṛśyadehālayabhogapratiṣṭhācintyaviṣaye deśyamāne nottrasati na saṃtrasati na saṃtrāsamāpadyate, veditavyam ayaṃ tathāgatayānābhisamayagotrakasya lakṣaṇam.*

(111) Cf. *Ibid.*, p. 28. 11-14: *aniyatagotrakaḥ punar mahāmate triṣv apy eteṣu deśyamāneṣu yatrānunīyate tatrānuyojyaḥ syāt. parikarmabhūmir iyaṃ mahāmate gotravyavasthā. nirābhāsabhūmyavakramaṇatayā vyavasthā kriyate. pratyātmālaye tu svakleśavāsanāśuddhasya dharmanairātmyadarśanāt samādhisukhavihāraṃ prāpya śrāvako jinakāyatāṃ pratilapsyate.....*

(112) According to *RGV*, I.41d, there is no category of *agotra: agotrāṇāṃ na vidyate.* This is in accordance with the *tathāgatagarbha* theory.

(113) Cf. *Mahāyānasūtrālaṃkāra*, IX. 37 and the commentary on it:

*sarveṣām aviśiṣṭāpi tathatā śuddhim āgatā /*

*tathāgatatvaṃ tasmāc ca tad garbhāḥ sarvadehinaḥ / /*

*sarveṣāṃ nirviśiṣṭā tathatā tad viśudhisvabhāvaś ca tathāgataḥ. ataḥ sarve sattvās tathāgatagarbhā ity ucyate;* also quoted in *RGVV*, p. 71.16-17; *Laṅkāvatārasūtra*, p. 29.3: *tathāgatānāṃ sarvasattvāḥ.*

(114) Obermiller (1932), p. 32, fn. 3.

(115) Ruegg (1976), n.6.

(116) There are actually five *mārgas*. Cf. *Abhidharmasamuccaya*, pp. 65.12-66.11: *punaḥ mārgaḥ pañcavidhaḥ. sambhāramārgaḥ prayogamārgaḥ darśanamārga bhāvanāmārgaḥ niṣṭhāmārgaś ca.*

*sambhāramārgaḥ katamaḥ. pṛthagjanānāṃ śīlam indriyadvārarakṣā bhojane mātrājñatā prathamarātrau tad uttararātriṣu vā nityam amiddhaṃ vīryabhāvanā śamathavipasyanā samprajanyavihāras' ca. yad vā punar anyad aupaniṣadaṃ kuśalaṃ śrutamayī prajñā cintāmayīprajñā. tad bhāvanayā abhisamayavimokṣasthānabhājanaṃ pratilabhate.*

*prayogamārgaḥ katamaḥ. yaḥ sambhāramārgaḥ sa prayogamārgaḥ. yas tu prayogamārgaḥ sa na sambhāramārgaḥ. sambhāramārgopacitāni nirvedhabhāgīyāni kuśalamūlāni ūṣmagataḥ mūrdhanaḥ satyānukūlakṣāntiḥ laukikāgradharmaś ca. ūṣmagataṃ katmat. pratyātmaṃ satyeṣv ālokalabdhaḥ samādhiḥ prajñā saṃyogaś ca. mūrdhānaṃ katamat. pratyātmaṃ satyeṣv ālokavṛddhaḥ samādhiḥ prajñā saṃyogaś ca. satyānukūlakṣāntiḥ katamā. pratyātmaṃ satyeṣv ekadeśapraviṣṭānusṛtaḥ samādhiḥ prajñā saṃyogaś ca. laukikāgradharmaḥ katamaḥ. pratyātmaṃ satyeṣv anantaryacittasamādhiḥ prajñā saṃyogaś ca.*

*darśanamārgaḥ katamaḥ. samāsato laukikāgradharmāntaram anupalambhaḥ samādhiḥ prajñā saṃyogaś ca. samasamālambyālambanajñānam api tat pratyātmam apanītasattvasaṃketasarvato 'panītobhayasaṃketālambanadharmajñānam api tat. prabhedaśaḥ punar darśanamārgo laukikāgradharmāntaraṃ duḥkhe dharmajñānakṣāntiḥ duḥkhe dharmajñānaṃ duḥkhe 'nvayajñānakṣāntiḥ duḥkhe 'nvayajñānaṃ samudaye dharmajñānakṣāntiḥ samudaye dharmajñānaṃ samudaye 'nvayajñānakṣāntiḥ samudaye 'nvayajñānaṃ nirodhe dharmajñānakṣāntiḥ nirodhe dharmajñānaṃ nirodhe 'nvayajñānakṣāntiḥ nirodhe 'nvayajñānaṃ marge dharmajñānakṣāntiṃ mārge dharmajñānaṃ mārge 'nvayajñānakṣāntiḥ mārge 'nvayajñānam. evaṃ ca ṣoḍaśa jñānakṣāntibhir darśanamārgaprabhedāḥ.*

Also see A. K. Chatterjee (1975), pp. 163-66.

(117) See Suzuki, p. 219. Also cf. *Laṅkāvatārasūtra*, p. 28.11-14: *aniyatagotrakaḥ punar mahāmate triṣv apy eteṣu deśyamāneṣu yatrānunīyate tatrānuyojyaḥ syāt. parikramabhūmir iyaṃ mahāmate gotravyavasthā. nirābhāsabhūmyavakramaṇatayā vyavasthā kriyate. pratyātmālaye tu svakleśavāsanāśuddhasya dharmanairātmyadarśanāt samādhisukhavihāraṃ prāpya śrāvako jinakāyatāṃ pratilapsyate.....*

(118) Cf. *Madhyāntavibhāgaśāstra*, p. 51.15-18: *tatra vyāpti kleśajñeyāvaraṇaṃ bodhisattvagotrakāṇām iti. vyāpnotīti vyāpti, sakalārthāvaraṇāt. sakalārtho hi svārthaḥ parārthaś ca. athavā dvividhaṃ kleśaṃ jñeyaṃ cāvaraṇaṃ bodhisattvasya vyāpnotīty upacārāt. kleśa evāvaraṇam ity āvaraṇasya kleśadharmatvena sārūpyādihopakleśo 'pi kleśaśabdena gṛhyate.*

(119) Cf. *Ibid.*, p. 52.1-4: *jñeya evāvaraṇam iti jñeyāvaraṇam. tena jñeyaprāvṛtatvāj jñānasya viṣaya eva nāsti. jñāne vā jñeyāvaraṇam, jñeyasya jñānotpattipratibandhakatvād iti jñeyāvaraṇam ity atra madhyamapadalopo draṣṭavyaḥ tailapātram iva.*

(120) Obermiller (1932), p. 33.

(121) Cf. *RGVV*, p. 28.1, and p. 36.12-13.

(122) Cf. *RGV*, I.41d: *agotrāṇāṃ na vidyate.*

(123) Ruegg (1977), p. 291.

(124) Suzuki, p. 219, fn.l.

(125) Cf. *Laṅkāvatārasūtra*, p. 28.24-27: *tatrecchantikānāṃ punar mahāmate anicchantikatāmokṣaṃ kena pravartate. yad uta sarvakuśalamūlotsargataś ca sattvānādikālapraṇidhānataś ca. tatrakuśalamūlotsarga katamaḥ. yad uta bodhisattvapiṭakanikṣepo 'bhyākhyānaṃ ca naite sūtrāntā vinayamokṣānukūlā iti bruvataḥ sarvakuśalamūlotsargatvān na nirvāyate.*

See *RGVV* on I.32, 33, 38, 41 (*aparinirvāṇadharmaka = aparinirvāṇagotraka*).

126. Cf. *Mahāyānasūtrālaṃkāra*, III.11 with commentary:

*ekāntiko duścarite 'sti kaścit kaścit samudghātitaśukladharmā|*
*amokṣabhāgīyaśubho 'sti kaścin nihīnaśuklo 'sty api hetuhīnaḥ||*

*aparinirvāṇadharmaka etasminn agotrastho 'bhipretaḥ. sa ca samāsato dvividhaḥ. tatkālāparinirvāṇadharmā atyantaṃ ca. tatkālāparinirvāṇadharmā caturvidhaḥ. duścaritaikāntikaḥ, samucchinnakuśalamūlaḥ, amokṣabhāgīyakuśalamūlaḥ, hīnakuśalamūlaś cāparipūrṇasambhāraḥ. atyantāparinirvāṇadharmā tu hetuhīno yasya parinirvāṇagotram eva nāsti.*

127. Cf. *Laṅkāvatārasūtra*, pp. 28.27-29.4: *dvitīyaḥ punar mahāmate bodhisattvo mahāsattva evaṃ bhavapraṇidhānopāyapūrvakatvānn aparinirvṛtaiḥ sarvasattvaiḥ parinirvāsyāmīti tato na parinirvāti. etan mahāmate aparinirvāṇadharmakāṇāṃ lakṣaṇam yenecchantikagatiṃ samadhigacchanti.*

*punar api mahāmatir āha – katamo 'tra bhagavan atyantato na parinirvāti. bhagavān āha – bodhisattvecchantiko 'tra mahāmate ādiparinirvṛtān sarvadharmān viditvā atyantato na parinirvāti. na punaḥ sarvakuśalamūlotsargecchantikaḥ. sarvakuśalamūlotsargecchantiko hi mahāmate punar api tathāgatādhiṣṭhānāt kadācit karhicit kuśalamūlān vyutthāpayati. tat kasya hetoḥ. yad uta aparityaktā hi mahāmate tathāgatānāṃ sarvasattvāḥ. ata etasmāt kāraṇān mahāmate bodhisattvecchantiko na parinirvātīti.*

# Bibliography

*Abhidharmasamuccaya* of Asaṅga, ed. by Pralhad Pradhan, Santiniketan, Visva-Bharati, 1950.

*AD, ADV – Abhidharmadīpa* with *Vibhāṣāprabhāvṛtti,* ed. by Padmanabh S. Jaini, K.P. Jayaswal Research Institute, Patna, 1977. (First ed. 1959)

*AK, AKB, AKV – Abhidharmakośa (AK)* of Vasubandhu, with his *Bhāṣya (AKB)* and Yaśomitra's *Vyākhyā (AKV),* ed. by D.D. Shastri, Varanasi, Bauddha Bharati, 4 volumes, 1970-73.

*Arthaviniścayasūtra and its Commentary (Nibandhana),* ed. by N. H. Samtani, Patna, K. P. Jayaswal Research Institute, 1971.

*Aṭṭhasālinī,* ed. by P.V. Bapat and R.D. Vadekar, Poona, 1942.

*Bodhicaryāvatāra* of Śāntideva with Prajñākaramati's Commentary, ed. by P. L. Vaidya, Darbhanga, 1960.

Chatterjee, A.K. (1971): *Readings on Yogācāra Buddhism,* Varanasi, Banaras Hindu University.

. . . . .(1975): *The Yogācāra Idealism,* Varanasi, Motilal Banarsidass. (First ed. 1962)

Conze, Edward (1967): *Buddhist Thought in India,* University of Michigan Press. (First ed. 1962)

*Encyclopedia of Buddhism,* ed. by G.P. Malalasekera, Ceylon, 1961-77, 3 volumes.

Guenther, Herbert V. (1974): *Philosophy and Psychology in the Abhidharma,* Delhi, Motilal Banarsidass. (First ed. 1957)

Jaini, Padmanabh S. (1959): "The Sautrāntika Theory of Bīja", in *Bulletin of the School of Oriental and African Studies,* Vol. 22, part.2, pp.236-49.

Kunst, Arnold (1977): "Some Aspects of the Ekayāna", in *Prajñāpāramitā and Related Systems* (Studies in Honour of Edward Conze), ed. by Lewis Lancaster, California, University of California, pp. 313-26.

*Laṅkāvatārasūtra,* ed. by P.L. Vaidya, Darbhanga, 1963.

*Madhyamaka-kārikā* of Nāgārjuna with Candrakīrti's *Prasannapadā,* ed. by P.L. Vaidya, Darbhanga, 1960.

*Madhyāntavibhāgaśāstra* with Maitreya's *Kārikās*, Vasubandhu's *Bhāṣya* and Sthiramati's *Ṭīkā*, ed. by R. C. Pandeya, Delhi, Motilal Banarsidass, 1971.

*Mahāyānasūtrālaṃkāra* of Asaṅga, ed. by S. Bagchi, Darbhanga, 1970.

Murti, T.R.V. (1970): *The Central Philosophy of Buddhism*, London, George Allen & Unwin. (First ed. 1955)

Nakamura, Hajime (1980): *Indian Buddhism, A Survey with Bibliographical Notes*, Tokyo, Kufs Publication.

Nakamura, Zuiryu, (1961), *A Study of Ratnagotravibhāga-Mahāyānottaratantra-śāstra based on a Comparison and Contrast between the Sanskrit Original and the Chinese Translations*, Tokyo.

Obermiller, E. (1931): "The Sublime Science of the Great Vehicle to Salvation being a Manual of Buddhist Monism", in *Acta Orientalia*, IX, pp.81-306. (Being reprinted herewith. In the notes, the original page numbers are quoted.)

. . . . .(1932), "The Doctrine of Prajñāpāramitā as Exposed in the Abhisamayālaṃkāra of Maitreya", in *Acta Orientalia*, XI, pp. 1-133, 334-58

Prasad, H.S. (1989): "Understanding Buddhist Epistemology", in *Amalā Prajñā: Aspects of Buddhist Studies* (P. V. Bapat Felicitation Volume), ed. by N. H. Samtani and H. S. Prasad, Delhi, Indian Books Centre, pp. 277-97.

*RGV, RGVV – The Ratnagotravibhāga Mahāyānottaratantraśāstra*, ed. by E. H. Johnson, Patna, 1950. (Being reprinted herewith. In the notes, the original page numbers are quoted.)

Ruegg, D. Seyfort (1976): "The Meaning of the Term Gotra and the Textual History of the Ratnagotravibhāga", in *Bulletin of the School of Oriental and African Studies*, Vol. 39, pp. 341-63.

. . . . .(1977): "The gotra, ekayāna and tathāgatagarbha theories of the prajñāpāramitā according to Dharmamitra and Abhayākaragupta", in *Prajñāpāramitā and Related Systems* (Studies in Honour of Edward Conze), ed. by Lewis Lancaster, California, University of California, pp. 283-312.

*Saddharmapuṇḍarīkasūtra*, ed. by P. L. Vaidya, Darbhanga, 1960.

Schmithausen, Lambert (1987): *Ālayavijñāna: (On the Origin and the Early Development of a Central Concept of Yogācāra Philosophy)*,

2 parts, Tokyo, The International Institute for Buddhist Studies.

Suzuki, D.T. (1981): *Studies in the Laṅkāvatāra Sūtra*, Boulder, Prajna Press. (First ed. 1930)

Takasaki, Jikido (1966): *A Study on the Ratnagotravibhāga (Uttaratantra). Being a Treatise on the Tathāgatagarbha Theory of Mahāyāna Buddhism*, Rome, Is. M. E. O.

*Triṃśikā* of Vasubandhu, see Chatterjee, A.K. (1971).

*Viṃśatikā* of Vasubandhu, see Chatterjee (1971).

Wayman, Alex and Hideko (1990): *The Lion's Roar of Queen Śrīmālā (A Buddhist Scripture on the Tathāgatagarbha Theory)*, Delhi, Motilal Banarsidass. (First ed. 1974)

# PART - II

# SANSKRIT TEXT

*Edited by*

**E.H. Johnston**

# The Ratnagotravibhāga Mahāyānottaratantrasāstra

*Edited by*

E.H. Johnson

The Bihar Research Society
Museum Building
PATNA

1950

# INTRODUCTORY NOTE

It is a matter of profound regret for the Bihar Research Society that the learned editor of the following pages did not live to see them in print. In his last letter to the General Secretary, dated the 14th December, 1941, Dr. Johnston expressed his concern over the insecurity of Indian mails during the continuity of war with Japan and communicated his decision to hold up the Script for the time being. Unfortunately, he passed away the next year, and it was not till September, 1946 that we received it through the courtesy of Mrs. Johnston and Sir Richard Burn. Non-availibility of a good press and suitable paper, to our great regret, made it impossible for us to undertake the work of publication until now, and we are happy that the difficulties are now overcome and this, probably the last, great work of a great scholar sees the light of day. The printing, we are glad to announce, has been done in absolute conformity with the instructions that he left for the press.

Unfortunately, Dr. Johnston's personal copy of the prepared text and notes and the MS. B were not available to me until nearly the whole of the text had been in print, while I could consult the MS. A only after the major portion had been printed off. This led to certain errors, owing to slips in the press-copy, which are now recommended for correction, viz., p. 1, line 1, *śro*°; p. 22, line 1, *prakṛtipariśuddhi*°; p. 25, line 8, p. 52, line 20, p. 97, line 15 and the captions of pp. 93, 95 and 97, *tritīya* ; p. 36, line 12, *icchāntikānām* ; p. 39, line 10, *jigarbho* ; p. 44, line 8, *mārṣā*; p. 50, line 13, *prajñāpāṛamita*°; and p. 64, fn.[3], *viṣaya.* A few other fairly obvious errors, too, have been similarly recommended for correction on the authority of the MSS., viz., p. 6, line 12, *ṣoḍaśākārī* to *ṣoḍaśākārā* (B) ; p. 50, line 14, °*dābhimukhyāṁ* to °*dabhimukhyāṁ* (A); p. 51, line 2, °*mābhimukhyāṁ* to °*mabhimukhyāṁ* (A, B); and p. 93, line 6, *nopekṣāpratisaṁkhyāya hāni*° to *nopekṣāpratisaṁkhyāpahāni*° (B).

A few apparent misreadings I felt myself called upon to correct owing to the exigencies of metre and sense, supported mostly by the authorities, viz., p. 26, line 4, *sarvadehino* to *saurve dehino* (metre and context); p. 61, line 18, *yatparibhoga°* to *yadvatparibhoga°* (metre and A); p. 63, line 6, *°madiśacchudhaye* to *°madiśattacchuddhaye* (metre, A and B); p. 67, line 4, *rāgādi-dviṁmoha°* to *rāgādidviḍmoha* (context and B, A apparently reading *°dviṇ°*); p. 68, line 21, *bhramarā* to *bhramarāḥ* (A, B); p. 78, line 20, *buddhatvam* to *buddhatām* (A, B); p. 81, fn.[3], *kṛpāmbhubhiḥ* to *kṛpāmbubhiḥ*; p. 87, line 18, *garbhākramaṇaṁ* to *garbhāvakramaṇaṁ* (Johnston's personal copy and B); p. 100, line 8, *mahītale nivāsinaḥ* to *mahītalanivāsinaḥ* (rhythm and B); p. 101, line 18, *cittān uyutpādayantī* to *citrāṇyutpādayanti* (B); p. 105, line 15, *°meti prajāsu* to *°meti tadvat prajāsu* (metre and B); p. 108, line 16, *vineyādriṁ tannipāto* to *vineyādritannipāto* (grammar and B); p. 111, line 16, *prakṛto'rtho* to *prakṛto'trārtho* (metre, A and B); and p. 116, line 11, *evaṁ guṇa°* to *evaṁguṇa°* (sense).

While handling the MSS. I came across a few other important readings, which I beg to present here for the consideration of scholars for whatsoever they are worth, e.g., p. 24, line 15, for *nirnītākāraṇam* B has *nirnānākāraṇaṁ*, A being illegible; p. 30, line 9, B adds *uktāḥ* after *viśuddhihetavaḥ*; p. 32, line 4, A and B both have *bodhisattvānām* before *nityapāramitā°*; p. 44, line 8, for the most obscure *kavi°* A appears to read *chavi°* [Note that *chavi* meant 'hide' or 'skin' in ancient usage, that 'darkness' has been termed *niśācarman*, 'skin of the night', and that T uses a term meaning 'darkness', which is also favoured by the context.][1]; p. 45, line 9, A and B both have *mūlaparicchinnāḥ* before *sarvadharmā*; p. 45, line 18, for the obscure *nirmamīkaraṇaṁ* A reads *nirmaṣīkuraṇaṁ*; p. 51, line 11, for *prativicya* B has *pratividhya*; and p. 87, line 17, for *jātakānyupapattiṁ* B appears to have *jātakādyupa°*.

The text remains unsatisfactory, to my mind, in a few more instances, viz., p. 47, line 18, *manāpo* (for *manaso* ?); p. 49,

1. For a similar use of *tvac.* 'skin', cf. RV. iv, 17, 14; ix, 41, 1 & 73, 5.

line 14, *nāvalīyanācittam* (for *na+abali+iyatā cittam* ?); p. 52, line 11, *gospada*, the only authority for which is B and which apparently deserves to be corrected to *goṣpada*; p. 74, lines 12-14 and 16, *satyuttaribhāvayitavye* (for *satyuttare bhāvayitavye*, which B seems to read in one or two of the instances, ?); and p. 106, line 6, the pāda lacks one short syllable like *ca* or *tu* after *kleśagatān*.

Dr. Johnston desired to prepare indexes after he had received paged proofs, but left no indications as to their precise contents. Judging him by his predilections, I have ventured to supply four indexes. Of these the *Index of Technical Terms* is not a register of all the occurrences of a term, but only of those that either define it or indicate the various aspects of its signification. It may, to some extent, serve the purpose of a general index.

Finally, let me take this opportunity of thanking the Council of the Bihar Research Society for entrusting me with the work of seeing the volume through the press and the Manager and Staff of the Svatantra Nava Bharat Press for carrying out my directions most ungrudgingly.

Patna,
*November* 1950

T. Chowdhury

## CONTENTS

| | PAGE |
|---|---|
| Introductory Note by T. Chowdhury | i—iii |
| Foreword | v—xiv |
| Abbreviations | xv |
| Corrections | xvi |
| Chapter I : *Tathāgatagarbhādhikāra* | 1—78 |
| Chapter II : *Bodhyadhikāra* | 79—90 |
| Chapter III : *Guṇādhikāra* | 91—97 |
| Chapter IV : *Tathāgatakṛtyakriyādhikāra* | 98—114 |
| Chapter V : *Anuśaṁsādhikāra* | 115—119 |
| I. Index of Metres | 120 |
| II. Index of Authorities | 121 |
| III. Index of Technical Terms | 122—128 |
| IV. Index of Rare Words and Uses | 129 |

# FOREWORD

Till quite recently nothing more was known of the text edited in this volume than that, under the title of *Uttaratantra*, it was included among the five chief works of Asaṅga by Tibetan tradition, which reported it to represent the Mādhyamika aspect of his teaching. In 1931 however a complete translation of it from Tibetan into English was published by E. Obermiller in Vol. IX, parts ii, iii and iv, of *Acta Orientalia*, under the title "The Sublime Science of the Great Vehicle to Salvation, being a Manual of Buddhist Monism, the work of Ārya Maitreya with a Commentary by Āryāsaṅga". A few years later Prof. Bailey discovered among the Central Asian finds a Śaka transliteration of a number of Sanskrit verses, among which I identified the first verse of chapter i and the opening verses of chapter iii.[1] The MS. gave the name of the work as *Ratnagotravibhāga*, thereby enabling me to adduce Chinese tradition about its authorship[2]. This tradition and the contents of the few verses thus restored caused me to doubt whether the treatise was really by Asaṅga at all and whether Obermiller had not in certain respects misrepresented its doctrinal tendencies by following modern Tibetan exegesis, which naturally endeavours to support the ascription to Asaṅga by reading his known views into the text. But while this paper was in the press, the Rev. Rāhula Sāṁkṛtyāyana published the first list of Sanskrit MSS. found by him in Tibet. These discoveries, whose importance for Buddhist learning can hardly be exaggerated, included

1. *Bull. LSOS*, VIII, pp. 77—89. My reconstruction was only partially successful, the transliteration being imperfect and leaving much to guesswork.

2. The full name is shown by the MSS. as well as by the Tibetan and Chinese translations to be *Ratnagotravibhāga Mahāyānottaratantraśāstra*; the second part is merely descriptive of the scope of the work, and the first, being the proper title, is used throughout hereafter in place of the hitherto accepted *Uttaratantra*.

according to him three MSS. of the *Uttaratantra*[1], and, as the work I had done on it had convinced me of its great value in filling a gap in our knowledge of Mahāyāna developments, I asked the Bihar and Orissa Research Society for permission to edit it, a request which was most generously granted. Owing to the defectiveness of the original photographs and the necessity of obtaining new ones on a later expedition, there was some delay in undertaking the work, and the war has further postponed preparation and publication of the text.

Of the three MSS. mentioned, one proved on examination not to be of the *Ratnagotravibhāga*. As at present constituted, it consists of three folios in a script, which is substantially older than that of the other two MSS., VIII century perhaps or even earlier,[2] and is hard to decipher in the photographs; it contains a brief summary of the *Ratnagotravibhāga*, as appears from the colophon, *Mahāyānottaratantropadeśaḥ kṛtiś ŚrīSatyajñānapādānām.* The author, Satyajñāna, is apparently not mentioned elsewhere, and I have not noted any passages which throw light on the text of the main work. The other two MSS. are as follows.

A, in an early Śāradā script, originally consisting of 26 leaves, of which eleven only are extant, viz., 7, 9, 12, 13, 15, 16, 17, 19, 20, 25, 26. Leaf 7 is mutilated at both ends, with the loss of about a third of the text. The handwriting is of a neat, spidery type, a further development of that in the MS. of the *Mahāyānottaratantropadeśa*, and dating perhaps to somewhere about the X century, so far as in the absence of comparable material it is possible to suggest a precise figure; when at all rubb ed, as it often is, it is hard to read, but in its original state was singu larly legible. It is a first-rate MS., and if it had been complete, there would have been no difficulty in editing the text. One of its peculiarities is not to elide *a* after *e* and *o*.

1. *JBORS*, XXI, pp. 31 and 33.

2. It is closely related to the handwriting of MS. A of the *Bhaiṣajyaguruvaidūryaprabhārājasūtra* as illustrated in *Gilgit Manuscripts*, I.

B, in a Nepali script of the XI century, was a MS. of 55 leaves, of which the last is now missing. The main authority for the greater part of the text, it does not reach the standard of accuracy of most Nepali MSS. of its period, and is particularly given to omitting single letters and even occasionally longer passages. The larger omissions have been made good in a later Nepali hand of the XIV or XV century, and the correctness of the additions proves that comparison was made with a good source. The copyist's ignorance is also shown by his having misplaced certain leaves of the original and copied them in the wrong order between leaves 46 and 50. Nevertheless with the help of the Chinese and Tibetan translations it affords a sound basis for the text, though, where A is also available, I have generally in cases of disagreement preferred that MS.

The Central Asian version of a few verses referred to above has been of no help, but another similar fragment, discovered by Prof. Bailey in Paris and containing verses iii, 19—22, helped me to make up my mind about one puzzling reading.

No Buddhist text in Sanskrit can be satisfactorily edited without detailed comparison with such Chinese and Tibetan versions as exist. For the Tibetan I have used the Narthang edition in the India Office copy, and Obermiller's translation shows that the Sde-dge edition, which he used, hardly ever differs from it in any substantial point. It is based on practically the same text as that found in A and B, though with sufficient differences to suggest that neither MS. was used by the translators, and it agrees with them against the Chinese in respect of omissions and additions. Of the former in one at least, at i, 64, for which A is missing, the text common to B and the Tibetan is certainly defective, from which it may be inferred that they go back to an archetype with the same omission. The facts about the Chinese translation are less simple. There are said to have been two translations, by Ratnamati and Bodhiruci respectively, who were fellow-workers under the Northern Wei at Lo Yang. The extant translation,

No. 1611 in the Taisho Issaikyo edition, is attributed to Ratnamati, but in fact it consists of two parts. After 18 introductory stanzas, which do not appear in the MSS. and may be the translator's work, the first part contains the verses only, confining itself largely to the pure *kārikās* and omitting most of the semi-*kāvya* verses which form the bulk of the text, with the two notable exceptions of i, 99-126, and iv, 14-76 and 88. The second consists of the verses together with the commentary as it exists in the Sanskrit; it omits a few verses not essential to the text, as well as the two long series just mentioned, giving in the latter case references to the previous part for them. It seems possible that the first part is the translation attributed to Ratnamati, and the second that of Bodhiruci; and there is a small point which affords slight corroboration of this presumption. Among the sūtra quotations in the commentary not identified by Obermiller are a number from the *Anūnatvāpūrṇatvanirdeśaparivarta*,[1] No. 668 of the Taisho Issaikyo edition, and the Chinese translator always gives the name of the sūtra in introducing the extract. Now this sūtra, which is possibly a section of some larger work and cannot be traced in the Kanjur under this name, was translated by Bodhiruci, and if he is the author of the second part of the translation, his knowledge of an otherwise little known sūtra is accounted for. The renderings of the verses common to both parts are practically identical, but in view of the close association between the two translators it might well have happened that, if Bodhiruci is the author of the second part, he would have used Ratnamati's versions when available, and that would explain the curious fact that separate translations should have been made of the same work by two men who were working together.[2] This point, however, does not affect the value of the Chinese text, which,

1. It is not quite clear from B whether this is the correct form of the name or whether it should be *Anūnāpūrṇatvanirdeśaparivarta*.

2. For some light on the complicated relationship between these two translators see P. Demiéville, 'Sur l'authenticité du Ta tch'eng k'i sin louen', in *Bull. de la Maison Franco-Japonaise*, II. pp. 32ff. of offprint.

as usual, is useful for the constitution of the text where other authorities disagree; in such cases I have as a rule given its evidence considerable weight, in view of its greater antiquity. I have not thought it safe to insert readings from it without corroboration, because, unlike the Tibetan, it is not a verbatim version, though keeping fairly close to the original. On the general contents of the work it suggests that one *kārikā* is missing from the other versions between i, 36, and 37, explaining the significance of *ātman* as applied to the Buddha, and two more at i, 64, while possibly it may be correct in adding a verse on the ten *vaśitās* in the commentary on i, 18. It is also valuable in that, as regards quotations from the sūtras, it usually, though not invariably, names the source, agreeing for the most part with Obermiller where he had traced them out and supplementing his information where he had failed.

Despite the difficulty of reading the MSS. in certain passages, the excellence in general of our authorities has permitted the constitution of a text which may be considered as sound except in a few minor points which nowhere affect the argument. The principles adopted in their exploitation appear clearly from the notes and need no discussion here. All variant readings in A and B have been noted, except those due to wrong spelling, of which the most important instance is the regular confusion between *śa* and *sa*. The spelling has been standardized, except that the sūtra quotations, where the rules of *saṁdhi* have not been observed, have been left as they stand. Thus I have written *pratipraśrabdha* etc. for °*srabdha* etc. in all the formations from the root *śrabh*, and *vaiḍūrya* for *vaidūrya*; the correct form of the latter appears only in the Tibetan, Buddhist MSS. usually, like many modern scholars, preferring the solecism of the dental for the cerebral. The MSS. occasionally have *anyathībhāva* for *anyathābhāva*, and *vinirbhoga* for *vinirbhāga*, both of which have been amended *sub silentio*. But alternances, such as *vālukā* and *vālikā*, *duṣprativedha* and *duṣprativedhya*, where either form would be possible, have been retained. The notes do not profess to contain a commentary on the text, which indeed the existence of Obermiller's translation and the simplicity of the Sanskrit make unnecessary.

The literary form of the work is somewhat unusual, consisting of a certain number of *kārikās*, supplemented by other verses either explaining them in detail or illustrating them by similes from the sūtra literature. The supplementary verses often attempt *kāvya* methods, but with only moderate success, and a curious feature of them is the way matter given in verses of shorter metres is repeated in a longer metre, e.g., i, 96ff., and ch. iii and iv, passim. A considerable variety of metres is employed, two of which appear not to occur elsewhere. The second half of ii, 38, is a triṣṭubh scanning ⏓ – ⏑ – – ⏑ – – ⏑ – –, a cross between Upajāti and Śālinī. More unusual is v, i, in which all four pādas scan – ⏑ – – – ⏑ – – . The commentary, which appears to be by the author of the verses and is called *Ślokasaṁgrahavyākhyāna*, is very detailed for the first chapter, but consists of little more than captions for the remainder. It contains quotations from seventeen sūtras, in addition to eight from unidentified sources and references to the *Saddharmapuṇḍarīka* and *Prajñāpāramitā*. Of the quoted sūtras we possess Sanskrit texts only of the *Kāśyapaparivarta* and *Vajracchedikā*. The largest number of quotations come from the *Āryaśrīmālādevīsiṁhanādasūtra* (whose name is cited in the notes in the shortened form *Āryaśrīmālāsūtra*), a work which appears to be the leading canonical authority for the Tathāgatagarbha theory; a translation of it into a European language is a desideratum for Buddhist studies.

So much for the technical aspects of this edition, but there remains to be answered the much more important question about the place which should be assigned to the treatise in the evolution of Mahāyāna doctrine, and that again depends to some extent on the authorship. On the latter point prolonged study of the original text has only strengthened my belief in the views put forward in the paper quoted above, p. v, n. 1, namely that Asaṅga has nothing to do with the *Ratnagotravibhāga*, and that, following Chinese tradition, it should be attributed to a certain Sthiramati, the author of a commentary on the *Kāśyapaparivarta*. Reminiscences of the phrasing of this sūtra are fairly frequent in it, and it may be noted that, whereas the author, like Āryadeva in the *Catuḥśataka*,[1] quotes a well-known passage from the sūtra in dealing with those who take a mistaken view of *śūnyatā*, Asaṅga in the *Bodhisattvabhūmi* (ed. Wogihara), p. 46, gives a different quotation in support of the same opinion. Differences in the use of terms such as *ratnagotra*, *yāvadbhāvikatā* and *yathāvadbhāvikatā*, are also to be found. Similarly in minor tenets, such as those of the number of Buddhadharmas, to the sixty-four of which in the *Ratnagotravibhāga*, ch. iii, Asaṅga adds the 80 *anuvyañjanas*, bringing the total up to 144 (*Bodhisattvabhūmi*, pp. 188-89). Naturally there are a number of parallels, particularly with ch. ix of the *Mahayānasūtrālaṁkāra*, and of the three verses that the latter work has in common with the *Ratnagotravibhāga*, one (*nāpaneyaṁ tataḥ kiṁcit*) is a Mādhyamika verse, and the other two, *Mahāyānasūtrālaṁkāra*, ix, 15 (*yathāmbaraṁ sarvagatam*), and 37 (*sarveṣām aviśiṣṭāpi*), were probably also taken by Asaṅga from earlier works, as the *āha* with which the present text introduces these and other quotations regularly implies canonical authority.[2] In general however this text knows nothing of the doctrines peculiar to Asaṅga and his school, thus not a word about *vijñaptimātratā* or the three *svabhāvas*[3] or the *ālayavijñāna*, no use made of the *Saṁdhinirmocanasūtra* etc. An interesting point is that the MSS. agree in using *āśrayaparivṛtti* for Asaṅga's *āśrayaparāvṛtti*, except at v, 7, where a long syllable is required and the original reading was probably °*parīvṛttau*. The difference in term corresponds to a difference in teaching; Asaṅga's *parāvṛtti* does not mean exactly 'metamorphosis'

1. See Bhattacharya, *The Catuḥśataka of Āryadeva*. p. 150. Quoted also at Laṅkāvatārasūtra, p. 146, line 1.

2. For an exact parallel note the quotation from the *Abhidharmamahāyānasūtra*, p. 72, lines 13-14.

3. See i, 144, for the only group of three *svabhāvas* mentioned, viz. *dharmakāya*, *tathatā* and *gotra*.

as often rendered, but refers to the view that the *āśraya* is merely an extension of the *vijñānālaya* without independent reality of its own and 'returns' to it, when the correct understanding of *vijñaptimātratā* is obtained.[1] Here on the other hand the term implies that, when the pure *cittaprakṛti* is freed from the sheaths of the *kleśas*, a metamorphosis of the *āśraya* takes place.

This point brings us close to the core of the *Ratnagotravibhāga*, the Tathāgatagarbha theory, of which it gives us at last a complete account in Sanskrit. The ultimate reality consists of an Absolute, called the *dharmakāya*, but which has several other names to indicate various aspects of it such as *Tathāgata*, *tathatā*, *dharmadhātu*; the *sattvadhātu*, the sphere of individual, phenomenal existence, is merely the *dharmadhātu* in its temporal aspect, which is to be found in each being of the *sattvadhātu* in the shape of the Tathāgatagarbha. The latter is defined as the *cittaprakṛti*, which is *pariśuddha*, that is, not only pure from all time but incapable of defilement, and *prabhāsvara*, 'radiant', implying presumably that it is spiritual, not material, in essence. In the case of an ordinary individual this spiritual entity is enclosed in innumerable sheaths of the *kleśas*, or, more properly, the *vāsanās* of the *kleśas*, which do not form part of its substance or enter into it in any way, but are mere 'accidents' (*āgantuka*); and the process of salvation, which consists in following the career of the Bodhisattva through the ten *bhūmis*, is effected by the gradual removal of these sheaths. There is no suggestion of any difference between the Tathāgatagarbha and the *dharmakāya*, and the parallelism between this monistic system and the *ātman* theories, particularly that of the *Gauḍapādakārikās* and other Vedāntin works, which reject the various *bhedābheda* explanations, is obvious and extends in the case of Gauḍapāda even to the use of identical phraseology. Our text emphasizes the likeness by the application to the Tathāgatagarbha at i, 80, of a well-

1. For the literature about this word see E. Lamotte, *La Somme du Grand Véhicule* (Louvain, 1936), note at end of tome II, i, on i, 57.

known line, which was used by Aśvaghoṣa at *Buddhacarita*, xii, 24, to describe the *ātman*; nor did it escape contemporary critics. For at *Laṅkāvatārasūtra*, pp. 77-79, the Buddha is made to explain the difference between the two theories against those who maintained their essential identity, but in a manner that is difficult to grasp; apparently the doctrine is not accepted there as the ultimate truth, but is said to be taught merely as a means of weaning certain classes of non-believers from their wrong views. This sūtra, whose doctrine is *cittamātra* rather than *vijñaptimātra*, equates the Tathāgatagarbha and the *ālayavijñāna* and discusses them in an interesting passage at pp. 220-24, which is avowedly based on the *Āryaśrīmālāsūtra* and, unlike the rest of the work, presents many analogies of wording with the *Ratnagotravibhāga*. The difference between the two doctrines is as obvious as the fact there is some genetic relationship between them. The *ālayavijñāna*, we now know, originated with the Sautrāntikas,[1] whose doctrinal position is halfway between the two Vehicles, but the conception was profoundly modified by the school of Asaṅga, possibly in part under the influence of the Tathāgatagarbha theory; the considerable differences that remain, particularly with regard to the potentialities of the Act, may be due to an attempt by Asaṅga to avoid the criticism that he was formulating a principle which was indistinguishable from the *ātman*.

This brief discussion of the points of interest presented by the text may be concluded with a few remarks on its handling of the 'Buddha-body' theory. The standard doctrine of the Mādhyamikas knows two such bodies corresponding to the *saṁvṛtisatya* and the *paramārthasatya*, that of the Vijñānavādins postulates three corresponding with the three *svabhāvas*.[2] The *Ratnagotravibhāga's* position is not so clear cut. At iii, 3, it propounds the Mādhyamika view, but at i, 150-152, ii, 21-22, and

1. See E. Lamotte, *Le Traité de l'Acte de Vasubandhu, Karmasiddhiprakaraṇa*, Introduction (Bruges, 1936).

2. For the views of the various schools see the masterly article in *Hobogirin* under *Busshin*.

iv, 61, and other passages it has the three regular bodies but under two heads, *dharmakāya* and *rūpakāya*, the latter covering the *sāmbhogika* and *nairmāṇika* bodies. Thus the connection with the older view is maintained, and it seems that in this matter also the present text stands midway between the two chief Mahāyāna schools.

Finally let me take this opportunity of expressing my gratitude to the Bihar Research Society for giving me the privilege of editing this important text and for undertaking the onerous task of its publication. To its learned Secretary, Dr. Banerji-Sastri, I am particularly indebted for the infinite trouble he has taken in procuring adequate photographs of the MSS. It is a pleasure to me to have a work published by the premier Society of a province in which I spent some of the best years of my life.

Oxford, E. H. JOHNSTON
*December*, 1941.

## ABBREVIATIONS

| | |
|---|---|
| A | Śāradā MS. of the *Ratnagotravibhāga* from Tibet. |
| B | Nepali Do. |
| Buddhac. | The *Buddhacarita* of Aśvaghoṣa, Panjab Un. Or. Publications, 31 and 32. |
| C | Chinese translation of the *Ratnagotravibhāga*, Taisho Issaikyo edition, No. 1611. |
| Daśabh. | *Daśabhūmikasūtra*, ed. J. Rahder. |
| Divy. | *Divyāvadāna*, ed. Cowell and Neil. |
| Kāś. P. | *Kāśyapaparivarta*, ed. von Staël-Holstein. |
| MBh. | *Mahābhārata*. |
| Mvy. | *Mahāvyutpatti*, ed. Sakaki. |
| O | Translation of the *Ratnagotravibhāga* from Tibetan into English, by E. Obermiller, *Acta Orientalia*, XI, ii, iii and iv. |
| PW | St. Petersburg Sanskrit Dictionary, by Böhtlingk and Roth. |
| PWK | Do., in kürzerer Fassung, by Böhtlingk. |
| S. | The *Saundarananda* of Aśvaghoṣa, Panjab Un. Or. Publications, 1928 and 1932. |
| T | Tibetan translation of the *Ratnagotravibhāga*, Bstaṅ-Ḥgyur (Narthang ed.), Mdo, XLV. |

## CORRECTIONS

P. 1, line 1, for श्रो° read श्री°.—P. 4, line 10, insert space after ततः ; line 11, close up space between °व्यूह[7] and निर्वृत्ति°; line 14, add a hyphen after °प्रभाव.—P. 6, line 12, for षोडशाकारी read षोडशाकारा.—P. 15, line 7, for दुष्प्रतिवधार्थं° read दुष्प्रतिवेधार्थं°.—P. 16, line 13, add a hyphen after शरण ; lines 19 and 20, interchange the first letters.—P. 21, line 1, insert space after °योनि[2].—P. 22, line 1, for प्रकृतिपरिशुद्धि° read प्रकृतिपरिशुद्ध°.—P. 27, line 6, close up space between °समृद्ध्यादि[3] and प्रभाव°.—P. 29, line 4, for उच्यत्ते read उच्यन्ते.—P. 31, line 5, for सम्यक read सम्यक्; line 14, for °रमभिप्राप्तः read °रभिप्राप्तः.—P. 36, line 12, for तदिच्छान्तिका° read तदिच्छन्तिका°.—P. 38, line 21, for '*hākaruṇā*' read '*hākaruṇā*'; line 27, for '*for*' read 'for'.—P. 39, line 11, for जिगर्भो read जिनगर्भा.—P. 43, line 22, insert a single inverted comma before '*Ayoniśoma*'-.—P. 44, line 8, for °मर्षि read °मर्षिः.—P. 45, line 16, for तेया read ज्ञेया.—P. 49, line 8, for पयदाप्येत read पर्यदाप्येत.—P. 50, line 5, for `शयिष्यामः read देशयिष्यामः; line 6, for कुशलमल° read °मूल°; line 13, for °प्रज्ञापारमित° read °प्रज्ञापारमिता°; line 14, for °दाभिमुख्यां read °दभिमुख्यां.—P. 51, line 2, for स्यामाभिमुख्यां read स्यामभिमुख्यां.—P. 54, line 3, for सख ल्वेष read स खल्वेष; line 13, insert space between पुत्र and धर्मकायो.—P. 56, line 1, for यथासंख्यमिम read यथासंख्यमिमे.—P. 64, line 3, for °त्वगन्तः read °त्वगन्तः[2]; line 23, for '*viṣaya*' read 'visarga'.—P. 70, line 3, for द्विधा read द्विधा.—P. 71, line 12, drop hyphen after तत्र-.—P. 74, line 19, for विपयासा° read विपर्यासा°.—P. 75, line 9, for भूता read भूत।.—P. 85, line 9, for स्वभाविक° read स्वाभाविक°; line 18, add a hyphen after '°*guṇa*'—P. 93, line 6, for °प्रतिसंख्याय हानि° read °प्रतिसंख्यापहानि°.—P. 97, lines 9 and 11, for द्वात्रिंश° read द्वात्रिंश°; line 12, for °कांय° read °काय°; line 14, for द्विधा read द्विधा.—P. 104, line 10, close up space between शास्ति and प्रातिहार्यम.

# रत्नगोत्रविभागो महायानोत्तरतन्त्रशास्त्रम्

——:)o(:——

## I

(1*b*) ओं नमः श्रीवज्रसत्त्वाय[1] ।

बुद्धश्च धर्मश्च गणश्च धातु-[2]
बोधिर्गुणाः कर्म च बौद्धमन्त्यम्[3] ।
कृत्स्नस्य शास्त्रस्य शरीरमेतत्
समासतो वज्रपदानि सप्त ॥ १ ॥

वज्रोपमस्याधिगमार्थस्य पदं स्थानमिति वज्रपदम् । तत्र श्रुतिचिन्तामयज्ञानदुष्प्रतिवेधादन[4]भिलाप्यस्वभावः प्रत्यात्मवेदनीयोऽर्थो वज्रवद्वेदितव्यः । यान्यक्षराणि तमर्थमभिवदन्ति तत्प्राप्त्यनुकूलमार्गाभिद्योतनतस्तानि तत्प्रतिष्ठाभूतत्वात् पदमित्युच्यन्ते[5] । इति दुष्प्रतिवेधार्थेन प्रतिष्ठार्थेन च वज्रपदत्वमर्थव्यञ्जनयोरनुगन्तव्यम् । तत्र कतमोऽर्थः कतमद्व्यञ्जनम् । अर्थ उच्यते सप्तप्रकारोऽधिगमार्थो यदुत बुद्धार्थो धर्मार्थः[6] संघार्थो धात्वर्थो बोध्यर्थो गुणार्थः

1. T has instead the usual invocation to all the Buddhas and Bodhisattvas.

2. *dhātu*, B.

3. *karma ca* (break) *ddham acintyaṁ*, B; *saṅs-rgyas phrin-las tha-ma-ste*, T.

4. The characters *dhād ana* are lost in the break in B, but C and T agree in the above reading.

5. The gap in B has destroyed the characters *bhūtatvāt padam i* and left the rest of the sentence doubtful; the remains look like *ty etad ucyate*, but T shows the text with *de-dag ni gnas zhes brjod-de*.

6. The characters *gamārtho yaduta buddhārtho dha* are lost in B's break and have been supplied from T and C.

कमर्थिंश्च । अयमुच्यतेऽर्थः । यैरक्षरैरेष सप्तप्रकारोऽधिगमार्थः सूच्यते प्रकाश्यत इदमुच्यते व्यञ्जनम् । स चैष[1] वज्रपदनिर्देशो विस्तरेण यथासूत्रमनुगन्तव्यः ।

अनिदर्शनो ह्यानन्द तथागतः । स न शक्यश्चक्षुषा द्रष्टुम् । अनभिलाप्यो ह्यानन्द धर्मः । स न शक्यः कर्णेन श्रोतुम्[2] । असंस्कृतो ह्यानन्द संघः । स न शक्यः कायेन वा चित्तेन वा पर्युपा(2a)सितुम् । इतीमानि त्रीणि वज्रपदानि दृढाध्याशयपरिवर्तानुसारेणानुगन्तव्यानि[3] ।

तथागतविषयो हि शारिपुत्रायमर्थस्तथागतगोचरः । सर्वश्रावकप्रत्येकबुद्धैरपि तावच्छारिपुत्रायमर्थो न शक्यः सम्यक् स्वप्रज्ञया × × × द्रष्टुं वा प्रत्यवेक्षितुं वा[4] । प्रागेव बालपृथ[5]ग्जनैरन्यत्र तथागतश्रद्धागमनतः । श्रद्धागमनीयो हि शारिपुत्र परमार्थः । परमार्थ इति शारिपुत्र[6] सत्त्वधातोरेतदधिवचनम् । सत्त्वधातुरिति शारिपुत्र तथागतगर्भस्यैतदधिवचनम् । तथागतगर्भ इति शारिपुत्र धर्मकायस्यैतदधिवचनम् । इतीदं चतुर्थं वज्रपदमनूनत्वापूर्णत्वनिर्देशपरिवर्ता[7]नुसारेणानुगन्तव्यम् ।

1. The characters *dam ucyate vyañjanam / sa cai* are lost in B's break and have been supplied from T and C; the latter adds a brief quotation from an unnamed sūtra in support of the statement.

2. The characters *ḥ sa na śakyate karṇena śro* are lost in B's break and have been supplied from T and C.

3. The characters *anugantavyāni / Tathāga* are lost in B's break and have been supplied from T. O gives the name of the sūtra as *Sthirādhyāśayaparivarta*.

4. B has a break here; T shows three infinitives, *śes-pa* (*jñātum?*), *blta-ba*, *brtag-pa*, but the second and the prepositions of the third are not quite certain in B, which is disfigured by a stain.

5. B omits *tha*.

6. B has a break and stain covering four or five characters after *Śāri*, and goes on with two of the hieroglyphics it uses to fill up a gap and then with *sattvadhātor*. T shows that only *putra* is to be supplied.

7. T omits *parivarta* in the title of the sūtra, possibly rightly; cf. below.

अनुत्तरा सम्यक्संबोधिरिति भगवन् निर्वाणधातोरेतदधिवचनम् । निर्वाणधातुरिति भगवन् तथागतधर्मकायस्यैतदधिवचनम् । इतीदं पञ्चमं वज्रपदमार्यश्रीमालासूत्रानुसारेणानुगन्तव्यम् ।

योऽयं शारिपुत्र तथागतनिर्दिष्टो धर्मकायः सोऽयमविनिर्भागधर्मा । अविनिर्मुक्तज्ञानगुणो यदुत गङ्गानदीवालिकाव्यतिक्रान्तैस्तथागतधर्मैः । इ(2*b*)तीदं षष्ठं वज्रपदमनूनत्वापूर्णत्व[1]निर्देशानुसारेणानुगन्तव्यम् ।

न मञ्जुश्रीस्तथागतः कल्पयति न विकल्पयति । अथवास्यानाभोगेनाकल्पयतोऽविकल्पयत इयमेवंरूपा क्रिया प्रवर्तते । इतीदं सप्तमं वज्रपदं **तथागतगुणज्ञानाचिन्त्यविषयावतारनिर्देशा**नुसारेणानुगन्तव्यम् । इतीमानि समासतः सप्त वज्रपदानि सकलस्यास्य शास्त्रस्योद्देशमुखसंग्रहार्थेन शरीरमिति वेदितव्यम् ।

स्वलक्षणेनानुगतानि चैषां
यथाक्रमं धारणिराजसूत्रे ।
निदानत[2]स्त्रीणि पदानि विद्या-
च्चत्वारि धीमज्जिनधर्मभेदात् ॥ २ ॥

एषां च सप्तानां वज्रपदानां स्वलक्षणनिर्देशेन यथाक्रम**मार्यधारणीश्वरराजसूत्रनिदानपरिवर्ता**नुगतानि त्रीणि पदानि[3] वेदितव्यानि । तत ऊर्ध्वमवशिष्टानि चत्वारि बोधिसत्त्वतथागतधर्मनिर्देशभेदादिति । तस्माद्यदुक्तम्[4] ।

भगवान् सर्वधर्मसमताभिसंबुद्धः सुप्रवर्तितधर्मचक्रोऽनन्तशिष्यगणसुविनीत इति । एभिस्त्रिभिर्मूलपदैर्यथाक्रमं त्रयाणां रत्नानामनुपूर्वसमुत्पादसमुदागमव्यव[5]स्थानं वेदितव्यम् । अवशिष्टानि चत्वारि पदानि त्रिरत्नोत्पत्त्यनुरूपहेतुसमुदा(3*a*)गमनिर्देशो वेदितव्यः । तत्र यतोऽष्टम्यां बोधिसत्त्वभूमौ वर्तमानः सर्व-

1. *anūnāpūrṇnatva°*, B, but cf. above. C gives a longer quotation from the sūtra.
2. B om. *ta*.
3. B om. *padāni*, which is given by T and C.
4. The characters *tasmā* (*de-las*, T) are lost in a break in B.
5. The characters *samutpāda* and *gamavya* are lost in two breaks in B, and have been supplied from T's *skye-ba ḥgrub-pa rnam-par bzhag-par*, with which C agrees in sense.

धर्मवशिताप्राप्तो भवति तस्मात् स बोधिमण्डवरगतः सर्वधर्मसमताभिसंबुद्ध इत्युच्यते । यतो नवम्यां बोधिसत्त्वभूमौ वर्तमानोऽनुत्तरधर्मभाणकत्वसंपन्नः[1] सर्वसत्त्वाशयसुविधिज्ञ इन्द्रियपरमपारमिताप्राप्तः सर्वसत्त्वक्लेश[2]वासनानुसंधिसमुद्घातनकुशलो भवति तस्मात् सोऽभिसंबुद्धबोधिः सुप्रवर्तितधर्मचक्र इत्युच्यते । यतो दशम्यां भूमाव[3]नुत्तरतथागतधर्मयौवराज्याभिषेकप्राप्त्यनन्तरमनाभोगबुद्धकार्याप्रतिप्रश्रब्धो भवति तस्मात् स सुप्रवर्तितधर्मचक्रोऽनन्तशिष्यगणसुविनीत इत्युच्यते । तां पुनरनन्तशिष्यगणसुविनीततां तद[4]नन्तरमनेन ग्रन्थेन दर्शयति । महता भिक्षुसंघेन सार्धं यावदप्रमेयेण च बोधिसत्त्वगणेन सार्धमिति । यथाक्रमं श्रावकबोधौ बुद्धबोधौ च सुविनीतत्वादेवंगुण[5]समन्वागतैरिति ।

ततःश्रावकबोधिसत्त्वगुणवर्णनिर्देशानन्तरमचिन्त्यबुद्धसमाधिवृषभितां[6]प्रतीत्य विपुलरत्नव्यूहमण्डलव्यूह[7] निर्वृत्तितथागतपरिषत्समावर्तनविविधदिव्यद्रव्य[8]पूजाविधानस्तुतिमेघाभिसंप्रव (3b) र्षणतो बुद्धरत्नगुणविभागव्यवस्थानं वेदितव्यम् । तदनन्तरमुदारधर्मासनव्यूहप्रभाधर्मपर्यायनामगुणपरिकीर्तनतो धर्मरत्नगुणविभागव्यवस्थानं वेदितव्यम् । तदनन्तरमन्योन्यं[9] बोधिसत्त्वसमाधिगोचरविषयप्रभावसंदर्शनतद्विचित्रगुणवर्णनिर्देशतः संघरत्नगुणविभागव्यवस्थानं वेदितव्यम् । तदन-

1. B omits *anuttaradharmabhāṇakatvasaṁpannaḥ*, which is supplied from T's *bla-na-med-paḥi chos smra-ba-ñid daṅ ldan-pa*, and appears also in C. For *dharmabhāṇakatva* in the ninth stage, cf. *Daśabh.*, p. 76, section M.

2. B omits *kleśa*, which is given by T and C.

3. *yato daśamyāv anuttara°*, B; *sa bcu-pa-la*, T.

4. B om. *tad*; *de ma-thag-tu*, T.

5. *eva guṇa°*, B; *de-lta-buḥi yon-tan*, T.

6. *vṛṣabhitāṁ* is probably a misreading for *vṛṣabhatāṁ*, which occurs repeatedly in the *Daśabh.*

7. For *maṇḍalavyūha*, a common phrase in this connection, T has *ḥkhor-gyi khyams*, which should stand for *maṇḍalamāla*.

8. B omits *dravya*, supplied from T's *rdzas*. *Samāvartana* in the sense of 'assembling' (so T and O) is unknown; but C suggests, much more probably, that it means 'presents' made to the Tathāgata, in accordance with the usual classical sense.

9. T seems to read *anyonyaṁ* as well as B; apparently it is to be construed as an adverb with *saṁdarśana*, but *anyonya°* would seem better. C translates it as 'various'.

न्तरं पुनरपि बुद्धरश्म्यभिषेकैरनुत्तरधर्मराजज्येष्ठपुत्रपरमवैशारद्यप्रतिभानोपकरणतां[1] प्रतीत्य तथागतभूतगुणपरमार्थस्तुतिनिर्देशतश्च महायानपरमधर्मकथावस्तूपन्यसनतश्च तत्प्रतिपत्तेः परमधर्मैश्वर्यफलप्राप्तिसंदर्शनतश्च यथासंख्यमेषामेव त्रयाणां रत्नानामनुत्तरगुणविभागव्यवस्थानं निदानपरिवर्तावसानगतमेव द्रष्टव्यम्।

ततः सूत्रनिदानपरिवर्तानन्तरं बुद्धधातुः षष्ट्याकारतद्विशुद्धिगुणपरिकर्मनिर्देशेन परिदीपितः। विशोध्येऽर्थे गुणवति तद्विशुद्धिपरिकर्मयोगात्। इमं चार्थवशमुपादाय दशसु बोधिसत्त्वभूमिषु पुनर्जातरूपपरिकर्मविशेषोदाहरणमुदाहृतम्[2]। अस्मिन्नेव च सूत्रे तथाग(4*a*)तकर्मनिर्देशानन्तरमविशुद्धवैडूर्यमणिदृष्टान्तः कृतः।

तद्यथा कुलपुत्र कुशलो मणिकारो मणिशुद्धिसुविधिज्ञः। स मणिगोत्रादपर्यवदापितानि मणिरत्नानि गृहीत्वा तीक्ष्णेन खारोदकेनोत्क्षाल्य[3] कृष्णेन[4] केशकम्बलपर्यवदापनेन[5] पर्यवदापयति। न च तावन्मात्रेण वीर्यं प्रश्रम्भयति। ततः पश्चात् तीक्ष्णेनामिषरसेनोत्क्षाल्य खण्डिकापर्यवदापनेन[6] पर्यवदापयति। न च तावन्मात्रेण वीर्यं प्रश्रम्भयति। ततः स[7] पश्चान्महाभैषज्यरसेनोत्क्षाल्य सूक्ष्मवस्त्रपर्यवदापनेन पर्यवदापयति[8]। पर्यवदापितं चापगतकाचम[9]भिजातवैडूर्य-

1. The characters between *prati* and *natāṁ* are uncertain in B, which is rubbed; *spobs-pa....ñe-bar bsgrub-pa-la*, T. I take *upakaraṇa* in the sense of 'conferring', but the reading should possibly be *upaharaṇatāṁ*. C affords no help.

2. T om. *punar* and *viśeṣa*.

3. B here and twice below has *unmīlya* which I conjecture to be a mistake for *utkṣālya* in view of T's *sbasṅ-nas* and C's 'wash'; cf. *suprakṣālita* of a jewel at *Kāś. P.*, 131, p. 188. Note the Prakrit form *khāra*.

4. T om. *kṛṣṇena*.

5. °*payavadānena*, B, but cf. below.

6. °*paryayadāpanena*, B. I cannot trace the word *khaṇḍikā* anywhere else; T translates *bal-gyi la-ba*, 'blanket of wool', but C, which I do not quite understand, appears to indicate a cloth of some vegetable fibre.

7. T om. *sa*.

8. °*dāpayayali*, B.

9. For *apagalakācam* see Rhys-Davids Stede, *Pali Dict.*, s. *kāca* and *kācin*. 'T' has *dri-ma* (*mala*).

मित्युच्यते । एवमेव कुलपुत्र तथागतोऽप्यपरिशुद्धं सत्त्वधातुं विदित्वानित्यदुःखानात्माशुभोद्वेगकथया संसाराभिरतान् सत्त्वानुद्वेजयति । आर्ये च धर्मविनयेऽवतारयति । न च तावन्मात्रेण तथागतो वीर्यं प्रश्रम्भयति । ततः पश्चाच्छून्यानिमित्ताप्रणिहितकथया तथागतनेत्री[1]मवबोधयति । न च तावन्मात्रेण तथागतो वीर्यं प्रश्रम्भयति । ततः पश्चादविवर्त्यधर्मचक्रकथया त्रिमण्डलपरिशुद्धिकथया च[2] तथागतविषये तान् सत्त्वानवतारयति नानाप्रकृतिहेतुकान् । अवती(4*b*)र्णाश्च समानास्तथागतधर्मतामधिगम्यानुत्तरा दक्षिणीया इत्युच्यन्त इति[3] ।

एतदेव विशुद्धगोत्रं तथागतधातुमभिसंधायोक्तम् ।

यथा पत्थरचुण्णम्हि[4] जातरूपं न दिस्सति ।
परिकम्मेण तद् दिट्ठं एवं लोके तथागता इति ॥

तत्र कतमे ते बुद्धधातोः षष्ट्याकारविशुद्धिपरिकर्मगुणाः । तद्यथा चतुराकारो बोधिसत्त्वालंकारः । अष्टाकारो बोधिसत्त्वावभासः । षोडशाकारी बोधिसत्त्वमहाकरुणा । द्वात्रिंशदाकारं बोधिसत्त्वकर्म ।

तन्निर्देशानन्तरं बुद्धबोधिः षोडशाकारमहाबोधिकरुणानिर्देशेन[5] परिदीपिता । तन्निर्देशानन्तरं बुद्धगुणा दशबलचतुर्वैशारद्याष्टादशावेणिकबुद्धधर्मनिर्देशेन परिदीपिताः । तन्निर्देशानन्तरं बुद्धकर्म द्वात्रिंशदाकार[6]निरुत्तरतथागतकर्मनिर्देशेन परिदीपितम् । एवमिमानि सप्त वज्रपदानि स्वलक्षणनिर्देशतो[7] विस्तरेण यथासूत्रमनुगन्तव्यानि । कः पुनरेषामनुश्लेषः ।

1. T translates *netrī* by *tshul*, i.e. as equivalent to *naya* or *nyāya*.

2. B om. *ca*, which is supplied from T.

3. *dakṣiṇī ity ucyante iti*, B; T translates *dakṣiṇīya* by *yon-gnas*, possibly a mistake for the more correct *sbyin-gnas*.

4. B om. *ttha*; *rdo-yi phyi-ma-la*, T; 'stone ore', C, which does not name the sūtra in which this Prakrit verse is found.

5. *ṣoḍaśākārā mahākaruṇānirdeśena*, B; *byaṅ-chub chen-poḥi sñiṅ-rjeḥi rnam-pa bcu-drug bstan-pas*, T; 'which has 16 kinds of *Buddha-bodhi mahākaruṇā* mind', C, which supports T's reading adopted in the text.

6. Possibly B reads *dvātriṁśadākāraṁ*, but C and T certainly as in text.

7. *bstan-paḥi sgo-nas* (*nirdeśamukhena* or °*mukhato*), T.

बुद्धाद्धर्मो धर्मतश्चार्यसंघः
संघे[1] गर्भो ज्ञानधात्वाप्तिनिष्ठः ।
तज्ज्ञानाप्तिश्चाग्रबोधिर्बलाद्यै-
र्धर्मैर्युक्ता सर्वसत्त्वार्थकृद्भिः ॥ ३ ॥

उक्तः शास्त्रसंबन्धः ।

इदानीं श्लोकानामर्थो वक्तव्यः । ये सत्त्वास्तथागतेन[2] विनीतास्ते तथागतं शरणं गच्छन्तो धर्मतानिष्यन्दा[3]भिप्रसादेन (5*a*) धर्मं च संघं च शरणं गच्छन्ति । अतस्तत्प्रथमतो बुद्धरत्नमधिकृत्य श्लोकः ।

यो बुद्धत्वमनादिमध्यनिधनं शान्तं विबुद्धः स्वयं
बुद्ध्वा चाबुधबोधनार्थमभयं मार्गं दिदेश ध्रुवम् ।
तस्मै ज्ञानकृपासिवज्रवरधृग्दुःखाङ्कुरैकच्छिदे[4]
नानादृग्गहनोपगूढविमतिप्राकारभेत्त्रे नमः ॥ ४ ॥

अनेन किं दर्शयति ।

असंस्कृतमनाभोगमपरप्रत्ययोदितम् ।
बुद्धत्वं ज्ञानकारुण्यशक्त्युपेतं द्वयार्थवत् ॥ ५ ॥

अनेन समासतो[5]ऽष्टाभिर्गुणैः संगृहीतं बुद्धत्वमुद्भावितम् । अष्टौ गुणाः कतमे । असंस्कृतत्वमनाभोगतापरप्रत्ययाभिसंबोधिर्ज्ञानं करुणा शक्तिः स्वार्थसंपत् परार्थसंपदिति ।

1. T (*tshogs-las*) and possibly C read *saṁghād*, but B's *saṁghe* gives the better sense, as the Tathāgatagarbha is in each member of the community and by its working leads to the acquisition of knowledge and the realization of the *dhātu* (=*dhatu*).

2. B adds *ca*, which T om.

3. °*niḥsyandā*°, B.

4. °*aikacchede*, B against the metre. T and C om. *eka*.

5. B om. *to*.

अनादिमध्यनिधनप्रकृतत्वादसंस्कृतम् ।
शान्तधर्मशरीरत्वादनाभोगमिति स्मृतम् ॥ ६ ॥
प्रत्यात्ममधिगम्यत्वादपरप्रत्ययोदयम् ।
ज्ञानमेवं त्रिधा बोधात् करुणा मार्गदेशनात् ॥ ७ ॥
शक्तिर्ज्ञानकृपाभ्यां तु दुःखक्लेशनिबर्हणात् ।
त्रिभिराद्यैर्गुणैः स्वार्थः परार्थः पश्चिमैस्त्रिभिः ॥ ८ ॥

संस्कृतविपर्ययेणासंस्कृतं वेदितव्यम् । तत्र संस्कृतमुच्यते यस्योत्पादोऽपि प्रज्ञायते स्थितिरपि भङ्गोऽपि प्रज्ञायते । तदभावाद्बुद्धत्वमनादिमध्यनिधनमसंस्कृतधर्मकाय[1]प्रभावितं द्रष्टव्यम् । सर्वप्रपञ्चविकल्पोपशान्तत्वादनाभोगम् । स्वयंभूज्ञानाधिगम्यत्वादपरप्रत्ययोदयम् । उ(5*b*)दयोऽत्राभिसंबोधोऽभिप्रेतोत्पादः[2] । इत्यसंस्कृतादप्रवृत्तिलक्षणादपि तथागतत्वाद[3]नाभोगतः सर्वसंबुद्धकृत्यमा संसारकोटेरनुपरतमनुपच्छिन्नं प्रवर्तते ।

इत्येवमत्यद्भुताचिन्त्यविषयं बुद्धत्वमश्रुत्वा परतः स्वयमनाचार्यकेण स्वयंभूज्ञानेन निरभिलाप्यस्वभावतामभिसंबुध्य तदनुबोधं प्रत्यबुधानामपि जात्यन्धानां परेषामनुबोधाय तदनुगाभिमार्गव्युपदेशकरणादनुत्तरज्ञानकरुणान्वितत्वं वेदितव्यम् । मार्गस्याभयत्वं लोकोत्तरत्वात् । लोकोत्तरत्वमपुनरावृत्तितश्च । यथाक्रमं परदुःखक्लेशमूलसमुद्घातं प्रत्यनयोरेव तथागतज्ञानकरुणयोः शक्तिरसिवज्रदृष्टान्तेन परिदीपिता । तत्र दुःखमूलं समासतो या काचिद्भवेषु नामरूपाभिनिर्वृत्तिः[4] । क्लेशमूलं या काचित्सत्कायाभिनिवेशपूर्विका दृष्टिर्विचिकित्सा च । तत्र नामरूपसंगृहीतं दुःखमभिनिर्वृत्तिलक्षणत्वादङ्कुरस्थानीयं वेदित-

1. °*dharmatraya*°, B. T and C as in text.

2. T's *ḥdod-kyi skye-ba ni ma-yin-no* shows that it read °*saṁbodho nābhipretotpādaḥ*, which does not mean 'here the word *udaya* is to be understood in the sense of thorough cognition, but not in that of origination', as O gives it. C's rendering is unrecognizable in the Sanskrit.

3. T's reading *de-bzhin gśegs-pa de-ñid-kyi phyir* (*Tathāgatatattvād*) is not supported by C.

4. Here and in the next sentence but one B has °*nivṛtti*°, but T's *grub-pa*, corresponding to the text, must be right.

व्यम् । तच्छेत्तृत्वे तथागतज्ञानकरुणयोः शक्तिरसिदृष्टान्तेनोपमिता वेदितव्या । दृष्टिविचिकित्सासंगृहीतो दर्शनमार्गप्रहेयः[1] क्लेशो लौकिकज्ञानदुरवगाहो दुर्भेदत्वाद्वनगहनोपगूढप्राकारसदृशः । तद्भेत्तृत्वात् तथागतज्ञानकरुणयोः शक्तिर्वज्रदृष्टान्तेनोपमिता वेदितव्या ।

(6*a*) इत्येते यथोद्दिष्टाः षट् तथागतगुणा विस्तरविभागनिर्देशतोऽनयैवानुपूर्व्या **सर्वबुद्धविषयावतारज्ञानालोकालंकारसूत्रा**नुसारेणानुगन्तव्याः । तत्र यदुक्तमनुत्पादोऽनिरोध इति मञ्जुश्रीस्तथागतोऽर्हन् सम्यक्संबुद्ध एष इत्यनेन तावदसंस्कृतलक्षणस्तथागत इति परिदीपितम् । यत्पुनरनन्तरं विमलवैडूर्यपृथिवीशक्रप्रतिबिम्बोदाहरणमादिं कृत्वा यावन्नवभिरुदाहरणैरेतमेवानुत्पादानिरोधतथागतार्थमधिकृत्याह[2] । एवमेव मञ्जुश्रीस्तथागतोऽर्हन् सम्यक्संबुद्धो नेञ्जते न विठपति[3] न प्रपञ्चयति न कल्पयति न विकल्पयति । अकल्पोऽविकल्पो[4]ऽचित्तोऽमनसिकारः शीतीभूतोऽनुत्पादोऽनिरोधोऽदृष्टोऽश्रुतोऽनाघ्रातोऽनास्वादितोऽस्पृष्टोऽनिमित्तोऽविज्ञप्तिकोऽविज्ञपनीय इत्येवमादिरुपशमप्रभेदप्रदेश[5]निर्देशः । अनेन स्वक्रियासु सर्वप्रपञ्चविकल्पोपशान्तत्वादनाभोगस्तथागत इति परिदीपितम् । तत ऊर्ध्वमुदाहरणनिर्देशादवशिष्टेन ग्रन्थेन सर्वधर्मतथताभिसंबोधमुखेष्वपरप्रत्ययाभिसंबोधस्तथागतस्य परिदीपितः[6] । यत्पुनरन्ते षोडशाकारां तथागतबोधिं निर्दिश्यैवमाह । तत्र मञ्जुश्रीस्तथागतस्यैवंरूपान् सर्वधर्मानभिसंबुध्य सत्त्वानां च धर्मधातुं व्य(6*b*)वलोक्याशुद्धमविमलं साङ्गनं विक्रीडिता नाम[7] सत्त्वेषु

1. T om. *mārga*, but C has it.

2. T om. *anutpādānirodhatathāgata*, but C supports B's reading. For the nine examples see iv, 13ff.

3. T translates *viṭhapati* by *sems-par byed-pa*, 'thinks'; C similarly. The *Mvy.* gives *rnam-par bsgrub-pa* as the equivalent.

4. B omits *akalpo 'vikalpo*, which are supplied from T, as C has one of them.

5. T om. *pradeśa*, and C translates it by the equivalent of *lakṣaṇa*, so that it should mean 'designation' therefore (Soothill and Hodous, *Dict. of Chinese Buddhist Terms*, 309*b*).

6. T om. *abhisaṁbodhas Tathāgatasya* and apparently read *aparapratyayatvaṁ paridīpitam*. C supports B's readings.

7. B om. *ma*; *zhes-bya-baḥi*, T. I can find no parallel to this use of *vikrīḍitā* as a feminine noun meaning 'taking compassion on'

महाकरुणा प्रवर्तंत इति । अनेन तथागतस्यानुत्तरज्ञानकरुणान्वितत्वमुद्भावितम् । तत्रैवंरूपान् सर्वधर्मानिति यथापूर्वं[1] निर्दिष्टानभावस्वभावात् । अभिसंबुध्येति यथाभूतमविकल्पबुद्धज्ञानेन ज्ञात्वा । सत्त्वानामिति नियतानियतमिथ्यानियतराशिव्यवस्थितानाम् । धर्मधातुमिति स्वधर्मताप्रकृतिनिर्विशिष्टतथागतगर्भम् । व्यवलोक्येति सर्वाकारमनावरणेन बुद्धचक्षुषा दृष्ट्वा । अशुद्धं क्लेशावरणेन बालपृथग्जनानाम् । अविमलं ज्ञेयावरणेन श्रावकप्रत्येकबुद्धानाम् । साङ्गनं तदुभयान्यतमविशिष्टतया बोधिसत्त्वानाम् । विक्रीडिता विविधा संपन्नविनयोपायमुखेषु[2] सुप्रविष्टत्वात् । सत्त्वेषु महाकरुणा[3] प्रवर्तंत इति समतया सर्व[4]सत्त्वनिमित्तमभिसंबुद्ध[5]बोधेः स्वधर्मताधिगमसंप्रापणाशयत्वात् । यदित ऊर्ध्वमनुत्तरज्ञानकरुणाप्रवृत्तेरसमधर्मचक्रप्रवर्तनाभिनिर्हारप्रयोगाश्रंसनमियमनयोः परार्थकरणे शक्तिर्वेदितव्या । तत्रैषामेव यथाक्रमं षण्णां तथागतगुणानामाद्यैस्त्रिभिरसंस्कृतादिभिर्योगः स्वार्थसंपत् । त्रिभिरवशिष्टैर्ज्ञानादिभिः[6] परार्थसंपत् । अपि खलु ज्ञानेन परमनित्योपशान्तिपदस्वाभिसंबोधिस्थान(*7a*)गुणात् स्वार्थसंपत् परिदीपिता । करुणाशक्तिभ्यामनुत्तरमहाधर्मचक्रप्रवृत्तिस्थान[7]गुणात् परार्थसंपदिति ।

अतो[8] बुद्धरत्नाद्धर्मरत्नप्रभावनेति तद[9]नन्तरं तदधिकृत्य श्लोकः ।

> यो नासन्न च सन्न चापि सदसन्नान्यः सतो नासतो[10]
> ऽशक्यस्तर्कयितुं निरुक्त्यपगतः प्रत्यातमवेद्यः शिवः ।

1. *go-rim ji-lta-ba* (*yathākramam*), T; but C, 'as said above'.
2. *gdul-byaḥi thabs-kyi sgo sna-tshogs-pa grub-pa-la* (*vividheṣu sampannavineyopāyamukheṣu* ?), T.
3. T om. *mahākaruṇā*, but C has it.
4. T om. *sarva*, but C has it.
5. T om. *buddha*, but C has it.
6. T adds here *yogaḥ* (*ldan-pa*), which can however equally well be understood from the previous sentence.
7. T om. *sthāna*.
8. B om. *ato*, supplied from T.
9. B om. *tad*, supplied from T. Cf. the introductory sentence to verse 13 below.
10. *nāsataḥ śakyas*, B; *mi-nus*, T, confirmed by C.

तस्मै धर्मदिवाकराय विमलज्ञानावभासत्विषे
सर्वारम्वण[1]रागदोषतिमिरव्याघातकर्त्रे नमः ॥ ९ ॥

अनेन किं दर्शितम् ।

अचिन्त्याद्वयनिष्कल्पशुद्धिव्यक्तिविपक्षतः ।
यो येन च विरागोऽसौ धर्मः सत्यद्विलक्षणः ॥ १० ॥

अनेन समासतोऽष्टाभिर्गुणैः संगृहीतं धर्मरत्नमुद्भावितम् । अष्टौ गुणाः कतमे । अचिन्त्यत्वमद्वयता निर्विकल्पता शुद्धिरभिव्यक्तिकरणं प्रतिपक्षता विरागो विरागहेतुरिति ।

निरोधमार्गसत्याभ्यां संगृहीता विरागिता ।
गुणैस्त्रिभिस्त्रिभिश्चैते[2] वेदितव्ये यथाक्रमम् ॥ ११ ॥

एषामेव यथाक्रमं षण्णां गुणानां त्रिभिराद्यैरचिन्त्याद्वयनिर्विकल्पतागुणैर्निरोधसत्यपरिदीपनाद्विरागसंग्रहो वेदितव्यः । त्रिभिरवशिष्टैः शुद्ध्यभिव्यक्तिप्रतिपक्षतागुणैर्मार्गसत्यपरिदीपनाद्विरागहेतुसंग्रह इति । यश्च विरागो निरोधसत्यं येन च विरागो मार्गसत्येन तदुभयमभिसमस्य व्यवदानसत्य (7b) द्वयलक्षणो विरागधर्म इति परिदीपितम् ।

अतर्क्यत्वादलाप्यत्वादार्यज्ञानादचिन्त्यता ।
शिवत्वादद्वयाकल्पौ शुद्ध्यादि त्रयमर्कवत् ॥ १२ ॥

समासतो निरोधसत्यस्य त्रिभिः कारणैरचिन्त्यत्वं वेदितव्यम् । कतमैस्त्रिभिः । असत्सत्सदसन्नोभयप्रकारैश्चतुर्भिरपि तर्कागोचरत्वात् । सर्वरुतरवितघोषवाक्पथनिरुक्तिसंकेतव्यवहाराभिलापैरनभिलाप्यत्वात् । आर्याणां च प्रत्यात्मवेदनीयत्वात् ।

1. In this text *ārambaṇa* replaces the more usual *ālambana*. Cf. Pali *ārammaṇa*.

2. *tribhis tribhir eva*, By, *di-dag dan yon-tan gsum gsum-kyis*, T. *Ete* is required to show that the line refers to the two Truths.

तत्र निरोधसत्यस्य कथमद्वयता निर्विकल्पता च वेदितव्या[1] । यथोक्तं भगवता[2] । शिवोऽयं शारिपुत्र धर्मकायोऽद्वयधर्माविकल्पधर्मा । तत्र द्वयमुच्यते कर्म क्लेशाश्च । विकल्प उच्यते कर्मक्लेशसमुदयहेतुरयोनिशोमनसिकारः । तत्प्रकृतिनिरोधप्रतिवेधाद् द्वयविकल्पासमुदाचारयोगेन यो दुःखस्यात्यन्तमनुत्पाद इदमुच्यते दुःखनिरोधसत्यम् । न खलु कस्यचिद्धर्मस्य विनाशाद्दुःखनिरोधसत्यं परिदीपितम् । यथोक्तम् । अनुत्पादानिरोधे मञ्जुश्रीश्चित्तमनोविज्ञानानि न[3] प्रवर्तन्ते । यत्र चित्तमनोविज्ञानानि न प्रवर्तन्ते तत्र न कश्चित्परिकल्पो येन परिकल्पेनायोनिशोमनसिकुर्यात् । स योनिशोमनसिकारप्र(8a)युक्तोऽविद्यां न समुत्थापयति । यच्चाविद्यासमुत्थानं तद् द्वादशानां भवाङ्गानामसमुत्थानम् । साजातिरिति विस्तरः[4] । यथोक्तम्[5] । न खलु भगवन् धर्मविनाशो दुःखनिरोधः । दुःखनिरोधनाम्ना भगवन्ननादिकालिकोऽकृतोऽजातोऽनुत्पन्नोऽक्षयः क्षयापगतः नित्यो ध्रुवः शिवः शाश्वतः प्रकृतिपरिशुद्धः सर्वक्लेशकोशविनिर्मुक्तो गङ्गा[6]वालिकाव्यतिवृत्तैरविनिर्भागैरचिन्त्यैर्बुद्धधर्मैः[7] समन्वागतस्तथागतधर्मकायो देशितः । अयमेव च भगवंस्तथागतधर्मकायोऽविनिर्मुक्तक्लेशकोशस्तथागतगर्भः सूच्यते । इति सर्वविस्तरेण यथासूत्रमेव दुःखनिरोधसत्यव्यवस्थानमनुगन्तव्यम् ।

अस्य खलु दुःखनिरोधसंज्ञितस्य तथागतधर्मकायस्य प्राप्तिहेतुरविकल्पज्ञानदर्शनभावनामार्गस्त्रिविधेन साधर्म्येण दिनकरसदृशः वेदितव्यः । मण्डलविशुद्धिसाधर्म्येण सर्वोपक्लेशमलविगतत्वात् । रूपाभिव्यक्तिकरणसाधर्म्येण सर्वाकारज्ञेयावभासकत्वात् । तमःप्रतिपक्षसाधर्म्येण च सर्वाकारसत्यदर्शन[8]विबन्धप्रतिपक्षभूतत्वात् ।

1. *veditavye* would be more regular.

2. From the *Anūnatvāpūrṇatvanirdeśaparivarta* according to C.

3. B om. *na*, which T has. C omits the sentence. The quotation is noted by O as from the *Jñānālokālaṁkārasūtra*.

4. T had *ityādi vistaraḥ*.

5. From the *Āryaśrīmālāsūtra*.

6. T reads *Gaṅgānadī*°, which is perhaps preferable.

7. C adds *amuktajñair* and another adjective ('not different' ?).

8. *sarvākāratv*(?)*adarśana*°, B; *dben mthoṅ-baḥi dgegs-kyiernam-pa thams-cad-kyi*, T. C om. *satya*.

विबन्धः पुनरभूतवस्तुनिमित्तारम्बणमनसिकारपूर्विका रागद्वेषमोहोत्पत्तिरनुशयपर्युत्थानयोगात् । अनुशयतो हि बालानाम(8b)भूतमतत्स्वभावं वस्तु शुभाकारेण वा निमित्तं भवति रागोत्पत्तितः । प्रतिघाकारेण वा द्वेषोत्पत्तितः । अविद्याकारेण वा मोहोत्पत्तितः । तच्च रागद्वेषमोहनिमित्तमयथाभूतमारम्बणं कुर्वतामयोनिशोमनसिकारश्चित्तं पर्याददाति । तेषामयोनिशोमनसिकारपर्यवस्थितचेतसां रागद्वेषमोहानामन्यतमक्लेशसमुदाचारो भवति । ते ततोनिदानं कायेन वाचा मनसा रागजमपि कर्माभिसंस्कुर्वन्ति । द्वेषजमपि मोहजमपि कर्माभिसंस्कुर्वन्ति । कर्मतश्च पुनर्जन्मानुबन्ध एव भवति । एवमेषां बालानामनुशयवतां निमित्तग्राहिणामारम्बणचरितानामयोनिशोमनसिकारसमुदाचारात्[1] क्लेशसमुदयः । क्लेशसमुदयात् कर्मसमुदयः । कर्मसमुदयाज्जन्मसमुदयो भवति । स पुनरेष सर्वाकारक्लेशकर्मजन्मसंक्लेशो बालानामेकस्य धातोर्यथाभूतमज्ञानाददर्शनाच्च[2] प्रवर्तते ।

स च तथा द्रष्टव्यो यथा परिगवेषयन्न तस्य[3] किंचि[4]न्निमित्तमारम्बणं वा पश्यति । स यदा न[5] निमित्तं नारम्बणं वा पश्यति तदा भूतं पश्यति । एवमेते धर्मास्तथागतेनाभिसंबुद्धाः समतया समा इति[6] । य एवमसतश्च निमित्तारम्बणस्यादर्शनात् सतश्च यथाभूत(9a)स्य परमार्थसत्यस्य दर्शनात् तदुभयोरनुत्क्षेपाप्रक्षेपसमताज्ञानेन सर्वधर्मसमताभिसंबोधः सोऽस्य सर्वाकारस्य तत्त्वदर्शनविबन्धस्य प्रतिपक्षो वेदितव्यो यस्योदयादितरस्यात्यन्तमसंगतिरसमवधानं प्रवर्तते । स खल्वेष धर्मकायप्राप्तिहेतुरविकल्पज्ञानदर्शनभावनामार्गो विस्तरेण यथासूत्रं प्रज्ञापारमितानुसारेणानुगन्तव्यः ।

अतो महायानधर्मरत्नादवैवर्तिकबोधिसत्त्वगणरत्नप्रभावनेति तदनन्तरं तदधिकृत्य श्लोकः ।

1. °*samudācārā*, B. T reads °*samudayāt* (*kun ḥbyuṅ-ba-las*).
2. T om. *adarśanāc ca*, but C gives it.
3. B om. *tasya*; *deḥi*, T. C implies the text reading.
4. *kaṁcin*, B.
5. B om. *na*, which is required by the context.
6. T om. *iti*, and B has an illegible hieroglyphic for the first *i*.

ये सम्यक् प्रतिविध्य सर्वजगतो नैरात्म्यकोटिं शिवां
तच्चित्तप्रकृतिप्रभास्वरतया क्लेशास्वभावेक्षणात् ।
सर्वत्रानुगतामनावृतधियः पश्यन्ति संबुद्धतां[1]
तेभ्यः सत्त्वविशुद्ध्यनन्तविषयज्ञानेक्षणेभ्यो नमः ।। १३ ।।

अनेन किं दर्शितम् ।

यथावद्यावदध्यात्मज्ञानदर्शनशुद्धितः ।
धीमतामविवर्त्यानामनुत्तरगुणैर्गणः ।। १४ ।।

अनेन समासतोऽवैवर्तिकबोधिसत्त्वगणरत्नस्य द्वाभ्यामाकाराभ्यां[2] यथावद्भाविकतया यावद्भाविकतया च लोकोत्तरज्ञानदर्शनविशुद्धितोऽ[3]नुत्तरगुणान्वितत्वमु[4]द्भावितम् ।

यथावत्तज्जगच्छान्तधर्मतावगमात् स च ।
प्रकृतेः परिशुद्धत्वात् क्लेशस्यादिक्षयेक्षणात्[5] ।। १५ ।।

तत्र यथावद्भाविकता कृत्स्न(9b)स्य पुद्गलधर्माख्यस्य[6] जगतो यथावन्नैरात्म्यकोटेरव[7]गमाद्वेदितव्या । स चायमवगमोऽत्यन्तादिशान्तस्वभावतया पुद्गलधर्माविनाशयोगेन समासतो द्वाभ्यां कारणाभ्यामुत्पद्यते । प्रकृतिप्रभास्वरतादर्शनाच्च[8] चित्तस्यादिक्षयनिरोधदर्शनाच्च[9] तदुपक्लेशस्य । तत्र या चित्तस्य

1. *sambaddhatāṁ*, B apparently.

2. T reads *kāraṇābhyām* (*rgyu*) for *ākārābhyam*. For *yathāvadbhāvikatā* and *yāvadbhāvikatā* see *Bodhisattvabhūmi* (ed. Wogihara), Index s.v., though used somewhat differently there. T translates them by *ji-lta-ba-bzhin yod-pa* and *ji-sñed yod-pa*.

3. °*visuddhi 'nuttara*°, B; *dag-paḥi phyir*, T.

4. °*ānvitam*, B; *ldan-pa-ñid*, T. C om. the entire sentence.

5. °*ādikṣaṇāt*, B (two syllables short); *gdoṅ-nas zad-phyir* (*ādikṣayāt*), T. That the two defective readings should be combined is shown by the third sentence of the commentary.

6. °*dharmākṣasya*, B; *chos daṅ gaṅ-zag ces-bya-baḥi*, T.

7. *koṭer anavagamād*, B; C and T om. the negative.

8. *pratiprabhāsvaratādarśāc ca*, B.

9. B om. *dha*.

प्रकृतिप्रभास्वरता यश्च तदुपक्लेश इत्येतद् द्वयमनास्रवे धातौ कुशलाकुशलयोश्चित्तयोरेकचरत्वाद् द्वितीयचित्तानभिसंधानयोगेन परमदुष्प्रतिवेध्यम् । अत आह[1] । क्षणिकं भगवन् कुशलं चित्तम् । न क्लेशैः संक्लिश्यते[2] । क्षणिकमकुशलं चित्तम् । न संक्लिष्टमेव तच्चित्तं क्लेशैः[3] । न भगवन् क्लेशास्तच्चित्तं स्पृशन्ति । कथमत्र भगवन्नस्पर्शनधर्मि चित्तं तमःक्लिष्टं भवति । अस्ति च भगवन्नुपक्लेशः । अस्त्युपक्लिष्टं चित्तम् । अथ च पुनर्भगवन् प्रकृतिपरिशुद्धस्य चित्तस्यो[4]पक्लेशार्थो दुष्प्रतिवेध्यः । इति विस्तरेण यथावद्भाविकतामारभ्य दुष्प्रतिवधार्थनिर्देशो[5] यथासूत्रमनुगन्तव्यः ।

यावद्भाविकता ज्ञेयपर्यन्तगतया धिया ।
सर्वसत्त्वेषु सर्वज्ञधर्मतास्तित्वदर्शनात्[6] ॥ १६ ॥

तत्र यावद्भाविकता सर्वज्ञेयवस्तुपर्यन्तगतया लोकोत्तरया प्रज्ञया सर्व-[7]सत्त्वेष्वन्तशस्ति[8]र्यग्योनिगतेष्वपि तथागतगर्भास्तित्वदर्शनाद्वेदितव्या । तच्च दर्शनं बोधिसत्त्वस्य प्रथमायामेव बोधिसत्त्वभूमावुत्पद्यते सर्वत्रगार्थेन[9] धर्मधातुप्रतिवेधात् ।

1. From the *Āryaśrīmālāsūtra.*

2. B om. *śya.*

3. B is not clear, reading these two sentences as one and having an illegible character after *citta,* which I take to be *nna* (i.e. *cittan na saṁkliṣṭam*). The text above agrees with T and C, except that T om. *tac.*

4. B om. from °*pakleśārtho* to *loko*° four lines below, and the passage has been added above in a xiv century hand.

5. T, if not corrupt, seems to read *duṣprativedhāntaranirdeśo* (*rtogs-par bkaḥ-baḥi bar bstan-pa*).

6. C treats this kārikā as prose and gives a very free rendering.

7. B om. *sarva,* supplied from T and rendered necessary by the kārikā.

8. *antaśa,* B.

9. °*gāthena,* B. T reads *sarvatragārthe* (*don-du*).

इत्येवं योऽवबोधस्तत्प्रत्यात्मज्ञानदर्शनम्[1] ।
तच्छुद्धिरमले धातावसङ्गाप्रतिघा ततः ॥ १७ ॥

इत्येवमनेन प्र(10*a*)कारेण यथावद्भाविकतया च यावद्भाविकतया च यो लोकोत्तरमार्गावबोधस्तदार्याणां प्रत्यात्ममनन्यसाधारणं लोकोत्तरज्ञानदर्शनमभिप्रेतम् । तच्च समासतो द्वाभ्यां कारणाभ्यामितरप्रादेशिकज्ञानदर्शनमुपनिधाय सुविशुद्धिरित्युच्यते । कतमाभ्यां द्वाभ्याम् । असङ्गत्वादप्रतिहतत्वाच्च । तत्र यथावद्भाविकतया सत्त्वधातुप्रकृतिविशुद्धविषयत्वादसङ्गम् यावद्भाविकतयानन्तज्ञेयवस्तुविषयत्वादप्रतिहतम् ।

ज्ञानदर्शनशुद्ध्या*[2] बुद्धज्ञानादनुत्तरात् ।
अवैवर्त्याद्भवन्त्यार्याः शरणं सर्वदेहिनाम् ॥ १८ ॥

इतीयं ज्ञानदर्शनशुद्धि[3]रविनिवर्तनीयभूमिसमारूढानां बोधिसत्त्वानामनुत्तरायास्तथागतज्ञानदर्शनविशुद्धेरुपनिषद्गतत्वादनुत्तरा वेदितव्या तदन्येभ्यो वा दान[4]शीलादिभ्यो बोधिसत्त्वगुणेभ्यो यद्योगादविनिवर्तनीया बोधिसत्त्वाः शरणभूता भवन्ति सर्वसत्त्वानामिति ।

श्रावकसंघरत्नाग्रहणं बोधिसत्त्वगणरत्नानन्तरं तत्पूजानर्हत्वात्[5] । न हि जातु पण्डिता बोधिसत्त्वश्रावकगुणान्तरज्ञा महाबोधिविपुलपुण्यज्ञानसंभारापूर्यमाणज्ञान[6]करुणामण्डलमप्रमेयसत्त्वधातुगणसंताना[7]वभासप्रत्युपस्थितमनुत्तरतथागत-

1. *pratyātmavedyajñāna*°, B (two syllables in excess). T om. *vedya* and appears to omit *iti*, reading *eva* (*ñid*) instead. C treats the verse as prose.

2. Pāda *a* is one syllable short in B; T has nothing to represent it and C is no help.

3. T om. °*śuddhir*, but C has it.

4. T om. *dāna*°, but C has it. These ablatives are governed by *anuttarā*. *Vā*, for which T has *ñid*, is here equivalent to *eva*.

5. *tatprajñānatatvāt*, B; *de mchod-par ḥos-pa ma-yin-paḥi-phyir*, T, which C corroborates. C adds after this sentence a kārikā enumerating the ten *vaśitās* of the Bodhisattva with a commentary on it.

6. *śes-rab daṅ sñiṅ-rje* (*prajñākaruṇā*°), T.

7. T om. *gaṇasaṁtāna*, which is required to balance *svasaṁtāna* below.

पूर्णचन्द्र(10*b*)गमनानुकूलमार्गप्रतिपन्नं बोधिसत्त्वनवचन्द्रमुत्सृज्य प्रादेशिकज्ञाननिष्ठागतमपि तारारूपवत् स्वसंतानावभासप्रत्युपस्थितं श्रावकं नमस्यन्ति। परहितक्रियाशयविशुद्धेः[1] संनिश्रयगुणेनैव हि प्रथमचित्तोत्पादिकोऽपि बोधिसत्त्वो निरनुक्रोशमनन्यपोषि[2]गण्यमनास्रवशीलसंवरविशुद्धिनिष्ठागतमार्यश्रावकमभिभवति। प्रागेव तदन्यैर्दशवशितादिभिर्बोधिसत्त्वगुणैः। वक्ष्यति हि।

यः शीलमात्मार्थकरं[3] विभर्ति
दुःशीलसत्त्वेषु दयावियुक्तः।
आत्मंभरिः[4] शीलधनप्रशुद्धो[5]
विशुद्धशीलं न तमाहुरार्यम्॥
यः शीलमादाय परोपजीव्यं
करोति तेजोऽनिलवारिभूवत्।
कारुण्यमुत्पाद्य परं परेषु
स शीलवांस्तत्प्रतिरूपकोऽन्य इति॥

तत्र केनार्थेन किमधिकृत्य भगवता शरणत्रयं प्रज्ञप्तम्।

**शास्तृशासनशिष्यार्थैरधिकृत्य त्रियानिकान्।**
**कारत्रयाधिमुक्तांश्च प्रज्ञप्तं[6] शरणत्रयम्॥ १९॥**

1. T reads *rnam-par ma-dag-paḥi phyir-ro* (°*āśayāviśuddheḥ*), taking it as an adjunct to the previous sentence; but C confirms B. But should not the reading be °*viśuddhisaṁniśraya*° ?

2. *Poṣin* is recorded by the *PW* only from the *Kathāsaritsāgara.*

3. *ātmārthikaraṁ*, B; *bdag-don byed-par*, T. The source of these two verses is not known.

4. This is perhaps the earliest recorded occurrence of *ātmaṁbhari*, which is known from the *Amarakośa* and the *Harṣacarita* (Schmidt, *Nachträge*).

5. °*dhanasaśuddha*, B against the metre; *nor-gyis rab dag-pa*, T. *Śudh* with *pra* is not recorded elsewhere, but *praśuddhi* occurs *MBh.* (Poona ed.), V, 37, 29, in exactly the same position in a triṣṭubh, having apparently been chosen for metrical reasons.

6. B om. *pra*, and T seems to read *vijñaptam* (*rnam-par bzhag-pa*); but the repeated use of *prajñaptam* in the commentary makes the text reading certain.

बुद्धः शरणमग्र्यत्वाद् द्विपदानामिति शास्तृगुणोद्भावनार्थेन बुद्धभावायोपगतान् बोधिसत्त्वान् पुद्गलान् बुद्धे च परमकारक्रियाधिमुक्तानधिकृत्य देशितं प्रज्ञप्तम् ।

धर्मः शरणमग्र्यत्वाद्विरागाणामिति शास्तुः शासन[1]गुणोद्भावनार्थेन स्वयं प्रतीत्य[2] गम्भीरधर्मानुबोधायोपगतान् प्र(11a)त्येकबुद्धयानिकान् पुद्गलान् धर्मे च परमकारक्रियाधिमुक्तानधिकृत्य देशितं प्रज्ञप्तम् ।

संघः शरणमग्र्यत्वाद्गणानामिति शास्तुः शासने सुप्रतिपन्नशिष्यगुणोद्भावनार्थेन परतः श्रवघोषस्या[3]नुगमायोपगतान् श्रावकयानिकान् पुद्गलान् संघे च परमकारक्रियाधिमुक्तानधिकृत्य देशितं प्रज्ञप्तम् । इत्यनेन समासतस्त्रिविधेनार्थेन षट् पुद्गलानधिकृत्य प्रभेदशो भगवता संवृतिपदस्थानेन सत्त्वानामनुपूर्वनया[4]वतारार्थमिमानि त्रीणि शरणानि देशितानि प्रज्ञप्तानि ।

त्याज्यत्वान् मोषधर्मत्वादभावात् सभयत्वतः ।
धर्मो द्विधा[5]र्यसंघश्च नात्यन्तं शरणं परम् ।। २० ।।

द्विविधो धर्मः । देशनाधर्मोऽधिगमधर्मश्च । तत्र देशनाधर्मः सूत्रादिदेशनाया[6] नामपदव्यञ्जनकायसंगृहीतः । स च मार्गाभिसमयपर्यवसानत्वात् कोलोपम[7] इत्युक्तः । अधिगमधर्मो[8] हेतुफलभेदेन द्विविधः । यदुत मार्गसत्यं निरोध-

1. T om. *śāsana*.

2. B reads *svayaṁ gambhīrapratītyadharmā°*, but T and C give the order followed above. C gives an expanded commentary at this point.

3. *sravaghoṣāyonu°*, B; *thos-paḥi sgraḥi rjesu*, T. The dative does not seem to be a possible construction.

4. T's *tsheg-pa-la rim-gyis* suggests *anupūrvayāna°*; C probably had the text reading.

5. *vidhā°*, B; *chos rnams* (for *rnam*) *gñis*, T. 'the twofold dharma', C.

6. The text is uncertain, though the meaning is clear. I follow B; but T runs *mdoḥi sde-la sogs-pa bstan-pa brjod-pa-ste min* etc. (apparently *sūtrāntādideśanocyate nāma*). C does not show the exact wording, but probably read *sūtrādi°*.

7. *kola*, 'boat', is only known from *Divy.*, 56, and the lexicons.

8. *°dhamo*, B.

सत्यं च । येन यदधिगम्यत इति कृत्वा । तत्र मार्गः संस्कृतलक्षणपर्यापन्नः[1] । यत् संस्कृतलक्षणपर्यापन्नं तन् मृषामोषधर्मि । यन् मृषामोषधर्मि तदसत्यम् । यदसत्यं तदनित्यम् । यदनित्यं तदशरणम् । यश्च तेन मार्गेण निरोधोऽधिगतः सोऽपि श्रावकनयेन प्रदीपोच्छेदवत् क्लेशदुःखाभावमात्रप्रभावितः । न चाभावः[2] शरणमशरणं वा (11*b*)भवितुमर्हति ।

संघ इति त्रैयानिकस्य गणस्यैतदधिवचनम् । स च नित्यं सभयस्तथागतशरणगतो[3] निःसरणपर्येषी शैक्षः सकरणीयः प्रतिपन्नकश्चानुत्तरायां सम्यक्संबोधाविति[4] । कथं सभयः । यस्मादर्हतामपि क्षीणपुनर्भवानामप्रहीणत्वाद्वासनायाः सततसमितं सर्वसंस्कारेषु[5] तीव्रा भयसंज्ञा प्रत्युपस्थिता भवति स्याद्यथापि नामोत्क्षिप्तासिके[6] वधकपुरुषे तस्मात्तेऽपि नात्यन्तसुखनिःसरणमधिगताः । न हि शरणं शरणं[7] पर्येषते । यथैवा[8]शरणाः सत्त्वा येन तेन भयेन भीतास्ततस्ततो निःसरणं पर्येषन्ते तद्वदर्हतामप्यस्ति तद्भयं यतस्ते भयाद्भीतास्तथागतमेव शरणमुपगच्छन्ति । यश्चैवं सभयत्वाच्छरणमुपगच्छत्यवश्यं भयान्निःसरणं स पर्येषते[9] । निःसरणपर्येषित्वाच्च भयनिदानप्रहाणमधिकृत्य शैक्षो भवति सकरणीयः । शैक्ष-

1. B omits many words in this passage, reading *mārgaḥ saṁskṛtalakṣaṇaparyāpannaṁ / tan mṛsāmoṣadharmi tad asatyaṁ / yad asatyaṁ nityaṁ tad aśaraṇaṁ*. I follow T, but C, which agrees with it in form, adds two extra terms, both meaning 'not true', which I cannot determine.

2. *ca bhāvaḥ*, B; C and T as in text.

3. °*śaragato*, B.

4. T's *zhugs-pa ma-yin-no* indicates the reading *sakaraṇīyo 'pratipannas*; it omits *iti* at the end.

5. °*saṁskāre*, B; T and C show the plural.

6. *nāmotkṣiptāstike*, B; *ral-gri gdeṅs-paḥi*, T. There is possibly an omission in the text here, as C attributes most of this sentence and probably those that follow to the *Āryaśrīmālāsūtra*; cf. O, p. 146, n. 5, for the reference. There should be some allusion to the fact that it is a quotation.

7. B om. one *śaraṇam*; C and T as in text.

8. The characters *thaiva* are uncertain in B, and I would have read *yadvad*, if the vowel of the first character had not been clearly *ai*.

9. B om. *niḥsaraṇaṁ sa paryeṣate*; *de ni..ṅes-par ḥbyuṅ-ba tshol-ba*, T, which is confirmed by C.

त्वात् प्रतिपन्नको भवत्यभयमार्षभस्थानमनुप्राप्तुं यदुतानुत्तरां सम्यक्संबोधिम् । तस्मात्सोऽपि तदङ्गशरणत्वा[1]न्नात्यन्तं शरणम् । एवमिमे द्वे शरणे पर्यन्तकाले शरणे इत्युच्येते ।

जगच्छरणमेकत्र बुद्धत्वं पारमार्थिकम् ।
मुनेर्धर्मशरीरत्वात् तन्निष्ठत्वाद्गणस्य च ॥ २१ ॥

अनेन तु पूर्वोक्तेन विधिनानुत्पादानिरोधप्रभावितस्य मुनेर्व्यवदानसत्यद्वय[2]-विरागधर्मकायत्वाद् धर्मकायविशुद्धिनि (12*a*) ष्ठाधिगमपर्यवसानत्वाच्च त्रैयानिकस्य गणस्य पारमार्थिकमेवात्राणेऽशरणे लोकेऽपरान्तकोटिसममक्षयशरणं नित्यशरणं ध्रुवशरणं[3] यदुत तथागता अर्हन्तः[4] सम्यक्संबुद्धाः । एष च नित्यध्रुवशिवशाश्वतैकशरणनिर्देशो[5] विस्तरेणार्यश्रीमालासूत्रानुसारेणानुगन्तव्यः ।

रत्नानि दुर्लभोत्पादान् निर्मलत्वात् प्रभावतः ।
लोकालंकारभूतत्वादग्रत्वान् निर्विकारतः ॥ २२ ॥

समासतः षड्विधेन रत्नसाधर्म्येणैतानि बुद्धधर्मसंघाख्यानि त्रीणि रत्नान्युच्यन्ते । यदुत दुर्लभोत्पादभाव[6]साधर्म्येण बहुभिरपि कल्पपरिवर्तैरनवाप्तकुशलमूलानां तत्समवधानाप्रतिल[7]म्भात् । वैमल्यसाधर्म्येण सर्वाचारमलविगतत्वात्[8] । प्रभावसाधर्म्येण षडभिज्ञाद्यचिन्त्यप्रभावगुणयोगात् । लोकालंकारसाधर्म्येण सर्वजगदाशयशोभानिमित्तत्वात् । रत्नप्रतिवर्णिकाग्र्यसाधर्म्येण लोकोत्तरत्वात् । स्तुतिनिन्दाद्यविकारसाधर्म्येणासंस्कृतस्वभावत्वादिति ।

1. B om. *ṇa*.
2. T adds *lakṣaṇa* (*mtshan-ñid*) after *dvaya*, but C has no trace of the word.
3. T adds *skyabs ni gcigs* (*śaraṇam ekam*).
4. *Tathāgatārhantaḥ*, B.
5. T om. *nirdeśo*.
6. T om. *bhāva*.
7. °*dhānaprati*°, B, but possibly the *ā* is added above the line after *n*; T shows the negative required by the context.
8. So B, but the text is uncertain. T has *rnam-pa thams-cad-du* (*sarvākāra*°), and C translates as if having *sarvasāsrava-dharmavigatatvāt*.

रत्नत्रयनिर्देशानन्तरं यस्मिन् सत्येव[1] लौकिकलोकोत्तरविशुद्धियोनि[2]रत्नत्रयमुत्पद्यते तदधिकृत्य श्लोकः ।

समला तथताथ निर्मला विमला बुद्धगुणा[3] जिनक्रिया ।
विषयः परमार्थदर्शिनां शुभरत्नत्रयसर्गको यतः ॥ २३ ॥

अनेन किं परिदीपितम् ।

गोत्रं रत्नत्रयस्यास्य विष(12*b*)यः सर्वदर्शिनाम् ।
चतुर्विधः स चाचिन्त्यश्चतुर्भिः कारणैः क्रमात् ॥ २४ ॥

तत्र समला तथता यो धातुरविनिर्मुक्तक्लेशकोशस्तथागतगर्भ इत्युच्यते । निर्मला तथता स एव[4] बुद्धभूमावाश्रयपरिवृत्तिलक्षणो यस्तथागतधर्मकाय इत्युच्यते । विमलबुद्धगुणा[5] ये तस्मिन्नेवाश्रयपरिवृत्तिलक्षणे तथागतधर्मकाये[6] लोकोत्तरा दशबलादयो बुद्धधर्माः । जिनक्रिया तेषामेव दशबलादीनां बुद्धधर्माणां प्रतिस्वमनुत्तरं कर्म यदनिष्ठितम[7]विरतमप्रतिप्रश्रब्धं[8] बोधिसत्त्वव्याकरणकथां नोपच्छिनत्ति । तानि पुनरिमानि चत्वारि स्थानानि यथासंख्यमेव चतुर्भिः कारणैरचिन्त्यत्वात् सर्वज्ञविषया[9] इत्युच्यन्ते । कतमैश्चतुर्भिः ।

शुद्ध्युपक्लिष्टतायोगात् निःसंक्लेशविशुद्धितः ।
अविनिर्भागधर्मत्वादनाभोगाविकल्पतः ॥ २५ ॥

तत्र समला तथता युगपदेककालं विशुद्धा च संक्लिष्टा[10] चेत्यचिन्त्यमेतत् स्थानं गम्भीरधर्मनयाधिमुक्तानामपि प्रत्येकबुद्धानामगोचरविषयत्वात् । यत

1. e.c.; *saty esta* (?), B; T om. *eva.*
2. *viśuddhiyāni*, B; *dag-pa skye-bahi gnas,* T.
3. *buddhaguṇa*, B.
4. T om. *sa eva.*
5. Should one not read *vimalā Buddha*° ?
6. °*kāya,* B; *sku de-ñid-la yod-pa* (°*kāye sthitā* ?), T.
7. B may read *aviṣṭhitam.* T has *med-par ma-gyur-zhin,* 'not becoming non-existent'.
8. B om. *bdhaṁ.*
9. T adds *ye-śes* (*jñāna*) after *sarvajña,* but C does not show it and verse 24 proves it not to be required.
10. T evidently read *viśuddhā yā saṁkliṣṭā yety.*

आह[1]। द्वाविमौ देवि धर्मौ दुष्प्रतिवेध्यौ। प्रकृतिपरिशुद्धिचित्तं दुष्प्रतिवेध्यम्। तस्यैव चित्तस्योपक्लिष्टता दुष्प्रतिवेध्या। अनयोर्देवि धर्मयोः श्रोता त्वं वा भवेरथवा महाधर्मसमन्वागता बोधिसत्त्वाः। शेषाणां देवि सर्वश्रावकप्रत्येकबुद्धानां तथागतश्रद्धागमनीया(13a)वेवैतौ[2] धर्माविति।

तत्र निर्मला तथता पूर्वमलासंक्लिष्टा पश्चाद्विशुद्धेत्यचिन्त्यमेतत् स्थानम्। यत आह[3]। प्रकृतिप्रभास्वरं चित्तम्। तत्तथैव ज्ञानम्। तत उच्यते। एकक्षणलक्षण[4]समायुक्तया प्रज्ञया सम्यक्संबोधिरभिसंबुद्धेति।

तत्र विमला बुद्धगुणाः पौर्वापर्येणैकान्तसंक्लिष्टायामपि पृथग्जनभूमावविनिर्भागधर्मतया निर्विशिष्टा विद्यन्त इत्यचिन्त्यमेतत् स्थानम्। यत आह[5]।

न स कश्चित्सत्त्वः सत्त्वनिकाये संविद्यते यत्र तथागतज्ञानं[6] न सकलमनुप्रविष्टम्। अपि तु संज्ञाग्राहतस्तथागतज्ञानं न प्रज्ञायते। संज्ञाग्राहविगमात् पुनः सर्वज्ञज्ञानं स्वयंभूज्ञानमसङ्गतः प्रभवति। तद्यथापि नाम भो जिनपुत्र त्रिसाहस्रमहासाहस्र[7]लोकधातुप्रमाणं महापुस्तं भवेत्। तस्मिन् खलु पुनर्महापुस्ते त्रिसाहस्रमहासाहस्रलोकधातुः सकलसमाप्त आलिखितो भवेत्। महापृथिवीप्रमाणेन महापृथिवी। द्विसाहस्रलोकधातुप्रमाणेन द्विसाहस्रलोकधातुः। साहस्रलोकधातुप्रमाणेन साहस्रलोकधातुः[8]। चातुर्द्वीपिक[9]प्रमाणेन चातुर्द्वीपिकाः। महासमुद्रप्रमाणेन महासमुद्राः। जम्बूद्वीपप्रमाणेन जम्बूद्वीपाः। पूर्वविदेहद्वीपप्रमाणेन पूर्वविदेहद्वीपाः। गो(13b)दावरीद्वीपप्रमाणेन गोदावरीद्वीपाः[10]। उत्तरकुरुद्वीपप्रमाणेनोत्तरकुरुद्वीपाः। सुमेरुप्रमाणेन सुमेरवः।

1. The quotation is from the *Āryaśrīmālāsūtra*.

2. B om. *vai*, supplied from T's *rtogs-par bya-ba-ñid*. C has 'only'.

3. From the *Dhāraṇīśvararājasūtra* according to O.

4. B om. *kṣaṇa* and T *lakṣaṇa*; C has both.

5. Neither C nor O say where this long quotation comes from.

6. B om. *naṁ*.

7. B repeats *mahāsāhasra*.

8. B om. *lokadhātu*, which T has.

9. B adds *lokadhātu* after *cāturdvīpika*°, but T omits it.

10. So B, but the name should be Godāna or Godānīya; T has *nub-kyi ba-laṅ spyod-kyi gliṅ*, equivalent to Aparagocaradvīpa. C does not give the names of the dvīpas.

भूम्यवचरदेवविमानप्रमाणेन भूम्यवचरदेवविमानानि । कामावचरदेवविमानप्रमाणेन कामावचरदेवविमानानि । रूपावचरदेवविमानप्रमाणेन रूपावचरदेवविमानानि । तच्च महापुस्तं त्रिसाहस्रमहासाहस्रलोकधात्वायामविस्तरप्रमाणं भवेत् । तत्खलु पुनर्महापुस्तमेकस्मिन् परमाणुरजसि प्रक्षिप्तं भवेत् । यथा चैकपरमाणुरजसि[1] तन्महापुस्तं प्रक्षिप्तं भवेत् तथान्येषु[2] सर्वपरमाणुरजःसु तत्प्रमाणान्येव महापुस्तान्यभ्यन्तरप्रविष्टानि भवेयुः । अथ कश्चिदेव पुरुष उत्पद्यते पण्डितो निपुणो व्यक्तो मेधावी तत्रोपगमिकया मीमांसया समन्वागतः । दिव्यं चास्य चक्षुः समन्तपरिशुद्धं प्रभास्वरं भवेत् । स दिव्येन चक्षुषा व्यवलोकयति । इदं महापुस्तमेवंभूतमिहैव[3] परीत्ते परमाणुरजस्यनुतिष्ठते[4] । न कस्यचिदपि[5] सत्त्वस्योपकारिभूतं भवति । तस्यैवं स्यात् । यन्न्वहं महावीर्यबलस्थाम्ना एतत्परमाणुरजो भित्त्वा एतन्महापुस्तं[6] सर्वजगदुपजीव्यं कुर्याम्[7] । स महावीर्यबलस्थाम संजनयित्वा सूक्ष्मेण वज्रेण तत्परमाणुरजो भित्त्वा यथाभिप्रायं तन्महापुस्तं सर्वजगदुपजीव्यं कुर्यात् । यथा चै(14a)कस्मात् तथाशेषेभ्यः[8] परमाणुभ्यस्तथैव कुर्यात् । एवमेव भो जिनपुत्र तथागतज्ञानमप्रमाणज्ञानं[9] सर्वस(VIIa)त्त्वोपजीव्यज्ञानं सर्वसत्त्वचित्तसंतानेषु सकलमनुप्रविष्टम् । सर्वाणि च तानि सत्त्वचित्तसंतानान्यपि[10] तथागतज्ञानप्रमाणानि[11] । अथ च पुनः संज्ञाग्राहविनि-

1. B om. *si*.

2. The reading °*ānyeṣu* is uncertain in B, and T and C have nothing to correspond.

3. *idaṁ khalu punar evaṁbhutam*, B; *ḥdi lta-bur gyur-paḥi dar-yug chen-po ḥdi*, T. C apparently had the text reading also.

4. Note *anutiṣṭhate* Ātmanepada, a usage not included in Pāṇini, i, 3, 22 ff.

5. B om. *api*; *yaṅ*, T.

6. I have left the two hiatuses as probably a peculiarity of the sūtra's style. T adds *vajreṇa* (*rdo-rjes*) before *bhittvā*; C has 'by some *upāya*'.

7. *kuryāt*, B.

8. T adds another epithet, *mthaḥ-dag*, something like *samasta*.

9. B repeats *apramāṇajñānam*.

10. B om. *api*, which A and T have.

11. T has a negative and read °*jñānāpramāṇāni*.

बद्धा बाला न जानन्ति न[1] प्रजानन्ति नानुभवन्ति न साक्षात्कुर्वन्ति तथागतज्ञानम् । ततस्तथागतोऽसङ्गेन तथागतज्ञानेन सर्वधर्मधातुसत्त्वभवनानि व्यवलोक्याचार्यसंज्ञी भवति । अहो बत इमे सत्त्वा यथावत् तथागतज्ञानं न प्रजानन्ति । तथागतज्ञानानुप्रविष्टाश्च । यन्न्वहमेषां सत्त्वानामार्येण मार्गोपदेशेन सर्वसंज्ञाकृतबन्धनापनयनं[2] कुर्यां यथा स्वयमेवार्यमार्ग[3]बलाधानेन महतीं संज्ञाग्रन्थिं विनिवर्त्य तथागतज्ञानं प्रत्यभिजानीरन् । तथागतसमतां चानुप्राप्नुयुः । ते तथागतमार्गोपदेशेन सर्वसंज्ञाकृतबन्धनानि[4] व्यपनयन्ति । अपनीतेषु च सर्वसंज्ञाकृतबन्धनेषु[5] तत् तथागतज्ञानम[6]प्रमाणं भवति सर्वजगदुपजीव्यमिति ।

तत्र जिनक्रिया युगपत्सर्वत्र सर्वकालमनाभोगेनाविकल्पतो[7] यथाशयेषु यथावैनयिकेषु[8] सत्त्वेष्वक्षूण[9]मनुगुणं प्रवर्तत इत्यचिन्त्यमेतत् स्थानम् । यत आह[10] । संक्षेपमात्रकेणावतारणार्थं सत्त्वानामप्रमाणमपि तथागतकर्म प्रमाण(14b)तो निर्दिष्टम् । अपि तु कुलपुत्र यत्तथागतस्य भूतं तथागतकर्म तदप्रमाणमचिन्त्यमविज्ञेयं सर्वलोकेन । अनुदाहरणमक्षरैः । दुःसंपादं परेभ्यः । अधिष्ठितं सर्वबुद्धक्षेत्रेषु । समतानुगतं सर्वबुद्धैः । समतिक्रान्तं सर्वाभोगक्रियाभ्यः । निर्विकल्पमाकाशसमतया । निर्नीताकारणं धर्मधातुक्रियया । इति[11] विस्तरेण यावद्विशुद्धवैडूर्यमणिदृष्टान्तं कृत्वा निर्दिशति । तदनेन कुलपुत्र पर्यायेणैवं वेदितव्यमचिन्त्यं तथागतकर्म समतानुगतं च सर्वतोऽनवद्यं च त्रिरत्नवंशानुपच्छेत्तृ च । यत्राचिन्त्ये तथागतकर्मणि प्रतिष्ठितस्त[12]थागत आकाशस्वभावतां च कायस्य न विजहाति

1. B om. *na*.
2. °*bandhanā apanayanaṁ*, B; A as in text.
3. T read *jñāna* (*ye-śes*) for *mārga*.
4. B om. *abandhan*, supplied from T.
5. B om. *sarva* and *abandhan*, supplied from T.
6. B om. *ma*; *ye-śes tshad-med-pa*, T; A begins line 3 *ānam apramāṇam*.
7. °*kalpayato*, B.
8. *yatha vainaikeṣu*, B; the two characters before *vainayikeṣu* in A are illegible, but do not look like *yathā*; *gdul-bya ji-lta-ba bzhin-du* (*yathāvadvineyeṣu* ?), T.
9. e.c.; *akṣūṇatvaṁ*, B; A illegible. Cf. *Mvy*., Andersen-Helmer Smith's *Pali Dict*. s. *akkhaṇavedhin*, and *Daśabh*., 69.
10. From the *Dhāraṇīśvararājasūtra* (O).
11. B om. *iti*, supplied from T. A is missing here.
12. B repeats *Tathāgatakarmaṇi pratiṣṭhitas*.

सर्वबुद्धक्षेत्रेषु च दर्शनं ददाति । अनभिलाप्यधर्मतां च वाचो न विजहाति यथारुतविज्ञप्त्या च सत्त्वेभ्यो धर्मं देशयति । सर्वचित्तारम्बणविगतश्च सर्वसत्त्वचित्तचरिताशयांश्च प्रजानातीति ।

बोध्यं बोधिस्तदङ्गानि बोधनेति यथाक्रमम् ।
हेतुरेकं पदं त्रीणि प्रत्ययस्तद्विशुद्धये ॥ २६ ॥

एषां खल्वपि चतुर्णामर्थपदानां सर्वज्ञेयसंग्रहमुपादाय प्रथमं बोद्धव्यपदं[1] द्रष्टव्यम् । तदनुबोधो बोधिरिति द्वितीयं बोधिपदम् । बोधेरङ्गभूता बुद्धगुणा इति त्रितीयं बोध्यङ्गपदम् । बोध्यङ्गैरेव बोधनं परेषामिति चतुर्थं बोधनापदम् । इतीमानि (15*a*) चत्वारि पदान्यधिकृत्य हेतुप्रत्ययभावेन रत्नत्रयगोत्रव्यवस्थानं वेदितव्यम् ।

तत्रैषां चतुर्णां पदानां प्रथमं लोकोत्तरधर्मबीजत्वात् प्रत्यात्मयोनिशोमनसिकारसंनिश्रयेण तद्विशुद्धिमुपादाय त्रिरत्नोत्पत्तिहेतुरनुगन्तव्यः । इत्येवमेकं पदं हेतुः । कथं त्रीणि प्रत्ययः । तथागतोऽनुत्तरां सम्यक्संबोधिमभिसंबुध्य दशबलादिभिर्बुद्धधर्मैर्द्वात्रिंशदाकारं तथागतकर्म कुर्वन्[2] परतो(VII*b*)घोषसंनिश्रयेण[3] तद्विशुद्धिमुपादाय त्रिरत्नोत्पत्तिप्रत्ययोऽनुगन्तव्यः । इत्येवं त्रीणि प्रत्ययः । अतः परमेषामेव चतुर्णां पदानामनुपूर्वमवशिष्टेन ग्रन्थेन विस्तरविभागनिर्देशो वेदितव्यः ।

तत्र समलां तथतामधिकृत्य यदुक्तं सर्वसत्त्वास्तथागतगर्भा[4] इति तत् केनार्थेन[5] ।

1. *bodhyavya*°, B.

2. B om. *kurva*, but the *n* still remaining shows the text to be the correct restitution of T's *mdzad-pa-na*. A is missing here.

3. *ghoṣayanniśrayeṇa*, B.

4. It is not clear if B intends °*garbha* or °*garbhā*, but cf. below in the first sentence after verse 28, where A and B both have °*garbhā*.

5. The order of the text is confused in T and C. A's order cannot be determined, as it has only a portion of the commentary from *trividhenā*° to *punas trayā*°. T is obviously wrong; it has verse 28 followed by the commentary as far as *Bhagavatā*, then verse 27 followed by the sentence *yenārthena* to *nirdekṣyāmi*, then the commentary from *yad uta* to *bhaviṣyati*, ending with *uddānam*. C inserts 27 after *uddānam*, which is impossible.

बुद्धज्ञानान्तर्गमात्[1] सत्त्वराशे-
स्तन्नैर्मल्यस्याद्वयत्वात् प्रकृत्या ।
बौद्धे गोत्रे तत्फलस्योपचारा-
दुक्ताः सर्वे देहिनो बुद्धगर्भाः ॥ २७ ॥

संबुद्धकायस्फरणात् तथताव्यतिभेदतः ।
गोत्रत[2]श्च सदा सर्वे बुद्धगर्भाः शरीरिणः ॥ २८ ॥

समासतस्त्रिविधेनार्थेन सदा सर्वसत्त्वास्तथागतगर्भा इत्युक्तं भगवता । यदुत सर्वसत्त्वेषु तथागतधर्मकायपरिस्फरणार्थेन तथागततथताव्यतिभेदार्थेन तथागतगोत्रसंभवार्थेन च । एषां पुनस्त्रयाणामर्थपदानामुत्तरत्र **तथागतगर्भसूत्रानुसा**रेण निर्देशो भविष्यति । (15*b*)पूर्वतरं तु येनार्थेन सर्वत्राविशेषेण प्रवचने सर्वाकारं तदर्थसूचनं भवति तदप्यधिकृत्य[3] निर्देक्ष्यामि । उद्दानम् ।

स्वभावहेत्वोः फलकर्मयोग-
वृत्तिष्ववस्थास्वथ सर्वगत्वे[4] ।
सदाविकारित्वगुणेष्वभेदे
ज्ञेयोऽर्थसंधिः परमार्थधातोः ॥ २९ ॥

समासतो दशविधमर्थमभिसंधाय परमतत्त्वज्ञानविषयस्य तथागतधातोर्व्यवस्थानमनुगन्तव्यम् । दशविधोऽर्थः कतमः[5] । तद्यथा स्वभावार्थो हेत्वर्थः फलार्थः कर्मार्थो योगार्थो वृत्त्यर्थोऽवस्थाप्रभेदार्थः सर्वत्रगार्थोऽविकारार्थोऽभेदार्थश्च । तत्र स्वभावार्थं हेत्वर्थं चारभ्य श्लोकः ।

सदा प्रकृत्यसंक्लिष्टः शुद्धरत्नाम्बराम्बुवत् ।
धर्माधिमुक्त्यधिप्रज्ञासमाधिकरुणान्वयः ॥ ३० ॥

1. e.c.; *jñānāt(?)ta*māt*, B; *sans-rgyas ye-śes..zhugs*, T; 'not separate', C.
2. B om. *ta*.
3. *api krtya*, B.
4. *avasthāneṣv atha sarvatve*, B (against the metre); *gnas-skabs de-bzhin kun-tu ḥgro-bahi don (...sarvagārthe)*, T; not in A.
5. B om. *katamaḥ*, found in A and T.

तत्र पूर्वेणं श्लोकार्धेन किं दर्शयति ।

प्रभावानन्यथाभावस्निग्धभावस्वभावतः ।
चिन्तामणिनभोवारिगुणसाधर्म्य[1]मेषु हि ॥ ३१ ॥

य एते त्रयोऽत्र[2] पूर्वमुद्दिष्टा एषु त्रिषु यथासंख्यमेव स्वलक्षणं सामान्यलक्षणं चारभ्य तथागतधातोश्चिन्तामणिनभोवारिविशुद्धिगुणसाधर्म्यं वेदितव्यम् । तत्र तथागतधर्मकाये तावच्चिन्तितार्थसमृद्ध्यादि[3] प्रभावस्वभावतां स्वलक्षणमारभ्य चिन्तामणिरत्नसाधर्म्यं वेदितव्यम् । तथतायामनन्यथाभावस्वभावतां स्वलक्षणमारभ्याकाशसाधर्म्यं वेदितव्यम् । तथागतगोत्रे सत्त्वकरुणास्निग्धस्वभावतां[4] स्वलक्षणमारभ्य (16*a*) वारिसाधर्म्यं वेदितव्यम् । सर्वेषां चात्र सदात्यन्तप्रकृत्यनुपक्लिष्टतां प्रकृतिपरिशुद्धिं सामान्यलक्षणमारभ्य तदेव चिन्तामणिनभोवारिवि[5]शुद्धिगुणसाधर्म्यं वेदितव्यम् ।

तत्र परेण श्लोकार्धेन किं दर्शितम् ।

चतुर्धावरणं धर्म[6]प्रतिघोऽप्यात्मदर्शनम् ।
संसारदुःखभीरुत्वं सत्त्वार्थं निरपेक्षता ॥ ३२ ॥
इच्छन्तिकानां तीर्थ्यानां[7] श्रावकाणां स्वयंभुवाम् ।
अधिमुक्त्यादयो धर्माश्चत्वारः शुद्धिहेतवः । ३३ ॥

समासत इमे त्रिविधाः सत्वाः सत्त्वराशौ संविद्यन्ते । भवाभिलाषिणो विभवाभिलाषिणस्तदुभयान[8]भिलाषिणश्च । तत्र भवाभिलाषिणो द्विविधा वेदितव्याः ।

1. B om. *dha*.

2. T om. *ya*, and A corrects on margin from the text to *ya ete trayo 'rthā atra*.

3. C has a lacuna from *samṛddhi* to the end of the commentary on verse 31.

4. °*svabhāvatāsvalakṣaṇam*, A, which has °*svabhāvatām* in the previous sentence.

5. B om. *vi*, but T shows it (*rnam-par*).

6. *dharme*, B; A as in text.

7. *tīrthānāṁ*, B; A as in text.

8. °*ubhayābhi*° B; but T, C and the explanation require the negative.

मोक्षमार्गप्रतिहताशा अपरिनिर्वाणगोत्रकाः सत्त्वा ये संसारमेवेच्छन्ति न निर्वाणं तन्नियतिपतिताश्चेहधार्मिका एव[1] । तदेकत्या महायानधर्मविद्विषो या[2]नधिकृत्यैतदुक्तं भगवता । नाहं तेषां शास्ता न ते मम श्रावकाः । तानहं शारिपुत्र तमसस्तमोऽन्तरमन्धकारान् महान्धकारगामिनस्तमोभूयिष्ठा इति वदामि ।

तत्र विभवाभिलाषिणो द्विविधाः । अनुपायपतिता उपायपतिताश्च । तत्रानुपायपतिता अपि त्रिविधाः । इतोबाह्या बहुनानाप्रकाराश्चरकपरिव्राजकनिर्ग्रन्थिपुत्र[3]प्रभृतयोऽन्यतीर्थ्याः । इहधार्मिकाश्च तत्सभागचरिता एव श्राद्धा अपि दुर्गृहीतग्राहिणः । ते च पुनः कतमे । यदुत पुद्गलदृष्टय(16*b*)श्च परमार्थानधिमुक्ता यान् प्रति भगवता शून्यतानधिमुक्तो निर्विशिष्टो भवति तीर्थिकैरित्युक्तम्[4] । शून्यतादृष्टयश्चाभिमानिका येषामिह तद्विमोक्षमुखेऽपि शून्यतायां माद्यमानानां शून्यतैव दृष्टिर्भवति यानधिकृत्याह । वरं खलु काश्यप सुमेरुमात्रा पुद्गलदृष्टिर्न त्वेवाभिमानिकस्य शून्यतादृष्टिरिति[5] । तत्रोपायपतिता अपि द्विविधाः । श्रावकयानीयाश्च सम्यक्त्वनियाममवक्रान्ताः प्रत्येकबुद्धयानीयाश्च ।

तदुभयानभिलाषिणः पुनर्महायानसंप्रस्थिताः परमतीक्ष्णेन्द्रियाः सत्त्वा ये नापि संसारमिच्छन्ति यथेच्छन्तिका[6] नानुपायपतितास्तीर्थिकादिवन् नाप्युपायपतिताः श्रावकप्रत्येकबुद्धवत् । अपि तु संसारनिर्वाणसमतापत्ति[7]मार्गप्रतिपन्नास्ते भवन्त्यप्रतिष्ठितनिर्वाणाशया निरुपक्लिष्टसंसारगतप्रयोगा दृढकरुणाध्याशयप्रतिष्ठितमूलपरिशुद्धा इति[8] ।

1. *ihadhārmika* means 'Buddhist'. A om. *eva*, which B and T have.

2. A's vii*b* ends with the character *ya*. C attributes the quotation to the *Anūnatvāpūrṇatvanirdeśaparivarta*.

3. B om. *putra*, which seems necessary; T's *gcer-bu-pa* leaves it vague. For *caraka* see *PW* s.v.

4. Quotation not identified by C or O.

5. The quotation is to be found with slight differences of wording in *Kāś. P.*, p. 95.

6. For the *icchantikas* see *Laṅkāvatārasūtra*, p. 65, line 16, to p. 66, line 9.

7. When this phrase is repeated lower down, B has the more natural *samatāpti°*, which perhaps should be read here.

8. T om. *iti*.

तत्र ये सत्त्वा भवाभिलाषिण इच्छन्तिकास्तन्नियतिपतिता[1] इहधार्मिका एवोच्यन्ते मिथ्यात्वनियतः[2] सत्त्वराशिरिति । ये विभवाभिलाषिणोऽप्यनुपायपतिता उच्यन्तेऽनियतः सत्त्वराशिरिति[3] । ये वि[4]भवाभिलाषिण उपायपतितास्तदुभयानभिलाषिणश्च[5] समताप्तिमार्गप्रतिपन्नास्त उच्यंते सम्यक्त्वनियतः सत्त्वराशिरिति । (17*a*)तत्र महायानसंप्रस्थितान् सत्त्वाननावरणगामिनः स्थापयित्वा य इतोऽन्ये सत्त्वास्तद्यथा । इच्छन्तिकास्तीर्थ्याः श्रावकाः प्रत्येकबुद्धाश्च । तेषामिमानि चत्वार्यावरणानि तथागतधातोरनधिगमायासाक्षात्क्रियायै संवर्तन्ते । कतमानि च चत्वारि । तद्यथा महायानधर्मप्रतिघ इच्छन्तिकाना[6]मावरणं यस्य प्रतिपक्षो महायानधर्माधिमुक्तिभावना बोधिसत्त्वानाम् । धर्मेष्वात्मदर्शनमन्यतीर्थानामा[7]वरणं यस्य प्रतिपक्षः प्रज्ञापारमिताभावना बोधिसत्त्वानाम् । संसारे दुःखसंज्ञा दुःखभीरुत्व श्रावकयानिकानामावरणं यस्य प्रतिपक्षो गगनगञ्जादिसमाधिभावना बोधिसत्त्वानाम् । सत्त्वार्थविमुखता सत्त्वार्थनिरपेक्षता प्रत्येकबुद्धयानिकानामावरणं यस्य प्रतिपक्षो महाकरुणाभावना बोधिसत्त्वानामिति ।

एतच्चतुर्विधमावरणमेषां चतुर्विधानां सत्त्वानां यस्य प्रतिपक्षानिमांश्चतुरोऽधिमुक्त्यादीन्[8] भावयित्वा बोधिसत्त्वा निरुत्तरार्थधर्मकायविशुद्धिपरमतामधिगच्छन्त्येभिश्च विशुद्धिसमुदागमकारणैश्चतुर्भिरनुगता[9] धर्मराजपुत्रा भवन्ति तथागतकुले । कथमिति ।

बीजं येषामग्रयानाधिमुक्ति-
र्माता प्रज्ञा बुद्धधर्मप्रसूत्यै ।

1. One would expect °*patitāś ceha*°, but neither B nor T have *ca*.
2. *niyatasattva*°, B, but cf. the other two sentences.
3. B om. *ri*.
4. B om. *vi*, but T and C rightly have it.
5. *tadubhayābhi*°, B
6. B om. *nā*.
7. B later on reads *anyatīrthya*, not *anyatīrtha* as here.
8. T adds *dharmān* (*chos*) after °*ādīn*, but this is not necessary and is not in C.
9. B adds *dharmakāya* before *dharmarāja* against C and T.

गर्भस्थानं ध्यानसौख्यं कृपोक्ता
धात्री पुत्रास्तेऽनुजाता मुनीनाम् ॥ ३४ ॥

तत्र फलार्थं कर्मार्थं[1] चारभ्य श्लोकः ।

शुभा(17*b*)त्मसुखनित्यत्वगुणपारमिता फलम् ।
दुःखनिर्विच्छमप्राप्तिच्छन्दप्रणिधिकर्मकः[2] ॥ ३५ ॥

तत्र पूर्वेण श्लोकार्धेन किं दर्शितम् ।

फलमेषां समासेन धर्मकाये विपर्ययात् ।
चतुर्विधविपर्यासप्रतिपक्षप्रभावितम् ॥ ३६ ॥

य एतेऽधिमुक्त्यादयश्चत्वारो धर्मास्तथागतधातोर्विशुद्धिहेतव एषां यथासंख्यमेव समासतश्चतुर्विधविपर्यासविपर्ययप्रतिपक्षेण चतुराकारा तथागतधर्मकायगुणपारमिता फलं द्रष्टव्यम् । तत्र या रूपादिके वस्तुन्यनित्ये नित्यमिति संज्ञा । दुःखे सुखमिति । अनात्मन्यात्मेति । अशुभे शुभमिति संज्ञा । अयमुच्यते चतुर्विधो विपर्यासः । एतद्विपर्ययेण चतुर्विध एवाविपर्यासो वेदितव्यः । कतमश्चतुर्विधः । या तस्मिन्नेव रूपादिके वस्तुन्यनित्यसंज्ञा । दुःखसंज्ञा । अनात्मसंज्ञा । अशुभसंज्ञा । अयमुच्यते चतुर्विधविपर्यासविपर्ययः । स खल्वेष नित्यादिलक्षणं तथागतधर्मकायमधिकृत्येह विपर्यासोऽभिप्रेतो यस्य प्रतिपक्षेण[3] चतुराकारा तथागतधर्मकायगुणपारमिता व्यवस्थापिता[4] । तद्यथा नित्यपारमिता सुखपारमितात्मपारमिता शुभपारमितेति । एष च ग्रन्थो विस्तरेण यथासूत्रमनुगन्तव्यः[5] । विपर्यस्ता भगवन् सत्त्वा उपात्तेषु पञ्चसूपादानस्कन्धेषु । ते भवन्त्यनित्ये नित्यसंज्ञिनः । दुःखे सुखसंज्ञिनः । अनात्मन्यात्मसंज्ञिनः । अशुभे शुभसं(18*a*)ज्ञिनः। सर्वश्रावकप्रत्येकबुद्धा अपि भगवन् शून्यताज्ञानेनादृष्टपूर्वे सर्वज्ञज्ञानविषये तथा-

1. B om. *karmārthaṁ*, which is required and is given by C and T.

2. °*dharmakaḥ*, corrected on margin to °*karmakaḥ*, B; C and T as in text.

3. *pratikṣepeṇa*, B; C and T as in text.

4. °*sthāpitāḥ*, B.

5. From the *Āryaśrīmālāsūtra*.

गतधर्मकाये विपर्यस्ताः । ये[1] भगवन् सत्त्वाः स्युर्भगवतः पुत्रा औरसा नित्यसंज्ञिन आत्मसंज्ञिनः सुखसंज्ञिनः शुभसंज्ञिनस्ते भगवन् सत्त्वाः स्युरविपर्यस्ताः[2] । स्युस्ते भगवन् सम्यग्दर्शिनः । तत् कस्माद्धेतोः । तथागतधर्मकाय एव भगवन् नित्यपारमिता सुखपारमिता आत्मपारमिता शुभपारमिता । ये भगवन् सत्त्वास्तथागतधर्मकायमेवं पश्यन्ति ते सम्यक् पश्यन्ति[3] । ये सम्यक पश्यन्ति ते[4] भगवतः पुत्रा औरसा इति विस्तरः ।

आसां पुनश्चतसृणां तथागतधर्मकायगुणपारमितानां हेत्वानुपूर्व्या[5] प्रतिलोमक्रमो वेदितव्यः । तत्र महायानधर्मप्रतिहतानामिच्छन्तिकानामशुचिसंसाराभिरतिविपर्ययेण बोधिसत्त्वानां महायानधर्माधिमुक्तिभावनायाः शुभपारमिताधिगमः फलं द्रष्टव्यम् । पञ्चसूपादानस्कन्धेष्वात्मदर्शिनामन्यतीर्थ्यानामसदात्मग्रहा[6]भिरतिविपर्ययेण प्रज्ञापारमिताभावनायाः परमात्मपारमिताधिगमः फलं द्रष्टव्यम् । सर्वे ह्यन्यतीर्थ्या रूपादिकमतत्स्वभावं वस्त्वात्मेत्युपगताः[7] । तच्चैषां वस्तु यथाग्रहमात्मलक्षणेन विसंवादित्वात् सर्वकालमनात्मा । तथागतः (18*b*) पुनर्यथाभूतज्ञानेन सर्वधर्मनैरात्म्यपरपा(IX*a*)रमभिप्राप्तः[8] । तच्चास्य नैरात्म्यमनात्मलक्षणेन यथादर्शनमविसंवादित्वात् सर्वकालमात्माभिप्रेतो नैरात्म्यमेवात्मनि कृत्वा । यथोक्तं स्थितोऽस्थानयोगेनेति[9] । संसारदुःखभीरूणां श्रावक-

1. In B the words *viparyastāḥ ye* are very faint and may be meant to be erased. The first occurs in T, which has *de daṅ* (*te ca*) for *ye*; this is apparently a mistake for *gaṅ* (*ye*), which O evidently read.

2. *syur viparyastāḥ*, B; T and C as in text.

3. B om. *te samyak paśyanti* against C and T.

4. T had *te sarve* (*de-dag thams-cad*).

5. *hetvānu°*, B.

6. Should one read *ātmagrāha* here and *yathāgrāham* below?

7. *upagatā*, B.

8. *Tathāgatavastu*... *°prāptaṁ*, B; T and C as in text; A has *°prāptaṁ*, which suggests that it too read *vastu*, but this reading seems to me inferior in sense.

9. *°yogenayati*, B. O misunderstands this sentence, which means that the paradox of treating *nairātmya* as *ātman* is parallel to the opposition between *sthita* and *asthāna* in the phrase quoted. This quotation, not necessarily from a sūtra and missing in C, has not been traced. C adds a verse with commentary to explain this view of *ātman*, and there is possibly a lacuna in the Sanskrit text.

यानिकानां संसारदुःखोपशममात्राभिरतिविपर्ययेण गगनगञ्जादिसमाधिभावनायाः सर्वलौकिकलोकोत्तरसुखपारमिताधिगमः फलं द्रष्टव्यम् । सत्त्वार्थनिरपेक्षाणां प्रत्येकबुद्धयानीयानामसंसर्गविहाराभिरतिविपर्ययेण महाकरुणाभावनायाः सततसमितमा संसारात् सत्त्वार्थफलिगोध[1]परिशुद्धत्वान् नित्यपारमिताधिगमः फलं द्रष्टव्यम् । इत्येतासां चतसृणामधिमुक्तिप्रज्ञासमाधिकरुणाभावनानां यथासंख्यमेव चतुराकारं[2] तथागतधर्मकाये शुभात्मसुखनित्यत्वगुणपारमिताख्यं फलं निर्वर्त्यते[3] बोधिसत्त्वानाम् । आभिश्च तथागतो धर्मधातुपरम आकाशधातुपर्यवसानोऽपरान्तकोटिनिष्ठ इत्युच्यते । महायानपरमधर्माधि[4]मुक्तिभावनया हि तथागतोऽत्यन्तशुभधर्मधातुपरमताधिगमाद्धर्मधातुपरमः संवृत्तः । प्रज्ञापारमिताभावनयाकाशोपमसत्त्वभाजनलोकनैरा(19a)त्म्यनिष्ठागमनाद् गगनगञ्जादिसमाधिभावनया च सर्वत्र परमधर्मैश्वर्यविभुत्वसंदर्शनादाकाशधातुपर्यवसानः । महाकरुणाभावनया सर्वसत्त्वेष्वपर्यन्तकालकारुणिकतामुपादायापरान्तकोटिनिष्ठ इति ।

आसां पुनश्चतसृणां[5] तथागतधर्मकायगुणपारमितानामधिगमायानास्रवधातुस्थितानामप्यर्हतां प्रत्येकबुद्धानां वशिताप्राप्तानां च बोधिसत्त्वानामिमे चत्वारः परिपन्था भवन्ति । तद्यथा प्रत्ययलक्षणं हेतुलक्षणं संभवलक्षणं विभवलक्षणमिति । तत्र प्रत्ययलक्षणमविद्यावासभूमिरविद्येव संस्काराणाम् । हेतुलक्षणमविद्यावासभू[6]मिप्रत्ययमेव संस्कारवद्[7]नास्रवं कर्म । संभवलक्षणमविद्यावासभूमिप्रत्ययानास्रवकर्महेतुकी च त्रिविधा[8] मनोमयात्मभावनिर्वृत्तिश्चतु[9]-

1. So A; *pariśodha* (for *parigodha*?), B; *yoṅs-su spyod-pa*, T. C does not translate the word. Its form is quite uncertain in the texts, and its meaning far from clear.

2. °*ākāre*, B.

3. *nirvattate*, B

4. B om. *dharma*.

5. T had *caturvidhānāṁ* (*rnam-par bzhi*).

6. °*vāsanābhūmi*°, B. The *Laṅkāvatārasūtra*, p. 220, line 14, has *avidyāvāsanabhūmi*.

7. C read either *saṁskārā iva vijñānasya* or *saṁskārapratyayam iva vijñānam*; the second perhaps is a better reading.

8. *tridhā*, A.

9. *nivṛtti catur*°, B.

रुपादानप्रत्यया सास्रवकर्महेतुकीव त्रिभवाभिनिर्वृत्तिः[1] । विभवलक्षणं त्रिविधमनोमयात्मभावनिर्वृत्ति[2]प्रत्यया जातिप्रत्ययमिव जरामरणमचिन्त्या पारिणामिकी[3] च्युतिरिति ।

तत्र सर्वोपक्लेशसंनिश्रयभूताया अविद्यावासभूमेर[4]प्रहीणत्वादर्हन्तः प्रत्येकबुद्धा वशिताप्राप्ताश्च बोधिसत्त्वाः सर्वक्लेशमलदौर्गन्ध्यवासनापकर्ष[5]पर्यन्तशुभपारमितां नाधिगच्छन्ति । तामेव चावि(19b)द्यावासभूमिं प्रतीत्य सूक्ष्मनिमित्तप्रपञ्चसमुदाचारयोगादत्यन्तमनभिसंस्कार[6]मात्मपारमितां नाधिगच्छन्ति । तां चाविद्यावासभूमिमविद्यावासभूमिप्रत्ययं च[7] सूक्ष्मनिमित्तप्रपञ्चसमुदाचारसमुत्थापितमनास्रवं कर्म प्रतीत्य मनोमयस्कन्धसमुदयात् तन्निरोधमत्यन्तसुखपारमितां नाधिगच्छन्ति । यावच्च निरवशेषक्लेशकर्मजन्मसंक्लेशनिरोधसमुद्भूतं तथागतधातुं न साक्षात्कुर्वन्ति तावदचिन्त्यपारिणामिक्याश्च्यु(IXb)तेरविगमाद[8]त्यन्तानन्यथाभावां नित्यपारमितां नाधिगच्छन्ति । तत्र क्लेशसंक्लेशवदविद्यावासभूमिः । कर्मसंक्लेशवदनास्रवकर्माभिसंस्कारः । जन्मसंक्लेशवत् त्रिविधा मनोमयात्मभावनिर्वृत्तिरचिन्त्यपारिणामिकी च[9] च्युतिरिति ।

एष च[10] ग्रन्थो विस्तरेण यथासूत्रमनुगन्तव्यः । स्याद्यथापि नाम भगवन्नुपादानप्रत्ययाः सास्रवकर्महेतुकास्त्रयो भवाः संभवन्ति । एवमेव भगवन्नविद्या-

1. A om. *tri*, which B and T have.
2. °*nivṛtti*°, B.
3. *pariṇāmikī*, B.
4. *bhūmir*, B
5. Text as in A; °*vāsanāprakarṣa*°, B, which does not make sense; T seems to have read °*vāsanāyogāt* (*bag-chags . . . . daṅ ldan-paḥi phyir*), which would bring the sentence into the same form as the following ones. C paraphrases and throws no light on the original it had.
6. *anabhisaṁskāram*, read by A and B, is difficult and has to be understood either as an adverb or a gerund in *-am*. C seems to have had *asaṁskṛtām* or *anabhisaṁskṛtām*, and T may have had the same. Possibly one should read °*saṁskārām*.
7. *bhūmiñ ca pratyayañ ca*, B.
8. *anapagamād*, B.
9. B om. *ca*, which is added above the line in A.
10. B om. *ca*. Quotation from the *Āryaśrīmālāsūtra*.

वासभूमिप्रत्यया अनास्रवकर्महेतुका अर्हतां प्रत्येकबुद्धानां वशिताप्राप्तानां च बोधिसत्त्वानां मनोमयास्त्रयः कायाः संभवन्ति । आसु भगवन् तिसृषु भूमिष्वेषां त्रयाणां मनोमयानां कायानां[1] संभवायानास्रवस्य च कर्मणोऽभिनिर्वृत्तये प्रत्ययो भव(20*a*)त्यविद्यावासभूमिरिति विस्तरः । यत एतेषु त्रिषु मनोमयेष्वर्हत्प्रत्येकबुद्धबोधिसत्त्वकायेषु शुभात्मसुखनित्यत्वगुणपारमिता न संविद्यन्ते तस्मात् तथागतधर्मकाय एव नित्यपारमिता सुखपारमितात्मपारमिता शुभपारमितेत्युक्तम् ।

स हि प्रकृतिशुद्धत्वाद्वासनापगमाच्छुचिः
परमात्मात्मनैरात्म्यप्रपञ्चक्षयशान्तितः ॥ ३७ ॥
सुखो मनोमयस्कन्धतद्धेतुविनिवृत्तितः ।
नित्यः संसारनिर्वाणसमताप्रतिवेधतः[2] ॥ ३८ ॥

समासतो द्वाभ्यां कारणाभ्यां तथागतधर्मकाये शुभपारमिता वेदितव्या । प्रकृतिपरिशुद्ध्या सामान्यलक्षणेन । वैमल्यपरिशुद्ध्या विशेषलक्षणेन । द्वाभ्यां कारणाभ्यामात्मपारमिता वेदितव्या । तीर्थिकान्तविवर्जनतया चात्मप्रपञ्चविगमाच्छ्रावकान्तविवर्जनतया च नैरात्म्यप्रपञ्चविगमात् । द्वाभ्यां कारणाभ्यां सुखपारमिता वेदितव्या । सर्वाकारदुःखसमुदयप्रहाणतश्च वासनानुसंधिसमुद्घातात् सर्वाकारदुःखनिरोधसाक्षात्करणतश्च मनोमयस्कन्ध[3]निरोधसाक्षात्करणात् । द्वाभ्यां कारणाभ्यां नित्यपारमिता वेदितव्या । अनित्यसंसारानपकर्षणत[4]श्चोच्छेदान्ता[5]पतनान् नित्यनिर्वाणसमारोपणतश्च शाश्वतान्तापतनात् । यथोक्तम्[6] । अनित्याः सं(20*b*)स्कारा इति चेद् भगवन् पश्येत सास्य स्यादु-

1. A om. *kāyānāṁ*, which B and T have.

2. C treats these two verses as prose.

3. T read *ātmabhāva* (*lus*) for *skandha*, and so also apparently C ('birth-bodies').

4. A read *saṁsārānupakarṣaṇa;*; T translates *ḥbrid-pas*, to which S. C. Das, *Tibetan Dict.*, attributes the meaping 'impose' (i.e. *upakarṣaṇa*), but which O renders 'suppress' (i.e. *apakarṣaṇa*). B and C as in text.

5. *cocchedāpatanāt*, B.

6. From the *Āryaśrīmālāsūtra*.

च्छेददृष्टिः । सास्य[1] स्यान्न सम्यग्दृष्टिः । नित्यं निर्वाणमिति चेद् भगवन् पश्येत सास्य स्याच्छाश्वतदृष्टिः । सास्य स्यान्न सम्यग्दृष्टिरिति ।

तदनेन धर्मधातुनयमुखेन परमार्थतः संसार एव निर्वाणमित्युक्तम् । उभयथाविकल्पनाप्रतिष्ठितनिर्वाणसाक्षात्करणतः[2] । अपि खलु द्वाभ्यां कारणाभ्यामविशेषेण सर्वसत्त्वानामासन्नदूरीभावविगमादप्रतिष्ठितपदप्राप्तिमात्रपरिदीपना[3] भवति । कतमाभ्यां द्वाभ्याम् । इह बोधिसत्त्वोऽविशेषेण सर्वसत्त्वानां नासन्नीभवति[4] प्रज्ञयाशेषतृष्णानुशयप्रहाणात्[5] । न दूरीभवति महाकरुणया तदपरित्यागादिति[6] । अयमुपायोऽप्रतिष्ठितस्वभावायाः सम्यक्संबोधेरनुप्राप्तये । प्रज्ञया हि बोधिसत्त्वोऽशेषतृष्णानुशयप्रहाणादात्महिताय निर्वाणगताध्याशयः[7] संसारे न प्रतिष्ठतेऽपरिनिर्वाणगोत्रवत् । महाकरुणया दुःखितसत्त्वा[8]परित्यागात् परहिताय संसारगतप्रयोगो निर्वाणे न प्रतिष्ठते शमैकयानगोत्रवत् । एवमिदं धर्मद्वयमनुत्तराया बोधेर्मूलं प्रतिष्ठानमिति ।

छित्त्वा स्नेहं प्रज्ञयात्मन्यशेषं
सत्त्वस्नेहान् नैति शान्तिं कृपावान् ।
निःश्रित्यैवं धीकृपे बोध्युपायौ
नोपैत्यार्यः संवृतिं निर्वृतिं वा ॥ ३९ ॥

तत्र पूर्वाधिकृ(21a)तं[9] कर्मार्थमारभ्य परेण श्लोकार्धेन किं दर्शितम् ।

बुद्धधातुः सचेन्न स्यान्निर्विद्दुःखेऽपि नो भवेत् ।
नेच्छा न प्रार्थना नापि प्रणिधिर्निर्वृतौ भवेत् ॥ ४० ॥

1. *sasya*, B.
2. C adds a gāthā here, and then omits everything up to the introductory sentence to verse 40.
3. °*parīdīpanā*, A.
4. B om. the negative.
5. °*ānuśaṃsayaprahāṇāt*, B; *bag-la ñal*, T.
6. *tad api parityāgād*, B.
7. A's f. ix ends here with *nirvāṇa*. B om. *nirvāṇagatādhyā*°, leaving a gap.
8. B repeats *sattva*.
9. B om. *taṃ*.

तथा चोक्तम् । तथागतगर्भश्चे[1]द् भगवन्न स्यान्न स्याद्दुःखेऽपि निर्विन्न निर्वाण इच्छा वा प्रार्थना वा प्रणिधिर्वेति[2] । तत्र समासतो बुद्धधातुविशुद्धिगोत्रं[3] मिथ्यात्वनियतानामपि सत्त्वानां द्विविध[4]कार्यप्रत्युपस्थापनं भवति । संसारे च दुःखदोषदर्शननिःश्रयेण निर्विदमुत्पादयति । निर्वाणे सुखानुशंसदर्शननिःश्रयेण च्छन्दं जनयति । इच्छां प्रार्थनां प्रणिधिमिति । इच्छाभिलषितार्थप्राप्तावसंकोचः । प्रार्थनाभिलषितार्थप्राप्त्युपायपरिमार्गणा । प्रणिधिर्याभिलषितार्थे चेतना चित्ताभिसंस्कारः[5] ।

भवनिर्वाणतद्दुःखसुखदोषगुणेक्षणम् ।
गोत्रे सति भवत्येतदगोत्राणां न विद्यते ॥ ४१ ॥

यदपि तत् संसारे च दुःखदोषदर्शनं भवति निर्वाणे च सुखानुशंसदर्शनमेतदपि शुक्लांशस्य[6] पुद्गलस्य गोत्रे सति भवति नाहेतुकं नाप्रत्ययमिति । यदि हि तद्गोत्रमन्तरेण[7] स्यादहेतुकमप्रत्ययं पापसमुच्छेदयोगेन[8] तदिच्छान्तिकानामप्यपरिनिर्वाणगोत्राणां स्यात् । न च भवति तावद्यावदागन्तुकमलविशुद्धिगोत्रं त्रयाणामन्यतमधर्मा[9]धिमुक्तिं न स(21*b*)मुदानयति सत्पुरुषसंसर्गादिचतुःशुक्लसमवधानयोगेन ।

यत्र ह्याह[10] । तत्र पश्चादन्तशो मिथ्यात्वनियतसंतानानामपि सत्त्वानां कायेषु[11] तथागतसूर्यमण्डलरश्मयो निपतन्ति * * * [12]अनागतहेतुसंजन-

1. *Tathāgarbhas*, B. Quotation from the *Āryaśrīmālāsūtra*.
2. e.c.; *nirvin nirvāṇecchā prārthanā va praṇi*(gap)*ti*, B; *mya-ṅan-las ḥdas-pa-la ḥdod-pa daṅ ḥdun-pa daṅ don-du gñer-pa smon-pa yaṅ med-par ḥgyur-ro zhes* (text, adding *chando vā*, which C omits), T.
3. °*dhātuḥ* (or *r*) *viśuddhi*°, B; T ambiguous.
4. *dvividhaṁ*, B; T as in text.
5. T om. either *cetanā* or *citta*; but C shows both.
6. *śuklasasya*, B; *dkar-po cha daṅ ldan-paḥi*, T.
7. T om. *gotram antareṇa*, but C apparently had it.
8. *ahetutvapratyayaṁ*, B; *rgyu-med rkyen med-par sdig-pa mi zad-pa daṅ ldan-paḥi tshul-gyis* (. . *pāpāsamucchedayogena*), T.
9. *Dharma* here stands for Vehicle.
10. C attributes the quotation to the *Avataṁsakasūtra*, O to the *Jñānālokālaṁkārasūtra*.
11. e.c.; *kāyena*, B (much rubbed and not clear); *lus-la*, T.
12. C and T agree that a phrase is missing in B here, meaning 'and they cause benefit (*hita*)'.

नतया संवर्धयन्ति च कुशलैर्धर्मैरिति । यत्पुनरिदमुक्तमिच्छन्तिकोऽत्यन्तमपरिनिर्वाणधर्मेति तन् महायानधर्मप्रतिघ इच्छन्तिकत्वे हेतुरिति महायानधर्मप्रतिघनिवर्तनार्थमुक्तं कालान्तराभिप्रायेण । न खलु कश्चित्प्रकृतिविशुद्धगोत्रसंभवादत्यन्ताविशुद्धिधर्मा[1] भवितुमर्हति । यस्मादविशेषेण[2] पुनर्भगवता सर्वसत्त्वेषु विशुद्धिभव्यतां[3] संधायोक्तम् ।

अनादिभूतोऽपि हि चावसानिकः
स्वभावशुद्धो ध्रुवधर्मसंहितः[4] ।
अनादिकोशैर्बहिर्वृतो न दृश्यते[5]
सुवर्णबिम्बं परिच्छादितं[6] यथा ॥

तत्र योगार्थमारभ्य श्लोकः ।

महोदधिरिवामेयगुणरत्नाक्षयाकरः ।
प्रदीपवदनिर्भागगुणयुक्तस्वभावतः ॥ ४२ ॥

तत्र पूर्वेण श्लोकार्धेन किं दर्शितम्[7] ।

धर्मकायजिनज्ञानकरुणाधातुसंग्रहात् ।
पात्ररत्नाम्बुभिः साम्यमुदधेरस्य दर्शितम् ॥ ४३ ॥

त्रयाणां स्थानानां यथासंख्यमेव त्रिविधेन महासमुद्रसाधर्म्येण तथागतधातोर्हेतुसमन्वागममधिकृत्य योगार्थो वेदितव्यः । कतमानि त्रीणि स्थानानि । तद्यथा धर्मकायविशुद्धिहेतुः[8] । बुद्धज्ञानसमु(22*a*)दागमहेतुः । तथागतमहाकरुणा-

1. T om. *dharma*.
2. *aviśeṣaṇa*, B.
3. °*bhavyatī*, B. C omits this sentence and the following verse.
4. °*śuddho hi dharma*°, B; *rtag-paḥi chos-can*, T. The verse is attributed by O to the *Āryaśrīmālāsūtra*.
5. e.c.; *anādikośai bahi vṛdo na dṛśyante* (?), B; *thog-med ñon-moṅs-kyis phyi bsgribs mi mthoṅ* (*anādikleśair bahir vṛto na dṛśyate*), T. °*kośair* is better metrically and to suit the simile; *bahir vṛto* is a syllable in excess. C omits the verse
6. *paricchāditaṁ* is unmetrical.
7. *darśita*, B.
8. *dharmakāviśuddhi*°, B; T om. *kāya*, but C has it.

वृत्तिहेतुरिति[1] । तत्र धर्मकायविशुद्धिहेतुर्महायानाधिमुक्तिभावना द्रष्टव्या । बुद्धज्ञानसमुदा[2]गमहेतुः प्रज्ञासमाधिमुखभावना । तथागतमहाकरुणाप्रवृत्ति[3]-हेतुर्बोधिसत्त्वकरुणाभावनेति । तत्र महायानाधिमुक्ति[4]भावनाया भाजनसाधर्म्यं तस्यामपरिमेयाक्षयप्रज्ञासमाधिरत्नकरुणावारिसमवसरणात् । प्रज्ञासमाधिमुख-भावनाया रत्नसाधर्म्यं तस्या निर्विकल्पत्वादचिन्त्यप्रभावगुणयोगाच्च । बोधि-सत्त्वकरुणाभावनाया वारिसाधर्म्यं तस्याः सर्वजगति परमस्निग्धभावैकरस-लक्षणप्रयोगादिति[5] । एषां त्रयाणां धर्माणामनेन त्रिविधेन हेतुना तत्संबद्धः समन्वागमो योग इत्युच्यते ।

तत्रापरेण श्लोकार्धेन किं दर्शयति ।

अभिज्ञाज्ञानवैमल्यतथताव्यतिरेकतः ।
दीपालोकोष्णवर्णस्य साधर्म्यं विमलाश्रये[6] ॥ ४४ ॥

त्रयाणां स्थानानां यथासंख्यमेव त्रिविधेन दीपसाधर्म्येण तथागतधातोः फल-समन्वागममधिकृत्य योगार्थो वेदितव्यः । कतमानि त्रीणि स्थानानि । तद्यथा । अभिज्ञा आस्रवक्षयज्ञानमास्रवक्षयश्चेति । तत्र पञ्चानामभिज्ञानां ज्वालासाधर्म्यं तासामर्थानुभवज्ञान[7]विपक्षान्धकारविधमनप्रत्युपस्थानलक्षणत्वात् । आस्रव-क्षयज्ञानस्योष्णसाधर्म्यं तस्य निरव(22*b*)शेषकर्मक्लेशेन्धनदहनप्रत्युपस्थान-लक्षणत्वात् । आश्रयपरिवृत्तेरास्रवक्षयस्य वर्णसाधर्म्यं तस्यात्यन्तविमलविशुद्ध-

1. C seems to have read *karuṇāprāptihetur*.

2. B repeats the characters *mudā*.

3. T does not show *pra* in *pravṛtti*, and has *bodhisattvamahākaruṇā*.

4. T reads *mahāyānadharmādhimukti*.

5. T om. *lakṣaṇapra*; C either as in text or reading °*lakṣaṇayogād*, which is perhaps preferable.

6. B reads *abhijñāvaimalyatathatādivyatirekataḥ / dīpāloṣṇatāvavarṇṇasya dharmamālāśraye*. T has *dri-med gnas-la mṅon-śes daṅ / ye-śes dri-med de-gñis (for ñid) daṅ / rnam-dbye med-phyir mar-me-yi / sna* (for *snaṅ*) *daṅ dro mchog chos-mtshuṅs-can*. C as in text, omitting *jñāna*; like T, it divides *tathatā-avyatirekataḥ*.

7. T om. *jñāna*, but C as in text. B adds here, *viśuddhaprabhāsvaralakṣaṇatvāt / tatra vimalakleśāvaraṇaprahāṇāt / viśuddho jñānāvaraṇaprahāṇāt*, which recur lower down and do not belong here.

प्रभास्वरलक्षणत्वात् । तत्र विमलः[1] क्लेशावरणप्रहाणात् । विशुद्धो ज्ञेयावरणप्रहाणात् । प्रभास्वरस्तदु[2]भयागन्तुकताप्रकृतितः । इत्येषां समासतः सप्तानामभिज्ञाज्ञानप्रहाणसंगृहीतानामशैक्षसान्तानिकानां धर्माणामनास्रवधातावन्योन्यमविनिर्भागत्वमपृथग्भावो धर्मधातुसमन्वागमो योग इत्युच्यते । एष च योगार्थमारभ्य प्रदीप[3]दृष्टान्तो विस्तरेण यथासूत्रमनुगन्तव्यः[4] । तद्यथा शारिपुत्र प्रदीपः । अविनिर्भागधर्मा । अविनिर्मुक्तगुणः । यदुत[5] आलोकोष्ण[6]वर्णताभिः । मणिर्वालोकवर्णसंस्थानैः । एवमेव शारिपुत्र तथागतनिर्दिष्टो धर्मकायोऽविनिर्भागधर्माविनिर्मुक्तज्ञानगुणो यदुत गङ्गानदीवालिकाव्यतिवृत्तैस्तथागतधर्मैरिति ।

तत्र वृत्त्यर्थमारभ्य श्लोकः ।

पृथग्जनार्यसंबुद्धतथताव्यतिरेकतः ।
सत्त्वेषु जिगर्भो[7]ऽयं देशितस्तत्त्वदर्शिभिः ॥ ४५ ॥

अनेन किं दर्शितम् ।

पृथग्जना विपर्यस्ता दृष्टसत्या विपर्ययात् ।
यथावदविपर्यस्ता निष्प्रपञ्चास्तथागताः ॥ ४६ ॥

यदिदं तथागतधातोः सर्वधर्मतथताविशुद्धिसामान्यलक्षणमुपदिष्टं **प्रज्ञापारमिता**दि(23*a*)षु निर्विकल्पज्ञानमुखाववादमारभ्य वोधिसत्त्वानामस्मिन् समासतस्त्रयाणां पुद्गलानां पृथग्जनस्यातत्त्वदर्शिन आर्यस्य तत्त्वदर्शिनो[8] विशुद्धिनिष्ठागतस्य तथागतस्य[9] त्रिधा भिन्ना प्रवृत्तिर्वेदितव्या[10] । यदुत विपर्यस्ता-

1. *vimala*, B.
2. *prabhāsvara tad°*, B.
3. T om. *pradīpa* and adds *uktam* after sentence. C omits the whole para.
4. C omits this quotation and O does not identify it; probably it comes from the *Anūnatvāpūrṇatvanirdeśaparivarta*.
5. T om. *yad uta*.
6. B om. *ṣṇa*; *snaṅ-ba daṅ dro-ba daṅ mdog-dag-gis*, T
7. e.c.; *jayagarbho*, B; *rgyal-baḥi sñiṅ-po*, T; 'Tathāgatagarbha', C.
8. *pudgalānām atatvadarśi* (*pṛthagjanasyatatvadarśi*, added on margin in second hand) *na āryasya tatvadarśina*, B.
9. B om. first *ta* in *Tathāgatasya*.
10. *pravṛtir*, B.

विपर्यस्ता सम्यगविपर्यस्ता[1] निष्प्रपञ्चा च यथाक्रमम् । तत्र विपर्यस्ता संज्ञाचित्तदृष्टिविपर्यासाद् बालानाम् । अविपर्यस्ता विपर्ययेण तत्प्रहाणादार्याणाम्[2] । सम्यगविपर्यस्ता निष्प्रपञ्चा च सवासनक्लेशज्ञेयावरणसमुद्घातात् सम्यक्संबुद्धानाम् ।

अतः परमेतमेव[3] वृत्त्यर्थमारभ्य तदन्ये चत्वारोऽर्थाः प्रभेदनिर्देशादेव[4] वेदितव्याः । तत्रैषां त्रयाणां पुद्गलानामवस्थाप्रभेदार्थमारभ्य श्लोकः ।

अशुद्धोऽशुद्धशुद्धोऽथ[5] सुविशुद्धो यथाक्रमम् ।
सत्त्वधातुरिति प्रोक्तो बोधिसत्त्वस्तथागतः ॥ ४७ ॥

अनेन किं दर्शितम् ।

स्वभावादिभिरित्येभिः षड्भि[6]रर्थैः समासतः ।
धातुस्तिसृष्ववस्थासु विदितो नामभिस्त्रिभिः ॥ ४८ ॥

इति ये केचिदनास्रवधातुनिर्देशा नानाधर्मपर्यायमुखेषु भगवता विस्तरेण निर्दिष्टाः सर्वे त[7] एभिरेव समासतः षड्भिः[8] स्वभावहेतुफलकर्मयोगवृत्त्यर्थैः संगृहीतास्तिसृष्ववस्थासु यथाक्रमं त्रिनामनिर्देशतो निर्दिष्टा वेदितव्याः । यदुताशुद्धावस्थायां सत्त्वधातुरिति । अशुद्धशुद्धावस्थायां बोधिसत्त्व इति[9] । (23*b*) सुविशुद्धावस्थायां तथागत इति । यथोक्तं भगवता[10] । अयमेव शारिपुत्र धर्मकायोऽपर्यन्तक्लेशकोशकोटिगूढः । संसारस्रोतसा उह्यमानोऽनवराग्रसंसारगतिच्युत्युपपत्तिषु संचरन् सत्त्वधातुरित्युच्यते । स एव शारिपुत्र धर्मकायः संसारस्रोतोदुःखनिर्विण्णो विरक्तः सर्वकामविषयेभ्यो दशपारमितान्तर्गतैश्चतुरशीत्या

1. *samyagviparyastā*, B; T and C as in text.
2. *ācāryāṇām*, B; T and C as in text.
3. T om. *etam eva*.
4. °*nirdeśād veva* B.
5. e.c.; B om. '*tha*; *daṅ*, T.
6. *ṣadbhir*, B.
7. *te*, B.
8. *ṣadbhiḥ*, B.
9. B repeats *śuddhāvasthāyām bodhisatva iti*.
10. From the *Anūnatvāpūrṇatvanirdésaparivarta* (C).

धर्मस्कन्धसहस्रैर्बोधाय[1] चर्यां चरन् बोधिसत्त्व इत्युच्यते । स एव पुनः शारिपुत्र धर्मकायः सर्वक्लेशकोशपरिमुक्तः सर्वदुःखातिक्रान्तः सर्वोपक्लेशमलापगतः शुद्धो विशुद्धः परमपरिशुद्धधर्मतायां स्थितः सर्वसत्त्वालोकनीयां भूमिमारूढः सर्वस्यां ज्ञेयभूमावद्वितीयं पौरुषं स्थाम प्राप्तोऽनावरणधर्माप्रतिहतसर्वधर्मैश्वर्य-बलतामधिगतस्तथागतोऽर्हन् सम्यक्संबुद्ध इत्युच्यते ।

[2]तास्वेव तिसृष्ववस्थासु तथागतधातोः सर्वत्रगार्थमारभ्य श्लोकः ।

सर्वत्रानुगतं यद्वन्निर्विकल्पात्मकं नभः ।
चित्तप्रकृतिवैमल्यधातुः सर्वत्रगस्तथा ॥ ४९ ॥

अनेन किं दर्शितम् ।

तद्दोषगुणनिष्ठासु व्यापि सामान्यलक्षणम् ।
हीनमध्यविशिष्टेषु व्योम रूपगतेष्विव ॥ ५० ॥

यासौ पृथग्जनार्य[3]संबुद्धानामविकल्पचित्तप्रकृतिः (24*a*) सा तिसृष्ववस्थासु यथाक्रमं दोषेष्वपि गुणेष्वपि गुणविशुद्धिनिष्ठायामपि सामान्यलक्षणत्वादाकाश-मिव मृद्रजतसुवर्णभाजनेष्वनुगतानुप्रविष्टा समा निर्विशिष्टा प्राप्ता सर्वकालम्[4] । अत एवावस्थानिर्देशानन्तरमाह[5] । तस्माच्छारिपुत्र नान्यः सत्त्वधातुर्नान्यो धर्मकायः । सत्त्वधातुरेव धर्मकायः । धर्मकाय एव सत्त्वधातुः । अद्वयमेतदर्थेन । व्यञ्जनमात्रभेद इति[6]

एतास्वेव तिसृष्ववस्थासु तथागतधातोः सर्वत्रगस्यापि तत्संक्लेशव्यवदाना-भ्यामविकारार्थं[7]मारभ्य चतुर्दश श्लोकाः । अयं च तेषां पिण्डार्थो वेदितव्यः ।

दोषागन्तुकतायोगाद् गुणप्रकृतियोगतः ।
यथा पूर्वं तथा पश्चादविकारित्वधर्मता ॥ ५१ ॥

1. *bodhādhāya*, B.
2. B has *iti* at beginning, which T omits.
3. *pṛthagjanasyārya*°, B.
4. *sasarvakālaṁ*, B.
5. °*nirdeśāntaram*, B; T as in text. From the *Anūnatvā-pūrṇatvanirdeśaparivarta* (C).
6. e. c. ; *vyañjanamātran nāpati* (for *nāmeti* ? ), B; *yi-ge. tsam daṅ tha-dad-pa yin-no zhes*, T; 'different in name', C.
7. *adhikārārtham*, B; C and T as in text.

द्वादशभिरेकेन च श्लोकेन यथाक्रममशुद्धावस्थायाम[1]शुद्धशुद्धावस्थायां च क्लेशोपक्लेशदोषयोरा[2]गन्तुकयोगांच्चतुर्दशमेन श्लोकेन सुविशुद्धावस्थायां गङ्गानदीवालुकाव्यतिवृत्तैरविनिर्भागैरमुक्तज्ञैरचिन्त्यैर्बुद्धगुणैः[3] प्रकृतियोगादाकाशधातोरिव पौर्वापर्येण तथागतधातोरत्यन्ताविकार[4]धर्मता परिदीपिता । तत्राशुद्धावस्थायामविकारार्थ[5]मारभ्य कतमे द्वादश श्लोकाः

यथा सर्वगतं सौक्ष्म्यादाकाशं नोपलिप्यते ।
सर्वत्रावस्थि(24*b*)तः सत्त्वे[6] तथायं नोपलिप्यते ॥५२॥
यथा सर्वत्र लोकानामाकाश उदयव्ययः ।
तथैवासंस्कृते धाताविन्द्रियाणां व्ययोदयः[7] ॥ ५३ ॥
यथा नाग्निभिराकाशं दग्धपूर्वं कदाचन ।
तथा न प्रदहत्येनं मृत्युव्याधिजराग्नयः ॥ ५४ ॥
पृथिव्यम्बौ जलं[8] वायौ वायुर्व्योम्नि प्रतिष्ठितः ।
अप्रतिष्ठितमाकाशं वाय्वम्बुक्षितिधातुषु ॥ ५५ ॥
स्कन्धधात्विन्द्रियं तद्वत्कर्मक्लेशप्रतिष्ठितम् ।
कर्मक्लेशाः सदायोनिमनस्कारप्रतिष्ठिताः ॥ ५६ ॥
अयोनिशोमनस्कारश्चित्तशुद्धिप्रतिष्ठितः ।
सर्वधर्मेषु चित्तस्य प्रकृतिस्त्वप्रतिष्ठिता[9] ॥ ५७ ॥
पृथिवीधातुवज्ज्ञेयाः[10] स्कन्धायतनधातवः ।
अब्धातुसदृशा ज्ञेयाः कर्मक्लेशाः शरीरिणाम् ॥ ५८ ॥

1. *yathākramaś aśuddhāvasthām*, B.
2. °*doṣaṣayor*, B; T om. *doṣa*; C as in text.
3. *saṅs-rgyas-kyi chos* (*Buddhadharmaiḥ*), T; C shows *guṇa*.
4. *atyantavikāra*°, B; T and C as in text.
5. *ḥgyur-ba med-paḥi mtshan-ñid-la* (*avikāralakṣaṇam*), T.
6. *satvo*, B; but T and C imply a locative.
7. Cf. *S.*, xviii, 16*ab*, for the phraseology.
8. e.c.; *pṛthivy ayā calaṁ*, B; *sa ni chu-la chu*, T; 'the earth rests on water, water again on the wind', C.
9. °*sthitāḥ*, B.
10. *jñeyā*, B.

अयोनिशोमनस्कारो विज्ञेयो वायुधातुवत् ।
तदमूलाप्रतिष्ठाना प्रकृतिर्व्योमधातुवत् ॥ ५९ ॥
चित्तप्रकृतिमालीनायोनिशो मनसः कृतिः ।
अयोनिशो[1]मनस्कारप्रभवे क्लेशकर्मणी ॥ ६० ॥
कर्मक्लेशाम्बुसंभूताः स्कन्धायतनधातवः ।
उत्पद्यन्ते निरुध्यन्ते तत्संवर्तविवर्तवत् ॥ ६१ ॥
न हेतुः प्रत्ययो नापि न सामग्री न चोदयः ।
न व्ययो न स्थितिश्चित्तप्रकृतेर्व्योमधातुवत् ॥ ६२ ॥
चित्तस्य यासौ प्रकृतिः प्रभास्वरा
न जातु[2] सा द्यौरिव याति विक्रियाम् ।
आगन्तुकै रागमला[3]दिभिस्त्वसा—
वुपैति संक्लेशमभूतकल्पजैः ॥ ६३ ॥

कथमनेनाकाशदृष्टान्तेन तथागतधातोर[4]शुद्धावस्थायामविकारधर्मता परिदीपिता । तदुच्यते ।

नाभिनिर्वर्तयत्येनं कर्मक्लेशाम्बुसंचयः
न निर्दहत्युदी (25*a*) र्णोऽपि मृत्युव्याधिजरानलः[5] ॥६४॥

1. e.c. ; B om. *manasaḥ kṛtiḥ/ayoniśo*; .*tshul-bzhin, ma-yin yid-byed ni..tshul-bzhin ma-yin yid-byed-kyis*, T ; C similarly.

2. e.c. ; *yā tu*, B ; T om.

3. *rāgamanādibhis*, B; *ḥdod-chags sogs..dri-mas*, T;'*kleśas*',C.

4. For °*dhātor* T has *sñiṅ-po* (°*garbhasya*): C as in text.

5. According to C two verses are missing here in B and T before 64 ; it gives the meaning as follows, *Ayoniśomanaskāra* is the wind, *karmakleśa* the water, and *cittaprakṛti* space, which is not produced in dependence on these two. *Śuddhacittaprakṛti* has the characteristics of space, as that which the wind of *ayoniśomanaskāra* cannot disperse'. It has the same extent of commentary as B and T, whose form seems to imply a mention of *ayoniśomanaskāra* in the kārikās. Possibly 64 is a quotation, however, not a kārikā. In 64*a* B

यद्वदयोनिशो[1]मनस्कारवातमण्डलसंभूतं कर्मक्लेशोदकराशिं प्रतीत्य स्कन्धधात्वायत[2]नलोकनिर्वृत्त्या चित्तप्रकृतिव्योमधातोर्विवर्तो[3] न भवति। तद्वदयोनिशोमनस्कारकर्मक्लेशवाय्वप्स्कन्धप्रतिष्ठितस्य[4] स्कन्धधात्वायतनलोकस्यास्तंगमाय मृत्युव्याधिजराग्निस्कन्धसमुदयादपि तदसंवर्तो वेदितव्यः। इत्येवमशुद्धावस्थायां भाजनलोकवदशेषक्लेश(XIIa)कर्मजन्मसंक्लेशसमुदयास्तंगमेऽप्याकाशवदसंस्कृतस्य तथागतधातोर[5]नुत्पादानिरोधादत्यन्तमविकारधर्मता परिदीपिता। एष च प्रकृतिविशुद्धिमुखं धर्मालोकमुखमारभ्याकाशदृष्टान्तो विस्तरेण यथासूत्रमनुगन्तव्यः। कविमर्षा[6] क्लेशाः। आलोको विशुद्धिः। दुर्बलाः क्लेशाः। बलवती विपश्यना[7]। आगन्तुकाः क्लेशाः। मूलविशुद्धा प्रकृतिः। परिकल्पाः क्लेशाः। अपरिकल्पा प्रकृतिः। तद्यथा मार्षा इयं महापृथिव्यप्सु प्रतिष्ठिता। आपो वायौ प्रतिष्ठिताः। वायुराकाशे प्रतिष्ठितः। अप्रतिष्ठितं चाकाशम्। एवमेषां[8] चतुर्णां धातूनां पृथिवीधातोरब्धातोर्वायुधातोराकाशधातुरेव बली यो दृढोऽचलोऽनुपचयो[9]ऽनपचयोऽनुत्पन्नोऽनिरुद्धः स्थितः स्वरसयोगेन। तत्र य[10] एते त्रयो धातवस्त उत्पादभङ्गयुक्ता अनवस्थिता अचिरस्थायिनः। दृश्यत एषां विकारो न पुनराकाशधातोः[11] (25b) कश्चिद्विकारः। एवमेव

has *nābhinirvṛttayaty* and T *mnon-par ḥgrub-min-te*, which indicate the text, but C has 'rot by wetting,' the Sanskrit equivalent of which is not obvious, and which is a more probable sense in view of the parallelism of *nirdahati* and *anala* in the second line.

1. *yadvad yoniśo*, B; T and C as in text.
2. B om. *ta*.
3. °*dhāto vivàrtte* B.
4. *prasthitasya*, B.
5. *de-bzhin gśegs-paḥi sñiṅ-po* (*Tathāgatagarbhasya*), T.
6. *māṣā*, B. I retain *kavir* in view of A and B's agreement, but can find no other authority for the word. T translates it by *mun-pa* (*tamas*); and C renders 'the *kleśas* are *asvabhāva* in origin'. C attributes the quotation to the *Dhāraṇīśvararājasūtra*, O to the *Gaganagañjasūtra*.
7. B om. *pa*.
8. *eteṣām*, B.
9. T om. *anupacayaḥ* and C has instead of it 'inactive' (*anīha* ?).
10. *tatra va ete*, B.
11. *āśadhātoḥ*, B.

स्कन्धधात्वायतनानि कर्मक्लेशप्रतिष्ठितानि । कर्मक्लेशा अयोनिशोमनस्कारप्रतिष्ठिताः । अयोनिशोमनस्कारः प्रकृतिपरिशुद्धिप्रतिष्ठितः । तत उच्यते प्रकृतिप्रभास्वरं चित्तमागन्तुकैरुपक्लेशैरुपक्लिश्यत[1] इति । तत्र पश्चाद्योऽयोनिशो[2]मनस्कारो ये च कर्मक्लेशा यानि च स्कन्धधात्वायतनानि सर्वे एते धर्मा हेतुप्रत्ययसंगृहीता उत्पद्यन्ते हेतुप्रत्ययविसामग्र्या निरुध्यन्ते । या पुनः सा प्रकृतिस्तस्या न हेतुर्न प्रत्ययो[3] न सामग्री नोत्पादो न निरोधः । तत्र यथाकाशधातुस्तथा प्रकृतिः । यथा वायुधातुस्तथायोनिशोमनसिकारः । यथाब्धातुस्तथा कर्मक्लेशाः । यथा[4] पृथिवीधातुस्तथा[5] स्कन्धधात्वायतनानि । तत उच्यन्ते सर्वधर्मा असारमूला अप्रतिष्ठानमूलाः शुद्धमूला अमूलमूला इति ।

उक्तमशुद्धावस्थायामविकारलक्षण[6]मारभ्य प्रकृतेराकाशधातुसाधर्म्यं तदाश्रितस्यायोनिशोमनसिकारस्य कर्मक्लेशानां च हेतुलक्षणमारभ्य वायुधातुसाधर्म्यमब्धातुसाधर्म्यं च तत्प्रभवस्य स्कन्धधात्वायतनस्य विपाकलक्षणमारभ्य पृथिवीधातुसाधर्म्यम् । तद्विभवकारणस्य तु मृत्युव्याधिजराग्नेरुपसर्गलक्षणमारभ्य तेजोधातुसाधर्म्यं नोक्तमिति तदुच्यते ।

त्रयोऽग्नयो युगान्तेऽग्निर्नारकः प्राकृतः क्रमात् ।
त्रयस्त उपमा तेया मृत्युव्याधिजराग्नयः ॥ ६५ ॥

त्रिभिः[7] (26*a*) कारणैर्यथाक्रमं मृत्युव्याधिजराणामग्निसाधर्म्यं वेदितव्यम् । षडायतननिर्ममीकरणतो विचित्रकारणानुभवनतः[8] संस्कारपरिपाकोपनयनतः । एभिरपि मृत्युव्याधिजराग्निभिरविकारत्वमारभ्य तथगतधातोरशुद्धावस्थायामिदमुक्तम्[9] । लोकव्यवहार एष भगवन् मृत इति वा जात इति

1. °*kliṣyata*, B.
2. *paścād yoniśo*, B; *paścā yoniśo*, A; *de-la tshul-bzhin ma-yin-paḥi yid-la byed-pas gan-yin-pa* (text, omitting *paś-cād*), T.
3. *hetuḥ/pratyayo*, B.
4. A adds *ca*, which T omits.
5. B om. *sta*. The quotation is unidentified.
6. '*avikalpalakṣaṇam*', C.
7. C om. these two sentences.
8. *kāraṇā*, 'suffering' (*sdug-bsṅal*).
9. From the *Āryaśrīmālāsūtra*.

वा । मृत इति भगवन्निन्द्रियोपरोध एषः । जात इति भगवन् नवानामिन्द्रियाणां प्रादुर्भाव एष । न पुनर्भगवंस्तथागतग(XII*b*)र्भो जायते वा जीर्यति वा म्रियते वा च्यवते वोत्पद्यते वा । तत्कस्माद्धेतोः । संस्कृतलक्षणविषयव्यतिवृत्तो भगवंस्तथागतगर्भो नित्यो ध्रुवः शिवः शाश्वत[1] इति ।

तत्राशुद्धशुद्धा[2]वस्थायामविकारार्थमारभ्य श्लोकः ।

निर्वृत्तिव्युपरमरुग्जराविमुक्ता[3]
अस्यैव प्रकृतिमनन्यथावगम्य ।
जन्मादिव्यसनमृतेऽपि तन्निदानं
धीमन्तो जगति कृपोदयाद्भ[4]जन्ते ॥ ६६ ॥

अनेन किं दर्शयति ।

मृत्युव्याधिजरादुःखमूलमार्यैरपोद्धृतम्[5] ।
कर्मक्लेशवशाज्जातिस्त[6]दभावान्न तेषु तत् ॥ ६७ ॥

अस्य खलु मृत्युव्याधिजरादुःख[7]वह्नेरशुद्धावस्थायामयोनिशोमनसिकार[8]कर्मक्लेशपूर्विका जातिरिन्धन[9]मिवोपादानं भवति । यस्य मनोमयात्मभावप्रतिलब्धेषु बोधिसत्त्वेषु शुद्धाशुद्धावस्थायामत्यन्तम[10]नाभासगमनादितर[11]स्यात्यन्तमनुज्ज्वलनं प्रज्ञायते ।

1. Note that *Laṅkāvatārasūtra*, p. 78, line 1, says that the sūtras attribute these four qualities to the Tathāgatagarbha.

2. *tatrāśuddhāsuddhā°*, B. T om. *artham.*

3. C seems to have read *°vimuktām*, a better reading ; T is ambiguous.

4. B om. *dbha.*

5. *apodṛtaṁ*, B.

6. *jāti tad*, B.

7. *dukha*, B: T om. *duḥkha*, but C has it.

8. B om. *ra.*

9. *jātir ivandhanam*, B.

10. *°sthāyām anatyantam*, B.

11. *itirasyā°*, B.

जन्ममृत्युजराव्याधीन् दर्शयन्ति कृपात्मकाः ।
जात्यादिवि(26*b*)निवृत्ताश्च[1] यथाभूतस्य दर्शनात् ॥६८॥

कुशलमूलसंयोजनाद्धि बोधिसत्त्वाः संचिन्त्योपपत्तिवशितासंनिःश्रयेण करुणया त्रैधातुके संश्लिष्यन्ते[2] । जातिमप्युपदर्शयन्ति जरामपि व्याधिमपि मरणमप्युपदर्शयन्ति । न च तेषामिमे जात्यादयो धर्माः संविद्यन्ते । यथापि[3] तदस्यैव धातोर्यथाभूतमजात्यनुत्पत्तिदर्शनात्[4] । सा पुनरियं बोधिसत्त्वावस्था विस्तरेण यथासूत्रमनुगन्तव्या । यदाह[5] । कतमे च ते संसारप्रवर्तकाः कुशलमूलसंप्रयुक्ताः क्लेशाः । यदुत पुण्यसंभारपर्येष्ट्यतृप्तता[6] । संचिन्त्यभवोपपत्तिपरिग्रहः । बुद्धसमवधानप्रार्थना । सत्त्वपरिपाकापरिखेदः । सद्धर्मपरिग्रहोद्योगः । सत्त्वकिंकरणीयोत्सुकता । धर्मरागानुशयानुत्सर्गः । पारमितासंयोजनानामपरित्यागः। इत्येते सागरमते कुशलमूलसंप्रयुक्ताः क्लेशा यैर्बोधिसत्त्वाः संश्लिष्यन्ते । न खलु क्लेशदोषैर्लिप्यन्ते । आह पुनः । यदा भगवन् कुशलमूलानि तत्केन कारणेन क्लेशा इत्युच्यन्ते । आह । तथा हि सागरमते एभिरेवंरूपैः क्लेशैर्बोधिसत्त्वास्त्रैधातुके श्लिष्यन्ते । क्लेशसंभूतं च त्रैधातुकम् । तत्र बोधिसत्त्वा उपायकौशलेन च कुशलमूलबलान्वाधानेन च संचिन्त्य त्रैधातुके श्लिष्यन्ते । तेनोच्यन्ते कुशलमूलसंप्रयुक्ताः क्लेशा इति । यावदेव[7] त्रैधातुके श्लेषतया न पुनश्चित्तोपक्लेशतया।

स्याद्यथापि नाम सागरमते श्रेष्ठिनो गृहपतेरेक(27*a*)पुत्रक इष्टः कान्तः[8] प्रियो मनापो[9]ऽप्रतिकूलो दर्शनेन स च दारको बालभावेन नृत्यन्नेव मीढकूपे प्रपतेत । अथ ते तस्य दारकस्य मातृज्ञातयः[10] पश्येयुस्तं दारकं मीढकूपे प्रपतितम् । दृष्ट्वा च गम्भीरं निश्वसेयुः[11] शोचेयुः परिदेवेरन् । न पुनस्तं मीढकूपमवरुह्य

1. T's *ḥdas-gyur* suggests *vyativṛttāś*.
2. e.c.; *saṁkliṣyante*, B; *saṁsliṣyante*, A apparently; *sbyar-ro*, T; 'they appear', C.
3. T apparently omits *yathāpi*.
4. C may have read *ajātyanirodhadarśanāt*.
5. From the *Sāgaramatiparipṛcchā*.
6. *sambhāraḥ / ryeṣṭatṛptatā*, B.
7. *yāvad evaṁ*, B.
8. T om. *iṣṭaḥ* or *kāntaḥ*.
9. *namāpo*, A.
10. *mātāpitṛjnātayaḥ*, A; so also C, which makes the rescuer someone else than the father.
11. B seems to read *viṣvaṣeyuḥ*.

तं दारकमध्यालम्बेरन् । अथ तस्य दारकस्य पिता तं प्रदेशमागच्छेत् । स पश्येतैकपुत्रकं मीढकूपं प्रपतितं दृष्ट्वा[1] च शीघ्रशीघ्रं त्वरमाणरूप एकपुत्रकाध्याशयप्रेमानुनीतो[2]ऽजुगु (XIII*a*) प्समानस्तं मीढकूपमवरुह्यैकपुत्रकमभ्युत्क्षिपेत् । इति हि सागरमते उपमैषा कृता यावदेवार्थस्य विज्ञप्तये । कः प्रबन्धो द्रष्टव्यः । मीढकूप इति सागरमते त्रैधातुकस्यैतदधिवचनम् । एकपुत्रक इति सत्त्वानामेतदधिवचनम् । सर्वसत्त्वेषु हि बोधिसत्त्वस्यैकपुत्रसंज्ञा प्रत्युपस्थिता भवति । मातृज्ञातय[3] इति श्रावकप्रत्येकबुद्धयानीयानां पुद्गलानामेतदधिवचनं ये संसारप्रपतितान् सत्त्वान् दृष्ट्वा शोचन्ति परिदेवन्ते न पुनः समर्था भवन्त्यभ्युत्क्षेप्तुम् । श्रेष्ठी गृहपतिरिति बोधिसत्त्वस्यैतदधिवचनं यः शुचिर्विमलो[4] निर्मलचित्तोऽसंस्कृतधर्मप्रत्यक्षगतः संचिन्त्य त्रैधातुके प्रतिसंदधाति सत्त्वपरिपाकार्थम् । सेयं सागरमते बोधिसत्त्वस्य महाकरुणा यदत्यन्तपरिमुक्तः सर्वबन्धनेभ्यः पुनरेव भवोपपत्तिमुपाददाति । उपायकौशल्यप्रज्ञापरिगृहीतश्च संक्लेशैर्न लिप्यते । सर्व (27*b*) क्लेशबन्धनप्रहाणाय[5] च सत्त्वेभ्यो धर्मं देशयतीति । तदनेन सूत्रपदनिर्देशेन[6] परहितक्रियार्थं वशिनो बोधिसत्त्वस्य संचिन्त्यभवोपपत्तौ कुशलमूलकरुणाबलाभ्या[7]मुपक्लेशादुपायप्रज्ञाबलाभ्यां च तदसंक्लेशादशुद्धशुद्धावस्था परिदीपिता ।

तत्र यदा बोधिसत्त्वो यथाभूताजात्यनुत्पत्तिदर्शनमागम्य तथागतधातोरिमां[8] बोधिसत्त्वधर्मतामनुप्राप्नोति तथा विस्तरेण यथासूत्रमनुगन्तव्यम्[9] । यदाह । पश्य सागरमते धर्माणामसारताम[10]कारकतां निरात्मतां निःसत्त्वतां

1. B om. *dṛṣṭvā*.
2. °*ādhyāśayapremānunīto* is a doubtful reading, A being blurred and B practically illegible; *ḥdon-par* (or *ḥdren-par*) *ḥdod-paḥi sred-pas byas-te*, T, for which, if correct, the equivalent is not clear; C is no help.
3. *mātāpitṛjñātaya*, A; 'father, mother and relations', C.
4. T om. *vimalo*.
5. B om. *ya*.
6. B om. *rde*, and T *nirdeśena*.
7. *bodhisatvasya mahākaruṇā yad atyantaparimuktaḥ karuṇābalābhyām*, B; T as in text, omitting *bala*, which C has.
8. °*dhātoḥ māṁ*, B.
9. *yathāsūtrasarttavyaṁ*, B; A om. *yathā*; T as in text.
10. *asārakatām*, B. The quotation, the first part of which C omits, is from the *Sāgaramatiparipṛcchā* (O).

निर्जीवतां निःपुद्गलतामस्वामिकताम् । यत्र हि नाम यथेष्यन्ते तथा विठप्यन्ते[1] विठपिताश्च समाना न चेतयन्ति न प्रकल्पयन्ति[2] । इमां सागरमते धर्मविठपनामधिमुच्य बोधिसत्त्वो[3] न कस्मिंश्चिद्धर्मे परिखेदमुत्पादयति । तस्यैव ज्ञानदर्शनं शुचि शुद्धं भवति । नात्र कश्चिदुपकारो वापकारो वा[4] क्रियत इति । एवं च धर्माणां धर्मतां यथाभूतं प्रजानाति । एवं च महाकरुणासंनाहं न त्यजति । स्याद्यथापि नाम[5] सागरमतेऽनर्घं वैडूर्यमणिरत्नं स्ववदापितं सुपरिशुद्धं सुविमलं कर्दमपरिक्षिप्तं वर्षसहस्रमवतिष्ठेत । तद्वर्षसहस्रात्ययेन ततः कर्दमादभ्युत्क्षिप्य लोड्येत[6] पर्यवदाप्येत । तत्सु[7]धौतं परिशोधितं पर्यवदापितं समानं तमेव शुद्धविमलमणिरत्नस्वभावं न जह्यात्[8] । एवमेव सागरमते बोधिसत्त्वः सत्त्वानां प्रकृतिप्रभास्वरतां चित्तस्य प्रजानाति । तां पुनरागन्तुको(28*a*)पक्लेशोपक्लिष्टां पश्यति । तत्र बोधिसत्त्वस्यैवं भवति । नैते क्लेशाः सत्त्वानां चित्तप्रकृतिप्रभास्वरतायां प्रविष्टाः । आगन्तुका एते क्लेशा अभूतपरिकल्पसमुत्थिताः । शक्नुयामहं पुनरेषां सत्त्वानामागन्तुक्लेशापनयनाय[9] धर्मं देशयितुमिति । एवमस्य नावलीयनाचित्तमुत्पद्यते । तस्य भूयस्या मात्रया सर्वसत्त्वानामन्तिके प्रमोक्षचित्तोत्पाद उत्पद्यते । एवं चास्य भवति । नैतेषां क्लेशानां[10] किंचिद्बलं स्थाम वा । अबला दुर्बला एते[11] क्लेशाः । नैतेषां किंचिद्भूतप्रतिष्ठानम् । अभूतपरि-

1. B repeats *pyante*; A om. *viṭhapi*; T om. *tathā viṭhapyante viṭhapitāś ca samānā.*

2. A om. *na prakalpayanti.*

3. *bodhisatva*, B. T translates *viṭhapanā* by *gzhan-du mi-ḥgyurba*, 'not developing elsewhere'. Cf. *Abhisamayālaṃkārāloka* (ed. Wogihara), p. 370, for this passage.

4. *kasyacid upakāro apakāro vā*, A ; *ḥdi-la ḥgaḥ yan phan ḥdogs-pa ḥam*, (*nātra kaścid apy upakāro vā*), T.

5. A om. *nāma.*

6. The root *luḍ* in the sense *manthane*, 'rub', does not appear to have been recorded elsewhere in literature.

7. B om. *tat.*

8. *tyahyāt* (for *tyajyāt*), B.

9. Reading uncertain. °*kleśāpanayāyaya*, B; °*kleśānāṃ panayanāya*, A; *ñe-bar ñon-moṅs-pa zhi-bar bya-baḥi phyir*, (*sattvānāṃ upakleśaśamanāya* ?), T. C understands, 'cause the beings to get rid of the *āgantukakleśamalas*'.

10. *saṃkleśānāṃ*, A.

11. *yate*, B.

कल्पिता।[1] एते क्लेशाः। ते यथाभू(XIII*b*)तयोनिशो[2]मनसिकारनिरीक्षिता न कुप्यन्ति। तेऽस्माभिस्तथा प्रत्यवेक्षितव्या[3] यथा न भूयः श्लिष्येयुः। अश्लेषो हि क्लेशानां साधुर्न पुनः श्लेषः। यद्यहं क्लेशानां श्लिष्येय तत्कथं क्लेशबन्धनबद्धानां सत्त्वानां क्लेशबन्धनप्रहाणाय धर्मं देशयेयम्। हन्त वयं[4] क्लेशानां च न श्लिष्यामहे क्लेशबन्धनप्रहाणाय च सत्त्वेभ्यो धर्मं देशयिष्यामः। ये पुनस्ते संसारप्रबन्धकाः कुशलमलसंप्रयुक्ताः क्लेशास्तेऽस्माभिः सत्त्वपरिपाकाय श्लेष्टव्यमिति।

संसारः पुनरिह त्रैधातुकप्रतिबिम्बकमनास्रवधातौ मनोमयं कायत्रयमभिप्रेतम्। तद्ध्यनास्रवकुशलमूलाभिसंस्कृतत्वात् संसारः। सास्रवकर्मक्लेशानभिसंस्कृतत्वान्निर्वाणमपि तत्। यदधिकृत्याह[5]। तस्माद्भगवन्नस्ति संस्कृतोऽप्यसंस्कृतोऽपि संसारः। अस्ति संस्कृतमप्यसंस्कृतमपि निर्वाणमिति[6]। (28*b*) तत्र संस्कृता[7]संस्कृतसंसृष्टचित्तचैतसिकसमुदाचारयोगादियमशुद्धशुद्धावस्थेत्युच्यते। सा पुनरास्रवक्षयाभिज्ञाभिमुख्य[8]सङ्गप्रज्ञापारमितभावनया महाकरुणाभावनया च[9] सर्वसत्त्वधातुपरित्राणाय तदसाक्षात्करणादाभिमुख्यां बोधिसत्त्वभूमौ प्राधान्येन व्यवस्थाप्यते।

यथोक्तमास्रवक्षयज्ञानमारभ्य नगरोदाहरणम्[10]। एवमेव कुलपुत्र बोधिसत्त्वो महता यत्नेन महता वीर्येण दृढयाध्याशयप्रतिपत्त्या[11] पञ्चाभिज्ञा उत्पादयति। तस्य ध्यानाभिज्ञापरिकर्मकृतचित्तस्यास्रवक्षयोऽभिमुखीभवति। स महाकरुणाचित्तोत्पादेन सर्वसत्त्वपरित्राणायास्रवक्षयज्ञाने परिजयं कृत्वा पुनरपि

1. *abhūtāparikalpitāḥ*, B.
2. A om. *yoniśo*.
3. *pratyavekṣitāḥ*, B.
4. *hetur ayam*, B; *ḥon-kyaṅ kho-bos*, T.
5. From the *Āryaśrīmālāsūtra*.
6. B adds *tatra saṁskṛtāsaṁ*(28*b*)*skṛtam api nirvāṇam iti*.
7. B om. *saṁskṛtā°*.
8. *°mukhyām asaṅga°*, B.
9. A om. *ca*.
10. *meḥi dper brjod-pa*, T (read *mi ḥi* and understand *narodāharaṇam* with O?). C quotes the parable in full and attributes it and the following passage to the *Ratnamālāsūtra*.
11. *dṛḍha adhyāśayaprapattyā*, B.

सुपरिकर्मकृतचेताः[1] षष्ठ्यामसङ्गप्रज्ञोत्पादादास्रवक्षयेऽभिमुखीभवति[2] । एवमस्यामाभिमुख्यां बोधिसत्त्वभूमावास्रवक्षयसाक्षात्करणवशित्वलाभिनो बोधिसत्त्वस्य विशुद्धावस्था परिदीपिता । तस्यैवमात्मना सम्यक्प्रतिपन्नस्य परानपि चास्यामेव सम्यक्प्रतिपत्तौ स्थापयिष्यामीति[3] महाकरुणया विप्रतिपन्नसत्त्वपरित्राणाभिप्रायस्य शमसुखानास्वादनतया तदुपायकृतपरिजयस्य संसारा[4]भिमुखसत्त्वापेक्षया निर्वाणविमुखस्य[5] बोध्यङ्गपरिपूरणाय ध्यानैर्विहृत्य पुनः कामधातौ संचिन्त्योपपत्तिपरिग्रहणतो यावदाशु सत्त्वानामर्थं कर्तुकामस्य विचित्रतिर्यग्योनिगतजातकप्रभेदेन पृथग्जनात्मभावसंदर्शनविभुत्वलाभिनोऽविशुद्धा-(29a)वस्था परिदीपिता ।

[6]अपरः श्लोकार्थः

धर्मतां प्रतिविध्येमामविकारां जिनात्मजः ।
दृश्यते यदविद्यान्धैर्जात्यादिषु तदद्भुतम् ॥ ६९ ॥
अत एव जगद्बन्धोरुपायकरुणे परे ।
यदार्यगोचरप्राप्तो दृश्यते बालगोचरे ॥ ७० ॥
सर्वलोकव्यतीतोऽसौ न च लोकाद्विनिःसृतः ।
लोके चरति लोकार्थमलिप्तो लौकिकैर्मलैः ॥ ७१ ॥
यथैव नाम्भसा पद्मं लिप्यते जातमम्भसि ।
तथा लोकेऽपि जातोऽसौ लोकधर्मैर्न लिप्यते[7] ॥७२॥

1. °*cetasaḥ*, B.

2. *āsraya āmukhībhavati*, B; T shows *abhi* (*mṅon-du*). C enlarges this passage, describing also the attainments of the fourth and fifth *bhūmis*.

3. *sthāsyāmīti*, B.

4. B om. *rā*.

5. *mya-ṅan-las ḥdas-pa-la mṅon-du phyogs-par* (*nirvāṇābhimukhasya*), T.

6. C omits from here up to verse 79. Verses 69-78 and the commentary on them may therefore be later additions; the heading to them is suspicious and their omission would improve the arrangement of the exposition. But verse 76 is in the first of C's translations.

7. Cf. *S.*, xiii, 4-6; *d*=6*d*.

नित्योज्ज्वलितबुद्धिश्च कृत्यसंपादनेऽग्निवत् ।
शान्तध्यानसमापत्तिप्रतिपन्नश्च सर्वदा ॥ ७३ ॥
पूर्वाविधवशात् सर्वविकल्पापगमाच्च सः ।
न पुनः कुरुते यत्नं[1] परिपाकाय देहिनाम् ॥ ७४ ॥
यो यथा येन वैनेयो मन्यतेऽसौ तथैव तत् ।
देशन्या रूपकायाभ्यां चर्ययेर्यापथेन वा[2] ॥ ७५ ॥
अनाभोगेन तस्यैवमव्याहतधियः सदा ।
जगत्याकाशपर्यन्ते सत्त्वार्थः संप्रवर्तते ॥ ७६ ॥
एतां गतिमनुप्राप्तो बोधिसत्त्वस्तथागतैः ।
समतामेति लोकेषु सत्त्वसंतारणं[3] प्रति ॥ ७७ ॥
अथ चाणोः पृथिव्याश्च गोस्पदस्योदधेश्च यत् ।
अन्तरं बोधिसत्त्वानां बुद्धस्य च तदन्तरम् ॥ ७८ ॥

एषां दशानां श्लोकानां यथाक्रमं नवभिः श्लोकैः प्रमुदिताया बोधिसत्त्वभूमेरधश्च संक्लेशपरमतां दशमेन श्लोकेन धर्ममेधाया बोधिसत्त्वभूमेरूर्ध्वं विशुद्धिपरमतामुपनिधाय समासतश्चतुर्णां बोधिसत्त्वानां दशसु बोधिसत्त्व[4]-भूमिषु विशुद्धिरविशुद्धिश्च परिदीपिता । चत्वारो बोधिसत्त्वाः प्रथमचित्तोत्पादिकः । चर्याप्रति(29*b*)पन्नः । अवैवर्तिकः । एकजातिप्रतिबद्ध इति । तत्र प्रथम[5]द्वितीयाभ्यां श्लोकाभ्यामनादिकालिकमदृष्टपूर्वप्रथमलोकोत्तरधर्मताप्रतिवेधात् प्रमुदितायां भूमौ[6] प्रथमचित्तोत्पादिकबोधिसत्त्वगणविशुद्धि[7]लक्षणं परिदीपितम् । त्रितीयचतुर्थाभ्यां श्लोकाभ्यामनुपलिप्तचर्याचरणाद्विमलां[8]

1. A's f.xiii*b* ends here.
2. *varyeryāpathena vā*, B (one syllable short); *spyod dan spyod-lam-gyis*, T.
3. *°sāṁtāraṇaṁ*, B.
4. T om. *bodhisattva*.
5. T om. *prathama*.
6. *sa dan-po rab-tu dgaḥ-ba-la* (*pramuditāyāṁ prathamabhūmau*), T.
7. *yons-su dag-paḥi* (*°pariśuddhi°*), T.
8. *vimalā*, B.

भूमिमुपादाय यावद्दूरंगमायां भूमौ चर्याप्रतिपन्नबोधिसत्त्वगुणविशुद्धि[1]लक्षणं परिदीपितम् । पञ्चमेन श्लोकेन निरन्तरमहाबोधिसमुदागम[2]प्रयोगसमाधिषु व्यवस्थितत्वादचलायां भूमाववैवर्तिकबोधिसत्त्वगुणविशुद्धिलक्षणं परिदीपितम् । षष्ठेन सप्तमेनाष्टमेन च श्लोकेन सकलस्वपरार्थसंपादनोपायनिष्ठागतस्य[3] बुद्धभूम्येकचरमजन्मप्रतिबद्धत्वादनुत्तरपरमाभिसंबोधिप्राप्तेर्धर्ममेघायां बोधिसत्त्वभूमावेक[4]जातिप्रतिबद्धबोधिसत्त्वगुणविशुद्धि[5]लक्षणं परिदीपितम् । नवमेन दशमेन च श्लोकेन परार्थमात्मार्थं चारभ्य निष्ठागतबोधिसत्त्वतथागतयोर्गुणविशुद्धेर्[6]विशेषो विशेषश्च परिदीपितः ।

तत्र सुविशुद्धा[7]वस्थायामविकारार्थमारभ्य श्लोकः ।

अनन्यथात्माक्षयधर्मयोगतो
जगच्छरण्योऽनपरान्तकोटितः ।
सदाद्वयोऽसावविकल्पकत्वतो
ऽविनाशधर्माप्यकृतस्वभावतः ॥ ७९ ॥

अनेन किं दर्शयति ।

न जायते न म्रियते बाध्यते नो न जीर्यते[8] ।
स नित्यत्वाद्ध्रुवत्वाच्च शिवत्वाच्छाश्वत (30a) त्वतः ॥८०
न जायते स नित्यत्वा[9]दात्मभावैर्मनोमयैः ।
अचिन्त्यपरिणामेन[10] ध्रुवत्वान् म्रियते[11] न सः ॥८१॥

1. *yons-su dag-paḥi* (°*pariśuddhi*°), T.
2. *bodhisatvasamudāgama*°, B; T om. *sattva*.
3. °*niryātasya*, B; *mthar phyin-pa*, T which does not show case-ending.
4. B adds *ekajātipratibaddhabodhisatvabhūmau*.
5. *yons-su dag-paḥi* (*pariśuddhi*), T.
6. T om. *viśuddher*.
7. *ta viśuddhā*°, B; *de-la śin-tu rnam-par dag-paḥi*, T; C as in text.
8. Cf. *Buddhac.*, xii, 22.
9. B om. *tvā*.
10. °*pariṇāmena macintyaś cyutya dhruva*°, B; possibly an old interpolation, as T also shows *cyuti* in *d*.
11. *mṛyate*, B.

वासनाव्याधिभिः सूक्ष्मैर्बाध्यते न शिवत्वतः ।
अनास्रवा[1]भिसंस्कारैः शाश्वतत्वान्न जीर्यते ॥८२॥

स खल्वेष तथागतधातुर्बुद्धभूमावत्यन्तविमल[2]विशुद्धप्रभास्वरतायां स्वप्रकृतौ स्थितः पूर्वान्तमुपादाय नित्यत्वान्न पुनर्जायते मनोमयैरात्मभावैः । अपरान्तमुपादाय ध्रुवत्वान्न पुनर्म्रियतेऽचिन्त्यपारिणामिक्या[3] च्युत्या । पूर्वापरान्तमुपादाय शिवत्वान्न पुनर्बाध्यतेऽविद्यावासभूमिपरिग्रहेण । यश्चैवमनर्थपतितः स शाश्वतत्वान्न पुनर्जीर्यत्य[4]नास्रवकर्मफलपरिणामेन ।

तत्र द्वाभ्यामथ द्वाभ्यां द्वाभ्यां द्वाभ्यां[5] यथाक्रमम् ।
पदाभ्यां नित्यताद्यर्थो विज्ञेयोऽसंस्कृते पदे ॥ ८३ ॥

तदेषामसंस्कृतधातौ चतुर्णां नित्यध्रुवशिवशाश्वतपदानां यथाक्रममेकैकस्य पदस्य द्वाभ्यां द्वाभ्यामुद्देशनिर्देश[6]पदाभ्यामर्थप्रविभागो यथासूत्रमनुगन्तव्यः[7] । यदाह । नित्योऽयं शारिपुत्र धर्मकायोऽनन्यत्वधर्माक्षयधर्मतया । ध्रुवोऽयं शारिपुत्रधर्मकायो ध्रुवशरणोऽपरान्तकोटिसमतया । शिवोऽयं शारिपुत्र धर्मकायोऽद्वयधर्माविकल्पधर्मतया । शाश्वतोऽयं शारिपुत्र धर्मकायोऽविनाशधर्माकृत्रिमधर्मतयेति ।

1. *anaśravā°*, B.

2. B om. *vimale*; *dri-med-ciṅ*, T; C shows *vimala* too.

3. *°pariṇāmikyā*, B.

4. B reads *jīryati* / *anāsrava°* here, though it reads *jīryate* in verse 80.

5. In *b* B om. one *dvābhyām* and has *svābhyām* for the other; C and T as in text.

6. *uddeśanideśanirdeśa°*, B; *bstan-pa dan bśad-pa*, T.

7. B and T add two verses here, which C omits and which must be interpolations, as the quotation from the sūtra clearly follows directly on the reference to it in the previous sentence. They are simply an enlargement of 79 and run as follows :

*Nityārtho'nanyathātmatvam akṣayyaguṇayogataḥ* /
*Dhruvārthaḥ śaraṇātmatvam antakoṭisamānataḥ* //
*Śivārtho'dvayadharmatvam avikalpasvabhāvataḥ* /
*Śāśvatārtho'vināśitvam akṛtrimaguṇatvataḥ* //

B om. *kr* in the last line. The quotation according to C is from the *Anūṇatvāpūrṇatvanirdeśaparivarta*.

अस्यामेव विशुद्धावस्थायामत्यन्तव्यवदा (30*b*) ननिष्ठागमनलक्षणस्य तथागतगर्भस्या[1]संभेदार्थमारभ्य श्लोकः ।

स धर्मकायः स तथागतो यत–
स्तदार्यसत्यं परमार्थनिर्वृतिः ।
अतो न बुद्धत्वमृतेऽर्करश्मिवद्
गुणाविनिर्भागतयास्ति निर्वृतिः ॥ ८४ ॥

तत्र पूर्वश्लोकार्धेन किं दर्शयति ।

धर्मकायादिपर्याया वेदितव्याः समासतः ।
चत्वारोऽनास्रवे धातौ चतुरर्थप्रभेदतः ॥ ८५ ॥

समासतोऽनास्रवे धातौ तथागतगर्भे चतुरोऽर्थानधिकृत्य चत्वारो नामपर्याया वेदितव्याः । चत्वारोऽर्थाः कतमे ।

बुद्धधर्माविनिर्भागस्तद्गोत्रस्य तथागमः ।
अमृषामोषधर्मित्वमादिप्रकृतिशान्तता ॥ ८६ ॥

बुद्धधर्माविनिर्भागार्थः । यमधिकृत्योक्तम्[2] । अशून्यो भगवंस्तथागतगर्भो गङ्गानदीवालुकाव्यतिवृत्तैरविनिर्भागैरमुक्तज्ञैरचिन्त्यैर्बुद्धधर्मैरिति । तद्गोत्रस्य प्रकृतेरचिन्त्यप्रकारसमुदागमार्थः । यमधिकृत्योक्तम्[3] । षडायतनविशेषः स तादृशः परंपरागतोऽनादिकालिको धर्मताप्रतिलब्ध इति । अमृषामोषार्थः । यमधिकृत्योक्तम्[4] । तत्र परमार्थसत्यं यदिदममोषधर्मि निर्वाणम् । तत्कस्माद्धेतोः । नित्यं तद्गोत्रं समधर्मतयेति[5] । अत्यन्तोपशमार्थः । यमधिकृत्योक्तम्[6] । आदिपरिनिर्वृत एव तथागतोऽर्हन् सम्यक्संबुद्धोऽनुत्पन्नोऽनिरुद्ध

1. *Tathāgatadhātor*, B; C and T as in text.

2. From the *Āryaśrīmālāsūtra*.

3. From the *Ṣaḍāyatanasūtra* (C).

4. Probably from the *Āryaśrīmālāsūtra* (O).

5. So B, but the reading is uncertain; *gtan-du zhi-baḥi chos-ñid-kyis-na* (*atyantaśamadharmatayā*), T; C suggests *śāśvatadharmatayā*.

6. From the *Jñānālokālaṁkārasūtra* (O).

इति । एषु चतुर्ष्वर्थेषु यथासंख्यमिम चत्वारो[1] नामपर्याया भवन्ति । तद्यथा धर्मकायस्तथागतः परमार्थसत्यं निर्वाणमिति । यत एवमाह[2] । तथागतगर्भ इति शारि(31*a*)पुत्र धर्मकायस्यैतदधिवचनमिति । नान्यो भगवंस्तथागतोऽन्यो धर्मकायः । धर्मकाय एव भगवंस्तथागत इति । दुःखनिरोधनाम्ना भगवन्नेवंगुणसमन्वागतस्तथागतधर्मकायो देशित इति । निर्वाणधातुरिति भगवंस्तथागतधर्मकायस्यैतदधिवचनमिति ।

तत्रापरेण श्लोकार्धेन किं दर्शयति ।

सर्वाकाराभिसंबोधिः सवासनमलोद्धृतिः ।
बुद्धत्वमथ निर्वाणमद्वयं परमार्थतः ॥ ८७ ॥

यत[3] (XV*a*) एते चत्वारोऽनास्रवधातुपर्यायास्तथागतधातावेकस्मिन्नभिन्नेऽर्थे[4] समवसरन्ति । अत एषामेकार्थत्वादद्वयधर्मनयमुखेन यच्च सर्वाकारसर्वधर्माभिसंबोधाद्बुद्धत्वमित्युक्तं यच्च महाभिसंबोधात् सवासनमलप्रहाणान्निर्वाणमित्युक्तमे[5]तदुभयमनास्रवे धातावद्वयमिति द्रष्टव्यमभिन्नमच्छिन्नम् ।

सर्वाकारैरसंख्येयैर[6]चिन्त्यैरमलैर्गुणैः ।
अभिन्नलक्षणो मोक्षो यो[7] मोक्षः स तथागत इति ॥

यदुक्तमर्हत्प्रत्येकबुद्धपरिनिर्वाणमधिकृत्य[8] । निर्वाणमिति भगवन्नुपाय एष तथा[9]गतानामिति । अनेन दीर्घाध्वपरिश्रान्तानामटवीमध्ये नगरनिर्माणवदविव[10]र्तनोपाय एष धर्मपरमेश्वराणां सम्यक्संबुद्धानामिति परिदीपितम् । निर्वा-

1. B om. *catvāro*; C and T as in text.
2. C gives the first sentence of the quotation to the *Anūnatvāpūrṇatvanirdeśaparivarta* and the rest to the *Āryaśrīmālāsūtra*.
3. B om. *ta*; *gaṅ-gi phyir*, T.
4. °*dhātā ekasminn abhinnārthe*, B; T om. *abhinna*; C not clear.
5. A and B om. *uktam*; T inserts it.
6. *asaṁkṣepair*, B. C attributes the verse to the *Mahāparinirvāṇasūtra*.
7. B om. *kṣo yo*.
8. From the *Āryaśrīmālāsūtra*.
9. B om. *ta* in *Tathāgatānām*.
10. *anivartano*°, B; *mi-ldog-pa*, T

णाधिगमाद् भग[1]वंस्तथागता भवन्त्यर्हन्तः सम्यक्संबुद्धाः सर्वाप्रमेयाचिन्त्यविशुद्धिनिष्ठागतगुणसमन्वागता इति । अनेन चतुराकारगुणनिष्पत्त्यसंभिन्नलक्षणं निर्वाणमधिगम्य तदात्मकाः सम्यक्संबुद्धा भवन्ती(31*b*)ति । बुद्धत्वनिर्वाणयोरविनिर्भागगुणयोगाद्बुद्धत्वमन्तरेण कस्यचिन्निर्वाणाधिगमो[2] नास्तीति परिदीपितम् ।

तत्र तथागतानामनास्रवे धातौ सर्वाकारवरोपेतशून्यताभिनिर्हारतश्चित्रकरदृष्टान्तेन गुणसर्वता वेदितव्या[3] ।

अन्योन्यकुशला यद्वद्भवेयुश्चित्रलेखकाः ।
यो यदङ्गं प्रजानीयात्तदन्यो नावधारयेत् ॥ ८८ ॥
अथ तेभ्यः प्रभू राजा प्रयच्छेद्दूष्यमाज्ञया ।
सर्वैरेवात्र युष्माभिः कार्या प्रतिकृतिर्मम ॥ ८९ ॥
ततस्तस्य प्रतिश्रुत्य युञ्जेरंश्चित्रकर्मणि ।
तत्रैको व्यभियुक्तानामन्यदेशगतो भवेत् ॥ ९० ॥
देशान्तरगते तस्मिन् प्रतिमा तद्वियोगतः ।
न सा सर्वाङ्गसंपूर्णा भवेदित्युपमा कृता ॥ ९१ ॥
लेखका ये तदाकारा दानशीलक्षमादयः ।
सर्वाकारवरोपेता शून्यता प्रतिमोच्यते[4] ॥ ९२ ॥

तत्रैषामेव दानादीनामेकैकस्य बुद्धविषयापर्यन्त[5]प्रकारभेदभिन्नत्वादपरिमितत्वं वेदितव्यम् । संख्याप्रभावाभ्यामचिन्त्यत्वम् । मात्सर्यादिविपक्षमलवासनापकर्षितत्वाद्विशुद्धिपरमत्वमिति । तत्र सर्वाकारवरोपेतशून्यतासमाधिमुखभावनयानुत्पत्तिकधर्मलाभादचलायां बोधिसत्त्वभूमा-

1. °*gamā Bhaga*°, B.

2. *nirvāṇabhigamo*, A; *thob-pa*, T.

3. According to C this parable is taken from the *Ratnamālāsūtra*, whose account it quotes immediately after the verses.

4. *pratiyocyate*, B.

5. °*viṣayaparyanta*°, A; but *yul-la mthaḥ-yas-par*, T, and 'unlimited', C.

सविकल्पनिश्छिद्रनिरन्तरस्वरसवाहिमार्गज्ञानसंनिश्रयेण तथागतानामनास्रवे धातौ गुणसर्वता समुदागच्छति । साधुमत्यां बोधिसत्त्वभूमावसंख्येयसमाधिधारणीमुखसमुद्रैरपरिमाणबुद्धधर्मपरि(32a)ग्रहज्ञानसंनिश्रयेण गुणाप्रमेयता समुदागच्छति । धर्ममेघायां बोधिसत्त्वभूमौ सर्वतथागतगुह्यस्थानाविपरोक्षज्ञानसंनिश्रयेण गुणाचिन्त्यता समुदागच्छति । तदनन्तरं बुद्धभूम्यधिगमाय सर्वसवासनक्लेशज्ञेयावरणविमोक्षज्ञान[1]संनिश्रयेण गुणविशुद्धिपरमता समुदागच्छति । यत एषु चतुर्षु भूमिज्ञानसंनिश्रयेष्वर्हत्प्रत्येकबुद्धा[2] न संदृश्यन्ते तस्मात्ते दूरी[3]भवन्ति चतुराकारगुणपरिनिष्पत्त्यसंभिन्नलक्षणान्[4] निर्वाणधातोरित्युक्तम् ।

प्रज्ञाज्ञानविमुक्तीनां दीप्तिस्फरणशुद्धि( xv*b* )तः ।
अभेदतश्च साधर्म्यं प्रभारश्म्यर्कमण्डलैः ॥ ९३ ॥

यया प्रज्ञया येन ज्ञानेन यया विमुक्त्या स[5] चतुराकारगुणनिष्पत्त्यसंभिन्नलक्षणो निर्वाणधातुः सूच्यते तासां यथाक्रमं त्रिभिरेकेन च[6] कारणेन चतुर्विधमादित्यसाधर्म्यं परिदीपितम् । तत्र बुद्धसान्तानिक्या लोकोत्तरनिर्विकल्पायाः परमज्ञेयतत्त्वान्धकारविधमनप्रत्युपस्थानतया प्रज्ञाया दीप्तिसाधर्म्यम् । तत्पृष्ठलब्धस्य सर्वज्ञज्ञानस्य[7] सर्वाकारनिरवशेषज्ञेयवस्तुप्रवृत्ततया रश्मिजालस्फरणसाधर्म्यम् । तदुभयाश्रयस्य चित्तप्रकृतिविमुक्तेरत्यन्तविमलप्रभास्वरतयार्कमण्डलविशुद्धिसाधर्म्यम् । तिसृणामपि धर्मधात्वसंभेदस्वभावतया तत्त्रयाविनिर्भागसाधर्म्यमिति ।

अतोऽनागम्य बुद्धत्वं निर्वाणं नाधिगम्यते ॥
न हि शक्यः प्रभारश्मी निर्वृज्य[8] प्रेक्षितुं रविः ॥ ९४ ॥

1. B om. *na*.
2. °*buddhāḥ*, B.
3. *dūre*, B.
4. A om. *lakṣaṇān*.
5. B om. *sa*.
6. B om. *ca*; *daṅ rnam-pa gcig-gis* (*ekena cākāreṇa*), T; C's equivalent is not clear (*i*, usually for *artha*).
7. *sarvajñeyajñānasya*, B; *ye-śes śes-bya thams-cad-kyi ye-śes* (*sarvajñānajñeyajñānasya*), T; C as in text.
8. *nivṛjya*, A; *spaṅs-nas*, T. Cf. *nibbajjayam* at *Theragāthā*, 1105.

यत एवमनादि(32*b*)सांनिध्यस्वभावशुभधर्मोपहिते धातौ तथागतानामविनिर्भागगुणधर्मत्वमतो न तथागतत्व[1]मसङ्ख्याप्रतिहतप्रज्ञा[2]ज्ञानदर्शनमनागम्य सर्वावरणविमुक्ति[3]लक्षणस्य निर्वाणधातोर[4]धिगमः साक्षात्करणमुपपद्यते प्रभारश्म्यदर्शिन इव सूर्यमण्डलदर्शनम् । अत एवमाह[5] । न हि भगवन् हीनप्रणीतधर्माणां निर्वाणाधिगमः । समधर्माणां[6] भगवन् निर्वाणाधिगमः । समज्ञानानां समविमुक्तीनां समविमु[7]क्तिज्ञानदर्शनानां भगवन् निर्वाणाधिगमः । तस्माद्भगवन् निर्वाणधातुरेकरसः समरस इत्युच्यते । यदुत विद्याविमुक्तिरसेनेति ।

जिनगर्भव्यवस्थानमित्येवं दशधोदितम्[8] ।
तत्क्लेशकोशगर्भत्वं पुनर्ज्ञेयं निदर्शनैः ॥ ९५ ॥

इत्येतदपरान्तकोटिसमध्रुवधर्मता[9]संविद्यमानतामधिकृत्य दशविधेनार्थेन तथागत[10]गर्भव्यवस्थानमुक्तम् । पुनरनादिसांनिध्यासंबद्ध[11]स्वभावक्लेशकोशतामनादिसांनिध्यसंबद्ध[12]स्वभावशुभधर्मतां[13] चाधिकृत्य नवभिरुदाहरणैरपर्यन्तक्लेशकोशकोटिगूढस्तथागत[14]गर्भ इति यथासूत्रमनुगन्तव्यम् । नवोदाहरणानि कतमानि ।

बुद्धः कुपद्मे मधु मक्षिकासु[15]
तुषेसु साराण्य[16]शुचौ सुवर्णम् ।

1. B om. *tva.*
2. T om. *prajñā.*
3. °*vinirmukti*°, B.
4. T om. *dhātor.*
5. From the *Āryaśrīmālāsūtra.*
6. B om. *sama.*
7. B om. *mu.*
8. *daśavidho*°, B.
9. B om. *tā.*
10. A om. *gata.*
11. *sāṁnidhyasambaddha*°, B; T as in text; C not clear.
12. A om. *saṁbaddha.*
13. *śubhakarmatām*, B.
14. A om. *gata.*
15. B om. *su.*
16. *sārany*, B.

निधिः क्षितावल्पफलेऽङ्कुरादि
प्रक्लिन्नवस्त्रेषु जिनात्मभावः ॥ ९६ ॥

जघन्यनारीजठरे नृपत्वं
यथा भवेन्मृत्सु च रत्नबिम्बम्[1] ।
आगन्तुकक्लेशमलावृतेषु
सत्त्वेषु तद्वत् स्थित एष धातुः ॥ ९७ ॥

पद्मप्राणितुषाशु(33*a*)चिक्षितिफलत्वक्पूतिवस्त्रावर–
स्त्रीदुःख[2]ज्वलनाभितप्तपृथिवीधातुप्रकाशा मलाः ।
बुद्धक्षौद्रसुसारकाञ्चननिधिन्यग्रोधरत्नाकृति–
द्वीपाग्राधिपरत्नबिम्बविमलप्रख्यः[3] स धातुः परः ॥ ९८ ॥

कुत्सितपद्मकोशसदृशाः क्लेशाः । बुद्धवत्तथागतधातुरिति ।

यथा विवर्णाम्बुज[4]गर्भवेष्टितं
तथागतं दीप्तसहस्रलक्षणम् ।
नरः समीक्ष्यामलदिव्यलोचनो
विमोचयेदम्बुजपत्त्रकोशतः ॥ ९९ ॥

विलोक्य तद्वत् सुगतः स्वधर्मता–
मवीचिसंस्थेष्वपि बुद्धचक्षुषा ।
विमोचयत्यावरणादनावृतो
ऽपरान्तकोटिस्थितकः कृपात्मकः ॥ १०० ॥

यद्वत् स्याद्विजुगुप्सितं जलरुहं संमिञ्जि(XVI*a*)तं दिव्यदृक्
तद्गर्भस्थितमभ्युदीक्ष्य सुगतं पत्त्राणि संछेदयेत् ।

1. *suvarṇabimbaṁ*, B.
2. *strīrupa*°, A; *stridusva*° (for °*kha* ?), B; *sdug-bsṅal..bud-med*, T.
3. B om. *ratna* and *vi*.
4. *suvārṇāmbuja*°, B; *mdog-ṅan padma*, T.

रागद्वेष[1]मलादिकोशनिवृतं संबुद्धगर्भं जगत्
कारुण्यादवलोक्य तन्निवरणं निर्हन्ति[2] तद्वन्मुनिः ॥ १०१ ॥

क्षुद्रप्राणकसदृशाः क्लेशाः । क्षौद्रवत्तथागतधातुरिति ।

यथा मधु प्राणिगणोपगूढं
विलोक्य विद्वान् पुरुषस्तदर्थी ।
समन्ततः प्राणिगणस्य तस्मा-
दुपायतोऽपक्रमणं प्रकुर्यात् ॥ १०२ ॥
सर्वज्ञचक्षुर्विदितं महर्षि-
र्मधूपमं धातुमिमं विलोक्य ।
तदावृतीनां भ्रमरोपमाना-
मश्लेषमात्यन्तिकमादधाति ॥ १०३ ॥

यद्वत् प्राणिसहस्रकोटिनियुतैर्मध्वावृतं स्यान्नरो
मध्वर्थी विनिहत्य तान्मधुकरान्मध्वा यथाकामतः ।
कुर्यात्कार्यम[3]नास्रवं मधुनिभं ज्ञानं तथा देहिषु
क्लेशाः क्षुद्रनिभा[4] जिनः पुरुषवत् तद्घातने कोविदः ॥१०४॥

बहिस्तुषसदृशाः क्लेशाः[5] । अन्तःसारवत्तथा (33*b*) गतधातुरिति ।

धान्येषु सारं तुषसंप्रयुक्तं
नृणां न य[द्व]त्परिभोगमेति ।
भवन्ति येऽन्नादिभिरर्थिनस्तु
ते तत्तुषेभ्यः[6] परिमोचयन्ति ॥ १०५ ॥

1. '*rāgakleśa*', C; the better reading perhaps.
2. *nirharanti*, B, against the metre.
3. *kuryāt tatvam*, A and B (reading doubtful in both); *bya byed-pa*, T.
4. *kṣudranibhāḥ*, B.
5. B om. *kleśāḥ*.
6. *[illegible]*, B.

सत्त्वेष्वपि क्लेशमलोपसृष्ट–
मेवं न तावत्कुरुते जिनत्वम् ।
संबुद्धकार्यं त्रिभवे न याव–
द्विमुच्यते क्लेशमलोपसर्गात् ॥ १०६ ॥

यद्वत् कङ्गुकशालिकोद्रवयवव्रीहिष्वमुक्तं तुषात्
सारं खाड्य[1]सुसंस्कृतं न भवति स्वादूपभोज्यं नृणाम् ॥
तद्वत् क्लेशतुषादनिःसृतवपुः सत्त्वेषु धर्मेश्वरो
धर्मप्रीतिरसप्रदो न भवति क्लेशक्षुधार्ते जने ॥ १०७ ।

अशुचिसंकार[2]धानसदृशाः क्लेशाः । सुवर्णवत्तथागतधातुरिति ।

यथा सुवर्णं व्रजतो नरस्य
च्युतं भवेत्संकरपूतिधाने ।
बहूनि तद्वर्षशतानि तस्मिन्
तथैव तिष्ठेदविनाशधर्मि ॥ १०८ ॥

तद्देवता दिव्यविशुद्धचक्षु–
र्विलोक्य तत्र प्रवदेन्नरस्य ।
सुवर्णमस्मिन्नवमग्ररत्नं
विशोध्य रत्नेन कुरुष्व कार्यम् ॥ १०९ ॥

दृष्ट्वा मुनिः सत्त्वगुणं तथैव
क्लेशेष्वमेध्यप्रतिमेषु मग्नम् ।

1. So B; *khyāḍyam asaṁskṛtam*, A; *gra-ma-can legs-par ma-grub(=śūky asusaṁskṛtam)*, T. *Khāḍin* is not recorded, but must mean 'husked' and is presumably related to *khaḍa*, known to the dictionaries in the sense of *laghutṛṇa*, and to Hindi *khaḍ* or *khar*, 'paddy straw', 'thatching grass'.

2. Note that the MSS. have *saṁkāra* here, as in Pali, but *saṁkara* in the verses.

तत्क्लेश[1]पङ्कव्यवदानहेतो-
धर्माम्बुवर्षं व्यसृजत् प्रजासु ॥ ११० ॥

यद्वत् संकर[2]पूतिधानपतितं चामीकरं देवता
दृष्ट्वा दृश्यतमं नृणामुपदिशेत् संशोधनार्थं मलात् ।
तद्वत् क्लेशमहाशुचिप्रपतितं संबुद्धरत्नं जिनः
सत्त्वेषु व्यवलोक्य धर्ममदिश[त्त]च्छुद्धये देहिनाम् ॥१११॥

पृथिवीतलसदृशाः क्लेशाः । रत्ननिधान[3]वत्तथागतधातुरिति ।

यथा दरिद्रस्य नरस्य वेश्म-
न्यन्तः पृथिव्यां निधिरक्षयः स्यात् ।
विद्यान्न चैनं स नरो न चास्मि-
न्नेषोऽहमस्मीति वदेन्निधिस्तम् ॥ ११२ ॥
तद्वन्मनोऽन्तर्गतमप्य[4] (34*a*) चिन्त्य-
मक्षय्यधर्मामलरत्नकोशम् ।
अबुध्यमानानुभवत्यजस्रं
दारिद्र्यदुःखं बहुधा प्रजेयम् ॥ ११३ ॥

यद्वद्रत्ननिधिर्दरिद्रभवनाभ्यन्तर्गतः स्यान्नरं
न ब्रूयादहमस्मि रत्ननिधिरित्येवं न विद्यान्नरः ।
तद्वद्धर्मनिधिर्मनोगृहगतः सत्त्वा दरिद्रोपमा-
स्तेषां तत्प्रतिलम्भकारणमृषिर्लोके समुत्पद्यते ॥ ११४ ॥

त्वक्कोशसदृशाः क्लेशाः । बीजाङ्कुरवत्तथागतधातुरिति ।

यथाम्रतालादिफले द्रुमाणां
बीजाङ्कुरः[5] सन्नविनाशधर्मी ।

1. *takleśa*°, B.
2. B om. *ra*.
3. B om. *na*.
4. B om. *apy*.
5. *bīje ṅkuraḥ*, B.

उप्तः[1] पृथिव्यां सलिलादियोगात्
क्रमादुपैति द्रुमराजभावम् ॥ ११५ ॥
सत्त्वेष्वविद्या (XVIb) दिफलत्वगन्तः–
कोशावनद्धः शुभधर्मधातुः ।
उपैति तत्तत्कुशलं प्रतीत्य
क्रमेण तद्वन्मुनिराजभावम् ॥ ११६ ॥

अम्ब्वादित्यगभस्तिवायुपृथिवीकालाम्बरप्रत्ययै–
र्यद्वत् तालफलाम्रकोशविवरादुत्पद्यते पादपः ।
सत्त्वक्लेशफलत्वगन्तरगतः संबुद्धबीजाङ्कुर–
स्तद्वद्वृद्धिमुपैति धर्मविटपस्तैस्तैः शुभप्रत्ययैः ॥ ११७ ॥

पूतिवस्त्रसदृशाः[2] क्लेशाः । रत्नविग्रहवत्तथागतधातुरिति ।

बिम्बं यथा रत्नम[3]यं जिनस्य
दुर्गन्धपूत्यम्बरसंनिरुद्धम् ।
दृष्ट्वोज्झितं वर्त्मनि देवतास्य
मुक्त्यै वदेदध्वगमेतमर्थम् ॥ ११८ ॥
नानाविधक्लेशमलोपगूढ–
मसङ्गचक्षुः सुगतात्मभावम् ।
विलोक्य तिर्यक्ष्वपि तद्विमुक्तिं
प्रत्यभ्युपायं विदधाति तद्वत् ॥ ११९ ॥

यद्वद्रत्नमयं तथागतवपुर्दुर्गन्धवस्त्रावृतं
वर्त्मन्युज्झितमेक्ष्य[4] दिव्यनयनो मुक्त्यै नृणां दर्शयेत् ।

1. e.c.; *uptaṁ*, A and B.
2. B om. *viṣaya*.
3. B om. *ma*.
4. *īkṣya*, B.

तद्वत् क्लेशविपूतिवस्त्रनिवृतं संसारवर्त्मोज्झितं
ति (34*b*) र्यक्षु व्यवलोक्य धातुमवदद्धर्मं विमुक्त्यै जिनः ॥१२०॥

आपन्नसत्त्वनारी[1]सदृशाः क्लेशाः । कललमहाभूतगतचक्रवर्तिवत्तथागत-धातुरिति ।

नारी यथा काचिदनाथभूता
वसेदनाथावसथे विरूपा ।
गर्भेण राजश्रियमुद्वहन्ती[2]
न सावबुध्येत नृपं स्वकुक्षौ ॥ १२१ ॥
अनाथशालेव भवोपपत्ति-
रन्तर्वतीस्त्रीवदशुद्धसत्त्वाः ।
तद्गर्भवत्तेष्वमलः स धातु-
र्भवन्ति यस्मिन्सति ते सनाथाः ॥ १२२ ॥

यद्वत् स्त्री मलिनाम्बरावृततनुर्बीभत्सरूपान्विता
विन्देद्दुःख[3]मनाथवेश्मनि परं गर्भान्तरस्थे नृपे ।
तद्वत् क्लेशवशादशान्तमनसो दुःखालयस्था जनाः
सन्नाथेषु च सत्स्वनाथमतयः स्वात्मा[4]न्तरस्थेष्वपि ॥ १२३ ॥

मृत्पङ्कलेपसदृशाः क्लेशाः । कनकबिम्बवत्त[5]थागतधातुरिति ।

हेम्नो यथान्तःक्वथितस्य पूर्णं
बिम्बं बहिर्मृन्मयमेक्ष्य[6] शान्तम् ।

1. B om. *nārī*.
2. Cf. *Buddhac.*, i, 5, in my translation.
3. *dukham*, B.
4. B om. *tmā*.
5. B om. *vat*.
6. *ikṣya*, B.

अन्तर्विशुद्ध्यै कनकस्य तज्ज्ञः
संचोदयेदावरणं बहिर्धा ॥ १२४ ॥
प्रभास्वरत्वं प्रकृतेर्मलाना-
मागन्तुकत्वं च सदावलोक्य ।
रत्नाकराभं जगदग्रबोधि[1]-
र्विशोधयत्यावरणेभ्य एवम् ॥ १२५ ॥

यद्वन्निर्मलदीप्तकाञ्चनमयं बिम्बं मृदन्तर्गतं
स्याच्छान्तं[2] तदवेत्य रत्नकुशलः संचोदयेन्मृत्तिकाम् ।
तद्वच्छान्तमवेत्य शुद्धकनकप्रख्यं[3] मनः सर्ववि-
द्धर्माख्याननयप्रहार[4]विधितः संचोदयत्यावृतिम् ॥ १२६ ॥

उदाहरणानां पिण्डार्थः ।

अम्बुजभ्रमरप्राणितुषोच्चारक्षितिष्वथ ।
फलत्वक्पूतिवस्त्रस्त्रीगर्भमृत्कोशकेष्व[5]पि ॥ १२७ ॥
बुद्धवन्मधुवत्सारसुवर्णनिधि[6]वृक्षवत् ।
रत्नविग्रहवच्चक्रवर्तिवद्धेमबिम्ब (35*a*) वत् ॥ १२८ ॥
सत्त्वधातोरसंबद्धं क्लेशकोशेष्वनादिषु ।
चित्तप्रकृतिवैमल्यमनादिमदुदाहृतम् ॥ १२९ ॥

समासतोऽनेन तथागतगर्भसूत्रोदाहरणनिर्देशेन कृत्स्नस्य सत्त्वधातोरनादिचित्तसंक्लेशधर्मागन्तुकत्वमनादिचित्तव्यवदानधर्म[7]सहजाविनिर्भागता च

1. *agrabuddhir*, A; but *byaṅ-chub mchog*, T, which supports B; C is ambiguous.
2. *śāntam*, 'cooled down'.
3. °*śuddhakañcanaka*°, B.
4. °*prāhāra*°, B. Cf. *Buddhac.*, i, 74; the phrase here shows that *tāḍa* in that passage means 'blow'.
5. *pūtigarbhastrīgarbhamṛtkopakeṣv*, B.
6. B om. *dhi*.
7. B om. *dharma*.

परिदीपिता । तत उच्यते । चित्तसंक्लेशात् सत्त्वाः संक्लिश्यन्ते[1] चित्तव्यवदानाद्विशुध्यन्त इति । तत्र कतमश्चित्तसंक्लेशो यमधिकृत्य नवधा पद्मकोशादिदृष्टान्तदेशना ।

रागद्विड्मोहतत्तीव्रपर्यवस्थान(xvii*a*)वासनाः ।
दृङ्मार्गभावनाशुद्धशुद्धभूमिगता मलाः ॥ १३० ॥
पद्मकोशादिदृष्टान्तैर्नवधा संप्रकाशिताः ।
अपर्यन्तोप[2]संक्लेशकोशकोट्यस्तु भेदतः ॥ १३१ ॥

समासत इमे नव क्लेशाः प्रकृतिपरिशुद्धेऽपि तथागतधातौ पद्मकोशादय इव बुद्धबिम्बादिषु सदागन्तुकतया संविद्यन्ते । कतमे नव । तद्यथा रागानुशयलक्षणः क्लेशः । द्वेषानुशयलक्षणः । मोहानुशयलक्षणः । तीव्ररागद्वेषमोहपर्यवस्थानलक्षणः । अविद्यावासभूमिसंगृहीतः । दर्शनप्रहातव्यः । भावनाप्रहातव्यः[3] । अशुद्धभूमिगतः । शुद्धभूमिगतश्च । तत्र ये लौकिकवीतरागसान्तानिकाः क्लेशा आनिञ्ज्य[4]संस्कारोपचयहेतवो रूपारूप्य[5]धातुनिर्वर्तका लोकोत्तरज्ञानवध्यास्त उच्यन्ते रागद्वेषमोहानुशयलक्षणा इति । ये रागादिचरितसत्त्वसान्तानिकाः पुण्यापुण्यसंस्कारोपचयहेतवः केवलकामधातुनिर्वर्तका अशुभादिभावज्ञानवध्यास्त उच्यन्ते तीव्रराग[6]द्वे(35*b*)षमोहपर्यवस्थानलक्षणा इति । येऽर्हत्सान्तानिका अनास्रवकर्मप्रवृत्तिहेतवो विमलमनोमयात्मभावनिर्वर्तकास्तथागतबोधिज्ञानवध्यास्त उच्यन्तेऽविद्यावासभूमिसंगृहीता इति । द्विविधः शैक्षः पृथग्जन आर्यश्च । तत्र ये पृथग्जनशैक्षसांतानिकाः प्रथमलोकोत्तरधर्मदर्श[7]नज्ञानवध्यास्त उच्यन्ते दर्शनप्रहातव्या

1. °*saṁkletsatvās saṁkliṣyante*, B. Neither C nor O identify the quotation, but the former may imply that it comes from the *Tathāgatagarbhasūtra*, for which see *Śikṣāsamuccaya* (ed. Bendall), pp. 368 and 407, note on 171, 13.

2. *aparyantopisaṁ*°, B.

3. B om. *bhāvanāprahātavyaḥ*.

4. °*rāgaśāṁtānikāyāḥ/āniñjya*°, B.

5. *rūpyārūpya*, B.

6. B om. *ga*.

7. *sa daṅ-po ḥjig-rten-las ḥdas-paḥi* (*prathamabhūmilokottara*°), T. B om. *dharma*.

इति । य आर्यपुद्गलशैक्षसान्तानिका यथादृष्टलोकोत्तरधर्मभावनाज्ञानवध्यास्त उच्यन्ते भावनाप्रहातव्या इति । येऽनिष्ठागतबोधिसत्त्वसान्तानिकाः सप्तविधज्ञानभूमिविपक्षा अष्टम्यादिभूमित्रयभावनाज्ञानवध्यास्त उच्यन्तेऽशुद्धभूमिगता इति । ये निष्ठागतबोधिसत्त्वसान्तानिका अष्टम्यादिभूमित्रयभावनाज्ञानविपक्षा वज्रोपमसमाधिज्ञानवध्यास्त उच्यन्ते शुद्धभूमिगता इति । एते[1]

नव रागादयः क्लेशाः संक्षेपेण यथाक्रमम् ।
नवभिः पद्मकोशादिदृष्टान्तैः संप्रकाशिताः ॥ १३२ ॥

विस्तरेण पुनरेत एव चतुरशीतिसहस्रप्रकारभेदेन[2] तथागतज्ञानवदपर्यन्ता भवन्ति यैरपर्यन्तक्लेशकोशकोटिगूढस्तथागतगर्भ उच्यते ।

बालानामर्हतामेभिः शैक्षाणां धीमतां क्रमात् ।
मलैश्चतुर्भिरेकेन द्वाभ्यां द्वाभ्यामशुद्धता ॥ १३३ ॥

यदुक्तं भगवता[3] । सर्वसत्त्वास्तथागतगर्भ इति । तत्र सर्वसत्त्वाः संक्षेपेणोच्यन्ते चतुर्विधास्तद्यथा पृथग्जना अर्हन्तः शैक्षा बोधिसत्त्वाश्चेति । तत्रैषामनास्रवे धातौ यथाक्रमं चतुर्भिरेकेन द्वाभ्यां द्वाभ्यां च क्लेशमलाभ्यामशुद्धिः (36*a*)परिदीपिता[4] ।

कथं पुनरिमे नव रागादयः क्लेशाः पद्मकोशादिसदृशा वेदितव्याः । कथं च तथागतधातोर्बुद्धबिम्बादिसाधर्म्यमनुगन्तव्यमिति ।

तत्पद्मं मृदि संभूतं पुरा भूत्वा मनोरमम् ।
अरम्यमभवत् पश्चाद्यथा रागरतिस्तथा ॥ १३४ ॥
भ्रमराः प्राणिनो यद्वद्दशन्ति कुपिता भृशम् ।
दुःखं ज (XVII*b*) नयति द्वेषो जायमानस्तथा हृदि ॥ १३५ ॥

1. It is doubtful if this verse is a *kārikā* at all; C treats it as prose, and *cd* is practically identical with 131*cd*. I have excluded *ete* from the verse for metrical reasons, T showing both *ete* and *nava*.
2. *rab-tu dbye-bas* (*prabhedena*), T.
3. C omits this quotation.
4. B om. *dī*.

शाल्यादीनां यथा सारमवच्छन्नं बहिस्तुषैः ।
मोहाण्डकोशसंछन्न[1]मेवं सारार्थदर्शनम् ॥ १३६ ॥
प्रतिकूलं यथामेध्यमेवं कामा विरागिणाम्[2] ।
कामसेवानिमित्तत्वात् पर्युत्थानान्यमेध्यवत् ॥ १३७ ॥
वसुधान्तरितं यद्वदज्ञानान्नाप्नुयुर्निधिम् ।
स्वयंभूत्वं तथाविद्यावासभूम्यावृता जनाः ॥ १३८ ॥
यथा बीजत्वगुच्छित्तिरङ्कुरादिक्रमोदयात् ।
तथा दर्शनहेयानां व्यावृत्तिस्तत्त्वदर्शनात् ॥ १३९ ॥
हतसत्कायसाराणामार्यमार्गानुषङ्गतः ।
भावनाज्ञानहेयानां पूतिवस्त्रनिदर्शनम् ॥ १४० ॥
गर्भकोशमलप्रख्याः सप्तभूमिगता मला ।
विकोशगर्भवज्ज्ञानमविकल्पं विपाकवत् ॥ १४१ ॥
मृत्पङ्कलेपवज्ज्ञेयास्त्रिभूम्यनुगता मलाः ।
वज्रोपमसमाधानज्ञानवध्या महात्मनाम् ॥ १४२ ॥
एवं पद्मादिभिस्तुल्या नव रागादयो मलाः ।
धातोर्बुद्धादिसाधर्म्यं स्वभावत्रयसंग्रहात् ॥ १४३ ॥

त्रिविधं स्वभावमधिकृत्य चित्तव्यवदानहेतोस्तथागतगर्भस्य नवधा बुद्धबिम्बादिसाधर्म्यमनुगन्तव्यम् । त्रिविधः स्वभावः कतमः ।

स्वभावो धर्मकायोऽस्य तथता गोत्रमित्यपि ।
(36*b*) त्रिभिरेकेन स ज्ञेयः[3] पञ्चभिश्च निदर्शनैः ॥ १४४ ॥

त्रिभिर्बुद्धबिम्बमधुसारदृष्टान्तैर्धर्मकायस्वभावः स धातुरवगन्तव्यः । एकेन सुवर्णदृष्टान्तेन तथतास्वभावः । पञ्चभिर्निधितरुरत्नविग्रहचक्र-

1. °*saśchannam*, B.
2. T takes *kāmāvirāgiṇām* as one word; C is not clear, but may have divided as in the text.
3. B om. the visarga.

वर्तिकनकबिम्बदृष्टान्तैस्त्रिविधबुद्ध[1]कायोत्पत्तिगोत्रस्वभाव इति । तत्र धर्मकायः कतमः

धर्मकायो द्विधा[2] ज्ञेयो धर्मधातुः सुनिर्मलः ।
तन्निष्यन्दश्च गाम्भीर्यवैचित्र्यनयदेशना ॥ १४५ ॥

द्विविधो बुद्धानां धर्मकायो[3]ऽनुगन्तव्यः । सुविशुद्धश्च धर्मधातोरविकल्पज्ञानगोचरविषयः । स च तथागतानां प्रत्यात्ममधिगमधर्ममधिकृत्य वेदितव्यः । तत्प्राप्तिहेतुश्च सुविशुद्धधर्मधातुनिष्यन्दो यथावैनयिक[4]परसत्त्वेषु विज्ञप्तिप्रभवः । स च देशनाधर्ममधिकृत्य वेदितव्यः । देशना पुनर्द्विविधा सूक्ष्मौदारिकधर्मव्यवस्थाननयभेदात् । यदुत गम्भीरबोधिसत्त्वपिटकधर्मव्यवस्थान[5]नयदेशना च परमार्थसत्यमधिकृत्य विचित्रसूत्रगेयव्याकरणगाथोदाननिदानादिविविध[6]धर्मव्यवस्थाननयदेशना च संवृतिसत्यमधिकृत्य ।

लोकोत्तरत्वाल्लोकेऽस्य दृष्टान्तानुपलब्धितः ।
धातोस्तथागतेनैव सादृश्यमुपपादितम् ॥ १४६ ॥
मध्वेक[7]रसवत् सूक्ष्मगम्भीरनयदेशना ।
नानाण्डसारवज्ज्ञेया विचित्रनयदेशना ॥ १४७ ॥

इत्येवमेभिस्त्रि[8]भिर्बुद्धबिम्बमधुसारदृष्टान्तैस्तथागतधर्मकायेन निरवशेषसत्त्व[9]धातुपरिस्फरणार्थमधिकृत्य तथागतस्येमे गर्भाः सर्वसत्त्वा इ(37*a*)ति परिदीपितम् । न हि स कश्चित्सत्त्वः सत्त्वधातौ संविद्यते यस्तथागतधर्मकायाद्बहिराकाशधातोरिव रूपम् । एवं ह्याह ।

1. B repeats *buddha*.
2. *dvividho*, B.
3. *dhamakāyo*, B.
4. *yathāvainainayika°*, A.
5. T om. *vyavasthāna*.
6. B om. one *dha*.
7. B om. *ka*.
8. *tṛbhir*, B.
9. *niraśeṣadharmadhātu°*, B; A, T and C as in text.

यथाम्बरं सर्वगतं सदा मतं
तथैव तत्सर्वगतं सदा मतम् ।
यथाम्बरं रूपगतेषु सर्वगं
तथैव त[1]त्सत्त्वगणेषु सर्वगमिति ॥

प्रकृतेरविकारित्वात् कल्याणत्वाद्विशुद्धितः ।
हेममण्डलकौपम्यं तथतायामुदाहृतम् ॥ १४८ ॥

यच्चित्तमपर्यन्तक्लेशदुःखधर्मा[2]नुगतमपि प्रकृतिप्रभास्वरतया विकारानुदाहृतेरतः[3] कल्याणसुवर्णवदन[4]न्यथाभावार्थेन तथतेत्युच्यते । स च सर्वेषामपि मिथ्यात्वनियतसंतानानां सत्त्वानां प्रकृतिनिर्विशिष्टानां सर्वागन्तुकमलविशुद्धिमागतस्तथागत[5] इति संख्यां गच्छति । एवमेकेन सुवर्णदृष्टान्तेन तथताव्यतिभेदार्थमधिकृत्य तथागतस्तथतैषां गर्भः सर्वसत्त्वानामिति परिदीपितम् । चित्तप्रकृतिविशुद्ध्यद्वयधर्मतामुपादाय यथोक्तं भगवता । तत्र मञ्जुश्रीस्तथागत आत्मोपादानमूलपरिज्ञातावी[6] । आत्मविशुद्ध्या सर्वसत्त्वविशुद्धिमनुगतः । या चात्मविशुद्धिर्या च सत्त्वविशुद्धिरद्वयैषाद्वैधीकारो ति[7] । एवं ह्याह ।

सर्वेषामविशिष्टापि तथता शुद्धिमागता ।
तथागतत्वं तस्माच्च तद्गर्भाः सर्वदेहिन इति[8] ॥

गोत्रं तद्द्विविधं[9] ज्ञेयं निधानफलवृक्षवत् ।
अनादिप्रकृतिस्थं च समुदानीतमुत्तरम् ॥ १४९ ॥

1. *tathaiva tsarva*, B. This verse recurs at *Mahāyānasūtrālaṁkāra*, ix, 15, which reads *rūpagaṇeṣu* in *c*.
2. T om. *dharma*, and C the whole sentence. A's f.xvii ends with *yac citta*.
3. *vikāranudāhṛteḥ*, B; *rnam-par ḥgyur-ba-la mi-ston-pa*, T.
4. B om. *an*.
5. B repeats *Tathāgata*.
6. T oddly takes the ending *-āvī* of *parijñātāvī* to the root *av* in the meaning 'protect'. C does not give the name of the sūtra (*Jñānālokālaṁkārasūtra*, O).
7. So B, which may reproduce a faulty saṁdhi of the original; but *kāreti* is perhaps preferable.
8. This verse recurs at *Mahāyānasūtrālaṁkāra*, ix, 37.
9. *ta dvividhaṁ*, B; *rigs de rnam-gñis*, T.

बुद्धकायत्रयावाप्तिरस्मादगोत्रद्वयान्मता[1] ।
प्रथमा[2]त्प्रथमः कायो द्विती (37b) याद्द्वौ तु पश्चिमौ ॥१५०॥
रत्नविग्रहवज्ज्ञेयः कायः स्वाभाविकः शुभः ।
अकृत्रिमत्वात् प्रकृतेर्गुणरत्नाश्रयत्वतः ॥ १५१ ॥
महाधर्माधिराजत्वात् साम्भोगश्चक्रवर्तिवत् ।
प्रतिबिम्बस्वभावत्वान्निर्माणं[3] हेमबिम्बवत् ॥ १५२ ॥

इत्येवमेभिरवशिष्टैः पञ्चभिर्नि[4]धितरुरत्नविग्रहचक्रवर्तिकनकबिम्बदृष्टान्तैस्त्रि[5]विधबुद्धकायोत्पत्तिगोत्रस्वभावार्थमधिकृत्य तथागतधातुरेषां गर्भः सर्वसत्त्वानामिति परिदीपितम् । त्रिविधबुद्धकायप्रभावितत्वं हि तथागतत्वम् । अतस्तत्प्राप्तये हेतुस्तथागतधातुरिति । हेत्वर्थोऽत्र धात्वर्थः । यत आह[6] । तत्र च सत्त्वे सत्त्वे तथागतधातुरुत्पन्नो गर्भगतः संविद्यते न च ते सत्त्वा बुध्यन्त इति । एवं ह्याह ।

अनादिकालिको धातुः सर्वधर्मसमाश्रयः ।
तस्मिन् सति गतिः सर्वा निर्वाणाधिगमोऽपि च[7] ॥

तत्र कथमनादिकालिकः । यत्तथागतगर्भमेवाधिकृत्य भगवता[8] पूर्वकोटिर्न प्रज्ञायत इति देशितं प्रज्ञप्तम् । धातुरिति । यदाह[9] । योऽयं भगवं-

1. e.c.; last two syllables uncertain. B seems to have °*dvayāt satā* (or *punā* ?), while T only shows *yan*, perhaps for °*dvayād api*.
2. B om. *mā*.
3. *nimāṇa*, B.
4. *ity evam aviśiṣṭai pañcabhi*, B; *de-ltar. .lhag-ma lṅa-bo ḥdi-dag-gis*, T; C as in text.
5. *dṛṣṭāntai tri* B.
6. C omits this quotation, and O has not identified it.
7. For this verse from the *Abhidharmamahāyānasūtra* see Lamotte, *Mélanges chinois et bouddhiques*, III, 171 and *La Somme du Grand Véhicule d'Asaṅga(Mahāyānasaṃgraha)*, II, p. 12. Note the difference of intepretation at the latter passage, where the verse is applied to the *ālayavijñāna*.
8. T om. *Bhagavatā*, but C has it.
9. This and the next three quotations are from the *Ārya-śrīmālāsūtra*.

स्तथागतगर्भो लोकोत्तरगर्भः प्रकृतिपरिशुद्धगर्भ इति । सर्वधर्मसमाश्रय इति[1] । यदाह । तस्माद्भगवंस्तथागतगर्भो निश्रय आधारः प्रतिष्ठा संबद्धानामविनिर्भागानाममुक्तज्ञानानामसंस्कृतानां धर्मणाम् । असंबद्धानामपि भगवन् विनिर्भागधर्माणां[2] मुक्तज्ञानानां संस्कृतानां धर्माणां निश्रय आधारः प्रतिष्ठा तथागतगर्भ इति । (38*a*)तस्मिन् सति गतिः सर्वेति । यदाह । सति भगवंस्तथागतगर्भे संसार इति परिकल्पमस्य वचनायेति । निर्वाणाधिगमोऽपि चेति । यदाह । तथागत[3]गर्भश्चेद् भगवन्न स्यान्न स्याद्दुःखेऽपि निर्विन्न[4] निर्वाणेच्छा प्रार्थना प्रणिधिर्वेति विस्तरः ।

स खल्वेष तथागतगर्भो धर्मकायाविप्रलम्भ[5]स्तथतासंभिन्नलक्षणो नियतगोत्रस्वभावः सर्वदा च सर्वत्र च निरवशेषयोगेन सत्त्वधाताविति द्रष्टव्यं[6] धर्मतां प्रमाणीकृत्य । यथोक्तम् । एषा[7] कुलपुत्र धर्माणां धर्मता । उत्पादाद्वा तथागतानामनुत्पादाद्वा सदैवैते सत्त्वास्तथागतगर्भा इति । यैव चासौ धर्मता सैवात्र युक्तिर्योग उपायः पर्यायः । एवमेव तत्स्यात्[8] । अन्यथा नैव[9] तत्स्यादिति । सर्वत्र धर्मतैव प्रतिशरणम् । धर्मतैव युक्तिश्चित्तनिध्यापनाय चित्तसंज्ञापनाय । सा न चिन्तयितव्या न विकल्पयितव्याधिमोक्तव्येति[10] ।

1. B repeats *sarvadharmasamāśraya iti.*
2. *rnam-par dbye-ba dan bcas-paḥi chos* (*savinirbhāga*..), T.
3. *Tathāgarbhaś*, B.
4. B om. *nna*. Cf. i, 40, above.
5. e.c.; *dharmakāyavipralambhas ta tathatā*°, B; *chos-kyi sku-ltar rgya-che-ba de-bzhin-gśegs-pa*, (*dharmakāyavipulas* (?) *Tathāgata*°), T; C has the equivalent of *abhinna* (for *avipralambha*) and of *tathatā*, which corresponds to the text, or perhaps preferably to *dharmakāyāvipralabdhas*...
6. e.c.; °*yogena saṁrvadyatanatija draṣṭavyaṁ*, B; T, which is partly illegible, seems to omit *sattvadhātau*; C shows something like *sattvakāya*.
7. *aśeṣa*, B; *ḥdi*, T.
8. Reading uncertain. *paryāyā eva vai tat syāt*, B. Several syllables are illegible in T, which seems to omit *upāyaḥ paryāyaḥ* and reads *evam eva* (*de-lta-bu kho-nar*). C shows *upāyaḥ*, but omits *paryāyaḥ*.
9. *naivai*, B.
10. T is difficult to read again here, but suggests that something is missing in B to separate *adhimoktavyā* from *vikalpayitavyā* (e.g. *adhimoktavyā tv iti*).

श्रद्धयैवानुगन्तव्यं परमार्थे[1] स्वयंभुवाम् ।
न ह्यचक्षुः प्रभादीप्तमीक्षते सूर्यमण्डलम् ॥ १५३ ॥

समासत इमे चत्वारः पुद्गलास्तथागतगर्भदर्शनं प्रत्यचक्षुष्मन्तो व्यवस्थिताः । कतमे चत्वारः । यदुत पृथग्जनः श्रावकः प्रत्येकबुद्धो नवयानसंप्रस्थितश्च बोधिसत्त्वः । यथोक्तम्[2] । अगोचरोऽयं भगवंस्तथागतगर्भः सत्कायदृष्टिपतितानां विपर्यासाभिरतानां शून्यताविक्षिप्तचित्तानामिति । तत्र सत्कायदृष्टिपतिता उच्यन्ते बालपृथग्जनाः । तथा हि तेऽत्यन्तसास्रवस्कन्धादी(38*b*)न्धर्मानात्मत आत्मीयत[3]श्चोपगम्याहंकारममकाराभिनिविष्टाः सत्कायनिरोधमनास्रवधातुमधिमोक्तुमपि नालम् । कुतः पुनः सर्वज्ञविषयं तथागतगर्भमवभोत्स्यन्त इति । नेदं स्थानं विद्यते । तत्र विपर्यासाभिरता उच्यन्ते श्रावकप्रत्येकबुद्धाः । तत्कस्मात् । तेऽपि हि नित्ये तथागतगर्भे सत्युत्तरिभावयितव्ये तन्नित्यसंज्ञाभावनाविपर्ययेणानित्यसंज्ञाभावनाभिरताः । सुखे तथागतगर्भे सत्युत्तरिभावयितव्ये तत्सुखसंज्ञाभावनाविपर्ययेण दुःखसंज्ञाभावनाभिरताः[4] । आत्मनि तथागतगर्भे सत्युत्तरिभावयितव्ये तदात्मसंज्ञाभावनावि[5]पर्ययेणानात्मसंज्ञाभावनाभिरताः । शुभे तथागतगर्भे सत्युत्तरिभावयितव्ये तच्छुभसंज्ञाभावनाविपर्ययेणाशुभसंज्ञाभावना[6]भिरताः । एवमनेन पर्यायेण सर्वश्रावकप्रत्येकबुद्धानामपि धर्मकायप्राप्तिविधुरमार्गाभिरतत्वादगोचरः स परमनित्यसुखात्मशुभलक्षणो धातुरित्युक्तम् । यथा च स विपर्यासाभिरतानामनित्यदुःखानात्माशुभसंज्ञानामगोचरस्तथा विस्तरेण **महापरिनिर्वाणसूत्रे** भगवता वापीतोयमणिदृष्टान्तेन प्रसाधितः ।

तद्यथापि नाम भिक्षवो ग्रीष्मकाले वर्तमाने सलिलबन्धनं बद्ध्वा स्वैः स्वैर्मण्डनकोपभोगैर्जनाः सलिले क्रीडेयुः । अथ तत्रैको जात्यं वैडूर्यमणिमन्तरुदके

1. *parārthe*, B; *don dam*, T.
2. From the *Āryaśrīmālāsūtra*.
3. e.c.; B om. *ātmīyata*; *bdag dan bdág-gi-ba-ñid-du*, T, which possibly represents *ātmato mamatvataś ca*.
4. B misplaces this sentence and inserts marks to correct the error.
5. B om. *vi*.
6. B om. *viparyayeṇāśubhasaṃjñābhāvanā*; T as in text.

स्थापयेत् । ततस्तस्य वैडूर्यस्यार्थे सर्वे ते मण्डनकानि त्य(39a)क्त्वा निमज्जेयुः । अथ यत्तत्रास्ति शर्करं कठल्यं वा तत्ते मणिरिति मन्यमाना गृहीत्वा मया लब्धो मणिरित्युत्सृज्योत्सृज्य वापीतीरे स्थित्वा[1] नायं मणिरिति संज्ञां प्रवर्तेयुः । तच्च वाप्युदकं मणिप्रभावेन तत्प्रभेव भ्राजेत । एवं तेषां[2] तदुदकं भ्राजमानं दृष्ट्वाहो मणिरिति गुणसंज्ञा प्रवर्तेत । अथ तत्रैक उपायकुशलो मेधावी मणिं तत्त्वतः प्रतिलभेत । एवमेव भिक्षवो युष्माभिः सर्वमनित्यं सर्वं दुःखं सर्वमनात्मकं सर्वमशुभ(XIXa)मिति सर्वग्रहणेन[3] भावितभावितं बहुलीकृतबहुलीकृतं धर्मतत्त्वम[4]जानद्भिस्तत्सर्वं घटितं निरर्थकम् । तस्माद्भिक्षवो वापीशर्करकठल्यव्यवस्थि[5]ता इव मा भूता उपायकुशला यूयं भवत । यद्यद्भिक्षवो युष्माभिः सर्वमनित्यं[6] सर्वं दुःखं सर्वमनात्मकं सर्वमशुभमिति सर्वग्रहणेन भावितभावितं बहुलीकृतबहुलीकृतं तत्र तत्रैव नित्यसुखशभात्मकानि सन्तीति विस्तरेण परमधर्मतत्त्वव्यवस्थानमारभ्य विपर्यासभूतनिर्देशो यथासूत्रमनुगन्तव्यः ।

तत्र शून्यताविक्षिप्तचित्ता उच्यन्ते[7] नवयान[8]संप्रस्थिता बोधिसत्त्वास्तथागतगर्भशून्यतार्थनयविप्रनष्टाः[9] । ये भावविनाशाय शून्यताविमोक्षमुखमिच्छन्ति सत एव धर्मस्योत्तरकालमुच्छेदो विनाशः परिनिर्वाणमिति । ये वा पुनः शून्यतोपलम्भेन शून्यतां प्रतिसरन्ति शून्यता नाम रूपादिव्यतिरेकेण कश्चिद्भा(39b)वोऽस्ति यमधिगमिष्यामो भावयिष्याम इति । तत्र कतमः स तथागतगर्भशून्यतार्थनय[10] उच्यते ।

1. Reading doubtful; *phyuṅ-no/phyuṅ-nas rdziṅ-buḥi ḥgram-du bltas-pa-na*, T, which suggests (*ity*) *unmajjeyuḥ/unmajjya vāpītīre paśyanto* (?, or *dṛṣṭvā*).

2. e.c.; *teṣaṁ teṣāṁ*, B, omitting *evam*; *de-dag de-ltar* (*evam* or *tathā*), T.

3. *savagrahaṇena*, B; *sarvasaṁjñāgrahaṇena*, A; T om. *saṁjñā*.

4. *chos-kyi don ni de-kho-na* (*dharmārthatattvam*?), T.

5. °*vyavasthāpitā*, A.

6. B om. *ḥ sarvam anityam*.

7. *utpadyante*, B.

8. B repeats *yāna*.

9. T om. *artha*. °*nayapraṇaṣṭāḥ*, B.

10. T om. *sa* and *artha*.

नापनेयमतः किंचिदुपनेयं न किंचन ।
द्रष्टव्यं भूततो भूतं भूतदर्शी विमुच्यते[1] ॥ १५४ ॥
शून्य आगन्तुकैर्धातुः सविनिर्भागलक्षणैः ।
अशून्योऽनुत्तरैर्धर्मैरविनिर्भागलक्षणैः[2] ॥ १५५ ॥

किमनेन परिदीपितम् । यतो न किंचिद[3]पनेयमस्त्यतः प्रकृतिपरिशुद्धात् तथागतधातोः संक्लेशनिमित्तमागन्तु[4]कमलशून्यताप्रकृतित्वादस्य । नाप्यत्र[5] किंचिदुपनेयमस्ति व्यवदाननिमित्तमविनिर्भाग[6]शुद्धधर्मप्रकृतित्वात् । तत उच्यते[7]। शून्यस्तथागतगर्भो विनिर्भागैर्मुक्तज्ञैः सर्वक्लेशकोशैः । अशून्यो गङ्गानदीवालिकाव्यतिवृत्तैरविनिर्भागैरमुक्तज्ञैरचिन्त्यैर्बुद्धधर्मैरिति । एवं यद्यत्र नास्ति तत्तेन शून्यमिति समनुपश्यति । यत्पुनरत्रावशिष्टं भवति तत्सदिहास्तीति यथाभूतं प्रजानाति । समारोपापवादान्तपरिवर्जनादपर्यन्तं शून्यतालक्षणमनेन श्लोकद्वयेन परिदीपितम् । तत्र येषामितः शून्यतार्थनयाद्बहिश्चित्तं विक्षिप्यते विसरति न समाधीयते नैकाग्रीभवति तेन ते शून्यताविक्षिप्तचित्ता उच्यन्ते । न हि परमार्थशून्यताज्ञानमुखमन्तरेण शक्यते[8]ऽविकल्पो धातुरधिगन्तुं साक्षात्कर्तुम् । इदं च संधायोक्तम्[9] । तथागतगर्भज्ञानमेव तथागतानां शून्यताज्ञानम् । तथागतगर्भश्च सर्वश्रावकप्रत्येकबुद्धैरदृष्टपूर्वोऽनधिगतपूर्व इति विस्तरः । स खल्वेष तथागतगर्भो (40*a*) यथा धर्मधातुगर्भस्तथा सत्कायदृष्टिपतितानामगोचर इत्युक्तं दृष्टिप्रतिपक्षत्वाद्धर्मधातोः । यथा धर्मकायो लोकोत्तरधर्म[10]गर्भस्तथा विपर्यासाभिरतानामगोचर इत्युक्तमनित्यादिलोकधर्मप्रतिपक्षेण लोकोत्तरधर्मपरिदीपनात् । यथा प्रकृतिपरिशुद्धधर्मगर्भस्तथा शून्यताविक्षिप्तानामगोचर इत्युक्तमागन्तुकमलशून्यताप्रकृति-

1. It is uncertain if this famous verse is to be taken as a kārikā. For its occurrence in literature see La Vallée Poussin, *Mélanges chinois et bouddhiques*, I, 394.
2. B om. this line and adds it in margin in the same hand.
3. *kamcid*, B.
4. °*nimittāyā āgantuka*°, B.
5. *nāpy anyatra*, B.
6. T inserts *dharma* (*chos*) between *avinirbhāga* and *śuddha*.
7. C attributes this quotation to the *Āryaśrīmālāsūtra*.
8. *sa śakyo*, B.
9. C attributes this quotation to the *Āryaśrīmālāsūtra*.
10. T om. *dharma*.

त्वाद्विशुद्धिगुणधर्माणामविनिर्भागलोकोत्तरधर्मकायप्रभावि (XIX*b*) तानामिति। तत्र यदेकनयधर्मधात्वसंभेदज्ञानमुख[1]मागम्य लोकोत्तरधर्म[2]कायप्रकृतिपरिशुद्धिव्यवलोकनमिदमत्र यथाभूतज्ञानदर्शनमभिप्रेतं येन दशभूमिस्थिता बोधिसत्त्वास्तथागतगर्भमीषत्पश्यन्तीत्युक्तम्। एवं ह्याह।

छिद्राभ्रे नभसीव[3] भास्कर इह त्वं शुद्धबुद्धीक्षणै-
रार्यैरप्यवलोक्यसे न सकलः प्रादेशिकीबुद्धिभिः।
ज्ञेयानन्तनभस्तलप्रविसृतं ते धर्मकायं तु ते
साकल्येन विलोकयन्ति भगवन्[4] येषामनन्ता मतिरिति॥

यद्येवमसङ्ग[5]निष्ठाभूमिप्रतिष्ठितानामपि परमार्याणामसर्वविषय एष दुर्दृशो धातुः। तत्किमनेन बालपृथग्जनमारभ्य[6] देशितेनेति। देशनाप्रयोजनसंग्रहे श्लोकौ। एकेन प्रश्नो द्वितीयेन व्याकरणम्।

शून्यं सर्वं सर्वथा तत्र तत्र
ज्ञेयं मेघस्वप्नमायाकृताभम्।
इत्युक्त्वैवं बुद्धधातुः[7] पुनः किं
सत्त्वे सत्त्वेऽस्तीति बुद्धैरिहोक्तम्॥ १५६॥
लीनं चित्तं हीनसत्त्वेष्ववज्ञा-
भू (40*b*) तग्राहो भूतधर्मापवादः।
आत्मस्नेहश्चाधिकः पञ्च दोषा[8]
येषां तेषां तत्प्रहाणार्थमुक्तम्॥ १५७॥

अस्य खलु श्लोकद्वयस्यार्थः समासेन दशभिः श्लोकैर्वेदितव्यः।

1. *jñāpanamukham*, A; T om. *jñāna*.
2. B om. *rma*.
3. B om. *bha*; *chidrābhena nabhasīva*, A. C does not give the source of this verse.
4. *Bhagavat*, B.
5. *evam anaṅga°*, B.
6. *byis-pa so-soḥi skye-bo* (*bālapṛthagjanam*), T.
7. *saṅs-rgyas sñin-po* (*buddhagarbhaḥ*), T.
8. *lhag-paḥi skyon lṅa* (*adhikāḥ pañca doṣā*), T.

विविक्तं संस्कृतं सर्वप्रकारं भूतकोटिषु ।
क्लेशकर्मविपाकार्थं मेघादिवदुदाहृतम् ॥ १५८ ॥

क्लेशा मेघोपमाः कृत्यक्रिया स्वप्नोपभोगवत् ।
मायानिर्मितवत् स्कन्धा विपाकाः[1] क्लेशकर्मणाम् ॥ १५९ ॥

पूर्वमेवं व्यवस्थाप्य तन्त्रे पुनरिहोत्तरे ।
पञ्चदोषप्रहाणाय धात्वस्तित्वं प्रकाशितम् ॥ १६० ॥

तथा ह्यश्रवणादस्य बोधौ चित्तं न जायते ।
केषांचिन्नीचचित्तानामात्मावज्ञानदोषतः ॥ १६१ ॥

बोधिचित्तोदयेऽप्यस्य श्रेयानस्मीति मन्यतः
बोध्यनुत्पन्नचित्तेषु हीनसंज्ञा प्रवर्तते ॥ १६२ ॥

तस्यैवंमतिनः सम्यग्ज्ञानं नोत्पद्यते ततः ।
अभूतं परिगृह्णाति भूतमर्थं न विन्दते ॥ १६३ ॥

अभूतं सत्त्वदोषास्ते कृत्रिमागन्तुकत्वतः ।
भूतं तद्दोषनैरात्म्यं[2] शुद्धिप्रकृतयो गुणाः ॥ १६४ ॥

गृह्णन् दोषानसद्भूतान् भूतानपवदन् गुणान् ।
मैत्रीं न लभते धीमान् सत्त्वात्मसमदर्शिकाम् ॥ १६५ ॥

तच्छ्रवाज्जायते[3] त्वस्य प्रोत्साहः शास्तृगौरवम् ।
प्रज्ञा ज्ञानं महामैत्री पञ्चधर्मोदयात्ततः ॥ १६६ ॥

निरवज्ञः समप्रेक्षी निर्दोषो गुणवानसौ ।
आत्मसत्त्वसमस्नेहः क्षिप्रमाप्नोति बुद्धताम् ॥ १६७ ॥

इति रत्नगोत्रविभागे महायानोत्तरतन्त्रशास्त्रे तथागतगर्भाधिकारः प्रथमः परिच्छेदः श्लोका[4]र्थसंग्रहव्याख्यानतः समाप्तः ॥१॥

—o—

1. *vipākaḥ*, B.
2. *nairātmya*, A; *tadoṣanairātmya*, B.
3. *tacchraddhāj jāyate tv asya*, B; *hdi-ltar de ni thos-pa-las* (*tacchravād evam*, omitting *jāyate*), T; 'hearing the *yathābhūta* nature', C.
4. °*ādhikāra prathama śloka*°, B.

## II

उक्ता समला तथता । निर्मला (41*a*)तथतेदानीं वक्तव्या । तत्र कतमा निर्मला तथता यासौ बुद्धानां भगवतामनास्रवधातौ सर्वाकारमलविगमादाश्रयपरिवृत्तिर्व्यवस्थाप्यते । सा पुनरष्टौ पदार्थानधिकृत्य समासतो वेदितव्या । अष्टौ पदार्थाः कतमे ।

शुद्धिः प्राप्तिर्विसंयोगः स्वपरार्थस्तदाश्रयः ।
गम्भीर्यौदार्यमाहात्म्यं यावत्कालं यथा च तत् ॥ १ ॥

इत्येतेऽष्टौ पदार्था यथासंख्यमनेन श्लोकेन[1] परिदीपिताः । तद्यथा स्वभावार्थो हेत्वर्थः फलार्थः कर्मार्थो योगार्थो वृत्त्यर्थो नित्यार्थोऽचिन्त्यार्थः । तत्र (XX*a*) योऽसौ धातुरविनिर्मुक्तक्लेशकोशस्तथागतगर्भ[2] इत्युक्तो भगवता । तद्विशुद्धिराश्रयपरिवृत्तेः स्वभावो वेदितव्यः । यत आह[3] । यो भगवन् सर्वक्लेशकोशकोटिगूढे तथागतगर्भे निष्काङ्क्षः सर्वक्लेशकोशवि[4]निर्मुक्तेस्तथागतधर्मकायेऽपि स[5] निष्काङ्क्ष इति । द्विविधं ज्ञानं[6] लोकोत्तरमविकल्पं तत्पृष्ठलब्धं[7] च । लौकिकलोकोत्तरज्ञानमाश्रयपरिवृत्तिहेतुः प्राप्तिशब्देन परिदीपितः । प्राप्यतेऽनेनेति[8] प्राप्तिः । तत्फलं द्विविधम् । द्विविधो विसंयोगः क्लेशावरणविसंयोगो ज्ञेयावरणविसंयोगश्च । यथाक्रमं स्वपरार्थसंपादनं कर्म । तदधिष्ठानसमन्वागमो योगः । त्रिभिर्गाम्भीर्यौदार्यमाहात्म्यप्रभावितैर्बुद्धकार्यैर्नित्यमा भवगतेर[9]चिन्त्येन प्रकारे(41*b*)ण वर्तनं वृत्तिरिति । उद्दानम् ।

स्वभावहेतुफलतः कर्मयोगप्रवृत्तितः ।
तन्नि[10]त्याचिन्त्यतश्चैव बुद्धभूमिष्ववस्थितिः ॥ २ ॥

1. A om. *ślokena*.
2. B om. *rbha*.
3. From the *Āryaśrīmālāsūtra*.
4. B om. *vi*.
5. B om. *sa*.
6. *dvividhaṁ kiṁ jñānaṁ*, B.
7. B adds *laukikam* after *tatpṛṣṭhalabdham*. A, T and C omit it, but Obermiller's version of T had it.
8. *anenepti*, B.
9. *ā bhagavater*, B.
10. B om. *tam*.

तत्र स्वभावार्थं हेत्वर्थं चारभ्य बुद्धत्वे तत्प्रा[1]प्त्युपाये च श्लोकः ।

बुद्धत्वं प्रकृतिप्रभास्वरमिति प्रोक्तं यदागन्तुक-
क्लेशज्ञेयघनाभ्रजालपटलच्छन्नं रविव्योमवत् ।
सर्वैर्बुद्धगुणैरुपेतममलैर्नित्यं ध्रुवं शाश्वतं
धर्माणां तदकल्पनप्रविचयज्ञानाश्रयादाप्यते ॥ ३ ॥

अस्य श्लोकस्यार्थः समासेन चतुर्भिः श्लोकैर्वेदितव्यः ।

बुद्धत्वमविनिर्भागशुक्लधर्मप्रभावितम् ।
आदित्याकाशवज्ज्ञानप्रहाणद्वयलक्षणम्[2] ॥ ४ ॥
गङ्गातीररजोऽतीतैर्बुद्धधर्मैः प्रभास्वरैः ।
सर्वैरकृतकैर्युक्तमविनिर्भागवृत्तिभिः ॥ ५ ॥
स्वभावापरिनिष्पत्तिव्यापित्वागन्तुकत्वतः ।
क्लेशज्ञेयावृतिस्तस्मान्मेघवत् समुदाहृता ॥ ६ ॥
द्वयावरणविश्लेषहेतुर्ज्ञानद्वयं पुनः ।
निर्विकल्पं च तत्पृष्ठलब्धं त[3]ज्ज्ञानमिष्यते ॥ ७ ॥

यदुक्तमाश्रयपरिवृत्तेः स्वभावो विशुद्धिरिति तत्र विशुद्धिः समासतो द्विविधा । प्रकृतिविशुद्धिर्वैमल्यविशुद्धिश्च । तत्र प्रकृतिविशुद्धिर्या विमुक्तिर्न च[4] विसंयोगः प्रभास्वरायाश्चित्तप्रकृतेरागन्तुक[5]मलाविसंयोगात् । वैमल्यविशुद्धिर्विमुक्तिर्विसंयोगश्च[6] वार्यादीनामिव रजोजलादिभ्यः प्रभास्वराया[7]श्चित्तप्रकृतेरनवशेषमागन्तुक(42*a*)मलेभ्यो विसंयोगात् । तत्र वैमल्यविशुद्धौ फलार्थमारभ्य द्वौ श्लोकौ ।

1. B om. *tat*; A and T have it.
2. C seems to have read *prahāṇadvaya*.
3. B om. *taj*.
4. *viśuddhir yā viddhir yā vimukti na ca visaṁyogaḥ*, B; T om. *yā*, and A may mean it to be cut out.
5. B om. *ka*.
6. °*viśuddhir vimuktiḥ* ! *sa ca visaṁyogaḥ* !, B; T om. *sa*.
7. B om. *yā*.

ह्रद इव विमलाम्बुः फुल्लपद्मक्रमाढ्यः[1]
सकल इव शशाङ्को राहुवक्त्राद्विमुक्तः[2] ।
रविरिव जलदादिक्लेशनिर्मुक्तरश्मि-
र्विमलगुणयुतत्वाद्भाति मुक्तं तदेव ॥ ८ ॥
मुनिवृषमधुसारहेमरत्न-
प्रवरनिधानमहाफलद्रुमाभम् ।
सुगतविमलरत्नविग्रहाग्र-
क्षितिपतिकाञ्चनबिम्बवज्जिनत्वम् ॥ ९ ॥

अस्य खलु श्लोकद्वयस्यार्थः समासतोऽष्टाभिः श्लोकैर्वेदितव्यः ।

रागाद्यागन्तुकक्लेशशुद्धिरम्बुह्रदादिवत् ।
ज्ञानस्य निर्विकल्पस्य फलमुक्तं समासतः ॥ १० ॥
सर्वाकारवरोपेतबुद्धभावनिदर्शनम् ।
फलं तत्पृष्ठलब्धस्य ज्ञानस्य परिदीपितम् ॥ ११ ॥
स्वच्छाम्बुह्रदवद्रागरजःकालुष्यहानितः ।
विनेयाम्बुरुहध्यानवार्यभिष्यन्दनाच्च तत् ॥ १२ ॥
द्वेषराहुप्रमुक्तत्वा (xx*b*) न्महामैत्रीकृपांशुभिः[3] ।
जगत्स्फरणतः पूर्णविमलेन्दूपमं च तत् ॥ १३ ॥
मोहाभ्रजालनिर्मोक्षाज्जगति ज्ञानरश्मिभिः ।
तमोविधमनात्तच्च बुद्धत्वममलार्कवत् ॥ १४ ॥
अतुल्यतुल्यधर्मत्वात् सद्धर्मरसदानतः ।
फल्गु[4]व्यपगमात्तच्च सुगतक्षौद्रसारवत् ॥ १५ ॥

1. So A and T; *phullapadmakramadrumādhyaḥ*, B (two syllables in excess).
2. *vinirmuktaḥ*, B (one syllable in excess).
3. C evidently read *kṛpāmbubhiḥ*.
4. For *phalgu* cf. Pali *pheggu* (properly the 'sapwood' of a tree which covers the valuable heartwood) and *Mvy.*, 433, 7636.

पवित्रत्वाद्गुणद्रव्यदारिद्र्यविनिवर्तनात् ।
विमुक्तिफलदानाच्च[1] सुवर्णनिधिवृक्षवत् ॥ १६ ॥
धर्मरत्नात्मभावत्वाद् द्विपदाग्राधिपत्यतः ।
रूपरत्नाकृतित्वाच्च तद्रत्ननृप( 42*b* )बिम्बवत्[2] ॥ १७ ॥

यत्तु[3] द्विविधं लोकोत्तरमविकल्पं तत्पृष्ठलब्धं[4] च ज्ञानमाश्रयपरिवृत्तेर्हेतुर्विसं[5]योगफलसंज्ञितायाः। तत्कर्म स्वपरार्थसंपादनमित्युक्तम्। तत्र कतमा स्वपरार्थसंपत् । या सवासनक्लेशज्ञेयावरणविमोक्षादनावरणधर्मकायप्राप्तिरियमुच्यते स्वार्थसंपत्तिः । या त[6]दूर्ध्वमा लोकादनाभोगतः कायद्वयेन संदर्शनदेशनाविभुत्वद्वयप्रवृत्तिरियमुच्यते परार्थसंपत्तिरिति । तस्यां स्वपरार्थसं[7]पत्तौ कर्मार्थमारभ्य त्रयः श्लोकाः ।

अनास्रवं व्याप्यविनाशधर्मि च
ध्रुवं शिवं शाश्वतमच्युतं पदम् ।
तथागतत्वं गगनोपमं सताम्
षडिन्द्रियार्थानुभवेषु कारणम् ॥ १८ ॥
विभूतिरूपार्थविदर्शने सदा
निमित्तभूतं सुकथाशुचिश्रवे ।
तथागतानां शुचिशीलजिघ्रणे
महार्यसद्धर्मरसाग्रविन्दने ॥ १९ ॥

1. So A; *ḥbras-bu smin-byed* (*phalapākāc ca*), T; 'it can give', C. *Smin* in T may be a corruption for *sbyin*.

2. *gser bzhin* (*hemavat*), T.

3. The I. O. copy of T has a sheet missing here, which goes down to half way through the commentary on verse 28; for the verses I have used the other translation of T.

4. *avikalpaṁ lokottara laukikaṁ vat tatpṛṣṭha*°, B; according to O T omitted *laukikam* here, and so does C.

5. °*hetu visaṁ*°, B.

6. B om. *ta*.

7. B repeats *parārthasaṁ*.

समाधिसंस्पर्शसुखानुभूतिषु
स्वभावगाम्भीर्यनया[1]ऽवबोधने ।
सुसूक्ष्मचिन्तापरमार्थगह्वरं[2]
तथागतव्योम निमित्तवर्जितम् ॥ २० ॥

अस्य खलु श्लोकत्रयस्यार्थः समासतोऽष्टाभिः श्लोकैर्वेदितव्यः ।

कर्म ज्ञानद्वयस्यैतद्वेदितव्यं समासतः ।
पूरणं मुक्तिकायस्य धर्मकायस्य शोधनम् ॥ २१ ॥
विमुक्तिधर्मकायौ च वेदितव्यौ द्विरेकधा ।
अनास्रवत्वाद्व्यापित्वाद[3]संस्कृतपदत्वतः ॥ २२ ॥
अनास्रवत्वं क्लेशानां[4] सदासननि( 43a )रोधतः ।
असङ्गाप्रतिघातत्वाज्ज्ञानस्य व्यापिता मता ॥ २३ ॥
असंस्कृतत्वमत्यन्तमविनाशस्व[5]भावतः ।
अविनाशि[6]त्वमुद्देशस्तन्निर्देशो ध्रुवादिभिः ॥ २४ ॥
नाशश्चतुर्विधो ज्ञेयो ध्रुवत्वादिविपर्ययात् ।
पूतिर्विकृतिरुच्छित्तिरचिन्त्यनमनच्युतिः ॥ २५ ॥
तदभावाद्ध्रुवं ज्ञेयं शिवं शाश्वतमच्युतम् ।
पदं तदमलज्ञानं शुक्लधर्मास्पदत्वतः ॥ २६ ॥
यथानिमित्तमाकाशं निमित्तं रूपदर्शने ।
शब्दगन्धरसस्पृश्यधर्माणां च श्रवादिषु ॥ २७ ॥

1. *gāmbhirya ca nayā°*, B (one syllable in excess).
2. For *gahvaram*, which was evidently read by C, T has *bde-mdzad*, *śaṁkaram*, a mistake which is quite natural palaeographically.
3. *anāsravād avyāpitvād*, B; A, T and C as in text.
4. B om. *nā*.
5. *atyantaviśanāsva°*, B.
6. B om. *śi*.

इन्द्रियार्थेषु धीराणामनास्रवगुणोदये ।
हेतुः कायद्वयं तद्वदनावरणयोगतः ॥ २८ ॥

यदुक्तमाकाशलक्षणो बुद्ध इति तत्पारमार्थिकमावेणिकं तथागतानां बुद्धलक्षणमभिसंधायोक्तम्। एवं ह्याह[1]। सचेद्द्वात्रिंशन्महापुरुषलक्षणैस्तथागतो द्रष्टव्योऽभविष्यत्तद्राजापि चक्रवर्ती तथागतोऽभविष्यदिति । तत्र परमार्थलक्षणे योगार्थमारभ्य श्लोकः ।

अचिन्त्यं नित्यं च ध्रुवमथ शिवं शाश्वतमथ
प्रशान्तं च व्यापि व्यपगतविकल्पं गगनवत् ।
असक्तं सर्वत्राप्रतिघपरुषस्पर्शविगतं
न दृश्यं न ग्राह्यं शुभमपि च बुद्धत्वममलम् ॥ २९ ॥

अथ खल्वस्य श्लोकस्यार्थः समासतोऽष्टाभिः श्लोकैर्वे[2]दितव्यः ।

विमुक्तिधर्मकायाभ्यां स्वपरार्थो निदर्शितः ।
स्वपरार्थाश्रये तस्मिन् योगोऽचिन्त्यादिभिर्गुणैः ॥ ३० ॥
अचिन्त्यमनुगन्तव्यं त्रिज्ञानाविषयत्वतः ।
(43b) सर्वज्ञज्ञानविषयं बुद्धत्वं ज्ञानदेहिभिः ॥ ३१ ॥
श्रुतस्याविषयः सौक्ष्म्याच्चिन्तायाः परमार्थतः ।
लौक्यादिभावनायाश्च धर्मतागह्वरत्वतः ॥ ३२ ॥
दृष्टपूर्वं न तद्यस्माद्बालैर्जात्यन्धकायवत् ।
आर्यैश्च सूतिकामध्यस्थित[3]बालार्कबिम्बवत् ॥ ३३ ॥
उत्पादविगमान्नित्यं निरोधविगमाद्ध्रुवम् ।
शिवमेतद्द्वयाभावाच्छाश्वतं धर्मतास्थितेः ॥ ३४ ॥

1. From the *Vajracchedikāsūtra* (ed. Anecd. Ox.), pp. 42-43, with a slight variation of wording.

2. A's xx*b* finishes here.

3. e.c.; *sūtikāmadhyasthita'*, B; *btsas-paḥi khyim-nas*, T.

शान्तं निरोधसत्यत्वादव्यापि सर्वाविबोधतः ।
अकल्पमप्रतिष्ठानादसक्तं क्लेशहानितः ॥ ३५ ॥
सर्वत्राप्रतिघं सर्वज्ञेयावरणशुद्धितः ।
परुषस्पर्शनिर्मुक्तं मृदुकर्मण्यभावतः ॥ ३६ ॥
अदृश्यं तदरूपित्वादग्राह्यमनिमित्ततः ।
शुभं प्रकृतिशुद्धत्वादमलं मलहानितः ॥ ३७ ॥

यत्पुनरेतदाकाशवदसंस्कृतगुणाविनिर्भाग[1]वृत्त्यापि तथागतत्वमा भवगतेर[2]-चिन्त्यमहोपायकरुणाज्ञानपरिकर्म[3]विशेषेण जगद्धितसुखाधाननिमित्तममलै स्त्रिभिः स्वभाविकसांभोगिकनैर्माणिकैः कायैर[4]नुपरतमनुच्छिन्नमनाभोगेन प्रवर्तत इति द्रष्टव्यमावेणिकधर्मयुतत्वादिति । तत्र वृत्त्यर्थमा[5]रभ्य वुद्धकायविभागे चत्वारः श्लोकाः ।

अनादिमध्यान्तमभिन्नमद्वयं
त्रिधा विमुक्तं विमलाविकल्पकम् ।
समाहिता योगिनस्तत्प्रयत्नाः
पश्यन्ति यं धर्मधातुस्वभावम्[6] ॥ ३८ ॥
अमेयगङ्गासिकतातिवृत्तै-
र्गुणैरचिन्त्यैरसमैरुपेतः ।

1. °*guṇāvirbhoga*, B; *yon-tan daṅ rnam-par dbye-bas* (°*guṇa vinirbhāga*), T; C as in text.

2. *a bhagavater*, B; *srid-pa ji-srid-kyi bar-du*, T.

3. *thabs chen-po daṅ śes-rab-kyi yoṅs-su spyod-paḥi* (*mahopāyaprajñāparikarma*°), T; C as in text.

4. B and T om. *kāyair*, supplied from C.

5. Reading not quite certain. *tatreme vṛttyartham* , B; *de-la ḥjug-paḥi don-las* (*tatra vṛtty*[or *pravṛtty*]*artham*), T.

6. *ya*(written over *sa*)*ddharma*°, B ; T's *gaṅ yin* requires *yaṁ*, corresponding to *sa* in 39. The change of metre in the second hemistich is odd; the metre does not appear to be known elsewhere.

सवासनोन्मूलितसर्व( 44*a* )दोष[1]-
स्तथागतानाममलः स धातुः[2] ॥ ३९ ॥
विचित्रसद्धर्ममयूखविग्रहै-
र्जगद्विमोक्षा[3]र्थसमाहृतोद्यमः ।
क्रियासु चिन्तामणिराजरत्नव-
द्विचित्रभावो न च तत्स्वभाववान् ॥ ४० ॥
लोकेषु यच्छान्तिपथावतार-
प्रपाचनाव्याकरणे निदानम् ।
बिम्बं तदप्यत्र सदावरुद्ध-
माकाशधाताविव रूपधातुः ॥ ४१ ॥

एषां खलु चतुर्णां श्लोकानां पिण्डार्थो विंशतिश्लोकैर्वेदितव्यः ।

यत्तद्बुद्धत्वमित्युक्तं सर्वज्ञत्वं स्वयंभुवाम् ।
निर्वृतिः[4] परमाचिन्त्यप्राप्तिः प्रत्यात्मवेदिता[5] ॥ ४२ ॥
तत्प्रभेदस्त्रिभिः कायैर्वृत्तिः[6] स्वाभाविकादिभिः ।
गाम्भीर्यौदार्यमाहात्म्यगुणधर्मप्रभावितैः ॥ ४३ ॥
तत्र स्वाभाविकः कायो बुद्धानां पञ्चलक्षणः ।
पञ्चाकारगुणोपेतो वेदितव्यः समासतः ॥ ४४ ॥
असंस्कृतमसंभिन्नमन्तद्वयविवर्जितम् ।
क्लेशज्ञेयसमापत्तित्रयावरणनिःसृतम् ॥ ४५ ॥

1. *doṣa tathā°*, B.
2. *amalo sau*, B (two syllables short); *dri-med dbyiṅs-pa de*, T.
3. B om. *kṣā*.
4. *nivṛttiḥ*, B; T and C as in text.
5. *pratyātmamadatā*, B; *so-soḥi bdag ḥgyur-ba*, T; 'experienced within the self', C.
6. *tatprabhedaḥ kāyair vṛttiḥ svābhāvikā°* , B (two syllables short); *de-dbye sku gsum-dag-gis ḥjug*, T.

वैमल्यादविकल्पत्वाद्योगिनां गोचरत्वतः ।
प्रभास्वरं विशुद्धं च धर्मधातोः स्वभावतः ॥ ४६ ॥
अप्रमेयैरसंख्येयैरचिन्त्यैरसमैर्गुणैः ।
विशुद्धिपारमीप्राप्तैर्युक्तं स्वाभाविकं वपुः ॥ ४७ ॥
उदारत्वादगण्यत्वात्[1] तर्कस्यागोचरत्वतः ।
कैवल्याद्वासनोच्छित्तेरप्रमेयादयः क्रमात् ॥ ४८ ॥
विचित्रधर्मसंभोगरूप[2]धर्मावभासतः ।
करुणाशुद्धिनिष्यन्दसत्त्वार्थास्रंसनत्वतः ॥ ४९ ॥
निर्विकल्पं निराभोगं यथाभिप्रायपूरितः ।
चिन्तामणिप्रभावर्द्धेः सांभोगस्य व्यव( 44b )स्थितिः॥५०॥
देशने दर्शने कृत्यास्रंसनेऽनभिसंस्कृतौ[3] ।
अतत्स्वभावाख्याने च चित्रतोक्ता च पञ्चधा ॥ ५१ ॥
रङ्गप्रत्ययवैचित्र्यादतद्भावो यथा मणेः ।
सत्त्वप्रत्ययवैचित्र्यादतद्भावस्तथा विभोः ॥ ५२ ॥
महाकरुणया कृत्स्नं लोकमालोक्य लोकवित् ।
धर्मकायादविरलं[4] निर्माणैश्चित्ररूपिभिः ॥ ५३ ॥
जातकान्युपपत्तिं[5] च तुषितेषु च्युतिं ततः ।
गर्भा[व]क्रमणं जन्म शिल्पस्थानानि कौशलम् ॥ ५४ ॥

1. *agamyatvāt*, B; *grañs-med phyir*, T; C supports T.

2. For *rūpa* T has *rañ-bzhin* (*saṁbhogamaya*? ?); but C appears to support the text.

3. *°sraṁsanenābhi°*, B; *mdzad-rgyun mi-ḥchad dañ mṅon-par ḥdu-byed med-pa*, T.

4. *ma g'yos-par* (*avicalaṁ*), T. C om. verse 53.

5. B's reading of the fourth letter is not quite certain; T evidently read *jātakābhyupapattiṁ* (*skye-ba mṅon-par skye-ba dañ*).

अन्तःपुररतिक्रीडां नैष्क्रम्यं दुःखचारिकाम्[1] ।
बोधिमण्डोपसंक्रान्तिं मारसैन्यप्रमर्दनम् ॥ ५५ ॥
संबोधिं धर्मचक्रं च निर्वाणाधिगमक्रियाम्[2] ।
क्षेत्रेष्वपरिशुद्धेषु दर्शयत्या भवस्थितेः ॥ ५६ ॥
अनित्यदुःखनैरात्म्यशान्तिशब्दैरुपायवित् ।
उद्वेज्य त्रिभवात् सत्त्वान् प्रतारयति निर्वृतौ ॥ ५७ ॥
शान्तिमार्गावतीर्णांश्च प्राप्यनिर्वाण[3]संज्ञिनः ।
सद्धर्मपुण्डरीकादिधर्मतत्त्वप्रकाशनैः ॥ ५८ ॥
पूर्वग्रहान्निवर्त्यैतान् प्रज्ञोपायपरिग्रहात् ।
परिपाच्योत्तमे याने व्याकरोत्यग्रबोधये ॥ ५९ ॥
सौक्ष्म्यात्[4] प्रभावसंपत्तेर्बालसार्था[5]तिवाहनात् ।
गाम्भीर्यौदार्यमाहात्म्यमेषु ज्ञेयं यथाक्रमम् ॥ ६० ॥
प्रथमो धर्मकायोऽत्र रूपकायौ तु पश्चिमौ ।
व्योम्नि रूपगतस्येव[6] प्रथमेऽन्त्यस्य वर्तनम् ॥ ६१ ॥

तस्यैव कायत्रयस्य जगद्धितसुखाधानवृत्तौ नित्यार्थमारभ्य श्लोकः ।

हेत्वानन्त्यात्[7] सत्त्वधात्वक्षयत्वात्
कारुण्यर्द्धि[8]ज्ञानसंपत्तियोगात् ।

1. *cārikā* in this sense is apparently confined to Buddhist texts.

2. B om. *dhi*; T does not show the preposition and read °*kriyāḥ* (*mdzad-rnams*).

3. T's *mya-ṅan ḥdas thob* suggests *prāptanirvāṇa*° ; C's version is free, but seems to imply the text.

4. So C; *saukhyāt*, B; *zab* (!, *gāmbhīryāt*), T.

5. *bālasārvā*°, B; *byis-pa don-mthun*, T; C may possibly have read *bālasattvā*°.

6. *śiṣyagatasyeva*, B; *gzugs gnas bzhin*, T; 'just as all forms are in space', C.

7. *hetvātyantyāt*, B; C and T as in text.

8. *kāruṇyar*(?)*di*°, B; *brtse daṅ ḥphrul*, T; C uncertain.

धर्मैश्वर्यान्मृत्युमारावभङ्गान्
नैःस्वा( 45a )भाव्याच्छाश्वतो लोकनाथः ॥ ६२ ॥

अस्य पिण्डार्थः षड्भिः श्लोकैर्वेदितव्यः ।

कायजीवितभोगानां त्यागैः सद्धर्मसंग्रहात् ।
सर्वसत्त्वहितायादिप्रतिज्ञोत्तरणत्वतः ॥ ६३ ॥
बुद्धत्वे सुविशुद्धायाः करुणायाः प्रवृत्तितः ।
ऋद्धिपादप्रकाशाच्च[1] तैरवस्थानशक्तितः ॥ ६४ ॥
ज्ञानेन भवनिर्वाणद्वयग्रहविमुक्तितः ।
सदाचिन्त्यसमाधानसुखसंपत्तियोगतः ॥ ६५ ॥
लोके विचरतो लोकधर्मैरनुपलेपतः ।
शमा[2]मृतपदप्राप्तौ मृत्युमाराप्रचारतः ॥ ६६ ॥
असंस्कृतस्वभावस्य मुनेरादिप्रशान्तितः ।
नित्यमशरणानां[3] च शरणाभ्युपपत्तितः[4] ॥ ६७ ॥
सप्तभिः कारणैराद्यैर्नित्यता रूपकायतः ।
पश्चिमैश्च त्रिभिः शास्तुर्नित्यता धर्मकायतः ॥ ६८ ॥

स चायमाश्रयपरिवृत्तिप्रभावितस्तथागतानां प्राप्तिनयोऽचिन्त्यनयेनानुगन्तव्य इति । अचिन्त्यार्थमारभ्य श्लोकः ।

अवाच्यवत्त्वात् परमार्थसंग्रहा-
दतर्कभूमेरुपमानिवृत्तितः ।

1. e.c. Pāda *c* is corrupt in B, which omits two characters, leaving a gap and reading *pādaprave*(?)*tuś*(?)*ca*; *rdzu-ḥphrul rkaṅ-ba ston-pa ni*, T, which may be tentatively reconstructed as in the text; C agrees with T in sense.

2. *samā°*, B; *zhi-ba*, T.

3. *nityatā śaraṇānām*, B; *rtag-pa skyabs-med-rnams-kyi*, T.

4. *skyabs-la-sogs-pa ḥthad-phyir* (*śaraṇādyupapattitaḥ*), T.

निरुत्तरत्वाद्भवशान्त्यनुद्ग्रहा-
दचिन्त्य आर्यैरपि बुद्धगोचरः ॥ ६९ ॥

अस्य पिण्डार्थश्चतुर्भिः श्लोकैर्वेदितव्यः ।

अचिन्त्योऽनभिलाप्यत्वादलाप्यः परमार्थतः ।
परमार्थोऽप्रतर्क्यत्वादतर्क्यो व्यनुमेयतः[1] ॥ ७० ॥
व्यनुमेयोऽनुत्तरत्वादानुत्तर्यमनुद्ग्रहात् ।
अनुद्ग्रहोऽप्रतिष्ठानादगुणदोषाविकल्पनात् ॥ ७१ ॥
पञ्चभिः कारणैः[2] सौक्ष्म्यादचिन्त्यो धर्मकायतः ।
षष्ठेनातत्त्वभावित्वादचिन्त्यो रूपकायतः ॥ ७२ ॥

अनुत्तरज्ञानमहाकृपादिभि-
र्गुणैरचिन्त्या गुणपारगा जिनाः ।
( 45*b* )अतः क्रमोऽन्त्योऽप्ययमपि स्वयंभुवो[3]
ऽभिषेकलब्धा न महर्षयो विदुरिति[4] ॥ ७३ ॥

इति रत्नगोत्रविभागे महायानोत्तरतन्त्रशास्त्रे[5] बोध्यधिकारो नाम द्वितीयः परिच्छेदः ॥२॥

---

1. C evidently read *'nupameyataḥ* or *vyupameyataḥ* against B and T.

2. O translates 'out of four motives', evidently a slip in view of *c*.

3. So T understands the line, taking *svayaṁbhuvo* as genitive, but the reading may be *yam*, 'which', not *'yam*.

4. T om. *iti*, and C the whole stanza. The reference in the last line is to the Bodhisattvas in the tenth stage.

5. °*tantrasāre*, B; *bstan-bcos*, T.

## III

उक्ता निर्मला तथता । ये तदाश्रिता मणिप्रभावर्णसंस्थानवदभिन्नप्रकृतयोऽनन्तनिर्मला गुणास्त इदानीं वक्तव्या इति । अनन्तरं बुद्धगुणविभागमारभ्य श्लोकः ।

स्वार्थः[1] परार्थः परमार्थकाय[2]-
स्तदाश्रिता संवृतिकायता च ।
फलं विसंयोगविपाकभावा-
देतच्चतुः[3]षष्टिगुणप्रभेदम् ॥ १ ॥

किमुक्तं भवति ।

आत्मसंपत्त्यधिष्ठानं शरीरं पारमार्थिकम् ।
परसंपत्त्यधिष्ठानमृषेः सांकेतिकं वपुः ॥ २ ॥
विसंयोगगुणैर्युक्तं वपुराद्यं बलादिभिः ।
वैपाकिकैर्द्वितीयं तु महापुरुषलक्षणैः ॥ ३ ॥

अतः परं ये च बलादयो यथा चानुगन्तव्यास्तथतामधिकृत्य ग्रन्थः ।

बलत्वमज्ञानवृतेषु वज्रव-
द्विशारदत्वं परिषत्सु सिंहवत् ।
तथागतावेणिकतान्तरीक्षवन्
मुनेर्द्विधादर्शनमम्बुचन्द्रवत् ॥ ४ ॥

बलान्वित इति ।

स्थानास्थाने विपाके च कर्मणामिन्द्रियेषु च ।
धातुष्वप्यधिमुक्तौ च मार्गे सर्वत्रगामिनि ॥ ५ ॥

1. *svārtha*, B.
2. *paramārthakāyatā*, B.
3. B om. visarga.

ध्यानादिक्लेशवैमल्ये निवासानुस्मृतावपि ।
दिव्ये चक्षुषि शान्तौ[1] च ज्ञानं दशविधं बलम् ॥ ६ ॥

वज्रवदिति ।

स्थानास्थानविपाकधातुषु जगन्नानाधिमुक्तौ नये
संक्लेशव्यवदान इन्द्रिय(46a)गणे पूर्वे निवासस्मृतौ ।
दिव्ये चक्षुषि चास्रवक्षयविधावज्ञानवर्मा[2]चल–
प्राकार[3]द्रुमभेदनप्रकिरणच्छेदाद्बलं वज्रवत्[4] ॥ ७ ॥

चतुर्वैशारद्यप्राप्त इति ।

सर्वधर्माभिसंबोधे विबन्धप्रतिषेधने ।
मार्गाख्याने निरोधाप्तौ वैशारद्यं चतुर्विधम् ॥ ८ ॥
ज्ञेये वस्तुनि सर्वथात्मपरयोर्ज्ञानात् स्वयंज्ञापना[5]–
द्धेये वस्तुनि हानिकारणकृतेः[6] सेव्ये विधौ सेवनात् ।
प्राप्तव्ये च निरुत्तरेऽतिविमले प्राप्तेः परप्रापणा–
दार्याणां स्वपरार्थसत्यकथनादस्तम्भितत्वं क्वचित् ॥ ९ ॥

सिंहवदिति ।

नित्यं वनान्तेषु यथा मृगेन्द्रो
निर्भीरनुत्त्रस्तगतिर्मृगेभ्यः ।

1. For *śāntau* T has *ldan-pa* (*yoge*); C as in text.
2. °*dharmā*°, B; *go-cha*, T; 'armour', C.
3. °*prakāra*°, B; *rtsig*, T; 'wall', C.
4. C puts verse 7 after verse 28.
5. e.c.; B's reading is uncertain, possibly *jñānātm*(or *s*) *ayajñāpanād*; T has nothing to represent the two doubtful syllables, and of the possibilities *svayam* alone makes any sort of sense. But the difficulty is that the sentence is complete without it, and neither T nor C give any clear indication of what their texts read.
6. *hānikāraṇakṣateḥ*, B; *spaṅs dan spoṅ-mdzad*, T.

मुनीन्द्रसिंहोऽपि तथा गणेषु
स्वस्थो निरास्थः[1] स्थिरविक्रमस्थः ॥ १० ॥

अष्टादशावेणिकबुद्धधर्मसमन्वागत इति ।

स्खलितं रवितं नास्ति शास्तुर्न मुषिता स्मृतिः ।
न चासमाहितं चित्तं नापि नानात्वसंज्ञिता ॥ ११ ॥
नोपेक्षाप्रतिसंख्याय हानिर्न च्छन्दवीर्यतः ।
स्मृतिप्रज्ञाविमुक्तिभ्यो विमुक्तिज्ञानदर्शनात् ॥ १२ ॥
ज्ञानपूर्वंगमं कर्म त्र्यध्वज्ञानमनावृतम् ।
इत्येतेऽष्टादशान्ये च गुरोरावेणिका गुणाः ॥ १३ ॥
नास्ति प्रस्खलितं रवो मुषितता चित्ते (48*a*) न संभेदतः[2]
संज्ञा न[3] स्वरसाध्युपेक्षणमृषे[4]र्हानिर्न च च्छन्दतः ।
वीर्याच्च स्मृतितो विशुद्धविमलप्रज्ञाविमुक्तेः सदा
मुक्ति[5]ज्ञाननिदर्शनाच्च निखिलज्ञेयार्थसंदर्शनात् ॥ १४ ॥
सर्वज्ञानपुरोजवानुपरिवर्त्यर्थेषु[6] कर्मत्रयं
त्रिष्वध्वस्वपराहता[7] सुविपुलज्ञानप्रवृत्तिर्ध्रुवम् ।

1. *svastho pi nirāsvasthaḥ*, B. C puts this verse after verse 30. For it cf. *Kāś. P.* 36, p. 65.

2. *na bhedataḥ*, B (one syllable short). B goes on from *citta* to iv, 9, and the text resumes in 48*a*, line 4. Evidently one or more leaves were displaced in the MS. from which B was copied.

3. B om. *na*.

4. *ṛṣe*, B.

5. *vimukti°*, B.

6. *artheṣu* is a doubtful reading in B, for which T's *gaṅ-gis* suggests a relative instead. C is no help.

7. B is not quite clear and might be read as *aparāvṛtā*, and C suggests a form from *vṛ*; T's *thogs-pa med-pa* agrees best with the text (e.g. *thogs-med*=*avyāhata* elsewhere).

इत्येषा जिनता[1] महाकरुणया युक्तावबुद्धा[2] जिनै–
र्यद्बोधाज्जगति प्रवृत्तमभय[3]दं सद्धर्मचक्रं महत् ॥ १५ ॥

आकाशवदिति ।

या क्षित्यादिषु धर्मता न नभसः सा धर्मता विद्य (48b) ते
ये चानावरणादिलक्षणगुणा व्योम्नो न ते रूपिषु ।
क्षित्यम्बुज्वलनानिलाम्बरसमा लोकेषु साधारणा
बुद्धावेणिकता न चाश्वपि पुनर्लोकेषु साधारणा[4] ॥ १६ ॥

द्वात्रिंशन्महापुरुषलक्षणरूपधारीति ।

सुप्रतिष्ठितचक्राङ्कव्यायतोत्सङ्ग[5]पादता ।
दीर्घाङ्गुलिकता जालपाणिपादावनद्धता ॥ १७ ॥
त्वङ्मृदुश्रीतरुणता सप्तोत्सदशरीरता ।
एणेयजङ्घता नागकोशवद्व[6]स्तिगुह्यता ॥ १८ ॥
सिंहपूर्वार्धकायत्वं निरन्तरचितांशता[7] ।
संवृत्तस्कन्धता वृत्तश्लक्ष्णानुन्नाम[8]बाहुता ॥ १९ ॥

1. *janatā*, B; *rgyal-ba-ñid*, T; '*Tathāgatatva*', C.

2. *brñes* (*avalabdhā*), T.

3. B repeats *ya*.

4. *na cāśva puna*, B (one syllable short); *sādhāraṇāḥ*, B. T has for the line *ma-ḥdres-ñid ni rdul dran tsam yaṅ ḥjig-rten-dag-na thun-moṅ min*, omitting Buddha and substituting a word which I cannot determine; it may have read *cāṇv* for *cāśv*. For *āśu* cf. *S.*, vi, 9, and note in text. C puts this verse after verse 34.

5. *ucchaṅka* is the more usual form, found in the *Mvy.* and *Abhisamayālaṁkārāloka*.

6. B om. *dva*; *glaṅ-po bzhin-du*, T.

7. *citāṅgatā*, B; *thal-gon. .rgyas-pa*, T. Cf. *Mvy.*, 251.

8. °*ślakṣṇanu*(?)*nnāma*°, B; *phyag ḥjam-riṅ zhum zhiṅ mthon dman-med*, T. Prof. Bailey has found verses 19*cd* to 22 transliterated in the Paris MS., Pelliot 2740; it reads here *ṡilaṣanau nāmabahūtta*, which supports the text.

प्रलम्बबाहुता शुद्धप्रभामण्डलगात्रता ।
कम्बुग्रीवत्वममलं मृगेन्द्रहनुता समा ॥ २० ॥
चत्वारिंशद्दशनता स्वच्छाविरलदन्तता ।
विशुद्धसमदन्तत्वं[1] शुक्लप्रवरदंष्ट्रता ॥ २१ ॥
प्रभूतजिह्वतानन्ताचिन्त्यरसरसाग्रता ।
कलविङ्करुतं[2] ब्रह्मस्वरता च स्वयंभुवः ॥ २२ ॥

नीलोत्पलश्रीवृषपक्ष्मनेत्र-
सितामलोर्णोदितचारुवक्त्रः ।
उष्णीषशीर्षव्यवदातसूक्ष्म-
सुवर्णवर्णच्छविरग्रसत्त्वः ॥ २३ ॥
एकैकविश्लिष्टमृदूर्ध्वदेह-
प्रदक्षिणावर्तसुसूक्ष्मरोमा ।
महेन्द्रनीलामलरत्नकेशो[3]
न्यग्रोधपूर्ण[4]द्रुममण्डलाभः ॥ २४ ॥
नारायणस्थामदृढात्मभावः
समन्तभद्रोऽप्रतिमो महर्षिः ।
द्वात्रिंशदेतान्यमितद्युतीनि
नरेन्द्रचिह्नानि वदन्ति शास्तुः ॥ २५ ॥

दकचन्द्रवदिति ।

व्यभ्रे यथा नभसि चन्द्रमसो विभूतिं
पश्यन्ति नीलशरदम्बुमहाह्र( 49*a* )दे[5] च ।

1. °*dantatā klapravara*°, B (one syllable short and unmetrical); *dkar-pa* (for *dkar-po*), T.
2. °*ruta*, B.
3. °*kośo*, B; *dbu-skra*, T.
4. °*pūrṇṇo*, B; *rdzogs-paḥi ljon-śiṅ*, T.
5. *hradeṣu*, B (one syllable in excess): T does not show the plural.

संबुद्धमण्डलतलेषु विभोर्विभूतिं
तद्वज्जिनात्मजगणा व्यवलोकयन्ति ॥ २६ ॥

इतीमानि दश तथागतबलानि चत्वारि वैशारद्यान्यष्टादशावेणिका बुद्धधर्मा द्वात्रिंशच्च महापुरुषलक्षणान्येकेनाभिसंक्षिप्य चतुःषष्टिर्भवन्ति ।

गुणाश्चैते चतुःषष्टिः सनिदानाः[1] पृथक् पृथक् ।
वेदितव्या यथासंख्यं **रत्नसूत्रानुसारतः** ॥ २७ ॥

एषां खलु यथोद्दिष्टानामेव चतुःषष्टेस्तथागतगुणानामपि यथानुपूर्व्या विस्तरविभागे निर्देशो **रत्नदारिकासूत्रानुसारेण** वेदितव्यः । यत्पुनरेषु स्थानेषु चतुर्विधमेव यथाक्रमं वज्रसिंहाम्बरदकचन्द्रोदाहरणमुदाहृतमस्यापि पिण्डार्थो द्वादशभिः श्लोकैर्वेदितव्यः ।

निर्वेधिकत्वनिर्दैन्यनिष्कैवल्यनिरीहतः ।
वज्रसिंहाम्बरस्वच्छदकचन्द्रनिदर्शनम् ॥ २८ ॥
बलादिषु बलैः षड्भिस्त्रिभिरेकेन च क्रमात् ।
सर्वज्ञेयसमापत्तिसवासनमलोद्धृतेः ॥ २९ ॥
भेदाद्विकरणा[2]च्छेदाद्वर्मप्राकारवृक्षवत् ।
गुरुसारदृढाभेद्यं वज्रप्रख्यमृषेर्बलम् ॥ ३० ॥
गुरु[3] कस्माद्यतः सारं सारं कस्माद्यतो दृढम् ।
दृढं कस्माद्यतोऽभेद्यमभेद्यत्वाच्च वज्रवत् ॥ ३१ ॥
निर्भयत्वान्निरास्थत्वा[4]त्स्थैर्याद्विक्रमसंपदः ।
पर्षद्गणेष्ववशारद्यं मुनिसिंहस्य सिंहवत् ॥ ३२ ॥

1. °*ṣaṣṭih anidānāḥ*, B; *rgyu bcas*, T; C also indicates the text.

2. *vikaraṇa* here is translated in T by the same word as *prakiraṇa* in iii, 7; possibly the correct reading is not *vikaraṇāc* nor *vikiraṇāc*, but *vidāraṇāc*.

3. B om. *ru*, and C the whole verse.

4. *nirāndhatvāt*, B; *ltos-med phyir*, T; '*svastha*', C.

सर्वाभिज्ञतया स्वस्थो विहरत्यकुतोभयः ।
निरास्थः शुद्धसत्त्वेभ्योऽप्यात्मनोऽसमदर्शनात् ॥ ३३ ॥
स्थि( 49*b* )रो नित्यसमाधाना[1]त् सर्वधर्मेषु चेतसः ।
विक्रान्तः परमाविद्यावासभूमिव्यतिक्रमात् ॥ ३४ ॥
लौकिकश्रावकैकान्तचारिधीमत्स्वयंभुवाम्[2] ॥
उत्तरोत्तरधीसौक्ष्म्यात् पञ्चधा तु निदर्शनम् ॥ ३५ ॥
सर्वलोकोपजीव्यत्वाद्भूम्यम्बवग्न्यनिलोपमाः ।
लौक्यलोकोत्तरातीतलक्षणत्वान्नभोनिभाः ॥ ३६ ॥
गुणा द्वात्रिंशदित्येते[3] धर्मकायप्रभाविताः ।
मणिरत्नप्रभावर्णसंस्थानवदभेदतः ॥ ३७ ॥
द्वात्रिंशल्लक्षणाः काये दर्शनाह्लादका गुणाः ।
निर्माणधर्मसंभोगरूपकायद्वयाश्रिताः ॥ ३८ ॥
शुद्धेर्दूरान्तिकस्थानां लोकेऽथ जिनमण्डले ।
द्विधा तद्दर्शनं शुद्धं[4] वारिव्योमेन्दुबिम्बवत् ॥ ३९ ॥

इति रत्नगोत्रविभागे महायानोत्तरतन्त्रशास्त्रे गुणाधिकारो नाम त्रितीयः परिच्छेदः ॥३॥

---

1. B om. *nā.*

2. *laukikai śrāvakaiḥ kānta°*.. *°bhuvā*, B; T and C indicate the text.

3. B om. *te.*

4. *dvidhātu ddarśanaṁ*, B; *de mthoṅ-ba*, T. C suggests the reading *śuddhavāri°*; T omits *śuddham*, unless *chu daṅ* is a mistake for *chu dag*, in which case it had the same text as C.

## IV

उक्ता विमला बुद्धगुणाः। तत्कर्म जिनक्रियेदानीं ववतव्या। सा पुनरनाभोगतश्चाप्रश्रब्धितश्च समासतो द्वाभ्यामाकाराभ्यां[1] प्रवर्तत इति । अनन्तरमनाभोगाप्रश्रब्धं[2] बुद्धकार्यमारभ्य द्वौ श्लोकौ ।

विनेयधातौ विनयाभ्युपाये
विनेयधातोर्विनयक्रियायाम् ।
तद्देशकाले गमने च नित्यं
विभोरनाभोगत एव वृत्तिः ॥ १ ॥

कृत्स्नं निष्पाद्य[3] यानं प्रवरगुणगणज्ञानरत्नस्वगर्भं
पुण्यज्ञानार्करश्मिप्रविसृतविपुला[4]नन्तमध्याम्बराभम् ।
बुद्धत्वं सर्वसत्त्वे विमलगुणनिधिं[5] निर्विशिष्टं विलोक्य
क्लेशज्ञेयाभ्रजालं विधमति करुणा वायुभूता जिनानाम् ॥२॥

(50*a*)एतयोर्यथाक्रमं द्वाभ्यामष्टाभिश्च श्लोकैः पिण्डार्थो वेदितव्यः ।

यस्य येन च यावच्च यदा च विनयक्रिया ।
तद्विकल्पोदयाभावादनाभोगः सदा मुनेः ॥ ३ ॥
यस्य धातोर्विनेयस्य येनोपायेन भूरिणा ।
या विनीतिक्रिया यत्र यदा तद्देशकालयोः ॥ ४ ॥
निर्याणे तदुपस्तम्भे तत्फले तत्परिग्रहे ।
तदावृतौ तदुच्छित्तिप्रत्यये चाविकल्पतः[6] ॥ ५ ॥

1. *akārābhyām*, B.

2. *apratisrabdham*, B, but *pra* is the regular preposition, or else *pratipra* combined.

3. *nirmathya*, B; *ṅes-par bsgrubs-te*, T; 'realizing', C.

4. B seems to read *vimalā°*; *rgya chen*, T; 'widespread', C.

5. °*nidhi*, B (against the metre). B omits *vi* in *vimala*; *dri-ma med*, T; C also as in text.

6. c.c.; *vāvikalpataḥ*, B; T does not show either *ca* or *vā*.

भूमयो दश निर्याणं तद्धेतुः संभृतिद्वयम् ।
तत्फलं परमा बोधिर्बोधेः सत्त्वः परिग्रहः[1] ॥ ६ ॥
तदावृतिरपर्यन्तक्लेशोपक्लेशवासनाः ।
करुणा तत्समु[2]द्घातप्रत्ययः सार्वकालिकः ॥ ७ ॥
स्थानानि वेदितव्यानि षडेतानि यथाक्रमम् ।
महोदधिरविव्योमनिधानाम्बुदवायुवत् ॥ ८ ॥
ज्ञानाम्बुगुणरत्नत्वादग्रयानं (46*a*) समुद्रवत् ।
सर्वसत्त्वोपजीव्यत्वात् संभारद्वयमर्कवत्[3] ॥ ९ ॥
विपुलानन्तमध्यत्वाद्बोधिराकाशधातुवत् ।
सम्यक्संबुद्धधर्मत्वात् सत्त्वधातुर्निधानवत् ॥ १० ॥
आगन्तुव्याप्त्यनिष्प (46*b*) त्तेस्तत्संक्लेशोऽभ्रराशिवत् ।
तत्क्षिप्तिप्रत्युपस्थानात् करुणोद्वृत्तवायुवत् ॥ ११ ॥
पराधि[4]कारनिर्याणात् सत्त्वात्मसमदर्शनात् ।
कृत्यापरिसमाप्तेश्च क्रियाप्रश्रब्धिरा भवात् ॥ १२ ॥

यदनुत्पादानिरोधप्रभावितं बुद्धत्वमित्युक्तं तत्कथमिहासंस्कृतादप्रवृ[5]त्तिलक्षणाद्बुद्धत्वादनाभोगाप्रतिप्रश्रब्धमा लोकादविकल्पं बुद्धकार्यं प्रवर्तत इति । बुद्धमाहात्म्यधर्म[6]तामारभ्य विमतिसंदेहजातानामचिन्त्यबुद्धविषयाधिमुक्तिसंजननार्थं तस्य माहात्म्ये श्लोकः ।

शक्रदुन्दुभिवन् मेघब्रह्मार्कमणिरत्नवत् ।
प्रतिश्रुतिरिवाकाशपृथिवीवत् तथागतः ॥१३॥

1. *satvaparigrahaḥ*, B.
2. B om. *mu*.
3. *dvayakarmavat*, B; *gñis-dag ni ñi-ma bzhin*, T; C as in text.
4. The syllable *dhi* is uncertain in B; *gzhan-gyi dbaṅ-gyis*, T. C omits the hemistich.
5. B om. *vṛ*.
6. B om. *rma*.

अस्य खलु सूत्रस्थानीयस्य श्लोकस्य यथाक्रमं परिशिष्टेन ग्रन्थेन विस्तरविभागनिर्देशो वेदितव्यः ।

शक्रप्रतिभासत्वादिति ।

विशुद्धवैडूर्यमयं यथेदं स्यान्महीतलम् ।
स्वच्छत्वात्तत्र दृश्येत देवेन्द्रः साप्सरोगणः ॥ १४ ॥
प्रासादो वैजयन्तश्च तदन्ये च दिवौकसः ।
तद्विमानानि चित्राणि ताश्च दिव्या विभूतयः ॥ १५ ॥
अथ नारीनरगणा महीतलनिवासिनः ।
प्रतिभासं तमालोक्य प्रणिधिं कुर्युरीदृशम् ॥ १६ ॥
अद्यैव न चिरादेवं[1] भवेमस्त्रिदशेश्वराः ।
कुशलं च समादाय वर्तेरंस्तदवाप्तये ॥ १७ ॥
प्रतिभासोऽयमित्येवमविज्ञायापि ते भुवः[2] ।
च्युत्वा दि[3]व्युपपद्येरंस्तेन शुक्लेन कर्मणा ॥ १८ ॥
प्रतिभासः स चात्यन्तमविकल्पो नि(47*a*)रीहकः ।
एवं च महतार्थेन भुवि स्यात्प्रत्युपस्थितः ॥ १९ ॥
तथा श्रद्धादिविमले[4] श्रद्धादिगुणभाविते ।
सत्त्वाः पश्यन्ति संबुद्धं प्रतिभासं[5] स्वचेतसि ॥ २० ॥
लक्षणव्यञ्जनोपेतं[6] विचित्रेर्यापथक्रियम् ।
चङ्क्रम्यमाणं तिष्ठन्तं निषण्णं शयनस्थितम् ॥ २१ ॥

1. Reconstruction uncertain; the first three syllables are illegible in B, and the fourth uncertain but not like *na*; *deṅ kyan riṅ-na mi-thogs-par*, T.
2. Pāda *b* is much rubbed in B, but the text seems certain.
3. B om. *di*.
4. B is not clear and may read *śravādivimale*; T as in text.
5. B om. anusvāra.
6. B om. anusvāra.

तै॰ भाषमाणं शिवं धर्मं तूष्णींभूतं[1] समाहितम् ।
चित्राणि प्रातिहार्याणि दर्शयन्तं महाद्युतिम् ॥ २२ ॥
तं च दृष्ट्वाभियुज्यन्ते बुद्धत्वाय स्पृहान्विताः ।
तद्धेतुं च समादाय प्राप्नुवन्तीप्सितं पदम् ॥ २३ ॥
प्रतिभासः स चात्यन्तमविकल्पो निरीहकः ।
एवं च महतार्थेन लोकेषु प्रत्युपस्थितः ॥ २४ ॥
स्वचित्तप्रतिभासोऽयमिति नैवं पृथग्जनाः ।
जानन्त्यथ च तत्तेषामवन्ध्यं बिम्बदर्शनम् ॥ २५ ॥
तद्धि दर्शनमागम्य क्रमादस्मिन्नये स्थिताः ।
सद्धर्मकायं[2] मध्यस्थं पश्यन्ति ज्ञानच[3]क्षुषा ॥ २६ ॥
भूर्यद्वत्स्यात् समन्तव्यपगतविषमस्थानान्तरमला
वैडूर्यस्पष्टशुभ्रा विमलमणिगुणा श्रीमत्समतला ।
शुद्धत्वात्तत्र बिम्बं सुरपतिभवनं माहेन्द्रमरुता-
मुत्पद्येत क्रमेण क्षितिगुणविगमादस्तं पुनरियात् ॥२७॥
तद्भावायोपवासव्रतनियमतया दानाद्यभिमुखाः
पुष्पादीनि क्षिपेयुः प्रणिहितमनसो नारीनरगणाः ।
वैडूर्यस्वच्छभूते मनसि मुनिपतिच्छायाधिगमने
चित्राण्युत्पादयन्ति प्रमुदितमनसस्तद्वज्जिनसुताः ॥२८॥
यथैव वैडूर्यमहीतले शुचौ
सुरेन्द्रकायप्रतिबिम्बसंभवः ।
तथा ज(47*b*)गच्चित्तमहीतले शुचौ
मुनीन्द्रकायप्रतिबिम्बसंभवः ॥ २९ ॥

1. *tūṣṇībhūtaṁ*, B.
2. °*kāya*, B.
3. B om. *ca*.

बिम्बोदयव्ययमनाविलताविलस्व-
चित्तप्रवर्तनवशाज्जगति प्रवृत्तम् ।
लोकेषु यद्वदवभासमुपैति बिम्बं
तद्वन्न तत्सदिति नासदिति[1] प्रपश्येत् ॥ ३० ॥

देवदुन्दुभिवदिति ।

यथैव दिवि देवानां पूर्वशुक्लानुभावतः ।
यत्नस्थानमनोरूपविकल्परहिता सती ॥ ३१ ॥
अनित्यदुःखनैरात्म्यशान्तशब्दैः प्रमादिनः ।
चोदयत्यमरान् सर्वानसकृद्देवदुन्दुभिः ॥ ३२ ॥
व्याप्य बुद्धस्वरणैवं विभुर्जगदशेषतः ।
धर्मं दिशति भव्येभ्यो यत्नादिरहितोऽपि सन् ॥ ३३ ॥
देवानां दिवि दिव्यदुन्दुभिरवो यद्वत् स्वकर्मोद्भवो
धर्मोदाहरणं मुनेरपि तथा लोके स्वकर्मोद्भवम् ।
यत्नस्थानशरीरचित्तरहितः शब्दः [2]स शान्त्यावहो
यद्वत् तद्वदृते चतुष्टयमयं धर्मः स शान्त्यावहः ॥ ३४ ॥
संग्रामक्लेशवृत्तावसुरबलजय[3]क्रीडाप्रणुदनं
दुन्दुभ्याः शब्दहेतुप्रभवमभयदं यद्वत् सुरपुरे ।
सत्त्वेषु क्लेशदुःखप्रमथनशमनं मार्गोत्तमविधौ
ध्यानारूप्यादिहेतुप्रभवमपि तथा लोके निगदितम् ॥ ३५ ॥

कस्मादिह धर्मदुन्दुभिरेवाधिकृता न तदन्ये दिव्यास्तूर्यप्रकाराः । तेऽपि हि दिवौकसां पूर्वकृत[4]कुशलकर्मवशादघट्टिता एव दिव्यश्रवणमनोहरशब्दमनुरुवन्ति ।

1. *tadvanna tatvād iti nāsati prapaśyet*, B (one syllable short); I reconstruct the text from T's *de-bzhin yod daṅ zhig ces de mi-lta*, though it is an incomplete rendering of the Sanskrit.
2. B om. *ya*.
3. B om. *jaya* and leaves a gap; *rgyal*, T.
4. *pūrvakṛtaṁ*, B.

तैस्तथागतघोषस्य चतुःप्रकारगुणवैधर्म्यात् । तत्पु(48*a*)नः कतमत् । तद्यथा प्रादेशिकत्वमहितत्वमसुखत्वमनैर्याणिकत्वमिति । धर्मदुन्दुभ्याः पुनरप्रादेशिकत्वमशेषप्रमत्तदेवगणसंचोदनतया[1] च तत्कालानतिक्रमणतया च परिदीपितम् । हितत्वमसुरादिपरचक्रोपद्रवभयपरित्राणतया चाप्रमादसंनियोजनतया च । सुखत्वमसत्कामरतिसुखविवेचनतया च धर्मारामरतिसुखोपसंहरणतया च । नैर्याणिकत्वमनित्यदुःखशून्यानात्मशब्दोच्चारणतया च सर्वोपद्रवोपायासोपशान्तिकरणतया च परिदीपितम् । एभिः समासतश्चतुर्भिराकारैर्धर्मदुन्दुभिसाधर्म्येण बुद्धस्वर[2]-मण्डलं विशिष्यत इति । बुद्धस्वरमण्डलविशेषणश्लोकः ।

सार्वजन्यो हितसुखः प्रातिहार्यत्रयान्वितः ।
मुनेर्घोषो यतो दिव्यतूर्येभ्योऽतो (50*a*) विशिष्यते ॥ ३६॥

एषां खलु चतुर्णामाकाराणां यथासंख्यमेव चतुर्भिः श्लोकैः समासनिर्देशो वेदितव्यः ।

शब्दा महान्तो दिवि दुन्दुभीनां
क्षितिस्थितेषु श्रवणं न यान्ति ।
संसारपातालगतेषु लोके
संबुद्धतूर्यस्य तु याति[3] शब्दः ॥ ३७ ॥
बह्व्योऽमराणां दिवि तूर्यकोट्यो
नदन्ति कामज्वलनाभिवृद्धौ ।
एकस्तु घोषः करुणात्मकानां
दुःखाग्निहेतुप्रशमप्रवृत्तः ॥ ३८ ॥
शुभा मनोज्ञा दिवि तूर्यनिस्वना
भवन्ति चित्तोद्धतिवृद्धि[4]हेतवः ।

1. B om. *ta*, but *bskul-ba-ñid*, T.
2. B repeats *svara*.
3. e.c.; *saṁbuddhabhūmer upayāti*, B, which is poor sense; *saṅs-rgyas rṅa sgra . . ḥgro*, T, which supports the text. C omits verses 36-40. Note that *tu* appears in 38*c* and 39*c*.
4. °*vṛtti*°, B; *ḥphel-bar gyur-paḥi*, T.

तथागतानां तु रुतं महात्मना[1]
समाधिचित्तार्पणभावचाचकम् ॥३९॥
समासतो यत्सुखकारणं दिवि
क्षितावनन्तास्व( 50b )पि लोकधातुषु[2] ।
अशेषलोकस्फरणावभासनं
प्रघोषमा[3]गम्य तदप्युदाहृतम् ॥४०॥

कायविकुर्वितेन दशदिगशेषलोकधातुस्फरणमृद्धिप्रातिहार्यमिति सूचितम् । चेतःपर्यायज्ञानेन तत्पर्यापिन्नं सर्वसत्त्वचित्तचरितगहनावभासनमादेशनाप्रातिहार्यम् । वाग्घोषोदाहरणेन नैर्याणिकीं[4] प्रतिपदमारभ्य तदववादानुशासनमनुशास्ति प्रातिहार्यम् । इत्येवमव्याहतगतेराकाशधातुवदपरिच्छिन्नवर्तिनोऽपि बुद्धस्वरमण्डलस्य यन्न सर्वत्र सर्वघोषो[5]पलब्धिः प्रज्ञायते न तत्र बुद्धस्वरमण्डलस्यापराध इति । प्रत्यायनार्थमतत्प्रहिताना[6]मात्मापराधे श्लोकः[7] ।

यथा सूक्ष्मान् शब्दाननुभवति न श्रोत्रविकलो
न दिव्यश्रोत्रेऽपि श्रवणपथमायान्ति निखिलम् ।
तथा धर्मः सूक्ष्मः परमनिपुणज्ञानविषयः
प्रयात्येकेषां तु श्रवणपथम[8]विलष्टमनसाम् ॥४१॥

मेघवदिति ।

प्रावृट्काले[9] यथा मेघः पृथिव्यामभिवर्षति ।
वारिस्कन्धं निराभोगो निमित्तं सस्यसंपदः ॥४२॥

1. *thugs-rjeḥi bdag-ñid* (*kṛpātmanām*), T.
2. Note *dhātu* feminine as in Pali.
3. *praghoṣa* is a rare word; T's *dbyaṅs-ñid* suggests *ghoṣatvam.*
4. *nairyāṇikī*, B.
5. B om. *ṣo.*
6. *atatprahināṃ*, B; *de ma-gtogs-pa-rnams-kyi*, T.
7. *ñes-pa-las brtsams-te* (*aparādham ārabhya*), T.
8. *sramaṇapatham*, B; *rna lam-du*, T.
9. *prāviṭkāle*, B.

करुणाम्बुदतस्तद्वत्[1] सद्धर्मसलिलं जिनः ।
जगत्कुशलसस्येषु निर्विकल्पं प्रवर्षति ॥४३॥

लोके यथा कुशलकर्मपथप्रवृत्ते
वर्षन्ति वायुजनितं सलिलं पयोदाः ।
तद्वत् कृपानिलजगत्कुशलाभिवृद्धेः[2]
सद्धर्मवर्षमभिवर्षति बुद्धमेघः[3] ॥४४॥

भवेषु संवित्करुणावभृत्कः[4]
क्षराक्षरासङ्गनभस्तलस्थः ।
समाधिधारण्यमला (51*a*) म्बुगर्भो
मुनीन्द्रमेघः शुभसस्यहेतुः ॥४५॥

भाजनविमात्रतायाम् ।

शीतं स्वादु प्रसन्नं मृदु लघु च पयस्तत्पयोदाद्विमुक्तं
क्षारादिस्थानयोगादतिबहुरसतामेति यद्वत् पृथिव्याम् ।
आर्याष्टाङ्गाम्बुवर्षं सुविपुलकरुणामेघगर्भाद्विमुक्तं
सन्तानस्थानभेदाद्बहुविधरसतामेति तद्वत् प्रजासु ॥४६॥

निरपेक्षप्रवृत्तौ ।

यानाग्रेऽभिप्रसन्नानां मध्यानां प्रतिघातिनाम् ।
मनुष्यचातकप्रेतसदृशा राशयस्त्रयः ॥४७॥

ग्रीष्मान्तेऽम्बुधरेष्वसत्सु मनुजा व्योम्न्यप्रचाराः खगा
वर्षास्वप्यतिवर्षणप्रपतना[5]त्प्रेताः क्षितौ[6] दुःखिताः ।

1. *karumveditas tatsad°*, B (two syllables short); *de-bzhin thugs-rjeḥi sprin-las*, T.

2. B is not clear and should possibly be read as *°vṛddhau*. T's *mnon ḥphel-phyir* can stand for *°vṛddheḥ* or *°vṛddhyai*.

3. *saṅs-rgyas-kyi sprin-las* (*Buddhameghāt*), T.

4. *°bhritkaḥ*, B.

5. *°pradahanāt* (or *°pradadanāt*), B, which cannot be satisfactorily explained; *ḥbab-pas-na*, T.

6. *khitau*, B.

अप्रादुर्भवनोदयेऽपि करुणामेघाभ्रधर्माम्भसो
धर्माकाङ्क्षिणि धर्मताप्रतिहते लोके च सैवोपमा ॥ ४८ ॥
स्थूलैर्बिन्दुनिपातनैरशनिभिर्वज्राग्निसंपातनैः
सूक्ष्मप्राणकशैलदेशगमिका[1]न्नापेक्षते तोयदः ।
सूक्ष्मौदारिकयुक्त्युपायविधिभिः प्रज्ञाकृपाम्भोधर-
स्तद्वत् क्लेशगतान्दृ[2]ष्ट्यनुशयान्नापेक्षते सर्वथा ॥ ४९ ॥

दुःखाग्निप्रशमने ।

संसारोऽनवराग्रजातिमरणस्तत्संसृतौ पञ्चधा
मार्गः पञ्चविधे च वर्त्मनि सुखं नोच्चारसौगन्ध्यवत् ।
तद्दुःखं ध्रुवमग्निशस्त्रशिशिरक्षारादिसंस्पर्शजं
तच्छान्त्यै च सृजन् कृपाजलधरः[3] सद्धर्मवर्षं महत् ॥५०॥
देवेषु च्युतिदुःखमित्यवगमात् पर्येष्टिदुःखं नृषु[4]
प्राज्ञा नाभिलषन्ति (51*b*) देवमनुजेष्वैश्वर्यमप्युत्तमम् ।
प्रज्ञायाश्च तथागतप्रवचनश्रद्धानुमान्यादिदं
दुःखं हेतुरयं निरोध इति च ज्ञानेन संप्रेक्षणात् ॥ ५१ ॥

व्याधिर्ज्ञेयो[5] व्याधिहेतुः प्रहेयः
स्वास्थ्यं प्राप्यं भेषजं सेव्यमेवम् ।
दुःखं हेतुस्तन्निरोधोऽथ मार्गो
ज्ञेयं हेयः स्पर्शितव्यो निषेव्यः[6] ॥ ५२ ॥

1. For *gamika* see *Mvy.*, 8747.
2. B om. *n*.
3. °*jaladhara*, B; *sprin-las* (*jaladharāt*), T.
4. Cf. *Buddhac.*, xiv, 45-46, in my translation.
5. *vyādhi jñeyo*, B.
6. e.c.; *heṣevyaḥ*, B; T gives no indication of the preposition before *ṣevyaḥ*.

महाब्रह्मवदिति ।

सर्वत्र देवभवने[1] ब्राह्म्यादविचलन् पदात् ।
प्रतिभासं यथा ब्रह्मा दर्शयत्यप्रयत्नतः ॥ ५३ ॥
तद्वन्मुनिरनाभोगान्निर्माणैः[2] सर्वधातुषु ।
धर्मकायादविचलन् भव्यानामेति दर्शनम् ॥ ५४ ॥
यद्वद् ब्रह्मा विमानान्न चलति सततं कामधातुप्रविष्टं
देवाः पश्यन्ति चैनं विषयरतिहरं दर्शनं तच्च तेषाम् ।
तद्वत् सद्धर्मकायान्न चलति सुगतः सर्वलोकेषु चैनं
भव्याः पश्यन्ति शश्वत्सकलमलहरं दर्शनं तच्च तेषाम् ॥५५॥

स्वस्यैव पूर्वप्रणिधानयोगान्
मरुद्गणानां च शुभानुभावात् ।
ब्रह्मा यथा भासमुपैत्ययत्नान्
निर्माणकायेन तथा स्वयंभूः ॥ ५६ ॥

अनाभासगमने ।

च्युतिं गर्भाक्रान्तिं जननपितृवेश्मप्रविशनं
रतिक्रीडारण्यप्रविचरणमारप्रमथनम् ।
महाबोधिप्राप्तिं प्रशमपुरमार्गप्रणयनं
निदर्श्याधन्यानां[3] नयनपथमभ्येति न मुनिः ॥ ५७ ॥

सूर्यवदिति ।

सूर्ये यथा तपति पद्मगणप्रबुद्धि-
(xxva) रेकत्र कालसमये कुमुदप्रसुप्तिः ।

1. B om. *bhava*; *lha-yi gnas*, T.

2. *agabhogān*, B; *ḥbad-med-par*, T.

3. *skal-med* (*abhavyānām*), T; C's '*sattvas* of mean fortune' supports the text.

बुद्धिप्रसुप्तिगुणदोषविधावक[1]ल्पः
सूर्योऽम्बुजेष्वथ च तद्वदिहार्यसूर्यः ॥ ५८ ॥

द्विविधः सत्त्वधातुरविनेयो विनेयश्च । तत्र यो विनेयस्तमधिकृ(52a)त्य पद्मोपमता स्वच्छजलभाजनोपमता च[2] ।

निर्विकल्पो यथादित्यः कमलानि स्वरश्मिभिः ।
बोधयत्येकमुक्ताभिः[3] पाचयत्यपराण्यपि ॥ ५९ ॥
सद्धर्मकिरणैरेवं तथागतदिवाकरः ।
विनेयजनपद्मेषु निर्विकल्पः प्रवर्तते ॥ ६० ॥
धर्मरूपश[4]रीराभ्यां बोधिमण्डाम्बरोदितः ।
जगत्स्फरति सर्वज्ञदिनकृज्ज्ञानरश्मिभिः ॥ ६१ ॥
यतः शुचिनि सर्वत्र विनेयसलिलाशये ।
अमेयसुगतादित्यप्रतिबिम्बोदयः सकृत् ॥ ६२ ॥

एवमवि[5]कल्पत्वेऽपि सति बुद्धानां त्रिविधे सत्त्वराशौ[6] दर्शनादेशनाप्रवृत्ति[7]-क्रममधिकृत्य शैलोपमता[8] ।

सदा सर्वत्र विसृते धर्मधातुनभस्तले ।
बुद्धसूर्ये विनेयाद्रितन्निपातो यथार्हतः ॥ ६३ ॥

1. B om. *ka*.

2. B omits a good deal here, reading *vineyas tam adhikṛtya padmatā / acchajalabhājanopamatā* followed by an unintelligible hieroglyphic. The text follows A and T.

3. The use of *raśmi* in the feminine is exceptional, but for the phrase cf. *Kāś. P.*, 35, p. 63, and *Mahāyānasūtrālaṁkāra*, ix, 33.

4. B om. *dharmarūpaśa*, leaving a gap.

5. B om. *vi*.

6. °*satvadhātau*°, B, against A and T.

7. °*pravṛtta*°, B.

8. *ñi-ma dan ḥdra-ba-ñid* (*sūryopamatā*), T.

उदित इह[1] समन्ताल्लोकमाभास्य यद्वत्
प्रततदशशतांशुः सप्तसप्तिः क्रमेण ।
प्रतपति[2] वरमध्यन्यूनशैलेषु तद्वत्
प्रतपति जिनसूर्यः सत्त्वराशौ क्रमेण ॥ ६४ ॥

प्रभामण्डलविशेषणे ।

सर्वक्षेत्रनभस्तलस्फरणता भानोर्न संविद्यते
नाप्यज्ञानतमोऽन्धकारगहनज्ञेयार्थसंदर्शनम् ।
नानावर्णविकीर्णरश्मिविसरैरेकैकरोमोद्भवै-
र्भासन्ते करुणात्मका जगति तु ज्ञेयार्थसंदर्शकाः ॥६५॥
बुद्धानां नगरप्रवेशसमये चक्षुर्विहीना जनाः
पश्यन्त्यर्थमनर्थजालविगमं विन्दन्ति तद्दर्शनात् ।
मोहान्धाश्च भवार्णवान्तरगता दृष्ट्यन्धकारावृता
बुद्धार्कप्रभयावभासितधियः पश्यन्त्यदृष्टं[3] पदम् ॥ ६६ ॥

चिन्तामणिवदिति ।

(52*b*) युगपद्गोचरस्थानां सर्वाभिप्रायपूरणम् ।
कुरुते निर्विकल्पोऽपि पृथक् चिन्तामणिर्यथा ॥ ६७ ॥
बुद्धचिन्तामणिं तद्व[4]त् समेत्य[5] पृथगाशयाः ।
शृण्वन्ति धर्मतां चित्रां न कल्पयति तांश्च सः ॥ ६८ ॥
यथाविकल्पं[6] मणिरत्नमीप्सितं
धनं परेभ्यो विसृजत्ययत्नतः ।

1. T read *iva* (*bzhin*) for *iha*.
2. *ḥbab* (*prapatati*), T, here and in the next line, agreeing with *nipāto* in verse 63.
3. *paśyanti dṛṣṭaṁ*, B.
4. A om *dva*.
5. *bsten-nas* (*saṁśritya*?), T.
6. So A; *yathā'vilpaṁ*, B (one syllable short); *ji-ltar yid-bzhin nor-bu* (*yathā cintāmaṇi°*), T.

तथा मुनिर्यत्नमृते यथार्हतः
परार्थमातिष्ठति नित्यमा भवात् ॥६९॥

दुर्लभप्राप्तभावास्तथागता इति ।

इह शुभमणिप्राप्तिर्यद्वज्जगत्यतिदुर्लभा
जलनिधिगतं पातालस्थं यतः स्पृहयन्ति तम् ।
न सुलभमिति ज्ञेयं तद्व[1]ज्जगत्यतिदुर्भगे
मनसि विविधक्लेशग्रस्ते तथागतदर्शनम् ॥ ७० ॥

प्रतिश्रुत्काशब्दवदिति ।

प्रतिश्रुत्कारुतं यद्वत् परविज्ञप्तिसंभवम् ।
निर्विकल्पमनाभोगं नाध्यात्मं न बहिः स्थितम् ॥ ७१ ॥
तथागतरुतं तद्वत् परविज्ञप्तिसंभवम् ।
निर्विकल्पमनाभोगं नाध्यात्मं न बहिः स्थितम् ॥ ७२ ॥

आकाशवदिति ।

निष्किंचने निराभासे निरालम्बे निराश्रये ।
चक्षुष्पथव्यतिक्रान्तेऽप्यरूपिण्यनिदर्शने ॥ ७३ ॥
यथा निम्नोन्नतं व्योम्नि दृश्यते न च तत्तथा ।
बुद्धेष्वपि तथा सर्वं दृश्यते न च तत्तथा ॥ ७४ ॥

पृथिवीव[2]दिति ।

सर्वे महीरुहा यद्वदविकल्पां वसुंधराम् ।
निश्रित्य[3] वृद्धिं वैरूढिं वैपुल्यमुपयान्ति च ॥ ७५ ॥
संबुद्धपृथिवीमेवमविकल्पामशेषतः ।
जगत्कुशलमूलानि वृद्धिमाश्रित्य यान्ति हि ॥७६॥

1. B om. *dva*.
2. B om. *va*.
3. *nisṛtya*, B.

उदाहरणानां पिण्डार्थः ।

न प्रयत्नमृते[1] कंश्चिद्‌दृष्टः कुर्वन् क्रि(xxv*b*)यामतः ।
विनेयसंशयच्छित्त्यै नवधोक्तं निदर्शनम् ॥ ७७ ॥
सूत्रस्य (53*a*) तस्य नाम्नैव दीपितं तत्प्रयोजनम्[2] ।
यत्रैते नव दृष्टान्ता विस्तरेण प्रकाशिताः ॥ ७८ ॥
एतच्छ्रुतमयोदारज्ञानालोकाद्यलंकृताः[3] ।
धीमन्तोऽवतरन्त्याशु सकलं बुद्धगोचरम् ॥ ७९ ॥
इत्यर्थं शक्रवैडूर्यप्रतिविम्बाद्युदाहृतिः ।
नवधोदाहृता तस्मिन्तत्पिण्डार्थोऽवधार्यते ॥ ८० ॥
दर्शनादेशना[4] व्याप्तिर्विकृतिर्ज्ञाननिःसृतिः ।
मनोवाक्कायगुह्यानि प्राप्तिश्च करुणात्मनाम् ॥ ८१ ॥
सर्वाभोगपरिस्पन्दप्रशान्ता निर्विकल्पिकाः ।
धियो विमलवैडूर्यशक्रबिम्बोदयादिवत् ॥ ८२ ॥
प्रतिज्ञाभोगशान्तत्वं हेतुर्धीनिर्विकल्पता ।
दृष्टान्तः शक्रबिम्वादिः प्रकृतार्थसुसिद्धये ॥ ८३ ॥
अयं च प्रकृतोऽत्रार्थो नवधा दर्शनादिकम् ।
जन्मान्तर्धिमृते[5] शास्तुरनाभोगात् प्रवर्तते ॥ ८४ ॥

1. B is only partially legible; *prayatnahm ṛte*, A.

2. O explains this by saying that the instances are taken from the *Sarvabuddhaviṣayāvatārajñānālokālaṁkārasūtra*; cf. the wording of verse 79.

3. So A apparently, except that the character *dya* is uncertain; *ādi* does not appear in T. B, mainly illegible, seems to have *dya*. The alternative is to read °*ālokāt svalaṁ*°.

4. A and B both read *darśanā*°, where one would expect *darśanaṁ deśanā*, but cf. the introductory sentence to verse 63 above. It is not clear if we are to divide *darśanā* and *deśanā* or to understand *ādesanā*.

5. C divides *janmāntardhim* into *janmānta* and *ṛddhi*, T into *janma* and *antardhi*.

एतमेवार्थमधि[1]कृत्योदाहरणसंग्रहे चत्वारः श्लोकाः ।

यः शक्रवद्दुन्दुभिवत् पयोदवद्
ब्रह्मार्कचिन्तामणिराजरत्नवत् ।
प्रतिश्रुतिव्योममहीवदा भवात्
परार्थकृद्यत्नमृते स योगवित् ॥ ८५ ॥

सुरेन्द्ररत्नप्रतिभासदर्शनः
सुदेशिको दुन्दुभिवद्विभो रुतम् ।
विभुर्महाज्ञानकृपाभ्रमण्डलः
स्फरत्यनन्तं जगदा भवाग्रतः ॥ ८६ ॥

अनास्रवाद्ब्रह्मवदच्युतः[2] पदा-
दनेकधा दर्शनमेति निर्मितैः ।
सदार्कवज्ज्ञानविनिःसृतद्युति-
र्विशुद्धचिन्तामणिरत्नमानसः ॥ ८७ ॥

प्रतिरव इव घोषोऽनक्षरोक्तो जिनानां
गगनमिव शरीरं व्याप्यरूपि ध्रुवं च ।
क्षितिरिव निखिलानां शुक्लधर्मौषधीनां[3]
जगत इह समन्तादास्प(53*b*)दं बुद्धभूमिः ॥ ८८ ॥

कथं पुनरनेनोदाहरणनिर्देशेन सततमनुत्पन्ना अनिरुद्धाश्च[4] बुद्धा भगवन्त उत्पद्यमाना निरुध्यमानाश्च संदृश्यन्ते[5] सर्वजगति चैषामनाभोगेन बुद्धकार्यप्रतिप्रश्रब्धिरिति परिदीपितम् ।

शुभं वैडूर्यवच्चित्ते बुद्धदर्शनहेतुकम् ।
तद्विशुद्धिरसंहार्यश्रद्धेन्द्रियविरूढिता ॥ ८९ ॥

1. B om. *m adhi*.
2. B om. *d acyutaḥ* and leaves a gap.
3. *śukladharmam auṣadhīnām*, B.
4. B om. *a* in *aniruddhāś*.
5. B om. *śyante*,

शुभोदयव्ययाद्बुद्धप्रतिबिम्बोदयव्ययः ।
मुनिर्नोदेति न व्येति शक्रवद्धर्मकायतः ॥ ९० ॥
अयत्नात् कृत्यमित्येवं[1] दर्शनादि प्रवर्तते ।
धर्मकायादनुत्पादानिरोधादा[2] भवस्थितेः ॥ ९१ ॥
अयमेषां समासार्थ औपम्यानां क्रमः पुनः ।
पूर्वकस्योत्तरेणोक्तो[3] वैधर्म्यपरिहारतः ॥ ९२ ॥
बुद्धत्वं प्रतिबिम्बाभं तद्वन्न च न[4] घोषवत् ।
देवदुन्दुभिवत् तद्वन्न च नो सर्वथार्थकृत्[5] ॥ ९३ ॥
महामेघोपमं तद्वन्न च नो सार्थबीजवत्[6] ।
महाब्रह्मोपमं तद्वन्न च नात्यन्तपाचकम् ॥ ९४ ॥
सूर्यमण्डलवत् तद्वन्न नात्यन्त[7]तमोऽपहम् ।
[8]चिन्तामणिनिभं तद्वन्न च नो दुर्लभोदयम् ॥ ९५ ॥
प्रतिश्रुत्कोपमं तद्वन्न च प्रत्यय[9]संभवम् ।
आकाशसदृशं तद्वन्न च शुक्लास्पदं च तत् ॥ ९६ ॥
पृथिवीमण्डलप्रख्यं तत्प्रतिष्ठाश्रयत्वतः ।
लौक्यलोकोत्तराशेषजगत्कुशलसंपदम्[10] ॥ ९७ ॥

1. *prayatnāt kṛtyam ity eva*, B.
2. B om. *da*.
3. O translates as if reading *brjod-pa min* for *yin* of the Narthang edition, i.e. *uttare nokto*.
4. *tadvane va na*, B.
5. *sarvathāsakṛt*, B.
6. e.c.; *na cantāmarthabījavat*, B; *na ca nārthabījavat*, A (one syllable short); *don-med-pahi sa-bon spoṅ min* (*nānarthabījavat*), T; C's indications agree with the text.
7. *na cātyanta*°, B.
8. B inserts *tam* at beginning.
9. *cāpratyaya*°, A.
10. *saṁpada*, n., is extremely rare; *PW* gives only one instance, from the *Kathāsaritsāgara*.

बुद्धानां बोधिमागम्य लोकोत्तरपथोदयात् ।
शुक्लकर्म[1]पथध्यानाप्रमाणारूप्यसंभव इति ॥ ९८ ॥

इति रत्नगोत्रविभागे महायानोत्तरतन्त्रशास्त्रे तथागतकृत्यक्रियाधिकारश्चतुर्थः (XXVI*a*)परिच्छेदः श्लोकार्थसंग्रहव्याख्यानतः समाप्तः ॥४॥

---

1. *śukladharma*°, B.

## V

अतः परमेष्वेव यथापरिकी(54*a*)र्तितेषु स्थानेष्वधिमुक्तानामधिमुक्त्यनुशंसे षट् श्लोकाः

बुद्धधातुर्बुद्धबोधिर्बुद्धधर्मा बुद्धकृत्यम् ।
गोचरोऽयं नायकानां शुद्धस[1]त्त्वैरप्यचिन्त्यः ॥१॥

इह जिनविषयेऽधिमुक्तबुद्धि-[2]
र्गुणगणभाजनतामुपैति धीमान् ।
अभिभवति स सर्वसत्त्वपुण्य-
प्रसवमचिन्त्यगुणाभिलाषयोगात् ॥२॥

यो दद्यान्मणिसंस्कृतानि कनकक्षेत्राणि बोध्यर्थिको
बुद्धक्षेत्ररजःसमान्यहरहो धर्मेश्वरेभ्यः सदा ।
यश्चान्यः शृणुयादितः पदमपि श्रुत्वाधिमुच्येदयं
तस्माद्दानमयाच्छुभाद्बहुतरं पुण्यं समासादयेत् ॥३॥

यः शीलं तनुवाङ्मनोभिरमलं रक्षेदनाभोगव-
द्धीमान् बोधिमनुत्तरामभिलषन् कल्पाननेकानपि ।
यश्चान्यः शृणुयादितः पदमपि श्रुत्वाधिमुच्येदयं
तस्माच्छीलमयाच्छुभाद्बहुतरं पुण्यं समासादयेत् ॥४॥

ध्यायेद्ध्यानमपीह यस्त्रिभुवनक्लेशाग्निनिर्वापकं
दिव्यब्रह्मविहारपारमिगतः संबोध्युपायाच्युतः ।
यश्चान्यः शृणुयादितः पदमपि श्रुत्वाधिमुच्येदयं
तस्माद्ध्यानमयाच्छुभाद्बहुतरं पुण्यं समासादयेत् ॥५॥

1. B om. *sa*. The metre of this verse is not given in the treatises on prosody.

2. T's *mos-pa sans-rgyas* suggests *adhimuktibuddho*, and B originally read *adhimukti* and has the final *i* erased.

दानं भोगानावहत्येव[1] यस्मा-
च्छीलं स्वर्गं भावना क्लेशहानिम् ।
प्रज्ञा क्लेशज्ञेयसर्वप्रहाणं
सातः श्रेष्ठा हेतुरस्याः श्रवोऽयम् ॥६॥

एषां श्लोकानां पिण्डार्थो नवभिः श्लोकैर्वेदितव्यः ।

आश्रये तत्परावृत्तौ[2] तद्गुणेष्वर्थसाधने ।
चतुर्विधे जिनज्ञानविषयेऽस्मिन् यथोदिते ॥७॥
धीमानस्तित्वशक्तत्वगुणवत्त्वा[3]धिमुक्तितः ।
तथागतपदप्राप्तिभव्यतामाशु गच्छति ॥८॥
अस्त्यसौ विषयोऽचिन्त्यः शक्यः प्राप्तुं स मादृशैः ।
प्राप्त एवंगुणश्चासाविति श्रद्धाधिमुक्तितः ॥९॥
छन्दवीर्यस्मृतिध्यानप्रज्ञादिगुणभाजनम् ।
बोधिचित्तं भवत्यस्य सततं प्रत्युपस्थितम् ॥१०॥
तच्चित्त[4]प्रत्युपस्था (54*b*) नादविवर्त्यो जिनात्मजः ।
पुण्यपारमिता[5]पूरिपरिशुद्धिं निगच्छति ॥११॥
पुण्यं पारमिताः पञ्च त्रेधा तदविकल्पनात् ।
तत्पूरिः परिशुद्धिस्तु तद्विपक्षप्रहाणतः ॥१२॥
दानं दानमयं पुण्यं शीलं शीलमयं स्मृतम् ।
द्वे भावनामयं क्षान्तिध्याने वीर्यं तु सर्वगम् ॥१३॥

1. *āmahaty*, B; A om. *nā*.
2. The original reading was probably °*parīvṛttau*.
3. °*guṇadatvā*°, B.
4. *tacitta*°, B.
5. *punā*(or *nya*)*pāramitā*, B.

त्रिमण्डलविकल्पो[1] यस्तज्ज्ञेयावरणं मतम् ।
मात्सर्यादिविपक्षो यस्तत् क्लेशावरणं मतम् ॥१४॥
एतत्प्रहाणहेतुश्च नान्यः प्रज्ञाभृते ततः ।
श्रेष्ठा प्रज्ञा श्रुतं[2] चास्य मूलं तस्माच्छ्रुतं परम् ॥१५॥

[3]इतीदमाप्तागमयुक्तिसंश्रया-
दुदाहृतं केवलमात्मशुद्ध[4]ये ।
धियाधिमुक्त्या कुशलोपसंपदा
समन्विता ये तदनुग्रहाय च ॥१६॥
प्रदीपविद्युन्मणिचन्द्रभास्करान्
प्रतीत्य पश्यन्ति यथा सचक्षुषः ।
महार्थधर्मप्रतिभा[5]प्रभाकरं
मुनिं प्रतीत्येदमुदाहृतं तथा ॥१७॥
यदर्थवद्धर्मपदोपसंहितं[6]
त्रिधातुसंक्लेशनि[7]बर्हणं वचः ।
भवेच्च यच्छान्त्यनुशंसदर्शकं
तदुक्तमार्षं विपरीतमन्यथा ॥१८॥
यत्स्यादविक्षिप्तमनोभिरुक्तं
शास्तारमेकं जिनमुद्दिशद्भिः ।

1. *rnam-rtog* (°*vikalpo*), T; but C supports the MSS.'s reading.
2. *śre prā śrutaṁ*, B (two syllables short).
3. The MSS. omit the headings to this and the following verses, which are found in T.
4. B om. *ddha*.
5. B om. *prabhā*.
6. °*saṁhṛtam*, B. Cf. *S.*; ix, 49*b*.
7. B repeats *ni*. This verse is quoted by Prajñākaramati in the *Bodhicaryāvatārapañjikā* (ed. Bibl. Ind.), p. 432, on *Bodhicaryāvatāra*, ix, 42.

मोक्षा(xxvi*b*)प्तिसंभारपथानुकूलं
मूर्ध्ना तदप्यार्षमिव प्रतीच्छेत् ॥१९॥

यस्मान्नेह जिनात् सुपण्डिततमो लोकेऽस्ति कश्चित्क्वचित्
सर्वज्ञः सकलं स वेद विधिवत्तत्त्वं परं नापरः ।
तस्माद्यत्स्वयमेव नीतमृषिणा सूत्रं विचाल्यं न तत्
सद्धर्मप्रतिबाधनं[1] हि तदपि स्यान्नीति[2]भेदान्मुनेः ॥२०॥

आर्यांश्चापवदन्ति तन्निगदितं धर्मं च गर्हन्ति यत्
सर्वः सोऽभिनिवेशदर्शनकृतः क्लेशो विमूढात्मनाम् ।
तस्मान्नाभिनिवेशदृष्टिमलिने तस्मिन्निवेश्या[3] मतिः
शुद्धं वस्त्रमुपैति रङ्गविकृतिं न स्नेहपङ्काङ्कितम् ॥२१॥

धीमान्द्यादधिमुक्तिशुक्लविरहान् मिथ्याभिमानाश्रयात्
सद्धर्मव्यसनावृतात्म[4]कतया नेयार्थतत्त्वग्रहात् ।
लोभग्रेधतया[5] च दर्शनवशाद्ध[6]र्मद्विषां सेवना-
दाराद्धर्मभृतां च हीनरुचयो धर्मान् क्षिपन्त्यर्हताम् ॥२२॥

नाग्नेर्नोग्रविषादहेर्न वधकान्नैवाशनिभ्यस्तथा
भेतव्यं विदुषामतीव तु यथा गम्भीरधर्मक्षतेः ।
कुर्युर्जीवितविप्रयोगमनलव्यालारिवज्राग्नय-
स्तद्धेतोर्न पुनर्व्रजेदतिभयामावीचिकानां गतिम् ॥२३॥

1. °*pratibodhanam*, B.

2. *syā nīti*°, B.

3. *naveśyā*, B.

4. So A; *saddharmavyavasananṛtātma*°, B; *bsgribs-paḥi bdag* (°*āvṛtātma*°), T; C read °*ānṛtātma*°.

5. *lobhāgredha*°, B; *rñed-lu* (?) *bsnom-phyir* (*lābhagrāhatayā*?), T; C ambiguous. For *gredha* cf. Pali *gedha*.

6. B ends with *vaśād dha*.

योऽभीक्ष्णं प्रतिसेव्य[1] पापसुहृदः स्याद्बुद्धदुष्टाशयो
मातापित्ररिहद्व[2]धाचरणकृत् संघाग्रभेत्ता नरः ।
स्यात्तस्यापि ततो विमुक्तिरचिरं धर्मार्थं[3] निध्यानतो
धर्मे यस्य तु मानसं प्रतिहतं तस्मै[4] विमुक्तिः कुतः ॥२४॥
रत्नानि व्यवदानधातुममलां बोधिं गुणान् कर्म च
व्याकृत्यार्थपदानि सप्त विधिवद्यत् पुण्यमाप्तं मया ।
तेनेयं जनतामितायुषमृषिं पश्येदनन्तद्युतिं
दृष्ट्वा चामलधर्मचक्षुरुदयाद्बोधिं परामाप्नुयात् ॥२५॥

एषामपि दशानां श्लोकानां पिण्डार्थस्त्रिभिः श्लोकैर्वेदितव्यः ।

यतश्च यन्निमित्तं च यथा च यदुदाहृतम् ।
यन्निष्यन्दफलं श्लोकैश्चतुर्भिः परिदीपितम् ॥२६॥
आत्मसंरक्षणोपायो[5] द्वाभ्यामेकेन च क्षतेः ।
हेतुः फलमथ द्वाभ्यां श्लोकाभ्यां परिदीपितम् ॥२७॥
संसारमण्डल[6]क्षान्तिर्बोधिप्राप्तिः समासतः ।
द्विधा धर्मार्थवादस्य फलमन्त्येन दर्शितम् ॥२८॥

इति रत्नगोत्रविभागे महायानोत्तरतन्त्रशास्त्रेऽनुशंसाधिकारो नाम पञ्चमः परिच्छेदः श्लोकार्थसंग्रहव्याख्यानतः समाप्तः ॥५॥

---

1. The only other recorded instance of *pratisev* in literature is in Sāyaṇa's Rigveda commentary, where also it retains the dental *s*; cf. *PWK*.
2. The form *arihat* is remarkable.
3. T read *dharmatā*° (*chos-ñid*).
4. A, which is far from clear on this page, seems to read *tasmād*; *de-la*, T.
5. *bdag-ñid dag-pa-yis thabs* (*ātmasaṁśodhanopāyo*?), T.
6. A is a syllable short in *a* and seems to read *hāryammaṇḍala*°; *ḥkhor-gyi dkyil-ḥkhor*, T.

# I. INDEX OF METRES

*The references are to chapters and verses.*


अनुष्टुभ् (=वितानभेद) V. 1.*

,, (=श्लोक) I. $\frac{2}{3}$(C.), 5-8, 10-12, 14-22, 24-26, 28, 30-33, 35-38, 40-62, 64, 65, 67-68, 80 83, 85-95, $\frac{87}{88}$(C.), 127 155, $\frac{118}{149}$(C.), $\frac{152}{153}$(C.), 158-167; II. 1, 2, 4-7, 10-17, 21-28, 30-37, 42-61, 63-68, 70-72; III. 2, 3, 5, 6, 8, 11-13, 17-22, 27-39; IV. 3-26, 31-33, 36, 42, 43, 47, 53, 54, 59-63, 67, 68, 71-84, 89-98; V. 7-15, 26-98.

इन्द्रवज्रा I. 1, 110, 119, 124; V. 19.

उपजाति (=इन्द्रवंशा+वंशस्थविल) I. 63; IV. 85.

,, (=इन्द्रवज्रा+उपेन्द्रवज्रा) I. 2, $\frac{18}{19}$(C.)[2], 29, 96, 97, 103, 105, 106, 112, 113, 115, 116, 119, 121, 122, 125; II. 41; III. 1, 10, 23-25; IV. 1, 37, 38, 58.

उपेन्द्रवज्रा I. 102, 108, 109; II. 39; IV. 45.

पुष्पिताग्रा II. 9; V. 2.

प्रहर्षिणी I. 66.

मालिनी II. 8; IV. 64, 88.

वंशस्थविल I. $\frac{41}{42}$(C.), 79, 99, 100, $\frac{147}{148}$(C.); II. 18-20, 38†, 40, 69, 73; III. 4; IV. 29, 39, 40, 69, 86, 87; V. 16-18

वसन्ततिलक III. 26, 30; IV. 44, 58.

शार्दूलविक्रीडित I. 4, 9, 13, 98, 101, 104, 107, 111, 114, 117, 120, 123, 126, $\frac{155}{156}$(C.); II. 3; III. 7, 9, 14-16; IV. 34, 48-51, 65, 66; V. 3-5, 20-25.

शालिनी I. 3, 27, 34, 39, 156, 157; II. 62; IV. 52; V. 6.

शिखरिणी II. 29; IV. 41, 57.

सुन्दरी I. 23.

सुवदना IV. 28, 35.

स्रग्धरा IV. 2, 46, 55.

हरिणी IV. 70.


* This particular variety of Vitāna could not be traced in the treatises on prosody.

† The second half is a Triṣṭubh scanning; the metre of *d* having been named Vidhvaṅkamālā, that of *c* may be named Upavidhvaṅkamālā after the manner of Indravajrā and Upendravajrā.

# II. INDEX OF AUTHORITIES

*Figures in bold type refer to pages and the others to lines.*


अनूनत्वापूर्णत्वनिर्देशपरिवर्त **2**, 13; **3**, 6; **12**, fn.[2]; **28**, fn.[2]; **39**, fn.[4]; **40**, fn.[10]; **41**, fn.[5]; **54**, fn.[7]; **56**, fn.[2]

(अभिधर्ममहायानसूत्र) **72**, fn.[7]

(अवतंसकसूत्र) **36**, fn.[10]

आर्यधारणीश्वरराजसूत्रनिदानपरिवर्त **3**, 16.

आर्यश्रीमालासूत्र **3**, 3; **12**, fn.[5]; **15**, fn.[1]; **19**, fn.[6]; **20**, 10; **22**, fn.[1]; **30**, fn.[5]; **33**, fn.[10]; **34**, fn.[6]; **36**, fn.[1]; **37**, fn.[4]; **45**, fn.[5]; **50**, fn.[5]; **55**, fn.[2,4]; **56**, fn.[2,8]; **59**, fn.[5]; **72**, fn.[9]; **74** fn.[2]; **76**, fn.[7,9]; **79**, fn.[6].

(काश्यपपरिवर्त) **28**, fn.[5]; **93**, fn.[1]; **108**, fn.[3]

(गगनगञ्जसूत्र) **44**, fn.[6]

(ज्ञानालोकालंकारसूत्र) **13**, fn.[3]; **36**, fn.[10]; **55**, fn.[6]; **71**, fn.[6]

तथागतगर्भसूत्र **26**, 9; **67**, fn.[1]

तथागतगुणज्ञानाचिन्त्यविषयावतारनिर्देश **3**, 9.

दृढाध्याशयपरिवर्त **2**, 7.

धारणिराजसूत्र **3**, 12.

(धारणीश्वरराजसूत्र) **22**, fn.[3]; **24**, fn.[10]; **44**, fn.[6]

प्रज्ञापारमिता **13**, 20; **39**, 15.

महापरिनिर्वाणसूत्र **56**, fn.[6]; **74**, 20.

(महायानसूत्रालंकार) **71**, fn.[1,8]; **108**, fn.[3]

रत्नदारिकासूत्र **96**, 8.

(रत्नमालासूत्र) **50**, fn.[10]; **57**, fn.[3]

रत्नसूत्र **96**, 6.

(वज्रच्छेदिकासूत्र) **84**, fn.[1]

(षडायतनसूत्र) **55**, fn.[3]

सद्धर्मपुण्डरीक **88**, 8.

सर्वबुद्धविषयावतारज्ञानालोकालंकारसूत्र **9**, 6; **111**, fn.[2]

सागरमत (परिपृच्छा) **47**, 11, 13; **48**, 4, 5, 11, 19; **49**, 2, 9

(स्थिराध्याशयपरिवर्त) **2**, fn.[3]

## III. INDEX OF TECHNICAL TERMS


अकल्प **85**, 2.

अक्षर **105**, 8.

अचला **53**, 3; **57**, 21.

अतत्त्वभाविन् **90**, 9.

अद्वय **53**, 12.

अधिगम: °धर्म **18**, 14, 16; **77**, 6. +अर्थ **1**, 6.

अधिप्रज्ञा **27**, 21.

अधिमुक्ति **27**, 16; **117**, 7; **118** 11. धर्म+**26**, 21.

अध्याशय **28**, 17; **48**, 2. °प्रतिपत्ति **50**, 17.

अध्वन् **93**, 15.

अनपरान्तकोटि **53**, 11.

अनाभोग **8**, 2, 9; **52**, 7; **98**, 7, 14.

अनावरण : °गामिन् **29**, 5.

अनास्रव **15**, 1: **54**, 2, 7; **55**, 9. °त्व **83**, 10. °धातु **32**, 14, 18; **50**, 8.

अनुद्ग्रह **90**, 1, 7.

अनुबन्ध **13**, 8.

अनुशंस **115**, 1; **117**, 15; **119**, 16.

अनुशय **13**, 2; **35**, 7; **47**, 10; **67**, 10. °वत् **13**, 9.

अन्त : अपर+**54**, 4. उच्छेद+**34**, 9. तीर्थिक+**34**, 14. पूर्व+**54**, 4. पूर्वापर+**54**, 5. शाश्वत+**34**, 19 श्रावक+**34**, 15.

अन्यतीर्थ **29**, 10.

अन्यतीर्थ्य **28**, 7.

अपरान्तकोटि: °सम **20**, 8; **54**, 13. °निष्ठ **32**, 8, 13. अन् **53**, 11.

अपरिनिर्वाणगोत्रक **28**, 1; **35**, 10.

अप्रतिघ **85**, 3.

अप्रश्रब्धि **98**, 2.

अभाव **19**, 4.

अभिज्ञा **38**, 14; **50**, 17. षड्° **20**, 16.

अभिनिर्हार **10**, 10; **57**, 6.

अभिनिवेश **8**, 19. °दर्शन **118**, 8, 9.

अभिमुखी **50**, 14; **51**, 2.

अभिसंस्कार **54**, 2.

अभिसमय **18**, 15.

अभिसंबोधि **7**, 17; **56**, 8.

अभूत **78**, 12, 13. °कल्पज **43**, 12. °ग्राह **77**, 17. °परिकल्प **49**, 12. °परिकल्पित **49**, 16.

अमुक्तज्ञ **42**, 3.

अमुक्तज्ञान **73**, 3.

अमृषामोष **55**, 17. °धर्मिन् **55**, 13.

अमोषधर्मिन् **55**, 18.

अयोनिशो–: °मनसिकार **12**, 3; **13**, 5. °मनस्कार **42**, 15, 16; **43**, 1.

अर्थ **1**, 10. °पद **119**, 6. पर+**8**, 6. स्व+**8**, 6.

अर्हत् **32**, 16.

अवलीयनाचित्त **49**, 14.

अववाद **39**, 16; **104**, 9.

अविद्या **12**, 8; **13**, 4; **64**, 3. +अन्ध **51**, 12. °वासभूमि **32**, 17; **54**, 6; **97**, 4. °समुत्थान **12**, 9.

अविनिर्भाग **42**, 3; **76**, 9; **77**, 1; **80**, 7. °धर्म **21**, 16. °लक्षण **76**, 4. °वृत्ति **80**, 10; **85**, 7.

अविवर्त्य **14**, 7.

अवीचि **60**, 17.

अवैवर्तिक **13**, 21; **14**, 8; **53**, 3.

अवैवर्त्य **16**, 10, 11, 13.

अष्टाङ्ग : आर्य+ **105**, 14.

अष्टादशावेणिकबद्धधर्म **6**, 15.

असंस्कृत **8**, 7.

असक्त **85**, 2.

असङ्ग **77**, 9.

असत् **10**, 7.

आजाति **12**, 9; **48**, 17.

आत्मन् **30**, 10, 12, 15; **31**, 12, 15. + ग्रह **31**, 10. + पारमिता **30**, 18; **31**, 4, 11. + भाव **32**, 19; **53**, 17; **60**, 2. + स्नेह **77**, 18; परम+ **31**, 11; **34**, 9.

आनिञ्ज्य **67**, 13.

आभास : अन्° **46**, 15.

आभोग : °क्रिया **24**, 14. अन्° **8**, 2, 9; **52**, 7: **98**, 7, 14.

आयतन **42**, 18; **43**, 5; **45**, 18.

आरम्बण **11**, 2; **13**, 1, 4, 9, 12.

आरूप्य **67**, 13; **102**, 19; **114**, 2.

आर्य : °श्रावक **17**, 4. °संघ **7**, 1. °सत्य **55**, 4. + अष्टाङ्ग **105**, 14.

आर्षभस्थान **20**, 1.

आवरण **10**, 5, 6; **27**, 13; **29**, 7, 9-11, 13. क्लेश+ **79**, 14. ज्ञेय+ **79**, 14. द्वय+ **80**, 13.

आवीचिक **118**, 18.

आवेणिक **85**, 10; **93**, 9. °ता **91**, 16; **94**, 7. °बुद्धधर्म **93**, 3.

आवेध : पूर्व+ **52**, 3.

आशय **20**, 17; **24**, 9; **25**, 3; **28**, 17.

आश्वासन **10**, 10.

आश्रयपरिवृत्ति **21**, 9, 10; **38**, 17; **79**, 2, 10, 13.

आस्वंसन **87**, 8, 11.

आस्रव **38**, 14. °धातु **39**, 3. अन्° **15**, 1; **32**, 19; **34**, 1. स+ **33**, 1, 17.

इच्छन्तिक **27**, 15; **28**, 7, 15.

इच्छा **36**, 5.

इतोबाह्य **28**, 6.

इन्द्रिय **42**, 9, 14; **46**, 1. + अर्थ **82**, 14; **84**, 1. + उपरोध **46**, 1.

ईर्यापथ **52**, 6; **100**, 18.

उदय **42**, 8, 9; **43**, 7.

उदान **70**, 11.

उद्दान **26**, 11.

उपक्लेश **12**, 18; **14**, 18; **15**, 5; **41**, 2. क्लेश+ **42**, 2; **45**, 3.

उपपत्ति **47**, 3, 8; **51**, 7. भव+ **48**, 12.

उपशम **9**, 13. अत्यन्त+ **55**, 19.

उपसर्ग **45**, 13.

उपादान **46**, 14. °प्रत्यय **33**, 16. °स्कन्ध **30**, 19; **31**, 10. चतुर्° **33**, 1.

एकान्तचारिन् **97**, 5.

करुणा **26**, 21.

कर्मन् **12**, 2; **13**, 7-10; **42**, 14, 15, 19; **43**, 4, 5. + त्रय **93**, 14. अनास्रव° **32**, 18; **54**, 7.

कामधातु **51**, 7; **67**, 16.

काय **18**, 15; **34**, 2, 3; **52**, 6; **85**, 9; **86**, 14. °त्रय **50**, 8; **72**, 1. °द्वय **84**, 2. धर्म° **2**, 13; **12**, 2; etc. परमार्थ° **91**, 4. मुक्ति° **83**, 7. रूप° **88**, 13. संवृति° **91**, 5. सत्° **8**, 19; **74**, 6.

कार : °क्रिया **18**, 2, 6. °बल **17**, 16.

क्लेश **9**, 2; **12**, 3; **13**, 6, 10; **42**, 14, 15, 19; **43**, 4, 5. °कोश **12**, 12, 14; **21**, 8; **40**, 17; **59**, 10, 14. °मूल **8**, 19. +उपक्लेश **42**, 2.
क्षर **105**, 8.
क्षेत्र **88**, 4. बुद्ध° **115**, 10.
गगनगञ्जादिसमाधि **28**, 12; **32**, 1.
गर्भ **7**, 2.
गाथा **70**, 10.
गेय **73**, 10.
गोचर : बुद्ध° **90**, 2; **111**, 7.
गोत्र **21**, 6; **25**, 9; **26**, 3, 6; **55**, 16; **69**, 19; **70**, 1; **71**, 18, अपरिनिर्वाण° **28**, 1; **35**, 10. मणि° **5**, 9. विशुद्ध° **6**, 8.
ग्रह : आत्म° **31**, 11. यथा° **31**, 13.
चतुर्वैशारद्य **6**, 15.
चतुष्टय **102**, 15.
चरक **28**, 6.
चरित : चित्त° **25**, 3. रागादि° **67**, 15.
चित्त **12**, 7; **14**, 16; **15**, 2-6; **40**, 2; **45**, 3; **71**, 7; **78**, 7-9 °चैतसिक **50**, 12. °प्रकृति **41**, 12; **43**, 8; **66**, 17; **80**, 17, 18. °शुद्धि **42**, 15. अवलीयना° **49**, 14. प्रमोक्ष° **49**, 14.
चैतसिक **50**, 12.
जन्मन् : +समुदय **13**, 10. +अनुबन्ध **13**, 8.
जाति **46**, 12.
जिन : °गर्भ **39**, 11; **59**, 9. °ज्ञानविषय **116**, 7.
ज्ञान **12**, 7; **13**, 19; **14**, 6; **79**, 12; **80**, 14; **81**, 11, 13. °देहिन् **84**, 15. °द्वय **80**, 13; **83**, 7. °भूमि **68**, 3. त्रि° **84**, 14. प्रादेशिक° **16**, 5; **17**, 1.
ज्ञेय **80**, 3. +आवरण **79**, 14.
तत्त्व : °ज्ञान **26**, 16. °दर्शन **13**, 17.
तथता **21**, 3; **26**, 5; **27**, 7; **71**, 8.
तथागत **40**, 8, 16: **41**, 5. °कुल **29**, 18. °गर्भ **2**, 12; **10**, 4; **12**, 14; **15**, 12; **21**, 8; **46**, 2-4. °गोत्र **27**, 8. °त्व **82**, 13. °धर्मकाय **3**, 2; **12**, 13, 14; **21**, 9; **27**, 6; **30**, 10; **31**, 3.
तमस् **12**, 19; **15**, 5; **28**, 4.
तीर्थिक **28**, 9, 15.
तीर्थ्य **27**, 15.
तृष्णा **35**, 7.
त्रिधातु **117**, 14.
त्रिभव **33**, 1; **62**, 3; **88**, 6.
त्रिमण्डल **6**, 5; **117**, 1.
त्रियानिक **17**, 14.
त्रैधातुक **47**, 4; **14**, 3. °प्रतिबिम्बक **50**, 8.
त्रैयानिक **19**, 6; **20**, 8.
त्र्यध्वज्ञान **93**, 9.
दर्शन **9**, 2; **12**, 17; **13**, 19; **14**, 6; **31**, 15. ज्ञान° **49**, 3.
दशपारमिता **40**, 9.
दशबल **6**, 15; **21**, 11.
दुःख : °निरोध **12**, 5, 10, 11, 16. °मूल **8**, 18.
दुष्प्रतिवेध **1**, 7, 9.
दुष्प्रतिवेध्य **22**, 1.
दूरंगमा **53**, 1.
दृष्टि **8**, 19; **9**, 2; **28**, 8, 10-12; **40**, 2. °प्रतिपक्ष **76**, 17. उच्छेद° **34**, 20. शाश्वत° **35**, 2. सम्यग्° **35**, 1, 2.
देशना : °धर्म **18**, 14.
देशनी **52**, 6.

दोष **77**, 18; **78**, 6.
द्वय **12** 2.
द्वेष **13**, 13; **67**, 6.
धर्म **11**, 1, 5; **18**, 14; **45**, 4, 9; **48**, 19. °काय **2**, 13; **12**, 2; **37**, 7; **40**, 18; **41**, 16; **55**, 3; **70**, 3; **74**, 18. °चक्र **3**, 17; **6**, 5; **88**, 3; **94**, 2. °धातु **10**, 4; **15**, 13; **24**, 15; **76**, 17. °मेघा **52**, 14; **53**, 5; **58**, 4. °स्कन्ध **43**, 1 +अधिमुक्ति **26**, 21. अधिगम° **18**, 14 देशना° **18**, 14.
धातु **1**, 1; **13**, 11; **42**, 13, 14, 18; **43**, 6.
धारणी **58**, 3; **105**, 9.
धीमत् **3**, 14; **14**, 7.
नय **18**, 11; **19**, 4; **21**, 18.
नामरूप **8**, 18, 20.
नाश **83**, 14.
निःसरण **19**, 6, 10, 12-14.
निकाय **22**, 10.
निदान **46**, 8; **70**, 11; **96**, 5. ततो° **13**, 7.
निमित्त **13**, 1, 9, 12. °प्रपञ्च **33**, 7, 8.
नियाम : सम्यक्त्व° **28**, 13.
निरोध **9**, 7; **19**, 3. °सत्य **11**, 9, 12, 13, 18; **12**, 1; **19**, 1; **85**, 1.
निर्ग्रन्थिपुत्र **28**, 6.
निर्माण **107**, 3. °काय **107**, 13.
निर्याण **98**, 17; **99**, 1.
निर्वाण **28**, 1, 16; **50**, 10; **56**, 9, 12. °धातु **3**, 1; **56**, 5. प्राप्य° **88**, 7.
निर्वृति 35, 16.
नेत्री **6**, 4.
नैरात्म्य **31**, 14, 15; **34**, 9. °कोटि **14**, 1, 13.
नैष्कर्म्य **88**, 1.
नैःस्वाभाव्य **89**, 2.
पंचदोष **78**, 6
पंचधर्म **78**, 18.
पदार्थ **79**, 3, 7.
परमात्मन् **31**, 11; **34**, 9.
परमार्थ **2**, 11; **28**, 8. °धातु **26**, 15. °निर्वृति **55**, 4. °सत्य **13**, 16; **55**, 18. +अनधिमुक्त **28**, 8.
परार्थ **8**, 6. °संपत् **10**, 12, 14.
परावृत्ति **116**, 6.
परिकर्मन् **50**, 18.
परिकल्प **12**, 7; **44**, 10; **73**, 6. अ° **44**, 10.
परिजय **50**, 19; **51**, 5.
परिणाम **53**, 18.
परिनिर्वाण **28**, 1; **75**, 15.
परिव्राजक **28**, 6.
परीत्त **23**, 9.
पर्युत्थान **69**, 4.
पर्येष्टि **106**, 12.
पारमिता **30**, 17, 18.
पारिणामिकी **33**, 2, 11, 14. अचिन्त्य° **54**, 5.
पुद्गल **18**, 2, 5, 8, 10; **36**, 11; **39**, 17. °दृष्टि **28**, 8. °धर्म **14**, 13, 14.
पुनर्भव **19**, 8.
पूरि **116**, 15, 17.
प्रकृति **42**, 17; **43**, 2; **44**, 9, 10; **45**, 6, 7; **55**, 16; **66**, 3. चित्त° **41**, 12; **43**, 3.
प्रणिधि **36**, 6.
प्रतिघ **13**, 3.
प्रतिपद् **10** 4, 9.
प्रतिपन्नक **19**, 7; **20**, 1.
प्रतिवेध **15**, 14; **34**, 11. दुष्° **1**, 7, 9.
प्रतिसंख्या **93**, 6.

प्रत्यय **25**, 5, 9, 13, 15; **34**, 3; **43**, 7; **64**, 7. °लक्षण **32**, 17.
प्रत्येकबुद्ध **18**, 5; **21**, 18. °यानीय **28**, 13; **32**, 3.
प्रथमचित्तोत्पादिक **52**, 16, 19.
प्रपञ्च **8**, 9; **9**, 14.
प्रपाचना **86**, 8.
प्रमुदिता **52**, 13, 19.
प्रमोक्षचित्तोत्पाद **49**, 14.
प्रयोग **10**, 10; **35**, 11; **53**, 2.
प्रातिहार्य **101**, 2. °त्रय **103**, 9. अनुशास्ति° **104**, 9. आदेशना° **104**, 8. ऋद्धि° **104**, 7.
प्रादेशिकीबुद्धि **77**, 6.
प्रार्थना **30**, 6.
बल **92**, 6. दश **21**, 11.
बुद्ध: कर्मन् **6**, 16. °गर्भन् **26**, 4, 6. °गुण **6**, 15. °त्व **7**, 9; **56**, 9, 12; **80**, 1, 7. °धातु **5**, 5; **77**, 14. °बोधि **6**, 14. °भूमि **79**, 19.
बोधि **1**, 3. °मण्ड **4**, 1; **88**, 2. बुद्ध° **4**, 9. श्रावक° **4**, 9; **6**, 14.
बोधिसत्त्व **40**, 8, 15; **41**, 1. °कर्मन् **6**, 13. °गणरत्न **16**, 15. °गुण **17**, 5. °भूमि **3**, 20; **5** 7; **15**, 13; **52**, 13-15. °महाकरुणा **61**, 2. +अलंकार **6**, 12. +अवभास **6**, 42.
भव **8**, 18: **27**, 17, 18; **33**, 16. +अङ्ग **12**, 9. त्रि° **33**, 1.
भाजन **105**, 11. °लोक **44**, 5.
भाव **75**, 14, 16.
भावना **12**, 17; **13**, 19; **29**, 9, 10, 12, 13.
भूत **76**, 2; **78**, 12, 14. °कोटि **78**, 1. °दर्शिन् **76**, 2. °धर्मापवाद **77**, 17. °प्रतिष्ठान **49**, 16. अ° **49**, 15.
मण्डल **12**, 17. त्रि° **6**, 6.
मनस् **12**, 7; **63**, 12, 18. +मय **32**, 19; **33**, 9; **46**, 14; **50**, 8.
मनसिकार **13**, 1. अ° **9**, 12. अयोनिशो° **12**, 3. योनिशो° **12**, 8; **25**, 11.
मनस्कार: अयोनिशो° **42**, 15, 16; **43**, 1.
मल **33**, 5; **43**, 11; **51**, 16; **60**, 8; **66**, 3: **67**, 5. सवासन° **56**, 8.
महाकरुणा **29**, 13; **48**, 11.
महाबोधि **6**, 14.
महाब्रह्मन् **113**, 10.
महायान **28**, 14. °धर्म **28**, 2.
मार **89**, 1. °सैन्य **88**, 2.
मार्ग **18**, 15; **19**, 1. °सत्य **11**, 9, 12, 14; **18**, 16. +उपदेश **24**, 4, 6. मोक्ष° **28**, 1. समाप्ति° **29**, 4.
मुक्तज्ञ **76**, 8. अ° **76**, 9.
मुक्तज्ञान **73**, 4.
मुक्तिकाय **83**, 7.
मृषामोषधर्मिन् **19**, 2.
मैत्री **78**, 16. महा° **78**, 18.
मोक्ष **56**, 15; **118**, 1. °मार्ग **28**, 1.
मोषधर्म **18**, 12.
मोह **13**, 1, 4.
यथावद्भाविकता **14**, 9, 11, 13; **15**, 7; **16**, 3, 7.
यान **88**, 10; **98**, 8. अग्र° **29**, 19; **99**, 7. नव° **74**, 5; **75**, 13. महा° **28**, 14; **29**, 5.
°यानिक: त्रि° **17**, 15. प्रत्येकबुद्ध° **18**, 5; **29**, 13. श्रावक° **18**, 8; **29**, 11.
°यानीय: प्रत्येकबुद्ध° **28**, 13; **32**, 3. श्रावक° **28**, 13.
यावद्भाविकता **14**, 9; **15**, 9, 11; **16**, 3, 7.

योनिशोमनसिकार **12**, 8; .**25**, 11.
रत्न **3**, 19; **4**, 12, 13,. 15; **20**, 13. °त्रय **21**, 6.
राग **13**, 1, 3; **43**, 11.
रूप **52**, 6. °काय **88**, 13.
रूपारूप्यधातु (रूप्या°, B) **67**, 13.
वज्रपद **1**, 5; **2**, 6, 13; **3**, 2, 6, 8.
वज्रसत्त्व **1**, 1.
वशिता **17**, 5; **32**, 15.
वासना **19**, 8; **33**, 5; **67**, 4. +अपगम **34**, 8. °व्याधि **54**, 1.
विकल्प **12**, 3; **52**, 3.
विक्रीडिता **9**, 18; **10**, 7.
विचिकित्सा **8**, 19; **9**, 2.
विज्ञान **12**, 7, 8.
विनय **10**, 7.
विनिर्भाग **76**, 8. अ°**21**, 16.
विपर्यस्त **30**, 19.
विपर्यास **30**, 13. +अभिरत **76**, 18.
विपश्यना **44**, 9.
विपाक **45**, 12; **78**, 2, 4.
विबन्ध **13**, 1.
विभव **27**, 17, 18. °कारण **45**, 13. °लक्षण **32**, 16; **33**, 1.
विमला **52**, 20.
विमुक्ति **58**, 10.
विराग **11**, 5, 13. °धर्म **11**, 15.
विवर्त **43**, 6; **44**, 2.
विसंयोग **79**, 14.
विसामग्री **45**, 5.
वैनयिक **24**, 10.
वैनेय **52**, 5.
वैशारद्य **92**, 10. चतुर्° **6**, 15.
व्यञ्जन **1**, 10; **2**, 2; **18**, 15; **41**, 16.
व्यनुमेय **90**, 5, 6.
व्यय **42**, 8, 9; **43**, 8.
व्यवदान **41**, 18; **55**, 1. °धातु **119**, 5. °निमित्त **76**, 7. °सत्य **11**, 14; **20**, 6.
व्याकरण **21**, 12; **70**, 10; **77**, 11; **86**, 8.
व्यापिता **83**, 11.
शम: °सुख **51**, 5. °एकयानगोत्र **35**, 11.
शरणत्रय **17**, 14, 16.
शाश्वत **84**, 21
शास्तृ **28**, 7.
शीतीभूत **9**, 12.
शील **17**, 4, 6-10.
शुक्ल **36**, 10; **118**, 11. चतुः° **36**, 14.
शुद्धसत्त्व **97**, 2; **114**, 4.
शून्य **76**, 3, 9; **77**, 12.
शून्यता **30**, 21; **57**, 17; **75**, 13-17. °ज्ञान **76**, 15. °दृष्टि **28**, 10. +अनधिमुक्त **28**, 9. °लक्षण **76**, 11. °विक्षिप्तचित्त **76**, 13. °विमोक्षमुख **75**, 14. परमार्थ° **76**, 13. सर्वाकारवरोपेत° **57**, 6.
शैक्ष **19**, 7, 14; **67**, 19. °सान्तानिक **39**, 3.
श्रद्धा **44**, 1.
श्राद्ध **28**, 7.
श्रावक **17**, 2; **27**, 15; **28**, 13. °यानिक **18**, 8; **29**, 11. °यानीय **28**, 13. °संघरत्न **16**, 15.
षडायतन **45**, 18; °विशेष **55**, 17.
संवर **17**, 4.
संवर्त्त **43**, 6. अ° **44**, 4.
संवृति **18**, 10; **35**, 16. °काय **91**, 5. °सत्य **70**, 11.
संसार **6**, 2; **28**, 1; **32**, 4; **50**, 8. °निर्वाणसमता **28**, 16; **34**, 11.

संस्कार **19**, 9; **32**, 17; **34**, 20. °परिपाक **45**, 18. °वत् **32**, 18.
संस्कृत **8**, 7; **19**, 2.
सकरणीय **19**, 7, 14.
संक्लेश **13**, 11; **33**, 10, 12, 13; **41**, 18; **43**, 12.
संघ **19**, 6.
सञ्चिन्त्य: °भवोपपत्ति **47**, 8; **48**, 14; **51**, 7. +उपपत्ति **47**, 3; **51**, 7.
संज्ञा **24**, 4, 5; **29**, 12-14; **40**, 2. °ग्राह **22**, 11; **23**, 16.
सत् **10**, 17; **76**, 10. °काय **8**, 19; **76**, 17. +असत् **10**, 17.
सत्त्व **10**, 3; **14**, 4; **15**, 12; **42**, 7: °धातु **2**, 11; **6**, 1; **16**, 7; **40**, 8, 15, 18; **41**, 16. °राशि **27**, 17; **29**, 2, 3, 5.
सत्य **11**, 5. निरोध° **11**, 9, 12, 13. परमार्थ° **70**, 10. मार्ग° **11**, 9, 13, 14. व्यवदान° **11**, 14. संवृति° **70**, 11.
संतान **16**, 17. चित्त° **23**, 15, 16. स्व° **17**, 2.
संनिश्रय : गुण° **17**, 3.
समवधान **47**, 9. अ° **13**, 18.
समाधि **26**, 21; **29**, 12.
समुदागम **53**, 2; **55**, 16.
समुदाचार **13**, 6, 9.
संपत्.: परार्थ° **10**, 12, 14. स्वार्थ° **10**, 12, 13.
सम्पत्ति : परार्थ° **82**, 9. स्वार्थ° **82**, 8.
संबोधि **88**, 3. सम्यक° **3**, 1.
संभवलक्षण **32**, 18.
संभार **118**, 1. °द्वय **99**, 8.
संभृतिद्वय **99**, 1.
सम्यक्संबुद्ध **41**, 5.
सर्वाकारवरोपेत-: °बुद्धभाव **81**, 12. °शून्यता **57**, 20.
साङ्गन **9**, 18; **10**, 6.
साधुमती **58**, 2.
°सान्तानिक : अर्हत्° **67**, 17 आर्यपुद्गलशैक्ष° **68**, 1. पृथग्जनशैक्ष° **67**, 20. बुद्ध° **58**, 14. बोधिसत्त्व° **68**, 2. रागादिचरितसत्त्व° **67**, 15. वीतराग° **67**, 13.
सामग्री **43**, 7; **45**, 6. वि° **45**, 5.
स्कन्ध **42**, 14, 18; **43**, 6; **78**, 4. उपादान° **30**, 19; **31**, 10. मनोमय° **33**, 9; **34**, 10.
स्थान **18**, 10; **21**, 13, 18; **37**, 16; **38**, 14; **74**, 10.
स्थिति **43**, 8.
स्वभाव **69**, 19. °त्रय **69**, 16.
स्वयंभू **27**, 15; **97**, 5.
स्वार्थ **8**, 6. °संपत् **10**, 12, 13.
हेतु **25**, 5, 9, 12, 13; **43**, 7. °लक्षण **32**, 17.

## IV. INDEX OF RARE WORDS AND USES


अक्षूण **24**, 10.
अण्डकोश : मोह+ **62**, 2.
अनुशास्ति **104**, 10.
अयोनिशोमनसिकुर्यात् **12**, 9.
अरिहत् **119**, 2.
अवभृत् **105**, 7.
अशारद्य **98**, 20.
आत्मंभरि **17**, 8.
आशय n. **108**, 11.
√इ : प्रतीत्य **44**, 1.
√इञ्ज : इञ्जते **9**, 10.
उत्सङ्ग **94**, 9.
उत्सद **94**, 11,
उपगमिका : तत्र+ **22**, 7.
एकत्य **28**, 2.
एकमुक्ता **108**, 6.
औदारिक **106**, 5.
कवि (for छवि?) **44**, 8.
काच **5**, 14.
कालसमय **107**, 21.
किंकरणीय **47**, 10.
कोल **18**, 16.
क्षुद्रप्राणक **61**, 3.
खण्डिका **5**, 12.
खाडिन् **62**, 6.
खार **5**, 10.
गमिक **106**, 4.
ग्रेध **118**, 13.
चारिका **88**, 1.
जिघ्रण **82**, 17.
√ठप् : विठपति **9**, 11; -विठपनाम् **49**, 2; विठपिता: **49**, 2, विठप्यन्ते **49**, 1.
दुर्दृश **77**, 9.
√दृश् A. **34**, 20; **35**, 1; **47**, 19; **48**, 1.
धातु f. **104**, 4.
निर्नीताकारण (निर्नानाकारण, B) **24**, 15.
निर्ममीकरण (निर्मंषी°, A) **45**, 18.
निष्पव् **57**, 2.
√पत् : प्र–Ā. **47**, 19.
°परिज्ञातावी **71**, 13.
परिपन्थ **32**, 16.
पर्यन्तकाल **20**, 2.
पारमि **31**, 14; **115**, 18.
पारमी **87**, 4.
°पोषिन् **17**, 4.
प्रघोष **104**, 6.
प्रणवन **102**, 16.
प्रतिश्रुत्का **110**, 9; **113**, 13.
प्रविशन **107**, 15.
प्रशुद्ध **17**, 8.
फलिगोध (परिशोध, B) **32**, 4.
फल्गु **81**, 21.
मुख **39**, 16; **44**, 7; **75**, 14; **76**, 13.
√मुच् : अधिमुच्येत् (°मुञ्चेत्, A) **115**, 11, 15, 19.
रश्मि f. **108**, 5.
√लुड् : लोड्येत **49**, 8.
°वरधक **7**, 11.
विकरण **96**, 15.
√विच् : प्रतिविच्य (for °विध्य ?) **51**, 11.
विटप **64**, 10.
विन्वन **82**, 18.
विमात्रता **105**, 11.
√वृ : नि– **61**, 1, 2; **65**, 2.
√वृज् : निर्वृज्य **58**, 21.
वैरुढि (वि°, A) **110**, 20.
व्यक्त **23**, 7.
सततसमित **19**, 9; **32**, 4.
समावर्त्तन **4**, 11.
सम्पद n. **113**, 16.
संमिञ्जित **60**, 20.
सूतिका **84**, 19.
√सेव् : प्रतिसेव्य **119**, 1.
√स्था : अनुतिष्टते **23**, 9.
स्पर्शितव्य **106**, 19.

# PART - III

# CORRECTIONS AND EMENDATIONS

*By*

**Jikido Takasaki**

# Correction and Emendation to the Sanskrit Text of the Ratnagotravibhāga

*by*

**Jikido Takasaki**

Reprinted from Jikido Takasaki, *A Study of the Ratnagotravibhāga (Uttaratantra)*, Rome, IsMEO, 1966, pp. 396-99.

# CORRECTION & EMENDATION TO THE SANSKRIT TEXT OF THE RATNAGOTRAVIBHĀGA

**(This table excludes those errata which were already corrected by the publisher).**

*Corrigenda*

| (Page, line) | for | read | (Source)*) |
|---|---|---|---|
| 2.9 | svaprajñayā draṣṭuṃ vā | svaprajñayā *jñātuṃ vā* draṣṭum | (T) |
| 3.2 | bhagava*n* tathā- | bhagava*ṃs* tathā- [vā | (grammar) |
| 3.4 | -dharmā / avi- | -dharm*ā*'vi- | (cf. S. 39.8) |
| 3.16 | -parivartānugatāni | -parivartā*d a*nugatāni | (C) |
| 4.14 | anyonyaṃ bodhisattva | anyonya-bodhisattva- | (context) |
| 5.1 | upa*k*araṇatāṃ | upa*h*araṇatāṃ | (C) |
| 5.10, 12 | utkṣālya | unmīlya ? | (Ms.) |
| 9.11 | viṭhapa*t*i | viṭhapeti | (cf. S. 49.1-2 |
| 10.2 | abhāvasvabhāvā*t* | abhāvasvabhāvā*n* (Acc.) | (T) |
| 10.7 | -anyatamâvi*ś*iṣṭa- | -anyatamâva*ś*iṣṭa- | (T, C) |
| 10.9 | abhisam*buddhabodeḥ* | abhisam*bodhibuddhyā* ? | (T) |
| 11.2 | sarvāram*v*aṇa | sarvāram*b*aṇa | (misprint) |
| 12.2 | -dharmā / | -dharm*atayeti* | (cf. S. 44.14) |
| 12.19 | -*satya*darśana- | -*tattva*darśana | (T, S. 13.17) |
| 15.4 | (after) spṛśanti / | *nâpi cittaṃ saṃkliṣṭam bhavati* / | |
| 15.5 | (before) katham | (should be inserted) | (T, C) |
| 15.6 | upakle*śâ*rtho | upakli*ṣṭâ*rtho | (cf. S. 22.2) |
| 16.9 | -śuddhy*ā* | -śuddhy*aiva* (or śuddhyā *hi*) | (T) |
| 16.10 | avaivarty*ād* bha- | avaivarty*ā* bha- | (T, C) |
| 18.2 | bodhisattvān | bodhisattv*ayānikān* | (context) |
| 18.5 | *pratītya gambhīra*-dh. | *gambhīra-pratītya*dharma | (Ms. B, T, C) |
| 19.9 | bhavati syād | bhavati / syād | (context) |
| 19.10 | vadhakapuruṣe tasmāt | vadhakapuruṣe / tasmāt | |
| 20.6-7 | vyavadānasatyadvaya- virāgadharma- | vyavadānasatyadvaya*lakṣaṇa*- virāgadharma- | (T, S. 11.14) |
| 20.8 | pāramārthikamevâtraṇe | pāramārthika*m ekam ev*âtraṇe | (T, C) |
| 20.15 | sarvâcāra | sarvâ*k*āra | (T) |
| 22.7 | *lakṣaṇa*- | (to be omitted) | (context) |
| 22.15 | (before) mahāpṛthivī- | (*mahācakravālapramāṇena mahācakravālaḥ* /) | (T) |

*) T. Tibetan Version of the Ratnagotravibhāga (Sde-dge Edition); C. Chinese Version of the Ratnagotravibhāga (Taisho Edition); Ms. A. & B. those Mss. used by Johnston for editing the Sanskrit Text.

*Corrigenda*

| (Page, line) | for | read | (Source) |
|---|---|---|---|
| 23.13 | tathâśeṣebhyaḥ | tathā śesebhyaḥ | (C) |
| 24.4 | *–āryeṇa–mārgô*padeśena | *–āryamārgô*padeśena | (T, C) |
| 24.10 | vain*a*yikeṣu | vain*e*yikeṣu | (vineya) |
| 24.15 | nir*nītākāraṇaṃ* | nir*nānākaraṇaṃ* | (T, C) |
| 24.17 | (before) triratnavaṃśa– | *tryadhvânubaddha* (to be inserted) | (T, C) |
| 25.9 | bodhan*ā*–padam | bodhan*a*–padam | (grammar) |
| 26.4–5 | after v. 27 | (*anena kiṃ darśitam*) | (context) |
| 27.14 | sattvârth*aṃ* nirapekṣatā | sattvâr*the* nirapekṣatā or sattvâr*thani*rapekṣatā | (T) |
| 28.7 | *tri*vidhāḥ | *dvi*vidhāḥ | (C.AAS, BGŚ) |
| 28.16 | –samatâp*atti* | –samatâp*ti*– | (T, context., S. p. 29.4) |
| 29.1 | –patitā ihadhārmikā | –patitā*ś ce*hadhārmikā | (C) |
| 29.6 | sattvās tadyathā | sattvā*ḥ caturvidhāḥ*/tadyathā | (T, C) |
| 30.4 | –pāramitā phala*m*/ | –pārami*tāphalaḥ* / (bahuvr.) | (context) |
| 30.9 | –hetava eṣāṃ | –hetava *uktā* eṣāṃ | (Ms. B, T, C) |
| 32.4 | (before nityapāramitā | insert) *bodhisattvānām* | (T. C) |
| 32.11 | sarvatra parama– | *sarvatraparama* | (T) |
| 34.19 | –nirvāṇa–samāropa– | nrvāṇâsamāropa– | (C) |
| 36.2–3 | *mithyātva–niyata–* | *a*niyata– | (C, BGŚ) |
| 36.5 | (after praṇidhim iti / | insert) *tatra cchando 'bhilāṣaḥ* / | (T, C) |
| 36.12 | pāp*a*samuccheda– | pāp*â*samuccheda– | (T) |
| 36.17 | nipatanti * * * anāgata– | nipatanti *tān upakurvanty* anāgata– | (T, C) |
| 37.13 | ki | ki*ṃ* | (misprint) |
| 38.17 | –sādharmya | –sādharmya*ṃ* | (misprint) |
| 39.6 | avinirbhāgadharmā / avinirmuktaguṇaḥ / yad– | avinirbhāgadharm*ā'vi*–nirmuktaguṇo yad– | (context) |
| 40.17 | –upagūḍhaḥ / saṃ– | –upagūḍhaḥ saṃ– | (context) |
| 42.11 | pradahati | *pradahanti* | (grammar) |
| 44.13 | bali yo | *balīyo* (comparative degree) | |
| 45.9 | (before sarvadharmā | insert) *mūlaparicchinnā* | (Mss., T) |
| 46.2 | eṣa / | eṣa*ḥ* / | (grammar) |
| 46.6 | –vimuktā | –vimukt*ā*– | » |
| 46.7 | asyaiva | *ma*syaiva (vimukt*ām* asya–) | (C) |
| 47.17 | sreṣṭhiṇo gṛhapater eka– | śreṣṭhiṇo *vā* gṛhapater *vai*ka– | (T, C) |
| 47.18 | darśanena sa ca | darśanena / sa ca | (context) |
| 48.2–3 | ekaputrakâdhyāśāya–premâ*nunīto* | –premâ*lambanataḥ* ? | (T) |
| 48.9 | śreṣṭhī gṛhapatir iti | śreṣṭhī *vā* gṛhapatir *v*eti | (T, C) |
| 50.13 | āsravakṣay*âbhijñābhi*–mukhy– | āsravakṣayâbhimukhy– | (C) |
| 50.17 | dṛḍhay*ā'*dhyāśayaprati–pattyā | dṛ*ḍhâdhyā*śayapratipattyā | (T, C) |
| 51.11 | prati*vicyê*mām– | prati*vedhye*mām– | (T) |
| 52.19 | bodhisattvag*aṇa* | bodhisattvag*uṇa*– | (T) |

## *Corrigenda*

| (Page, line) | for | read | (Source) |
|---|---|---|---|
| 55.2 | tathāgata*garbhasya* | tathāgata*dhātor* | (Ms. B) |
| 55.7 | ki | kiṃ | (misprint) |
| 55.19 | *sama*dharmatayā | *śama*dharmatayā | (T) |
| 56.3 | tathāgato 'nyo | tathāgato *nânyo* | (context) |
| 57.2 | niṣpatsv–asaṃ– | niṣpat*ty*–asaṃ– | (S. 58.9) |
| 58.13 | ekena ca *kāraṇena* | ekena *câkāreṇa* | (T) |
| 61.1 | jagat | jagat– | (misprint) |
| 64.21 | ujjñitam– | uj*jh*itam– | (misprint) |
| 67.4 | rāgâdidviḍmoha | rāgâdi*dviṁ*moha | (misprint) (Ms. A) |
| 67.16 | aśubhâdi*bhāva*jñāna– | aśubhâdi*bhāvanā*jñāna– | (T, C) |
| 68.6–7 | (v. 132 | into prose) | (C, context) |
| 68.13 | tathāgatagarbh*a* iti | tathāgatagarbh*ā* iti | (context) |
| 69.6 | -āvṛ*tā* | –āvṛ*tam* | (T, C, con.) |
| 70.3 | d*b*idhā | *dv*idhā | (misprint) |
| 70.3 | vain*a*yika– | vain*e*yika– | (<vineya) |
| 70.5 | dharmadhāt*or* avi– | dharmadhāt*ur* avi– | (T, C) |
| 71.8 | vikārā | vikārā– | (misprint) |
| 71.9 | sarve | sarve– | (misprint) |
| 71.12 | tatra– | tatra | (misprint) |
| 71.14 | +advaidhikāro ti | –advaidhikā*reti* | (gram.) |
| 72.5 | mahādharmâdhir*āja*tvāt | mahādharm*âdhirājya*tvāt | (T) |
| 73.6 | iti parikal*pam* asya vacanāyeti | iti parikal*pitam* asya *vacanam iti* | (context) |
| 73.15 | vikalpayitavyā'dhimoktavyā | vikalpayitavyā *kevalam tv* adhimoktavyā | (T, C) |
| 74.7 | te'tyantasāsrava– | te ' tyan*ta*ṃ sāsrava– | (T) |
| 74.19 | | (change the pargraph from 'yathāca sa...' and connect 'tad yathā'pi nāma...' after 'prasādhitah/ 'without changing paragraph.) | (context) |
| 75.11 | -*śa*bha– | *śu*bha | (misprint) |
| 76.11 | –*aparyantaṃ* śūnya– | *aviparyastaṃ* śūnya– | (T, C) |
| 79.15 | tatphalaṃ dvividham / | tatphalaṃ *visamayogaḥ* / | (context) |
| 79.16 | –visaṃyogaś ca / yathākramaṃ | –visaṃyogaś ca yathākrama*m* / | (C, context) |
| 79.7 | g*a*mbhīryaudārya– | *gāmbhīryau*dārya | (context) |
| 79.12 | –vinirmuk*test*athāgata– | –vinirmuk*te ta*thāgata– | (context) |
| 79.13 | (after)–pṛṣṭhalabdhaṃ | (insert) *laukikaṃ* | (T, Ms.B) |
| 84.18 | jātyandha*kāya*vat | jātyandha*rūpa*vat | (T, C) |
| 84.19 | sūtikā*madhya*sthita | sūtikā*sadma*sthita | (T) |
| 85.8 | –amalai stribhiḥ | –amalai*s tr*ibhiḥ (to be connected in Devanāgarī) | (context) |
| 86.13 | acintya*prāptiḥ* pratyātmaveditā | acinty*ârhattvaṃ* pratyātmavedita*m* | (T, C) |
| 88.7 | prā*pya*nirvāṇa– | *prāpta*nirvāṇa– | (T, C) |

## *Corrigenda*

| (Page, line) | for | read | (Source) |
|---|---|---|---|
| 90.5 | vy*anu*meyataḥ | *vyupameyataḥ* | (C, context) ... v. 69 |
| 90.6 | vy*anu*meyo | *vyupameyo* | (C, context) ... v. 69 |
| 91.14 | *tathatām*adhikṛtya | *tathā–tad*–adhikṛtya | (T) |
| 91.15 | (before v. 4) | (add) *uddānam* / | (T, C) |
| 92.11 | svayaṃjñāpanā | svayaṃ jñāpanā– | |
| 93.6 | apratisaṃkhy*āpa*hānir acc. to J's correction) | apratisaṃkhyāya hānir (as in the text) | (context) |
| 93.10 | muṣitatā citte | muṣita*tâ*citte | (T, context) |
| 94.2 | abhayadaṃ | *abhayam* | (metre) |
| 98.9 | –arkaraśmipravisṛta– | –arkaraśmi pravisṛta– (to be separated) | (context) |
| 100.3 | *–tvād* iti | *–vad* iti | |
| 100.10 | *adyaiva* na cirād | *vayam apy a*cirād | (T) |
| 101.11 | –sthānāntaramalā | –sthān*ā'*ntaramalā | (context) |
| 102–21 | –vaśād aghaṭṭitā | –vaś*ād gha*ṭṭitā | (T, context) |
| 103.16 | saṃbuddha*tūrya tu* yāti | saṃbuddha*bherer upa*yāti | (T, ms. B, context) |
| 104.14 | āy*ā*nti nikhilam / | āy*ā*ti nikhilam / | (context) |
| 106.6 | kleśagat*ān* dṛṣṭy– | kleśagat*âtmad*ṛṣṭy– | (T, C) |
| 108.15 | visṛt*e* | visṛt*o* | (T) |
| 108.16 | buddhasūrye | buddhasūry*o* | (T) |
| 108.16 | vineyâdr*i*–tannipāto | vinetâdr*au t*annipāto | (T) |
| 111.6 | –ālokādy–alaṃkṛtāḥ | –ālokā*d*–alaṃkṛt*āḥ* | (T) |
| 115.1 | (before sthāneṣv–) | (insert) *caturṣu* | (T, C) |
| 116.14 | tac*citta*pratyupasthānād | ta*nnitya*pratyupasthānād | (T, C) |
| 117.4 | câsy*a* mūlaṃ | *câsyā* mūlaṃ | (context) |

(The following headings had better be inserted:)

| | | | |
|---|---|---|---|
| 117.5 | (before v. 16) | tatra yadāśraye yannimittaṃ côdāhṛtaṃ tadārabhya ślokaḥ / | (C) |
| 117.9 | (before v. 17) | yathôdāhṛtam tadārabhya ślokaḥ / | (T) |
| 117.13 | (before v. 18) | yadudāhṛtaṃ tadārabhya ślokaḥ / | (T) |
| 117.17 | (before v. 19) | yenôdāhṛtaṃ tadārabhya ślokaḥ / | (T) |
| 118.3 | (before v. 20) | ātmarakṣaṇôpāyam ārabhya dvau ślokau / | (T) |
| 118.11 | (before v. 22) | kṣatihetum ārabhya ślokaḥ / | (T) |
| 118.15 | (before v. 23) | kṣatiphalam ārabhya dvau ślokau / | (T, C) |
| 119.5 | (before v. 25) | āptapuṇyapariṇamane ślokaḥ / | (C) |

# PART - IV

# ENGLISH TRANSLATION

*By*

**E. Obermiller**

# The Sublime Science of the Great Vehicle to Salvation
# Being
# A Manual of Buddhist Monism

The Work of Ārya Maitreya with a Commentary by Āryāsaṅga

*Translated from the Tibetan with*
*Introduction and Notes by*

**E. Obermiller**

Reprinted from *Acta Orientalia*, IX,
1931, pp. 81-306.

# The Sublime Science of the Great Vehicle to Salvation Being A Manual of Buddhist Monism

## The Work of Ārya Maitreya with a Commentary by Āryāsanga.

Translated from the Tibetan with introduction and notes

by

E. Obermiller, Leningrad.

## Introduction.

### I. The 5 Treatises of Maitreya and their Subject-matter.

According to the Tibetan tradition, the foundation of all the exegetical literature connected with the Buddhist Scripture of the latest and, partly, of the intermediate period[1] is contained in the 5 treatises ascribed to the Bodhisattva Maitreya. These are:—

1) The *Sūtrālaṁkāra*,[2]
2) „ *Madhyānta-vibhanga*,[3]
3) „ *Dharma-dharmatā-vibhanga*,[4]
4) „ *Abhisamayālaṁkāra*,[5] and
5) „ *Uttaratantra*.[6]

---

[1] Tib. *ḥkhor-lo-tha-ma* = *antya-cakra-(pravartuna)* and *ḥkhor-lo-bar-ba* = *madhya-cakra-(pravartuna)*. These are regarded in general as the foundation of the two branches of the Mahāyānistic literature, viz. 1) the idealistic, maintaining the unreality of the external world (*bāhya-artha-śūnyatā*) i.e. the Yogācāra system of Āryāsanga (IV—V century A. D.) and 2) the monistic teaching of universal non-substantiality (*sarva-dharma-śūnyatā*) i.e. the Mādhyamika system founded by Nāgārjuna (II century A. D.). The ideas expressed in these 2 branches of Mahāyāna are much older than Āryāsanga and Nāgārjuna who have only established regular philosophical systems.

[2] Tib. Mdo-sde-rgyan.

[3] Tib. Dbus-mthaḥ-rnam-ḥbyed.

[4] Tib. Chos-daṅ-chos-ñid-rnam-ḥbyed.

[5] Tib. Mṅon-rtogs-rgyan.

[6] Tib. Rgyud-bla-ma.

Of these 5 treatises the original Sanskrit text of the *Sūtrālaṁkāra* has been edited by Prof. Sylvain Lévi, who has likewise given a French translation of it. The Sanskrit text of the *Abhisamayālaṁkāra* and its Tibetan translation have been recently edited by Prof. Th. Stcherbatsky and by myself in the Bibliotheca Buddhica and will be followed by an analysis of the 8 subjects and the 70 topics which form its contents. The 3 other works have not, till now, met with the full appreciation of European scholars. The reason perhaps is that we possess only their Tibetan translations in the Tangyur (MDO XLIV), the original Sanscrit texts having not, up to this time, been discovered. An investigation of this branch of Buddhist literature according to the Tibetan sources enables us to ascertain the exclusive importance of the said 3 treatises as containing, in a very pregnant form, the idealistic and monistic teachings of later Buddhism. In particular the Tibetan works draw our attention to the *Uttaratantra*, the translation and analysis of which forms the subject-matter of the present work. It is indeed the most interesting of the three, if not of all the five, being the exposition of the most developed monistic and pantheistic teachings of the later Buddhists and of the special theory of the Essence of Buddhahood,[1] the fundamental element[2] of the Absolute, as existing in all living beings. Before we commence an investigation of this theory, it is necessary to give a general summary review of the contents of all the 5 treatises. The Lamaist monasteries of Tibet and Mongolia possess separate block-print editions (independently from the Tangyur) of all of them.[3] We have moreover works of diverse Tibetan scholars containing a special analysis of them *en regard*.[4] Both these circumstances greatly facilitate a sum-

[1] *tathāgata-garbha = de-bžin-gšegs-paḥi-sñiṅ-po.* [2] *dhātu = khams.*

[3] In Transbaikalia we have two such editions, one issued by the Bde-chen-lhun-grub-gliṅ (Aga), and the other by the Gusinoozersky Monastery.

[4] Among these works it will be sufficient to mention two, viz. 1) The Commentary on the Abhisamayālaṁkāra by Jam-yaṅ-gā-bᵃi-lo-ḍö (Ḥjam-dbyaṅs-dgaḥ-baḥi-blo-gros, edition of the Lo-sä-liṅ section of the Bräbuṅ Monastery of Tibet), and 2) the investigation of the contents of the 3 Prajñā-pāramitā-sūtras by the celebrated Loṅ-dol (Kloṅ-rdol) Lama.

mary investigation of the works in question and of the theories contained in them. According to the earlier Tibetan writers,[1] the *Sūtrālaṁkāra*, *Uttaratantra*, *Madhyānta-vibhanga* and *Dharma-dharmatā-vibhanga* are all of them written from the standpoint of the Yogācāra-vijñānavāda school. The *Abhisamayālaṁkāra*, as an interpretation of the Prajña-pāramitā-sūtras, is regarded by the said authorities as referring to the Scripture of the intermediate period, i.e. as a Mādhyamika work. The Tibetan authors of the later period, Tsoṅ-kha-pa, &c., have another opinion as regards this subject. They admit, as their predecessors, that the *Sūtrālaṁkāra* and the two *Vibhangas* contain an exposition of the specific Yogācāra teachings. But the *Uttaratantra* is according to them not a Yogācāra, but a Mādhyamika-Prāsangika[2] work, since it expresses the extreme monistic views peculiar to that school. As to the *Abhisamayālaṁkāra*, it is regarded as belonging to that branch of the Mādhyamika school which is called Yogācāra-Mādhyamika-Svātantrika,[3] the representatives of which are the great authorities in the Prajñā-pāramitā,—Ārya-Vimuktasena, Bhadanta-Vimuktasena, and Haribhadra. As we shall see later on, this standpoint of the Tibetan writers belonging to Tsoṅ-kha-pa's school may in general be regarded as correct.

We shall now make an attempt to give a summary analysis of all the 5 treatises. We begin with the *Sūtrālaṁkāra*, which is the best known owing to the edition and translation of it by Prof. Sylvain Lévi. It is to be regarded as a systematical exposition of the teachings contained in the sūtras of the later period expressing

---

[1] Cf. Bu-ton's Index of the Tangyur in his "History of Buddhism" 180 a. 3. —Bu-ton has even the tendency of viewing all the 5 treatises of Maitreya as forming one separate branch of literature belonging to the Yogācāra school. He says that this literature consists altogether of 20 treatises viz. the 5 works of Maitreya, the 5 divisions of Āryāsanga's Yogacaryā-bhūmi, the Abhidharma-samuccaya and Mahāyāna-saṁgraha and the 8 treatises of Vasubandhu. Cf. Prof. Stcherbatsky's article in the Muséon "La littérature Yogācāra d'après Bou-ston" and my translation of Bu-ton's History p. 57.

[2] Tib. Dbu-ma-thal-ḥgyur-ba.

[3] Tib. Rnal-ḥbyor-spyod-pahi-dbu-ma-raṅ-rgyud-pa.

the Yogācāra views.[1] The whole work is characterized as a detailed exposition of the methods by means of which the Bodhisattva has to act on his Path toward Enlightenment.[2] The division of the subjects and chapters is as follows:—

First comes the exposition of the basis on which the Bodhisattva has to act.[3] Accordingly we have:—

Chapter I.[4]—A vindication of the Mahāyānistic Scripture and an attempt to prove it to be the true Teaching of Buddha.—

Chapter II.[5] The search of a refuge in the 3 Jewels, Buddha, the Doctrine, and the Congregation.—The individual who has obtained faith in the Mahāyānistic Teaching and in the 3 Jewels becomes able to enter the Path toward Salvation.[6]—

Chapter III.[7] The Germ of Enlightenment or the element of the saintly lineage[8] which is the source of all the virtuous qualities of a living being.—It must be first awakened to life in order to become the foundation of spiritual progress on the Path.[9]—

Chapter IV.[10] The Creative Mental Effort for Enlightenment,[11] the production of a special state of the mind connected with the desire of attaining Buddhahood in order to lead others to Salvation.— The person in whom the Germ of Enlightenment is aroused to life and who has made the Creative Effort can now begin his course of training.[12]

---

[1] According to the Siddhānta (Grub-mtḫaḥ) of Jam-yaṅ-źad-pa, the sūtras which are regarded as the foundation of the Yogācāra system, are:—a) the Saṁdhinirmocana (tib. Dgoṅs-pa-ṅes-par-ḫgrel-pa), b) the Laṅkāvatāra, c) the Ghana-vyūha.

[2] Jam-yaṅ-gā-bᵃi-lo-ḍö, 8 a. 2.

[3] Jam-yaṅ-gā-bᵃi-lo-ḍö, 8 b. 2.

[4] Mahāyāna-siddhy-adhikāra. In the later Tibetan editions this chapter is divided into two parts viz. a general introduction (verses 1—6) and the vindication of Mahāyāna (v. 7—21).

[5] Śaraṇa-gamana-adhikāra.

[6] Jam. 8 b. 3.

[7] Gotra-adhikāra.

[8] *gotra* = *rigs*.

[9] *pratipatter ādhāraḥ* = *sgrub-paḥi-rten.*

[10] Citta-utpāda-adhikāra.

[11] *bodhi-citta-utpāda* = *byaṅ-chub-tu-sems-bskyed.*

[12] Jam. 8 b. 4.

Next comes the exposition of the topics in which the Bodhisattva must become instructed. Accordingly we have:—

Chapter V.[1]—The activity of the Bodhisattva in pursuit ot one's own weal and of that of others.[2] The causes of this activity are exposed in:—

Chapter VI.[3]—On the Absolute Truth and its cognition by the Saint. The teaching of the Absolute is given here from the standpoint of the Yogācāra system, i.e. as the negation of the imaginary[4] external world opposed to the relative[5] reality of the individual ideas and the unique, undifferentiated Absolute Reality.[6]—

Chapter VII.[7]—On the attainment of exclusive power by the Bodhisattva.—

Chapter VIII.[8]—The methods of attaining complete maturity oneself and of conveying the same to others.[9]—

Chapter IX.[10]—The teaching about Supreme Enlightenment and the 3 Bodies of the Buddha.—

Then follows the teaching about the way, how the Bodhisattva must undergo his course of training:—[11]

Chapter X.[12]—Faith in the Mahāyānistic Doctrine and adherence to it.—

Chapter XI.[13]—A search for the full knowledge of this Doctrine. Here we again meet with the typical Yogācāra theories concerning the 3 aspects of reality, &c.—[14]

Chapter XII.[15]—The preaching of the Doctrine by the Bodhisattva.—

Chapter XIII.[16]—Action according to the Doctrine.—

---

[1] Pratipatty-adhikāra (1).
[2] Jam. 8 b. 5.
[3] Tattva-adhikāra.
[4] *parikalpita = kun-btags.*
[5] *paratantra = gźan-dbaṅ.*
[6] *pariniṣpanna = yoṅs-grub.*
[7] Prabhāva-adhikāra.
[8] Paripāka-adhikāra.
[9] Jam. 8 b. 5.
[10] Bodhy-adhikāra.
[11] Jam. 8 b. 7.
[12] Adhimukty-adhikāra.
[13] Dharma-paryeṣṭy-adhikāra.
[14] XI. 13 sqq., 38—41.
[15] Deśana-adhikāra.
[16] Pratipatty-adhikāra (2).

Chapter XIV.[1]—The precepts and instructions received by the Bodhisattva at the time of his abiding on the Path. The different stages of the latter, as the 4 degrees of the Path of Training,[2] &c.

Chapter XV.[3]—The skilful acts of the Bodhisattva. Thereafter we have an exposition of these acts in detail:—

Chapter XVI.[4]—The 6 highest transcendental virtues and the four methods of obtaining adherents.[5]

Chapter XVII.[6]—On the worship of the Buddha and the limitless noble feelings.[7]

Chapter XVIII.[8]—The characteristic properties harmonizing with Enlightenment.[9] The Accumulations of Virtue and Wisdom,[10] &c.

Chapter XIX[11].—The different virtuous properties of the Bodhisattva.

Chapter XX—XXI.[12]—The termination of the Bodhisattva's activity at the time of final Enlightenment.—

The *Sūtrālaṁkāra* is thus, as we have just seen, an exposition of Yogācāra theories in connexion with the religious practice and conduct of the Bodhisattva. In the next two works, viz. the *Madhyānta-vibhanga* and *Dharma-dharmatā-vibhanga*, the philosophical part predominates. These treatises are regarded as special interpretations of that part of Scripture which contains the Yogācāra Doctrine in its purest and most pregnant form, such as the *Saṁdhinirmocana-sūtra.*[13] A special characteristic feature of this doctrine is, besides its idealistic character, the discrimination between the 3 aspects of reality which we have slightly mentioned above. The *Madhyānta-vibhanga* exposes the Yogācāra theories from the stand-

---

[1] Avavāda-anuśāsanī-adhikāra. [2] *nirvedha-bhāgīya*, XIV. 23—27.

[3] Upāya-sahita-karma-adhikāra. [4] Pāramitā-adhikāra.

[5] *catvāri saṁgraha-vastūni = bsdu-baḥi-dṅos-po-bźi.*

[6] Pūjā-sevā-apramāṇa-adhikāra. [7] *apramāṇa = tshad-med-pa.*

[8] Bodhipakṣa-adhikāra.

[9] *bodhipakṣika-dharma = byaṅ-chub-kyi-phyogs-daṅ-mthun-paḥi-chos.*

[10] *puṇya-jñāna-saṁbhāra.* [11] Guṇa-adhikāra. [12] Caryā-pratiṣṭhā-adhikāra.

[13] Tib. Dgoṅs-pa-ṅes-par-ḥgrel-pa, otherwise called Mdo-sde-dgoṅs-ḥgrel, Kg. MDO. V.

point of their being the middle way,[1] the negation of the two extremities of Eternalism[2] and Materialism,[3] or otherwise, of Realism and Nihilism.[4] As the external world is regarded as unreal and allowed only an imaginary, fancied[5] existence, the extremity of Realism becomes rejected. But, on the other hand, there is neither any room for nihilistic views, since the relative[6] reality of the individual ideas from the empirical standpoint[7] and their ultimate Absolute Reality[8] are both admitted.

The subject-matter of the *Madhyānta-vibhanga* is divided into 7 topics which are as follows:—

1) The 3 aspects of reality,—Chapter I.
2) The various forms of obscurations which are to be removed,—Chapter II.
3) The Absolute Truth according to the Yogācāra theory,—Chapter III.—It is defined as "that which, being cognized, makes impossible the origination of views maintaining the reality of the separate elements or of the personality[9] as a whole, of subject and object[10] and of ens and non-ens.—
4) The antidotes against the defiling elements, and
5) The concentration of mind upon these antidotes,—Chapter IV.
6) The basis for this concentration and
7) The activity on the Mahāyānistic Path,—Chapter V.

In the *Dharma-dharmatā-vibhanga* the theory of the 3 aspects of reality is the basis on which the elements (*dharma*) of the Phenomenal World and their ultimate Absolute Essence (*dharmatā*)

---

[1] *madhyama-pratipad = dbu-maḥi-lam.*

[2] *śāśvata-anta = rtag-mthaḥ.* [3] *uccheda-anta = chad-mthaḥ.*

[4] Tib. *yod-mthaḥ* and *med-mthaḥ* (= *sad-anta* and *asad-anta*). Cf. my translation of Bu-ton's History p. 54.

[5] *parikalpita = kun-btags.* [6] *paratantra = gźan-dbaṅ.*

[7] Cf. Bu-ton, Lhasa block-print, 79 a. 6.—*gźan-dbaṅ kun-rdzob-tu yod = paratantram asti saṁvṛtyā.*

[8] *pariniṣpanna = yoṅs-grub.*

[9] *pudgala = gaṅ-zag*

[10] *grāhya-grāhaka = gzuṅ-ḥdzin.*

are investigated.[1]—The relative[2] entities, as modifications of one conscious principle, are the elements which call forth the illusion of an independently existing external world; they are thus the factors by which the seeming existence in the Saṁsāra is conditioned. These elements, being separated from their imputed nature, disclose their true Absolute Essence (*dharmatā*). In the aspect of the latter they appear as unique and undifferentiated, as merged for ever in Nirvāṇa.[3] Thus from another standpoint, being viewed correctly, the same relative individual ideas are represented as that from which the true essence of all things, Nirvāṇa, may be conjectured.[4] Accordingly the *Dharma-dharmatā-vibhanga* is a treatise demonstrating the Phenomenal World and the Absolute, Saṁsāra and Nirvāṇa in regard of each other.[5] It is said that the aim of such an exposition is to bring about the cognition and rejection of the false, imputed, and defiled[6] character of the elements as constituting the Phenomenal World on one side, and to lead to the realization of Nirvāṇa through the cognition of the true, pure,[7] and absolute nature of the same elements, on the other.[8]

The contents of the *Abhisamayālaṁkāra* forms the subject of a special investigation,—the analysis of its 8 subjects and 70 topics which is now in the press. It is here only necessary to point to some characteristic features of this work owing to which the Tibetan authors maintain it to be a Mādhyamika and not a Yogācāra treatise. In fact, we do not find in it anywhere the discrimination between

---

[1] Cf. Bu-ton, translation p. 54. [2] *paratantra = gźan-dbaṅ.*

[3] *prakṛti-parinirvṛtta = raṅ-bźin-gyis-yoṅs-su-mya-ṅan-las-ḥdas-pa.*

[4] Jam. 7 b. 2—3. [5] Ibid.

[6] *sāṁkleśika = kun-nas-ñon-moṅs-pa.*

[7] *vaiyavadānika = rnam-par-byaṅ-ba.*

[8] Jam. 7 b. 3—4.—As the plurality of the elements influenced by defiling agencies is declared to be an illusion which in reality does not exist and has never existed before, we see that the Yogācāras likewise maintain the absence of a real difference between Saṁsāra and Nirvāṇa and that they consider the transition from the former into the latter to consist only in a change of the point of view, acc. to Abhisamayālaṁkāra V. 21.—*nā'paneyam ataḥ kiṁcit*, &c.

the 3 aspects of reality with the view of the imputed as being unreal and of the relative and absolute as having an independent reality. There is likewise nothing about the "store-consciousness,"[1] this characteristic tenet of the elder branch of the Yogācāra school. The main standpoint of the *Abhisamayālaṁkāra* is that of universal Non-substantiality and Relativity, i.e. the Mādhyamika view. Moreover, in respect of the fundamental element or Germ of Enlightenment,[2] the *Abhisamayālaṁkāra* likewise adheres to the Mādhyamika standpoint. The fundamental element is regarded as identical with the Absolute,[3] unique and undifferentiated,[4] and not as a special force, though derived from the Absolute, but nevertheless differing from it, as the Yogācāras admit.

[The Uttaratantra and its Sources.]

Finally, we have the *Uttaratantra* to which the present investigation is devoted. The principal subject-matter of this treatise is the special theory of the fundamental element[5] of the Absolute, otherwise called the Essence of the Buddha[6] or the element of his lineage.[7] In the *Abhisamayālaṁkāra* we have only a brief indication of this subject, as being the foundation for the activity on the Path toward Salvation. Here, on the contrary, we have it as the main, the central topic. All the other subjects are represented in their relation to it as the causes and the result of its development. The whole contents of the work is divided into 7 subjects:—

Buddha (1), the Doctrine (2), and the Congregation (3),—the 3 Jewels.

---

1 *ālaya-vijñāna = kun-gźi-rnam-par-śes-pa.*

2 *dhātu = gotra.*

3 Cf. Abhisamayālaṁkāra. I. 5. *ādhāraḥ pratipatteś ca dharma-dhātu-svabhāvakaḥ.*

4 Ibid. I. 39—*dharma-dhātor asaṁbhedād gotra-bhedo na yujyate.*

5 *dhātu = khams.*

6 *tathāgata-garbha = de-bźin-gśegs-paḥi-sñiṅ-po.*

7 *gotra = rigs.*

The fundamental element of the Absolute, the Essence of the Buddha as it exists in every living being, obscured by the accidental[1] defiling elements (4).[2]

The state of Supreme Enlightenment, that of the same element as delivered from all the Obscurations (5).

The properties of the Buddha possessed by him after the attainment of this state of complete Illumination (6).

The acts performed by the Buddha in pursuit of the welfare of all living beings (7).

The first four subjects are included in Chapter I,—"On the Essence of Buddhahood" (165 verses). The latter 3 are treated separately. So we have Chapter II—"On Supreme Enlightenment" (72 verses), Chapter III—"The Properties of the Buddha" (38 verses), and Chapter IV—"The Buddha's Acts" (101 verses).

The fifth and last chapter 28 verses has for its subject-matter the advantages and the merit of studying the Doctrine concerning the Essence of Buddhahood.

We possess a Commentary on the *Uttaratantra* by Āryāsanga called *Uttaratantra-vyākhyā* (Tangyur, MDO. XLIV), a separate block-print edition of which has been issued by the Aga (Bde-chen-lhun-grub-gliṅ) Monastery. It is known in the Tibetan tradition by the abriged title *Thogs-ḥgrel* (i.e. *Thogs-med-kyi-ḥgrel-pa* = *Asanga-vṛtti*). Among the detailed Tibetan Commentaries, the best known is that of Tsoṅ-kha-pa's pupil Gyal-tshab-dar-ma-rin-chen (*Dar-ṭīk*).[3] We give below a translation of the main text with the whole of Āryāsanga's Commentary, supplying it with explanations from Gyal-tshab's work when necessary.

---

[1] *āgantukā-mala* = *glo-bur-gyi-dri-ma.*

[2] Jam. 4 b. 4—5. — The Uttaratantra proves the existence of the unique undifferentiated Absolute Essence of all relative entities, the negation of all separate illusionary reality as existing from the outset and representing the essential nature of a living being.

[3] Vol. III of the full collection of his works (*gsuṅ-ḥbum*), Labraṅ edition.

The title *Uttaratantra* has been interpreted in two ways:—1) as the highest or 2) as the latest of the Mahāyānistic teachings.[1] The work is regarded as the interpretation of 5 Sūtras relating to the Scripture of the later period. These are:—1) The *Tathāgata-mahā-karuṇā-nirdeśa-sūtra* alias *Dhāraṇīśvara-rāja-paripṛcchā*,[2] 2) the *Śrī-mālā-devī-siṁhanāda-sūtra*,[3] 3) the *Tathāgata-garbha-sūtra*[4] containing the 9 examples which illustrate the Essence of the Buddha, as it exists in all living beings, 4) the *Sarva-buddha-viṣaya-avatāra-jñāna-āloka-alaṁkāra-sūtra*,[5] illustrating the inconceivable character of the Buddha's acts, and 5) the *Ratna-dārikā-paripṛcchā* on the 64 properties of the Buddha. The *Uttaratantra-vyākhyā*[6] contains numerous quotations from all these Sūtras, mostly without mentioning their titles. Sometimes even the quotation looks like an ordinary passage of Āryāsanga's Commentary without any allusion whatever to the Sūtra quoted.[7] The identification of such passages with their sources is of course exceedingly difficult.

Besides the Sūtras just mentioned, we have in the *Uttaratantra-vyākhyā* likewise quotations from other canonical works, such as the *Sāgaramati-paripṛcchā*,[8] the *Gaganagañja-sūtra*,[9] the *Mahāparinirvāṇa-sūtra*, &c. All these can be identified with their sources.

---

[1] Cf. Bu-ton, translation p. 54.

[2] Tib. Gzuṅs-kyi-dbaṅ-phyug-rgyal-pos-źus-paḥi-mdo. Kg. MDO. XV. Translated into Chinese by Ku-fa-hu (Dharmarakṣa) 265—316 A.D. (Nanjio's Catalogue No. 79).

[3] Tib. Dpal-phreṅ-gi-mdo. Kg. DKON. VI. Chinese translation by Guṇabhadra 420—479 A.D. and Bodhiruci 618—907 A.D. (Nanjio No. 23, 59).

[4] Tib. De-bźin-gśegs-paḥi-sñiṅ-poḥi-mdo. Kg. MDO. XXII. Chinese translations by Buddhabhadra 317—420 A.D. and by an unknown translator 350—431 A.D. (Nanjio No. 384, 443).

[5] Tib. Saṅs-rgyas-kyi-yul-thams-cad-la-ḥjug-pa-ye-śes-snaṅ-ba-rgyan-gyi-mdo. Kg. MDO. III. Chinese translations by Fa-hu (1004—1058) and others (960—1127, Nanjio No. 1013).

[6] The Uttaratantra itself has been translated into Chinese by Ratna-mati 508 A.D. (Nanjio, 1236).

[7] Cf. Vyākhyā, f. 9 b. 6. sqq.

[8] Tib. Blo-gros-rgya-mtshos-źus-paḥi-mdo. Kg. MDO. XIV.

[9] Tib. Nam-mkhaḥi-mdzod-kyi-mdo. Kg. MDO. XIII.

In several places the main text of the *Uttaratantra* itself represents nothing but a summary of different passages of the Sūtras, as for instance in Chapter I, on the 9 examples illustrating the Essence of the Buddha according to the *Tathāgata-garbha-sūtra.*

## II. The Authorship of the Treatises of Maitreya.

It is here that we meet again with the problem of the authorship of the 5 Treatises of Maitreya. Prof. Ui in his article expresses the opinion that Maitreya was a historical person, the teacher of Āryāsanga and the founder of the Yogācāra school. Now, as regards this last point, we have an interesting statement in the *Siddhānta* (Grub-mthaḥ) of Jam-yaṅ-źad-pa, where it is said:[1]—The teacher Nāgārjuna, having been inspired by the Bodhisattva Mañjuśrī, has laid the foundation to the Mādhyamika system in accordance with the *Akṣayamati-nirdeśa-sūtra.* The same has been done by the teacher Āryāsanga in regard of the Yogācāra system through the inspiration of Maitreya and on the basis of the *Saṁdhi-nirmocana-sūtra.*—A similar statement is to be found in Bu-ton's Commentary on the Abhisamayālaṁkāra called *Luṅ-gi-sñe-ma.*[2]—From this we may draw the conclusion that both the systems were evidently considered to have had each their own divine, legendary inspirer, from whom the Doctrine was said to have been obtained through revelation. In Bu-ton's History of Buddhism[3] it is moreover said that Āryāsanga has written down the 5 treatises after having heard them from Maitreya in the Tuṣita heavens. This might be simply interpreted in the sense that Āryāsanga and no other was the actual author of the 5 works. As the latter represent the foundation of the exegetical literature connected with the new conceptions of Buddhism, it is

[1] I quote the passage of the Grub-mthaḥ-rtsa-baḥi-tshig-ṭik-śel-dkar-me-loṅ, a short Commentary on the work of Jam-yaṅ-źad-pa by the Lama Blo-bzaṅ-dkon-mchog; Labraṅ edition 24 b. 3—5.

[2] Aga Monastery edition 114 b. 6 and 115 b. 2.

[3] Lhasa edition, 116 b. 3—*byams-chos-sde-lṅa yi-ger-bkod-do.*

quite natural that the adherents of these conceptions ascribed to the 5 treatises a divine, supermundane origin.—

Now, as a matter of fact, the 5 treatises show a great resemblance with each other as regards style. This resemblance may be noticed even in the Tibetan translations. We meet with many verses which have nearly the same contents,[1] and one which is exactly the same in both the *Abhisamayālaṁkāra* and the *Uttaratantra*.[2] As concerns the relation of the latter to its Commentary, there are some points which can prove that both must have been composed by the same author. In Chapter I the fundamental element, the Essence of Buddhahood is investigated from 10 points of view viz. the essence, the cause of purification, the result of the latter, &c. The main text does not contain a direct indication of everyone of these points as forming a new paragraph, and this we have only in the Commentary. Some verses are quite incomprehensible by themselves and only the Commentary makes clear their meaning and relation. Moreover, we must point to an interesting feature of the Commentary itself. It is only the first chapter which is commented in detail, forming almost 3 quarters of the whole work. The other four chapters contain almost exclusively the verses of the main text with a very few indications mostly like "the meaning of this verse is rendered clear by the following eight," &c. This fact may be understood in the sense that the author considered the text of the verses to be sufficiently clear by itself without needing an exposition in detail. If the Commentary had been composed by a writer other than the author of the main work, one could hardly understand the sense of his having merely copied the verses of the *Uttaratantra* in 4 chapters,

---

[1] We give here a few examples:—

a) Sūtrālaṁkāra IX. 60. *svābhāviko'tha sāṁbhogyaḥ kāyo nairmāṇiko' paraḥ kāya-bhedā hi buddhānāṁ prathamas tu dvayāśrayaḥ* and Abhisamayālaṁkāra VIII. 17. *svābhāvikaḥ sasaṁbhogo nairmāṇiko' paras tathā*, &c. b) Sūtrālaṁkāra IV. 11 and Uttaratantra I. 33., c) Sūtrālaṁkāra IX. 37 and Uttaratantra I. 27.

[2] Abhisamayālaṁkāra V. 21 and Uttaratantra I. 152.—
*nā' paneyam ataḥ kiṁcit prakṣeptavyaṁ na kiṁ ca na* &c.

after having given a detailed and brilliant exposition of the first. We may affirm that the principal aim of Āryāsanga in his Commentary was to enlarge upon the teaching of the Essence of Buddhahood and to put it forth as a special and quite new theory. This he has done in the first chapter of the work.

Now, if all the 5 treatises have been composed by one author, how can we explain the fact that they have been written from different points of view. It is said in the Commentary of Gyal-tshab[1] that the first 3 works (i.e. the *Sūtrālaṁkāra*, *Madhyānta-vibhanga*, and *Dharma-dharmatā-vibhanga*) contain an exposition of the teaching of the Absolute Truth as modified in accordance with the understanding of some of the converts, and not in its complete form, i.e. as the theory of the Relativity and Non-substantiality of all elements of existence. On the foundation of the said 3 treatises and in accordance with the discrimination between the conventional[2] and the direct[3] meaning in the *Saṁdhinirmocana-sūtra*, the teacher (Āryāsanga) has composed the 5 divisions of the *Yogacaryā-bhūmi* and the two summary works,[4] in which he has laid the foundation to the Yogācāra-vijñānavāda system.[5] The *Abhisamayālaṁkāra* in its turn exposes repeatedly the theory of universal Relativity and Non-substantiality; the main subject-matter is here however the process of Illumination[6] of the Saint, the Path toward Enlightenment, as being the hidden meaning of the *Prajñā-pāramitā-sūtras*. As to the *Uttaratantra*, it is said that it is to be subsequently exposed to those who have first attained maturity on the foundation of the Vijñānavāda Doctrine and to those members of the Mahāyānistic family who are endowed with the most acute intellectual faculty. It demonstrates the teaching of the Absolute as the unique undifferentiated principle, being the negation of the separate reality of

---

[1] 4 a. 5. sqq. [2] *neyārtha* = *draṅ-don.* [3] *nītārtha* = *ṅes-don.*

[4] The Mahāyāna-saṁgraha and Abhidharma-samuccaya. Cf. Bu-ton, translation p. 56.

[5] Lit. "has opened the passage for the Vehicle of Vijñānavāda".

[6] *abhisamaya* = *mṅon-rtogs.*

all the elements in their plurality, in accordance with the *Prajñā-pāramitā* and the *Tathāgata-garbha-sūtra.* This teaching is the principal subject-matter of the work and represents the real point of view of the teacher.

All this may perhaps be taken as an allusion to the fact that there might have been a gradual evolution in the conceptions of Āryāsanga.[1] It is probable that he started from the main Yogācāra standpoint with its extreme idealism and its theory of a store-consciousness,[2] and of the 3 aspects of reality. Then, on the foundation of the *Prajñā-pāramitā,* he has composed the *Abhisamayālaṁkāra,* giving up his extreme Yogācāra views and drawing near to the monistic conception of the Mādhyamikas. Indeed, as we have mentioned above, the *Abhisamayālaṁkāra* contains nothing about the store-consciousness or the other typical tenets of the Yogācāra school. It may be that at that time Āryāsanga was not quite certain in regard of his main standpoint, since we possess in Tsoṅ-kha-pa's Gser-phreṅ[3] an indication that his Commentary on the *Abhisamayālaṁkāra* and the *Pañca-viṁśati-sāhasrikā* was written from the Yogācāra point of view. Finally, in the *Uttaratantra* he may be considered to have attained the highest point of development in adopting a theory of purest, extreme monism. It is owing to this circumstance that the later Tibetan authors consider the *Uttaratantra* to be a Mādhyamika-Prāsangika work. At the same time we find Āryāsanga attempting to give a substitution for the idea of an individual soul. The conception of a store-consciousness containing the seeds of all the elements was replaced by him by the idea of the Essence of Buddhahood, the fundamental element of the Absolute as existing in every living being. This element which had before been regarded by Āryāsanga[4] as an active force,[5] was now viewed

---

[1] Cf. Prof. Th. Stcherbatsky, Conception of Buddhist Nirvāṇa, p. 34.

[2] *ālaya-vijñāna = kun-gźi-rnam-par-śes-pa.*

[3] Aga edition, I. 19 a. 1—5.

[4] In the Sūtrālaṁkāra, Śrāvaka-bhūmi, Bodhisattva-bhūmi, &c.

[5] *bīja = sāmarthya.*

es eternal, quiescent, and unalterable, as the true essence of every living being and the source of all the virtuous qualities. Once, in his Commentary,[1] Āryāsanga returns to his old conception of the element of the lineage of Buddhahood[2] as a force, governing the 6 internal bases of cognition.[3] This however refers only to the fundamental element taken in the aspect of Empirical Reality,[4] as the Germ of Enlightenment which becomes developed.[5]

We do not, however, exclude the possibility that Āryāsanga could have written different works from different points of view, without changing his main standpoint. We know that such a practice was familiar to the Indian scholars belonging to diverse philosophical systems, as for instance Vācaspatimiśra who has written works from the Nāyāyika, Yoga, and Vedānta standpoint. The great Tibetan writers, as Tsoṅ-kha-pa, &c., have likewise composed their Commentaries in accordance with the texts explained by them; so we have works expressing the Mādhyamika-Prāsangika, Mādhyamika-Svātantrika, Yogācāra, Sautrāntika and Vaibhāṣika (on the Abhidharmakośa) standpoint, all having been written by one author.

## III. The different Theories regarding the Fundamental Element or Germ of Enlightenment.

Thus, as we see, the main subject-matter of the Uttaratantra and the Commentary thereon is the teaching of the fundamental element[6] of the Absolute, otherwise called the Essence of the Buddha or the element of his lineage (*gotra*). Before we begin an investigation of this subject in accordance with the most developed Mādhyamika conception of it, we must give a brief account of the theories of other Buddhist schools concerning it likewise. In the celebrated Commentary of Tsoṅ-kha-pa on the *Abhisamayālaṁkāra*, called Gser-phreṅ, as well as in the manual[7] on the same work by the Grand

---

[1] Cf. p. 206. [2] *gotra = rigs.* [3] *ṣaḍ-āyatana = skye-mched-drug.*
[4] *saṁvṛtyā = kun-rdzob-tu.* [5] *paripuṣṭa* or *samudānita-gotra.*
[6] *dhātu = khams.* [7] *yig-cha.*

Lama Jam-yaṅ-źad-pa[1] we possess a thorough analysis of the teaching about *dhātu* or *gotra* from the standpoint of the 4 principal Buddhist schools. It is on the basis of these 2 Tibetan works that we now make an attempt to give a systematical review of the different theories concerning the element of the saintly lineage. We shall strictly follow the order in which the subject is investigated by the Tibetan Commentaries. First comes the standpoint of the Hīnayānistic schools, the Vaibhāṣikas and Sautrāntikas, then that of the Yogācāras, and, finally, the theory of the Mādhyamikas, or that which is contained in the *Uttaratantra* and *Abhisamayālaṁkāra*.

### a) The Term *gotra* and its Interpretation in Hīnayāna.

In the Vinaya and Abhidharma the term *gotra* is to be found in the sense of a special element which is regarded as the principal factor for the attainment of Arhatship, or otherwise, as that element which forms, so to say, the essential nature or character of a Saint.[2] Among the psychical elements,[3] there are 3, viz. absence of desire,[4] absence of enmity,[5] and absence of infatuation[6] which are called the 3 principal roots of virtue.[7] Of these three, the element of absence of desire is that which represents the essential character of the Saint and the element conducive to Salvation.[8] This element manifests itself in the contentment with every kind of clothing, food, dwelling, and couch, however poor and bad they might be,[9] and in a feeling of satisfaction with the practice of profound meditation and the removal of the defiling elements,[10] which likewise shows the Saint's aversion to all worldly matters. The first three characteristics

---

[1] Phar-phyin-skabs-brgyad-ka, Chilūtai (Dgaḥ-ldan-dar-rgyas-gliṅ) Monastery block-print edition.

[2] *ārya-pudgala.*

[3] *caitta* = *sems-byuṅ.*

[4] *alobha* = *chags-med-pa.*

[5] *adveṣa* = *że-sdaṅ-med-pa.*

[6] *amoha* = *gti-mug-med-pa.*

[7] *triṇi kuśala-mūlāni* = *dge-rtsa-gsum.*

[8] Cf. Bu-ton's Luṅ-gi-sñe-ma, Aga edition 203. a. 4.

[9] Gser-phreṅ I. 242 b. 2. (as a quotation from the Vinaya) and Skabs-brgyad-ka I. 232 b. 5.

[10] Gser. I. 242 b. 3. and Skabs. I. 232 b. 5–6.

refer to the nature of the Saint as securing the Path toward Salvation, whereas the fourth represents the essence of the Saint's activity on the Path.[1] Moreover, the element of absence of desire, as manifesting itself in the contentment with every kind of clothing, food, &c. is to be viewed as an antidote against every kind of attachment regarding one's property; being taken in the aspect of the satisfaction with the removal of defilement it is that which puts an end to every kind of consideration of "Ego" and "Mine."[2] Consequently, as the element of absence of desire represents such an important, predominant factor for the attainment of Salvation and the annihilation[3] of all worldly elements, it is the *gotra*, the fundamental element of the saintly lineage.[4]

Such is the conception of the *gotra* according to the Vaibhāsika school. The standpoint of the other branch of the Hīnayānists, that of the Sautrāntikas is quite different. This school admits the existence of a special force[5] governing the element of consciousness. It belongs to the so-called "pure forces"[6] and gives origination to the pure transcendental wisdom[7] of the Saint at the time of final Enlightenment. This force represents the fundamental element, the *gotra* of the Saint,[8] and is regarded as existing from the outset in every living being. According to the Sautrāntikas this force can be annihilated and the attainment of Enlightenment made impossible, this being the case with an individual in whom the roots of virtue are prevented to grow.[9] As we shall see further on, this point of view forms a link between the Hīnayānistic and the Mahāyānistic conceptions

---

[1] Gser. I. 242 b. 3—4.

[2] Gser. I. 242 b. 4—5. Both these aspects of the element of saintly lineage are mentioned in the Abhidharmakośa VI. 7, 8, Tsugol Monastery edition 85b. 5—86a. 2.

[3] *nirodha* = *ḥgog-pa*.

[4] Abhidharmakośa-bhāṣya, Aga edition.

[5] *bīja* = *sāmarthya*.

[6] *viprayukta-saṁskāra* = *ldan-min-ḥdu-byed*.

[7] *anāsrava-jñāna* = *zag-med-ye-śes*.

[8] Skabs-brgyad-ka I. 233 a. 1. and 238 b. 1, as a quotation from Yaśomitra's Abhidharmakośa-vyākhyā.

[9] *samucchinna-kuśala-mūla* = *dge-baḥi-rtsa-ba-kun-tu-chad-pa*.

of the *gotra*, since the theory of the Yogācāras which is to be discussed presently, represents only a more developed form of the Sautrāntika standpoint.

### b) The Yogācāra Theories concerning *dhātu* or *gotra*.

Before we begin an investigation of the *gotra* as viewed by the Yogācāras it is necesssary, in short, to point to the principal subdivisions of this school. The elder branch are the Yogācāras or Vijñānavādins basing upon Scripture,[1] the school of Āryāsanga and Vasubandhu. They maintain the theory of the store-consciousness[2] containing, so to say, the seeds of all the elements constituting a personality.[3] The other subdivision is that of the Logician Vijñānavādins,[4] the younger school founded by Dignāga. This branch of the Yogācāras does not admit the existence of the store-consciousness, the functions of which are according to this school divided among the six internal bases of cognition.

In accordance with these 2 varieties of the Yogācāras the conception of the *gotra* differs in some points, being, in regard of the main one, essentially the same. Those who maintain the theory of the store-consciousness define the "gotra" as a force which governs[5] this store-consciousness and which brings about the origination of pure transcendental knowledge, the removal of the defiling agencies and the transformation[6] of all the elements constituting a personality into component parts of the 3 Bodies of the Buddha. With the logicians it is respectively a force governing the internal bases of cognition, its functions being exactly the same as those maintained

---

[1] Tib. luṅ-gi-rjes-ḥbraṅs-sems-tsam-pa = āgama-anusāriṇo vijñānavādinaḥ.

[2] *ālaya-vijñāna* = *kun-gźi-rnam-par-śes-pa.*

[3] It is interesting to note that in the Lamaist schools it is maintained that the Yogācāras hold the store-consciousness to be *gaṅ-zag-rdzas-yod-pa* = *dravya-sat-pudgala* i.e. "the real personality" (!).

[4] rigs-paḥi-rjes-ḥbraṅs-sems-tsam-pa = nyāya-anusāriṇo vijñānavādinaḥ.

[5] Lit. "stands above" (*kun-gźiḥi-steṅ-du* = *ālayasya upari*).

[6] *parāvṛtti* = *yoṅs-su-gyur-pa.*

7*

by the elder school. The *gotra* is regarded by both the subdivisions of the Yogācāra school as manifesting itself in 2 aspects, viz. the fundamental, existing in every living being from the outset, and that which undergoes the process of development.[1] Thus, the standpoint of the Yogācāras regarding the very essence of the *gotra* itself agrees with that of the Sautrāntikas. It is held to be a pure force and an active[2] mutable element. This active character is very pregnantly expressed in the *Gūḍhārtha*[3] where it is said that the Absolute Reality[4] manifests itself in 2 forms, viz. the active and the immutable.[5] The first of these forms has again 2 varieties,—the pure Transcendental Wisdom of the Buddha[6] and the seed, the germ of this Transcendental Wisdom.[7] This seed is the *gotra*, the fundamental element and the original cause[8] of Enlightenment. It is, as has been mentioned before, of 2 kinds, viz. the primordial and that which becomes developed. Remarkable is the theory of the Yogācāras regarding the metamorphose[9] of the elements constituting the personality of an ordinary individual into component parts of the 3 Bodies of the Buddha at the time of final Enlightenment. This metamorphose is produced by the agency of the *gotra*, which is accordingly viewed as the force bringing about the transformation of the internal bases of cognition (and of the store-consciousness with the elder school) into the elements of Buddhahood. The process of transformation is viewed differently by the Yogācāra authorities. In general, the 3 Bodies of the Buddha are put in correspondence with the 8 or the 6 kinds of consciousness which are: 1) the store-consciousness,[10] 2) the intellect as the substratum of defiling forces,[11]

---

[1] *prakṛtistha* and *paripuṣṭa-gotra* = *raṅ-bźin-gnas-rigs* and *rgyas-ḥgyur-gyi-rigs*.

[2] *saṁskṛta* = *ḥdus-byas*.

[3] Tib. Don-gsaṅ, a commentary on the first chapter of the Mahāyāna-saṁgraha Tg. MDO. XVI. Quoted in Gser. I. 243 a. 3.

[4] *pariniṣpanna* = *yoṅs-grub*. [5] *nitya* = *rtag-pa*.

[6] A synonym of the Buddha's Body of Absolute Wisdom (*jñāna-dharma-kāya*).

[7] Gser. I. 243 a. 4. [8] *upādāna-kāraṇa* = *ñer-len-gyi-rgyu*.

[9] *parāvṛtti*. [10] *ālaya-vijñāna*.

[11] *kliṣṭa-manas* = *ñon-yid*. As a synonym of *mana-āyatana* (No. 6).

and the 6 forms corresponding to the 6 internal bases of cognition,—the 5 forms of sensious consciousness and the mental.[1] Candragomin[2] says that some are of the opinion that the store-consciousness becomes transformed into the Cosmical Body[3] of the Buddha, the intellect as the substratum of defiling forces—into the Body of Bliss,[4] and the 5 forms of sensuous consciousness[5]—into the Apparitional Body.[6] Otherwise, in correspondence with the 5 forms of the Divine Transcendental Wisdom of the Buddha, the transformation is to be viewed as follows:—

| | | |
|---|---|---|
| The store-consciousness | Becomes transformed into | The Cosmical Body as the perfectly pure Absolute[7] and the Transcendental Wisdom resembling a mirror.[8] |
| The intellect as the substratum of defiling forces | Becomes transformed into | The Body of Bliss i.e. the Altruistic[9] and the Discriminative Wisdom.[10] |
| The 5 forms of sensuous consciousness | Become transformed into | The active Wisdom[11] pursuing the welfare of living beings i.e. the Apparitional Body. |

According to those Yogācāras who do not accept the theory of the store-consciousness,—the 5 varieties of sensuous consciousness

[1] *mano-vijñāna = yid-kyi rnam-par-śes-pa.* [2] Quoted in Skabs I. 239b. 1–4.

[3] *dharma-kāya = chos-sku.*

[4] *saṁbhoga-kāya = loṅs-spyod-rdzogs-paḥi-sku (loṅs-sku).*

[5] *pañca-dvāra-vijñāna = sgo-lṅaḥi-rnam-śes.*

[6] *nirmāṇa-kāya = sprul-sku.*

[7] *dharma-dhātu-viśuddhi = chos-dbyiṅs-rnam-par-dag-pa.*

[8] *ādarśa-jñāna = me-loṅ-lta-buḥi-ye-śes.*

[9] *samatā-jñāna = mñam-ñid-ye-śes.*

[10] *pratyavekṣaṇa-jñāna = so-sor-rtog-paḥi-ye-śes.*

[11] *kṛtya-anuṣṭhāna-jñāna = bya-ba-sgrub paḥi-ye-śes.*

become transformed into the Body of Bliss, and the mental consciousness—into the Apparitional Body.[1] Thus we see the tendency of viewing the *gotra* as a special element, an active, transforming principle. It cannot be regarded as identical with the store-consciousness or as included in the internal bases of cognition. It is a force "standing above" the store-consciousness, dominating it and bringing about the transformation of it into the pure Transcendental Wisdom of the Buddha. According to Āryāsanga's Mahāyāna-saṁgraha it is the seed of the Cosmical Body in a living being which can be of a high, intermediate, and low degree. It is, so to say, a counter-agent[2] of the store-consciousness, inasmuch as it brings about its transformation.[3]—It would be likewise incorrect to view the *gotra* as quite identical with all the 6 internal bases of cognition, as do some of the Tibetan authorities.[4] The *gotra* is a force governing these bases of cognition, and in such an aspect cannot be considered as equal to them, because its function, that of bringing about the transformation of the elements and the attainment of Buddhahood, is other than the functions of the sense-organs and the intellect. On the other hand it is not something totally different from the internal elements.[5] Here we see that the standpoint of the Yogācāras is indefinite, resembling that of the Vātsiputrīyas in regard of the *pudgala*,—the individual viewed as a separate reality. It is clear that if the Germ of Enlightenment, at the same time the fundamental essence of a personality, were viewed as a separate element, essentially differing from the internal bases of cognition, the Yogācāras would run the danger of admitting the existence of a special substance which, though mutable, could be viewed as the Ego, as something resembling an individual soul. This they try to avoid by stating that the internal elements which represent a substratum and the

---

[1] Skabs-brgyad-ka, I. 239 a. 6—b 1.
[2] *pratipakṣa* = *gñen-po.*
[3] Gser. I. 243 b. 1—2.
[4] Skabs-brgyad-ka, I. 234 a. 5. sqq.
[5] Gser. I. 244 b. 3—4, as a quotation from the Śrāvaka-bhūmi and ibid. 244 b. 6—245 a. 1, as a quotation from Sāgaramegha's Bodhisattva-bhūmi-vyākhyā (Tg. MDO. LV).

*gotra* which governs them are not to be viewed as quite different from each other. The 6 bases of cognition are not the *gotra* itself, but they are neither something quite apart from it.

In Haribhadra's *Abhisamayālaṁkārālokā* [1] it is stated that the *gotra* as existing in every individual is beginningless and an outflow of the Absolute. The Yogācāras have the same opinion, but they do not admit the *gotra* to be the Absolute itself, as Haribhadra does.[2] Tsoṅ-kha-pa and Jam-yaṅ-źad-pa [3] rightly remark that if the *gotra* is taken to be an active element, it is quite impossible to regard it as identical with the Absolute, which is immutable. Moreover, as the Yogācāras maintain the annihilation of the force of the *gotra* with the Hīnayānist at the time of final Nirvāṇa [3] and with one in whom all the roots of virtue have perished, the *gotra* cannot be viewed as the Absolute, which is eternal and indestructible. That the *gotra* is derived from the Absolute means according to the Yogācāras that it exists from the outset, forming an inherent property of the stream of elements [4] constituting a personality. Neither in its fundamental, nor in its thriving state, it ever loses the character of a force, an active element.

As regards the principal varieties of the *gotra* as viewed by the Yogācāras, these are held to be three in correspondence with the 3 Vehicles,—of the Śrāvakas, Pratyekabuddhas and Bodhisattvas,[5] with the activity of these 3 different kinds of Saints and the forms of Enlightenment attained by them.[6] These 3 forms are held to be

---

[1] MS. Minaev, 59 a. 4—*anādi-kāla-āyāta-dharmatā-pratilabdham.*

[2] Ibid. 59 b. 2.—*dharma-dhātur gotram.*

[3] Gser. I. 234 b. 5—6 and Skabs I. 234 b. 5.

[4] *saṁtāna = rgyud.*—This concerns the majority of the Yogācāras. There are however followers of this system who agree with the Mādhyamikas in the opinion that the gotra is identical with the Absolute. Such is the standpoint of Ratnākaraśānti, the author of the Commentary on the Abhisamayālaṁkāra *en regard* Pañcaviṁśatisāhasrikā called Śuddhimatī (Tg. MDO. IX).

[5] Cf. Vasubandhu on Sūtrālaṁkāra III. 2.—*asti yāna-traye gotra-bhedaḥ.*

[6] Ibid.—*phala-bhedaś co' palabhyate hīna-madhya-viśiṣṭā bodhayaḥ so' ntareṇa gotra-bhedaṁ na syāt; bīja-anurūpatvāt phalasya.*

essentially different and not, as with the Mādhyamikas who maintain the theory of the Unique Vehicle,[1] as having one ultimate result which is the Supreme Enlightenment of the Buddha.

## IV.

### c) The Standpoint of the Mādhyamikas. The Teaching of the Element of Buddhahood according to the Uttaratantra.

The central point of this most developed theory is the teaching that the fundamental element of Buddhahood, the Essence of the Buddha[2] in a living being represents an eternal, immutable[3] element, which is identical with the monistic Absolute and is unique and undifferentiated in everything that lives. This is the main standpoint of the Uttaratantra. It is expressed likewise in the *Abhisamayālamkāra,*[4] in Haribhadra's Commentary thereon and in numerous other works. The definition of the Germ or the Essence of the Buddha given by Jam-yaṅ-źad-pa in his manual[5] is as follows:—It is the Absolute[6] (as the true essence of every living being) which at the time of final Enlightenment becomes the Body of Absolute Existence[7] of the Buddha. In the Commentary of Tsoṅ-kha-pa we have numerous quotations which especially point to the eternal immutable nature of the fundamental element. The most pregnant of these is that of the *Ratnakūṭa*:[8]—That in which there is absolutely nothing caused and conditioned[9] is (the element) which is eternal and immutable. This element is that of the saintly lineage;[10] it has a resemblance with space, being unique and undifferentiated. It is the true essence[11] of all the elements, is uniform[12] and eternal.[13]—As we have frequently stated above, it is considered to exist in all the living beings without

[1] *eka-yāna.* Cf. below.
[2] *tathāgata-garbha = de-bźin-gśegs-paḥi-sñiṅ-po.*
[3] *asaṁskṛta = ḥdus-ma-byas.*
[4] I. 39.
[5] Skabs-brgyad-ka I. 240 a. 1.
[6] *dharma-dhātu = chos-kyi-dbyiṅs.*
[7] *svabhāva-kāya = ṅo-bo-ñid-sku.*
[8] Quoted Gser-phreṅ, I. 246 b. 4—5.
[9] *saṁskṛta = ḥdus-byas.*
[10] *gotra = rigs.*
[11] *tathatā = de-bźin-ñid.*
[12] Lit. "of one taste" (*eka-rasa = ro-gcig-pa*).
[13] *nitya = rtag-pa.*

exception and forms the true essence, the background of all the elements constituting a personality.[1] At the same time it is considered to be of a pure spiritual nature[2] and as the element of the spirit of the Buddha. Only it, and nothing else, is real and persistent in an individual; it is beginningless and knows no end. In its essence it does not differ from the Cosmical Body of the Buddha, which is accordingly characterized as pervading everything that exists.[3] All the other elements constituting a personality as classified into the 5 groups,[4] the 12 bases of cognition,[5] and the 18 component elements of an individual[6] as well as the defiling agencies[7] and the Biotic Force[8] which produce them are regarded as totally unreal by themselves, and called forth by the force of illusion.[9] They are always spoken of as the occasional, the accidental defiling elements[10] which cannot affect or alter the element of the Absolute. The latter, as we have it with every individual, excepting the Buddha, is represented as concealed under the coverings of this accidental defilement, but by no means damaged by it. The whole process of the liberation of the Absolute Essence from the worldly elements which ends with the attainment of Buddhahood, that is to say the Path of a Saint, is to be viewed as an uninterrupted practice of mind-concentration upon the non-substantiality of the elements. Through this concentration, the illusion of the reality of the separate entities disappears, the desires, &c. in regard of the worldly objects cease to exist, and the Biotic Force called forth by these desires can no more exercise its activity. Consequently, the origination of new

---

[1] Skabs. I. 238 a. 4.

[2] *citta-svabhāva* = *sems-kyi-ran-bźin.*

[3] Cf. the quotation of Jñānagarbha's Satya-dvaya-vibhanga and Commentary in Skabs. VIII. 22 b. 2.—*chos thams-cad-kyi lus-ni ḥgro-ba-thams-cad de-bźin-gśegs-paḥi ṅo-bo-las mi-ḥdaḥ-baḥi-phyir* = *sarva-dharmāṇāṁ kāyaḥ, sarva-jagatas tathāgata-svabhāva-anatikramāt.* Cf. also Sutrālaṁkāra IX. 15.—*yathāmbaraṁ sarvagataṁ . . .*

[4] *skandha* = *phuṅ-po.*

[5] *āyatana* = *skye-mched.*

[6] *dhātu* = *khams.*

[7] *kleśa* = *ñon-moṅs.*

[8] *karma* = *las.*

[9] *avidyā-vāsanā* = *ma-rig-paḥi-bag-chags.*

[10] *āgantukā-malā* = *glo-bur-gyi-dri-mā.* –

groups of elements is made impossible, the remaining are gradually annihilated and the element of Buddhahood is delivered. This represents the attainment of the real, the true Nirvāṇa. Now, in the process of purification the element of Buddhahood remains essentially the same; its final metamorphose represents nothing but the removal of the occasional defiling elements. We see that Āryāsanga in his last work has come to a fully monistic and pantheistic conception. The statement that "the fundamental element of a living being and the Cosmical Body of the Buddha are the same, there being a difference only in the names," is a very pregnant expression of his standpoint. Another remarkable passage concerns the properties of the Buddha. It is said that these properties represent the attributes of the Absolute Essence as it is with the Buddha. But, as we read immediately after, this Essence is unique and indivisible with everything that lives. The difference is thus caused only by the presence of the defiling elements. But these have only an Empirical, a surface reality; they are not something which is to be really rejected. Absolutely real, eternal, and unalterable is only the element of Buddhahood.

This pantheist theory of the Uttaratantra and its development in the Kāla-cakra Doctrine were adopted by the famous Tibetan Lama Dolbopa-śeirab-gyal-tshan (1292–1391), the founder of the Jo-naṅ-pa sect, who interpreted them in a still more extreme way. Tsoṅ-kha-pa and his school rightly saw in this Doctrine a contradiction with the main principles of Buddhism. We find, accordingly, in their works an attempt to modify it. They accuse the Jo-naṅ-pa with having wrongly interpreted the Uttaratantra and say:[1]—There are such who (like the Jo-naṅ-pa) maintain that the Supreme Buddha, endowed with the powers and all the other attributes, exists in every living being from the outset. These do not in the least differ from the Brahmanists,[2] who adhere to the conception of a

[1] Dar. 12 b. 6—13 a. 1.

[2] *tīrthika* = *mu-stegs-pa.*

Supreme God[1] existing eternally.—In Gyal-tshab's Commentary[2] we find a discussion on the subject that the element of Buddhahood in a living being and the Cosmical Body of the Buddha cannot be regarded as completely identical. We have likewise many other passages in which the student is warned from confounding the teaching of the Uttaratantra with the Brahmanical systems.—In spite of all this it is quite clear that the *Uttaratantra* contains a full-blown pantheistic theory, the teaching of an eternal Buddha whose miraculous activity free from effort[3] manifests itself in everything that exists, and of the unique eternal element of Buddhahood or of the saintly lineage.

It has been stated above that, according to the Yogācāra point of view, the element of the lineage appears in two varieties, viz. as the primordial[4] and as that which becomes developed.[5] In the *Uttaratantra* we have likewise these 2 varieties, with the difference that the primordial represents, as we know, the eternal and immutable element of the Absolute. The Germ of Enlightenment which becomes developed is in its turn regarded as the reflection, the counterpart of the main aspect in the Phenomenal World. Accordingly, in the *Tathāgata-garbha-sūtra,* containing the 9 examples on the Essence of Buddhahood, the primordial element is characterized as resembling gold which always remains unalterable, and the Germ which becomes developed is compared with a real seed which brings fruit.

We must now mention another characteristic feature of the teaching about the element of the lineage as we have it in the *Uttaratantra.* This is the standpoint that, owing to the eternal character of this element, it can never be annihilated in a living being. This means that every living being has the chance of attaining Salvation. Moreover as the fundamental element is unique and undifferentiated

---

[1] ***iśvara = dbaṅ-phyug.***

[2] Dar. 12 b, 2. sqq.

[3] ***anābhoga = lhun-gyis-grub-pa.***

[4] ***prakṛti-stha-gotra = raṅ-bźin-gnas-rigs.***

[5] ***paripuṣṭa-gotra = rgyas-ḥgyur-gyi-rigs.***

in everything that lives, and as it is the Essence of the Buddha,[1] the ultimate result of its purification from defilement can be only one,—the attainment of Buddhahood. In accordance with this point of view it is maintained that the true Nirvāṇa is only that of the Buddha.[2] As concerns the Nirvāṇa of the Hīnayānist Saints,—the Śrāvakas and Pratyekabuddhas, it is considered to be a state of temporary pacification after the removal of the Obscuration of Moral Defilement.[3] The Hīnayānist Saint may abide for many æons in a state of perpetual trance in the so-called Unaffected Sphere,[4] having a spiritual, non-physical existence.[5] He is however at length aroused from this state by the grace of a Buddha, whereupon he enters the Mahāyānistic Path that ends with his attainment of Buddhahood.[6] Thus the varieties of the element of saintly lineage and the different results of its purification are to be viewed as conventional and temporary.

In close connexion with the theory of the Essence of the Buddha, the Uttaratantra gives us the teaching about the Cosmical Body[7] of the Buddha, the attainment of which is the result of the saintly Path. At the time of the termination of the latter, all the defiling elements which had hitherto obscured the Essence of the Absolute are completely removed, the illusion of the Empirical World vanishes and there remains the full and uninterrupted intuition of the unique Absolute with which the mind completely coalesces, there being no more a differentiation of subject and object and of separate entities. It is in such a sense that we have to understand the quotation from Scripture in the *Vyākhyā* that "the cessation, the negation of Phenomenal Existence[8] is the Cosmical Body of the Buddha." The

[1] *tathāgata-garbha.*

[2] Uttaratantra, I, verse 83.

[3] *kleśa-āvaraṇa = ñon-moṅs-kyi-sgrib-pa (ñon-sgrib).*

[4] *anāsrava-dhātu = zag-med-kyi-dbyiṅs.*

[5] *manomaya-kāya = yid-kyi-raṅ-bźin-gyi-lus.*

[6] This is the theory of the "Unique Vehicle" (*eka-yāna*).

[7] *dharma-kāya = chos-sku.*

[8] *nirodha-satya = ḥgog-bden.*

Ultimate Substance now viewed as the true Essence of the Buddha and his properties is called the Cosmical Body, or more precisely, the Body of Absolute Existence.[1]

The unique undifferentiated character of Buddhahood from the standpoint of Ultimate Reality is very pregnantly expressed in the works of Maitreya-Asanga and elsewhere. So we have in the Sūtrālaṁkāra IX. 4. the statement that all the elements of existence are identical with Buddhahood, since the Absolute is one undifferentiated whole; there exists no element whatever as a separate, differentiated reality.[2] In the same work (IX. 62 and Comm.) it is said that the Body of Absolute Existence is one and the same with all the Buddhas, being an undifferentiated whole.[3] And IX. 77. we have:—The Buddhas cannot be viewed as a unity from the standpoint of their previous bodily existence, their accumulations of merit, &c. But in the immaculate plane of Absolute existence they do not represent a plurality since the Cosmical Body is unique and undifferentiated.[4] In the *Jñāna-āloka-alaṁkāra-sūtra*[5] it is said that the Supreme Buddha represents the Ultimate Limit in the aspect of which all the elements are equal and uniform and do not appear (as separate entities).[6] He is always the same, free from constructive thought[7] and differentiation. Here in the Uttaratantra this Ultimate Cosmical Body of the Buddha is spoken of as endowed with the four absolute transcendental properties of Purity, Bliss, Eternity, and of being the Ultimate Essence of all the elements (*paramātman*).[8]

---

[1] *svabhāva-kāya* = *ṅo-bo-ñid-sku.* The active reflex of it is the Body of Absolute Wisdom (*jñāna-kāya*).

[2] *sarvadharmāś ca buddhatvaṁ tathatāyā abhinnatvāt tadviśuddhi-prabhāvitatvāc ca buddhatvasya, na ca kaścid dharmo'sti parikalpitena dharma-svabhāvena.*

[3] *svābhāvikaḥ (kāyaḥ) sarva-buddhānāṁ samo nirviśiṣṭatayā.*

[4] *bahutvam api ne'ṣyate buddhānāṁ dharma-kāyasya abhedād anāsrave dhātau.*

[5] Kg. MDO. III. 289 b. 6—7.

[6] This refers evidently to the teaching that all elements are for ever merged in Nirvāṇa (*prakṛti-parinirvṛtta*).

[7] *vikalpa* = *rnam-par-rtog-pa.*

[8] Tib. *dam-paḥi-bdag.*

Such is the Buddha in the aspect of the Absolute, called the true Ultimate Refuge. But, as we read in the *Sūtrālaṁkāra*, the accumulation of merit of the Buddha in the Empirical World cannot remain fruitless. This his activity is the moral Biotic Force [1] which must produce ultimately the highest and most blissful mundane existence. Moreover the Buddha has a double outlook facing both the Absolute [2] and the Empirical Reality [3] and has for his chief aim the salvation of other living beings. It is owing to these motives that the Buddha manifests himself in the Empirical World in his corporeal forms, [4] viz. the Body of Bliss, [5] eternally abiding in the region Akaniṣṭha and in the numerous Apparitional Bodies [6] which are its emanations, and are working for the weal of all living beings as long as the world exists. But in the aspect of the Absolute these corporeal forms are mere reflections and have no real essence of their own.

These are, in short, the main ideas expressed in the *Uttaratantra*. Their detailed exposition is contained in the translation which is now to follow. The paragraphs in the Commentaries of Tsoṅ-kha-pa and Jam-yaṅ-źad-pa concerning the teaching of *gotra* or *dhātu* with the different Buddhist schools will be translated separately and form an appendix to the present work. In the translation the greatest care has been bestowed on a faithful rendering of all technical terms of which the work is full. This has been made in accordance with the method adopted by Prof. Stcherbatsky. Not a single term is left without translation, but in order to facilitate control, the original term (Sanscrit and Tibetan) is always given in the note.

It now remains for me to express my gratitude to my revered teacher Prof. Th. Stcherbatsky at whose instigation and with whose help this work has been carried out and has assumed its present form, and to Prof. Sten Konow owing to whose kind attention it is now published. My deepest thanks are likewise due to the Khambo

---

[1] *karma = las.*
[2] *paramārtha = don-dam-pa.*
[3] *saṁvṛti = kun-rdzob.*
[4] *rūpa-kāya = gzugs-sku.*
[5] *saṁbhoga-kāya.*
[6] *nirmāṇa-kāya.*

(Mkhan-po) Lama Agvan (Ṅag-dbaṅ) Dorjeev who took such a keen interest in my Buddhist studies in Transbaikalia and has greatly furthered them, to the Abbot of the Chilūtai[1] Monastery, Lha-rampa [2] Donḍub Buddhayin with whom I undertook a systematical study of the *Uttaratantra* and *Vyākhyā* (July–August 1929), and to my friends the Lamas Galdan Jamsaranu and Gyamtsho Gomboyin who have supplied me with many valuable instructions.

# The Sublime Science of the Great Vehicle to Salvation.

## I. The Contents of the Work.

1. The Buddha, the Doctrine, the Congregation,
The Germ (of Buddhahood), Supreme Enlightenment,
The attributes of the Buddha and last of all his acts,—
These are the seven adamantine topics,
In which the compass of this treatise can be summarized.[3]

---

[1] Dgaḥ-ldan-dar-rgyas-gliṅ.

[2] The highest degree of learning in the Monasteries of Lhasa.

[3] Cf. Dar. 6a. 3—6b. 3. These 7 points appear in 2 aspects, namely from the standpoint of the Absolute (*paramārtha = don-dam-pa*) and from that of Empirical Reality (*saṁvṛti = kun-rdzob*). The Buddha in the aspect of the Absolute is the Cosmical Body (*dharma-kāya = chos-sku*),—the complement of purity and wisdom (*prahāṇa-jñāna-saṁpatti = spaṅs-pa daṅ ye-śes phun-sum-tshogs-pa*). The Buddha from the Empirical Standpoint is the corporeal form (*rūpa-kāya = gzugs-sku*). The Doctrine from the standpoint of the Absolute represents the Extinction (of Phenomenal Life *nirodha = ḥgog-pa*) and the Path (*mārga = lam*) of the Mahāyānist Saint. As to the Doctrine viewed empirically, it will be the collection of sermons (*pravacana = gsuṅ-rab*). The Congregation from the Ultimate Standpoint represents the elements of Wisdom and final Deliverance with the Mahāyānist Saint. The Congregation viewed empirically is the assembly of the Saints of the Great Vehicle.

The fundamental element (or Germ,—*dhātu = khams*) from the point of view of Ultimate Reality is the Absolute Essence (*tathatā = de-bźin-ñid*) forming the background of the consciousness of the living beings, the Absolute itself, only obscured by defiling elements (*āvaraṇa = sgrib-pa*). The same element viewed empirically is a force which governs the spirit of the living beings and makes possible the origination of the saintly (*lokottara = ḥjig-rten-las-ḥdas-pa*) elements.

## The Explanation of the Verse by Aryāsanga.

The subject that is to be cognized[1] has a resemblance with a diamond, and the (words that demonstrate it)[2] may be compared with diamond-mines, since they represent the receptacles (of this subject). The subject which is accessible (only) to the inward conviction (or introspection) of the Saint and is of an inexpressible, unutterable character, resembles a diamond (that is hard and unpenetrable), since it cannot be "pierced" by the (ordinary) knowledge, which is a result of study and investigation.[3] [2 a.] The words which express this subject and afford a means for its cognition are spoken of as the (diamond)-mines, since they represent a foundation for this (cognition). Thus the unpenetrable character (of the subject) and the nature of the words, as being a support of it, let us know the former as a diamond and the latter as its repository. Now, of what kind is the subject and of what kind are the words (expressing it)? (Answer):—The subject consists of the 7 points that are to be cognized. These are as follows:—1) the Buddha, 2) the Doctrine,

---

Enlightenment (*bodhi* = *byaṅ-chub*) viewed sub specie aeternitatis is the Cosmical Body, and, taken empirically, represents the corporeal forms of the Buddha (the Body of Bliss—*saṁbhoga-kāya* = *loṅs-sku* and the Apparitional Body—*nirmāṇa-kāya* = *sprul-sku*). The difference between this subject and the first which is Buddhahood, is that here Enlightenment is viewed as something to be attained (by the person proceeding) on the Path himself, whereas before it has been taken from the standpoint of the element already attained by another personality. The attributes of the Buddha in the aspect of the Absolute are the 10 Powers (*daśa-bala* = *stobs-bcu*) and the other distinctive features which are the result of the removal of the Obscurations. The attributes, being viewed empirically, are the 32 corporeal marks. The acts of the Buddha from the standpoint of Ultimate Reality represent the Wisdom acting in behalf of others (*kṛtya-anuṣṭhāna-jñāna* = *bya-ba-sgrub-paḥi-ye-śes*). Empirically they are contained in the collection of the Buddha's sermons.

[1] Dar. 9a. 3. The sevenfold subject that is to be intuited, that is to say, revealed by introspection (*pratyātma-vedya* = *so-so-raṅ-gis-rig-par-bya-ba*) to the Saint.

[2] Ibid.

[3] *śrutimayī prajñā* = *thos-pa-las-byuṅ-baḥi-śes-rab* and *cintāmayī prajñā* = *bsam-pa-las-byuṅ-baḥi-śes-rab*.

3) the Congregation, 4) the Fundamental Germ (of Buddhahood),[1] 5) Enlightenment, 6) the attributes, and 7) the acts (of the Buddha). [2 b.] The words are those by means of which these 7 topics are demonstrated and made clear.

A detailed exposition of the (7) adamantine subjects is contained in the Sūtras.[2] It is said there as follows:—O Ānanda, the (real)[3] Buddha is indemonstrable. He cannot be seen by the eye. O Ānanda, the (true) Doctrine[4] is unutterable.[5] It cannot be heard by the ear. O Ānanda, the (true) Congregation is of an immutable character. It cannot be worshipped, neither by body nor mind. Such are the (first) 3 adamantine topics as we have them in the *Adhyāśaya-parivarta.*[6]

It is said further on:—O Śāriputra, this topic[7] is the object[8] that is the sphere[9] of the Buddha (alone). O Śāriputra, all the

---

[1] Cf. Dar. 6b. 6—7a. 4. If there were no fundamental Germ perfectly pure by itself, the purification from the casual (*āgantuka = glo-bur-ba*) defiling forces would be impossible. Thus this Germ is put forth as the necessary condition for the attainment of Enlightenment, and is metaphorically spoken of as the natural cause (*upādāna-kāraṇa = ñer-len-gyi-rgyu*) of the latter. It is not however a real producing cause, since it is an eternal, immutable element (*asaṁskṛta = ḥdus-ma-byas*). (The Germ) which becomes developped (*paripuṣṭa = rgyas-ḥgyur* or *samudānīta = yaṅ-dag-par-bsgrub-pa*) is to be regarded as the actual producing cause. As concerns the cooperating causes and conditions, these are Enlightenment as attained by another individual with the corresponding attributes and acts. On the basis of the teaching delivered by another who has attained Supreme Enlightenment, it is possible to purify one's own stream of elements (*saṁtāna = rgyud*) from defilement.

[2] Sthira-adhyāśaya-parivarta, Kg. MDO. XIX 172b. 2—3.

[3] Dar. 10b. 4. The Buddha in the aspect of the Absolute, unreal as a separate entity (differing from the unique Essence of the Cosmos) and free from all the additional defiling elements. He is inaccessible to empirical (*vaiyavahārika = tha-sñad-pa*) knowledge.

[4] The Doctrine viewed as Extinction and the Path. Cf. above.

[5] Dar. 10 b. 5. It is unutterable in the sense of its not being an object of thought-construction (*kalpanā = rtog-pa*) connected with speech.

[6] Tib. *lhag-paḥi-bsam-pa-brtan-paḥi-leḥu.*

[7] That is the Absolute as forming the fundamental germ of the living beings and mingled with defiling elements. Dar. 11 a. 6.

[8] *viṣaya = yul.* [9] *gōcara = spyod-yul.*

Śrāvakas as well as the Pratyekabuddhas are now unable to cognize, perceive, and investigate this subject by means of their own analytic wisdom, independently. If this be so, what is there to say of the ordinary, worldly beings.[1] This however does not concern the cognition which is inspired by the faith in the Buddha. O Śāriputra, the Absolute Truth may be perceived (by the Śrāvaka and Pratyekabuddha Saints)[2] as a result of their faith. O Śāriputra, the Absolute (in its defiled form)[3] is a name[4] of the fundamental element of the living beings. O Śāriputra, this fundamental element of the living beings (partly purified)[5] is a name for the essence, the pith of Buddhahood.[6] O Śāriputra, this pith of Buddhahood (being completely free from all defilement)[7] is a name of the Cosmical Body.[8] Such do we know to be the fourth adamantine topic which is not subjected to augmentation and decrease as it is demonstrated in Scripture.

(It is said further on):—O Lord, the perfect Supreme Enlightenment[9] is a name for the essence of Nirvāṇa.[10] O Lord, the essence of Nirvāṇa is a name for the Cosmical Body of the Buddha. Such is the 5th adamantine subject according to the *Śrī-mālā-siṁhanāda-sūtra.*[11] (It is said):—O Śāriputra, of what kind is the Cosmical

---

[1] *bāla = byis-pa* and *pṛthagjana = so-soḥi-skye-bo.*

[2] Dar. 12 a. 3.—*ñan-thos daṅ raṅ-saṅs-rgyas ḥphags-pa-rnams-kyis* &c.

[3] Ibid. 12 a. 6.—The Absolute mingled with defilement, when it is not in the least purified from the defiling elements.

[4] *adhivacana = tshig-bla-dvags.*

[5] Dar. 12 a. 6—b. 1.—When it is to some extent purified from the defiling forces, but nevertheless still connected with some of them.

[6] *tathāgata-garbha = de-bźin-gśegs-paḥi-sñiṅ-po.*

[7] Dar. 12 b. 1. *dri-ma mthaḥ-dag-gis-dben-pa-na = sakala-mala-vivikta.*

[8] Ibid. 12 b. 2. Thus the Absolute when it is in a defiled state is termed the fundamental element of the living beings and the Essence of Buddhahood. On the other hand, when it is completely free from all defilement, it is called the Cosmical Body.

[9] *anuttarā samyaksaṁbodhiḥ = yaṅ-dag-par-rdzogs-paḥi-byaṅ-chub.*

[10] *nirvāṇa-dhātu = mya-ṅan-las-ḥdas-paḥi-dbyiṅs.*

[11] Kg. DKON. VI. 274 b. 5—6.

Body of the Buddha? It is endowed with the attributes of the Buddha which are greater in number than the sands of the Ganges, the attributes which are inseparable (from the Essence of the Buddha),[1] the distinctive features peculiar to the Wisdom (of the Buddha) who never becomes destitute of any of them. The 6th diamond subject is thus demonstrated as something which can neither increase, nor become diminished. (We have further on):[2]—O Manjuśrī, the Buddha does not search, nor does he reflect (about the character of the work to be done). However, he does act, and this his activity free from search and reflection manifests itself miraculously and without effort.[3] Thus we have the 7th point as the manifestation of the Buddha's attributes and of his Transcendental Wisdom [3 b.], directed toward the objects that are inaccessible to ordinary human knowledge. Thus, in short, these 7 adamantine topics are to be regarded as forming the contents, the "body" of the whole of this work, since, to speak briefly, their elucidation has been the motive for the composition (of this treatise).

**The 7 Subjects according to the Dhāraṇīśvara-rāja-paripṛcchā.**[4]

2. Their essential character and mutual connexion
   Is, in gradual order, (shown) in the *Dharaṇīśvara-rāja-sūtra.*
   (The first) 3 topics are to be known from (its) introduction,[5]

---

[1] Dar. 13 a. 6. The attributes of the Buddha, the 10 forces &c. are the qualities which are inseparable (from the Cosmical Body) as the colour and shine of a precious stone are inseparable from the latter itself.

[2] Cf. below.

[3] *anābhogam* = *lhun-gyis-grub-par*. Dar. 13 b. 1—2. As every kind of exertion is, with the Buddha, pacified, he, in acting for the sake of other living beings, has no thought-construction as regards the essence of the work to be done, the agent and the object. Neither does he enter upon a close examination of the details.

[4] Tib. *gzuṅs-kyi-dbaṅ-phyug-rgyal-pos-žus-paḥi-mdo.* Kg. MDO. XV. In the Kg. it is called the Tathāgata-Mahākaruṇā-nirdeśa-sūtra. I have found out this sūtra with the help of Bu-ton's index to the Kangyur, f. 166 b. 3, where we have both names.

[5] *nidāna-parivarta* = *gleṅ-gžiḥi-leḥu.*

8*

And the (remaining) 4—from the analysis of the Buddha's[1] and the Bodhisattva's[2] attributes.

The elucidation of the particular essence[3] of these 7 subjects and their interconnexion is demonstrated in the *Dhāraṇīśvara-rāja-sūtra* in the order (in which the subjects have just been described). From the introductory chapter we come to know the first 3 subjects; then come the remaining 4 which are contained in the description of the various attributes peculiar to the Buddhas and the Bodhisattvas. We read as follows:[4]—

"The Lord has attained the Perfect Supreme Enlightenment,—(the intuition) of all the elements in their unity."[5] "He has duly demonstrated his Doctrine."[6] "He has obtained the illimited power of converting the multitude of disciples."—These 3 main aphorisms show us in gradual order the 3 Jewels[7] and the process of their origination.[8] The remaining 4 subjects are demonstrated as having the character of causes and conditions conformable with this origination. On the 8th Stage of the Bodhisattva the controlling power over all the elements[9] is attained. [4 a.] Through this one comes to the highest essence of Enlightenment[10] and the full Illumination, that is to say

---

[1] *rgyal-ba* = *jina.*

[2] *blo-ldan* = *dhīmat*—(the Wise).

[3] *svalakṣaṇa* = *raṅ-gi-mtshan-ñid.*

[4] Kg. MDO. XV. 142 a. 4—5.

[5] Dar. 14 b. 3—4. "as devoid of the character of real plurality."

[6] Lit. "has duly swung the Wheel of the Doctrine."

[7] *ratna-traya* = *dkon-mchog-gsum.*

[8] According to the following passage and Dar. 8 a. 3 sqq. and 14 b. 6 sqq. the 3 last Stages of the Bodhisattva (*acalā* = *mi-gyo-ba, sādhumatī* = *legs-paḥi-blo-gros* and *dharma-meghā* = *chos-kyi-sprin*) contain the most proximate causes of the 3 Jewels. The Bodhisattva on the 8th Stage is called "the Buddha in the conventional sense—*aupacāriko buddhaḥ* = *saṅs-rgyas-btags-pa-pa,*" inasmuch as he has obtained the controlling power over the elements. The 9th and 10th Stages, respectively, contain the proximate causes of the Jewel of the Doctrine and that of the Congregation.

[9] The 10 controlling powers—*daśa-vaśitāḥ* = *dbaṅ-bcu.* Cf. M. V. § 27.

[10] *bodhi-maṇḍa* = *byaṅ-chub-kyi-sñiṅ-po.* According to Dar. 15 a. 4 *bodhi-maṇḍa* means here the Bodhi tree.

the intuition of the ultimate unity[1] of all the elements. He who abides on the 9th Stage of the Bodhisattva becomes endowed with the faculty of preaching the Highest of Doctrines.[2] He comes to know the intellectual faculties of all the living beings,[3] brings to the highest development all the faculties (that of faith and the rest), and becomes skilful as regards the annihilation of the continuance of the defiling forces[4] in every living being. On account of this he who has attained Supreme Enlightenment can duly expound the Doctrine. (The Bodhisattva abiding) on the 10th Stage becomes consecrated[5] as the successor to (the Buddha's) religious kingdom and, immediately after, begins to perform the acts of the Buddha without effort and uninterruptedly. As a consequence, he who duly expounds the Doctrine has the illimited power of converting the circle of his disciples (who become members of the Congregation). It is said further on:[6]—"he who has the unlimited power of converting the assembly of disciples abides (after having brought about this conversion) in the company of the great Congregation of ascetics," and so on up to—"and in the company of an unmeasurable multitude of Bodhisattvas.[7] Being endowed with such merits"... &c. The indication (of the assembly of the ascetics and Bodhisattvas)[8] respectively refers to the (power of) completely converting [4 b.] to the Enlighten-

---

[1] *sarva-dharma-samatā = chos-thams-cad-mñam-pa-ñid.*

[2] Dar. 15 b. 1.—Through the attainment of the 4 methods of Intense Penetration (*pratisaṁvid = so-so-yaṅ-dag-par-rig-pa.* M. V. § 13).

[3] Ibid.—The spiritual lineage of the living beings, their religious fervour, and different intellectual faculties.

[4] *vāsanā = bag-chags.*

[5] *abhiṣikta = dbaṅ-bskur-ba.* Cf. Nāgārjuna's Ratnāvalī Tg. MDO. XCIV. 150 a. 8—b. 1. *bcu-pa chos-kyi-sprin yin-te. dam-pa chos-kyi char ḥbebs-phyir. byaṅ-chub-sems-dpaḥ saṅs-rgyas-kyi. ḥod-zer-dag-gis dbaṅ-bskur-phyir.* The 10th Stage is that of the Clouds of the Truth (*dharma-meghā*). It is (called) so, because the rain of the Highest Truth descends upon the saints, and the Bodhisattvas are consecrated with the light of the Buddha.

[6] Kg. MDO. XV. 142 a. 6.

[7] Ibid. 142 b. 1—2—143 a. 1.

[8] Dar. 15 b. 6—16 a. 1.

ment of the Śrāvaka and that of the Mahāyānist Saint, which (power) forms an attribute of the Buddha. Then comes a glorification of the virtues of the Śrāvakas and the Bodhisattvas. After that the Sūtra[1] relates how the Buddha, on the basis of the highest forms of trance[2] peculiar to him, has constructed a circular court-yard adorned with precious jewels, how the adherents of the Buddha assembled,[3] how the Gods offered various sacrifices, and how the rain of glory descended (upon the Buddha). Here we have an indication of all the virtues of the Jewel of the Buddha in their variety. Then it is described how the great throne[4] (for preaching) was erected, how streams of light (ejected from the head of the Buddha) and how the various names of the divisions of the Doctrine[5] and their qualities were made known. (This passage represents) a description of the virtues of the Jewel of the Doctrine. Next we have an indication of the sphere of the Bodhisattva's trance and of its power, and the praise of the Bodhisattva's merits in various forms, the whole passage containing, accordingly, a description of the various attributes peculiar to the Jewel of the Congregation. Thereafter we have 1) a glorification[6] of the highest absolute virtues of the Buddha (by Dhāraṇīśvara-rāja), after the latter had received the consecration of the light of the Buddha and had through this attained the intrepidity[7] and intelligence[8] peculiar to the eldest heirs to the Kingdom of the Highest Doctrine; this is followed by 2) an ascertainment [5 a. 1.] of the Highest Mahāyānistic Doctrine and 3) the demonstration of the result of apprehending this Doctrine, namely the power of governing the elements.[9] (These 3 points) respectively show us the varieties

[1] Acc. to the Dar. the following passages render the contents of the Sūtra condensed. The passage concerning the Buddha—Kg. MDO. XV. 143 a. 6.

[2] Tib. *tiṅ-ṅe-ḥdzin-khyu-mchog* = *samādhi-ṛṣabha.*

[3] Sic according to Āryāsanga's Commentary (*ḥdus-pa*); the Dar. has *bsdus-pa.*

[4] Dar. 18 a. 1. the throne supported by lions—*siṁhāsana* = *seṅ-geḥi-khri.*

[5] *dharma-paryāya* = *chos-kyi-rnam-graṅs.* [6] Dar. 19 a. 2.

[7] *vaiśāradya* = *mi-ḥjigs-pa.* [8] *pratibhāna* = *spobs-pa.*

[9] *chos-kyi-dbaṅ-phyug-dam-pa.* Dar. 19 b. 4—5.—*chos-kyi-dbaṅ-phyug-ni chos thams-cad-la dbaṅ thob-paḥo.*

of the highest virtues peculiar to each of the 3 Jewels. This forms the conclusion of the introductory chapter.

## The Germ of Buddhahood and the other 3 Subjects according to the Dhāraṇīśvara-rāja-paripṛcchā.

Directly after we have a description of the 60 appliances[1] (for the purification of the Germ of Buddhahood), the factors purifying (the essence of the Absolute mingled with defilement). Through this the character of the Germ of Buddhahood itself[2] is made clear, for (the existence of) purifying factors is admissible, (only) if there exists an object which is in need of purification. Having in view this object,[3] (the *Daśabhūmaka-sūtra*[4]) illustrates (the process of purification of the Germ) on the 10 Stages of the Bodhisattva by the comparison with the process of purifying grains of gold found in the sand. In this Sūtra[5] the subject is discussed immediately after the description of the Buddha's acts, (the Germ of Buddhahood) being compared with an impure stone of lapis-lazuli. (It is said as follows):[6]—O noble youth, take for instance a skilful jeweller who knows well the methods of polishing precious stones. He gets from a jewel-mine a stone, completely impure,[7] and, having washed it with acrid salt water, polishes it by wiping with a cloth made of hair. But he does not give up his task after having merely accomplished this. He then washes the stone with an acrid fluid of vitriol[8] and cleanses it with

---

[1] *parikarman* = *yoṅs-su-sbyoṅ-ba.*

[2] Dar. 20 a. 2—3. The Germ of Buddhahood in the aspect of Empirical Reality and in its character of the Absolute as mingled with defiling elements.

[3] Dar. 21 b. 5—6. Having in view this object, that is the mind of the living beings and its essence—the Absolute mingled with defilement and in the beginning completely impure, which through the contemplation of the antidotes of defilement gradually becomes purified.

[4] Dar. 21 b. 5.

[5] The Dhāraṇīśvara-rāja-paripṛcchā.

[6] Kg. MDO. XV. 215 b. 1—7.

[7] Dar. 22 a. 3. "through mud and dust."

[8] Tib. *zaṅs-kyi-khu-ba.* In the Dar. (22 a. 4.) we have *zas-kyi-khu-ba* which is explained as *ña-khu*—a fluid from boiled fish.(?)

a woollen cloth. But even here his efforts do not cease. Having washed again (the stone) with a medicinal fluid,[1] the jeweller completely purifies it with a very fine cloth [5 b.]. That which is thus purified and made completely free from all the stains is the precious essence of lapis-lazuli. O noble youth, in the same way the Buddha, having perceived the fundamental element of the living beings obscured by defilement, arouses aversion in those who love this worldly existence, by speaking so as to present before their minds the evanescence,[2] suffering, impersonality,[3] and impurity (of the Phenomenal World).[4] In such a way he induces them to embrace the Doctrine and submit to the discipline of the (Hīnayānist) Saint. But the Buddha does not give up his task with merely accomplishing this. He then speaks of Non-substantiality, Non-differentiation and Absence of Desire[5] and through this causes to apprehend the true essence[6] of the Buddha. But the energy of the Buddha does not cease here. After that he expounds the Doctrine of the Irretrievable State[7] and speaks of the perfect purity (that is the separate unreality) of subject, object and act,[8] and through this induces the different living beings to penetrate into the sphere of the Buddha.[9] It is said that those who have

---

[1] *dṅul-chu*—quicksilver.

[2] *anityatā* = *mi-rtag-pa-ñid.*

[3] *nairātmya* = *bdag-med-pa.*

[4] Acc. to Dar. 22 a. 6 sqq. this refers to the Hīnayānists. The Buddha speaks of evanescence, that is of the momentary change peculiar to Phenomenal Existence, of the uneasiness accompanying perpetual origination, of the unreality of the individual and of the Phenomenal World as a whole being like an impure pit.

[5] *śūnyatā* = *stoṅ-pa-ñid, animitta* = *mtshan-ma-med-pa* and *apraṇihita* = *smon-pa-med-pa.* These are called the 3 Gates of Deliverance and represent the unreality of the elements from the standpoint of their essence, cause, and result.

[6] Dar. 23 a. 3. "The nature, the essential character of the Buddha which is the Absolute."

[7] *avaivartika-dharma-cakra* = *phyir-mi-ldog-paḥi-chos-kyi-ḥkhor-lo.* Dar. 24 b. 1. "which prevents the origination of egoistic thoughts, that is the desire of attaining Salvation merely for oneself without caring for other living beings."

[8] *trimaṇḍala-pariśuddhi* (or *viśuddhi*) = *ḥkhor-gsum-yoṅs-su-dag-pa.*

[9] Dar. 24 b. 3.—"the cognition of Non-substantiality" (*śūnyatā* = *stoṅ-pa-ñid*).

entered (the Great Vehicle)[1] and cognized the true essence of Buddhahood become possessed of the highest merits. In regard of this Germ of the Buddha, the substance (of the living beings) which becomes purified, it has moreover been said:—

Just as fine grains of gold, invisible among stones and sand,
Come to be seen if they are duly purified,
In the same way, in the world of living beings
(The manifestation of) the Buddha (is perceived).

Now, what are the 60 appliances, [6 a. 1.] the factors for purifying the Germ of the Buddha? They are as follows:—The 4 Ornaments of the Bodhisattva,[2] the 8 kinds of lustre[3] illuminating his (Path), the 16 forms of the Bodhisattva's Great Commiseration[4] and his 32 acts.[5]

After this comes a description of the 16 forms of Great Commiseration,[6] the distinctive features of Supreme Enlightenment,

---

[1] Sic according to Dar. 24 b. 3—4.—*theg-pa-chen-po-la źugs-par-gyur ciṅ* &c.

[2] Dar. 26 b. 3—4. "the 3 Disciplines (*adhiśila-śikṣā* = *tshul-khrims-kyi-bslab-pa*, *adhicitta-śikṣā* = *sems-kyi-bslab-pa* and *adhiprajñā-śikṣā* = *śes-rab-kyi-bslab-pa*) and power of memory (*dhāraṇī* = *gzuṅs*) by which the activity of the Bodhisattva is "decorated."

[3] Dar. 26 b. 4—5. The 8 kinds of lustre which, being devoid of the darkness of ignorance, make clear the way (for the apprehension) of the Doctrine. They are:—1) the Lustre of Memory, 2) that of Discrimination, 3) Intuition, 4) the Doctrine, 5) the Knowledge (of it), 6) the Truth, 7) Supernatural Perception, and 8) Highest Activity.

[4] Ibid. 26 b. 5—27 a. 1. "consisting in the desire of removing the suffering of the living beings, with a view to the various false views, the 4 kinds of error, the consideration of Ego and Mine, the 5 Obscurations, attachment to the objects of the senses, the 5 kinds of pride, deviation from the Path of the Saint, dependence on others, wrath and sinful deeds, absence of the wisdom peculiar to a Saint, ignorance with regard to the profound doctrine of Causality, continuance of the force of Transcendental Illusion, non-deliverance from the burden of suffering, craft and deceit, and forfeiture of a blissful existence and Salvation."

[5] Cf. Appendix.

[6] Dar. 27 b. 4—28 a. 2. Manifesting itself with a view to the living beings who do not understand the essence of the Great Enlightenment and its 16 distinctive features, which are:—the Absence of foundation, Absence of a definite place,

which elucidates the nature of the latter as the Illumination of the Buddha.[1] Then the 10 Powers,[2] the 4 kinds of Intrepidity,[3] and the 18 Exclusive Attributes of the Buddha[4] are demonstrated, all his distinctive features being thus described. Thereupon[5] (the Sūtra) speaks of the highest forms of the Buddha's activity and thus makes clear the character of his 32 acts. In such a way the essential character of all the 7 adamantine subjects is made known by the Sūtra in detail.

### The Connexion between the 7 Subjects.

Now, what is the connexion between them?

3. From the Buddha comes the Doctrine, from the Doctrine—the Congregation of the Saints,
From the Congregation—the (desire of purifying) the Germ till the attainment of the quintessence of Wisdom.
This Wisdom being attained, one comes to Supreme Enlightenment,
Becomes endowed with it and the other attributes, through which one acts for the sake of all living beings.[6]

Finished the explanation of the connexion between (the parts of) the treatise.—

---

Quiescence, perfect Pacification, immaculate (radiant) nature, absence of increase and loss, absence of distinctive marks, impossibility of being an object of cognition, unity in the present, past and future, the incorporeal and immutable character, absence of differentiation and substratum, the fact of not being an object of corporeal or mental (receptive faculty), imperceptibility, absence of a definite aspect, non-substantiality, analogy to space, the fact of being the real substratum (of all things), absence of form, absence of defilement and of the causes of Phenomenal Life, purity, absence of every kind of Obscuration and of Passion.

[1] Ibid. 27 b. 3—4.—as pure by nature and devoid of every kind of additional defilement.

[2] *daśa-bala* = *stobs-bcu* M. V. § 7.

[3] *catvāri vaiśāradyāni.* Ibid. § 8.

[4] *aṣṭādaśa āveṇika-dharmāḥ.* Cf. M. V. § 9.

[5] Kg. MDO. XV. 185 a. 6—215 a. 2.

[6] Dar. 28 b. 1—29 a. 6.

## The Jewel of the Buddha. [6 b. 1.]

Now we have to explain the meaning of the following verses. The living beings who are converted by the Buddha seek their refuge in him. Being full of that faith which is a natural outflow of their belief in the Cosmical Body of the Buddha,[1] they likewise seek their refuge in the Doctrine and the Congregation. Therefore, as the Buddha is the first (and principal refuge), we begin with the verse referring to him.—

4. I bow before him, who has neither beginning, middle, nor end,[2]
Who is quiescent[3] and fully enlighted, (perceiving) his own (Cosmical) Essence of Buddhahood,[4]
Who, himself illuminated, shows to the ignorant
The Path sure and free from danger, in order that they might know (the Truth),[5]
Who, raising high the sword and the thunder-bolt of Mercy and Wisdom
Cuts down the sprout of Phenomenal Life,
And breaks the wall of Doubt surrounded

---

[1] Ibid. 29 b. 6. *chos-ñid-kyi-ste sans-rgyas-kyi chos-kyi-sku-la dan-bahi dad-pahi rgyu-mthun-pahi-hbras-bu (nisyanda-phala) yin-pahi-phyir-ro.* This passage is an extract from the Śrī-mālā-devī-siṁhanāda-sūtra. Kg. DKON. VI. 275 b. 3—4.

[2] Dar. 30 a. 4—5. The original purity of the Buddha. He represents the Absolute (*paramārtha-satya* = *don-dam-bden-pa*), devoid of all plurality (*sarva-prapañca-anta-vinirmukta* = *spros-pahi-mthah-thams-cad-dan-bral-ba*) and has no beginning, middle and end.

[3] The additional purity. The Buddha has brought to pacification all the defiling forces by means of their antidotes. Through this he exercises his activity without any effort.

[4] Dar. 30 a. 6. The Buddha is fully enlightened as regards his own Essence, the Unity of the Cosmos devoid of all plurality.

[5] Dar. 30 b. 2—3. The Commiseration of the Buddha. He shows the Path to the converts in order that the living beings, ignorant of the absolute and empirical character of the things cognizable, might come to know such. The Path is free from danger through its transcendental (*lokottara* = *hjig-rten-las-hdas-pa*) character and through the fact of its referring to the Irretrievable State.

By the dense thickets of the different heresies.[1]—

Now, what is shown here?

5. Immutable,[2] free from effort,[3]
Incognizable from without,[4]
Endowed with Wisdom, Love, and Power,[5]
And pursuing a twofold aim—such is Buddhahood.

This passage, in short, speaks of the Essence of Buddhahood, as possessed of 8 distinctive features. What are these 8? (They are as follows):—1) Immutability, 2) Action without effort, 3) The fact of being incognizable from without, 4) Wisdom, 5) Commiseration, 6) Power, 7) The complement of the Buddha's own aim, and 8) The complement of the aim of others.[6]

6. Having by nature no beginning,
Middle, nor end, (the Buddha) is immutable.[7]

---

[1] Ibid. 30 b. 3—5. The power of the Buddha. Having raised the sword of Commiseration and Wisdom he cuts down the sprout of Phenomenal Existence as it is contained in the 12-membered Causal Chain and, particularly, in its fourth member—that of the physical and mental elements (*nāma-rūpa* = *miṅ-daṅ gzugs*). Raising high the thunder-bolt of Mercy and Wisdom, he breaks down the wall of doubt which is surrounded by the dense thickets of the various false doctrines.

[2] The character of the Cosmical Body as the primary substance in its original purity,—the immutable Absolute.

[3] *anābhoga* = *lhun-gyis-grub-pa*. Dar. 31 a. 1. The additional purity of the Cosmical Body. It acts without effort through the perfect pacification of every kind of exertion.

[4] The Absolute Transcendental Wisdom. The Buddha cannot be cognized from without (*para-pratyaya-agamya* = *gźan-gyi-rkyen-gyis-rtogs-min-pa*), being an object of the inward cognition of the Buddha himself.

[5] Dar. 31 a. 2. The other attributes of the Buddha, his Wisdom in regard of the Empirical World, his Commiseration and Power relate to the corporeal form (*rūpa-kāya* = *gzugs-sku*) of the Buddha, through which he acts for the sake of others.

[6] *svārtha-saṁpatti* = *raṅ-gi-don-phun-sum-tshogs-pa*. the Cosmical Body and *parārtha-saṁpatti* = *gźan-gyi-don-phun-sum-tshogs-pa*. the corporeal forms of the Buddha.

[7] *asaṁskṛta* = *ḥdus-ma-byas*. Dar. 31 b. 1—2. The original purity of the Buddha's Cosmical Body. As it, essentially, has neither beginning, middle, nor end, that is to say, is not liable to origination (*jāti* = *skye-ba*), stability (*sthiti* = *gnas-pa*), and destruction (*vināśa* = *ḥjig-pa*), we call it an immutable element.

Being, in his Cosmical Essence, quiescent,
He is spoken of as acting without effort.[1]
7. Being perceived through inward conviction[2]
He is incognizable from without,
[7 a. 1.] He is (the personified) Wisdom as he knows himself in these 3 forms,[3]
Commiseration,—as he shows the Path,[4]
8. And Power, since through Wisdom and Love
He puts an end to Phenomenal Life and Defilement.
In the first 3 (attributes) lies the aim of oneself,
And in the latter 3—the aim of others.

## Āryāsanga on the Jewel of the Buddha.

"Immutable"[5] we know to be the reverse of that which is caused or conditioned.[6] Now, caused (or conditioned) is that with which origination, stability, and destruction are experienced.[7] The Buddha,[8] being devoid of these (3 distinctive features) is eternal,

---

[1] Ibid. 31 b. 2—3. He is free from every kind of effort in its activity for the sake of others, as he represents the Cosmical Body, the perfect pacification of every kind of exertion.

[2] Ibid. 31 b. 3. As it can be cognized only by the Introspective, Concentrated Transcendental Wisdom, he is inaccessible to the cognition from without by means of words, thought-construction, and the like.

[3] Dar. 31 b. 3—4. As he cognizes (objectively) the original purity, the additional purity, and the Absolute Transcendental Wisdom (as his own distinctive features).

[4] Ibid. 31 b. 6—32 a. 1. By showing the Path that leads to the intuition of this unthinkable object to those who are ignorant of it.

[5] *asaṁskṛta* = *ḥdus-ma-byas.*

[6] *saṁskṛta* = *ḥdus-byas.*

[7] Acc. to Dar. 32 a. 4. "The beginning," "the middle," and "the end" are synonyms of Origination, Stability, and Destruction (*jāti, sthiti, vināśa*). Cf. Conception of Buddhist Nirvāṇa, Index 7.

[8] Dar. 32 a. 5.—*don-dam-bden-pas-bsdus-paḥi-saṅs-rgyas-ñid* = *paramārthena saṅgṛhītaṁ buddhatvām*—Buddhahood as representing the Absolute.

immutable, that which has neither beginning, middle, nor end. As such he represents the Unity of the Cosmos.[1]

Through the perfect Quiescence of all Plurality[2] and the Extinction of all thought-construction,[3] (this Cosmical Body) is motionless and without effort. As it can be cognized only by means of the Introspective Transcendental Wisdom, it is not accessible to the cognition from without. Here the word "*udaya*" is to be understood in the sense of "thorough cognition," but not in that of "origination." The Buddha, having such an immutable and motionless character, nevertheless exercises his activity as long as the world exists, without effort, unhindered and uninterruptedly.[4]

The Buddha has thus come to the full Supreme Enlightenment, (the intuition) of this marvellous, unthinkable sphere of Buddhahood, this by means of his introspective Transcendental Wisdom, himself, without hearing from others and without the help of a teacher, and has cognized it in its unutterable nature.[5] After that, in order that the other living beings who, being deprived of this knowledge, are like born blind,[6] [7 b. 1.] may likewise perceive the Truth, he has demonstrated the Path leading to this perception. On account of this we know him to be possessed of the Highest Wisdom and Commiseration. The Path (shown by him) is free from danger, as it leads out of this world and (is peculiar to one who attains) the Irretrievable State.[7] The examples of a sword and a thunder-bolt

---

[1] Ibid. 32 a. 5. *chos-kyi-sku-yaṅ-dag-paḥi-mthas-rab-tu-phye-ba* = *dharma-kāya-bhūta-koṭi-prabhāvita*—representing the Cosmical Body, the Ultimate Essence of Existence.

[2] Dar. 32 b. 2. Plurality as the differentiation into subject and object (*grāhya-grāhaka* = *gzuṅ-ḥdzin*).

[3] Cf. "Conception of Buddhist Nirvāṇa," page 190—*sarva-kalpanā-kṣaya*.

[4] Dar. 32 b. 6.—through the efficiency of his previous vows (*pūrva-praṇidhāna* = *sṅon-gyi-smon-lam*). Cf. Abhisamayālaṁkāra VIII. 34.

[5] Dar. 33 a. 5.—has come to full Enlightenment in regard of the Absolute the essence of which is inexpressible by words.

[6] Tib. *mus-loṅ-du-gyur-pa* = *jātāndha-bhūta*.

[7] Dar. 33 b. 1—A characteristic of the Path that is demonstrated. It is free from danger, that is to say, from the 5 kinds of fear(?) The Buddha shows the Transcendental Path of the Saint as it begins with the first Stage of the Bodhisattva

illustrate both the Wisdom and the Commiseration of the Buddha as having the power of, respectively, annihilating the source of Phenomenal Life and that of Moral Defilement.[1] Now, the root of Phenomenal Existence are the physical and the mental elements,[2] as they become originated[3] in the (3) spheres of this world.[4] The root of Moral Defilement are the false doctrines and doubt which are preceeded by the views maintaining the existence of a real individuality.[5] Here the Phenomenal Life, as consisting of the physical and mental elements, has the character of growth and can through this be compared with a sprout. The power of the Buddha's Wisdom and Commiseration cuts down this sprout; it may accordingly be illustrated by the example of a sword. (The Obscuration of) Moral Defilement which is to be removed by means of intuition[6] and which consists in doubt and incorrect views, cannot be pierced, that is to say cognized by the ordinary worldly knowledge.[7] It is therefore like a wall surrounded by dense thickets, and the Buddha's Wisdom and Commiseration which break down this wall have here the resemblance with a thunder-bolt. [8 a. 1.]

## Reference to the Jñāna-āloka-alaṁkāra-sūtra.

A detailed exposition of the 6 distinctive characteristics of the Buddha, in the order given above, is contained in the *Sarva-buddha-*

---

(*pramuditā* = *rab-tu-dgaḥ-ba*). He who ventures on this Path never becomes devoid of the mind directed toward Enlightenment (*bodhicitta* = *byaṅ-chub-kyi-sems*) and has attained the Irretrievable State through the annihilation of the seed of imputed Realism.

[1] *kleśa-āvaraṇa* = *ñon-moṅs-kyi-sgrib-pa.*

[2] *nāma-rūpa* = *miṅ-daṅ-gzugs.* [3] *abhinirvṛtta* = *mṅon-par-grub-pa.*

[4] Dar. 34 a. 5.—An individual existing at present in the Immaterial Sphere (*arūpa-dhātu* = *gzugs-med-khams*) may be reborn in the world of Carnal Desire (*kāma-dhātu* = *ḥdod-khams*) or in that of Pure Matter (*rūpa-dhātu* = *gzugs-khams*). Accordingly, although the material elements do not exist with such an individual now, still the latter possesses the seed of them for a future existence.

[5] *satkāya-dṛṣṭi* = *ḥjig-tshogs-la-lta-ba.* [6] *dṛṣṭi-heya* = *mthoṅ-bas-spaṅs-pa.*

[7] Dar. 35 a. 1—2.—The ordinary worldly knowledge cannot directly cognize the true character of defilement and is incapable of annihilating it.

*viṣaya-avatāra-jñāna-āloka-alaṁkāra-sūtra,*[1] as follows:—O Mañjuśrī, "he with whom there can be neither origination nor destruction,"[2]—is an epithet[3] of the Tathāgata, the Arhat, the Perfect, Supreme Buddha.—This passage demonstrates the immutable essence of the Buddha. Then come the 9 examples (illustrating the miraculous character of the Buddha's deeds), beginning with the reflection of the immaculate form of Indra on a surface of lapis-lazuli.[4] With regard to the meaning of these examples it is said:—O Mañjuśrī, in a like way the Tathāgata, the Arhat, the Perfect Supreme Buddha is motionless, he does not reflect, nor does he speak, nor search, nor investigate.[5] He neither searches, nor investigates (the past),[6] nor does he reflect (about the present), nor has he any thoughts (and desires regarding the future). He is perfectly calm,[7] he knows no origination (anew), nor can he disappear. He cannot be seen, nor heard, nor smelt, nor tasted, nor touched. He has no characteristic marks (by which he may be cognized by ordinary wordlings),[8] he is not an absolute cognizing principle,[9] nor is he something cognizable.[10] [8 b. 1.] This and the following passage show the various (meanings) of

---

[1] Tib. *saṅs-rgyas-thams-cad-kyi-yul-la-ḥjug-pa-ye-śes-snaṅ-ba-rgyan-gyi-mdo.* Kg. MDO. III. 287 b. 6 sqq.

[2] Dar. 35 a. 6.—The Cosmical Body of the Buddha which represents the Absolute and neither becomes originated nor disappears.

[3] *adhivacana* = *tshig-bla-dvags.*

[4] Cf. below, the Acts of the Buddha.

[5] "Conception of Buddhist Nirvāṇa," page 210, quotation from the Tathāgata-guhya.

[6] Sic acc. to Dar. 35 b. 6—36 a. 1. Kg. MDO. III. 280 a. 4—6.

[7] Lit. "cool" *śīti-bhūta* = *bsil-bar-gyur-pa.* Cf. Lalita-Vistara, ed. Lefman, 405. 21.

[8] Dar. 36 a. 2—3.—*so-so-skye-bo raṅ-dgaḥ-baḥi-rtags-kyis dpag-par-bya-ba-ma-yin-pa.*

[9] Ibid. 36 a. 3. *śes-paḥi-ṅo-bor raṅ-bźin-gyis-ma-grub-pa rnam-par-rig-pa-med-pa* —he cannot be defined as having the essence of pure consciousness from the standpoint of the Absolute.

[10] Ibid. *śes-byaḥi-ṅo-bor raṅ-bźin-gyis-ma-grub-pa rnam-par-rig-par-bya-ba-ma-yin-pa*—he is not something cognizable, that is to say he is unreal as a separate object of cognition.

the words "perfectly quiescent." They likewise show the Buddha as free from effort while exercising his activity, inasmuch as he represents the Quiescence of all Plurality and Differentiation. Thereafter, the remaining text (of the Sūtra) demonstrates, by means of examples, the fact of the Buddha's being inaccessible to cognition from without. Indeed, the Absolute Essence of all the elements (which is identical with the Buddha who is constantly merged in it) is the only medium for Supreme Enlightenment. Then comes a description of the 16 aspects of the latter, as peculiar to the Buddha. At the end it is said:[1]—O Mañjuśrī, having attained Supreme Enlightenment, (the intuition of) all the elements in this their true essence, the Buddha has perceived in the living beings the Germ of the Absolute, completely impure (with some), not fully purified (with others), and (partly) defective (with still others).[2] He has become full of compassion[3] and has manifested the power of his Great Commiseration.—This passage demonstrates the Buddha as possessed of Wisdom and Love. "All the elements in this their true essence" means "in their character of Non-substantiality." "Having attained Supreme Enlightenment" signifies—"after having cognized (the elements) in their true state by means of the Transcendental Wisdom free from thought-construction, which is peculiar to the Buddha." "In the living beings" means "in those who definitely belong (to one of the 3 spiritual families[4] [9 a. 1.], those of an indefinite character, and those definitely rooted in error."[5] "The Germ of the Absolute"

[1] Kg. MDO. III. 298 a. 6—7.

[2] Cf. below.

[3] Tib. *rnam-par-brtse-ba*. Acc. to Dar. 36 b. 4.—*rnam-par-brtson-pa*—"manifests his energy." It is said that "some texts" (*kha-cig-tu*) have the reading *rnam-par-brtse-ba* "since the energy mentioned here is another name for Commiseration."

[4] Cf. M. V. § 61.

[5] Dar. 36 b. 6 sqq. Those rooted in error are the individuals whose Germ is for a time prevented to grow. This does not however mean that it is alltogether annihilated and that such living beings are incapable of attaining Enlightenment. Acc. to the Mādhyamikas, all living beings are sure of attaining Enlightenment, and their Germ cannot perish, since it is an immutable element, identical with the Absolute.

means the pith of the Buddha which, essentially, does not differ from his own true nature. "Has perceived" means that he has seen by means of the eyes which are peculiar to the Buddha[1] and to which nothing is obscure. (The Germ of the Absolute) is completely impure with the ordinary worldlings, since they are obscured by Moral Defilement.[2] It is not fully purified with the Śrāvakas and Pratyekabuddhas, who are possessed of the Obscuration of Ignorance. It is (partly) defective with the Bodhisattvas, in whom the residues of both (the Obscurations) still exist.[3] (The Buddha) is full of compassion[4] since he starts an activity for the realization of the means (of purifying the stream of elements) with the converts. He manifests himself in the living beings, since it has been his intention to attain Enlightenment, and, consequently, the intuition of his own essential nature, in order that other living beings (might attain a position) equal to that of his own.[5] Thereafter, having manifested his highest Wisdom and Commiseration, he has uninterruptedly exercised his activity in swinging the incomparable Wheel of the Doctrine. This is to be regarded as (the manifestation of) the power of both (Wisdom and Mercy) pursuing the welfare of other living beings.[6]—Now, of these 6 virtues of the Buddha, taken respectively, the first 3, beginning with the immutable character, represent the complement of (the Buddha's) own aim, and

[1] *buddha-cakṣuḥ = saṅs-rgyas-kyi-spyan.*

[2] *kleśa-āvaraṇa = ñon-moṅs-kyi-sgrib-pa.* Acc. to the Mādhyamika-Prāsangika School—Realism (*bden-ḥdzin*) relates to the Obscuration of Moral Defilement. The Obscuration of Ignorance (*jñeya-āvaraṇa = śes-sgrib*) consists in the differentiation into subject and object and the views maintaining a difference between Saṁsāra and Nirvāṇa. Cf. Grub-mthaḥ-rin-chen-phreṅ-ba of Ḥjigs-med-dbaṅ-po, 24 b. 6–25 a. 1 (Aga).

[3] Acc. to the Prāsangikas the Obscuration of Moral Defilement is removed on the first 7 Stages (of the Bodhisattva), and that of Ignorance—on the last 3 (Dar. 36 b. 6.).

[4] Acc. to Dar. 37 a. 6. as before *rnam-par-brtson-pa*—"Great energy."

[5] Dar. 37 b. 1.—*sems-can thams-cad-kyis raṅ-gi-go-ḥphaṅ-brñes-paḥi rgyu-mtshan-du mṅon-par-rdzogs-par-byaṅ-chub-pas-na.*

[6] Dar. 37 b. 4.—If he were deprived of Great Commiseration, he would, after the attainment of Nirvāṇa, have remained merged in the plane of complete Quiescence and would not have swung the Wheel of the Doctrine.

the latter 3, beginning with Transcendental Wisdom—the complement of the aim of other living beings. [9 b. 1.] Otherwise, Divine Transcendental Wisdom may represent the complement of one's own aim, inasmuch as it is the foundation for the eternal and quiescent character which both depend on one's own Enlightenment. The Buddha's Commiseration and Power are the complement of the aim of others, since they manifest themselves in teaching the Highest Doctrine.—

### The Jewel of the Doctrine.

From the Jewel of the Buddha comes the Jewel of the Doctrine.[1] Accordingly, next we have a verse concerning the latter.—

9. I bow before that which cannot be investigated
Neither as a non-ens, nor an ens,
Nor both ens and non-ens together, nor neither of both,[2]
Which has no name, is revealed by introspection,[3] and perfectly quiescent;
And before the sun of the Highest Doctrine,[4] immaculate,
Shining with the lustre of Divine Wisdom,
And vanquishing the darkness of Ignorance, Hatred,
And the Attachment toward all (worldly) objects.—

Now, what is shown here?—

10. Unthinkable, free from both (the causes of Phenomenal Life)[5] and from Differentiation,
Pure, illuminating, and the Antidote[6] (of defilement),
The deliverance from passions and that which leads to such,
Contained in the 2 (last) Truths—such is the Doctrine.—

---

[1] Dar. 38 a. 6.—The Doctrine in its absolute form as Extinction (*nirodha* = *ḫgog-pa*) and the Path (*mārga* = *lam*).

[2] Cf. Sūtrālaṁkāra VI. 1.—*na san na cāsan na tathā* &c.

[3] Dar. 39 a. 6. It is revealed by introspection to the Saint in the state of intense concentration in its undifferentiated, monistic character.

[4] The comparison with the sun refers only to the Doctrine viewed as the Path (Dar. 38 b. 2.).

[5] The Biotic Force (*karma* = *las*) and the passions (*kleśa* = *ñon-moṅs*).

[6] *pratipakṣa* = *gñen-poḥi-phyogs*.

9*

This passage, in short, speaks of the Jewel of the Doctrine, as endowed with 8 dinstinctive attributes. What are these 8?—1) Inaccessibility to discursive thought, 2) absence of the 2 (chief causes of Phenomenal Existence), 3) absence of differentiation, 4) purity, 5) illumination, 6) the fact of being an antidote (against defilement),[1] 7) the liberation from passions, and 8) the cause of the latter. [10 a. 1.]

11. The freedom from passions consists
In the Truths of Extinction and of the Path;
These 2, taken respectively,
Are each known by 3 distinctive features.—

Of 6 distinctive attributes, the unaccessibility to discursive thought, the absence of the 2 (factors of Phenomenal Life) and that of differentiation characterize the Truth of Extinction and are therefore included in the idea of deliverance from passion. The remaining 3 attributes, purity, illumination and the fact of being an antidote against defilement refer to the Path and, consequently, to the cause of liberation (from passion). That which represents this liberation is the Extinction (of Phenomenal Existence). That by means of which this liberation from the passions is attained, is the Path. It is thus said that these 2, combined together, represent the Doctrine delivering from passion[2] which thus bears the character of the 2 purifying[3] Truths of the Saint.

12. It is unthinkable, since it cannot be analysed,[4]
Is unutterable and revealed (only) to the Saint,
It is quiescent by being devoid of the two (causes of Phenomenal
Existence);

---

[1] *pratipakṣa* = *gñen-poḥi-phyogs.*

[2] Cf. M. V. § 267. 2. *dharmaṁ śaraṇaṁ gacchāmi virāgāṇām agryam.*

[3] *vaiyavadānika* = *rnam-par-byaṅ-ba.* Dar. 40 a. 2.—of the 4 Truths of the Saint—the first 2 (*duḥkha* and *samudaya*) contain the defiling (*sāṁkleśika* = *kun-nas-ñon-moṅs-pa*), and the latter two (*nirodha* and *mārga*)—the purifying elements. The 2 "purifying" Truths thus form the essence of the Doctrine.

[4] Dar. 40 b. 2.—analysed within the compass of the 4 limitations.

The other 3 attributes, purity and the rest
(Suggest) a resemblance with the sun.

In shorth, we know the Truth of Extinction to be inaccessible to our thought for 3 motives. What are these 3? (Answer):—1) (The Truth of Extinction) cannot be an object of discursive thought[1] which could be viewed in the compass of the 4 limitations which are: a) non-ens, b) ens, c) both ens and non-ens together, and d) neither ens, nor non-ens; 2) It cannot be expressed by means of words,[2] through such and such language [10 b. 1],[3] as a murmur of the mind,[4] in a sentence, by means of a name with a special etymology,[5] by a word having a conventional meaning,[6] as an object of conversation,[7] or in a special figurative form; 3) It can (only) be revealed by introspection to the Saint.[8]

## Reference to Scripture concerning Extinction.

Now, for what reason do we know the Truth of Extinction to be the absence of both (the Biotic Force and Desire) and of all differentiation. It has been said by the Lord as follows:– O Śāriputra, that which we call the Extinction (of Phenomenal Existence)[9] is the Cosmical Body. It has the character of being devoid of the 2 (causes of Phenomenal Life) and of every kind of differentiation.—Here "the 2 (causes)" mean the Biotic Force and Desire, and "differentiation" is used in the sense of the wrong appreciation (of objects by the mind)[10] which puts in motion both the Biotic Force and Desire. The

---

[1] Tib. *rtog-geḥi-yul-ma-yin-pa* = *na tarkasya viṣayaḥ*. Cf. Sūtrālaṁkāra I. 12.

[2] The bearers of such and such an idea (*vācaka-śabda* = *rjod-byed-kyi-sgra*).

[3] Dar. 40 b. 6—41 a. 1. *yul-mi-so-soḥi-skad*.

[4] Ibid. 41 a. 1. *yid-kyi-brjod-pa* = *mano-jalpa*.

[5] *nirukti* = *ṅes-tshig*. [6] *saṁketa* = *brda*. [7] *vyavahāra* = *tha-sñad*.

[8] Dar. 41 a. 2.—It is to be cognized in its monistic character as not differentiated into subject and object.

[9] Dar. 41 a. 4.—*glo-bur-gyi dri-ma mthaḥ-dag zad-paḥi ḥgog-pa*—Extinction as the annihilation of all the casual defiling elements.

[10] *ayoniśo manasikāraḥ* = *tshul-bźin-ma-yin-paḥi-yid-la-byed-pa*.

Saint has an introspective intuition that (the causes of Phenomenal Existence, are by their nature, essentially, annihilated. Therefore, the Truth of Extinction appears to him as that which is the complete absence of any new origination of Phenomenal Life. Indeed, at that time there are no constructions of the thought, no forces creating Phenomenal Existence, and no desires. But nowhere is this Extinction spoken of as the destruction of some of the elements of existence. It is said:[1]—O Mañjuśrī, there cannot be any activity of the mind,[2] the intellect,[3] and consciousness[4] regarding that which is neither originated, nor disappears.[5] That in regard of which there can be no activity of the mind, the intellect, and consciousness, is devoid of every kind of differentiation, that is to say, wrong appreciation.[6] On the contrary, the mind being directed upon the right point, it is impossible for ignorance[7] to arise. The non-origination of ignorance means the same in regard of the (whole) 12-membered chain of Phenomenal Life [11 a.]. There will be thus no (repeated) origination (in the Saṁsāra any more). This and more has been said (in Scripture). (We have next):[8]—O Lord, the destruction of the elements does not mean the Extinction of Phenomenal Existence.[9] O Lord, that which

---

[1] Jñāna-āloka-alaṁkāra-sūtra, Kg. MDO. III. 297 a. 7—b. 2.

[2] *citta* = *sems*. [3] *manas* = *yid*.

[4] *vijñāna* = *rnam-par-śes-pa* = (*rnam-śes*). Dar. 42 a. 1—2. The mind is that over which the different active forces (*vāsanā* = *bag-chags*) exercise their activity, the intellect is taken in the sense of a support or substratum (*āśraya* = *rten*—of the different faculties), and consciousness is to be understood as that which is founded on the said substratum. Otherwise the 3 are viewed as synonymous. Cf. Prof. Th. Stcherbatsky, Conception of Buddhist Nirvāṇa, p. 31.

[5] I.e. the Absolute. Dar. 41 b. 6. *skye-ba-med-ciṅ ḥgag-pa-med-pa don-dam-paḥi bden-pa-la.*

[6] Cf. p. 133 note 10.

[7] *avidyā* = *ma-rig-pa*. Dar. 42 a. 4. *bden-par-ḥdzin-paḥi ñon-moṅs-can-gyi-ma-rig-pa*—Ignorance connected with defilement and consisting in realistic views. Cf. Conception of Buddhist Nirvāṇa, Index 7. s. v. *avidyā*.

[8] Śrī-mālā-siṁhanāda-sūtra. Kg. DKON. VI. 278 a. 6—b. 2.

[9] This passage very pregnantly expresses the Mahāyānistic idea that the Extinction of Phenomenal Life, that is to say the attainment of Nirvāṇa, does not mean an actual annihilation of the elements constituting a personality, but that it

is called the Extinction of Phenomenal Existence manifests itself as the Cosmical Body of the Buddha which is beginningless, is neither created,[1] nor born (by itself),[2] nor has it an origination (from both self and not-self).[3] It cannot be destroyed (by anything else), nor can it disappear (by itself). It is eternal, persistent, quiescent, indestructible, perfectly pure by nature,[4] delivered from all the bonds of the passions, and endowed with the attributes of the Buddha which are inseparable (from it), inconceivable and greater in number than the sands of the Ganges.—O Lord, this very Cosmical Body of the Buddha, when it is not delivered from the bonds of the passions, is called the Germ of the Buddha.[5]—All this is to be regarded as a detailed characteristic of the Truth of Extinction as we have it in Scripture.

### The Path as the Cause of Extinction.

The cause for the realization of this Cosmical Body of the Buddha which is called the Extinction of Phenomenal Life, is the direct Transcendental Intuition which represents the Paths of Illumination[6] and Contemplation.[7] The Path (as a whole) may be compared with the sun, since it has 3 points of resemblance with it. 1) (First of all) it is akin to the disc of the sun which is perfectly pure, inasmuch as it (the Path) is completely free from the stains of passion. 2) Just as the sun casts its light on all the visible objects, in the same way the Path makes clear everything cognizable in all the different aspects. 3) Finally, it has a resemblance with the sun by being a counterpart of darkness [11 b.], since it appears as the antidote of all the impediments to the perception of the Absolute Truth.

---

means only a change of the point of view with regard to the Universe, which is intuited in the monistic sense.

[1] Dar. 42 b. 1. *rkyen gźan-gyis-ma-byas-pa* = *para-pratyayair akṛta.*

[2] Ibid. *raṅ-ñid ma-skyes-pa* = *svato'nutpanna.*

[3] Ibid. *gñis-ka-la-brten-nas-ma-byuṅ-ba* = *ubhaya-āśritatvena-anutpanna.*

[4] *raṅ-bźin-gyis-dag-pa* = *svabhāva-śuddha.*

[5] Dar. 42 b. 4.—The Absolute mingled with defilement, which is the Essence of the Buddha.

[6] *darśana-mārga* = *mthoṅ-lam.* [7] *bhāvanā-mārga* = *sgom-lam.*

The impediments are (caused) by the rise of passion,[1] hatred,[2] and infatuation,[3] since (all living beings) are possessed of these defiling forces in a dreaming,[4] or developped state. The origination of passion &c. is preceeded by an activity of the mind directed toward the illusionary objects which are a cause (for the origination of realistic views). As the dreaming defiling forces produce in the ordinary living beings desire, hatred and infatuation, inasmuch as (the objects) appear (respectively) in an attractive, repulsive, and utterly false aspect, these (forces) are the cause (of wrong appreciation).[5] The illusionary views which are the cause of passion, hatred, and infatuation, being directed toward such and such objects (give rise) to the wrong appreciation which completely takes possession of the mind. In the latter, which thus abides in a state of error, the different forms of defilement, be it desire, hatred or infatuation, begin to exercise their influence. On this foundation are done the deeds of body, speech, and mind, which have their origin in the 3 sources of evil. From the deeds, in its turn, comes the succession of births (in the Phenomenal World). Thus the ordinary wordly beings, possessed of the residues and seeds of the defiling forces and clinging to the reality of separate entities,[6] are directed toward the (illusionary wordly) objects. Accordingly this gives rise to the wrong appreciation which is the origin of the passions. [12 a.] The latter in their turn call forth the deeds and these are the cause of (repeated) births. All these different forms of defilement peculiar to the worldlings, those of passions, deeds and repeated birth,[7] manifest themselves in this world owing to the ignorance of the unique Germ (of Buddhahood) in its true character.

---

[1] *rāga* = *ḥdod-chags.* [2] *dveṣa* = *źe-sdaṅ.*

[3] *moha* = *gti-mug.* [4] *anuśaya* = *bag-la-ñal.*

[5] Dar. 43 b. 4. *tshul-min-yid-byed-kyi rgyu-mtshan-du bag-la-ñal de ḥgyur-ro.*

[6] *mtshan-mar-ḥdzin-pa-can* = *nimitta-grāhiṇaḥ.*

[7] *kleśa-saṁkleśa* = *ñon-moṅs-paḥi-kun-nas-ñon-moṅs-pa, karma-saṁkleśa* = *las-kyi-kun-nas-ñon-moṅs-pa,* and *jāti-saṁkleśa* = *skye-baḥi-kun-nas-ñon-moṅs-pa.* Cf. my translation of Bu-ton's "History of Buddhism," note 56.

Now, how are we to search (for the Absolute Truth)? (Answer):— It is to be perceived through the complete negation (of the separate reality) of every object and characteristic feature. As soon as we cease to perceive the (separate unreality) of the objects or their characteristic marks, we come to perceive the Absolute Truth.[1] In such a way the Lord has viewed all the elements and has come to Supreme Enlightenment, (the intuition of) their unity. Through the non-perception of the separate elements on account of their unreality, and through the intuition of the Absolute as the true reality (—the essence of everything cognizable), comes the Transcendental Wisdom perceiving the unity of the elements. For this wisdom both (the imputed reality of the separate elements and their ultimate Non-substantiality) are not something to be, respectively, rejected or established anew. Through this one comes to Supreme Enlightenment, the full intuition of the monistic essence of the elements. Here the Transcendental Wisdom which, thus arising, cognizes the points to be shunned as completely annihilated and (essentially) unreal, is to be viewed as the antidote against all the impediments to the perception of the Absolute Truth.[2] This Transcendental Wisdom which represents the Paths of Illumination and Contemplation, is the cause for the attainment of the Cosmical Body. It is to be known in detail from the Prajñāpāramitā-Sūtras.—

### The Jewel of the Congregation.

From the precious jewel of the Mahāyānistic Doctrine comes the precious Congregation of the Bodhisattvas who have attained the Irretrievable State. [12 b.] Accordingly, immediately after we have a verse referring to the Jewel of the Congregation:—

13. I bow before those who perceive the pure, radiant essence of the Spirit and the nullity of all defilement,

[1] Dar. 45 a. 1. At the time when we no more perceive a differentiation into subject and object, we come to the intuition of the Absolute Truth (*yaṅ-dag-pa-don-dam-paḥi-bden-pa*).

[2] Correct *dē-kho-na-mthoṅ-baḥi-gegs* for *kho-na-mthoṅ* &c. (12 a. 5.)

Who, knowing the background of the unreality of all that exists,
(the Absolute in its) quiescent nature,[1]
Perceive in all living beings the reflex of the Supreme Buddha,[2]
The powerful minds free from Obscuration and endowed with the sight of Divine Wisdom,
The object of which is the immaculate and infinite essence of all that lives.

Now, what is shown here?—

14. Through the perfect purity of their insight,
The Absolute and the Empirical, both being Introspective,[3]
The Congregation of the Sages abiding in the Irretrievable State
Is endowed with the highest merits.—

This verse, in short, shows us the Jewel of the Congregation,—the Bodhisattvas who have attained the Irretreivable State as possessed of merits higher than which there are none. Indeed, they have a pure transcendental intuition of existence in its Absolute and Empirical character.

### The Saint's Knowledge of the Absolute Truth.

15. As they know the quiescent nature of all that exists,[4]
They have the intuition of the Absolute Truth,
This owing to (their knowledge) of the pure nature (of the Spirit),
And of the essential nullity of the defiling forces.[5]

---

[1] The saint's intuition of the Absolute. Dar. 46 a. 5.—The background of the unreality of the Individual (*pudgala-nairātmya* = *gaṅ-zag-gi-bdag-med*) and of the separate elements (*dharma-nairātmya* = *chos-kyi-bdag-med*) is the Absolute quiescent by nature (in the aspect of which all separate entities are) unreal.

[2] The empirical knowledge of the Saint. He perceives in all living beings the reflex of the Buddha (which is the fundamental Germ). Cf. Bu-ton, Commentary on the Abhisamayālaṁkāra (*Luṅ-gi-sñe-ma*) 150 b. 3—4.—"perceives in all living beings the Essence of the Buddha."

[3] Lit. the "internal" (*naṅ-gi*). Dar. 46 b. 6—*naṅ-gi-ni-ste de gñis so-so-raṅ-gis-rig-paḥi ye-śes-kyi-gzigs-pa.*

[4] Dar. 47 a. 3—4. As they have a direct intuition of all that exists,—the personality and the separate elements,—in its quiescent character, that is to say, in the aspect of Universal Relativity and Non-Substantiality.

[5] Lit. "of the defiling forces as essentially annihilated."

Here the (intuition of the) Absolute Truth is to be understood as the knowledge of the background of the unreality of all that exists,[1] that is to say the separate elements and the individualities. This knowledge[2] of the (ultimate) imperishable nature of the individuality and the separate elements which is for ever quiescent[3] from the outset, has 2 causes for its origination. These are:—1) The perception of the mind in its pure, radiant character, and [13a. 1.] 2) the intuition of the defiling elements as essentially annihilated and unreal from the outset. Now, these 2 points, namely the mind as perfectly pure and brilliant by nature, and the defiling elements which affect it, are very hard to be correctly cognized in the aspect of the Absolute which is uninfluenced by defilement.[4] Indeed, when one of the 2 forms of the Spirit, either the defiled or the undefiled, manifests itself, it has no (real) contact with the other (its counterpart).[5] Accordingly, it has been said:[6]—O Lord, the undefiled Spirit represents one single moment. It cannot be affected by the defiling forces. The defiled spirit is also one single moment; the passions cannot really take possession of it. O Lord, if the passions do not really influence the spirit, and the latter does not (really) become defiled, how then, O Lord, does the spirit, which is uninfluenced, still become obscured

---

[1] Cf. above.

[2] Dar. 47 b. 3. *theg-chen-ḥphags-pas mṅon-sum-du-rtogs-pa*—the direct intuition of the Mahāyānist Saint.

[3] *ādi-śānta* = *gzod-ma-nas-źi-ba.*

[4] *anāsrava-dhātu* = *zag-pa-med-paḥi-dbyiṅs.*

[5] Dar. 48 a. 4–6. If it is supposed that the spirit arises in an undefiled form and is then influenced by the passions, the subsequent form of the spirit which is influenced will represent a result, and the influencing defiling agencies will be the cause (of it). Now, if both the influenced and the influencing are essentially unreal, it will be very difficult to put them forth as object and agent. If on the contrary they are viewed as real, they have to appear simultaneously and ought to be in contact with each other. Therefore it is very difficult to understand the state of things here, namely the fact that, when one form of the two manifests itself, it has at that very time no contact with the other; the idea of a cause and effect and of object and agent is therefore inadmissible.

[6] In the Śrī-mālā-siṁhanāda-sūtra. Kg. DKON. VI. 282 a. 1–5.

by the passions? The passions, O Lord, exist, and the spirit which becomes affected by them, likewise exists.[1] O Lord, although this[2] be so, it is still very hard to cognize the meaning of the perfectly pure spirit, which nevertheless becomes obscured by defilement.— The whole of this passage, beginning with the cognition of the Absolute and ending with the difficulty of cognizing (the spirit as unaffected by defilement), is demonstrated by the Sūtra[3] in detail.

### The Empirical Knowledge of the Saints.

16. Through the Wisdom which penetrates into the background of everything cognizable,
They perceive the Essence of the Omniscient [13 b. 1.]
As it exists in all living beings.
This is their knowledge of the Empirical Reality.

Here the (perception of)[4] the Empirical Reality (with the Mahāyānist Saint) is known to (have the following character):—On the basis of the cognition of the Ultimate Essence of all things, (the Saint), by his Transcendental Wisdom, perceives the existence of the Germ of Buddhahood in all the living beings without exception, even in those who are born in the form of beasts. The origination of this intuition of the Bodhisattvas dates from the first Stage,[5] since there they (first) perceive the all-pervading character of the Absolute.[6]

---

[1] Sic acc. to Dar. 49 b. 2. The Aga ed. of the Comm. has *ñe-bar-ñon-moṅs-par-ḥgyur-baḥi-sems-ni ma-mchis-so*—the spirit which becomes influenced by defilement does not exist.

[2] Dar. 49 b. 2.—that is the unreality of the influencing and the influenced (from the standpoint) of the Absolute and their reality from the Empirical standpoint.

[3] The Śrīmālā-devī-siṁhanāda.

[4] Dar. 49 b. 6—*ji-sñed-pa-yod-pa-ñid-gzigs-pa-ni.*

[5] *pramuditā* = *rab-tu-dgaḥ-ba.* Is identical with the Path of Illumination (*darśana-mārga* = *mthoṅ-lam*).

[6] Dar. 50 a. 4—5.—Because there (on the first Stage) they for the first time have an intuition of the Absolute Essence of everything cognizable which had not been perceived by them before. They have thus an intuition of the Absolute as pervading all the objects of cognition. This intuition coincides with the first moment

## The Perception of the Saints is Introspective Knowledge.

17. Thus, the intuition (of the Bodhisattvas)
Is their direct Transcendental Introspection.
It is perfectly pure, being free from attachment
Within the plane of the Immaculate Absolute,
And completely free from all impediments.—

That which thus represents the Transcendental Intuition, the Path (of the Saints) is to be viewed as the Divine, superhuman, introspective perception, peculiar to the (Mahāyānistic) Saints which has nothing in common with (the knowledge) of other people. In short, this introspection, being compared with other (ordinary) [1] and incomprehensive [2] knowledge, is spoken of as being perfectly pure out of 2 motives. What are these 2? (Answer:)—1) It is free from attachment [3] and 2) it (penetrates into the essence of everything cognizable) [4] through being unimpeded. Now (the knowledge of the Bodhisattva) is free from attachment since it has for its object the Germ of the living beings in its perfectly pure nature, this through the intuition of the Absolute. (At the same time) [14 a. 1.] as (the Saint) possesses the complete knowledge of Empirical Reality he has for his object everything cognizable without any limits. On account of this, his cognition is completely free from impediments.

18. Through their immaculate Transcendental Intuition,
They (are near) to the Divine Wisdom of the Buddha.[5]

---

of the Path of Illumination (*darśana-mārga*). Cf. Vasubandhu on Sutrālaṁkāra VI. 7—*dharma-dhātoḥ pratyakṣato gamane dvaya-lakṣaṇena viyukto grāhya-grāhaka-lakṣaṇena. iyaṁ darśana-mārga-avasthā.*

[1] Dar. 50 b. 3—4.—that which does not perceive the Non-substantiality of existence.

[2] *ñi-tshe-ba* = *prādeśika*. Ibid.—that which does not penetrate into the essence of everything cognizable.

[3] Dar. 50 b. 4—5. As they possess an intuition of the Absolute and through this have for their object the Germ of the living beings in its perfectly pure nature, they are free from attachment caused by realistic views.

[4] Sic acc. to Dar. 50 b. 5. [5] Cf. Abhisamayālaṁkāra III. 2 b.

Therefore the Saints that have attained the Irretrievable State
Are the refuge of all living beings.—

The Transcendental Intuition of the Bodhisattva who abides on the Irretrievable State[1] stands near to the perfectly pure Divine Perception of the Buddha, higher than which there is none. Moreover, the Bodhisattva, being possessed of such a knowledge, is a refuge for all living beings. For this reason the said intuition is to be regarded as superior to all the other virtues of the Bodhisattva, as morality and the rest.

## The Hīnayānistic Congregation is not worthy of being worshipped.

After the Congregation of the Bodhisattvas, that of the Śrāvakas has not been mentioned, since it is not worthy of being worshipped. As concerns the difference between the merits of the Bodhisattvas and those of the Śrāvakas, we know that the latter do not care for (the Path of) the Bodhisattva, which is like that of the ascending moon, and appear like stars that cast light only on their own form. Therefore they ought not to be worshipped, since they are not completely pure as regards the intention of helping other living beings. [14 b. 1.] On the contrary the Bodhisattvas bring to accomplishment the great Accumulations for the attainment of Supreme Enlightenment, they are possessed of the lustre of Wisdom and Commiseration, bring about Illumination regarding the essence of all the innumerable living beings and venture on the Path for the attainment of the state of a Buddha, which resembles that of the full moon. (Such are they) in comparison with the Hīnayānists, who possess only a limited[2] ultimate knowledge, and (having no desire of removing the suffering of all living beings), only further the Illumination of their own stream of elements. Even the Bodhisattva who, on a correct foundation, makes his first Creative Effort, beats the highest form of pure morality

---

[1] Dar. 51 a. 3. The Bodhisattva abiding on the 3 highest Stages, beginning with the 8th (*acalā*).

[2] *ñi-tshe-ba* = *prādeśika*. Cf. Abhisamayālaṁkāra. V. 11.

peculiar to the Hīnayānist Saint, who has no compassion (with others) and is not possessed of a wide (mind caring for all living beings). If this be so, what is there to say of the other (Bodhisattvas who are possessed of) such virtues as the 10 Controlling Powers[1] and the rest. Indeed it has been said:—

He who becomes great in morals for the sake of his own Salvation,
Who has no compassion with the living beings whose morals are impure,
Is possessed of the treasure of that morality (which only leads to) self-magnification.
Such a Saint cannot be called pure in his morals.
He in whom the Highest Commiseration toward others is aroused,
Who, having embraced the true Morality,
Is of help to others like fire, air, earth, and water,—
This one is really virtuous, whereas the other has only a resemblance of morality.—

### The 3 Jewels in their Character of a Refuge.

Now, what aim did the Lord pursue when he established the 3 Refuges?[2]

19. In order to make known the virtues[3]
Of the Teacher, the Teaching, and the Disciples,
For the sake of (the adherents of) the 3 Vehicles
And those devoted to the 3 forms of religious observance,[4]—
The 3 Refuges have been proclaimed (by the Lord). [15 a. 1.]

### The Motives for the Establishment of the 3 Refuges from the Empirical Standpoint as explained by Āryāsanga.

*In order to show the virtues of the Teacher*, with a view to those individuals who adhere to the Vehicle of the Bodhisattvas and

[1] *daśa vaśitāḥ* = *dbaṅ-bcu*.

[2] *trīṇi śaraṇāni* = *skyabs-gsum*. [3] Sic acc. to Comm. below.

[4] Dar. 56 b. 1—2.—for the sake of those who, though they have not entered the Path, are still devoted to the performance of the acts of religious observance, worship, &c., in regard of each of the 3 Jewels respectively.

wish to attain the character of a Buddha, as well as those who, (though they have not entered the Path), are devoted to the performance of religious observances which have the Buddha for their object, it has been spoken and ascertained:—the Buddha is the refuge, since he is the Highest of Men.[1]

*In order to make known the virtues of the Doctrine*, for the sake of those who belong to the Pratyekabuddha Vehicle and start an activity for an independent apprehension of the profound Doctrine of Causality,[2] as well as those whose religious fervour is directed toward the Doctrine (exclusively), it has been declared:—The Doctrine is the Refuge, since it is the highest for those who become dispassionate.[3]

*In order to show the virtues of the Disciples*,[4] who have embraced the Doctrine of the Teacher, with regard to the individuals who adhere to the Vehicle of the Śrāvakas and proceed on the Path in order to attain (the fruit of Arhatship) on the basis of the instructions heard of others, as well as those who are devoted to the worship of the Congregation, it has been proclaimed:—The Congregation is a refuge, since it is the highest of communities.[5]—Thus, in short, for 3 motives, and having in view 6 kinds of individuals, the Lord has proclaimed the 3 Refuges and shown them in their variety. This has been done in order to promote the living beings to the 3 Vehicles respectively, the matter being viewed from the Empirical standpoint.[6]

## The Doctrine and the Congregation are not Refuges in the Ultimate Sense.

20. The Doctrine in its two forms and the Congregation of the Saints
Are not by themselves the highest, absolute Refuge.[7]

---

[1] Cf. M. V. § 267. 1. *buddhaṁ śaraṇaṁ gacchāmi dvipadānām agryam.*

[2] *pratītya-samutpāda-dharma = rten-ḥbrel-gyi-chos.*

[3] M. V. § 267. 2. *dharmaṁ śaraṇaṁ gacchāmi virāgāṇām agryam.*

[4] The Arhats and Bodhisattvas.

[5] M. V. § 267. 3. *saṁghaṁ śaraṇaṁ gacchāmi gaṇānām agryam.*

[6] *saṁvṛti = kun-rdzob.*

[7] Dar. 56 a. 3.—*mthar-thug-paḥi chos daṅ dge-ḥdun-gyi-tshogs mṅaḥ-ba saṅs-rgyas-dkon-mchog-tu bsdus*—as the Doctrine and the Congregation in their Ultimate form are included in the idea of the Buddha.

Indeed, (the former) is (ultimately) given up, is illusionary and of a negative character,
(And the latter) is not devoid of fear (and error).—

Now, the Doctrine appears in 2 forms:—1) as the Teaching,[1] and 2) as the practical part.[2] The Doctrine as the Teaching (of Buddha) we call the aphorisms and the other (parts of Scripture)[3] which are included in the complex of letters, words, and sentences. This form is spoken of as resembling a ship (which is left) when the shore of the full apprehension (of the Truth) on the Path is reached. As regards the practical side of the Doctrine, it appears in 2 varieties, namely as the Extinction (of Phenomenal Existence) and the Path,—that which is practically attained and the means of attainment. Now, the Path is to be viewed as having the character of being caused (or conditioned).[4] That which is viewed as having the character of being caused, is false and illusionary. That which is false and illusionary is not true, that which is not true is—evanescent, and that which is evanescent cannot be a refuge.

The Extinction (of Phenomenal Life) which is attained by means of this Path, represents, according to the Hīnayānistic standpoint, the mere absence of Phenomenal Existence and of the defiling forces, being compared with a light that is extinguished. But, a Non-ens can neither be a refuge, nor its reverse.

"The Congregation" is a name for the assembly (of the Saints belonging to) the 3 Vehicles. These, being constantly possessed of fear, seek their refuge in the Buddha [16 a. 1.], search for a means of deliverance, have still (different) subjects to apprehend[5] and have not yet attained the Perfect, Supreme Enlightenment. Why are they possessed of fear? (Answer):—"Even the Arhats, though they are

---

[1] *deśanā-dharma* = *bstan-paḥi-chos*. Is the same as *āgama-dharma* = *luṅ-gi-chos*.

[2] *adhigama-dharma* = *rtogs-paḥi-chos*.

[3] The 12 classes of Sacred Texts (*dvādaśāṅga-dharma-pravacana*).

[4] *saṁskṛta* = *ḥdus-byas*. The whole passage is an extract from the Śrī-mālā-devī-siṁhanāda-sūtra. Kg. DKON. VI. 279 a. 3—4.

[5] Dar. 62 a. 2.—to attain by means of the Path.

rid of Phenomenal Existence, cannot remove the force (of Transcendental Illusion).[1] Therefore they perpetually abide in a state of mighty fear (caused by) the active forces[2] (of existence), just as a man over whom the executioner has raised his sword. For this reason even they cannot attain that deliverance which is fully blissful. That which is itself an Absolute Refuge[3] has no need to seek refuge (in others). Just as those living beings who have no refuge and, being full of fear with regard to this or that object, seek a means of deliverance, in the same way the Arhats are also possessed of fear. As they are thus afraid (of this or that object arousing their) fear, they seek their refuge in the Buddha. Now, one who being thus full of fear, seeks his refuge (in others), necessarily seeks (a means of) deliverance (from his fear). As he seeks deliverance, he undergoes a course of training in order to get rid of the sources of fear.[4] Through this training he proceeds (on the Path) for the attainment of the highest position of one who is completely free from fear. This means that he proceeds toward the perfect Supreme Enlightenment. [16 b. 1.] For this reason the Congregation of the Saints, as it represents only a partly refuge, cannot be such in the absolute sense." —Thus it is said that these 2 refuges (the Doctrine and the Congregation) are no more such at the time of final (Enlightenment).[5]

### The Buddha is the Unique Absolute Refuge.

21. In the absolute sense, the refuge
 Of all living beings is only the Buddha.
 Indeed, the Lord is possessed of the Cosmical Body,[6]
 And the multitudes of Saints, too, have their issue in the latter.

---

[1] *vāsanā* = *bag-chags*. Has here the meaning of *avidyā-vāsanā* = *ma-rig-paḥi bag-chags*.

[2] *saṁskāra* = *ḥdu-byed*.

[3] Dar. 62 a. 5.—*don-dam-paḥi-skyabs*.

[4] Dar. 62 b. 2.—the sources of fear, that is to say the subtle dreaming forces which give origination to sinful deeds.

[5] The whole passage is a reproduction of the sermon in the Śrī-mālā-devī-siṁhanāda-sūtra. Kg. DKON. VI. 268 b. 2—8. and 275 a. 7—b. 3.

[6] As the true Essence of Existence.

This (has the following meaning):—The Buddha, as has been said before, is characterized as neither becoming originated, nor disappearing, and is endowed with the Cosmical Body which represents the deliverance from passions and bears the character of the 2 purifying Truths (of the Saint).[1] The Congregation of the Saints belonging to the 3 Vehicles, too, attains its final goal, when it has coalesced with the ultimate, pure Cosmical Body. Therefore, for the living beings who have no other protection and refuge, the Imperishable Refuge that is like a last instance,[2] the Eternal Refuge,[3] the Undestructible Refuge,[4] and the Absolute Refuge[5] is only one.—It is the Tathāgata, the Arhat, the Perfect Supreme Buddha. This unique, indestructible, quiescent, and persistent refuge is to be known in detail from the *Ārya-śrī-mālā-sūtra.*[6]

## The Meaning of "The 3 Jewels."

22. They appear rarely, they are immaculate,
Are powerful, are an ornament of this world,
Are the highest (point of excellence), and cannot change,—
Therefore they have the character of jewels.

In short, the 3 highest and most precious subjects which are the Buddha, the Doctrine and the Congregation, are spoken of as being like jewels, since they have 6 points of resemblance (with such). [17 a.] These are as follows:—

1) (They are like jewels) since they appear very rarely. Indeed, those beings who have not fostered the roots of virtue,[7] do not come in contact with them, even during a long succession of æons.

---

[1] *nirodha* and *mārga*. Cf. above.

[2] Dar. 63 b. 1. He is like a last instance, beause he assists the living beings as long as the world exists.

[3] Ibid. 63 b. 2. He is an Eternal Refuge, since his stream of elements never ceases.

[4] Tib. *gyuṅ-druṅ* = *svastika*—here the symbol of all that is indestructible.

[5] *pāramārthikaṁ śaraṇam* = *don-dam-paḥi-skyabs.*

[6] Kg. DKON. VI. 275 a. 5—6.

[7] Cf. Abhisamayālaṁkāra IV. 6. *kṛtādhikārā buddheṣu teṣū'pta-śubha-mūlakāḥ.* The Tib. as here *dge-baḥi-rtsa-ba bskrun-pa.*

10*

2) They (resemble jewels) by their purity, since they are completely free from every kind of defilement.

3) They are powerful (like the wish-fulfilling gem),[1] since they are possessed of the power of the 6 Supernatural Faculties[2] and other inconceivable virtues.

4) They (have the character of jewels, being) the ornament of this world, as they are the cause of the virtuous thoughts of all living beings.[3]

5) Just as real jewels are greatly superior to the artificial, (the Buddha, the Doctrine and the Congregation) are superior (to everything that exists), since they are of a transcendental character.

6) As the wish-fulfilling gem never changes (in its faculty of bringing forth the desired objects), whether praised or reviled, so are (the 3 Refuges), since they are bearers of an eternal, immutable essence.—

## The Germ, Enlightenment, the Attributes and the Acts of the Buddha in their inconceivable Nature.

After the description of the 3 Jewels we have a verse concerning those (elements) the existence of which conditions the origination of the said Jewels, since they represent the source of all the purifying qualities, the mundane,[4] and the transcendental.[5]

23. The Absolute mingled with defilement,
The Absolute free from all the stains,
The immaculate attributes and the acts of the Buddha,

---

[1] *cintāmaṇi* = *yid-bźin-nor-bu.* Sic acc. to Dar. 64 a. 3.

[2] *abhijñā* = *mṅon-par-śes-pa.*

[3] Dar. 64 a. 4—5.—The desire of a blissful existence (*abhyudaya* = *mṅon-mtho*) and of the superbliss of Salvation (*niḥśreyasa* = *ṅes-legs*). Acc. to the Mahāyānists all the virtuous thoughts of the living beings are produced by the grace of the Buddha. Cf. Bodhicaryāvatāra I. 5. *rātrau yathā megha-ghanāndhakāre vidyut kṣaṇaṁ darśayati prakāśam, buddhānubhāvena tathā kadācil lokasya puṇyeṣu matiḥ kṣaṇaṁ syāt.*

[4] *laukika* = *ḥjig-rten-pa.*

[5] *lokottara* = *ḥjig-rten-las-ḥdas-pa.*

(These elements) from which the 3 illustrious Jewels arise,
(These 4 items) are only accessible to him who perceives the
Absolute Truth.

Now, what is elucidated here?

24. The source of these 3 Jewels[1] [17 b.]
Is accessible only to the Omniscient;
It has four varieties
And is inconceivable for four motives, respectively.

The Absolute mingled with defilement is the fundamental element which is not delivered from the bonds of the passions and is called the Essence of Buddhahood (as it exists in all the living beings). The Immaculate Absolute is the same thing as the exclusive property of the Buddha and consisting in a total metamorphose[2] (of all the elements of existence). As such it is called the Cosmical Body of the Buddha.[3] The immaculate attributes of the Buddha, which, essentially, are likewise nothing but a metamorphose of the elements, are the distinctive features of the Cosmical Body. Such are the 10 Powers and the other qualities which are all of a transcendental nature. The deeds of the Buddha are the sublime forms of his activity, (the manifestations) of the 10 Powers and the other attributes. These acts never cease and have no break in their continuance. Therefore the prophecies[4] (delivered by the Buddha and) concerning the Bodhisattvas (who are to attain Enlightenment by the grace of the Buddha in future times) have no end.[5] These 4 subjects, taken respectively, are inconceivable for 4 motives. Therefore it is said that they are

---

[1] Dar. 65 a. 2. *rigs-rgyu-rkyen-ma-lus-pa yoṅs-su-rdzogs-pa*—the full complex of causes (*hetu*) and conditions (*pratyaya*).

[2] *parāvṛtti* = *yoṅs-su-gyur-pa*.

[3] Cf. Abhisamayālaṁkāra VIII. 1. *sarvākārāṁ viśuddhim ye dharmā prāptā nirāsravāḥ, svābhāviko muneḥ kāyas teṣāṁ prakṛtilakṣaṇaḥ.*

[4] *vyākaraṇa* = *luṅ-bstan-pa.*

[5] Since all the run of the world's moral progress i.e. the attainment of Saintliness is nothing but a manifestation of the Buddha's Cosmical Body.

accessible only to the Divine Wisdom of the Omniscient. What are the 4 motives?

25. Because—

(The Absolute as the Germ) is pure, but nevertheless in contact with the defiling (worldly) elements, (1)

(The Absolute as the Cosmical Body) is on the other hand quite free from every defilement, (2)

The attributes of the Buddha are essentially identical with the Absolute as contained even in every ordinary being, (3)

(And the Buddha's acts) are free from effort[1] and (dialectical) constructions.[2]

The Absolute mingled with defiling elements is at the same time [18 a.] perfectly pure and nevertheless in contact with the defiling forces. For this reason the point is inconceivable; it is not accessible even to the Pratyekabuddhas who have faith in the profound Doctrine (of Monism).[3] It is accordingly said:[4]—O Goddess, these 2 points are very hard to be cognized. It is difficult to understand that (there exists) the spirit completely pure by nature, and it is difficult to understand that this very spirit is nevertheless influenced by the defiling elements. O Goddess, those who can teach this contradiction are either thyself or the Bodhisattvas who call the Highest Doctrine their own. O Goddess, the others, that is the Śrāvakas and Pratyekabuddhas, may cognize these 2 points (only) through their faith in the Buddha.

The Absolute in its undefiled form was not influenced by defilement before, and has nevertheless become purified subsequently. This point is inconceivable! It is said:[5]—The Spirit is pure and

---

[1] *anābhoga* = *lhun-grub* (*lhun-gyis-grub-pa*).

[2] *nirvikalpaka* = *rnam-par-mi-rtog-pa*.

[3] Dar. 66 b. 5. *stoṅ-ñid* (= *śūnyatā*) *spros-bral* (= *niṣprapañca*) *zab-moḥi chos-kyi tshul-la mos-pa* (= *gambhīra-dharma-adhimukta*).

[4] In the Śrī-mālā-siṁhanāda-sūtra. Kg. DKON. VI. 282 a. 7—b. 1.

[5] Dhāraṇīśvara-rāja-paripṛcchā, Kg. MDO. XV. 210 b. 6—7.

radiant by nature and can in its true form be intuited (by the Saints through introspection). In such a way the Lord has, by his momentary Divine Wisdom[1] attained the Perfect Supreme Enlightenment and has become a Buddha.

The immaculate attributes of the Buddha (are completely free from all defilement) and at the same time they have one essence (with the Absolute) as contained even in the ordinary wordly beings[2] who are totally obscured by defilement. As there is thus no (essential) difference between the former (the Absolute with the Buddha and his attributes) and the latter (the Absolute as the Germ of the living beings) [18 b. 1.], the subject is inaccessible to (discursive) thought. Indeed, there absolutely exists no living being in whom the Spirit of the Buddha does not fully manifest itself.[3] But as one has a conception[4] (of separate entities), the Spirit of the Lord is not perceived. (On the contrary) when one has got rid of this conception, the Divine Spirit of the Omniscient appears without hindrance to one's own transcendental introspection.

## The Parable of the Cloth of Silk.

It is said in Scripture:—O Bodhisattva, such is the state of things. Suppose there exists one great cloth of silk equal in size to the 3 thousand thousands of worlds,[5] and on this great cloth of silk all the 3 thousand thousands of worlds would be painted in full size. The Great Horizon,[6] the Great Earth, the 2 thousand worlds,[7] the

---

[1] This is the Intuition at the final moment of the Path (*eka-kṣaṇa-abhisaṁbodha*).

[2] *pṛthagjana = so-soḥi-skye-bo.* [3] Cf. Sūtrālaṁkāra IX. 15.—
*yathā 'mbaraṁ sarvagataṁ sadā mataṁ tathaiva tat sarvagataṁ sadā matam,*
*yathā'mbaraṁ rūpa-gaṇeṣu sarvagaṁ tathaiva tat sattva-gaṇeṣu sarvagam.*

[4] *saṁjñā = ḥdu-śes.*

[5] *trisāhasra-mahāsāhasra-lokadhātu = stoṅ-gsum-gyi-stoṅ-chen-poḥi-ḥjig-rten-gyi-khams.*

[6] *mahā-cakravāla = khor-yug-chen-po.*

[7] *dvisāhasro madhyamo lokadhātuḥ = stoṅ-gñis-paḥi ḥjig-rten-gyi-khams.* M. V. § 153. 2.

thousand worlds,[1] the World of 4 Continents,[2] the Great Ocean, the Continent of Jambudvīpa, the Eastern Continent Videha,[3] the Western Continent Godhanya,[4] the Northern Continent Kuru,[5] the Mount Sumeru,[6] [19 a. 1.] the abode of the gods who live on earth, that of the gods living in the World of Desire,[7] and that of the denizens of the Ethereal Sphere,[8]—all these would be painted there, each in its own size. (Suppose now) this great cloth of silk, the area of which is equal to the 3 thousand thousands of worlds, were (folded) and put into a grain of sand as small as an atom. Just as the great cloth of silk would be placed in one grain of sand of the size of an atom, in the same way it could be put into all such grains without exception. Thereafter a person, wise, skilful, clear-minded, attentive, and possessed of analytic thought, would appear. His faculty of vision would become supernatural like that of the gods, perfectly pure and radiant. He would see with his divine eyes the great cloth of silk hidden in the small grain of sand (not larger than) an atom and being in such a state of no use to anyone. He would think:—oh, if I were to apply the force of my great energy and pierce this grain of sand, as small as an atom, by a diamond-cutter, this great cloth of silk would become useful to all living beings. Accordingly, he would manifest the power of his great energy [19 a. 1.] and open the grain of sand with a small diamond. The great cloth of silk would, as he had thought, become of use to all the living beings, and he would do the same with all the other atoms without exception, as he did it with one.

O Bodhisattvas, in the same way the Divine Spirit of the Lord, the limitless Spirit, the Spirit helping all living beings is fully contained in everyone of them. And as the Spirit of the Buddha, so are the spiritual streams of the living beings, without limits. Although this

---

[1] *sāhasracūḍiko lokadhātuḥ* = *stoṅ-gi-ḥjig-rten-gyi-khams.* Ibid. § 153. 1.

[2] *cāturdvīpako lokadhātuḥ* = *gliṅ-bźiḥi-ḥjig-rten-gyi-khams.* Ibid. § 154. 1.

[3] Tib. *śar-gyi-lus-ḥphags-kyi-gliṅ.*

[4] Tib. *nub-kyi-ba-laṅ-spyod-kyi-gliṅ.*

[5] Tib. *byaṅ-gi-sgra-mi-sñan-gyi-gliṅ.*

[6] Tib. *ri-rab.*

[7] *kāma-dhātu* = *ḥdod-khams.*

[8] *rūpa-dhātu* = *gzugs-khams.*

be so, the ordinary worldlings, bound by the conception (of separate entities) do not know about the Spirit of the Lord (that exists within them), do not feel it and are incapable of realizing it. Therefore the Buddha, through his Divine Knowledge, free from every kind of attachment, perceives the Absolute Essence, as it has its abode in all living beings, and becomes possessed of the thoughts peculiar to a (spiritual) teacher.[1] He thinks:—Alas, these living beings have no right knowledge about the Spirit of the Buddha (that exists with them), though they are all reflections of this spirit. What if I show to these living beings the Path of the Saint and remove the bonds caused by (realistic conception).—Himself, he has exercised the power of his saintly wisdom, has loosened the great knot of spiritual delusion,[2] has introspectively intuited the Spirit of Buddhahood (within himself), and has attained the full identity with this Spirit, (has coalesced with it in its Cosmical Unity). In accordance with this, he shows the Path of Buddhahood to the living beings and through this removes all the bonds caused by the (false realistic) conceptions. In those who have become delivered from these bonds, the limitless Spirit of the Buddha, (manifesting itself), becomes of help to all living beings.

## The Acts of the Buddha in their inconceivable Character.

The acts of the Lord manifest themselves simultaneously in all living beings at all times, free from effort and (dialectical) thought-construction, in accordance with the needs of the converts and their constitution, and are performed fully with all living beings, furthering their weal. For this reason they are inaccessible to discursive thought. Indeed, it has been said:[3]—In order to lead the living beings (to

---

[1] *ācārya-saṁjñā* = *slob-dpon-gyi-ḥdu-śes.*

[2] Dar. 71 b. 2.—has loosened the great knot of (false) conception—naive realism and the force of Transcendental Illusion. *bag-chags* = *vāsanā* stands here for *ma-rig-paḥi-bag-chags* = *avidyā-vāsanā.*

[3] Dhāraṇīśvara-rāja-paripṛcchā (Tathāgata-mahākaruṇā-nirdeśa), Kg. MDO XV. 215 a, 3—6.

Enlightenment), the Wisdom of the Buddha, though it is (really) unlimited, is spoken of as having a definite character, being summarized (in the 32 attributes). Although this be so, still, O noble youth, the true acts of the Buddha are inconceivable,[1] immeasurable, incognizable for all the world and inexpressible by words. They cannot be performed by others, they manifest themselves in all the Spheres of the Buddhas,[2] are realized by all the Buddhas in a similar way [20 b. 1.], are free from all exertion and effort, are uniform like space and therefore free from all (dialectical) constructions, are the acts peculiar to the Buddha as the Absolute, and, accordingly, inseparable from the latter:—Then comes the example of the perfectly pure stone of lapis-lazuli and, thereafter, a detailed exposition as follows:[3]—O noble youth, by the following characteristics art thou to know this subject.—The acts of the Buddha are inaccessible to discursive thought, are attained (in the process of intense concentration upon) the Unity (of the Universe), are completely free from every kind of defect, are connected with the present, past, and future, and bring forth the 3 Jewels in their uninterrupted continuance. The form of the Buddha which manifests itself in these inconceivable acts, does not lose its (all-pervading) character which is analogous to space. (Therefore) he can manifest himself in all the Spheres of Buddhaic activity (simultaneously). He likewise does not give up the inconceivable character of his Word. Indeed, he exposes the Doctrine to all living beings in accordance with (their faculty of) understanding the (meaning of) words. Being free from (the attachment to) every kind of object on which his mind could become fixed, he (at the same time) perfectly knows the mental disposition[4] and the thoughts of all living beings.—

---

[1] Dar. 72 a. 3.—through their profound character and grandeur.

[2] *buddha-kṣetra* = *saṅs-rgyas-kyi-źiṅ*.

[3] Dhāraṇīśvara-rāja-paripṛcchā, Kg. MDO. XV. 215 b. 7—216 a. 3.

[4] *citta-caryā* = *sems-kyi-spyod-pa*—"the spiritual conduct." Cf. Abhisamayālaṁkāra IV. 14.

## The Germ and the 3 other Subjects as the Causes and Conditions of Buddhahood.

26. The object to be intuited,[1] the intuition,[2]
The distinctive features of the latter,
And the (acts) which bring it about,—
As such respectively (appear the said 4 subjects),
One as the cause of purification and the other 3 as its conditions.—

Of these 4 subjects, the first is to be regarded as the point that is to be intuited, inasmuch as it includes everything cognizable.[3] [21 a. 1.] The final introspection of it is the second subject—Enlightenment which is the (full immaculate) intuition. The distinctive features of Enlightenment[4] which form the 3d subject are such, inasmuch as they represent the attributes of the Buddha. The 4th subject (—the acts) are the (factors) bringing about the intuition, since, through the component parts of Enlightenment, others are caused to perceive (the Truth). (This passage) thus refers to the 4 subjects (beginning with the Germ of the Absolute) and represents a characteristic (of them) as the sources of the 3 Jewels, inasmuch as they act as the causes[5] and conditions[6] (of the latter).

---

[1] Dar. 72 b. 3—5.—The object that is to be cognized is the Absolute mingled with the defiling elements. When it is directly intuited (by the Saint), all the attributes of the Buddha become originated. If, on the contrary, there is no intuition of it, the deliverance from the Saṁsāra will be impossible. It is thus the ultimate object that is to be cognized. Although it is no real producing cause (since it is an immutable element—*asaṁskṛta* = *ḥdus-ma-byas*) still, as it is the object of the Saint's concentrated Transcendental Wisdom which is the principal cause for the origination of the Wisdom of the Buddha and is thus an invariable condition of the latter, it is metaphorically called a cause.

[2] Ibid. 72 b. 5—6.—Enlightenment, i. e. the ultimate, direct intuition of the Absolute.

[3] Ibid. 73 a. 2—3.—*śes-bya thams-cad-kyi gnas-lugs-mthar-thug-pa-bsdus-paḥi phyir*—because the Absolute represents the Ultimate Essence of all things.

[4] *bodhy-anga* = *byaṅ-chub-kyi-yan-lag.*

[5] *hetu* = *rgyu.*

[6] *pratyaya* = *rkyen.*—

Now, the first of the 4 subjects is the seed of the saintly elements;[1] it is therefore to be made known as the cause of the 3 Jewels. (As such it appears), if the introspective correct mental activity is directed toward it and (appreciates it) in its perfectly pure nature. Thus, one subject is the cause. Now, why are the other 3 regarded as conditions? (Answer:—) The Lord, having attained the perfect Supreme Enlightenment and become a Buddha, has performed his 32 acts through the efficiency of the 10 Powers and the other attributes peculiar to him. (These 3 facts)[2] are to be viewed as the conditions for the origination of the 3 Jewels. Indeed, (the Teaching of the Buddha) being relied upon as the word of another (who has already attained Enlightenment), there arises the correct appreciation of the Absolute in its perfectly pure form. (Enlightenment, the attributes and the acts of the Buddha) ought thus to be viewed as the conditions for the origination of the 3 Jewels. For this reason the 3 (last subjects are spoken of as) cooperating conditions. The following text is to be regarded as a detailed exposition of all the 4 subjects mentioned in gradual order. [21 b. 1.]

## The Germ of the Absolute.

With regard to the Absolute mingled with defilement (= the Essence of Buddhahood in the living beings) it has been said:[3]— All living beings are endowed with the Essence of the Buddha.— What is the meaning of this?

27. The Body of the Supreme Buddha is all-pervading,[4]
The Absolute is (one) undifferentiated (Whole)[5]

---

[1] *lokottara-dharma = ḥjig-rten-las-ḥdas-paḥi-chos.*

[2] The fact of attaining Enlightenment, of becoming possessed of the attributes of the Buddha, and the manifestation of the Sublime Activity.

[3] In the Tathāgata-garbha-sūtra. Kg. MDO. XXII. 248 b. 6.

[4] Dar. 80 a. 1—2. The acts of the Cosmical Body manifest themselves in all living beings, therefore the latter, all without exception, are such in whom the Buddha exercises his activity.

[5] Ibid. 80 a. 2. The Absolute as it is with the Buddha and with the living beings is essentially the same.

And the Germ (of Buddhahood) exists (in every living being).
Therefore, for ever and anon, all that lives
Is endowed with the Essence of the Buddha.[1]

In short, the Lord had in view 3 aims when he declared:—
"All living beings are possessed of the Essence of Buddhahood."—

28. The Spirit of the Buddha manifests itself in the multitudes of living beings,
It is immaculate by nature and unique (with all),
And Buddhahood is the fruit of the Germ.
Therefore the whole animate world bears the Essence of the Buddha.

This subject, in all its different aspects is to be explained in that sense in which it is invariably demonstrated throughout the whole of Scripture, namely as follows:—(All living beings are endowed with the Essence of the Buddha) in the sense that the Buddha's Cosmical Body manifests itself in all living beings, that the Absolute, (the true essence) of the Buddha represents an undifferentiated whole,[2] and that the Germ[3] of the Buddha exists in everything that lives. These 3 subjects are to be explained below in accordance with the *Tathāgata-garbha-sūtra*.

## Analysis of the Germ from 10 Points of View.

### Summary.

29. The essence (of the Germ).
The causes and the result (of its purification),

---

[1] Cf. Sūtrālaṁkāra IX. 37. *sarveṣām aviśiṣṭāpi tathatā śuddhim āgatā tathāgatatvaṁ tasmāc ca tadgarbhāḥ sarva-dehinaḥ.* And Commentary:—*sarveṣāṁ nirviśiṣṭā tathatā tad-viśuddhi-svabhāvaś ca Tathāgataḥ. ataḥ sarve sattvās Tathāgata-garbhā ity ucyate.*

[2] Cf. Sūtrālaṁkāra IX. 15. *yathāmbaraṁ sarvagataṁ* &c.

[3] *gotra* = *rigs*. Dar. 82 a. 3—4. The Fundamental Germ (*prakṛtistha-gotra* = *raṅ-bžin-gnas-rigs*) the final metamorphose of which is the Cosmical Body, and the Germ as it becomes developped (*paripuṣṭa-gotra* = *rgyas-gyur-gyi-rigs* or *samudānīta* = *yaṅ-dag-par-blaṅs-pa*) which becomes transformed into the corporeal forms of the Buddha.

Its functions, relations, and manifestations [22 a. 1.]
Its different states, its all-pervading character,
Its eternal, unchangeable, and indivisible nature,—
Such are the (10) points with respect to the Absolute Essence.

In short, the characteristic of the Germ of the Buddha is given from 10 points of view. What are these 10? (Answer):—

1) The essence of the Germ.[1]
2) The causes (of its purification).[2]
3) The result (of this purification).[3]
4) The functions (of the Germ).[4]
5) Its relations.[5]
6) The manifestations (of the Germ in general).
7) The varieties (of the Germ) in correspondence with the different states.
8) The all-pervading character (of the Absolute).
9) The unalterable character (of it).
10) The indivisible character.

## The Essence of the Germ (1) and the Causes of its Purification (2).

Now, let us begin with (the first 2 points), that of the essence (of the Germ) and the causes (of its purification). We have here the following verse:—

30. (The Essence of Buddhahood in its 3 aspects)
Is, respectively, like a jewel, like space, and like water,
And always, by its nature, undefiled.

---

[1] Dar. 81 a. 1.—In the 3 aspects just mentioned, namely that of the Cosmical Body as being all-pervading, of the Absolute as an undifferentiated Whole, and of the Germ as existing in all living beings.

[2] Ibid. 81 a. 2.—The factors for the purification of the Germ, faith (*adhimukti*) &c.

[3] Ibid. 81 a. 4.—The attainment of the Highest Transcendental Purity, Supreme Bliss &c.

[4] The act of arousing the desire of attaining Nirvāṇa &c.

[5] The possession of the 4 attributes characterizing the cause (of purification), aith &c.

It arises (to life) through faith and the Doctrine, through
 Highest Wisdom,
Through concentrated trance, and Great Commiseration.—

Now, what is shown in the first half of this verse?

31. Being essentially powerful,
Unalterable and moist by nature,
It has a resemblance, in its distinctive features,
With the wish-fulfilling gem, with space, and water.

The 3 characteristics of the Absolute have been mentioned before.[1] Having in view, respectively, their particular[2] and general[3] essence, we come to know the Germ of the Buddha as having a resemblance with a wish-fulfilling gem, with space and with water, by its distinctive qualities. [22 b. 1.] Indeed, if we take the special essential character of the Buddha's Cosmical Body, that of possessing the power of accomplishing the desired aim (of the living beings), we shall find it to have a resemblance with a wish-fulfilling gem. If we take in consideration the particular essence of the Absolute, namely its unique unalterable character, we shall see that it bears a likeness with space. And, if we have in view the particular essence of the Germ of the Buddha, that is its moist, soft nature, this on account of the Commiseration toward all living beings, we shall know it as being akin to water. Again, if we take the general essence (of all the 3), namely that of being, by their very nature, perfectly pure and devoid of every kind of defilement, we shall (likewise) find a resemblance with the wish-fulfilling gem, with space, and with water, through the quality of perfect purity.

## The Impediments and the Causes of Purification.

32. Enmity toward the Doctrine, views clinging to Ego and Mine,[4]
Fear caused by the sufferings of Phenomenal Life,

[1] In Kār. 27. [2] *svalakṣaṇa = raṅ-gi-mtshan-ñid.*

[3] *sāmānya-lakṣaṇa = spyiḥi-mtshan-ñid.*

[4] Tib. *bdag-lta = ātma-dṛṣṭi = satkāya-dṛṣṭi.*

And want of care for (other) living beings,—
Such are the 4 impediments, respectively,
With (the worldlings) endowed with great desires, with the heretics,
The Śrāvakas and those of self-sprung (Wisdom).[1]
As to the cause of purity, such is great faith,
And the other virtues, all of them being four.[2]

In short, among the multitudes of living beings there exist the following 3 varieties:—

1) Those who love this Phenomenal Life,
2) Those who wish to become delivered from it, and
3) Those who desire neither the one, nor the other.[3]

Now, those who are attached to worldly existence appear in two varieties. There is that kind of living beings who are hostile to the Path (leading to) Salvation [23 a. 1.] and do not strive for Nirvāṇa; they have no desire of attaining the latter, being exclusively attached to this worldly existence. Then there are such who, though they are followers of this our Doctrine, have likewise fallen (into the whirlpool of Saṁsāra). Of these there are some who hate the Doctrine of the Great Vehicle.[4] With regard to these the Lord has said:—I am not their teacher and they are not my disciples. O Śāriputra, I say—these are obscured by darkness, proceed toward

---

[1] Tib. *raṅ-byuṅ* = *svayambhū*—the Pratyekabuddhas. Cf. Abhisamayālaṁkāra II. 6—*paropadeśa-vaiyarthyaṁ svayaṁ-bodhāt svayaṁbhuvām.*

[2] Dar. 82 a. 6—b. 1. The highest faith in the Doctrine of the Great Vehicle, the Highest Wisdom of the Bodhisattva which bears the character of the Climax of Wisdom (*prajñāpāramitā*) the medium of limitless trance (*samādhi-mukha* = *tiṅ-ṅe-ḥdzin-gyi-sgo*) of the Bodhisattva, and his Great Commiseration. These are respectively compared with the seed, the mother, the womb, and the nurse. Cf. below.

[3] Cf. Abhisamayālaṁkāra I. 10. *prajñayā na bhave sthānaṁ kṛpayā na śame sthitiḥ.*

[4] Dar. 84 b. 3.—being the followers of the Hīnayānistic Code (*piṭaka* = *sde-snod*). They depreciate (the Doctrine of the Great Vehicle) saying:—The Mahāyānistic Sūtras are not the Word of Buddha.

still greater darkness and become finally possessed of the greatest darkness.—

As concerns those who wish to become free from Phenomenal Life, such, likewise, are of 2 kinds, namely those who use incorrect means and those whose methods are right. Those acting according to incorrect methods have in their turn 3 varieties. (First of all) there are the different varieties of heretics standing apart from this (our Teaching). These are the Cārvākas,[1] the Parivrājakas,[2] the Jains,[3] and many others.[4] Next come those who, though they are adherents of this our Doctrine and possessed of faith, still, by their principles, are akin to (the said) heretics, namely those who have an incorrect conception (of the Truth).[5] Now, who are these? They are those who, having a misconception of the Absolute, maintain the reality of the Individual (as an independent Whole).[6] With regard to these the Lord has said:—Those who do not maintain the Non-substantiality (of existence) do not differ from the heretics. —There are moreover those who, being full of pride, cling to the conception of the Universal Relativity and Non-substantiality[7] as an absolute principle.[8] According to these even the medium of Salvation is regarded as essentially non-substantial. (The Lord) had these persons in view when he said:[9]—O Kāśyapa, the views maintaining

---

[1] The Aga ed. of the Comm. and Dar. have both *tsa-ra-ka* (*caraka*?).

[2] Tib. *kun-tu-rgyu.* [3] Tib. *gcer-bu-pa*—"the naked."

[4] Those who deny a future existence (*abhyudaya*) and those who, though they admit it, deny the idea of a final salvation.

[5] Sic acc. to Dar. 85 a.

[6] *pudgala-vādinaḥ* = *gaṅ-zag-tu-smra-ba.* Dar. 85 a. 3.—Those who do not consider the Individual to be a nominal reality (*prajñapti-sat* = *btags-yod*) included in the complex of the 5 groups (*skandha* = *phuṅ-po*) and in the stream of elements, but maintain the existence of the Individual as an independent reality (*dravya-sat* = *rdzas-yod*); they are thus the followers of a system clinging to the conception of the Ego. These are the Vātsiputrīyas.

[7] *śūnyatā* = *stoṅ-pa-ñid.*

[8] Dar. 85 b. 4. *stoṅ-ñid bden-par-źen-pa.* Cf. Conception of Buddh. Nirvāṇa, page 49—50.

[9] Dar. 86 b. 1. Ḥod-sruṅs-kyis-źus-paḥi-mdo-las in the Kāśyapa-paripṛcchā.

the existence of real individuals are a blunder as great as the mount Sumeru. [23 b. 1.] However those who, being full of pride, cling to the conception of Non-substantiality (as an absolute principle) commit an error still greater.

Those who act according to correct means have also 2 varieties. There are the followers of the Śrāvaka Vehicle who proceed (on the Path) having a firm and settled conviction, and there are the adherents of the Vehicle of the Pratyekabuddhas.

Now, those who are neither attached to Phenomenal Existence, nor have a desire of attaining Salvation in the egoistic sense[1] are the living beings who constantly and firmly abide in the Great Vehicle and are possessed of the most acute faculties. These have neither an inclination toward this worldly life, as it is the case with the worldlings who are possessed of great desires, nor do they proceed toward Salvation using incorrect methods, as do the heretics. (On the other hand) their cognition is not that of the Śrāvakas and Pratyekabuddhas, though the methods (of both the latter) are correct. They proceed on that Path through which the (introspection of the) identity of Saṁsāra and Nirvāṇa is attained. Their minds are directed toward the Altruistic Nirvāṇa (which does not adhere to either of the 2 extremities),[2] and their activity bases upon the Phenomenal World, but without passions and desires.[3] They have a firm stand in sublime, altruistic thoughts,[4] and the foundation of their Path is perfectly pure.[5]

Now, those living beings who are full of great desires and love this worldly existence, as well as the adherents to this (our) Doctrine who have inevitably fallen (into the Saṁsāra) are called

---

[1] Dar. 87 a. 5. Those who have no desire of either being born in the Phenomenal World through the force of previous deeds and passions or of attaining that kind of Nirvāṇa which represents a mere cessation of births in the Saṁsāra.

[2] *apratiṣṭhita-nirvāṇa* = *mi-gnas-paḥi-myaṅ-ḥdas*.

[3] Acc. to Dar. 87 b. 2.— through the efficiency of previous vows and Great Commiseration.

[4] *adhyāśaya* = *lhag-paḥi-bsam-pa*.

[5] The Mahāyānistic Creative Effort (*citta-utpāda* = *sems-bskyed*).

" the category of living beings who are definitely rooted in error." Those who, being desirous of getting free from Phenomenal Existence, act according to incorrect methods are characterized as " the category of living beings who are not certain (as regards the means of Salvation)." Finally, those who wish to be delivered from Phenomenal Life and take recourse to the right means (of deliverance), as well as those who have no desire of both (the Phenomenal World and egoistic salvation) [24 a. 1.] and proceed on the Path in order to attain (the intuition of) the identity (of Saṁsāra and Nirvāṇa) are called " the category of living beings who have a definite knowledge of that which is right." If we except the living beings who abide in the Great Vehicle and whose cognition is not obscured, there are the following 4 varieties:—1) The worldlings endowed with great desires, 2) the heretics,[1] 3) the Śrāvakas, and 4) the Pratyekabuddhas. With these there exist (respectively) 4 kinds of impediments through which they are incapable of intuiting and realizing the Germ of the Buddha. (These impediments) are as follows:—

1) The Obscuration peculiar to the ordinary worldlings who are possessed of great desires and are hostile to the Mahāyānistic Doctrine. The antidote[2] against this is the concentration upon the faith[3] in the Teaching of the Great Vehicle as practised by the Bodhisattvas.

2) The Obscuration of the heretics who in the (complex of the) separate elements perceive a (real independent) Ego.[4] It has its antidote in the Bodhisattva's concentration upon the Climax of Wisdom[5] (in the aspect of which both the Individual and the separate elements are unreal).

3) The Obscuration of the Śrāvakas who cognize the Phenomenal World as being mere suffering and are afraid of it. Its antidote is the Gaganagañja[6] and other forms of trance peculiar to the Bodhisattva.

---

[1] *tīrthika = mu-stegs-pa.* [2] *pratipakṣa = gñen-po.* [3] *adhimukti = mos-pa.*
[4] *svatantra-ātman = raṅ-dbaṅ-can-gyi-bdag.* Cf. Abhisamayālaṁkāra I. 35.
[5] *prajñā-pāramitā.* [6] Tib. *nam-mkhaḥi-mdzod.*

11*

4) The Obscuration of the Pratyekabuddhas who have no regard for the welfare of the living beings and turn away [1] from the needs of others.[2] [24 b. 1.] Here the antidote will be the concentration upon the Great Mercy and Love as it is manifested by the Bodhisattva.

Such are these 4 kinds of impediments which are peculiar to the 4 varieties of individuals (mentioned). Their antidotes are, (as we have just seen), the 4 virtuous qualities beginning with faith. Through the concentrated contemplation of them the Bodhisattvas attain the highest aim, that is the immaculate, ultimate Cosmical Body. He who is endowed with these 4 factors for the attainment of the 4 kinds of Absolute Purity which are to be mentioned presently, becomes a son of the King of the Doctrine, a (true) member of the family of the Buddha. How that?

33. Those are the sons of the Lord,
Whose seed is the faith in the Highest of Vehicles,
Whose mother is the Wisdom [3] that gives birth to the properties
of the Buddha,
Who abide in the blissful womb of meditative trance and are
nursed by Great Commiseration.[4]

## The Result of Purification (3) and the Functions of the Germ (4).

Now, let us take the (next two) subjects—the result (of the purification of the Germ) and (its) functions. We have here the following verse:

34. The result are the Absolute, Transcendental Properties
Of Purity, Unity,[5] Bliss, and Eternity.

---

[1] Tib. *rgyab-kyis-phyogs-pa* = *vimukha.*

[2] Dar. 88 a. 5.—since they do not undertake the task of delivering other living beings from suffering.

[3] *prajñā* = *śes-rab* in the sense of *prajñā-pāramitā.*

[4] Cf. Sūtrālaṁkāra IV. 11.
*dharmādhimukti-bījāt pāramitā-śreṣṭha-mātṛto jātaḥ*
*dhyāna-maye sukha-garbhe karuṇā saṁvardhikā dhātrī.*

[5] *ātma-pāramitā* = *bdag-gi-pha-rol-tu-phyin-pa* or *paramātma-pāramitā. ātman* is to be understood in the sense of the unique essence of the Universe.

And the functions (of the Germ) manifest themselves
In the aversion toward this worldly life,
In the desire of Quiescence and the will[1] of attaining it.
Now, what is said in the first half of the verse?

35. In short, the fruit of these (4 virtues)[2]
Is (contained) in the Cosmical Body,
Representing (its properties) which are antidotes
And the reverse of the 4 kinds of error.

The 4 virtuous qualities, beginning with faith, have been just spoken of as the causes, the factors for the purification of the Germ of the Buddha. The result (of this purification) consists in the 4 Absolute Properties of the Cosmical Body. These (properties), taken respectively, are the counterparts, the reverse of the 4 kinds of error. [25 a. 1.] Now, the conception of Matter[3] and other evanescent[4] things as being enduring,[5] the conception of (Phenomenal Life which is) mere suffering as something blissful, the conception of the impersonal elements as constituting a real Ego, and the conception of the world's impurity as pure,—these are called the 4 kinds of error.[6] Their reverse are the 4 correct points of view, the conceptions of the evanescence, suffering, impersonality, and impurity regarding matter and the other (elements of the Phenomenal World). Now, with regard to the Cosmical Body of the Buddha, the properties of which are Eternity, &c., these 4 "correct" views we esteem to be wrong.[7]

---

[1] *praṇidhāna* = *smon-pa*. Cf. below.

[2] Dar. 89 b. 3.—of the faith in the Mahāyānistic Doctrine, &c.

[3] *rūpa* = *gzugs*. [4] *anitya* = *mi-rtag-pa*. [5] *nitya* = *rtag-pa*.

[6] Dar. 89 b. 5.—the 4 kinds of error regarding the Empirical Reality (*saṁvṛti* = *kun-rdzob*). Cf. the following note.

[7] They are the 4 kinds of error concerning the Absolute (*paramārtha* = *don-dam-pa*). In the Abhisamayālaṁkāra I. 27 Evanescence, &c. are spoken of as the object (*ālambana* = *dmigs-pa*) of concentration, and the aspect (*ākāra* = *rnam-pa*) in which they are to be viewed is the negation of the reality of these characteristics of the elements in the aspect of the unique Absolute. Cf. Haribhadra's Abhisamayālaṁkāra-ālokā, MS. 36 a. 9—14. *tat kena ākāreṇa ālambanīyam ity āha* ... *dharmatā-mukhenā anabhinivesādy-ākāreṇa iti yāvat. idam uktam bhavati. śrāvako*

Their counterparts are the 4 Absolute Transcendental Properties of the Buddha's Cosmical Body which are:—1) Absolute Eternity,[1] 2) Absolute Bliss,[2] 3) Absolute Unity,[3] and 4) Absolute Purity.[4] This theory is to be known in detail from Scripture. It is said:[5]— O Lord, the living beings are full of error, as regards the 4 groups of elements constituting Phenomenal Existence, as far as manifesting themselves in an individual.[6] That which is evanescent they hold to be eternal, the suffering (of the Phenomenal World) they consider to be happiness, that which is impersonal they imagine to have a relation to a real Ego, and the impure they mistake for pure. [25 b. 1.] The Śrāvakas and the Pratyekabuddhas, O Lord, are, in their turn, all of them deprived of the Transcendental Intuition of the Universal Relativity (and Non-Substantiality).[7] Therefore they have a misconception of the Cosmical Body of the Buddha, accessible only to the Divine Perception of the Omniscient. (On the other hand), O Lord, those living beings who have a conception (of the Cosmical Body) as eternal, as the Supreme Bliss, as the Absolute Unity and Absolute Purity are the Sons of the Lord born from his Spirit. O Lord, these living beings do not commit any error. These living beings perceive the Truth. How that?—Because the essence of this Cosmical Body of the Buddha is Absolute Eternity, Absolute Bliss, Absolute Unity, and Absolute Purity. O Lord, those living beings who perceive the Cosmical Body of the Buddha in such an aspect, perceive (through this) the Absolute Truth. And all those who perceive the Absolute Truth are the spiritual sons of the Buddha.—

---

*rūpaṇādi-lakṣaṇaṁ vastv ālambate tasya anityādaya ākārā bhavanti, ātma-darśana-pratipakṣatvāt. bodhisattvaḥ punar anityādi-lakṣaṇaṁ vastv ālambate tasya anabhiniveśādaya ākārā bhavanti.*

[1] *nitya-pāramitā = rtag-paḥi-pha-rol-tu-phyin-pa.*

[2] *sukha-pāramitā = bde-baḥi-pha-rol-tu-phyin-pa.*

[3] *ātma-pāramitā = bdag-gi-pha-rol-tu-phyin-pa.*

[4] *śuddhi-* (or *śuci-*) *pāramitā = gtsaṅ-baḥi-pha-rol-tu-phyin-pa.*

[5] In the Śrī-mālā-devī-siṁhanāda-sūtra. Kg. DKON. VI. 280 a. 4—b. 2.

[6] Tib. *ñin-paḥi-ñe-bar-len-paḥi-phuṅ-po-lṅa = upātta-pañca-upādāna-skandha.*

[7] *śūnyatā = stoṅ-pa-ñid.*

## Concordance between the 4 Absolute Properties and the 4 Causes of Purification.

These 4 Absolute Properties of the Buddha's Cosmical Body are known to have a correspondence with the (4) causes (of purification) in the reverse order.[1] Indeed, if we take the counterpart of the attachment to this impure worldly life, as it is peculiar to those that are hostile to the Mahāyānistic Doctrine and possessed of great desires [26 a. 1.], such is the concentration upon the faith in the Doctrine of the Great Vehicle. The result of this will be the attainment of Absolute Purity.

[The Absolute Transcendental Unity.]

The attachment to the conception of a non-existing Ego is peculiar to the heretics who in the 5 groups (of elements) perceive a real individual. The reverse (of such an attachment) is the concentration upon the Climax of Wisdom (which is the direct perception of the total unreality of the Individual and the groups of elements in the aspect of the unique Cosmical Essence).[2] Its result is (the introspection of) the Absolute Unity.[3] Indeed, all the heretics admit the existence of an Ego, either as identical with Matter and the other (component) elements or as something differing from them.[4] This substance which they maintain is illusionary in its character of an Ego; in reality no such Ego ever existed. Now, the Buddha, by means of his Absolute Wisdom perceiving the Truth, has attained the (intuition of the) ultimate, transcendental unreality of all the

---

[1] Dar. 91 b. 5—92 a. 1.
**The faith in the Mahāyānistic Doctrine is the cause of Absolute Purity,**
**The concentr. upon the Climax of Wisdom is the cause of the Absolute Unity**
**The Climax of transic meditation is the cause of the Supreme Bliss,**
**The concentration upon Highest Mercy is the cause of Absolute Eternity.**

[2] Sic acc. to Dar. 92 a. 4.

[3] Dar. 92 a. 4—5. The Supreme Transcendental Unity,—that of the Cosmical Body which is identical with the Absolute, and in the aspect of which both the Individual and the separate elements are unreal in their (seeming) Plurality.

[4] Cf. M. V. § 208.

separate elements. The unreality thus perceived,[1] is true and uncontradictory in its character of a negation of substantiality (with the separate entities and discloses itself as their ultimate monistic essence). It is therefore to be regarded as (that which reveals) the Supreme Absolute Unity of the Universe.[2] The non-substantiality (of the Individual and the separate elements) thus turns to be the (unique universal) substance, as we read (in Scripture):—"Taking one's stand in the non-attachment (to separate entities)."

[The Absolute Bliss and Absolute Eternity.]

The adherents to the Vehicle of the Śrāvakas, being afraid of the sufferings of the Phenomenal World, are desirous of attaining merely the pacification of these sufferings. The reverse (of such a desire) [26 b. 1.] are the forms of meditative trance, such as the Gaganagañja-samādhi and the like; their result is the attainment of the Supreme Bliss, the mundane[3] and the supermundane.[4]

The adherents to the Vehicle of the Pratyekabuddhas find the highest delight in the attainment of a solitary position (separated from all mankind). The reverse of this is the Bodhisattva's concentration upon (the idea of) Highest Mercy and Love. Through this he attains the perfect purification as regards the activity for the sake of other living beings which is to be exercised, perpetually and uninterruptedly, as long as the world exists. The result will, for this last reason, be the Absolute, Transcendental Eternity.[5] Thus, the faith, Wisdom, meditative trance, and Commiseration of the

---

[1] Dar. 92 b. 2.—as it is intuited by the Buddha in his meditative trance.

[2] Cf. Vasubandhu's Commentary on Sūtrālaṁkāra IX, 23.—*tatra ca anāsrave dhātau buddhānāṁ paramātmā nirdiśyate. kim kāraṇam? agra-nairātmya-ātmakatvāt. agram nairātmyam viśuddhā tathatā sa ca buddhānām ātmā svabhāva-arthena, tasyām viśuddhāyām agram nairātmyam ātmānam buddhā labhante śuddham. ataḥ śuddha-ātma-lābhitvād buddhā ātma-māhātmyam prāptā ity anena abhisaṁdhinā buddhānām anāsrave dhātau paramātmā vyavasthāpyate.*

[3] *laukika* = *ḥjig-rten-pa.*

[4] *lokottara* = *ḥjig-rten-las-ḥdas-pa.*

[5] Cf. Abhisamayālaṁkāra VIII. 11. *iti kāritra-vaipulyād buddho vyāpī nirucyate | akṣayatvāc ca tasyaiva nitya ity api kathyate.* and VIII. 34.—*tathā karmā 'py anucchinnam asyā 'saṁsāram iṣyate.*

Bodhisattvas, having become the objects of intense concentration, have as their result, respectively, the four Absolute Transcendental Properties of the Cosmical Body of the Buddha, those of Purity, Unity, Supreme Bliss, and Eternity. It is said that the Buddha, through the efficiency of these (4 factors, faith, &c.), represents the culminating point of existence—the Absolute, is infinite like space and has reached the ultimate limits (of time).[1] Indeed, in the process of concentration characterized by the faith in the highest Mahāyānistic Doctrine, the perfectly pure Ultimate Essence of the Buddha, which is the Absolute, is realized. This means the attainment of the culminating point (of existence in) the Absolute. The concentration upon (the idea of) the Climax of Wisdom brings about the (final) introspective intuition of (the Absolute as) the background of the unreality of the animate [27 a. 1.] and inanimate world[2] and as being infinite like space. The Gaganagañja and similar forms of trance have for their result the manifestation of the Supreme Power of governing the elements which is of an all-pervading character. (Owing to these 2 characteristics, the Buddha) is all-embracing like space. (Finally), through the concentration upon (the idea of) Highest Mercy one becomes possessed of that Commiseration and Love with regard to all living beings, which is not bound by time. For this reason the Buddha has neither limits nor end.

## The Impediments to the Attainment of the 4 Absolute Properties.

Now, with the Arhats and Pratyekabuddhas who abide in the Unaffected Sphere[3] and with the Bodhisattvas who have attained the

---

[1] Sic acc. to Dar. 93 a. 5.

[2] *sattva-loka* = *sems-can-gyi-ḥjig-rten* and *bhājana-loka* = *snod-kyi-ḥjig-rten.*

[3] *anāsrava-dhātu.* According to the theory of the "Unique Vehicle" (*ekayāna*) the termination of the Hīnayānistic Path does not represent the real Nirvāṇa, but merely the cessation of repeated births in the 3 Spheres of the Phenomenal World and a non-physical (*manomaya*) existence in the so-called Unaffected Sphere, a motionless, dreaming state. From this the Arhats are ultimately aroused by the Buddhas, whereupon they enter the Mahayānistic Path, having made the Creative

(10) Controlling Powers[1] there exist the 4 kinds of impediments to the attainment of the 4 Absolute Properties of the Buddha's Cosmical Body. These are:—

1) (The impediment) which has the character of a condition,[2]
2) That which bears the essence of a cause,[3]
3) That which is characterized by origination, and
4) That representing destruction.

(The first of these impediments), that which bears the character of a condition, is the elementary force of Transcendental Illusion.[4] The latter is akin to Ignorance[5] (as the first member of the Causal Chain) which gives origination to the active forces[6] (of Phenomenal Life).

(The impediment) which has the essence of a cause is the Biotic Force[7] uninfluenced by defiling agencies, which is conditioned by the elementary force of Transcendental Illusion. It corresponds to the active forces (in the Causal Chain).

(The impediment) which has the character of origination is the Non-physical Body[8] in its 3 forms (corresponding to the 3 kinds of individuals).[9] It is conditioned by the elementary force of Transcendental Illusion and its cause is the Biotic Force uninfluenced by the defiling elements. It has a correspondance with the origination in the 3 Spheres of Existence, caused by the Biotic Force which is influenced by defilement and conditioned by the 4 Egocentristic Properties.[10] [27 b. 1.]

(Finally, the impediment) bearing the character of destruction is that constant change which inevitably takes place in some incon-

---

Effort for Supreme Enlightenment. This is detailed by Haribhadra in his Abhisamayālaṁkāra-ālokā. Cf. Appendix.

[1] Dar. 94 a. 3. The Bodhisattvas who have attained the 10 Controlling Powers and abide on the 3 last Stages (*acalā*, *sādhumatī* and *dharmameghā*).

[2] *pratyaya* = *rkyen*. [3] *hetu* = *rgyu*.

[4] *avidyā-vāsanā* = *ma-rig-paḥi-bag-chags*. [5] *avidyā* = *ma-rig-pa*.

[6] *saṁskāra* = *ḥdu-byed*. [7] *karma* = *las*.

[8] *manomaya-kāya* = *yid-kyi-raṅ-bžin-gyi-lus*.

[9] The Arhats, the Pratyekabuddhas, and the Bodhisattvas on the 3 last Stages.

[10] *upādāna* = *ñe-bar-len-pa*. Dar. 94 b. 4.—Desire, incorrect views, bigotry, and the conception of an Ego.

ceivable manner.[1] It corresponds to Decrepitude and Death[2] which are conditioned by (preceding) birth.

Now, the Arhats, the Pratyekabuddhas and the Bodhisattvas who have attained the (10) Controlling Powers, have not extirpated the force of Transcendental Illusion which is a foundation of all the defiling elements. On account of this they are possessed of all those forces which attract the impurity of the passions. Therefore they cannot attain the culminating point of Absolute Purity.

On the foundation of this force of Transcendental Illusion the differentiation of separate entities (Pluralism)[3] manifests itself, though in a very subtle form. (The Arhats, &c.) being possessed (of this differentiation), cannot attain the Absolute Unity which is not produced by causes and conditions,[4] (a motionless Whole where no room is left for the manifestation of the active forces of the Phenomenal World).

Now, the subtle manifestations of Plurality (in the consciousness of the Arhats, &c.) and the force of Transcendental Illusion by which this is conditioned, call forth the undefiled Biotic Force. On the basis of the latter the groups of elements[5] of a non-physical nature[6] become originated. On account of this (separate spiritual existence which, though far from the sufferings of Phenomenal Life, still bears the character of uneasiness[7] accompanying every kind of origination), the perfect Absolute Bliss which is the cessation of (even) such (a separate existence) cannot be attained.

(Finally), as long as the essence of the Buddha which is the cessation of all the defiling forces, those of passions, of the Biotic Force and of (repeated) origination, is not fully realized,[8] one does not become free from the constant changes of existence which are of

---

[1] Cf. Abhidharmakośa IX. [2] *jarā-maraṇa = rga-śi.*

[3] *prapañca = spros-pa.* [4] *asaṁskṛta = ḥdus-ma-byas.* [5] *skandha = phuṅ-po.*

[6] This "non-physical" existence is not to be confounded with the existence in the immaterial Sphere (*arūpya-dhātu*).

[7] *duḥkha = sdug-bsṅal.*

[8] Dar. 95 a. 5—6.—through perpetual concentrated trance.

an inconceivable character. Consequently, (the Arhats, &c.) are incapable of attaining the Absolute Eternity where there is no change. Here the elementary force of Transcendental Illusion corresponds to the moral defilement [28 a. 1.], the production of the undefiled Biotic Force—to the defilement of the latter (in general), and the origination of the 3 forms of non-physical existence as well as the changes of the states of existence, a constant transformation taking place in an inconceivable manner,—to the defilement of repeated birth.

### Reference to Scripture.

This theory is to be known in detail from Scripture. It is said:[1] O Lord, the existence in the 3 (worldly) Spheres is conditioned by the Egocentristic Properties and has for its cause the Biotic Force which is influenced by defilement. In the same way, O Lord, the spiritual forms of the Arhats, the Pratyekabuddhas and the Bodhisattvas who have attained the (10 Controlling) Powers arise, being conditioned by the elementary force of Transcendental Illusion and having for their cause the undefiled Biotic Force. O Lord, the elementary force of Transcendental Illusion is thus the condition for the origination of the non-physical forms of existence and for the activity of the undefiled Biotic Force.—So we have it in detail. These 3 forms of non-physical existence, peculiar to the Arhats, the Pratyekabuddhas, and the Bodhisattvas who have attained the (10 Controlling) Powers, have not the Absolute Properties of Purity, Unity, Bliss, and Eternity. Therefore, only the Cosmical Body of the Buddha represents Absolute Eternity, Absolute Bliss, Absolute Unity, and Absolute Purity.

### The Motives of the 4 Absolute Properties.

36. (The Cosmical Body of the Buddha)[2] is perfectly pure, [28 b. 1.]
Being immaculate by nature and free from all the defiling forces.

---

[1] In the Śrī-mālā-devī-siṁhanāda-sūtra. Kg. DKON. VI. 271 a. 3—6.

[2] Dar. 96 b. 1.

It represents the Unity (of the Cosmos), the perfect Quiescence
Of all Plurality, of the Individuals as well as their impersonal
elements.

37. Through the extirpation of even the non-physical elements
And of their causes, it is the Supreme Bliss,
And, through the intuition of the identity of Saṁsāra and Nirvāṇa,
It is eternal (being free from the limits of both).

In short, the Cosmical Body of the Buddha is known as the Absolute Purity out of 2 motives:—1) It is perfectly pure by nature, this being its general essence[1] (through all the seeming varieties of being), and 2) it has the special essence[2] of being quite pure by stripping off all the defilement of Phenomenal Life (at the time of becoming a Buddha by coalescing with the Cosmical Body).

It is to be known as the Absolute Unity likewise for two motives:—1) It is the negation of the Plurality of the Individuals, through the rejection of the extremity peculiar to the Brāhmaṇical heretics,[3] and 2) it is the negation of the Plurality of the (separate) impersonal (elements), this being a result of shunning the Hīnayānistic extremity.

Furthermore, two causes make it the Supreme Transcendental Bliss, namely 1) the extirpation of the Phenomenal Elements[4] and their causes,[5] and through this the annihilation of the continuance of the defiling forces[6] and 2) the full realization of the Extinction[7] of Phenomenal Life and thus the cessation of the (highest separate) non-physical existence.[8]

[The Unstable, Non-dialectical Nirvāṇa.][9]

(Finally) two motives make it known in its character of Absolute Eternity:—1) It neither represents a fall into the Nihilistic

---

[1] *sāmānya-lakṣaṇa = spyiḥi-mtshan-ñid.*
[2] *viśeṣa-lakṣaṇa = khyad-par-gyi-mtshan-ñid.*
[3] *tīrthika = mu-stegs-pa.*
[4] *duḥkha = sdug-bsṅal.*
[5] *samudaya = kun-ḥbyuṅ.*
[6] *vāsanā-anusaṁdhi = bag-chags-kyi-mtshams-sbyor.*
[7] *nirodha = ḥgog-pa.*
[8] *manomaya-kāya = yid-kyi-raṅ-bźin-gyi-lus.*
[9] *apratiṣṭhita-nirvāṇa = mi-gnas-paḥi-myaṅ-ḥdas.*

Extremity,[1] because Phenomenality must not be suppressed (as being additional to the Absolute), 2) nor can it be regarded as a fall into the (opposite) Eternalistic Extremity,[2] since Nirvāṇa (or Eternality) is not something which can be added (to Phenomenal Existence).[3]

[Reference to Scripture.]

It is said:[4]—O Lord, if we cling to the conception that all the active elements of existence[5] are evanescent [29 a. 1.], it will be a nihilistic point of view which is incorrect. If (on the other hand) Nirvāṇa is considered to be (a separate reality which is) eternal, this will be an eternalistic conception which is likewise false.—

From the standpoint of this our theory of a monistic Absolute, the Phenomenal World itself, taken in the aspect of Ultimate Reality, is to be called Nirvāṇa.[6] The reason is, that the Saint has a direct intuition of the non-dialectical Nirvāṇa.[7] Now, though this be so, still, for 2 motives, we have merely an indication of this unstable stability as a state in which the Saint is neither immediately involved in the Phenomenal Life of the living beings (because he becomes identical with the Absolute), nor remote (from the living beings, owing to his intense love.[8] What are the 2 motives?—(Answer:—) The Bodhisattva is not involved in the life of the living beings,

---

[1] *uccheda-anta* = *chad-paḥi-mthaḥ.*

[2] *śāśvata-anta* = *rtag-paḥi-mthaḥ.*

[3] Cf. Abhisamayālaṁkāra V. 21. *nāpaneyam ataḥ kiṁcit prakṣeptavyaṁ na kiṁcana | draṣṭavyaṁ bhūtato bhūtaṁ bhūta-darśī vimucyate.*

[4] In the Śrī-mālā-sutra. Kg. DKON. VI. 279 b. 6—7. The version of Kg. is slightly different.

[5] *saṁskāra* = *ḥdu-byed* in the sense of *saṁskṛta-dharma.*

[6] Cf. Conception of Buddhist Nirvāṇa, p. 205.

[7] *apratiṣṭhita-nirvāṇa.* The Saint realizes that form of Nirvāṇa which does not represent a residence, either in the Phenomenal World, or egoistic peace, since he has no dialectical thought-construction, no differentiation of both Saṁsāra and Nirvāṇa as separate entities.

[8] Cf. Abhisamayālaṁkāra I. 16. *prajñayā na bhave sthānaṃ kṛpayā na śame sthitiḥ,* and III. 16. *nā 'pare na pare tīre nāntarāle tayoḥ sthitā.*

since he rejects all the residues[1] of Phenomenal Life by his High Wisdom. On the other hand he is not remote from them, since he does not forsake them, owing to his Great Commiseration. This[2] is the means for attaining, subsequently, the Perfect Supreme Enlightenment, an essential character of which is this Unstable Stability. Through the rejection of all the residues of Phenomenal Existence by means of Highest Wisdom, the Bodhisattva helps himself. Indeed, having his thoughts directed toward Nirvāṇa, he does not abide in the Phenomenal World, as do those living beings whose intentions are not those of attaining Salvation. On the other hand, as he does not forsake the suffering living beings[3] out of Great Commiseration, he administers help to others. [29 b. 1.] For this reason his activity is founded upon the Phenomenal World, and he does not reside in Nirvāṇa in the manner of those who have only the one tendency of attaining Quiescence. Therefore, these 2 qualities (of the Bodhisattva) are spoken of as the principal foundation of Supreme Enlightenment:—

38. (The Saint) by his great wisdom rejects all selfish (worldly)
inclinations,
But, being merciful and attached to the cause of the living
beings, he does not attain Quiescence.
Thus, having his stand in Wisdom and Love, these means of
Supreme Enlightenment,
The Saint neither resides in this world, nor does he depart to
(egoistic) peace.

### The Functions of the Germ of the Buddha (4).

Now, what shows the second half of verse (34) referring to the subject of the functions (of the Essence of Buddhahood) which has been taken in consideration before?—

---

[1] *anuśaya* = *bag-la-ñal.*

[2] The special forms of Wisdom and Commiseration (Dar. 98 b. 4.).

[3] Cf. Abhisamayālaṁkāra V. 3. *aparītyakta-sattva-artha.*

39. If the Germ of the Buddha[1] did not exist,
The aversion to the suffering (of this world) would not arise;
There would be no desire of Nirvāṇa,
And there would be no effort[2] for attaining it.

It is accordingly said:[3]—O Lord, if the Essence of the Buddha were not existing, there would be no aversion to (this) Phenomenal Existence. Accordingly, there would be no desire of Nirvāṇa, no inclination[4] (toward it), no request[5] (of it) and no efforts (made for its attainment). In short, the Essence of the Buddha, the perfectly pure Germ which has its abode even in those living beings who are definitely rooted in error, exercises its activity in two ways:— 1) It arouses the aversion (to this worldly existence) through the perception of the sufferings of Phenomenal Life and the harm caused by them, and 2) it calls forth inclination, desire, request, and efforts (directed toward the attainment of) Nirvāṇa, all of which are founded upon the contemplation of the bliss of the latter and its advantages.[6] Here "inclination" has the meaning of a clearly expressed wish. [30 a. 1.] "Desire" means a direction (of the mind) toward the attainment of the aim proposed. "Request" is used in the sense of a search of the means of attaining the desired aim, and "effort" is a manifestation of the will[7] directed toward this attainment.

40. This contemplation
Of the sufferings of Phenomenal Life and the bliss of Nirvāṇa,
Of the defects (of the former) and the advantages (of the latter)
Is (conditioned) by the existence of the Germ. Therefore,
With those in whom there is no Germ,[8] this contemplation does not exist.

---

[1] Dar. 99 b. 3.—The Germ of the Buddha, that is the seed perfectly pure by nature and uninfluenced by the defiling elements.

[2] *praṇidhāna* = *smon-pa*. Cf. below.

[3] In the Śrī-mālā-siṁhanāda-sūtra. Kg. DKON. VI. 281 a. 8—b. 1.

[4] *chanda* = *ḥdun-pa*. [5] *prārthanā* = *don-du-gñer-ba*.

[6] *anuśaṁsa* = *phan-yon*. [7] *citta-abhisaṁskāra* = *sems-mṅon-par-ḥdu-byed-pa*.

[8] The absence of the Germ is to be understood in a conventional sense. Cf. below.

The individual possessed of virtuous elements[1] perceives the harm and suffering of Phenomenal Existence and the bliss and advantages of Nirvāṇa. This perception is called forth by the existence of the Germ (of the Buddha); it is not something uncaused and unconditioned. Why that?—If (the said perception) were without causes and conditions and were not brought about through the extirpation of sin, it would likewise exist with the living beings who are possessed of vain desires and cannot attain Nirvāṇa. (In reality) as long as the Germ (of a living being has not been aroused to life)[2] by means of the 4 conditions,[3] beginning with the reliance upon a saintly personage,[4] and as long as the faith in either of the 3 Vehicles has not been obtained,—(the perception in question) cannot arise.

## The Annihilation of the Germ is to be understood in a Conventional Sense.

It is however said:[5]—After that the rays of the Divine Wisdom[6] of the Buddha which resembles the disc of the sun hit the bodies of even those living beings who were definitely rooted in error and administer help to them. They produce the causes of future (bliss) and cause to thrive all that is virtuous. (In the *Mahāparinirvāṇa* and other Sūtras)[7] we read: "he who is possessed of vain desires cannot attain Nirvāṇa altogether." This has been said in order to convert those who hate the Mahāyānistic Doctrine, this hatred being the cause of all the sinful inclinations, and refers only to a certain period

---

[1] *śukla-dharma* = *dkar-poḥi-chos.*

[2] Sic acc. to Dar. 100 b. 6—101 a. 1.

[3] Dar. 100 b. 5—6.—The reliance upon a saintly personage (1), the accumulation of virtue (2), a favourable dwelling-place (3), sublime vows and correct appreciation (4).

[4] *satpuruṣa* = *skyes-bu-dam-pa.*

[5] In the Jñāna-āloka-alaṁkāra-sūtra. Kg. MDO. III. 285 b. 6—7.

[6] Dar. 101 a. 3. After having taken recourse to the study of the Highest Doctrine.

[7] Dar. 101 a. 6.

of time.[1] As the Germ (of the Buddha) which is perfectly pure by nature exists (in every living being), it is impossible that there could exist some (living being) who would never become purified. Indeed, the Lord, having in view the fact that all the living beings, without any difference, have the possibility of attaining perfect purification, has said:[2]—

(The elements of Phenomenal Life)
Have no beginning, but they have an end.
The Absolute Essence,[3] eternal and pure by nature,
Is (only) obscured by defilement which is beginningless;
Therefore it cannot be perceived,
Just as gold buried (in mud and dust).—

## The Relations of Germ to the Factors and the Result of Purification (5).

Now let us take (the Germ of the Absolute) from the point of view of its (different) relations. We have here the following verse:—

[The Relation to the Causes of perfect Purity.]

41. (The Essence of the Buddha) is like the Great Ocean
Being the inexhaustible repository of jewels—its sublime properties;
It is (moreover) like a light, since, by its nature
It is endowed with properties indivisible (from it).

Now, what shows the first half of the verse?—

42. As it contains the sources
Of the Cosmical Body, of the Buddha's Wisdom and Commiseration,

[1] Dar. 101 b. 3.

[2] Cf. Śrī-mālā-simhanāda-sūtra. Kg. DKON. VI. 280 b. 8—281 a. 1.

[3] Tib. *chos-can* = *dharmin.* The Dar. (107 a. 3.) gives the synonym *de-bžin-ñid* = *tathatā.*

It appears as being akin to the ocean,
Since (the causes of purity to which it relates
Bear a resemblance) with a receptacle, with jewels, and with water.

The "relation" of the Germ of the Buddha is to be understood (first of all) in the sense of its relation to the causes (of perfect purity). (From such a point of view) 3 distinctive features give it a resemblance with the great ocean in 3 ways, respectively. [31 a. 1.] What are the 3 distinctive features?—They are as follows:—(The Germ of the Buddha) is connected with the cause of the perfectly pure Cosmical Body, of the factors for the attainment of the Wisdom of the Buddha, and of the causes for the manifestation of the Buddha's Mercy and Love. Now, the cause of the perfectly pure Cosmical Body we know to be the concentration upon the Faith in the Mahāyānistic Doctrine. The factors for the attainment of the Wisdom of the Buddha is the concentration upon the Climax of Wisdom and the medium of transic meditation.[1] The cause for the manifestation of the Buddha's Great Mercy and Love is the concentration upon Great Commiseration as the property of the Bodhisattva.[2]

Here the concentration upon the faith in the Mahāyānistic Doctrine has a resemblance with a receptacle,[3] since the jewels of Wisdom and transic meditation which are numberless and have no end, as well as the waters of Great Commiseration are included in it. The concentration upon Highest Wisdom and transic meditation may be compared with a wish-fulfilling gem, because they are possessed of the quality (of bringing about the desired aim) without dialectical thought-construction.[4] Finally, the concentration upon the Bodhisattva's

[1] *samādhi-mukha* = *tiṅ-ṅe-ḥdzin-gyi-sgo.*

[2] The word *mahā-karuṇā*—Great Commiseration is, in the Tibetan, rendered in 2 ways. As a property of the Buddha it appears in the honorific form *thugs-rje-chen-po,* and as the property of the Bodhisattva it is translated in the ordinary way—*sñiṅ-rje-chen-po.* Cf. Conception of Buddhist Nirvāṇa, p. 83.

[3] *bhājana* = *snod.*

[4] Dar. 108 a. 5.—without thinking "it is necessary to bring forth such and such a result."

12*

Great Mercy and Love bears a similarity with water, having a uniform, soft, moist character with regard to all that lives.[1] The 3 causes mentioned correspond to the 3 distinctive properties (of the Buddha).[2] The relation (of the Germ) to the causes of purification and their distinctive features,[3] is the "relation" spoken of here.

[The Relation of the Germ to the Result.]

What is shown in the second half of verse (41)?

43. (When) the state of Perfect Purity (is attained),
One is possessed of the supernatural faculties,[4]
Of the Wisdom bringing about the extirpation of defilement,
And this extirpation itself, which are indivisible.
Therefore (the Essence of the Buddha in the aspect of the result)
Suggests a resemblance with the rays, the heat, and the colour of a light.

Here the "relation" is to be understood as the relation of the Essence of the Buddha to the result (of purification). The 3 characteristic features (of this result) have resemblance respectively with the distinctive properties of a light. [31 b. 1.] What are the 3 characteristic features? Answer:— The (5) supernatural faculties, the Transcendental Wisdom bringing about the extirpation of the defiling forces,[5] and this extirpation itself. The 5 forms of supernatural perception have here a resemblance with the rays of a light, since they appear in their faculty of dispelling the darkness caused by all the impediments to the perception of the truth. The Transcendental Wisdom removing the defiling forces bears a likeness with heat, since it appears as consuming the fuel of the Biotic Force[6] and the passions. The removal of all

[1] Cf. Meghadūta, Uttaramegha, 30.—*prāyaḥ sarvo bhavati karuṇā-vṛttir ārdrāntarātmā.*

[2] Dar. 108 a. 6.—The Cosmical Body, Highest Wisdom and Highest Commiseration.

[3] Dar. 108 b. 1.

[4] *abhijñā = mṅon-par-śes-pa.*

[5] *āsrava-kṣaya-jñāna = zag-pa-zad-paḥi-ye-śes.*

[6] *karma = las.*

defilement which is a metamorphose[1] (of the elements) may be compared with the colour of a light, since it is, essentially, immaculate, perfectly pure, and radiant. It is immaculate through the removal of the Obscuration of Moral Defilement,[2] it is perfectly pure through the extirpation of that of Ignorance,[3] and it is radiant, since it never has the character of being, occasionally, obscured by either (of these) 2 (obscurations). Thus, the (5) supernatural faculties uninfluenced by the defiling forces, the Wisdom extirpating all defilement, and the removal[4] (of the Obscurations)—these 7 are the properties of the individual who has finished the course of Training (on the Path)[5] and are mutually indivisible within the immaculate monistic Absolute (the metamorphose of the elements) of such an individual. The relation (of the Germ) to this indivisible Absolute in the sense of its being identical with it,—this is the relation meant in this case.

### Reference to Scripture.

These examples referring to the subject of the relations (of the Germ) are to be known in detail from Scripture. It is said:— O Śāriputra, take for instance a light [32 a. 1.] or a precious stone. The properties (of the former), its rays, heat, and colour, (as well as of the latter),—its shine, colour, and form, are indivisible and inseparable. In the same way, o Śāriputra, the Cosmical Body manifested by the Buddha is possessed of the properties of the Buddha which are greater in number than the sands of the Ganges and are indivisible, and is, moreover endowed with the spiritual attributes inseparable (from it).—

### The Manifestations of the Germ (6).

Next we have a verse referring to the subject of the manifestations (of the Germ of the Buddha):—

---

[1] *parāvṛtti = yoṅs-su-ḥgyur-ba.* [2] *kleśa-āvaraṇa = ñon-moṅs-kyi-sgrib-pa.*
[3] *jñeya-āvaraṇa = śes-byaḥi-sgrib-pa.*
[4] *prahāṇa = spaṅs-pa.* [5] *aśaikṣa = mi-slob-pa.*

44. The Absolute manifests itself differently
In the worldlings,[1] the Saints, and the Supreme Buddha.
Having perceived this, (the Lord) has declared
That the Essence of Buddhahood exists in all that lives.

What is said here?

45. With the ordinary beings (the Absolute) is obscured by error,
And with those who perceive the Truth [2] it is the reverse.
As to the Buddha who has the full and perfect intuition,—
With him it is completely free from error and differentiation.[3]

In the Prajñāpāramitā and elsewhere, in connexion with the teaching about the medium of direct intuitive knowledge, the Lord has demonstrated to the Bodhisattvas the general character [4] of the Absolute Essense of all the elements, perfectly pure (by nature), as being the Germ of the Buddha. This (Absolute) is to be known as manifesting itself in 3 different ways:—in the ordinary (worldly) beings who do not perceive the Truth, in the Saints who have an intuition of the latter, and with the Buddha who has attained the culminating point of the perfectly pure introspection of the Ultimate Reality. Accordingly, it may be either obscured by error, or (partly) free from it, [32 b. 1.] or completely devoid of every kind of error and differentiation, respectively. Now, it is obscured by error with the ordinary worldlings, since the conceptions and views of the latter are totally incorrect. The reverse, that is a (partly) unerring character, is to be found with the Saints, since they have rejected these (false views). Finally, (the Absolute) completely free from all error and differentiation is the form peculiar to the Supreme Buddha, since he has completely annihilated the passions and the residues, as well as the Obscuration of Ignorance.

---

[1] *pṛthagjana = so-soḥi-skye-bo.*
[2] The Saints (*ārya-pudgala*).
[3] *prapañca = spros-pa.*
[4] *sāmānya-lakṣaṇa = spyiḥi-mtshan-ñid.*

### The different States of the Germ (7).

After that, in connexion with the subject of the manifestations (of the Germ), we have the remaining 4 subjects[1] and their varieties demonstrated. First of all we have a verse referring to the different states of the Germ corresponding to the 3 kinds of individuals just mentioned:—

46\. Impure, (partly) pure and (partly) impure,
And perfectly pure—(the Absolute).
Is called (the Germ of) ordinary beings, (that of) the Bodhisattvas,
And the Perfect Supreme Buddha,[2] respectively.

What is said here?—

47\. The Germ (of the Buddha) considered
From the 6 points of view beginning with (its) essence,
Is, in accordance with its 3 states,
Designated by 3 different names.

The undefiled Germ (of the Buddha) has been demonstrated by the Lord in detail, in many divisions of Scripture, having been discussed from 6 points of view,—that of its essence, the cause (of its purification), the result (of the latter), its functions, relations, and manifestations. All this, in short, refers to the 3 different states (of the Germ) which have, respectively, 3 different names, viz.:—1) in the impure [33 a. 1.] state (the Germ) is called "the fundamental element of a living being;" 2) in the state which is (partly) pure and (partly) impure, it bears the name of "the (Essence of the) Bodhisattva."[3] 3) Finally, in the state of perfect purity (the Absolute which is no more a Germ) is called "the Buddha."[4]

---

[1] The different states, the all-pervading character, the inalterable, and the indivisible character (of the Germ).

[2] I.e. the Absolute is in the last case identical with the Cosmical Body of the Buddha.

[3] Lit. "bears the name of the Bodhisattva." Cf. Abhis. āloka. MS. *dharma-dhātu-svabhāvenaiva bodhisattvena ...*

[4] *Tathāgata.* The word is here taken in the sense of *tathatām gata iti tathāgataḥ* "He who has coalesced with the Absolute."

## Reference to Scripture concerning the 3 different States of the Germ.

The Lord has said:—O Śāriputra, this Cosmical Body[1] when it is concealed by the innumerable coverings of defilement, carried by the stream of Phenomenal Life, and subjected to a beginningless and endless migration through death and birth,—is called the fundamental element of a living being. O Śāriputra, when this same Cosmical Body has become averse to the suffering (experienced) in the stream of Saṁsāra, when it is free from attachment to all the objects arousing desire, firmly rooted in the 10 Transcendental Virtues, and, with the help of the analysis of innumerable elements of existence,[2] acts in order to attain Enlightenment, then it is called (the essence of) the Bodhisattva. O Śāriputra, when this very Cosmical Body is completely free from all the bonds of defilement, delivered from Phenomenal Existence,[3] devoid of all the stains of the passions, is merged in the pure, the stainless, the universally immaculate Absolute, abides in a state that is looked to by all living beings, has attained the power of the one-without-a-second perceiving everything cognizable, is free from all the Obscurations, and has the illimited power of the Supreme Lord governing all the elements of existence,—then it is called the Tathāgata, [33 b. 1.] the Arhat, the Perfect Supreme Buddha.—

## The All-pervading Character of the Germ (8).

Now comes a verse referring to the Germ of the Buddha as having in its 3 different states an all-pervading character:—

48. Just as, being essentially free from (dialectical) thought-construction,
The element of space is ubiquitous,
In the same way the Immaculate Essence which is of spiritual nature, pervades all that exists.[4]

---

[1] Is to be understood in the sense of "the Germ of the Absolute, the final metamorphose of which is the Cosmical Body."

[2] Lit. the 84,000 classifications (*dharma-skandha*). [3] *duḥkha.*

[4] Cf. Sūtrālaṁkāra IX. 15. *yathā 'mbaraṁ sarvagataṁ sadā matam,* &c.

What is said by this?

49. It penetrates, in its general essence,
The defective, the virtuous, and the ultimate point (of perfection),
Just as space embraces all visible forms,
The base, the intermediate, and the sublime.

The spiritual Essence of the ordinary worldlings, the saints, and Perfect Supreme Buddha, being devoid of (dialectical) thought-construction is, with regard to the 3 states (of the living beings),— that which is thoroughly defective, that characterized by virtuous properties, and that which represents the culminating point of perfection,—all-pervading, all-embracing, equal (with all), and eternally the same. It has accordingly a resemblance with space (which is the same) whether included in an earthen, brazen, or golden vessel, respectively.

## Reference to Scripture concerning the All-pervading Character.

For this reason it has been said, immediately after the demonstration of the 3 different states:—Therefore, O Śāriputra, the fundamental Germ of a living being is not one separate element, and the Cosmical Body—another (quite different from it). The Germ of a living being is the Cosmical Body, and the Cosmical Body in its turn is the Germ of a living being. They are essentially identical, and only the words expressing them are different.

## The Germ in its unalterable Character (9).

The Germ of the Buddha, being in its 3 different states all-pervading [34 a. 1.] is, moreover, unchangeable, (since it cannot be really influenced) neither by the defiling,[1] nor by the purifying[2] elements. The following 14 verses all refer to this subject. This (first) one is to be regarded as a summary of their contents:—

50. It is possessed of occasional defects
And of virtuous properties relating to its essence;

[1] *sāṁkleśika = kun-nas-ñon-moṅs-pa.*

[2] *vaiyavadānika = rnam-par-byaṅ-ba.*

But in the initial[1] and in the subsequent[2] states
It remains the unalterable Absolute.

12 verses refer to (the Germ) in its impure state, and one (the 13th) to that state which is (partly) impure and (partly) pure. In both these cases (the Germ appears as) possessed of the primary[3] and the secondary[4] defiling elements, all of which are of a casual character. The 14th verse relates to (the Absolute) in the state of complete purification, when it is essentially endowed with all the properties of the Buddha, indivisible, inseparable, and greater in number than the sands of the Ganges. In the former (2) cases, as well as in the latter, the Germ of the Buddha is demonstrated as completely inalterable and as having (from this point of view) an analogy with space. Now, what (is said in) the 12 verses referring to the inalterable character (of the Germ) when it is in an impure state?

[The Germ of the Buddha cannot be affected by the defiling elements.]

51. Just as space fills everything,[5]
And, owing to its subtle (transcendental) character,[6] cannot be polluted,
In the same way this (perfectly pure Germ) has its abode
In all living beings, but remains undefiled (by their passions).

[The Germ is not affected by Origination and Destruction.]

52. Just as, in space, the worlds and all their elements
Become originated and are destroyed,
In the same way, in the Eternal[7] Substance,
The forces of Phenomenal Life appear and disappear.

---

[1] In the state of an ordinary worldly being. Dar. 114 a. 2.

[2] With the Śrāvaka and the Pratyekabuddha Saint, as well as with the Bodhisattva. Ibid.

[3] *mūla-kleśa* = *rtsa-baḥi-ñon-moṅs-pa.*

[4] *upakleśa* = *ñe-baḥi-ñon-moṅs-pa.*

[5] Dar. 114 b. 6. penetrates the whole of the Receptacle-world (*bhājana-loka*).

[6] Ibid. 115 a. 1. It is subtle, since it is not accessible to the perception by the sense-organs.

[7] *asaṁskṛta* = *ḥdus-ma-byas.*

53. Just as space will never be destroyed
By the (destructive) fires (at the end of the world) [34 b. 1.],
In a like way this (Essence of the Buddha)
Is not consumed by the fires of death, of illness, and decrepitude.

54. The earth is supported by water, the water is supported by air,
And air is supported by space;
But space (in its turn) has no support,
Neither in air, nor in water, nor in the earth.

55. In a similar manner the elements of life (classified into) groups,[1] component elements,[2] and bases of cognition[3]
Have their foundation in the Biotic Force and Desire,[4]
And the latter (two) are always supported
By the naive appreciation (of existence).[5]

56. This naive, incorrect evaluation
Is supported by the Spirit that is perfectly pure;
But the true Essence of the Spirit (which is the Absolute)
Has not its support in any (of the worldly elements).

57. We know that the elements of life (classified in) groups, component elements, and bases of cognition, are similar to the earth;
We know that the Biotic Force and the defiling elements of the living beings are akin to water.

58. And the naive appreciation (of existence)
Bears a likeness with the element of air;
The Spiritual Essence[6] is like space, having no foundation and no substratum.

---

[1] *skandha* = *phuṅ-po.*

[2] *dhātu* = *khams.*

[3] *āyatana* = *skye-mched.* Lit. "the sense-organs (*dbaṅ-po* = *indriya*)." Dar. 115 b. 1—2. *mig-gi-dbaṅ-po-la-sogs-paḥi skye-mched-rnams.*

[4] Ibid.—which are the cause of these elements.

[5] *ayoniśo-manasikāra* = *tshul-bźin-ma-yin-paḥi-yid-la-byed-pa.* Dar. 115 b. 2—perceiving the reality of the individual and the separate elements.

[6] Dar. 116 a. 6. The Absolute which is of spiritual nature (*sems-kyi-raṅ-bźin dōn-dam-paḥi-bden-pa* = *citta-svābhāva-pāramārtha-satya*).

59. The wrong appreciation (of existence)
Is supported by the spiritual essence.
This naive, incorrect evaluation
Calls forth the Biotic Force and the passions.

60. From the waters of the Biotic Force and Desire
Arise the elements of life (as classified into) groups, component elements, and bases of cognition;
And just as (the element of water), which is destroyed and formed anew,
Do (the elements of life) appear and disappear again.

61. But the Spiritual Essence is like space,
Being uncaused and unconditioned;
It is devoid of the complex (of producing factors)
And knows no birth, destruction, and (temporary) stability.

62. The Spiritual Essence which is pure and radiant
Is inalterable like space
And cannot be polluted by the occasional stains
Of Desire and the other (defiling forces)
Which arise from the wrong conception (of existence).

[35 a. 1.] The Essence of the Buddha in the impure state is thus demonstrated as being the inalterable Absolute, by means of this comparison with space. This is (moreover) expressed in the following verse:—

63. It does not become produced
By the waters of the Biotic Force, of Desire and the rest,
And it cannot be consumed by the violent fires
Of death, of illness, and infirmity.

The (5) groups, the (18) component elements of an individual, and the (12) bases of cognition (may be compared with) a world (that is formed anew). They become originated on the foundation of the water of the Biotic Force and the defiling factors, which in their turn arise from the naive appreciation of existence, this appreciation having a resemblance with the sphere of air.[1] This origination (of the elements of Phenomenal Life) does not affect the Spiritual Essence (of the Absolute), which is analogous to space. This (newly formed) world of groups, component elements, and bases of cognition has (as we have just seen) its support in the naive appreciation, in the Biotic Force and Desire, of which (the first has a resemblance) with air, and (the latter two) are akin to water. It (subsequently) becomes destroyed through death, illness, and decrepitude (which bear a likeness) with (destructive) fires. But, (just as the origination of the worldly elements does not add anything to the pure Spiritual Essence), in a like way it is not liable to destruction (through death, illness and decrepitude). It is thus shown that, in the impure state (of the living beings), all the defiling elements, those of Desire, of the Biotic Force, and Origination, which are like the Receptacle-world, appear and disappear, but that the Eternal Essence of the Buddha is, like space, not liable to origination and destruction and has a totally inalterable character.

[Reference to Scripture.]

We have this example of space enlarged upon in Scripture,[2] where it stands in connexion with (the subject of) the medium of perfect purification. This medium is, to speak otherwise, the means of (perceiving) the light of the essence of the Buddha. [35 b. 1.] (It is said):—O great Sage, the defiling forces are like darkness, and purification is light. The defiling forces are feeble in strength; the transcendental perception of the Truth,[3] on the contrary, is powerful. The defiling forces are casual, whereas the perfectly pure (Absolute) is the true fundamental Essence (of all that exists).[4] The defiling forces are imputed[5] (and essentially unreal, whereas the

---

[1] *vāyu-maṇḍala* = *rluṅ-gi-dkyil-ḥkhor*.

[2] In the Gaganagañja-Sūtra. Kg. MDO. XIII. 320 a. 6—321 a. 7.

[3] *vipaśyanā* = *lhag-mthoṅ*.

[4] Dar. 118 b. 5. *raṅ-bżin-gyis-rnam-par-dag-pa-ni chos thams-çad-kyi rtsa-baḥo* --the foundation, the root of all the elements.

[5] *parikalpita* = *kun-tu-brtags-pa*.

Absolute is the true (essence of all the elements) and not a construction (of the mind). O great Sage, such is the state of things.— This great earth is supported by water, water reposes in the air, and air is supported by space. But space itself has no support. Moreover, of these 4 elements, that of space is, in comparison with the elements of earth, water, and air, the most powerful.[1] It is stable, motionless, knows no decrease, no origination, and no destruction. It is enduring by its very nature. Now, the 3 (other) elements are liable to origination and destruction; they are not stable and have no long duration. With everyone of them a constant change may be perceived. But space (on the contrary) does not undergo the slightest change.

In a similar way the (5) groups (of elements), the (18) component elements (of an individual), and the (12) bases of cognition have their foundation in the Biotic Force and Desire. These two are founded upon incorrect appreciation, and the latter has its support in the (spiritual) essence, which is perfectly pure. This essence is (by itself) pure and radiant and cannot (really) become polluted by the occasional defiling forces. [36 a. 1.]

Now, the incorrect appreciation, the Biotic Force and the defiling factors, as well as the groups, component elements, and bases of cognition are all of them originated by the complex of their causes and conditions; as soon as these causes and conditions cease to exist, (the elements of life) are all of them annihilated. On the other hand, that which represents the (Absolute, Spiritual) Essence is uncaused, unconditioned, is not a product (of both causes and conditions); it neither becomes originated, nor does it disappear. Now, the (spiritual) Essence is like the element of space. The incorrect appreciation is akin to the element of air. The Biotic Force in the passions are like the element of water, and the groups, the component elements, and the bases of cognition bear a likeness with the element of the earth. Therefore, it is said:—The foundation of

[1] In the sense of its being indestructible.

all the elements is to be cognized as follows: they are completely devoid of any real foundation, their foundation is not essential and is not stable. (At the same time) they have a foundation that is perfectly pure and are founded on the absence of a real foundation.[1] Thus, with regard to its inalterable character even in the impure state (of a living being),—the Absolute is represented as resembling space. The wrong appreciation which is founded upon (this Spiritual Essence), the Biotic Force, and the defiling factors are, as concerns their character of causes (producing Phenomenal Existence), spoken of as having a similarity with the elements of air[2] and water.[3] Finally, with reference to the character of a result[4] peculiar to the groups, the component elements, and the bases of cognition,—these are all shown in their similarity with the element of the earth.

[The Indestructible Character of the Germ.]

Now, the factors bringing about the destruction (of the Phenomenal Elements) viz. death [36 b. 1.], illness, and decrepitude, have the character of the greatest calamities, (being like destructive) fires. They have, accordingly, a resemblance with the element of fire. (This resemblance) has not yet been spoken of; it is to be demonstrated presently.

64. The 3 fires,—those of death, illness, and decrepitude,
Are known to have a resemblance with 3 (other) fires,—
That (which arises) at the end of the world,[5] the fire of hell,
And the ordinary fire, respectively.

Death, illness, and decrepitude are known to bear a likeness with fire for 3 motives respectively. (The first) completely destroys

---

[1] As the elements of Phenomenal Life have no real connexion with the Absolute Essence.

[2] The wrong appreciation of existence.

[3] The Biotic Force and the defiling elements.

[4] *vipāka* = *rnam-par-smin-pa*.

[5] Dar. 119 b. 5. The fire which destroys the external world (*bhājana-loka*).

the 6 (internal) bases[1] as constituting an individual. (The second) produces the feeling of suffering in many different forms, and (the third) brings to full development[2] the forces[3] (which produce the changes in a state of existence). Now the Germ of the Buddha, even in the impure state, does not undergo any change through these 3 fires of death, illness, and decrepitude. With respect to this unchangeable character it has been said:[4]—O Lord, "Death" and "Birth"—these are but worldly names.[5] O Lord, that which we call "Death" is the annihilation of the bases of cognition. That which is called "Birth" is the fact of assuming these bases anew. As to the Essence of the Buddha, O Lord, it is not subjected to birth, death, decrepitude, and rebirth (anew). Why that? Because, O Lord, the Essence of the Buddha does not belong to the objects that are caused and conditioned.[6] It is eternal, persistent, quiescent, and indestructible.—

### The Germ of the Buddha with the Saints (partly pure and partly impure).

Now, let us take the inalterable character of the Germ in the state which is partly pure and partly impure (that is as it exists in the Saint). We have here the following verse:—

65. Being delivered from birth, death, illness, and old age,[7]
The Sage[8] is not subjected to the misery of either of them; [37 a. 1.]
However, as he knows the true nature (of the Germ within him),
And is full of mercy toward the living beings,
He continues to reside (in this world in order to help them).

---

[1] *abhyantara-āyatana.*

[2] Lit. "maturity" (*paripāka = yoṅs-su-smin-pa*).

[3] *saṁskāra = ḥdu-byed.*

[4] In the Śrī-mālā-sūtra. Kg. DKON. VI. 281 a. 3—6.

[5] *laukika-vyavahāra = ḥjig-rten-gyi tha-sñad.*

[6] *saṁskṛta = ḥdus-byas.*

[7] Dar. 120 b. 2.—which are caused by the Biotic Force and the defiling factors.

[8] The Mahāyānistic Saint.

What is said here?

66. The Saint has rooted out the suffering
Of death, of illness, and old age.
He is not subjected to the birth conditioned by the Biotic Force and Desire;
Therefore the sufferings of the Phenomenal World which follow (such a birth)[1]
Are not experienced by him.

In the state which is completely impure, the *causa materialis*[2] of the fires of death, illness, and old age, the fuel for these fires is the birth[3] which is preceded by the Biotic Force and the defiling elements, and by incorrect appreciation. In the state which is partly pure and partly impure we know that with the Bodhisattvas, who have attained the non-physical existence,[4] the birth conditioned by the Biotic Force and the passions is not experienced at all. Followingly, the fires of death, &c., are altogether incapable of blazing forth.[5]

67. As he has perceived the Absolute Truth,
He is delivered from birth and the other (stages of Phenomenal Life);[6]
But being full of Great Commiseration,
He appears as (being subjected to) birth, death, decrepitude, and illness.

The Bodhisattvas act in the Phenomenal World (furthering) the roots of virtue (of the living beings). They have the controlling

---

[1] Sic acc. to Dar. 121 a. 2.

[2] *upādāna-kāraṇa* = *ñer-len-gyi-rgyu.*

[3] Dar. 121 b. 6. *miṅ-gzugs-kyis-bsdus-paḥi-skye-ba* = *nāma-rūpa-saṁgṛhīta-janma*—the birth (existence) included in the physical and the mental elements.

[4] *manomaya-kāya* = *yid-kyi-raṅ-bźin-gyi-lus.*

[5] Sic acc. to Dar. 122 a. 1. Lit.—"as the one (the birth conditioned by the Biotic Force and Desire) is not experienced at all, the others (the fires of death, &c.) are altogether incapable of blazing forth.

[6] Cf. Abhisamayālaṁkāra V. 21. *draṣṭavyaṁ bhūtato bhūtaṁ bhūta-darśī vimucyate.*

power over their own birth (as they can assume this or that form of existence) according to their desire. On the foundation of this their power, (the Bodhisattvas), guided by Commiseration toward all living beings, exercise their activity in the 3 Spheres of Existence. They appear as being subjected to birth, old age, illness, and death. (In reality) the elements of birth,[1] &c., are not experienced with them, since they have the (introspective) intuition of the Absolute Essence[2] in its true nature as neither appearing nor disappearing (anew).

[Reference to Scripture.]

This state of the Bodhisattvas is to be known in detail from Scripture, where it is said:[3]—What are the virtuous Desires[4] which cause them to reside in the Phenomenal World? [37 b. 1.] They are as follows:—Non-satisfaction in the search of the Accumulations of Virtue,[5] (the will of) assuming an existence in the Phenomenal World in accordance with the intention (of assisting other living beings),[6] the desire of an encounter with a Buddha,[7] the absence of an aversion (toward Phenomenal Existence) owing to the intention of bringing other living beings to complete maturity,[8] the efforts for perfectly apprehending the Highest Doctrine, the energy in acting for the sake of other living beings in every possible way, the fact of never becoming deprived of virtuous thoughts, and the non-reluctance from the practice of the Highest Virtues.[9] Such, O Sāgaramati, are the Desires connected with the roots of virtue, owing to which the Bodhisattvas act (in the Phenomenal World) without however becoming polluted by the

---

[1] Dar. 122 a. 6.—as conditioned by the Biotic Force and the defiling factors.

[2] Ibid. *don-dam-paḥi-bden-pas-bsdus-paḥi-khams* = *paramārtha-satyena saṁgṛhītadhātuḥ.*

[3] Sāgaramati-paripṛcchā, Kg. MDO. XIV. 85 b. 5—86 a. 1.

[4] *dge-baḥi-rtsa-ba-daṅ-mtshuṅs-par-ldan-paḥi-ñon-moṅs-pa* = *kuśala-mūla-saṁprayukta-kleśa* (!)

[5] *puṇya-saṁbhāra* = *bsod-nams-kyi-tshogs.*

[6] Dar. 122 b. 3. [7] *buddha-samavadhāna* = *saṅs-rgyas-daṅ-phrad-pa.*

[8] *paripācana* = *yoṅs-su-smin-pa.* [9] *pāramitā.*

defilement of the passions.—It is said further on:[1]—(Sāgaramati asked):—O Lord, if (thou speakest of) the roots of virtue, how can their causes be called Desires? The Lord answered:—O Sāgaramati, such is the state of things.—Owing to the desires of such a nature the Bodhisattva exercised his activity in the 3 spheres of this world. Now, as the (existence in these) 3 Spheres is (as a general rule) conditioned by Desire, and as the Bodhisattvas, manifesting their skill and the power of their virtue, voluntarily assume this or that state of existence, the factors (which bring it about) are called "the Desires connected (with the roots of virtue)."—Thus the Bodhisattvas continue to abide in the 3 Spheres of this World, but their existence is not conditioned by a mind which is influenced by defilement.

## The Parable of the Householder.

O Sāgaramati, let us take the following example. Suppose a rich merchant or householder [38 a. 1.] had an only son, beloved, handsome, affectionate, and having nothing displeasing in his appearance. Suppose now that this boy, having grown older, would, whilst playing, fall into a pit filled with impurities. Thereupon the child's mother and her relatives would behold the boy fallen into the impure pit. Upon seing this they would become distressed, weep and lament, but would not make an effort to enter the pit and draw the boy out. After that the father of the child would come to the place and, seing his only son fallen into the impure pit, would become resolved to draw him out in the most speedy manner. Accordingly he, without any feeling of disgust, would descend into that impure pit and rescue his only son from it.—O Sāgaramati, this example has been made in order to illustrate a special subject.—What is this subject?—The impure pit, O Sāgaramati, is a name for the 3 Spheres of Existence. The only son is a name for the living beings (in general), since the Bodhisattvas have for every living being the consideration as for an only child. The mother and the relatives,—this is a name for the

---

[1] Sāgaramati-paripṛcchā, Kg. MDO. XIV. 86 a. 1—b. 4.

individuals who belong to the Vehicles of the Śrāvakas and the Pratyekabuddhas. These behold the living beings fallen into the Saṁsāra, are distressed and lament, but have not the power of rescuing (the living beings). The great merchant or householder,— this is a name for the Bodhisattva. It is he who is possessed of a spirit pure, immaculate, and completely free from defilement [38 b. 1.], directly perceives the eternal Absolute Essence, and, in order to convert the living beings, by his own will assumes a continuance of births in the 3 Spheres of Existence. O Sāgaramati, such is the Great Commiseration of the Bodhisattvas that, being free from all the successions (of births), they nevertheless become born in the Phenomenal World (for the sake of others). Owing to their skill and wisdom they cannot be harmed by the defiling forces; in order to deliver other living beings from the bonds of these forces, they demonstrate the Doctrine to them.—This fragment of Scripture thus shows how the Bodhisattva who is possessed of the power of helping other living beings, voluntarily assumes this or that form of existence (in the Phenomenal World) being at the same time free from all defilement owing to his wisdom and skill. It accordingly demonstrates the state (of the Essence of Buddhahood) which is partly pure [1] and partly impure.[2]

Now, the Bodhisattva, having come to the correct intuition of the Germ of the Buddha as being neither born nor conditioned, finally attains (the full realization) of this Absolute Essence (within him). A detailed exposition of this subject is to be found in Scripture. It is said (in the *Sāgaramati-paripṛcchā*):[3]—O Sāgaramatī, perceive thou, with the separate elements, the absence of any real essence of their own,[4] the absence of a creator, the absence of (a real individual who is) their owner, of a real living being (constituted by them), of an individual soul,[5] [39 a. 1.] of the personality[6] (as an independent

[1] Dar. 123 b. 5.—through the absence of the defiling elements.

[2] Ibid.—through the fact of being born in the Phenomenal World.

[3] Kg. MDO. XIV. 85 a. 2—b. 5.

[4] Dar. 124 a. 3.—The separate unreality of the elements (*dharma-nairātmya*).

[5] *jīva* = *srog*. [6] *pudgala* = *gaṅ-zag*.

whole), and of the Ego. Indeed, do not think of them and do not interprete them volubly. O Sāgaramatī, the aversion toward the separate elements, whatever they might be, will never arise in the Bodhisattva who is full of faith in the inalterable essence (of the Unique Absolute). He will become possessed of the pure transcendental perception, that not one (of the separate elements) can be (really) favourable or harmful. Thus, he will perfectly cognize the true essence of the elements and will not cast off the armour of Great Commiseration. O Sāgaramati, take thou for instance a stone of lapis lazuli of immeasurable value, finely polished, perfectly pure and completely free from every stain. Suppose it were thrown in a mire where it would remain for many thousands of years. Then, after these thousands of years would have passed away, it would be extracted from the mire, and purified, being well-washed, wiped and polished. Through all this it would not lose its essence of a precious stone. In a similar manner, O Sāgaramati, the Bodhisattva cognizes the spirit of the living beings as perfectly pure and radiant by nature, and at the same time perceives that it is obscured by the defiling forces which are of an occasional character. He thinks as follows:—These defiling forces do not affect the essence of the Spirit which is pure and radiant. They are only occasional and a product of incorrect imputation.[1] [39 b. 1.] I have the power of demonstrating the Doctrine in order to pacify the defiling forces of the living beings. Having once thought so, he never becomes depressed (whilst accomplishing his task), and is possessed of the intention of going into the world of living beings repeatedly. He has moreover the following thoughts:—These defiling forces have no efficiency and power. These defiling forces have no strength, they are feeble, and there is nothing real and true about them. They are produced by incorrect imputation and, being examined and appreciated correctly, cannot excite anger (on account of their unreality). I, myself, have no relation to them; therefore I can investigate them accurately. There exists no contact, no real connex-

[1] *parikalpanā = kun-tu-rtog-pa.*

ion with the defiling elements. Now, if I had some relation to the Desires, how could I teach the Doctrine in order that the living beings who are fettered by the bonds of Desire could cast them off. In reality I have no connexion with the Desires; therefore, in order to deliver the living beings from their bonds, I shall teach the Doctrine to them. But, in order to convert the living beings, I must become possessed of those Desires which, though they are connected with the roots of virtue, still produce a relation to the Phenomenal World. Here "Phenomenal World, Saṁsāra" is to be understood (metaphorically) [40 a. 1.] in the sense of the non-physical existence[1] in the Unaffected Plane,[2] of which there are 3 forms corresponding to the 3 spheres of this world. It is Phenomenal Existence inasmuch as it is induced[3] by the pure roots of virtue. At the same time, as it is not conditioned by the Biotic Force influenced by defiling agencies and by Desire, it represents Nirvāṇa. In regard of this it has been said:[4]—O Lord, for this reason there is a conditioned and unconditioned Saṁsāra and a conditioned and unconditioned Nirvāṇa. —Now, as we thus have a manifestation of the Spirit of a mixed nature, both conditioned and unconditioned,—this state is called partly pure and partly impure. This state is, in its principal features, characterized as the manifestation of the character of the Bodhisattva. Indeed, through the concentration upon Highest Wisdom[5] free from impediments and the contemplation of Highest Mercy and Love, (the Bodhisattva) gets close to (the attainment of) the supernatural faculty of extirpating the defiling elements.[6] But, in order to save the Germs of all the living beings, he does not realize this last result[7] (i.e. he does not pass away into egoistic Nirvāṇa).

---

[1] *manomaya-kāya = yid-kyi-raṅ-bžin-gyi-lus.*

[2] *anāsrava-dhātu = zag-med-kyi-dbyiṅs.*

[3] *abhisaṁskṛta = mṅon-par-ḥdus-byas-pa.*

[4] In the Śrī-mālā-siṁhanāda-sūtra. Kg. DKON. VI. 277 b. 4—5.

[5] *prajñā-pāramitā.*

[6] *āsrava-kṣaya-jñāna = zag-pa-zad-paḥi-ye-śes.*

[7] Cf. Abhisamayālaṁkāra IV. 28. *phalāsākṣātkriyātmakam* (*kāritram*).

With reference to the Transcendental Wisdom extirpating defilement, it has been said, in connexion with the parable of the man,[1] as follows:—O noble youth, in the same way the Bodhisattva, having manifested his great efforts, his great energy, and his firm altruistic intentions,[2] attains the 5 supernatural faculties.[3] Through concentrated trance and supernatural perception his mind becomes purified [40 b. 1.], and he gets close to the full extirpation of defilement. In order to save all living beings he makes his Creative Effort full of Great Commiseration,[4] and purifies the Wisdom through which all defilement is annihilated. Having then purified his mind again, he causes the Transcendental Wisdom which is free from all attachment to arise, this whilst abiding on the 6th Stage.[5] Owing to (the said Wisdom) he draws near to the extirpation of defilement. Thus on the Stage of the Bodhisattva called Abhimukhī, he attains the power of making manifest the annihilation of the passions. This shows (the Bodhisattva and his Germ) in the state which is perfectly pure. (On the other hand) he who has assumed such a character is desirous to save the living beings who are on the wrong way, owing to his Great Commiseration, (as he thinks):—I must bring others to that true knowledge which I have attained myself.—He has thus no taste for the bliss of (egoistic) peace and looks to the living beings that abide in the Phenomenal World. The latter is made sublime by him as a means (of saving others). Being directed toward Nirvāṇa, he, in order to bring to accomplishment the factors for the attainment of Supreme Enlightenment, descends from the worlds of trance,[6] and again, voluntarily, assumes an existence in the world of Carnal Desire.[7] As he is desirous of acting for the sake

---

[1] Cf. Appendix. [2] *dṛḍha-adhyāśaya* = *lhag-paḥi-bsam-pa-brtan-pa.*

[3] *abhijñā* = *mṅon-par-śes-pa* (= *mṅon-śes*).

[4] Cf. Abhis. āloka. MS. 17 a. 11—12. *śūnyatā-karuṇā-garbhaṁ bodhicittaṁ praṇidhi-prasthāna-svabhāvaṁ dvividham utpādya.*

[5] *abhimukhī* = *mṅon-du-gyur-pa.* The name of the 6th Stage refers, as we clearly see, to the fact of the Bodhisattva's being close to the extirpation of defilement.

[6] Dar. 126 b. 3. — [7] *kāma-dhātu* = *ḥdod-khams.*

of living beings as speedily as possible, he becomes born in many varieties of forms, including that of animals, and thus shows himself in the state of an ordinary worldly being. This his faculty alludes to the character (of the Bodhisattva) which is not perfectly pure (inasmuch as he continues to exist in the Phenomenal World).

## The partly pure and partly impure State of the Bodhisattva as compared with the ordinary being and the Buddha.

Another meaning of verse (65 is shown in the following verses):—

66. The son of the Buddha[1] directly perceives
This immutable Absolute Essence;
Nevertheless, he is to be seen [41 a. 1.]
As one of those obscured by ignorance,
Subjected to birth and the like;
This is really wonderful!

67. He has attained the position of a Saint,[2]
And nevertheless appears in the state of a worldly being,
Manifesting thus, for all that lives
The help of a friend and Highest Commiseration.[3]

68. He has drawn far from all that is worldly,
And nevertheless he does not leave the world;
For the sake of the world he acts in the world,
Unaffected by the world's impurity.

69. Just as a lotus flower growing in the water
Is not rendered impure by the latter,
In the same way he, though abiding in the world,
Is not influenced by the worldly elements.

---

[1] *jinātmaja* = *rgyal-sras.*

[2] Dar. 127 b. 1.—completely delivered from the sufferings of birth, death, &c.

[3] Cf. Abhisamayālaṁkāra IV. 27. *hitaṁ sukhaṁ ca trāṇaṁ ca śaraṇaṁ layanaṁ nṛṇām | parāyaṇaṁ ca dvīpaṁ ca pariṇāyakasaṁjñakam* (*kāritram*).

70. His Wisdom pursuing the welfare (of others),
Constantly blazes up like a flame;
At the same time he is always merged
In the quiescent trance and mystic absorption.

71. Being completely free from all constructive thought,
And of effort,—owing to his previous vows,
He does not use any exertion,
In bringing the living beings to maturity.

72. By teaching, by (various) apparitions,
By (demonstrating such and such) acts and means,—
Who, how, and by what means is to be converted,—
All this (the Bodhisattva) perfectly knows.

73. In such a way, among the living beings,
Who, (in their number), are infinite like space,
The Sage, constantly, withouth effort and hindrance,
Exercises his activity for the sake of all that lives.

74. This character of the Bodhisattva
Bears a similarity with (the activity of) the Buddhas in this world,
Which they undertake after the attainment (of Enlightenment)
In order to bring deliverance to all living beings.

75. Though this be so, still the Buddha and the Bodhisattva
Differ from each other (in the greatness of their acts)
Like the great Earth and a grain of sand,
Or like the ocean and (a pool of water)
Left in a foot-print of a bull.

Of these 10 verses taken respectively, 9 refer to the sublime Desires of the Bodhisattva after the attainment of the Stage of Joy[1] [41 b. 1.], and the 10th,—to the state of perfect purity peculiar to the Bodhisattva on the Stage of the Clouds of the Truth.[2] In short the 4 kinds of the Bodhisattvas on the 10 Stages, in the state which is partly pure and partly impure, are demonstrated in these verses.

---

[1] *pramuditā = rab-tu-dgaḥ-ba.* [2] *dharma-meghā = chos-kyi-sprin.*

The 4 kinds of the Bodhisattvas are:—1) He who has made the first Creative Effort (as a Saint),[1] 2) he who exercises the activity of a Saint, 3) he who has attained the Irretrievable State,[2] and 4) he who is separated (from Buddhahood) only by one birth.[3] The first and the second verse (66 and 67) show the perfectly pure nature of the properties of the Bodhisattva who makes the first Creative Effort (of a Saint) on the Stage of Joy, as he has (for the first time) the intuition of the Transcendental Absolute Essence which had not been perceived by him before from the outset. The third and fourth verses (68 and 69) show the same with regard to the Bodhisattva who exercises the activity (of a Saint) beginning with the Immaculate Stage[4] and up to the Motionless,[5] as he acts without being affected (by the defiling elements). The fifth verse (70) demonstrates the perfectly pure character of the properties of the Bodhisattva who has attained the Irretrievable State, as he, abiding on the Motionless Stage, is constantly merged in trance in order to attain Supreme Enlightenment. The sixth, the seventh and the eighth verses (71, 72 and 73) show the perfectly pure character of the properties of the Bodhisattva when he, abiding on the Stage called the Clouds of the Truth, has reached the uttermost limits of skill in fulfilling his own aim and that of others, and is separated from the attainment of the Stage of the Buddha and the Perfect Supreme Enlightenment only by one birth. [42 a. 1.] Finally, the ninth and the tenth verses (74 and 75) make known the similarity of the properties of the Bodhisattva who has fully attained his own aim and that of others, with those of the Buddha, and the difference between them.

---

[1] The so-called Absolute Creative Effort on the Path of Illumination (*darśana-mārga*), not to be confounded with the Initial Creative Effort at the beginning of the Path.

[2] *avaivartika* or *avinivartanīya* = *phyir-mi-ldog-pa*.

[3] *eka-jāti-pratibaddha* = *skye-ba-gcig-gis-thogs-pa*.

[4] *vimalā* = *dri-ma-med-pa*.

[5] *acalā* = *mi-gyo-ba*.

### The Absolute in the State of Perfect Purification.

Now we shall take in consideration the unalterable character of the Absolute in the state of complete purification. We have here the following verse:—

76. (The Cosmical Body of the Buddha is eternal),[1]
Being the unalterable Ultimate Essence of Existence possessed of imperishable properties,
The refuge of living beings, infinite and extending beyond all limits,
Always unique and free from (dialectical) thought-construction,
Of undestructible nature, and not produced (by causes).

What is said here?

77. It is not born, nor does it die,
It knows neither harm nor decrepitude,
As it is enduring and stable,
Quiescent and undestructible.

78. Being eternal, it is not subjected
Even to the origination peculiar to the non-physical body.[2]
It knows no death, since it is stable,
And does not migrate in an inconceivable way.

79. Being quiescent, it is unharmed
By the fever of the subtle defiling forces,
And, indestructible, it is not liable to decrepitude
Through the undefiled active forces of life.

If we take the Essence of Buddhahood as it is on the Stage of the Buddha, immaculate, perfectly pure and radiant, from the standpoint of its beginning, (we shall find that) it does not become originated anew, not even in the manner of the non-physical body (of the Arhat, &c.),[3] because it is eternal. [42 b. 1.] As regards the end, we see that it is not liable even to the inconceivable change

[1] Sic acc. to Dar. 130 b. 2.

[2] *manomayā-kāya* = *yid-kyi-raṅ-bžin-gyi-lus*. [3] Cf. below.

of the states of existence i.e. the form of death (of the non-physical body), owing to its stability. Being taken in the aspect of both beginning and end, it proves to be unaffected by the agency of the force of Transcendental Illusion,[1] since it is perfectly quiescent. It is not, moreover, subjected to that decrepitude which is the result, the product of the undefiled Biotic Force. Indeed, it cannot be affected by anything harmful, owing to its indestructible nature.

80. Here two words and the following two
(Are explained) by two and again two, respectively,
Making known, in regard of the Absolute Essence,
The meaning of "Eternal" and the rest.

The words "Eternal," "Stable," "Quiescent," and "Indestructible" (are all of them epithets) of the immutable Essence of the Absolute. The subject designated by each of these words, is, respectively, explained by 2 and again 2 sentences which, taken separately, are to be known from Scripture.

81. It is possessed of properties which never take an end,—
This is the meaning of "the Eternal, Inalterable Essence,"
It is like the Supreme Limit of existence,—
Such is the sense of "a stable, essential refuge."

82. It is by nature devoid of (dialectical) construction,—
This shows the meaning of "the undialectical quiescent Absolute,"
Its properties are real, inartificial,—
By this the meaning of "indestructible" (is explained).[2]

It is accordingly said:—O Śāriputra, being possessed of properties which never take an end, this inalterable Cosmical Body is eternal.—O Śāriputra, being similar with the Supreme Limit of existence, this Cosmical Body, a firm persistent refuge, bears the character of stability.—O Śāriputra, owing to the absence of dialectical opposition, this non-dialectical Cosmical Body is perfectly quiescent.—

---

[1] *avidyā-vāsanā = ma-rig-paḥi-bag-chags.*

[2] Sic acc. to Dar. 132 b. 4.

O Śāriputra, [43 a. 1.] being possessed of a true unartificial essence, this Cosmical Body is imperishable and indestructible.—

**The Essence of Buddhahood in its indivisible Character.**

The Essence of the Buddha which represents the culminating point of purity has, in this state of perfect purification, an indivisible nature. With reference to the latter we have the following verse:—

83. It is the Cosmical Body,[1] it is the (Buddha),—one with the Absolute[2]
It is the Highest Truth and point of saintliness,[3] and it is Nirvāṇa,
Just as the sun and its rays, so are its properties, indivisible;
Therefore there is no Nirvāṇa apart from Buddhahood.[4]

Now, what is shown in the first half of this verse?

84. In short, the Immaculate Absolute Essence,
Taken from 4 different points of view,
Is to be known by 4 synonyms,—
That of the Cosmical Body and the rest.[5]

In short, the undefiled Absolute, the Essence of the Buddha, being considered from 4 points of view, is designated by 4 synonyms. What are these 4 points?—

85. (It is the Cosmical Body, since)
The properties of the Buddha are indivisible (manifesting themselves in all that exists).[6]

---

[1] Dar. 133 a. 5. The Cosmical Body which is completely pure from the outset.

[2] *tathāgata*. Cf. below.

[3] *ārya-satya* = *ḥphags-paḥi-bden-pa*. Dar. 133 a. 6.—The Truth of Extinction (of Phenomenal Existence) representing the Absolute Truth (*paramārtha-satya* = *don-dam-bden-pa*).

[4] This is a very pregnant expression of the idea of the Unique Vehicle (*ekayāna*) and the Unique Nirvāṇa.

[5] The Buddha, the Highest Absolute Truth, and Nirvāṇa.

[6] Dar. 124 a. 2—3. Being the characteristic property of the stream of elements of a living being, the (Absolute as the) Germ is at the same time indivisible (from the Universal Whole).

(It is the Buddha)—

Because the Germ has developped in him into the Absolute.[1]

(It is the Highest Truth), being neither error nor illusion,

(And it is Nirvāṇa), being by nature quiescent from the outset.

With regard to the indivisible properties of the Buddha it has been said:[2]—O Lord, the Essence of the Buddha never becomes devoid of the properties of the Buddha which are indivisible, inexhaustible, inconceivable, and greater in number than the sands of the Ganges.—With reference to the Germ as being in an inconceivable manner derived from the Absolute[3] (and as becoming finally developed into the latter) it is said:—This (Germ) derived from the Absolute, beginningless and transferred from one existence to another,[4] [43 b. 1.] is as if it were a special property of the 6 (internal) bases of cognition.—As concerns the true, undeluding character (of the Cosmical Body) we have:[5]—The Absolute Truth is the real (not-seeming) Nirvāṇa. How that?—Because this Germ of Buddhahood is eternal owing to its perfectly quiescent nature.—With respect to this perfect Quiescence, (Scripture) says:[6]—The Tathāgata, the Arhat, the Perfect Supreme Buddha is, from the outset, merged in Nirvāṇa. He neither becomes originated anew, nor does he disappear.—In correspondence with these 4 points we have respectively 4 synonymous appellations (for the Essence of the Buddha), viz. the Cosmical Body, the Buddha, the Absolute Truth, and Nirvāṇa. It is accordingly said:[7]—1) O Śāriputra, the Essence of the Buddha is a name for the Cosmical Body,—

---

[1] *tathatām prāptam*. Cf. below.

[2] Śri-mālā-siṁhanāda-sūtra. Kg. DKON. VI. 278 b. 5—6.

[3] Cf. Abhis. āloka. MS. 59 a. 3—5. *idaṁ prakṛtisthaṁ gotram anādi-kāla-āyāta-dharmatā-pratilabdham*.

[4] *paraṁparayā* = *brgyud-nas*.

[5] A similar passage is to be found in the Śri-mālā-sūtra. Kg. DKON. VI. 279 a. 6—7.

[6] Jñāna-āloka-alaṁkāra-sutra. Kg. MDO. III. 283 a. 3.

[7] Cf. above.

2)[1] O Lord, it is impossible that the Buddha should be one entity and the Cosmical Body—another. The Cosmical Body, O Lord, is no other but the Buddha.

3)[2] O Lord, the Extinction of Phenomenal Existence is represented as the Cosmical Body of the Buddha endowed with all his properties.

4)[3] O Lord, "the Essence of Nirvāṇa" is a name for the Cosmical Body of the Buddha. [44 a. 1.]

Now, what is said in the second half of verse (83)?

86. The Perfect Supreme Enlightenment,
And the rejection of all defilement with its residues,—
The Buddha and his Nirvāṇa
Are one in the aspect of the Absolute.

The 4 synonymous appellations of the undefiled Absolute are all comprised in the one meaning of the Essence of the Buddha. For this reason, as they have all of them one sense, that which is called Buddhahood on account of the Perfect Supreme Enlightenment with regard to all the elements of existence in all their aspects from the standpoint of the unique Absolute, and that which is called Nirvāṇa owing to the removal of all defilement and its residues[4] which takes place simultaneously with the complete Enlightenment, these 2 are, within the Immaculate Plane, indivisible, inseparable, and identical. So are they to be viewed.

87. The properties complete, innumerable,
Inconceivable and immaculate,
All of which are of an indivisible character, represent Salvation,
And this Salvation is (no other but) the Buddha.

It has been said, with regard to the Nirvāṇa of the Arhats and the Pratyekabuddhas:[5] O Lord, that which is called Nirvāṇa

[1] Śrī-mālā-siṁhanāda-sūtra. Kg. DKON. VI. 274 b. 6—7.

[2] Cf. above. [3] Ibid. 274 b. 5—6.

[4] Cf. Abhis. āloka. MS. 100 b. 4 *nirvānty asmin sarva-vikalpā iti nirvāṇaṁ tathatā.*

[5] Śrī-mālā-siṁhanāda-sūtra. Kg. DKON. VI. 269 b. 2—3.

(of the Hīnayānists) is a means used by the Buddhas. Just as if amidst a wilderness a town were produced by magic (as a resting-place) for travellers tired of a long journey, such is this means used by the Supreme Buddha, the High Lord governing the elements. It prevents a relapse (into Phenomenal Existence). [44 b.] O Lord, the Tathāgatas, the Arhats, the Perfect Supreme Buddhas have attained the (true) Nirvāṇa. Therefore they are possessed of all the complete, the immeasurable, the inconceivable and the perfectly pure properties.— So we have the 4 characteristics of the properties demonstrated. And:—through the attainment of Nirvāṇa which is of a unique indivisible character, one becomes a Buddha. Accordingly, as the Buddha and Nirvāṇa are possessed of properties which are indivisible from each other, there can be no attainment of Nirvāṇa whatever apart from Buddhahood.—

## The Parable of the Painters.

Now the absolute character of the properties of the Buddha is due to the full realization, within the Immaculate Absolute, of the Highest Essence of all relative entities.[1] This is illustrated by the example of the painters:—

88. Suppose there were some painters,
Skilful (in painting) various (parts of the body),
And each of them, knowing his own special member,
Would not be able (to paint) the rest.

89. (Suppose then) a mighty king would bid to them—
On this (cloth) ye all must draw my portrait,—
And hand the cloth to them with this commandment.

---

[1] *rnam-pa-thams-cad-kyi-mchog-daṅ-ldan-paḥi-stoṅ-pa-ñid* = *sarva-ākāra-vara-upeta-śūnyatā.* Acc. to Dar. 135 b. 5—6. it is the Transcendental Wisdom perceiving the universal Relativity and the Absolute forming the background of this Wisdom. It is moreover said (Ibid. 136 b. 1—2) that it represents 1) the true Essence of the Buddha (*buddha-dharmatā*) which is attained on the foundation of the Accumulations of Virtue and Wisdom (*puṇya-jñāna-saṁbhāra*), 2) the Transcendental Wisdom of the Buddha constantly merged in the Absolute and 3) the Transcendental Intuition of the Bodhisattva, whilst abiding on the Path.

And (the painters), having heard (his word),
Would start their work of painting.

90. (Suppose again), of these (painters) engaged in the work,
One should go abroad and, owing to his absence,
Their number being incomplete, the portrait
Could not be accomplished in all its parts. [45 a. 1.]

91. The painters who are meant here
Are Charity, Morals, Patience, and the rest,[1]
And that which is the highest point of excellence,
The essence of all relative entities,—this is the picture.

Now, of (the 6 virtues)—Charity and the rest, each appears in an endless variety of forms in correspondence with the objects of the Buddha's activity, which are infinite. It is therefore to be regarded as illimited. (If we take the properties of the Buddha) from the point of view of number and power, they prove to be inconceivable. As they remove the residues[2] of envy[3] and the other negative counterparts[4] (of the 6 virtues), they represent the highest point of Purity.

Through the contemplation of the Highest Essence of all relative entities, the (steadfastness in regard of the) teaching about the non-origination (of the elements)[5] is attained. On account of this, on the Stage of the Bodhisattva called the Motionless,[6] (one is possessed of the direct knowledge of the Path which is free from (dialectical) construction[7] and from all defilement, and manifests itself uninterruptedly by its own force. On the basis of this knowledge, the complement of the Buddha's properties within the pale of the Immaculate Absolute is attained. On the Stage of the Bodhisattva called That of Perfect

[1] The 6 Transcendental Virtues (*pāramitā*).

*vāsanā* = *bag-chags.*

[3] *mātsarya* = *ser-sna.*

[4] *vipakṣa* = *mi-mthun-phyogs.*

[5] *anutpattika-dharma-kṣānti* = *mi-skye-baḥi-chos-la-bzod-pa.*

[6] *acalā* = *mi-gyo-ba.*

[7] *nirvikalpakā* = *rnam-par-mi-rtog-pa.*

Wisdom,[1] by means of innumerable hundreds and thousands of forms of transic meditation and magic formulas,[2] one (becomes endowed with) the knowledge for assuming all the illimited properties of the Buddha. On the foundation of this kind of knowledge, the Bodhisattva realizes the limitless character of the said properties. On the Stage of the Bodhisattva called the Clouds of the Truth,[3] basing upon the knowledge revealing the secret characteristics of all the Buddhas, (the Bodhisattva) realizes the inconceivable character of the properties, [45 b. 1.] Thereafter, in order to attain the Stage of a Buddha, he takes recourse to the knowledge through which one becomes completely delivered from the Obscurations of Moral Defilement[4] and of Ignorance[5] with their residues, and through this attains the Highest Point of Purity. The Arhats and the Pratyekabuddhas do not possess the intuition of these 4 spiritual foundations of the (highest) stages (of perfection). Therefore they are far from attaining the 4 kinds of properties and the unique indivisible essence of Nirvāṇa.

92. The Analytic Wisdom, the Highest knowledge and the Deliverance (from passion)
Are (respectively) clear, radiant, pure, and indivisible.
Therefore they are similar to the light,
The rays, and the disc of the sun.

The Analytic Wisdom, the Highest Knowledge, and the Deliverance (from all defilement), through which the 4 kinds of properties are attained, and which all characterize the unique indivisible essence of Nirvāṇa, appear as having a resemblance with the sun in 3 and in 1 aspect, respectively, there being altogether 4 points of resemblance. The Transcendental Wisdom free from all dialectical constructions[6]

---

[1] *sādhumatī* = *legs-paḥi-blo-gros.*

[2] *dhāraṇī* = *gzuṅs.* Cf. Sutrālaṁkāra XII. 23 and comment. *samādhi-mukhatā dhāraṇī-mukhatā ca.*

[3] *dharma-meghā* = *chos-kyi-sprin.*

[4] *kleśa-āvaraṇa* = *ñon-moṅs-kyi-sgrib-pa* (= *ñon-sgrib*).

[5] *jñeya-āvaraṇa* = *śes-byaḥi-sgrib-pa* (= *śes-sgrib*).

[6] *nirvikalpaka* = *rnam-par-mi-rtog-pa.*

appears as removing the darkness (that hides) the true absolute essence of everything cognizable; it has accordingly a resemblance with the light of the sun. The Divine Knowledge of all the objects of cognition which is attained subsequently[1] penetrates into all the objects cognizable in all their forms; it is thus akin to the net of (the sun's) rays which is spread (over everything perceptible). The deliverance of the Spiritual Essence which is the foundation of both these (kinds of Wisdom), being completely immaculate and brilliant, [46 a. 1.] bears a likeness with the perfectly pure disc of the sun. All these properties constitute the indivisible essence of the Absolute, therefore they resemble (the light, the rays, and the disc of the sun) in their indivisible character.

93. Therefore, without the attainment of Buddhahood,
The (ultimate)[2] Nirvāṇa cannot be reached,
Just as it is impossible to see the sun
Separated from its light and rays.

The Germ (of the Buddha), the Essence which exists without beginning and is possessed of (the sources of) all the virtuous properties, contains the essence of all the indivisible attributes of the Buddha. Therefore, without the attainment of (the state of) the Buddha who is possessed of the Divine Transcendental Intuition free from attachment and impediments, it is not possible to realize the full intuition of Nirvāṇa, the essence of which is the deliverance from all the Obscurations, just as it is impossible to see the sun without perceiving its rays and light. For this very reason it has been said:[3]—O Lord, the intuition of the (real, the ultimate) Nirvāṇa does not relate neither

---

[1] *pṛṣṭha-labdha = rjes-su-thob-pa.* The Wisdom of a Saint abiding on the Path is of 2 kinds:—1) The Wisdom at the time of intense concentration (*samāhita-jñāna = mñam-bźag-ye-śes*) having for its object the unique Absolute and 2) the Wisdom that is acquired subsequently, after the termination of the trance (*pṛṣṭha-labdha = rjes-thob*), and is directed upon the objects of the Empirical World.

[2] Dar. 139 b. 3. *mya-ṅan-las-ḥdas-pa-mthar-thug-pa.*

[3] Śrī-mālā-siṁhanāda-sūtra. Kg. DKON. VI. 272 b. 1—3.

to the base elements (of the Phenomenal World), nor to the perfection[1] (of Hīnayānistic Nirvāṇa).[2] O Lord, the intuition of the final Nirvāṇa is the attainment of the properties identical with the Highest Wisdom (of the Buddha). The (true) Nirvāṇa is (moreover the attainment of) the properties which are one with Divine Knowledge, with Deliverance and the intuition of the latter.[3] Therefore, O Lord, (as all these properties are indivisible), the Essence of Nirvāṇa is spoken of as unique and of one taste,[4] that is the taste [46 b. 1.] of Wisdom and Salvation.—

## The 9 Examples illustrating the Essence of Buddhahood in the living beings.

94. In such a way, the Essence of the Lord
Is characterized from 10 points of view.[5]
Now, this essence, as concealed by the coverings of defilement,
Is made known by the following examples.—

Thus, in order to make known the Eternal Absolute Essence, identical with the Ultimate Point of Existence, this Germ of the Buddha has been characterized from 10 points of view. Now we shall take into consideration "the coverings of defilement" which, existing without beginning, are essentially unconnected (with the pure Spiritual Essence),[6] and the Absolute Essence which likewise has no beginning, but is perfectly pure and connected (with the spirit of every living being). Here, in accordance with the *(Tathāgata-garbha)-sūtra*, we have the Essence of the Buddha, as it is concealed by the innumerable coverings of defilement, illustrated by 9 examples. What are these nine?

---

[1] *praṇīta* = *gya-nom-pa.*

[2] Sic. acc. to Dar. 140 a. 2.

[3] *vimukti-jñāna-darśana* = *rnam-par-grol-baḥi-ye-śes-mthoṅ-ba.*

[4] *eka-rasa* = *ro-gcig-pa.*

[5] Cf. above.

[6] Dar. 140 b. 1—2. *sems-kyi-raṅ-bźin-la-ma-źugs-par-ma-ḥbrel-paḥi* . . .

94. Like the Buddha in an ugly lotus flower,
Like honey (concealed by) a swarm of bees,
Like a kernel of a fruit in the bark, and like gold buried in impurities,
Like a treasure in the ground, and like a sprout hidden in a small seed,
Like the image of the Lord covered by a tattered garment,

95. Like the Chieftain of men[1] in the womb of a miserable woman,
And like a precious statue covered by dust,
In such a way does this Germ abide
In the living beings obscured by the occasional stains.

96. These stains are like a lotus,[2] like bees,[3]
Like the bark,[4] like impurities,[5] and like the ground,[6]
Like a seed,[7] like a tattered garment[8],
Like a woman tormented by violent pain,[9] and like dust.[10]
The Immaculate Germ has a resemblance
With the Buddha,[11] with honey,[12] with the kernel of a fruit,[13]

---

[1] The Universal Monarch (*cakravarti-rājā*).

[2] The example illustrating Desire (*rāga = ḥdod-chags*). Dar. 141 a. 4—6.

[3] The example illustrating Hatred (*dveṣa = že-sdaṅ*). Ibid. 141 a. 6.

[4] The example illustrating Infatuation (*moha = gti-mug*). Ibid.

[5] The example illustrating the 3 Sources of Evil in a developed state. Ibid. 141 b. 1.

[6] The example illustrating the Force of Transc. Illusion (*avidyā-vāsanā = ma-rig-paḥi-bag-chags*). Ibid. 141 b. 2.

[7] The example illustrating the Obscurations extirpated by Intuition (*dṛṣṭi-heya*). Ibid.

[8] The example illustrating the Obscurations extirpated by Concentration (*bhāvanā-heya*).

[9] The example illustrating the Obscurations on the 1st seven Stages of the Bodhisattva.

[10] The example illustrating the Obscurations on the 3 last Stages.

[11] As the source of the Cosmical Body. Dar. 141 b. 5.

[12] The Word of the Buddha demonstrating the Absolute Truth. Ibid. 141 b. 6.

[13] The Word demonstrating the Empirical Reality. Ibid.

With gold,[1] with a treasure,[2] with the Nyagrodha tree,[3] and a precious image,[4]
With the Highest Lord of the Universe,[5] and with a golden statue.[6] [47 a. 1.]

I. The defiling forces are like the petals of an ugly lotus flower, and the Germ has a resemblance with the Buddha himself.[7]

97. Suppose, in a lotus flower of ugly form,
The Buddha, shining with a thousand marks of beauty, were abiding,
And a man possessed of immaculate divine sight[8] would perceive him
And draw him out from the petals of the water-born lotus;

98. In the same way the Lord perceives with his sight of a Buddha[9]
His own essence even in those that abide in the lowest of hells,[10]
And, endowed with the uttermost Commiseration, free from impediments,
Delivers the living beings from the Obscurations.

99. Just as a person possessed of divine sight
Sees in an ugly lotus flower with folded leaves
The Buddha who abides in its interior,
And rends asunder the petals (in order to release him),
In the same way the Lord perceives the Essence of the Supreme Buddha
Existing in all that lives, but obscured by lust, hatred and other coverings of defilement,
And, full of mercy, vanquishes these Obscurations.

---

[1] The Absolute in its inalterable nature. Ibid. 142 a. 1.

[2] The Germ as the fundamental element of a living being as existing by itself (*prakṛtistha-gotra* = *raṅ-bźin-gnas-rigs*). Ibid. 142 a. 1—2.

[3] The Germ as becoming developed (*samudānīta-gotra*). Ibid.

[4] The Cosmical Body. [5] The Body of Bliss. [6] The Apparitional Body.

[7] Tathāgata-garbha-sūtra. Kg. MDO. XXII. 248 a. 3—249 a. 6.

[8] *divya-cakṣuḥ* = *lhaḥi-mig*. [9] *buddha-cakṣuḥ* = *saṅs-rgyas-kyi-spyan*.

[10] *avīci* = *mnar-med*.

II. The defiling forces are like bees, and the Essence of the Buddha is like honey.[1]

100. Suppose some honey were encircled by a swarm of bees,
And a skilful person, desirous to obtain this honey,
Would perceive it and, by using clever means,
Would separate the honey from the swarm.

101. Similarly, the Greatest of Sages with his vision of Omniscience,
Sees this fundamental Essence, resembling honey,
And brings about the complete removal
Of the Obscurations that are like the bees.

102. A man who is desirous of obtaining honey
Hidden by thousands and millions of bees,
Removes the latter and disposes of the honey as he wishes.
[47 b. 1.] The undefiled Spirit that exists in the living beings is like the honey,
The defiling forces are like the bees,
And the Lord who is skilful in vanquishing them
Is like the man (that obtains the honey).

III. The defiling forces are like the husk of a fruit, and the Germ of the Buddha is like the kernel contained within.[2]

103. The kernel of a fruit covered by a husk
Cannot be enjoyed by any man. Therefore
They who are desirous of eating it and the like
Extract it from the husk (that hides it).

104. In a similar way the (Essence of the) Buddha
Exists in the living beings, mingled with defilement,
And as long as it is not free from the contact with the stains of the passions,
It cannot perform the acts of the Buddha in the 3 Spheres.

---

[1] Tathāgata-garbha-sūtra. Kg. MDO. XXII. 249 a. 6—250 a. 2.

[2] Ibid. 250 a. 2—b. 2.

105. The kernel of a grain of rice, of buckwheat or barley, unextracted from its husk and covered with bristles
And not duly prepared, cannot become sweat food enjoyed by man.
Similar is the Body of the Lord of the elements,
Existing in the living beings and undelivered from the coverings of defilement,
It does not grant to the living beings affected by the passions
The delightful flavour of the Truth.

IV. The defiling forces are like a place filled with impurities, and the Germ of the Buddha has a resemblance with gold.[1]

106. Suppose that the gold belonging to a certain man
Were, at the time of his departure, cast into a place filled with impurities.
Being of an indestructible nature, this gold
Would remain there for many hundreds of years.

107. Then a god possessed of pure divine vision
Would see it there and say to men:—
The gold which is to be found here, this highest of precious things,
I shall purify and return to it its precious form. [48 a. 1.]

108. In a like way the Lord perceives the true virtues of the living beings
Sunk amidst the passions that are like impurities,
And, in order to wash off this dirt of Desire,
Lets the rain of the Highest Doctrine descend on all that lives.

109. Just as a god, seeing gold falling into a pit of impurities,
Would zealously show it to men in its beautiful nature in order to gladden them,
In a like way the Lord sees in the living beings

[1] Tathāgata-garbha-sūtra. Kg. MDO. XXII. 250 b. 2—251 a. 3.

The jewel of the Supreme Buddha fallen amidst the great impurities of the passions,
And shows the Doctrine in order to purify it.

V. The defiling forces are like the depths of the earth, and the Germ of the Buddha is like a treasure of jewels.[1]

110. Suppose in a poor man's house, deep under the ground,
An inexhaustible treasure were concealed.
The man would know nothing about it,
And the treasure itself could not say to him
That it is to be found here in this place.

111. Similar to this is the treasure contained in the Spirit,
The Immaculate Essence which neither diminishes nor increases;
The living beings that know nothing about it
Constantly experience manifold suffering that is like poverty.

112. As a treasure of jewels concealed in a poor man's house
Does not make it known to that man,—
I, the treasure am here,—and the man does not know about it,—
Such is the treasure of the Highest Truth abiding in the dwelling-place of the Spirit,
And the living beings possessed of it are like beggars;
In order to secure for them this treasure
The Sage makes his apparition in this world.

VI. The defiling forces are the rind of a seed, and the Essence of the Buddha is like the germ contained within.[2] [48 b. 1.]

113. The germ of a seed, contained in the fruit
Of the Mango-tree and the like, is of an imperishable nature,
And through cultivation of the ground, water and other (agencies),
Gradually attains the form of a lordly tree.

114. In a like way the Sublime Absolute Essence
Is concealed under the coverings of the fruit

---

[1] Tathāgāta-garbha-sūtra. Kg. MDO. XXII. 251 a. 3—252 a. 1.

[2] Ibid. Kg. MDO. XXII. 252 a. 1—252 b. 3.

Of a living being's ignorance and the like,
(But) on the foundation of this and that form of virtue,
It gradually assumes the character of the King of Sages.

115. Conditioned by water, the light of the sun,
By air, soil, time, and space,
From the rind of the Mango's and Palmyra's fruit
There springs forth a tree;
Like that the Germ of the seed of the Buddha,
Concealed in the peal of the fruit of a living being's passions,
Can thrive when the Highest Truth is revealed by this and that condition.

VII. The defiling forces are like a tattered garment, and the Germ of the Buddha is like a precious image.[1]

116. Suppose the image of the Lord made of precious jewels
Were covered by a tattered foul-smelling garment,
And a god travelling that way would see it
And, in order to free it (from that covering),
Would explain the meaning of its abiding on the path
To the people that are met with there.

117. In a like way the Buddha perceives his own Essence
As it exists even in animals,
Covered by the various forms of defilement which are beginningless,
And, in order to release it, shows the means (of deliverance).

118. As the precious image of the Buddha covered by a foul-smelling garment
Is seen by a god with divine vision who shows it to men in order to release it,
In the same way the Lord perceives, even in the beasts,
The Germ covered by the tattered garment of defilement

---

[1] Tathāgata-garbha-sūtra. 252 b. 3—253 b. 1.

And abiding on the path of worldly existence,—
And expounds his Doctrine in order to deliver it.

VIII. [49 a. 1.] The defiling forces are like a pregnant woman, and the Germ of the Buddha is like a Universal Monarch abiding in an embryonal state.[1]

119. Suppose a woman of miserable appearance and helpless
Were abiding in a place without shelter and protection,
And, bearing in her womb the glory of royalty,
Would not know that the Lord (who could protect her) were in her own body.

120. The birth in this world is like the house without shelter,
And the impure living beings are like that pregnant woman;
The Immaculate Germ through which one is protected
Is like (the king) abiding in the womb.

121. As a woman of ugly appearance, covered with a foul-smelling garment
Experiences the greatest suffering in a place without shelter,
Though the Lord of the Earth abides in her own womb;
In a like way the living beings whose spirit is helpless,
Though the protection exists within themselves,
Abide amidst sufferings, their minds being troubled by the passions.

IX. The defiling forces are like a covering of mud and dust, and the Germ of the Buddha is like a golden statue.[2]

122. Suppose a great statue of melted gold from within,
And from without covered by mud and dust that hides (the gold),
Were seen by some, who, knowing its nature,
Would remove the outward cover in order to purify the gold within;

[1] Tathāgata-garbha-sūtra. Kg. MDO. XXII. 253 b. 1—254 a. 5.

[2] Ibid. 254 a. 5—255 a. 4

123. In a like way the Buddha perceives
That the Essence[1] is pure and radiant and that the stains,
Are only occasional (and not real),
And leads (the living beings) to Supreme Enlightenment
Which purifies from all the Obscurations
The living beings resembling jewel-mines.

124. Just as a statue wrought of pure, shining gold and covered by earth [49 b. 1.]
Is seen by one who, knowing its true nature, removes the earth,—
In the same way the Omniscient perceives
The quiescent Spirit which is like gold,
And, by teaching the Doctrine, produces a cisel
Through which he removes all the Obscurations.
The meaning of all these examples is in short as follows:—

125. Within a lotus, amidst a swarm of bees,
Within the husk of a fruit, impurities, and the ground,
Within a seed, within a tattered garment,
The womb of a woman, and the covering of earth, respectively,

126. Like the Buddha, like honey, like the kernel of a fruit,
Like gold, like a treasure, and like a tree,
Like a precious image, like the sovereign
Of the Universe, and like a golden statue,—

127. The Immaculate Essence of the Spirit in the living beings
Is unaffected by the coverings of defilement;
As such it exists eternally,
Being spoken of as having no beginning.

In short, these examples given in the *Tathāgata-garbha-sūtra* illustrate the fact that all the defiling forces are accidental in every living being containing the element of Buddhahood which is the beginningless spiritual element. They are also an indication that all the purifying forces are innate and inseparable from the beginningless

[1] Of the living beings. Dar. 148 a. 2.

spiritual element. Therefore it is said:—Owing to the Desires, &c., the living beings are affected by defilement, and, owing to the undefiled Essence of the Spirit, they become purified.—

## The Varieties of the Defiling Elements illustrated by the 9 Examples.

128. Passion, hatred, infatuation,
Their outburst in a violent form,
The force of Transcendental Illusion,[1]
The defilement that is extirpated by intuition,[2]
And that removed by transic meditation,[3]
[50 a. 1.] The stains relating to the impure,[4]
And to the pure[5] Stages (of the Bodhisattva).

129. These 9 forms (of defilement) are illustrated
By the example of the petals of the lotus and the rest;
But all the coverings of defilement
In their variety extend beyond millions and millions.

In short 9 forms of defilement are, with regard to the element of Buddhahood, perfectly pure by nature, of an accidental character. They are thus like the coverings of the lotus with respect to the form of the Buddha (contained within) and the like. Now, what are these 9 forms? Answer: 1) The defilement consisting in the dormant residue[6] of Passion, 2) the defilement which has its essence in the dormant residue of Hatred, 3) the defilement which represents the dormant residue of Infatuation, 4) the violent outburst of all the three, 5) the defilement contained in the Force of Transcendental Illusion, 6) the defilement that is to be extirpated by means of

---

[1] *vāsanā* = *bag-chags* stands here for *avidyā-vāsanā* (Dar. 145 a. 5).

[2] *dṛṣṭi-heya* = *mthoṅ-spaṅ.*

[3] *bhāvanā-heya* = *sgom-spaṅ;* lit. — that which is to be removed on the Paths of Illumination and Concentrated Trance.

[4] The first 7 Stages beginning with *pramuditā* and ending with *dūraṅgamā.*

[5] The 3 last Stages — *acalā, sādhumatī,* and *dharma-meghā.*

[6] *anuśaya* = *bag-la-ñal.*

direct intuition, 7) that which is to be removed by concentrated trance, 8) the defiling elements peculiar to the impure, and 9) those relating to the pure Stages (of the Bodhisattva). Now, first of all we have the defilement which is contained in the stream of elements of one who is free from worldly passion. It is the cause of the forces[1] producing a motionless state of existence in the Ethereal[2] and the Immaterial[3] Spheres, and is to be extirpated by means of Transcendental Knowledge.[4] This defilement represents the dormant residues of Passion, Hatred and Infatuation. Then we have the defiling forces which exist in the living beings that indulge in passion and the like. They are the cause of virtuous and sinful deeds, &c., produce an existence only in the world of Carnal Desire,[5] [50 b. 1.] and are to be overcome by the Contemplation of Impurity[6] (of the objects of Desire, &c.). These represent a violent outburst of Passion, Hatred and Infatuation. Next come the defiling elements which are to be found with the Arhat. These are the cause for the manifestation of the undefiled Biotic Force,[7] produce the non-physical existence[8] (of the Arhat), and are to be removed by the Transcendental Wisdom, the Supreme Enlightenment of the Buddha. The said defiling elements are those which are included in the Force of Transcendental Illusion.

The individuals that undergo training (on the Path)[9] are of 2 kinds, viz. the ordinary beings[10] and the Saints.[11] Now, the defilement which exists in the stream of elements[12] of an ordinary being abiding on the Path and which is to be suppressed by the

---

[1] *saṁskāra* = *ḥdu-byed.*

[2] *rūpa-dhātu* = *gzugs-khams.*

[3] *ārūpya-dhātu* = *gzugs-med-khams.*

[4] *lokottara-jñāna* = *ḥjig-rten-las-ḥdas-paḥi-ye-śes.*

[5] *kāma-dhātu* = *ḥdod-khams.*

[6] *aśubha-bhāvanā* = *mi-sdug-paḥi-sgom-pa.*

[7] *anāsrava-karma* = *zag-pa-med-paḥi-las.*

[8] *manomaya-kāya* = *yid-kyi-raṅ-bźin-gyi-lus.*

[9] *śaikṣa* = *slob-pa.*

[10] *pṛthagjana* = *so-soḥi-skye-bo.*

[11] *ārya* = *ḥphags-pa.*

[12] *saṁtāna* = *rgyud.*

first intuitive Transcendental Perception of the Truth is said to be "extinct through the intuition of the Truth." (The defiling forces) which exist in the saintly individual on the Path and are to be extirpated through transic meditation over the perceived Transcendental Truth are said to be "removed by means of Concentrated Meditation."

(Thereafter we have) that defilement which is to be found with the Bodhisattva who has not attained the uttermost limits of perfection. It consists of the hostile elements[1] on the first 7 Stages of (the Bodhisattva's) intuition, and is to be suppressed by the transic meditation on the 3 (last) Stages, beginning with the eighth. We call this "the defilement relating to the impure Stages." (Finally, there are the Obscurations) that exist with the Bodhisattva who *has* attained the uttermost limits of perfection. These are the impediments to the Transcendental Intuition on the 3 last Stages beginning with the eighth, and are to be removed by means of the transic meditation called "the Diamond-cutter."[2] We call these defiling forces "those relating to the pure Stages."

130. These 9 forms of defilement, Passion and the rest, [51 a. 1.]
Being taken in short, respectively,
Are illustrated by 9 examples,—
That of the coverings of a lotus and the rest.

It is said that the Essence of the Buddha is concealed under the coverings of defilement of which there are innumerable millions. To speak in detail (these innumerable defiling elements) which are classified into 84,000 groups, are as infinite as the knowledge of the Buddha (which cognizes them).

131. The ordinary beings, the Arhats,
Those undergoing training, and the Sages[3]
Are rendered impure by four, by one, by two,
And again two forms of these defiling forces (respectively).

---

[1] *vipakṣa* = *mi-mthun-phyogs.*

[2] *vajropamā-samādhi* = *rdo-rje-lta-bu-hi-tiṅ-ṅe-ḥdzin.*

[3] The Bodhisattvas.

The Lord has declared:—All the living beings are endowed with the Essence of the Buddha.—Here the living beings, in short, are presented in four varieties, viz. the ordinary beings, the Arhats, the individuals undergoing training (on the Path), and the Bodhisattvas (on the 10 Stages). These, taken respectively, are spoken of as rendered impure by four, by one, by two, and again two forms of defilement, owing to which they cannot become for ever merged in the immaculate Absolute Essence.[1]

## The Concordance between the Examples illustrating the Obscurations and the Points expressed by them.

Now, what do we know to be the points of resemblance between the 9 forms of defilement and the petals of the lotus, &c. Likewise, what similarity is there between the Element of Buddhahood and the form of the Buddha (abiding in the lotus) and the other (examples illustrating it)?

132. The water-born lotus flower
At the first appearance causes delight,
But later on (when it withers) it no more excites joy,
Similar to it is the delight of sensual passion.

133. Just as the bees, [51 b. 1.]
Being disturbed, sting painfully,
In a like way hatred, being aroused,
Produces suffering of the heart.

134. As the kernel of a fruit and the like
Is concealed by the outward peal,
In a like way the perception of the Truth which is essential
Is hindered by the covering of ignorance.

135. Just as impurities are something repulsive,
In a like way with those that are possessed of desire,
The outburst of their passions, being the cause
For giving way to the desires, is abhorrent like impurities.

---

[1] *anāsrava-dhātu* = *zag-pa-med-paḥi-dbyiṅs.* Sic. acc. to Dar. 154 a. 5—6.

136. As riches, being hidden in the ground,
Are not known of and cannot be obtained,
Similarly, in the living beings, the self-sprung (essence)
Is obscured by the elementary force of illusion.

137. As a sprout and the like, growing gradually,
Rend asunder the peal of the seed,
In the same way, the perception of the Truth
Removes all those forms of defilement
That are to be extirpated by direct intuition.

138. The Obscurations which are to be removed
By the Wisdom on the Path of Concentrated Trance
Of those who, acting on the Path of a Saint,
Have done away with the views of a real personality,—
Are shown as resembling a tattered garment.

139. The stains relating to the first 7 Stages
Are like the impurities in the interior of a womb,
And the non-dialectical wisdom[1] resembles the mature form
Delivered from the coverings of the womb.

140. The stains connected with the last 3 Stages
Are known as being like the covering of muddy ground.
They are to be suppressed by the concentrated trance
Called "the diamond-cutter" which is of most sublime nature.

141. Thus the 9 forms of defilement, passion and the rest
Have a resemblance with a lotus flower and the other forms.
And the Essence of the Buddha, which of is threefold nature,[2]
Bears a similarity with the Buddha, &c.

If we take into consideration the Essence of the Buddha, the perfectly pure spiritual element in its threefold nature [52 a. 1.], we

---

[1] *nirvikalpaka-jñāna.* Dar. 155 a. 6. The Wisdom of him who has attained the 8th Stage.

[2] As the source of the Cosmical Body, as the Absolute, and as the element of Buddhahood in a living being. Kār. 27.

shall find a resemblance with the 9 examples mentioned, the form of the Buddha and the rest. Now, what is the threefold nature?

142. Its nature is that of the Cosmical Body,
Of the Absolute, and the lineage[1] of the Buddha;
These are to be known by three,
By one, and by five examples (respectively).

The (first) 3 examples, those of the form of the Buddha, honey, and the kernel of a grain, make known the element of Buddhahood in its nature of (being identical with) the Cosmical Body. Then one example, that of gold, illustrates the nature of the (inalterable) Absolute. Finally, the (last) 5 examples, those of the treasure, the tree, the precious image, the universal monarch, and the golden statue, show (the Essence of the Buddha) in its character of the source from which the 3 Bodies of the Buddha take their origin.

Now, of what nature is the Cosmical Body?

143. The Cosmical Body is to be known in 2 aspects:—
It is the Absolute perfectly immaculate,
And its natural outflow, the Word[2]
Which speaks of the profound (Highest Truth)[3]
And (of the elements of the Empirical World) in their variety.[4]

The Cosmical Body of the Buddha appears in 2 forms. It is (first of all) the perfectly pure Absolute accessible only to the non-dialectical[5] intuition. As such it is to be known in its character of the Absolute Truth revealed to the Buddhas by introspection. The cause bringing about the attainment of it is (the Word which is) the

---

[1] *gotra* = *rigs.*

[2] Dar. 156 a. 6.—The Word which is the natural outflow (*niṣyanda-phala* = *rgyu-mthun-paḥi-ḥbras-bu*) of the direct introspection of the Absolute by the Buddha.

[3] Ibid. The discourses of direct meaning (*nītārtha* = *ṅes-don*) demonstrating the profound Absolute Truth.

[4] Ibid. The discourses of conventional meaning (*neyārtha* = *draṅ-don*) demonstrating in a variety of forms the Empirical Reality, the individual, and the component elements.

[5] *nirvikalpaka* = *rnam-par-mi-rtog-pa.*

natural outflow of (the intuition of) this very Absolute. (This Word) instructs the living beings in accordance with the character of (every) convert taken separately. Such do we know to be (the Cosmical Body) in the aspect of the Doctrine, the Teaching (of the Buddha).[1]

Now, this Teaching is of 2 kinds inasmuch as there is a difference in the exposition of the Truth, viz. the subtle, and the extensive. There are the following (varieties):—[52 b. 1.] 1) The Code of the Bodhisattvas[2] which teaches the profound Doctrine referring to the Absolute Truth, and 2) the exposition of various teachings in many different forms (of style), as the Aphorisms,[3] the Sing-song,[4] the Prophecies,[5] the Verses,[6] the Solemn Utterances,[7] the Introductions,[8] &c.

144. (The Cosmical Body) is of unworldly nature,
And in this world there is absolutely nothing
With which it can be compared.
Therefore it can be shown only in its similarity
With the (corporeal form of) the Buddha himself.

145. The Teaching of the profound and subtle Doctrine
Is like honey that has only one taste,[9]
And the other, Empirical, Teachings, in their various forms,
Are like the interior (of different grains)
Covered by various kinds of peel.

Thus, these 3 examples,—of the form of the Buddha, of honey, and the interior (of a grain), refer to the Cosmical Body of the Buddha as it pervades all the living beings without exception, since it is said:—All the sentient beings are possessed of the Essence of the Buddha.—Indeed, among the categories of living beings, there exists absolutely none standing apart from the Cosmical Body

---

[1] *deśanā-dharma* = *bstan-paḥi-chos.*

[2] *bodhisattva-piṭaka* = *byaṅ-chub-sems-dpaḥi-sde-snod*, **i.e. the Mahāyānistic Doctrine as a whole.**

[3] *sūtra* = *mdo-sde.*

[4] *geya* = *dbyaṅs-kyis-bsñad-pa.*

[5] *vyākaraṇa* = *luṅ-du-bstan-pa.*

[6] *gāthā* = *tshigs-su-bcad-pa.*

[7] *udāna* = *ched-du-brjod-pa.*

[8] *nidāna* = *gleṅ-gźi.*

[9] *eka-rasa* = *ro-gcig-pa.*

of the Buddha, (not pervaded by it). (This Cosmical Body) has accordingly a resemblance with space that fills up all physical forms.[1] It is said:[2]—

As space is considered to be always all-embracing,
In a like way it[3] is held to be all-pervading for ever and anon.
Just as space fills up all visible forms,
Similarly it pervades all the multitudes of living beings.

146. Being by nature inalterable,
Sublime, and perfectly pure, [53 a. 1.]
This Absolute is spoken of
As having a resemblance with gold.

That which represents the spiritual element is, notwithstanding, its contact with innumerable forms of defilement and the miseries (of Phenomenal Existence), perfectly pure and radiant by nature. Therefore it cannot be spoken of as being alterable and, for this very reason, since it is unchangeable like fine gold, it is called the Absolute,[4] the true Essence (of existence). This (Absolute) exists without any difference even in all those living beings who are possessed of the factors for becoming definitely rooted in error. But, (every time) when it attains the full purification from all the accidental defiling forces, (he in whom this has taken place) is called "the Buddha."[5] Therefore, with regard to the indivisible character of the Absolute, we have the comparison with gold which illustrates the fact that the Absolute Essence of the Buddha is (at the same time) the fundamental element of the living beings. Having in view this unique, perfectly pure Absolute Essence which is of spiritual nature, the Lord has said:[6]—O Mañjuśrī, the Buddha has a direct knowledge of the root, the foundation of all the ego-centristic

---

[1] Dar. 157 b. 1. Like space in the interior of a vessel, &c.

[2] Sūtrālaṁkāra IX. 15. *yathāmbaraṁ sarvagataṁ sadā matam*, &c.

[3] The Essence of the Buddha. [4] *tathatā = de-bźin-ñid.* [5] *tathāgata.*

[6] In the Jñāna-āloka-alaṁkāra-sūtra. Kg. MDO. III. 297 a. 5—6.

properties.[1] Through this (knowledge) he protects (the living beings) from egoistic views. As the true Unique Essence has become perfectly pure (in him), he cognizes the perfectly pure essence of the living beings (identical with his own). That which represents the pure Unique Essence and that which is the pure element of Buddhahood in the living beings are the same thing; they cannot be separated from each other. It is moreover said:[2]—

The Absolute, though unique with all,
Is, every time that it becomes purified, [53 b. 1.]
No other but Buddhahood; therefore
All the living beings are endowed with the element of the Buddha.

147. Being like a treasure and like (the germ of) a tree in a seed,
The source (of Buddhahood) is known to be of 2 kinds,—
The Fundamental[3] that exists without beginning,
And that which undergoes the highest process of development.[4]

148. From these 2 forms of the source of Buddhahood
The 3 Bodies of the Buddha take their origin,
From the first arises the first of the Bodies,[5]
And from the second,—the latter two.

149. The Body of Absolute Existence[6]
Is like a beautiful, precious image,
Since, by nature, it is not wrought (by human hands)
And is the treasury of all the virtuous properties.

150. The Body of Supreme Bliss[7] is like a universal monarch,
Being endowed with the sovereignty over the Grand Doctrine,[8]

---

[1] *upādāna = ñe-bar-len-pa.*

[2] Sūtrālaṁkāra IX. 37. *sarveṣām aviśiṣṭā'pi tathatā śuddhim āgatā | tathāgatatvaṁ tasmāc ca tadgarbhāḥ sarvadehinaḥ.*

[3] *prakṛtistha-gotra = raṅ-bźin-gnas-rigs.*

[4] *samudānīta-gotra = yaṅ-dag-par-blaṅs-paḥi-rigs.*

[5] The Cosmical Body. [6] *svabhāva-kāya = ṅo-bo-ñid-sku.*

[7] *saṁbhoga-kāya = loṅs-sku.*

[8] Cf. Abhisamayālaṁkāra VIII. 12.—*sāṁbhogiko mataḥ kāyo mahāyānopabhogataḥ.*

And the Apparitional Form[1] is like a golden statue,
As it has the nature of being an image.

Therefore, these 5 remaining examples,—of a treasure, a tree, a precious image, the universal monarch, and the golden statue, refer to the source that gives rise to the 3 Bodies of the Buddha, as it exists (in all living beings). They illustrate the fact that (from this point of view likewise) the element of Buddhahood is the fundamental element of all the living beings.[2] Now, Buddhahood manifests itself in the 3 Bodies of the Buddha. Therefore, the source of Buddhahood in its 2 forms is the cause for the attainment (of these 3 Bodies). The word *dhātu* (element or essence) has here accordingly the special meaning of "a cause." It is accordingly said:—In every living being there exists the Essence of the Buddha as the element owing to which (the properties of the Buddha) are attained, but the living beings do not know about it. We have it, moreover, as follows:[3]—

The Essence that has no beginning
Is the foundation of all the elements,
Owing to its existence, all the Phenomenal Life,
And Nirvāṇa, likewise, is made manifest [54 a. 1.]

Now, how is it that there is no beginning?—It has been said and ascertained:—An initial limit is not to be perceived (with the Absolute Essence). This "Essence" is spoken of as follows:[4]—O Lord, that which is the Essence of the Buddha is likewise the Essence of all the supermundane and perfectly pure elements.—As concerns "the foundation of all the elements" it is said:[5]—O Lord, for this reason the Essence of the Buddha is the foundation, the support, and the

---

[1] *nirmāṇa-kāya* = *sprul-sku.*

[2] Dar. 160 a. 2—3.—The word *dhātu* has the sense of a cause, the essence, and an element. The *dhātu* of Buddhahood is to be understood in the sense of a cause.

[3] Dar. 160 a. 6. Chos-mṅon-paḥi-mdo-las—in the Abhidharma-sūtra.

[4] In the Śrī-mālā-sūtra. Kg. DKON. VI. 281 b. 6—8.

[5] Ibid. 281 a. 6—8.

substratum of the immutable[1] elements which are united (in one motionless whole), indivisible, and inseparable. (At the same time), O Lord, this very Essence of the Buddha is the foundation, the substratum, and the support of the elements that are produced by causes and conditions,[2] which are disunited (in their plurality), are differentiated and separated from each other. "All the Phenomenal Life" is spoken of as follows:[3]—O Lord, as the Essence of the Buddha exists, one can conventionally call it "The Phenomenal World."—"And Nirvāṇa is made manifest."—Here we have:[4]—O Lord, if the Essence of the Buddha did not exist, there would be no aversion to Phenomenal Existence, and there would be no desire, no effort, and no will of attaining Nirvāṇa.

This Essence of the Buddha is great and extensive like the Cosmical Body, and is by its very nature identical with the Buddha [54 b. 1.]. It has the character of the fundamental element which invariably exists in all the living beings, and is to be viewed in such an aspect, its measure being its own essential nature (i.e. the Absolute). It is said:[5]—O noble youth, such is the true essence of the elements.—May the Buddhas appear in this world, or may they not,[6] all the living beings are possessed of the Essence of Buddhahood.—That which represents the true essence of the elements acts here as the argument, the mode of proof, and the means (of cognition), since such is the state of things and there is no other. In every case, for the accurate investigation of the spiritual element and a correct knowledge about it, the Absolute Essence must be resorted to, and represents a logical foundation. This Essence itself is not accessible to discursive thought and to investigation. It can only be the object of faith.

---

[1] *asaṁskṛta* = *ḥdus-ma-byas.*

[2] *saṁskṛta* = *ḥdus-byas.*

[3] In the Śrī-mālā-sūtra. Kg. DKON. VI. 281 a. 1—2.

[4] Ibid. 281 a. 8—b. 1.

[5] Tathāgata-garbha-sūtra. Kg. MDO. XX. 248 b. 6.

[6] *utpāde vā tathāgatānām anutpāde va.*

151. The Absolute Essence of the Buddhas
Can be cognized only by faith.
The blazing disk of the sun
Cannot be seen by those who have no eyes.

In short, four kinds of individuals are characterized as not being possessed of the faculty of vision perceiving the Essence of the Buddha. Who are these four?—The ordinary worldly beings, the Śrāvakas, the Pratyekabuddhas, and the Bodhisattvas who have recently entered the Vehicle. It is accordingly said:[1]—O Lord, this Essence of the Buddha is not accessible to those who have fallen into the error of maintaining the existence of real individuals, to those who have a false conception (of the Absolute Truth), and those whose mind deviates from the principle of Relativity[2] [55 a. 1.].—Here "those who are fallen into the error of maintaining the existence of real individuals" are the ordinary worldly beings. Indeed, the latter admit that the elements influenced by defilement,[3] the (5) groups and the rest, constitute a real Ego and belong to it. They thus cling to the conception of "Ego" and "Mine", and, owing to this conception, cannot have any faith in the immaculate Absolute Essence which represents a negation of the principle of separate individuality. Therefore, they cannot cognize the Essence of the Buddha which is accessible only to the Omniscient. "Those who indulge in a misconception (of the Absolute Truth)" are the Śrāvakas and the Pratyekabuddhas. How that?—Answer:—These (the Hīnayānists), instead of repeatedly meditating upon the idea of Eternity with regard to the Essence of the Buddha which must be contemplated as eternal, indulge in the contemplation of the evanescence (of the separate elements). Further on, instead of repeatedly meditating upon the idea of bliss with respect to the Essence of the Buddha which is the Supreme Bliss, they find pleasure in concentrating

---

[1] In the Śrī-mālā-sūtra. Kg. DKON. VI. 281 b. 5—6.

[2] *śūnyatā* = *stoṅ-pa-ñid*. Cf. below.

[3] *sāsrava* = *zag-bcas*.

their mind upon the idea of the suffering (of Phenomenal Life). Being far from the concentration upon the idea of the Unity (of the Universe),—the Essence of the Buddha having to be contemplated as this Unity,—they take delight in meditating upon the idea of the absence of a unity, (the impersonality) of the elements. And, averse to the concentration upon the idea of Absolute Purity with regard to the Essence of the Buddha which is to be contemplated as such [55 b. 1.], they find satisfaction in fixing their mind upon the impurity (of the Phenomenal World).

## Reference to the Mahāparinirvāṇa-sūtra.

Thus, in such a form, we have it stated that the Essence which is characterized as the Absolute Eternity, Bliss, Unity, and Purity, is not accessible to any of the Śrāvakas and Pratyekabuddhas, since they find pleasure in (venturing on) the Path that is not favourable to the attainment of the Cosmical Body. This fact, that (the Absolute) cannot be the object of those who indulge in false views and cling to the conception of Evanescence, Suffering, Impersonality, and Impurity,—is discussed in detail in the *Mahāparinirvāṇa-sūtra*[1] where the Lord makes it clear by the comparison with a stone of lapis lazuli in a pond. The passage runs as follows:—O brethren, suppose, in the hot season, the people, having washed and tied up their garments, begin to play in the water with their ornaments and objects of pastime. Suppose then, someone would cast into the water a valuable stone of lapis lazuli, and then, in order to get that stone, they all would leave their ornaments and begin to search for it. They would consider the pebbles and the gravel in the pond to be precious stones, seize them and draw them out, thinking:—I have got a precious stone.— Having thus extracted (the pebbles) they would look at them on the bank of the pond and become convinced that they are not precious stones. (The mistake would be caused) by the water of the pond, which, owing to the efficiency of the real stone would appear as

[1] Tib. Yoṅs-su-mya-ṅan-las-ḥdas-pa-chen-poḥi-mdo.

similar to it in its shine and colour. Therefore, the person thinking: Oh, this is a precious stone,—when it is really only the water (that is so coloured), will be possessed of the idea of the quality (of the stone transferred to the water). Thereafter one who is experienced [56 a. 1.] and attentive would really get hold of the stone. O brethren, in a similar manner, ye who are ignorant of the true essence of the elements, which is like a precious jewel, maintain that all things are evanescent, that there is only suffering, and that everything is impersonal and impure. Ye all meditate upon (this idea) and, contemplating it repeatedly, many times, fix (your mind upon it). In reality, all this is of no use. Therefore, O brethren, ye must become experienced (in order that these ideas) should not become for you like the pebbles and the gravel of that pond. O brethren, with those elements which ye maintain to be all of them evanescent, suffering, impersonal, and impure, and repeatedly contemplate as such, there exists (an essence which represents) Eternity, Bliss, Purity, and Unity.—Such is in detail the passage referring to the true Supreme Essence of the elements and showing the incorrectness (of clinging to the conception of evanescence, &c.), as we have it in Scripture.

## The true Conception of Relativity and Non-substantiality.

Now, "the individuals whose mind deviates from the true principle of Relativity" are the Bodhisattvas who have recently entered the Vehicle and who are deprived of (the cognition of) the Essence of the Buddha in the aspect of Universal Relativity. There are those who say that the subsequent annihilation, the destruction of elements which did really exist, represents Nirvāṇa. They thus understand "the Medium of Liberation of Non-substantiality"[1] as the destruction of real entities[2] [56 b. 1.]. Then there are such who say that the Non-substantiality[3] that is to be cognized and contem-

[1] *śūnyatā-vimokṣa-mukha* = *stoṅ-pa-ñid-kyi-rnam-thar-gyi-sgo.*

[2] Acc. to Dar. 164 a. 6. the Bodhisattvas who have not abandoned Hīnayānistic views.

[3] *śūnyatā* = *stoṅ-pa-ñid.*

plated, is some separate reality, differing from Matter and the other (elements). They thus, in their contemplation of Non-substantiality, cling to it as an absolute principle.[1] Now, what is the Essence of the Buddha, as it presents itself in the aspect of Relativity, (the true meaning of Non-substantiality).

152. Here there is nothing that is to be rejected,
And absolutely nothing to be added;
The Truth must only be directly perceived,
And he who sees the Truth becomes delivered.[2]

153. The element of Buddhahood is by nature devoid
Of the accidental (defiling forces), which are different from it,
But it is by no means devoid of the highest properties,
Which are, essentially, indivisible from it.

What is said by this?—There exists absolutely no real defiling element that is to be removed from the Essence of the Buddha, since it is from the outset devoid of all the accidental defilement, this being its nature. There exists likewise not the least purifying element that could be added to it, because it is itself the true essence of all the perfectly pure properties which are indivisible. Therefore it is said that the Essence of the Buddha is devoid of all the coverings of defilement which can be separated (from the spiritual element)[3] and stand apart from it, and that on the other hand it is not devoid of the properties of the Buddha, which are indivisible, inseparable, inconceivable, and greater in number than the sands of the Ganges. We know that an object is "devoid"[4] of something, if this does not exist with it [57 a. 1.], and that if something is added to it, it must always exist. These 2 verses demonstrate the essence of the

---

[1] Dar. 164 b. 1.—the Yogācāras.

[2] This verse is exactly the same as in the Abhisamayālaṁkāra (V, 21).
*nā'paneyam ataḥ kiṁcit prakṣeptavyaṁ na kiṁ ca na*
*draṣṭavyaṁ bhūtato bhūtaṁ bhūta-darśī vimucyate.*

[3] Dar. 166 b. 6. *sems-kyi-raṅ-bźin-las-rnam-par-dbye-ba-yod-pa ḥbral-bar ṅes-par-ḥbral-śes-pa.*

[4] *śūnya = stoṅ-pa.*

true Relativity, free from the extremities of imputed Realism and Nihilism.[1] Now, (the individuals) whose mind turns away from this principle, is distracted and not-concentrated upon it, we call "those that deviate from the principle of Relativity." Now, without the transcendental knowledge of the Relativity of the Ultimate Reality[2] it is impossible to intuit and realize the non-dialectical[3] Absolute. With regard to this subject it has been said:—The Transcendental Wisdom cognizing the Essence of the Buddha is the knowledge about the Relativity of the Buddhas. This essence of the Lord cannot be perceived and cognized by the Hīnayānists. As the Essence of the Buddha is the Essence of the Cosmical Body, it is spoken of as not being accessible to those who have fallen into the conception of a real individuality.[4] Indeed, (the intuition of) the unique Absolute is an antidote against such erroneous views. As the Cosmical Body represents the Transcendental Essence (of the Universe), it cannot be the object of those who indulge in a wrong view (regarding the Absolute Truth), since the Cosmical Body in its transcendental nature is put forth as the antidote of all the worldly properties as evanescence and the rest [57 b. 1.]. Then it is said that, as the Cosmical Body is the essence of all the purified elements,[5] it is not accessible to those whose mind deviates from the true principle of Relativity. Indeed, owing to their perfectly pure nature, the properties which are indivisible and characterize the Transcendental Cosmical Body are by their nature devoid of all the accidental defiling elements. Through the cognition of the unique spiritual medium which is inseparable from the Absolute in the aspect of monism, the perception of the Transcendental Cosmical Body, perfectly pure by nature, is

---

[1] *samāropa* = *sgro-ḥdogs* and *apavāda* = *skur-ḥdebs*. Cf. Abhisamayālaṁkāra IV. 52—*samāropāpavādānta-muktatā sā gabhīratā*.

[2] *paramārtha-śūnyatā* = *don-dam-pa-stoṅ-pa-ñid*.

[3] *nirvikalpaka* = *rnam-par-rtog-pa-med-pa*.

[4] *satkāya-dṛṣṭi* = *ḥjig-tshogs-kyi-lta-ba*.

[5] Cf. Abhisamayālaṁkāra VIII. 1. *sarvākārāṁ viśuddhiṁ ye dharmāḥ prāptā nirāsravāḥ | svābhāviko muneḥ kāyas teṣāṁ prakṛtilakṣaṇaḥ.*

attained. As regards this perception it has been said that the Bodhisattvas abiding on the 10 Stages may slightly perceive the Essence of the Buddha. They are considered to intuit it by means of their Absolute Transcendental Wisdom.[1] We have it accordingly in Scripture:—

Thou hast here only a partly knowledge of the Truth[2]
Which is perceived like the sun in the sky covered with clouds;
Even the Saints possessed of pure spiritual vision cannot see it at all times.
O Lord, only they whose Wisdom is illimited, perceiving the Cosmical Body,
And pervades the Essence of everything cognizable that is infinite like space,—
They can perceive the Truth at all times.

### Controversy.

It is said:—This Essence of the Buddha is thus not always accessible even to the Highest of Saints that abide on the Stages characterized by the full absence of Desire. If this be so, it is something exceedingly hard to be cognized. Therefore, what is the use of this teaching about it to the ordinary worldly beings?—[58 a. 1.] The necessity of this teaching is in short expressed in 2 verses, one containing the question, and the other being the reply given to it.

154. It has been said in these and those (parts of Scripture)[3]
That all the things cognizable are essentially unreal,
Being like clouds, like visions in a dream, and like an illusion.
Wherefore then has the Lord declared here[4]
That the Essence of the Buddha exists in all living beings.

---

[1] At the time of intense concentration.

[2] Dar. 168 a. 4.—perceiving it only at the time of intense concentration.

[3] Dar. 169 a. 4 and 172 a. 5.—in the Scripture of the intermediate period, the Śatasāhasrikā, Aṣṭasāhasrikā, &c.

[4] In the Scripture of the later period.

155. There are 5 kinds of defects (in a living being):—
Depression of the mind, contempt regarding those that are inferior,
Evaluation of the unreal, nihilistic views regarding the Absolute Truth.
(The teaching about the element of Buddhahood) has been exposed
In order that those with whom these defects exist
Might become rid of them.

The meaning of these 2 verses is, in short, explained by the following ten:—

156. The Ultimate Reality (is the Essence of the Buddha),
It is devoid of all the elements that are conditioned[1] in all their forms;
The passions, the Biotic Force and their consequences
Are described as resembling the clouds and the like.

157. The passions, they are like the clouds,
The Biotic Force that is produced (by ignorance)
Is (unreal) as the objects of enjoyment in a dream,
The consequence of the passions and of the Biotic Force,—
The groups of elements, they are like illusionary forms produced by magic.

158. So has it been ascertained before.[2]
Then, subsequently, in this Highest of Teachings,[3]
In order to remove the 5 kinds of defects (in a living being),
It is shown that the Essence of the Buddha exists.

159. Indeed, if one has not heard about it,
There may arise the defect of self-depreciation,[4]

[1] *saṁskṛta*. Dar. 173 b. 3—4. The Absolute Reality that is the spiritual element of a living being, perfectly pure by nature, is the Essence of the Buddha that is spoken of here. It is devoid of all the elements of Phenomenal Existence and their causes (*duḥkha-samudaya*).

[2] In the Scripture of the intermediate period. Dar. 174 b. 4.

[3] Or "the latest Teaching" (Uttaratantra = the Scripture of the latest period).

[4] Dar. 175 a. 2.—thinking oneself incapable of attaining Buddhahood.

Owing to which the mind becomes depressed in some,
And the spirit directed toward Enlightenment[1]
Is not aroused in them.

160. (There are others) who, having made the Creative Effort,
Are full of pride, thinking that they are the highest,
And have thoughts of extreme contempt
For those in whom the will of Enlightenment is not aroused.

161. With him who thinks like that [58 b. 1.]
Correct knowledge does not arise;
He perceives that which is unreal,[2]
And does not know the true state of things.

162. (Indeed), the defects of the real beings are unreal,
Since they are not-genuine and accidental.
As the defects are thus imputed,
Only the virtuous properties are pure by nature.

163. He who is possessed of a mind having regard for the defects that are unreal,
And depreciating the virtuous properties that are true,
Cannot perceive the equality of oneself and other living beings[3]
And become full of love for them.

164. Therefore, having heard about this[4]
(One can become possessed of) zeal,
Of regard (for all living beings)[5] as for the Teacher,
Of Highest Wisdom, Transcendental Intuition, and great Love.
These 5 properties having become originated,

---

[1] *bodhi-citta = byaṅ-chub-kyi-sems.*

[2] Dar. 175 a. 6.—He considers that which is unreal, i.e. the defects of the living beings, to have a real essence of its own.

[3] Dar. 173 b. 3.—In the sense of being possessed of the element of Buddhahood and of being capable of attaining the state of a Buddha.

[4] Ibid. 173 b. 4—5.—about the existence of the element of Buddhahood in all the living beings.

[5] Ibid. 173 b. 5. *saṅs-rgyas thob-ḥdod-kyi spro-ba daṅ sems-can gźan-la ston-pa-bźin-du-gus-pa.*

165. One becomes free from the defect (of self-depreciation),
Perceives the equality (of oneself and others),
Is devoid of (real)[1] defects and possessed of virtuous properties,
And having made one's aim the weal of others,
One attains Buddhahood at an early date.

Finished the explanation of Essence of Buddhahood, the summary of which is to be found in the first verse (concerning the subject).[2] So we have it, as a part of the investigation of the sources of the 3 Jewels as contained in the Treatise on the Sublime Science of the Great Vehicle.

End of the exposition of the Absolute mingled with defiling elements.

## II. Enlightenment and the Absolute free from Defilement.

Now we shall speak of the undefiled Absolute. What is this undefiled Absolute?—It is the condition of a complete metamorphose[3] (of the elements of existence) which become fully merged in the unaffected Absolute Essence[4] of the Buddhas. This is brought about through the removal of the defiling elements in all their forms. In short, this (undefiled Absolute Essence) is to be considered from 8 points of view. What are these 8?—

1. Perfect purity,[5] the factors that bring it about,[6]
The removal (of all the stains,[7] the action in behalf of oneself and others,

[1] Ibid. 174 a. 1. *skyon-ran-bžin-gyis-grub-pa-med-ciṅ-yon-tan-ḥbyuṅ-ruṅ-du ldan-pa.*

[2] I.e. verse 27.

[3] *parāvṛtti* = *yoṅs-su-gyur-pa.*

[4] *anāsrava-dhātu* = *zag-pa-med-paḥi-dbyiṅs.*

[5] Dar. 176 b. 6.—Perfect purity, the essence of Enlightenment.

[6] The causes of Enlightenment. Dar. 176 b. 6.—The Transcendental Wisdom at the time of intense concentration (*samāhita-jñāna*), and the wisdom acquired after (the termination of the trance—*pṛṣṭha-labdha*).

Dar. 177 a. 1. Enlightenment taken from the standpoint of the result.

And the foundation of these kinds of action,
The Profound,[1] the Magnificent,[2] and the Magnanimous[3] [59 a. 1.]
(The 3 Bodies) that endure as long as the world exists[4]
And manifest themselves in accordance (with the needs of the converts).[5]

This verse indicates, respectively, 8 subjects which are as follows:—1) the essence, 2) the cause, 3) the result, 4) the functions, 5) the relations, 6) the manifestations, 7) the eternal, and 8) the inconceivable character (of Buddhahood).

Now, we know that the fundamental element, when it is not delivered from the coverings of defilement, is called "the Essence of the Buddha." This same essence, in the state of complete purification, has the character of a metamorphose (of all the elements). It is accordingly said:[6] O Lord, those who have no doubt as regards the Essence of the Buddha as it is concealed under all the millions of coverings of defilement, shall likewise not be doubting of the Cosmical Body of the Buddha delivered from all the bonds of the passions.

(The cause which brings about the attainment of Enlightenment is) the Highest Wisdom (of a Saint), which is of two kinds, viz. the supermundane,[7] non-dialectical,[8] and the mundane[9] that is acquired after (the termination of the trance).[10] This mundane and supermundane knowledge is the cause of the metamorphose (of the

[1] The Cosmical Body. Dar. 177 a. 3. *zab-pa-chos-kyi-sku* (= *dharma-kāya*).

[2] The Body of Bliss. Ibid. *rgya-che-ba-loṅs-spyod-rdzogs-paḥi-sku* (= *sambhoga-kāya*).

[3] The Apparitional Body (*nirmāṇa-kāya* = *sprul-sku*).

[4] Dar. 177 a. 3. The eternal character of Buddhahood.

[5] Ibid. 177 a. 4. The inconceivable character of Buddhahood.

[6] Śrī-mālā-siṁhanāda-sūtra. Kg. DKON. VI. 277 a. 5—6.

[7] *lokottara* = *ḥjig-rten-las-ḥdas-pa*.

[8] *nirvikalpaka* = *rnam-par-rtog-pa-med-pa*.

[9] *laukika* = *ḥjig-rten-pa*.

[10] *pṛṣṭha-labdha* = *rjes-las-thob-pa*.

elements).[1] The idea of the cause is expressed by the word ("factors for the) attainment,"—"that by which something is attained."[2]

The result (produced by) these (factors) is of 2 kinds, viz. the removal of the Obscuration of Moral Defilement,[3] and the removal of the Obscuration of Ignorance.[4]

The accomplishment of one's own aim and of that of others,— these are the functions (of the supermundane and the mundane Wisdom) respectively.

The connexion of the foundation of these 2 forms of activity with its properties is the relation (spoken of here) [59 b. 1.]. The manifestations are those of the 3 Bodies of the Buddha which are respectively characterized by profundity, magnificence, and magnanimity. They are realized in an inconceivable manner and endure as long as the world exists.

### Summary.

2. The essence, the cause, and the result,
The functions, the relations, and the manifestations,
The eternal and the inconceivable character,—
By these the state of the Buddha is characterized.

Now, (first of all) we have a verse referring to Buddhahood and the means for the attainment of it, that is to say, the essence and the causes (of Enlightenment)—

3. Buddhahood[5] is that which is called pure and radiant,
(Shining) like the sun and (immaculate) like the sky,
Which was darkened by the Obscurations
Of defilement and ignorance as by dense multitudes of clouds,

---

[1] Cf. Sutrālaṁkāra IX. 12 and Vasubandhu thereon—*suviśuddha-lokottara-jñāna-mārga-lābhāt tat-pṛṣṭha-labdha-ananta-jñeya-viṣaya-jñeya-mārga-lābhāc ca.*

[2] *ḥdis thob-pas-na thob-paḥo = prāpyate anena iti prāptiḥ.*

[3] *kleśa-āvaraṇa = ñon-moṅs-paḥi-sgrib-pa.*

[4] *jñeya-āvaraṇa = śes-byaḥi-sgrib-pa.*

[5] In its essence.

And is now perfectly pure, possessed of all the properties of
the Buddha,
Is eternal, firm and indestructible.
It is attained on the foundation of the knowledge of the Truth,
Which is free from dialectical thought-construction,
And the knowledge analyzing (the elements of existence).[1]

The meaning of this verse is in short explained by the following 4—

4. The state of the Buddha is characterized
By the indivisible purest properties.
It has a resemblance with the sun and the sky
In its character of wisdom and of purity.[2]

5. It is radiant and uncreated,[3]
It manifests itself in its indivisible essence,[4]
And is possessed of all the properties of the Buddha,
Which excel in their number the sands of the Ganges.

6. Being by their very essence unreal,
Pervasive and occasional,
The Obscurations of Defilement and of Ignorance
Are spoken of as resembling clouds.

7. The causes for the removal of these 2 Obscurations
Are the two kinds of Highest Wisdom,—
That which is free from (dialectical) construction,
And that which follows (the concentrated trance).

[60 a. 1.] It is said that the state of perfect purity represents the complete metamorphose (of the elements). Now, this purity, to speak briefly, appears in 2 forms, viz. the natural purity, and the

[1] Sic acc. to Dar. 178 b. 3.

[2] Lit. the removal (of the Obscurations—*prahāṇa* = *spaṅs-pa*).

[3] Dar. 179 a. 3—4.—It is not produced anew by causes and conditions.

[4] Dar. 179 a. 4. *raṅ-bźin-rnam-dag-gi-chos-ñid-la-ño-boḥi sgo-nas dbyer-med-par ḥjug-pa-can.*

16*

purification from (the accidental) defilement.[1] As regards the natural purity, it represents (the Absolute as the beginningless fundamental element), which is essentially free (from every real contact with the defiling elements), but is not separated from the (accidental) Obscurations. Indeed, this spiritual essence, being pure by nature, is at the same time not necessarily devoid of the stains of an occasional character. The purification from these occasional defiling forces is complete deliverance and the removal of all the stains, as water is purified from dust and the like. Indeed, the spiritual essence which is pure and radiant finally becomes devoid of all the accidental defilement. Now, with regard to the purification from defilement which represents the result, we have the following verse:—

8. Like a lake full of the purest water
And covered by lotuses that have developed gradually,[2]
Like the full moon delivered from the jaws of Rāhu,[3]
Like the sun free from all obscuration
Caused by the dense multitude of clouds,[4]
It is possessed of immaculate properties,
Is radiant and illuminating.

9.[5] Like the Highest of Sages,[6] like honey, and like the kernel (of a fruit),
Like precious gold, like a treasure and like a tree,
Like the immaculate images of the Buddha,
Like the ruler of the earth and like a golden statue—such is Buddhahood.

---

[1] Cf. Sūtrālaṁkāra, XII. 15.—*svabhāva-śuddhaṁ mala-śuddhitaṁ ca.*

[2] Dar. 179 b. 5—6.—being possessed of immaculate properties, owing to the complete extirpation of desire (*rāga*).

[3] Ibid. 179 b. 6.—being endowed with the light of immaculate love and Commiseration, owing to the removal of hatred (*dveṣa*).

[4] Ibid. 179 b. 6.—180 a. 1.—being possessed of the immaculate lustre of wisdom through the complete removal of infatuation (*moha*).

[5] The 9 examples illustrating the fundamental element now applied to Buddhahood.

[6] *muni-ṛṣabha* = *thub-paḥi-khyu-mchog.*

The meaning of these two verses is, in short, explained by the following 8:—

10. Similar to the waters of a lake and the like[1]
Is the state of perfect purity, (the liberation)
From desire and the other occasional defiling forces.
It is, in short, spoken of as the result
Of the Wisdom free from thought-construction. [60 b. 1.]

11. The certain attainment of the (3) Bodies of the Buddha
Possessed of the highest of all the forms of existence
Is demonstrated as being the result
Of the Wisdom following the transcendental contemplation.

12. Through the removal of the dust of Desire,
And by pouring forth the waters of transic meditation,
To the converts that resemble lotuses,
(Buddhahood) is like a lake of purest water.

13. Being delivered from the Rāhu of enmity,
It pervades all that exists
By the rays of Commiseration and Highest Love.
Therefore it is like the immaculate full moon.

14. Being free from the clouds of infatuation,
Buddhahood removes all darkness in the living beings
By the rays of its Divine Wisdom,
Having thus a resemblance with the sun free from every stain.

15. It is possessed of properties incomparable (with others)
And equal (only with the Buddhas),
It spreads the flavour of the Highest Doctrine
And is free from the coverings (of the Obscurations),
Therefore it is like the Body of the Buddha,[2]
Like honey and like the kernel of a fruit.

---

[1] Dar. 180 b. 2.—the moon delivered from Rāhu and the sun freed from the clouds.

[2] As incomparable with anything else.

16. It is pure; by the richness of its properties
It removes all (moral) poverty,
And brings to maturity the fruit of deliverance.
It is thus like gold, like a treasure, and like a tree.

17. As it represents the precious Cosmical Body,
Is the Highest Lord of all the bipeds,
And appears in the most precious of forms,
It is like a precious image, a king and a golden statue.

## The Functions of Enlightenment.

The supermundane, non-dialectical knowledge, and the knowledge which is acquired after the transcendental contemplation are the causes of the metamorphose (of the elements) which is called "the result consisting in the separation" (from the defiling forces).[1] The functions of these (2 kinds of wisdom) is that which we call the complement of one's own weal and of that of others. Now, what is this complement of one's own weal and of that of others?—(Answer): That which represents the attainment of the undefiled Cosmical Body and the deliverance from the Obscurations of passion and of ignorance [61 a. 1.] is called "the complement of one's own weal." That which, being founded on the latter, consists in a twofold manifestation, viz. the activity free from effort[2] by appearing in (either of the) two (corporeal) forms[3] as long as the world exists and the miraculous power of teaching,[4]—is the complement of the weal of other living beings. With reference to these functions we have the following 3 verses:—

[1] *visaṁyoga-phala* = *bral-baḥi-ḥbras-bu*, i.e. the Extinction of the elements of Phenomenal Life (*nirodha-satya*). Cf. Abhidharmakośa I. 6.

[2] *anābhoga* = *lhun-gyis-grub-pa*.

[3] The Body of Bliss and the Apparitional Body.

[4] Dar. 181 b. 2.—The act of teaching the Doctrine in such a manner that, being communicated in one way, it is understood by all the different converts, each in his own language.

18. Immaculate, of all-pervading Wisdom, imperishable,
Firm, quiescent, eternal, and motionless,
The Buddha (in his corporeal forms) is the cause
That the pure faculties of sense perceive their objects
As space is the receptacle for all things.[1]

19. He conveys the perception of (his) miraculous apparitions,
The pure audition of the most sublime words,
The pure scent of the Buddha's morality,
The relish of the flavour of the Highest Doctrine,
The enjoyment of the felicitous feeling of transic meditation,

20. And the cognition of the subject profound by its very nature.[2]
But, if closely investigated,
The Buddha who grants thus the true and highest bliss
Is (in his Cosmical Essence) uncaused and unconditioned.

The meaning of these 3 verses is, in short, made known by the following eight:—

21. In short, such do we know to be the functions
Of the 2 kinds of Highest Wisdom,—
The attainment of the fully accomplished Cosmical Body
Which is free (from all defiling elements)
And the activity of this Cosmical Body.

22. The perfectly delivered Cosmical Body and its manifestations[3]
Are to be known in two aspects and in one,
Being free from all defilement, all-pervading,
And the substratum of eternal properties.[4]

23. They are undefiled owing to the extirpation
Of all the passions and their residues,

---

[1] Dar. 181 b. 6. As, on the background of space, the 6 forms of consciousness of the living beings perceive each their own object.

[2] The meaning of universal Relativity and Non-substantiality.

[3] Dar. 182 b. 6.

[4] Sic acc. to Dar. 183 a. 1—2.

Being free from every attachment and hindrance[1]

[61 b. 1.] They are all-pervading in their wisdom.

24. They are eternal, being
Of a totally indestructible nature;
This imperishable character, being demonstrated in short,
Is expressed by the ideas of firmness and the rest.

25. Now, evanescence is known to be of 4 kinds,
Which are the reverse of firmness, &c.,—
Putrification, the changes caused by illness, birth,
And migration which takes place in an inconceivable way.

26. Owing to the absence of these, (the Cosmical Body) is firm and quiescent,
It is eternal and knows no migration.
This immaculate spiritual element, being the support
Of all the purest properties,[2] represents their substratum.

27. As space, being itself uncaused,
Is the cause for the perception of visible forms,
And, with regard to the sounds, smells, tangibles and mental elements,[3]
The cause of their audition and the rest.

28. So the 2 Bodies,[4] in their unimpeded activity,
Represent the cause for the origination
Of all the purest virtuous properties
Accessible to the perception of the Bodhisattvas.

It is said:[5]—The Buddha has the character of space.—This refers to the special absolute character of the Buddha, which has nothing in common with anything else. Indeed, if we were to recognize the Buddha only by the 32 corporeal marks of a super-

[1] *asakta* = *chags-pa-med-pa*, and *apratihata* = *thogs-pa-med-pa*.

[2] *śukla-dharma* = *dkar-poḥi-chos*.

[3] *dharma-āyatana* or *dharma-dhātu*.

[4] The Body of Bliss and the Apparitional Body.

[5] In the Jñāna-āloka-alaṁkāra-sūtra.

man,[1] the universal monarch[2] would turn to be a Buddha as well.— Now, with reference to the relations (of Buddhahood to the properties) of an absolute character, we have the following verse:—

29. Inconceivable, eternal, quiescent, indestructible,
Perfectly pacified, all-pervading, free from (dialectical) construction, and akin to space,
Free from attachment and impediments whatever, and devoid of rough sensation,
Imperceptible, incognizable, sublime, immaculate,—such is the Buddha [62 a. 1.].

The meaning of this verse is, in short, made known by the following eight:—

30. The Cosmical Body, perfectly delivered, and its manifestations
Represent the fulfilment of one's own aim and of that of others.
This support of the twofold aim
Is possessed of properties inconceivable and the like.

31. Buddhahood is accessible only to the Wisdom of the Omniscient,
Is not the object of the 3 (kinds of ordinary) knowledge,[3]
Therefore those, endowed with spiritual bodies[4]
Cognize it as being inconceivable.

32. Owing to its subtle transcendental character,
It cannot be made the object of study,
Being the Absolute Truth, it cannot be investigated,[5]
And, as the profound Ultimate Essence, it is not accessible
To mundane meditation and the like.

33. Indeed, as the visible forms for those that are born blind,
It is not accessible to the perception of ordinary beings;

---

[1] *mahā-puruṣa-lakṣaṇa.*

[2] *cakravarti-rāja = ḥkhor-los-bsgyur-baḥi-rgyal-po.*

[3] The knowledge which is a result of study, analysis, and meditation (*śruti-cintā-bhāvanā-mayī prajñā*).

[4] The Saints who have not attained the final Enlightenment.

[5] Cf. Bodhicaryāvatāra IX. 2. *buddher agocaras tattvam.*

And even to the Saints who, though they perceive it (a little),
Are with respect to it like new-born infants
Perceiving the sun from the house where they are kept.

34. It is eternal, as it is not subjected to birth,
And firm, since it does not disappear;
It is quiescent, being free from both (search and thought-construction),[1]
And indestructible as the Ultimate Essence (of the elements).

35. It represents the Perfect Peace, being the negation (of Phenomenal Existence),[2]
It is all-pervading, as it cognizes everything,
It is free from thought-construction through the non-insistence (upon the reality of the elements),[3]
Devoid of all attachment, owing to the extirpation of defilement.

36. Through the complete removal of the Obscuration of Ignorance,
It is free from impediments regarding everything (cognizable),[4]
And devoid of both (languor and distraction),[5] and duly purified,
It is free from every rough sensation.

37. Being immaterial, it is not perceptible,
And, as it has no real characteristic marks,
It cannot be cognized by inference.
It is sublime, being perfectly pure by nature,
And free from every stain through the complete removal of defilement.

Now, Buddhahood [62 b. 1.] manifests itself as indivisible from its properties and as being (unique and undifferentiated) like space. At the same time it applies, as long as the world exists, in an inconceivable manner, great skill, commiseration and Highest Wisdom, being the cause for the realization of the welfare and happiness of

---

[1] *vitarka-vicāra* (Dar. 185 a. 2.). [2] *nirodha-satya* = *ḥgog-bden.*
[3] Sic acc. to Dar. 185 a. 4. [4] Ibid. [5] Cf. below.

all living beings. (In this activity) it is to be viewed as manifesting itself, uninterruptedly and free from effort and hindrance, in the 3 immaculate forms, viz. the Body of Absolute Existence,[1] the Body of Bliss,[2] and the Apparitional Body.[3] This is due to the fact of its being endowed with the (18) exclusive properties.[4] With reference to these manifestations we have the following 4 verses, which describe the 3 Bodies of the Buddha:—

### The Body of Absolute Existence.

38. It has neither beginning, middle, nor end, is indivisible,[5]
Devoid of the 2 (extremities), delivered from the 3 (Obscurations),
Immaculate and free from thought-construction,
Is that which represents the Essence of the Absolute, and is perceived
By the Saint,[6] who cognizes it in concentrated trance.

39. Possessed of properties, inconceivable, unequalled,
Immeasurable, and excelling the sands of the Ganges,
This immaculate Essence of the Buddha
Is devoid of all defects and defiling forces.[7]

40. The Body endowed with the numerous rays of the Highest Doctrine
Exerts itself in working for the salvation of all that lives;
In its acts it is like the king of wish-fulfilling gems,[8]
Appearing in various forms, which, however, are not identical with it.

41. Acting on the Path that leads to the pacification of worldly existence,

---

[1] *svabhāva-kāya* = *ṅo-bo-ñid-sku.* [2] *saṁbhoga-kāya* = *loṅs-sku.*

[3] *nirmāṇa-kāya* = *sprul-sku.* [4] *āveṇika-dharma* = *ma-ḥdres-paḥi-chos.*

[5] From the Unique Absolute (*dharma-dhātu*). Dar. 188 b. 6—189 a. 1. *chos-dbyiṅs-las ṅo-bo tha-dad-paḥi-tshul-du rnam-par-dbyer-med-pas tha-mi-dad-pa.*

[6] *yogin* = *rnal-ḥbyor-pa.* [7] *vāsanā* = *bag-chags.* [8] *cintāmaṇi-ratna-rāja.*

The Body,[1] which is the cause of Salvation and of the Highest
Teaching,
Abides here in this world, uninterruptedly
As the visible forms in the element of space. [63 a. 1.]

The meaning of these 4 verses is explained by the following twenty:—

42. The Omniscience of the Divine is
That which is called the state of the Buddha,
The Ultimate, Highest Nirvāṇa,
The Buddha's inconceivable introspection;—

43. Its varieties are the Profound,[2] the Magnificent,[3]
And the Magnanimous;[4] owing to these
It manifests itself in the 3 Bodies,—
The Body of Absolute Existence and the rest.

44. Now, the Body of Absolute Existence of the Buddhas,[5]
Characterized by 5 distinctive features,
Is, in short, known to be possessed
Of 5 kinds of virtuous properties.

45. It is eternal and indivisible,
Is devoid of the 2 extremities,[6]
And completely free from the 3 Obscurations,
Of defilement, ignorance, and distraction.[7]

46. Free from all stains and thought-construction,
Accessible to the introspection of the Saints,
Representing the Essence of the Absolute,
Immaculate by nature,—it is pure and radiant.

---

[1] The Apparitional Body of the Buddha (*nirmāṇa-kāya*).

[2] The Body of Absolute Existence (*svabhāva-kāya*).

[3] The Body of Bliss (*saṁbhoga-kāya*). [4] The Apparitional Body.

[5] The Body of Absolute Existence is unique and undifferentiated with all the Buddhas. Cf. Vasubandhu on Sūtrālaṁkāra IX. 62. *svābhāvikaḥ sarva-buddhānāṁ samo nirviśiṣṭatayā.*

[6] Of imputed Realism and Nihilism (*samāropa-apavāda*).

[7] *samāpatty-āvaraṇa* = *sñoms-ḥjug-gi-sgrib-pa.*

47. Immeasurable, innumerable, inconceivable,
Incomparable, and representing the highest point of purity,—
With these kinds of virtuous properties
The Body of Absolute Existence is fully endowed.

48. Being great, extensive, and numberless,
Inaccessible to discursive thought,
Unique and devoid of the force of Illusion,
It is immeasurable and so on, respectively.

## The Body of Bliss.

49. By its nature enjoying the Doctrine in its various forms,
It appears uninterruptedly, as this Doctrine enjoyed by it,
Being the natural outflow of purest Commiseration,
It works uninterruptedly for the weal of all that lives.

50. Free from constructive thought and without effort,
[63 b. 1.] Fulfilling the desired aim (of the converts),[1]
It abides, enjoying the miraculous power[2]
Similar to that of the wish-fulfilling gem.

51. Teaching, manifesting itself, and acting uninterruptedly,
Devoid of a will (connected with exertion)[3]
It appears here in various forms,
Without demonstrating its true nature;—
Such are its 5 distinctive features.

52. Just as if a precious stone,
Being dyed with various colours,
Does not make manifest its real essence,
In a like way (the Buddha), pervading all that lives in various forms,
Is not perceived in his true nature.

53. Full of Commiseration, with a perfect knowledge of the world,
He has (mercifully) looked down upon the living beings,

---

[1] Dar. 191 a. 4. [2] *ṛddhi = rdzu-ḥphrul.*
[3] Cf. Abhisamayālaṁkāra II. 25. *sarvasyā̆nabhisaṁskṛtiḥ.*

And, without stirring from his Cosmical Body,
Has manifested himself in various emanations.

### The 12 Acts of the Buddha as a mere Manifestation of His Apparitional Body.

54. He became born (in the form of Śvetaketu)[1],
Descended from the abode of Tuṣita,
Entered (his mother's) womb, and was born (again);
He showed his skill in dexterous acts,

55. Led a merry life in the circle of noble women,
(Then) departed from home, practised asceticism,
Made his apparition at Bodhimaṇḍa,
Vanquished the hosts of the Evil-One,

56. Attained the Perfect Supreme Enlightenment,
Swung the Wheel of the Doctrine,
And departed into Nirvāṇa.—
Such acts he exhibits in the impure spheres,
As long as dures this world's existence.

57. He perfectly knows the means of conversion,
By teaching about Evanescence, Uneasiness,
About Impersonality and Quiescence,[2]
He creates aversion in the living beings
With regard to the 3 Spheres of Existence
And directs them toward Nirvāṇa.

58. To those who have entered the Path
That leads to the (egoistic) Quiescence,
And think they have attained (the true) Nirvāṇa,
He teaches about the true essence of the elements[3]
As in the White Lotus of the Highest Doctrine,[4] &c.

[1] Dar. 192 a. 3.
[2] The 4 main aphorisms of the Doctrine.
[3] The separate unreality of subject, object, and act (*trimaṇḍala-viśuddhi*).
[4] The Saddharma-puṇḍarīka.

59. He diverts them thus from their selfish desires,
And, using his Highest Wisdom and Skill,[1]
[64 a. 1.] Converts them to (the teaching of) the Highest Vehicle,
And prophecies Supreme Enlightenment for them.

60. Profound, displaying manifold power,
And guiding the ordinary beings, making his aim their weal,
(The Buddha is known) in these 3 forms, respectively,
As the Profound, the Magnanimous, and the Magnificent.

61. The first of these is the Cosmical Body,
And the latter two are the corporeal forms;
As visible matter abides in space,
So are the latter two supported by the former.[2]

**The Eternal Character of the 3 Bodies.**

The 3 Bodies (of the Buddha) manifest themselves by working for the weal of all living beings and having as such an eternal character. With reference to this subject we have the following verse:—

62. Called forth by causes that are infinite,[3]
Having an endless number of living beings to convert,[4]
Possessed of mercy, miraculous power, wisdom and of the complement of Bliss,
Governing all the elements,[5] vanquishing the demon of Death,
And transcendental by nature,[6]—the Lord of the World is eternal.[7]

The subject spoken of here in short is explained by the following 6 verses:—

---

[1] *prajñā-upāya.*

[2] Cf. Sūtrālaṁkāra IX. 60.—*prathamas tu dvayāśrayaḥ.*

[3] Dar. 195 b. 1.—The Accumulations of Virtue and Wisdom (*puṇya-jñāna-saṁbhāra*).

[4] Dar. 195 b. 2. [5] *dharmeśvara = chos-kyi-dbaṅ-phyug.*

[6] Lit. unreal as an empirical, worldly entity (*niḥsvabhāva*).

[7] Cf. Abhisamayālaṁkāra VIII. 11.

63. Giving up his body, his life and his property,
He has preserved the Highest of Doctrines;
He administers help to all living beings,
And fully accomplishes his previous vows.

64. The Buddha thus makes manifest
His Commiseration, pure and immaculate,
And shows his miraculous activity,
Which he applies in his acts, abiding eternally.

65. Owing to his Wisdom, he is free from the conception
Of Saṁsāra and Nirvāṇa (as 2 separate entities);
As he constantly partakes of the complement of bliss
Of the inconceivable concentrated trance,
He, whilst acting in this world,
Is unaffected by the worldly elements.

66. He has attained the state of immortality and quiescence,
Leaving no room for the activity of the Demon of Death;
[64 b. 1.] Therefore, the Lord, being of an immutable[1] nature,
Is perfectly quiescent from the outset.

67. Thus, eternal, he is fit to be
A refuge for the helpless and the like.—
The first 7 of these motives show
The eternal character of the corporeal forms,
And subsequent 3 demonstrate
The Eternity of the Cosmical Body.

### The inconceivable Character of Buddhahood.

This character of the Buddha, representing the complete metamorphose (of the elements of existence) we avow to be inconceivable. The following verse refers to the fact of its being such:—

[1] *asaṁskṛta* = *ḥdus-ma-byas.* Dar. 196 b. 1.—merged for ever in the immutable Absolute.

68. Unutterable, representing the Absolute Truth,
Inaccessible to constructive thought and incomparable,[1]
Being the highest point of perfection,
Relating neither to the Phenomenal World,
Nor to the (Hīnayānistic) Nirvāṇa,
The sphere of Buddhahood is inconceivable even for the Saint.

The subject expressed here in short is to be known from the following 4 verses:—

69. (The Buddha) is inconceivable, since he is unutterable,
He is unutterable, being the Absolute Truth,[2]
He is the Absolute Truth, being inaccessible to thought-construction,
And is inaccessible to thought-construction, since
He cannot be cognized through inference.

70. He cannot be made the object of inference,
Being the Highest Point of Perfection standing above all,
And he is highest of all, since he is not included
(Neither in the elements of the world, nor in Hīnayānistic Nirvāṇa),
He is such, as he does not abide (in either of them),
Having no view for the defects (of the former) and the merits (of the latter).

71. The Cosmical Body is inconceivable,
Being subtle and transcendental out of 4 motives,
And the corporeal forms are likewise beyond the reach of human intellect,
This owing to a sixth motive, (as they represent
Mere reflections of the Cosmical Body),[3]
Which have no real essence of their own.

---

[1] Dar. 197 a. 2.—he cannot be cognized on the foundation of dist. marks.
[2] Cf. Bodhicaryāvatāra IX. 2. *buddher agocaras tattvam.*
[3] *pratibimbā* = *gzugs-ornan.*

72. Being possessed of Wisdom, higher than which there is none,
Of greatest Commiseration and all the other properties,
The Lord, who has attained the highest point of perfection,
Is inaccessible to human thought.
Therefore this Ultimate Essence of the Buddha
Cannot be cognized even by the highest sages
Who have attained the controlling power[1] over the elements.
[65 a. 1.]

Finished the exposition of Supreme Enlightenment, the second chapter of the Analysis of the sources of the 3 Jewels, called "The Sublime Science of the Great Vehicle." Finished the description of the Absolute free from defilement.

## III. The Properties of the Buddha.

Now we have to describe the properties (of the Buddha, which are perfectly immaculate by nature). (These properties) have for their foundation (Supreme Enlightenment), with which they form one inseparable whole, like the form and the colour of a precious stone. Therefore, after (the exposition of the Immaculate Absolute)—we have a verse referring to the varieties of the properties of the Buddha:—

1. The ultimate aim of oneself and of others (respectively)
(Consists in) the Body which represents the Absolute Reality,[2]
And the worldly emanations which are founded upon it.[3]
These Bodies are the result of purity[4] and perfection,[5]
Possessed of the properties that appear in 64 varieties.—
What is said here?

2. The position of perfect bliss for one's own self
Is the Body which represents the Absolute Truth,[6]

---

[1] *vaśitā-prāpta* = *dbaṅ-thob*—the Bodhisattvas on the 3 last Stages.

[2] The Cosmical Body as the attainment of one's own aim Dar. 198 b. 1—2.

[3] The corporeal forms of the Buddha as the complement of the weal of others. Ibid.

[4] *visaṁyoga* = *bral-ba*—the removal (of the Obscuration).

[5] *vipāka* = *rnam-par-smin-pa*.

[6] Dar. 198 b. 3—4.—The immutable Body of Absolute Existence (*svabhāva-kāya*) and the Body of Absolute Wisdom (*jñāna-dharma-kāya*).

And the foundation for the complement (of the weal) of others
Are the emanational[1] forms of the Divine.

3. The first of these Bodies is possessed
Of the Powers and other attributes of perfect purity,
And the latter two (Bodies) are endowed
With the properties of perfection,—the marks of the super-man.

The following text refers to the character of the (10) Powers and the other properties, and the manner in which they are to be cognized.

## Summary.

4. The Powers (of the Buddha) are like a thunderbolt,
Breaking the impediments caused by ignorance;
His intrepidity in the circle of hearers is like that of a lion;
The Buddha's exclusive properties are like space,
And the corporeal forms of the Lord are like
The moon and its reflection in the water.

## The 10 Powers.

It is said that the Buddha is possessed of the (10) Powers.[1]

5. These are the 10 Powers of Cognition—
Of the possible and the impossible,[2]
Of the fruit of one's former deeds,[3] and of the faculties,[4]
[65 b. 1.] Of the component elements (of the Universe),[5]
And of the inclinations (of the converts),[6]
Of all the different paths,[7] of that which is defiling and purifying

---

[1] *sāṁketika-kāya = brdaḥi-sku*—"the conventional Bodies."

[1] Cf. M. Vyutp. § 7.

[2] *sthāna-asthāna-jñāna-bala = gnas-daṅ-gnas-min-mkhyen-paḥi-stobs.*

[3] *karma-vipāka-jñāna-bala = las-rnams-kyi-rnam-smin-mkhyen-paḥi-stobs.*

[4] *indriya-parāpara-jñāna-bala = dbaṅ-po-mchog-daṅ-mchog-ma-yin-pa-mkhyen-paḥi-stobs.*

[5] *nānā-dhātu-jñāna-bala = khams-sna-tshogs-mkhyen-paḥi-stobs.*

[6] *nānā-adhimukti-jñāna-bala = mos-pa-sna-tshogs-mkhyen-paḥi-stobs*

[7] *sarvatra-gāminī-pratipaj-jñāna-bala = kun-tu-ḥgro-baḥi-lam-mkhyen-paḥi-stobs.*

In the states of mystic absorption and the like,[1]
The power of remembering the place of former residence,[2]
The Divine Vision[3] and the Wisdom that pacifies (all the
defiling forces).[4]

It is said that (these Powers) resemble a thunderbolt.—

6. The cognition of that which is possible and impossible,
Of the fruit of former deeds, of the elements,
Of the paths, and the different inclinations,
Of the defiling and purifying, of the complex of faculties,
And the remembrance of the place of former residence,
The Divine Vision, and the means of removing defilement,—
These powers pierce, break, and cut down
The armour, the massive wall, and the tree of ignorance.—
Therefore they have resemblance with a thunderbolt.

## The 4 Forms of Intrepidity.[5]

It is said that (the Buddha) has attained the 4 kinds of intrepidity.—

7. The intrepidity (of the Buddha) is of 4 kinds:
That of cognizing all elements of existence,
Of removing all the impediments,
Of showing the Path, and the annihilation of defilement.

8. He knows himself and makes known to others
All the things cognizable in all their forms,

[1] *sarva-dhyāna-vimokṣa-samādhi-samāpatti-saṁkleśa-vyavadāna-vyutthāna-jñāna-bala* = *bsam-gtan daṅ rnam-par-thar-pa daṅ tiṅ-ṅe-ḥdzin daṅ sñoms-par-ḥjug-paḥi kun-nas-ñon-moṅs-pa-daṅ-rnam-par-byaṅ-ba-mkhyen-paḥi-stobs.*

[2] *pūrva-nivāsa-anusmṛti-jñāna-bala* = *sṅon-gyi-gnas-rjes-su-dran-pa-mkhyen-paḥi-stobs.*

[3] The power of premonition of birth and death by means of supernatural perception—*cyuty-upapatti-jñāna-bala* = *ḥchi-ḥpho-daṅ-skye-ba-mkhyen-paḥi-stobs.*

[4] *āsrava-kṣaya-jñāna-bala* = *zag-pa-zad-pa-mkhyen-paḥi-stobs.*

[5] *vaiśāradya* = *mi-ḥjigs-pa.* M. Vyutp. § 8.

He has removed all the Obscurations and causes others to
remove them,
Has entered the Path and induces others to do the same,
And has attained himself and causes to attain
The purest and highest of all aims.
Thus, teaching the Truth for himself and for others,
The Sage, wherever he might be, meets with no opposition.

It is said that (this intrepidity of the Buddha) is akin to (that of) the lion.—

9. As the king of beasts in the forest is always free from fear,
And, fearless, roams about amidst the other animals,
Similarly, in the multitude of hearers, that lion who is the
Lord of Sages,
Abides without depending on others,
And endowed with firmness and dexterity.

### The 18 Exclusive Properties.[1]

It is said that he is possessed of the 18 Exclusive Properties peculiar only to the Buddha.—

10. (With the Buddha) there is no error,[2] and no ill-sounding
speech,[3] [66 a. 1.]
The Teacher knows no loss of memory,
He is not possessed of a non-concentrated mind,
Nor has he a pluralistic outlook.[4]

11. He has no ill-considered indifference,[5]
Knows no bereavement of his zeal, his energy, and his memory,
Of Highest Wisdom, of his freedom (from the Obscurations),
And of the intuition of this freedom.

12. His acts preceded by Divine Wisdom,
His unimpeded knowledge regarding time,

---

[1] *āveṇika-dharma = ma-ḥdres-paḥi-chos.* [2] *skhalita = ḥkhrul-ba.*
[3] *ravita = ca-co.* [4] *nānātva-saṁjñā = sna-tshogs-paḥi-ḥdu-śes.*
[5] *apratisaṁkhyāyopekṣā = ma-brtags-btaṅ-sñoms.*

These 18 are the properties of the Teacher
Which have nothing in common with anyone else.

13. Error, unmelodious speech, forgetfulness,
A distracted mind, a pluralistic outlook,
And ill-considered indifference—these do not exist with the Sage;
He is not deprived of zeal, of energy,
Of pure, immaculate Wisdom,
Of eternal freedom (from all the bonds),
And of the intuition of one who has attained this freedom,
And the perception of the true essence of all things.

14. He makes manifest the 3 kinds of acts
Which are preceded by Transcendental Knowledge,[1]
And of the Knowledge great, extensive and certain,
Regarding present, past and future.
The position of the Lord who, possessed of these properties,
Free from fear, swings the Wheel of the Highest Doctrine
For the sake of all living beings
And is endowed with the Highest Commiseration,—
This is attained by the Buddha.

It is said that (these properties) have a resemblance with space.—

15. The properties which characterize
The elements of Matter, the solid[2] and the rest,
Are absent in the element of space.
And the property of space which consists in its being penetrable[3]
Does not exist with the elements of Matter.
However the solid, the liquid,[4] the hot,[5] the moving,[6] elements and that of Space likewise,

---

[1] *jñāna-pūrvaṁgama-jñāna-anuparivarti (kāya-vāṅ-manas-karma).*

[2] *pṛthivī-dhātu = saḥi-khams.*

[3] Cf. Abhidharmakośa. I. 5. *tatrā'kāśam anāvṛtiḥ.*

[4] *ab-dhātu = chuḥi-khams.* [5] *tejo-dhātu = meḥi khams.*

[6] *vāyu-dhātu = rluṅ-gi-khams.*

Are common to all the (material) worlds,
But the Exclusive Properties have not in the leas.
Anything in common with the worldly elements.

## The Body of Bliss.

## The 32 Characteristics of the Super-man.[1]

It is said that the Buddha is possessed of the corporeal form endowed with the 32 marks of the super-man. [66 b. 1.]

16. Firm and steady feet,[2] palms and soles marked by circles,[3]
Broad (heels),[4] and ancles with invisible joints,[5]
Fingers long,[6] and hands and feet likewise long,
(The fingers and the toes) connected by a web,[7]

17. With fine, soft, and juvenile skin,[8]
Seven spans in stature,[9] legs like those of the deer,[10]
The private parts concealed as with the elephant,[11]

18. The upper part of the body is like that of the lion,[12]
His shoulders and his breast are broad,
He has well-rounded shoulders,[13] long and tender arms,

19. The (body) standing upright, and not bending,[14]
Perfectly pure and surrounded by a nimb,
His neck is pure and resembles a shell,
His jaws are like those of the king of beasts,[15]

20. The teeth are 40 in number and equal,
Well arranged and closely set;
These pure and uniform teeth
Are above all of an exceeding whiteness.

---

[1] M. Vyutp. § 17. These marks evidently refer to the statue of the Buddha.
[2] *supratiṣṭhita-pāda.* [3] *cakrāṅkita-hasta-pāda-tala.*
[4] *āyata-pāda-parṣṇi.* [5] *ucchankha-pāda.* [6] *dīrghānguli.*
[7] *jāla-avanaddha-hasta-pāda.* [8] *mṛdu-taruṇa-hasta-pāda-tala.*
[9] *saptotsada.* [10] *aiṇeya-jangha.* [11] *kośa-gata-vasti-guhya.*
[12] *siṁha-pūrvārdha-kāya.* [13] *susaṁvṛtta-skandha.*
[14] *sthita-anavanata-pralamba-bāhutā.* (?) [15] *siṁha-hanu.*

21. A long tongue, the best taste, infinite and unthinkable,
A voice self-originated and clear like that of the Kalavinka;
22. His eyes are beautiful like a lotus with eyelashes like those of a bull,[1]
His face is handsome and has the immaculate hair of treasure,[2]
His head is adorned with a crest,[3] and the skin
Of the highest of beings is delicate and gold-like.[4]
23. The hairs (on his body) are fine and soft,
Each of them turning upward and to the right,
The hair on his head is pure and like precious sapphires,
And rounded like the full-grown Ṇyagrodha-tree
24. Is the sublime and incomparable body of the Sage,
Which is firm and possessed of the power of Vishṇu.[5]

[67 a. 1.] These 32 inconceivable features
The Teacher has declared to be the marks of the Lord of Men.

It is said that (these 32 marks) are like the reflection of the moon in the water—

25. As the form of the moon in a cloudless sky
Is seen in the blue waters of a lake in autumn,
In a similar way the Body that is surrounded by the multitudes of Bodhisattvas
Can be perceived (in its reflected form on earth)
Within the circle of adherents of the Supreme Buddha.[6]

Thus, the 10 Powers, the 4 kinds of intrepidity, and the 18 exclusive properties of the Buddha, as well as the 32 marks of the super-man, being united under one head, make up the number sixty-four.

---

[1] *atinīla-netra gopakṣma.* [2] *ūrṇā-keśa.*

[3] *uṣṇīṣa-mūrdhā.* [4] *sūkṣma-suvarṇa-cchaviḥ.* [5] Tib. *sred-med-bu.*

[6] Dar. 204 b. 2—3.—In a like way this Body of Bliss which is surrounded by the multitude of Bodhisattvas can be perceived in its reflected form, as the Apparitional Body, in the circle of adherents of the Supreme Buddha, by the Śrāvaka and Pratyekabuddha Saints, and by some of the ordinary beings.

26. These 64 distinctive features
Each taken separately with their causes
Are in gradual order to be known
From the Ratna-dārikā-sūtra.

These 64 properties of the Buddha in their variety are contained in the *Ratna-dārikā-sūtra*,[1] being indicated in the same order in which they have just been described. These points are spoken of as resembling, respectively, a thunderbolt, the lion, space, and the moon, and her reflection in the water. This subject which has been indicated in short is explained in the following 10 verses:—

27. (Being respectively) unbreakable, knowing no failure,
Incomparable and unchangeable,
(The Buddha's properties) are illustrated
By the examples of the thunderbolt, the lion,
Of space, and of the moon with her reflection in the water.

28. Of the complex of the Buddha's powers, six,
Three, and one, taken respectively, [67 b. 1.]
Remove (the Obscurations of) Ignorance, Distraction,
And (that of Defilement) with its residues,

29. As if they were piercing an armour,
Breaking a wall, and cutting down a tree.
The powers of the Sage are like a thunderbolt,
Being steady, essential, firm, and unbreakable.

30. Why are they steady?—Because they are essential.
Why are they essential?—Because they are firm.
Why are they firm?—Because they are unbreakable.
And being unbreakable, they are like a thunderbolt.

31. Being free from fear and independent,
Being firm and (possessed of) the highest dexterity,
The Lion of Sages is like a (real) lion,
Always fearless within the circle of hearers.

---

[1] Tib. Bu-mo-rin-po-chehi-mdo.

32. He has a clear knowledge of everything,
Therefore he abides without fearing anything, whatever it might be,
And he is fully independent,
Since his perception is by nature incomparable
Even with that of those who are purified.[1]

33. He is firm (in his knowledge) since his mind
Is always concentrated upon all the elements of existence,
And as he has overcome the force of illusion,[2]
He is possessed of the highest dexterity.

34. With the worldlings, with the Śrāvakas,
With those that act in solitude,[3] with the Sages,[4]
And with those of self-originated knowledge,[5]
The wisdom is (respectively) higher and higher,
And is of a more and more subtle character;
It is therefore illustrated by 9 examples.

35. (The first four)[6] are common in these worlds,
They are therefore similar to the solid,
The liquid, the hot, and the moving elements.
(But the properties of the Buddha), as they surpass
Everything mundane and supermundane,
Have a resemblance with the element of space.

36. Of these properties, thirty-and-two
Represent the Buddha's Cosmical Body,
Being inseparable from it like the form,
The shine, and the colour of a precious stone.

37. The other 32 distinctive features,
Which, being perceived, arouse delight,

---

[1] Sic acc. to Dar. 205 b. 5.

[2] *avidyā-vāsanā = ma-rig-paḥi-bag-chags.*

[3] The Pratyekabuddhas. [4] The Bodhisattvas. [5] The Buddhas.

[6] Dar. 206 a. 1—2.—The properties of the first four.

Are those peculiar to the Apparitional Body
And to that which completely enjoys the Truth,[1]

38. To those that are far and near from purification
[68a. 1.] Abiding in the circle of the Victor of the World,
These Bodies appear in two forms,
Like the moon's reflection in the water,
And like her true form in the skies.

Finished the exposition of the properties of the Buddha, the 3rd chapter of the analysis of the sources of the 3 Jewels called "The Sublime Science of the Great Vehicle." Described the immaculate attributes of the Buddha.

## IV. The Acts of the Buddha.

Now we have to speak of the functions (peculiar to the Buddha's Properties, viz. the acts) of the Lord. These acts, in short, manifest themselves in 2 ways,—without effort,[2] and uninterruptedly.[3] Therefore, after (the description of the properties of the Buddha), we have a verse referring to the Buddha's acts performed without effort and interruption:—

1. The constitution of the converts, the means of conversion,
The benefit of the convert in accordance with his nature,
The place and time at which he is to act,—
The Lord pervades (by his Wisdom)
And constantly manifests himself without effort.[4]

2. The ocean of Wisdom bearing the most precious jewels—his sublime properties,
Endowed with the light of the sun
Of Virtue and of Highest Wisdom,
Realizing the Paths of all the Vehicles,

---

[1] The Body of Bliss (*saṁbhoga-kāya*).

[2] *anābhoga* = *lhun-gyis-grub-pa.* [3] *anucchinna* = *rgyun-mi-ḥchad-pa.*

[4] Cf. Abhisamayālaṁkāra VIII. 9.—*paripākaṁ gate hetau yasya yasya yadā yadā* [1] *hitaṁ bhavati kartavyaṁ prathate tasya tasya saḥ.*

Having neither middle nor end,
Extensive and all-pervading like space,—
The Buddha perceives the treasury
Of immaculate virtues in all that lives,[1]
And, by the wind of his Divine Commiseration,
Disperses that web of clouds,—the Obscurations of Defilement and of Ignorance.

The summary given in these 2 verses is respectively explained in the following eight and ten:—

3. Who and by what means is to be converted,
What is to be the aim,[2] and at what place and time,—
Without having any constructive thought regarding all of this,
[68 b. 1.] The Sage always acts completely free from effort.

4. Indeed he does not give himself up to thoughts
As to what may be the constitution of the convert,
Which of the many means of conversion is to be used,
Where and when it is to be accomplished, the place and the time,

5. And, as concerns the factors of deliverance[3] and their foundation,
Their result and the favourable object,[4]
The Obscurations and the conditions for their removal.

6. The factors of deliverance are the 10 Stages,
And the 2 Accumulations[5] are their cause,
The result—it is Supreme Enlightenment,
And the living being (fit for the attainment of it)
Represents the favourable sphere.

7. The Obscurations are the innumerable forms of defilement,
The secondary defiling forces[6] and their residues,[7]

---

[1] The fundamental element or Essence of the Buddha.
[2] Of the conversion.
[3] *nairyānika* = *ṅes-ḥbyin.* [4] *parigraha* = *yoṅs-ḥdzin.*
[5] Of virtue and wisdom (*puṇya-jñāna-saṁbhāra*).
[6] *upakleśa* = *ñe-baḥi-ñon-moṅs.* [7] *vāsanā* = *bag-chags.*

And the factor which always suppresses them
Is the great Commiseration (of the Buddha).

8. These 6 points, taken respectively,
Are known to have a resemblance
With the ocean, with the sun, with space,
With a treasure, with clouds, and with the wind.

9. Being endowed with the waters of Wisdom,
And with the jewels of virtuous properties,
The stages of perfection resemble the ocean;
By administering help to all living beings,
The two accumulations are akin to the sun.

10. Great and extensive, without middle or end,
Supreme Enlightenment is like the element of space;
Being the Essence of the Supreme Buddha,
The element of the living beings resembles a treasure.

11. Accidental, pervasive, and essentially unreal,
The defiling elements are like a multitude of clouds,
And, bringing about the removal of these,
The Great Commiseration is like a mighty wind.

12. Performing acts of deliverance for the sake of others,
Perceiving the identity of himself and the living beings,
And, knowing no termination in his (altruistic) work,
The Buddha acts uninterruptedly, as long as the world exists.[1]

**The 9 Examples illustrating the Acts of the Buddha.**

It is said[2] that the Buddha is characterized as neither becoming originated nor disappearing (anew). Being thus immutable, he cannot be regarded as acting (in the ordinary sense) [69 a. 1.]. But, free from all (dialectical) thought-construction, he, without any effort, uninterruptedly exercises the special activity of the Buddha. Such

---

[1] *āsaṁsāram = ḥkhor-ba-ji-srid-du.*

[2] **In the Jñāna-āloka-alaṁkāra sūtra. Kg. MDO. III. 278 b. 6.** —

is his magnanimous nature. The following verse illustrates this magnanimity (of the Buddha) by examples in order to arouse faith in the inconceivable sphere of the Buddha with those who are free from doubt and error.—

13. Like Indra,[1] like the celestial drum,[2] like a cloud,[3] and like
Brahma,[4]
Like the sun,[5] and like the wish-fulfilling gem,[6]
Like the echo,[7] like space,[8] and like the earth,[9]—
Such is the Buddha in his acts.

This verse has a resemblance with a main aphorism. The variety (of examples) is now to be demonstrated in detail. This we have in successive order in the remaining part of the text:—

I. It is said that the Buddha appears like the form of Indra.[10]—

14. Suppose here were a surface
Of the purest Vaiḍūrya stone,
And, owing to its purity, the chief of the gods,
With the multitude of the daughters of the gods,

15. The great palace of Vijaya,
And the other abodes of the gods,
With all their various dwellings,
And their manifold objects of enjoyment
Were to be perceived on that surface.

---

[1] The example illustrating the miraculous essence of the Buddha's Body. Dar. 211 a. 2—4.

[2] Ditto—of the Buddha's Word. Ibid.

[3] Ditto—of the Buddha's Mind. Ibid.

[4] Ditto—of the corporeal and oral acts. Ibid.

[5] Ditto—of the mental acts. Ibid.

[6] Ditto—of the inconceivable nature of the Mind. Ibid.

[7] Ditto—of the inconceivable nature of the Word. Ibid.

[8] Ditto—of the inconceivable nature of the Body. Ibid.

[9] Ditto—of the foundation of the Buddha's activity. Ibid.

[10] Jñana-āloka-alaṁkāra-sūtra. Kg. MDO. III. 278 b. 6—280 b. 1.

16. Suppose then, that multitudes of men and women,
Abiding on that surface of the earth,
Would come to see the vision,
And utter the following entreaty:

17. May we, at an early date
Become like that chieftain of the gods!—
And, in order to attain such a state,
They would abide in the practice of virtue.

18. Owing to these their virtuous deeds,
They, without having a notion
That (the form perceived by them) was only a vision,
Would, after passing away from this earth,
Become reborn in the realm of the gods. [69 b. 1.]

19. That vision (of Indra), by itself,
Would be devoid of thought and motionless;
Nevertheless, (appearing) on the surface of the earth,
It would aid in the attainment of a great aim.

20. Similarly, if one is possessed of purest virtue, faith, &c.,
Conditioned by the practice of these virtues,
Appearing in one's mind, the Supreme Buddha,
Endowed with all his marks and features,

21. Walking and rising,
Sitting and lying,
Exercising different forms of activity,
Preaching the Doctrine of Quiescence,

22. Silent and abiding in concentrated trance,
Showing many miraculous apparitions,[1]
Possessed of majesty and glory in his acts,
Can be perceived by the living beings.

23. Having seen him, one becomes full of desire,
And acts for the attainment of Buddhahood;

---

[1] *prātihārya* = *cho-ḥphrul.*

And, having brought to development all the factors,
One comes to attain the desired position.

24. Thus, the apparition of the Buddha,
Completely free from constructive thought and motionless,
Abides, nevertheless, here in this world,
And aids in the attainment of the highest aim.

25. The ordinary beings, they do not know
That this is a reflection of their own mind,[1]
But they perceive the form (of the Buddha),
And this leads to the fulfilment of their aim.

26. Gradually, on the foundation of this perception,
Those that abide in this (great) Vehicle
Come to see, by transcendental vision,
The sublime Cosmical Body within themselves.

27. Suppose the whole of the earth would become
Free from all unevenness and stain,
And grow smooth, shining and pure
Like a clear and beautiful Vaiḍūrya stone.
And, owing to its purity, the numerous abodes of the gods
And the form of Indra would appear on it;
But, as this surface would gradually lose its smoothness,
The vision (thereon) would subsequently disappear.

28. However, anxious to attain (the desired state),
Devoting themselves to worship,
To obeissances, charity and the like, [70 a. 1.]
The multitudes of men and women
Would offer flowers with minds full of sublime desire.
Like that, in order to attain (the state of) the Lord of Sages,
Whose form appears in the mind as in a pure Vaiḍūrya stone,
The sons of the Buddha, with minds full of delight,
Direct their minds toward Supreme Enlightenment.

---

[1] A very pregnant expression of Āryāsanga's idealistic views.

29. As on the pure surface of Vaiḍūrya
The reflection of the highest god's body is perceived,
Similarly on the pure surface of a living being's mind
There appears the reflection of the Body of the Highest Sage.

30. The appearance and disappearance of this reflection of the living beings
Proceeds in accordance with their own mind,
Which can be either serene or turbid;
And as the reflection (of Indra)
Only appears as arising and vanishing,
So the existence and disappearance (of the Buddha's form)
Is not to be perceived as a reality.

II. It is said that (the Word of the Buddha) has a resemblance with the celestial drum.[1]

31. Just as, amongst the gods,
By the force of their previous virtues,
Without effort, without a special place,
Without form, without consciousness,
And without any constructive thought,

32. The drum of the Doctrine, again and again,
Summons the inattentive gods
By the sounds of "evanescence," of "suffering,"
Of "impersonality," and of "quiescence."[2]

33. In a similar way, being all-pervading
And free from effort and the like,
The Buddha comprises all living beings by his Word,
And shows his Doctrine to the worthy.

34. As, amidst the gods, the sound of their drum
Arises as the result of their own virtuous deeds,
In a like way, in this world, the Doctrine of the Lord,

---

[1] Jñāna-āloka-alaṁkāra-sūtra. Kg. MDO. III. 280 b. 1—282 a. 4.

[2] The 4 main aphorisms of the Doctrine.

Is, though preached by him, a result
Of the (virtuous) deeds of the living beings.

35. Devoid of effort, place, form, and constructive thought,
[70 b. 1.] The sound (of the celestial drum) is conducive to quiescence,
Similarly the Doctrine, devoid of these 4 (properties),
Conveys the realization of Nirvāṇa.

36. In the city of the gods the sound of their drum,
Beating uninterruptedly, arouses their fearlessness,
And at the time of their starting to battle with the passionate (Asuras)
Vanquishes these and keeps off distraction.
In a similar way, in this world, the Word of the Buddha,
Speaks of the Path for overcoming the passions
And the sufferings of a living being,
Which Path is conditioned by profound meditation
And mystic absorption in the Immaterial Sphere.[1]

Now, why has the drum of the Doctrine only been referred to (as an example), and not the cymbals and the other forms (of celestial music). These are likewise a product of the previous (virtuous) deeds of the gods, and appear in this Sūtra as accompanying the drum which is delightful to the ears of the gods.—(We answer:—They are not referred to, since) they have 4 points of dissimilarity with the voice of the Buddha. What are these?—(The fact of) being limited,[2] of not affording help, of not causing (real) felicity, and of not being conducive to deliverance. On the other hand, the drum of the Doctrine summons all the multitudes of inattentive gods, and its sound never ceases. For this reason it is demonstrated as not being limited (or local). Then it protects from the fear of being harmed by the Asuras and the other hosts of adversaries, and directs toward the sphere of attention. Therefore it appears as administering real help. Further-

[1] *catvāri dhyānāni* and *ārūpya-samāpattayaḥ*.

[2] *prādeśika* = *ñi-tshe-ba*.

more, it puts an end to the impure joy of sensual desire and is conducive to the true bliss, the supreme delight of the Doctrine. It thus brings about the attainment of (real) felicity. And, (finally) it utters the sounds, the words "evanescence," "suffering" [71 a. 1.], "impersonality," and "non-substantiality," and brings about the pacification of all harm and misfortune. Consequently, it appears as being conducive to deliverance. In short, the sphere of the voice of the Buddha has a resemblance with the drum of the Doctrine through these 4 characteristic properties, and is superior (to all other sounds). Accordingly, we have now a verse referring to the spherial potency of the Buddha's voice:—

37. As it has regard for all living beings,
Administers help, grants the Highest Bliss,
And manifests the 3 miraculous powers,[1]
The voice of the Lord is superior
To the sounds of the celestial music.

These 4 points of superiority are in short demonstrated in the 4 following verses in successive order:—

38. The tremendous sound of the celestial drum
Does not reach the ears of the inhabitants of the earth,
But the drum-like voice of the Buddha
Reaches the living beings who abide
Even in the lowest spheres of the world.

39. In the region of the gods, the celestial music,
Of which there are many millions of forms,
Sounds only in order to kindle the flames of desire,
But the unique voice of those
Whose essence is Highest Mercy
Sounds in order to calm the fire of suffering.

40. Amongst the gods, the sweet and pleasant sounds of their music
Only enhance the emotion of the mind,

---

[1] *prātihārya* = *cho-ḥphrul*. Cf. below.

(On the contrary) the voice of the merciful Buddha
Summons one to give up the mind
To the practice of profound meditation.

41. In short, that which is the cause of bliss,
In all the regions of the world, the celestial and the earthly,
Is said to have its foundation in the unique voice
Which pervades the whole of the world without exception.
[71 b. 1.]

Now, (as regards the miraculous manifestations of the Buddha) we have first of all the corporeal manifestation; as it pervades all the regions of the world in the 10 quarters of the sky, it is called "the manifestation of the Buddha's miraculous power."[1] Then there is the miraculous manifestation of (the faculty of) revealing the secret mental acts of the living beings.[2] It is due to the knowledge of all the varieties of the spiritual element. And finally we have the miraculous manifestations of (the Buddha's Teaching). These are the precepts and instructions[3] delivered by utterances of the Buddha's voice, which refer to the Path conducive to deliverance. Thus, the unimpeded voice of the Buddha manifests itself as illimited, akin to the element of space. It cannot however be heard in all its forms and everywhere. The reason consists in the defects of the living beings, but not in those of the voice (since there are none). The following verse demonstrates this, and shows that the defects are to be found only with those who are not able to hear:—

42. Those that are deprived of the faculty of audition
Cannot hear the subtle sounds,
And, likewise not all the sounds can reach,
Even the ears of those who are possessed
Of divine, superhuman audition.

---

[1] *ṛddhi-prātihārya = rdzu-ḥphrul-gyi-cho-ḥphrul.* M. V. § 16. 1.

[2] *ādeśanā-prātihārya = kun-brjod-paḥi-cho-ḥprul.*

[3] *anuśāsanī-prātihārya = rjes-su-bstan-paḥi-cho-ḥphrul.*

43. In a similar way the Doctrine, exceedingly subtle,
As it is the object of Transcendental Knowledge,
Can reach only the ear of one
Whose mind is free from defilement.

III. It is said that (the mind of the Buddha in its activity) is like a cloud.[1]—

44. As, in summer-time, the clouds,
The cause of an abundant harvest,
Discharge, without any effort,
Their torrents of water upon the earth,—

45. In a like way, from the clouds of Commiseration
The rain of the waters of the Lord's Highest Doctrine
Is the cause of the harvest of virtue with living beings,
And descends without any searching thought.

46. [72 a. 1.] As, amidst the living beings
Who venture on the path of virtue,
The clouds, agitated by the wind,
Discharge their torrents of rain;
Similarly, as the virtues of the living beings
Grow through the wind of Commiseration,
The rain of the Highest Doctrine
Descends from that cloud which is the Buddha.

47. Representing Highest Wisdom and Mercy
Abiding in the inalterable pure celestial sphere,
And having for his essence the immaculate waters of concentration and memory,
The Lord of Sages is like a cloud
The cause of the harvest of virtue in this world.

With regard to the varieties of the "receptacles"[2] (of the waters of the Doctrine), we have:—

---

[1] Jñāna-āloka-alaṁkāra-sūtra. Kg. MDO. III. 282 a. 4—283 a. 5.
[2] *bhājana = snod.*

48. Cool, sweet, soft, and light
Is the water descending from the clouds,
But having touched on earth such places
That are filled with salt and the like,
It becomes possessed of many different tastes.

49. Similar is the rain of the Doctrine
Concerning the eightfold Path of the Saint;[1]
Abundant, it issues from the clouds of mercy,
But, owing to its repositories, the hearts of the living beings,
It subsequently assumes a variety of forms.

With regard to the manifestations (of the Buddha's mind), which are independent (from the character of the converts), we have:—

50. The three categories of living beings,
Those that have faith in the Great Vehicle,
Those of intermediate character, and the hostile,
Are (respectively) like men, like the peacocks,
And like the ghosts[2] (with regard to the rain).

51. When, at the end of spring, there are no clouds,
The human beings and the birds that do not move in the skies
are distressed,
And, on the contrary, when, in summer-time,
The rain descends on earth, the ghosts are suffering;
Similar is the state of the living beings
Desirous of the Doctrine and hostile to it,
When, from the clouds of Commiseration,
The waters of the Doctrine descend or not.

52. Discharging thick drops of rain, hail and lightening,
The clouds have no special regard
[72 b. 1.] For the small insects and the inhabitants of the caves,
Similar are the clouds of Wisdom and Mercy
With their subtle and their grand methods and means.

---

[1] *ārya-aṣṭāṅga-mārga = ḥphags-paḥi-lam-yan-lag-brgyad.*

[2] *preta = yi-dvags.*

They (eject the rain of the Doctrine) independently
From those that are purified from passion
And those who indulge in egoistic views.

As concerns the fact that (the rain of the Doctrine) quenches the fire of suffering, it is said:—

53. Five are the paths by which one travels
Through beginningless and endless birth and death in the Saṁsāra,
And there is no happiness in these 5 states of existence,
As there cannot be a sweet odour with impurities.
The suffering is constant, it is like the feeling
Which is produced through the contact with fire,
With weapons, ice, salt,[1] and the like;
But the rain of the Doctrine which descends
From the clouds of mercy can pacify it.

54. With the gods,—transmigration, and with men—
The constant search of objects of desire—,
This is suffering; having come to this conviction,
Even the highest of gods and men,
Grown wise, will have no desires;
Guided by wisdom and by the Word of the Buddha,
They perceive: "This is suffering, this its cause,
And this is its extinction."

55. The illness is to be cognized, its cause removed,
The state of happiness attained, and the remedy used;
Like that, Phenomenal Life, its Cause, Extinction, and the Path[2]
Are to be cognized, removed, realized, and resorted to.

IV. It is said that (the Buddha in his acts) is like the great Brahma:[3]—

---

[1] Dar. 118 b. 1.—Like salt put on a wound.

[2] The 4 Truths of the Saint.

[3] Tib. *tshaṅs-pa-chen-po*. Jñāna-āloka-alaṁkāra-sūtra. Kg. MDO. III. 284 b. 5—286 a. 7.

56. As Brahma, without moving from his abode,
In all the regions of the gods
Demonstrates his apparition without effort,

57. In a similar way, in all the regions of the world,
The Lord, though motionless in his Cosmical Body,[1]
Shows himself in apparitional forms
Without effort to those that are worthy. [73 a. 1.]

58. Just as Brahma, never moving from his abode,
Manifests himself in the World of Desire,[2]
Is seen by the gods, and this perception
Pacifies the desire of the objects (of enjoyment),—
Similarly the Lord, though motionless in his Cosmical Body,
Is seen by the worthy in all the regions of the world,
And this his vision removes for ever all defilement.

59. As owing to the vows of Brahma himself[3]
His vision is perceived without effort,
So is the Apparitional form (of the Buddha),
Which becomes originated by itself.

With regard to the fact of the Buddha's being invisible (for some) we have:—

60. Manifesting the descent from Tuṣita, the entrance into the womb,[4]
Birth, and the arrival at his father's palace,
His merry life (amongst noble women),
His existence in solitude, the victory over the Evil One,
The attainment of Supreme Enlightenment,
And the teaching of the Path that leads to the city of Peace,
The Lord is inaccessible to the eyes of the unworthy.

V. It is said (that the Buddha in his mental acts) is akin to the sun:[5]—

---

[1] Cf. above.
[2] *kāma-dhātu* = *ḥdod-khams.*
[3] Dar. 120 a. 1.
[4] *garbha-avakrānti* = *lhums-su-ḥjug-pa.*
[5] Jñana-āloka-alaṁkāra-sūtra. Kg. MDO. III. 284 b. 5—286 a. 7.

61. Warmed by the sun, at one and the same time,
The lotus flower expands and the Kumuda folds its leaves;
But the sun, it has no searching thought
About the qualities and the defects
Of the water-born flowers as they open and fold.
Similar to that is the Saint (in his acts).

The living beings are by nature of 2 kinds, viz. the converts and the non-converts. Now, as concerns the converts, they appear as similar to a lotus flower and to a receptacle of pure water:—

62. Free from any searching thought,
The sun, expanding its light, simultaneously, everywhere
Makes the lotus flower unfold its leaves
And causes to ripen (other kinds of plants).

63. Similar is that sun which is the Buddha
With its rays—the Highest of Doctrines;
Free from a searching thought, they are directed
Upon the converts resembling lotus flowers.

64. Arising in the heavens of Enlightenment
As the Cosmical Body and the visible forms, [73 b. 1.]
The Sun of Omniscience casts the rays
Of Divine Wisdom over all living beings.

65. Indeed, in (the minds of) all the converts
That are like receptacles of purest water
The innumerable reflections of that sun
Which is the Lord simultaneously appear.

Thus, the Buddhas, though they are free from dialectical thought-construction, appear to the 3 categories of living beings,[1] and teach their Doctrines. With respect to this their character they have a resemblance with the sun:—

---

[1] Dar. 221 a. 3.—Those who have a firm conviction regarding that which is right, those that are uncertain, and those who are definitely rooted in error.

66. Being always all-pervading
In the sphere of the Absolute, infinite like space,
The sun of the Buddha casts (its rays) on the converts,
As if they were mountains, in accordance with their merit.

67. The sun, great, radiant, and shining,
And illuminating the whole of the world,
Gradually casts (its rays) on the high,
The intermediate, and the lower mountains;
Similar is the sun of the Buddha which gradually
Casts its rays on the multitudes of living beings.

The light of the Buddha is superior to that of the sun. Indeed—

68. (The power of) penetrating into all the different worlds
And all the regions of the sky does not exist with the sun,
And it likewise cannot remove the darkness of ignorance
And demonstrate the essence of everything cognizable;
But the multitudes of rays which, in a variety of colours,
Emanate from him who is endowed with Highest Mercy.—
They illuminate and show the essence of all things.

69. The living beings who, at the time of the arrival of the Buddha,
Are like blind, obtain sight and, free from all harm,
Cognize the truth by this perception,
And those blinded by ignorance,
Who have fallen into the sea of worldly existence,[1]
And are obscured by the darkness of false views,
Have their minds illuminated by the light of the sun of the Buddha
And come to perceive the Truth unseen before.

VI. It is said that the Buddha in his acts is like the wish-fulfilling gem:[2]—

---

[1] *bhava-ārṇava* = *srid-paḥi-mtsho.*

[2] Jñāna-āloka-alaṁkāra-sūtra. Kg. MDO. III. 286 a. 7—287 a. 4.

70. Just as the wish-fulfilling gem [74 a. 1.]
Free from a searching thought, simultaneously,
Fulfills, in every case separately, all the desires
Of those who have in view a special aim,—

71. In a similar way, through reliance upon the Buddha,
Those possessed of different thoughts and inclinations
Come to hear the Doctrine in its various forms.—
But the Buddha has no searching thought regarding them.

72. As the jewel fulfilling all wishes, without effort,
Grants to others the objects desired by them,
Similarly the Sage abides as long as the world exists,
Acting without effort for the sake of others in accordance with their merits.

It is said that the appearance of the Buddha (in this world) occurs very rarely. Indeed:—

73. Just as precious jewels, concealed
Under the ground or in the depths of the ocean,
Are hard to be obtained here by those who are desirous of them;
Similarly we know that with the living beings
Who are unworthy and overpowered by the passions
The perception of the Buddha by their mind
Is exceedingly hard to be secured.

VII. It is said that (the voice of the Buddha) is like the sound of the echo.[1] Indeed:—

74. Just as the sound of the echo
Arising from vocal intimation[2]
Is free from searching thought, is not articulated,
And has no real foundation, neither external nor internal,

[1] Ibid. 287 a. 4—288 a. 5.
[2] *vijñapti* = *rnam-rig.*

75. Similar to it is the voice of the Buddha.
It arises through the intimations of others,[1]
Is devoid of searching thought, is inconceivable,
And has no real foundation, neither within, nor without.

VIII. It is said that (the inconceivable character of the Buddha's Body) has a resemblance with space:[2]—

76. Immaterial, invisible,
Inaccessible to the senses,
Without support and without foundation,
Formless and incapable of being pointed to—such is space.

77. Although it is experienced (as divisible)
In higher and in lower (parts),
This is not its true nature,
Which is that of being one whole. [74 b. 1.]
Similarly, though the Buddha is seen in all his different forms,
He is not such as we perceive him
(Being unique and undifferentiated).

IX. It is said that (the true Essence of the Buddha as the foundation for his activity) is like the earth:[3]—

78. As all that is produced by the earth,
Being, unconsciously, supported by it,
Can thrive, show (its growth), and expand,
In a like way, having, without any searching thought,
Their foundation in that soil which is the Supreme Buddha,
The roots of virtue of the living beings
Can thrive in all their different forms.

The meaning of all these examples is in short as follows:—

79. The performance of these and those acts without effort
Is not to be perceived (by us). Therefore,

---

[1] Dar. 222 b. 5. The acts of worship and reverence produced by faith, &c.

[2] Jñāna-āloka-alaṁkāra-sūtra. Kg. MDO. III. 288 b. 4—289 a. 5.

[3] Ibid. 288 a. 5—288 b. 4.

For the sake of clearing the doubts of the converts,
These 9 examples have been demonstrated.

80. And the discourse in which these examples
Are shown in detail, by its very name,[1]
Shows the necessity of their indication.

81. Adorned[2] by this magnificent light[3]
Of the knowledge[4] which is the result of study,
The wise will speedily penetrate[5]
Into the whole of the sphere of Buddhahood.[6]

82. The subject discussed is illustrated
By the form of Indra on the Vaiḍūrya surface,
And the other examples, nine in number;
Apprehend thou, in short, their meaning.

83. The apparition, teaching, and the all-pervading character,
The miraculous manifestations (of the corporeal and mental acts),
The emanation of the Highest Wisdom,
The inconceivable nature of body, speech, and mind,
And the character of Great Commiseration
All this is demonstrated here.

84. The mind of the Buddha with which all exertion
Is completely purified, since it is free
From every kind of thought-construction,
Is like the apparition of the reflected form
Of Indra on the surface of the Vaiḍūrya stone.

85. The proposition[7] is here the pacification of effort,
And the mind free from searching thought is the logical reason,[8]

---

[1] Sarva-buddha-viṣaya-avatāra-jñāna-āloka-alaṁkāra-sūtra.
[2] *alaṅkṛta = brgyan-pa.* [3] *āloka = snaṅ-ba.*
[4] *jñāna = śes-pa* or *ye-śes.* [5] *avatariṣyanti = ḥjug-par-ḥgyur.*
[6] *sarva-buddha-viṣaye = saṅs-rgyas-kyi-psyod-yul-kun-la.*
[7] *pratijñā = dam-bcaḥ.* [8] *hetu = gtan-tshigs.*

And, in order to prove its analytical character,[1]
The examples[2] of the form of Indra, &c., are given.

86. Here the meaning of the subject is as follows:—
The apparition of the Buddha's Body and the other aspects
Are manifested without any effort whatever,
Since the Teacher is not liable to birth and death.

[75 a. 1.] Now, with reference to this subject, we have moreover the following 4 verses which contain the summary of all the examples:—

87. He who appears like Indra,
Like the celestial drum, and like a cloud,
Like Brahma, the sun, and the king of wish-fulfilling gems,
Like the echo, like space, and like the earth,
And acts without effort for the sake of others
As long as dures this world's existence,—
He is cognized by the Saint in meditation.

88. The apparition is like the reflected form
Of the chief of the gods on a precious stone,
And the excellent teaching is like the celestial drum,
The all-penetrating Wisdom and Love, they are like clouds,
Pervading all that lives up to the highest limits of existence.[3]

89. Like Brahma, the Lord is motionless in the immaculate plane,
But shows himself in many apparitional forms,
Like the sun is the Divine Wisdom that ejects its light,
And similar to the pure wish-fulfilling gem is the Buddha's mind.

90. Like the echo, the Buddha's Word is not produced by effort,
His Body is, like space, all-pervading and eternal,
And the state of Buddhahood[4] is like the earth,

---

[1] *svabhāva-hetu* = *raṅ-bžin-gtan-tshigs.* As this verse shows, the *svabhāva-hetu* and the syllogism founded upon it were already known to Āryāsanga.

[2] *dṛṣṭānta* = *dpe.*

[3] *bhavāgra* = *srid-rtse.*

[4] *buddha-bhūmi* = *saṅs-rgyas-kyi-sa.*

Being the ground for the growth of those remedies
Which are the virtuous elements of the living beings.

Now, according to these examples, Buddha the Lord is, for ever, unsubjected to birth and disappearance. How is that? We perceive (the Buddha) as becoming born and disappearing, and in such a form he makes manifest, without effort and uninterruptedly, his activity amongst the living beings. To this we say:—

91. The causes for the perception of the Buddha
In the mind, pure like the Vaiḍūrya stone,
Is the intensity of the faculty of faith
Owing to which this purity of the mind is preserved.

92. In accordance with the origination and bereavement of virtue
[75 b. 1.] The form of the Buddha appears and disappears;
But, similar to Indra, the Lord
In his Cosmical Body neither becomes born, nor does he vanish.

93. Thus, without any exertion and effort,
(Emanating) from the Cosmical Body which neither arises nor disappears anew,
He manifests as long as the world exists
The apparition (of his body) and his other acts.

## The Points of Dissimilarity between the Examples and the Manifestations of the Buddha.[1]

94. Such is the meaning of all these examples,
And such the order (in which they are given);
However the subject has not been discussed
With regard to the dissimilarity that exists
Between the examples and the topics expressed by them.

95. (Indeed), the Buddha is like a reflected form,
But the latter, being voiceless, cannot match him;
He is like the drum of the gods, but this one

---

[1] The following verses contain the so-called *vyatireka-alaṁkāra*.

Is not like him in every respect,
Since it is not always efficient.

96. (His mind) resembles a great cloud,
But (the cloud) is not completely like it,
Since it does not remove the seed of all that is harmful;
He has a similarity with the great Brahma,
But the latter is not perfectly akin to him,
Since he does not bring (all living beings) to maturity.

97. He is similar to the form of the sun, but as the sun
Does not completely dispel all darkness, it cannot match him;
He appears like the jewel that fulfills all wishes,
But this jewel is not completely like him, as it is not so hard
to be obtained.

98. He resembles the echo, but as the latter
Is a product of causes, there is no perfect similarity;
He is like space, but space is not the foundation
Of virtue; therefore it is not akin to him.

99. (The Buddha) is like the surface of the earth,
But as he is the support for the continuance
Of the welfare of all that lives, mundane and supermundane,
(There is no perfect similarity between them).

100. Indeed, on the foundation of the Buddha's Enlightenment,
The Path that leads out of this world takes its origin,
And, by the deeds of virtue, the saintly Path,
The degrees of mystic trance,[1] the immeasurable feelings,[2]
And the absorption in the Immaterial Sphere[3] is conditioned.

Finished the exposition of the acts of the Buddha, the 4th chapter of the investigation of the sources of the 3 Jewels called "The Sublime Science of the Great Vehicle to Salvation." [76 a. 1.] Finished the explanation of the subjects contained in the verses.

---

[1] *dhyāna = bsam-gtan.* [2] *apramāṇa = tshad-med-pa.*
[3] *ārūpya-samāpatti = gzugs-med-kyi-sñoms-ḥjug.*

## V. The Merits of Founding one's Belief in the Doctrine of the Essence of Buddhahood.

After this we have 6 verses referring to the merits of those who found their belief in the 4 topics[1] which have been described:—

1. The element of Buddhahood, the Enlightenment of the Buddha,
The Buddha's properties, and the Buddha's acts,—
They are inaccessible even to the purest minds,
Being the exclusive sphere of the Leaders (of the world).

2. But the Sage[2] who is full of faith in these features of Buddhahood
Becomes a receptacle of all the mass of the Buddha's properties,
And, experiencing the highest delight in these unthinkable virtues,
Surpasses the merits of all other living beings.

3. One, being desirous to attain Enlightenment,
And possessed of gold and jewels
Equal in number to the sands in all the worlds of the Buddhas,
Daily offers them to the Lord of the Doctrine;
Another, if he hears but one word (of this Teaching)
And through this attains faith, will reap merit
Greater than that of such an offering.

4. One, wise and striving for Supreme Enlightenment
During numerous æons, without effort,
Preserves body, speech and mind in stainless chastity,—
Another, if he hears but a word of this teaching
And through this comes to faith, can reap
Merit, greater than that of the purest morals.

5. One gives himself up to mystic absorption
Suppressing the fire of passion in the 3 spheres of this World,

[1] The Essence of Buddhahood, Supreme Enlightenment, the Properties and the acts of the Buddha.

[2] The Bodhisattva.

And, transferred to the limits of the abode of the gods and
of Brahma,
Meditates upon the means of attaining
The inalterable state of Supreme Enlightenment;
Another, if he hears but one word (of this teaching)
And through it comes to faith, will reap [76 b. 1.]
Merit, greater than that of deepest meditation.

6. Charity, it secures objects of worldly enjoyment,
Morality leads to blissful existence,[1]
And deep meditation is conducive to the removal of defilement;
But Highest Wisdom completely removes all defilement and
ignorance,
Therefore it is superior (to all other virtues),
And its source is the study (of the Doctrine).

The meaning of these verses is explained in the following nine:—

7. The fundamental element, its metamorphose,[2]
The properties, and the acts pursuing the welfare (of the
living beings)
These are the 4 points discussed,
Which are accessible only to the Wisdom of the Buddha.

8. But the Sage who becomes full of faith,
As regards their existence, power, and virtuous qualities,
Becomes worthy of attaining the position
Of the Buddha at an early date.

9. Indeed, he is full of devotion and faith
That this inconceivable sphere exists,
That one like himself can realize it,
And, having once attained it, becomes endowed with such
properties.

---

[1] *svarga* = *mtho-ris.*

[2] *parāvṛtti* i. e. the metamorphose of the element of Buddhahood througa the purification from all defilement (Dar. 229 b. 4).

10. One becomes a receptacle of zeal,
Of energy, faith, and concentration,
Of Highest Wisdom and all the other virtues,
And the mind directed toward Enlightenment[1]
Is always extant with such (a Saint).

11. And, owing to its constant presence,
The son of the Buddha cannot be diverted (from his aim),[2]
Brings to accomplishment the Highest Virtues,
And becomes possessed of perfect purity.

12. The Highest Virtues are 5 in number,[3]
And there being no thought-construction
With regard to their 3 aspects,
Their accomplishment represents perfect Purification,
Since all hostile elements are completely removed.

13. The Highest Charity[4] consists of all the virtues of granting gifts,[5]
The Highest Morality represents (the quintessence of) moral merit,[6]
Patience and concentration of mind arise from deepest meditation,[7]
And energy is peculiar to all of them.[8] [77 a. 1.]

14. That which represents constructive thought
Regarding the 3 aspects of activity[9]
Is considered to be the Obscuration of Ignorance,[10]

---

[1] *bodhi-citta* = *byaṅ-chub-kyi-sems.*

[2] *avaivartika* = *phyir-mi-ldog-pa.*

[3] I.e. the first 5 Transcendental Virtues, representing the Accumulation of Virtue (*puṇya-saṁbhāra*; Dar. 231 a. 5).

[4] *dāna-pāramitā.*

[5] *dānamaya-puṇyakriyā-vastu.*

[6] *śīlamaya-puṇyakriyā-vastu.*

[7] *bhāvanāmaya-puṇyakriyā-vastu.*

[8] Cf. Sūtrālaṁkāra XVI. 7. and Commentary.

[9] Dar. 231 b. 5.—The habit of maintaining the separate reality of subject, object and act (*trimaṇḍala*).

[10] *jñeya-āvaraṇa.*

And the thoughts concerning the reality of envy and the like
We esteem to be the Obscuration of Moral Defilement.[1]

15. But, without Highest Wisdom,[2] all the other virtues
Are not possessed of the factors for removing (both) the Obscurations.
Therefore Highest Wisdom is superior (to all),
And, as the source of it is study (of the Doctrine),
It is this study which is most important.

16. Thus, on the foundation of authoritative Scripture[3] and of Logic
I have expounded (this treatise) in order to attain
Perfect purification, for myself, exclusively,
And to assist those whose mind is full of faith
And of the complement of highest virtue.

Next we have a verse concerning the way how (the treatise) explains (the subject-matter):—

17. As, with the aid of a lamp, of lightning,
Of a precious stone, the sun, and the moon,
Those possessed of vision are able to see,—
Similarly, I have explained all this,
Relying upon the Lord, who illuminates
By (his perfect knowledge of) the meaning,
The words, and the elements, and by his flashes of idea.[4]

Then comes a verse regarding that which has been explained:[5]—

18. The word which is connected with the Doctrine
That pursues the (ultimate) aim (of mankind),

---

[1] Acc. to the Tibetan authors, this is the standpoint of the Prāsangikas, who consider realism in general to be the Obscuration of Moral Defilement.

[2] *prajñā* = *śes-rab* in the sense of *prajñā-pāramitā*.

[3] *āgama* = *luṅ*. Dar. 232 a. 6.—The Sūtras commented by the Uttaratantra.

[4] The 4 methods of intense penetration (*pratisaṁvid*).

[5] The Word of the Buddha (*pravacana*).

Is conducive to the removal of defilement in the 3 spheres of this world,
And demonstrates the bliss of Quiescence,—
Is that of the Great Sage; all that disagrees with it is of other origin.

Next we have a verse concerning that by means of which (this Word of the Buddha) is explained:[1]—

19. That which, referring exclusively to the Teaching of the Lord,
Is an explanation (of this Teaching) by one
Whose mind is completely free from distraction,
And agrees with the Path leading to Salvation
Is to be revered as if it were
The Word of the Great Sage himself.

With regard to the means of preserving oneself from becoming deprived (of this Doctrine) we have the following verses:—

20. In this world there is absolutely none wiser than the Buddha,
No other who were omniscient and perceiving
All that exists and the essence of all things;
Therefore, do not have any confusion regarding
The discourses held by the Sage himself;[2]
Otherwise, the precepts of the Lord will be subverted,
And the Highest Doctrine will undergo harm. [77 b. 1.]

21. The depreciation of a Saint by those possessed of passion and ignorance,[3]
And the contempt regarding the Doctrine taught by him
Is always produced by erroneous views;
Therefore let not your mind become mingled

---

[1] The Exegetical Treatises (*śāstra*) interpreting Scripture. Cf. my translation of Bu-ton pp. 25 and 42.

[2] Dar. 233 b. 5—6. The consideration of the discourses of conventional meaning to express the direct one and the reverse, and the depreciation of some of the precepts by saying: "This is not the Word of Buddha."

[3] Dar. 234 a. 4.—who say that the Hīnayānist is not a Saint, &c.

With the defilement of these views.—
Only clean a garment may be dyed,
But not one that is smeared with grease.

Concerning the causes for becoming deprived (of the Doctrine) we have:—

22. Want of intelligence, want of faith in the virtuous (Doctrine),
Indulgence in ill-suited pride,
Obscurity through the rejection of the Teaching,
Apprehension of the conventional[1] meaning as direct,[2]
Love of gain, adherence to false views,
Reliance upon one who insults the Doctrine,
The fact of being distant from those that maintain it,
And insufficient devotion,—through all this
One becomes deprived of the Doctrine of the Saints.

With reference to the result of this loss of the Doctrine we have:—

23. The wise, they need not be afraid
Of fire, of the violent poison of serpents,
Of murderers, and of thunder and lightning,
As are those who have rejected this profound Doctrine.
Indeed, fire, serpents, foes, and lightning,
They only deprive one of (this) life,
But they cannot inspire the fear
Of being reborn in the lowest of hells.[3]

24. Even one who, repeatedly relying on bad friends,
Is hostile to the Buddha and commits the vilest of sins[4]
In killing father, mother and the Saints,
And sowing dissention among the Highest Congregation,—
Even that man can speedily become delivered (from sin),

[1] *neyārtha = draṅ-don.*
[2] *nitārtha = ṅes-don.*
[3] *avīci = mnar-med.*
[4] *anantarya = mtshams-med-pa.*

If he reflects over the Absolute Essence.
But where is Salvation for one
Who in his mind is hostile to the Doctrine?—

**Conclusion.**

25. I have thus duly expounded the 7 subjects,—
The 3 Jewels, the perfectly pure element (of Buddhahood),
The immaculate Supreme Enlightenment,
And the Buddha's properties and acts.
May, by the merit I have acquired through this,
All these living beings come to perceive
The Lord Amitāyus[1] endowed with boundless light,
And, having seen him, may they become possessed
Of the sublime vision of the Highest Truth
And attain Supreme Enlightenment.

The meaning contained in these 10 verses is again explained by the following three:—[78 a. 1.]

26. Owing to what cause and for what motive,[2]
What and in what manner has been expounded,[3]
And what is the natural outflow[4] (of the Doctrine),[5]
This is demonstrated by 4 verses.

27. Two verses[6] refer to the means of self-purification,
And one[7]—to the cause of the bereavement of the Doctrine,
And then, the following 2 verses[8]
Demonstrate the consequences (of this).

28. And finally, the sphere (in which the converts are to be born),[9]
Their steadfastness (regarding the Teaching),
Their attainment of Enlightenment,

[1] Tib. *tshe-dpag-med.*
[2] Verse 16.
[3] Verses 17 and 18.
[4] *niṣyanda-phala.*
[5] The treatises commenting Scripture, verse 19.
[6] 20 and 21.
[7] Verse 22.
[8] 23 and 24.
[9] The circle of Amitāyus or Amitābha.

And the preaching of the Doctrine (by them),
In short the 2 forms of the result
Are spoken of in the last verse.[1]

Finished the exposition of the advantages (of being possessed of faith in the 7 sublime subjects),[2] the 5th chapter of the investigation of the sources of the 3 Jewels entitled "The Sublime Science of the Great Vehicle to Salvation."—End of the explanation of the meaning contained in the verses.—

Through this explanation
Of the precious Highest Doctrine of the Great Vehicle
I have reaped inconceivable merit;
May, by the force of it, all living beings become the receptacles
Of the immaculate jewels of this Highest Sublime Teaching.

Finished the teacher Āryāsanga's explanation of "The Sublime Science of the Great Vehicle," the work of the Lord Maitreya.—

[1] Verse 25.
[2] Sic acc. to Dar. 236 a. 5—6.

# Technical Terms.


*acalā* = *mi-gyo-ba*, 116, 142, 170, 202, 209, 221.

*adveṣa* = *źe-sdaṅ-med-pa*, 97.

*adhigama-dharma* = *rtogs-paḥi-chos*, 145.

*adhicitta-śikṣā* = *sems-kyi-bslab-pa*, 121.

*adhiprajñā-śikṣā* = *śes-rab-kyi-bslab-pa*, 121.

*adhimukti* (= *mos-pa*), 158, 163, 164.

*adhivacana* = *tshig-bla-dvags*, 114, 128.

*adhiśīla-śikṣā* = *tshul-khrims-kyi-bslab-pa*, 121.

*adhyāśaya* = *lhag-paḥi-bsam-pa*, 102.

*anantarya* = *mtshams-med-pa*, 294.

*anabhiniveśa* = *mṅon-par-ma-źin-pa*, 165, 166.

*anādi-kāla-āyāta-dharmatā-pratilabdham* = *gotram*, 103, 206.

*anābhoga* = *lhun-gyis-grub-pa*, 107, 115, 124, 150, 246, 267.

*anāsrava-karma* = *zag-pa-med-paḥi-las*, 222.

*anāsrava-jñāna* = *zag-med-ye-śes*, 98.

*anāsrava-dhātu* = *zag-med-kyi* (*zag-pa-med-paḥi*)-*dbyiṅs*, 108, 139, 168, 169, 198, 224, 240.

*anitya* = *mi-rtag-pa*, 165.

*anityatā* = *mi-rtag-pa-ñid*, 120.

*animitta* (-*vimokṣa-mukha*) = *mtshan-ma-med-pa*(*ḥi-rnam-thar-gyi-sgo*), 120.

*anucchinna* = *rgyun-mi-ḥchad-pa*, 267.

*anuttarā samyaksaṁbodhi* = *yaṅ-dag-par-rdzogs-paḥi-byaṅ-chub*, 114.

*anutpattika-dharma-kṣānti* = *mi-skye-baḥi-chos-la-bzod-pa*, 209.

*anuśaṁsa* = *phan-yon*, 176.

*anuśaya* = *bag-la-ñal*, 136, 175, 221.

*anuśāsanī-prātihārya* = *rjes-su-bstan-paḥi-cho-ḥphrul*, 276.

*antya-cakra*(-*pravartana*) = *ḥkhor-lo-tha-ma*, 81.

*apavāda* = *skur-ḥdebs*, 236, 252.

*apraṇihita* (-*vimokṣa-mukha*) = *smon-pa-med-pa*(*ḥi-rnam-thar-gyi-sgo*), 120.

*apratiṣṭhita-nirvāṇa* = *mi-gnas-paḥi-myaṅ-ḥdas*, 162, 173, 174.

*apratisaṁkhyāyopekṣā* = *ma-brtags-btaṅ-sñoms*, 261.

*apratihata* = *thogs-pa-med-pa*, 248.

*apramāṇa* = *tshad-med-pa*, 86, 288.

*ab-dhātu* = *chuḥi-khams*, 262.

*abhijñā* = *mṅon-par-śes-pa*, 148, 180, 199.

*abhinirvṛtta* = *mṅon-par-grub-pa*, 127.

*abhimukhī* = *mṅon-du-gyur-pa*, 199.

*abhiṣikta* = *dbaṅ-bskur-ba*, 117.

*abhisaṁskṛta* = *mṅon-par-ḥdus-byas-pa*, 198.

*abhisamaya* = *mṅon-rtogs*, 94.

*abhyantara-āyatana* (= *naṅ-gi-skye-mched*), 192.

*abhyudaya* = *mṅon-mtho*, 148, 161.

*amoha* = *gti-mug-med-pa*, 97.

*ayoniśo manasikāra* = *tshul-bźin-ma-yin-paḥi-yid-la-byed-pa*, 133, 187.

*arūpa* (*ārūpya*)-*dhātu* = *gzugs-med-khams*, 127.

*alobha* = *chags-med-pa*, 97.

*avidyā* = *ma-rig-pa*, 134, 170.

*avidyā-vāsanā* = *ma-rig-paḥi-bag-chags*, 105, 146, 153, 170, 204, 213, 221, 266.

*avinivartanīya* = *phyir-mi-ldog-pa*, 202.

*avīci* = *mnar-med*, 214, 294.

*avaivartika* = *phyir-mi-ldog-pa*, 202, 291.

*avaivartika-dharma-cakra* = *phyir-mi-ldog-paḥi-chos-kyi-ḥkhor-lo*, 120.
*aśubha-bhāvanā* = *mi-sdug-paḥi-sgom-pa*, 222.
*aśaikṣa* = *mi-slob-pa*, 181.
*aṣṭadaśa-āveṇika-dharmāḥ* (= *ma-ḥdres-paḥi-chos-bco-brgyad*), 122.
*asaṁskṛta* = *ḥdus-ma-byas*, 104, 113, 124, 125, 155, 171, 186, 231, 256.
*asakta* = *chags-pa-med-pa*, 248.
*asad-anta* = *med-mthaḥ*, 87.
*ākāra* = *rnam-pa*, 165.
*ākāśam anāvṛtiḥ* (= *nam-mkhaḥ ma-sgrib-pa*), 262.
*āgantuka* = *glo-bur-ba*, 113.
*āgantuka-mala* = *glo-bur-gyi-dri-ma*, 90, 105.
*āgama* (= *luṅ*), 292.
*āgama-dharma* = *luṅ-gi-chos*, 145.
*ācārya-saṁjñā* = *slob-dpon-gyi-ḥdu-śes*, 153.
*ātma-dṛṣṭi* = *bdag-lta* (= *satkāya-dṛṣṭi*), 159.
*ātma-pāramitā* = *bdag-gi-pha-rol-tu-phyin-pa* (= *paramātma-pāramitā*), 164, 166.
*ātman* (= *bdag*), 164.
*ādarśa-jñāna* = *me-loṅ-lta-buḥi-ye-śes*, 101.
*ādi-śānta* = *gzod-ma-nas-ži-ba*, 139.
*ādeśanā-prātihārya* = *kun-brjod-paḥi-cho-ḥphrul*, 276.
*āyatana* = *skye-mched*, 105, 187.
*ārūpya-dhātu* = *gzugs-med-khams*, 171, 222.
*ārūpya-samāpatti* (= *gzugs-med-kyi-sñoms-ḥjug*), 274, 288.
*ārya* = *ḥphags-pa*, 222.
*ārya-aṣṭāṅga-mārga* = *ḥphags-paḥi-lam-yan-lag-brgyad*, 278.
*ārya-pudgala* (= *ḥphags-paḥi-gaṅ-zag*), 97, 182.
*ārya-satya* = *ḥphags-paḥi-bden-pa*, 205.
*ālambana* = *dmigs-pa*, 165.
*ālaya-vijñāna* = *kun-gži-rnam-par-śes-pa*, 89, 95, 99, 100.
*āvaraṇa* = *sgrib-pa*, 111.
*āvenika-dharma* = *ma-ḥdres-paḥi-chos*, 251, 261.
*āśraya* = *rten*, 134.
*āsaṁsāram* = *ḥkhor-ba-ji-srid-du*, 168, 269.
*āsrava-kṣaya-jñāna* = *zag-pa-zad-paḥi-ye-śes*, 180, 198.
*āsrava-kṣaya-jñāna-bala* = *zag-pa-zad-pa-mkhyen-paḥi-stobs*, 260.
*indriya-parāpara-jñāna-bala* = *dbaṅ-po-mchog-daṅ-mchog-ma-yin-pa-mkhyen-paḥi-stobs*, 259.
*īśvara* = *dbaṅ-phyug*, 107.
*uccheda-anta* = *chad-mthah*, 87, 174.
*udāna* = *ched-du-brjod-pa*, 227.
*upakleśa* = *ñe-baḥi-ñon-moṅs-pa*, 186, 268.
*upātta-pañca-upādāna-skandha* = *zin-paḥi-ñe-bar-len-paḥi-phuṅ-po-lṅa*, 166.
*upādāna* = *ñe-bar-len-pa*, 170, 229.
*upādāna-kāraṇa* = *ñer-len-gyi-rgyu*, 100, 113, 193.
*ṛddhi* = *rdzu-ḥphrul*, 253.
*ṛddhi-prātihārya* = *rdzu-ḥphrul-gyi-cho-ḥphrul*, 276.
*eka-kṣaṇa-abhisaṁbodha* (= *skad-cig-ma-gcig-gi-mṅon-par-rdzogs-par-byaṅ-chub-pa*), 151.
*eka-jāti-pratibaddha* = *skye-ba-gcig-gis-thogs-pa*, 202.
*eka-yāna* (= *theg-pa-gcig*), 104, 108, 169, 205.
*eka-rasa* = *ro-gcig-pa*, 104, 212, 227.
*aupacārika buddha* = *saṅs-rgyas-btags-pa-pa*, 116.
*karma* = *las*, 105, 110, 131, 170, 180.
*karma-vipāka-jñāna-bala* = *las-rnams-kyi-rnam-smin-mkhyen-paḥi-stobs*, 259.
*karma-saṁkleśa* = *las-kyi-kun-nas-ñon-moṅs-pa*, 136.
*kāma-dhātu* = *ḥdod-khams*, 127, 152, 199, 222, 280.

*kuśala-mūla-samprayukta-kleśa* = *dge-baḥi-rtsa-ba-daṅ-mtshuṅs-par-ldan-paḥi-ñon-moṅs-pa*, 194.
*kṛtya-anuṣṭhāna-jñāna* = *bya-ba-sgrub-paḥi-ye-śes*, 101, 112.
*kliṣṭa-manas* = *ñon-yid*, 100.
*kleśa* = *ñon-moṅs*, 105, 131.
*kleśa-āvaraṇa* = *ñon-moṅs-kyi-sgrib-pa* (= *ñon-sgrib*), 108, 127, 130, 181, 210, 242.
*kleśa-saṁkleśa* = *ñon-moṅs-paḥi-kun-nas-ñon-moṅs-pa*, 136.
*garbha-avakrānti* = *lhums-su-ḥjug-pa*, 280.
*gāthā* = *tshigs-su-bcad-pa*, 227.
*geya* = *dbyaṅs-kyis-bsñad-pa*, 227.
*gocara* = *spyod-yul*, 113.
*gotra* = *rigs*, 84, 89, 96, 97, 98, 99, *passim*.
*grāhya-grāhaka* = *gzuṅ-ḥdzin*, 87, 126, 141.
*cakravarti-rājan* (= *ḥkhor-los-bsgyur-baḥi-rgyal-po*), 213, 249.
*catvāri dhyānāni* (= *bsam-gtan-bźi*), 274.
*catvāri vaiśāradyāni* (= *mi-ḥjigs-pa-bźi*), 122.
*catvāri saṁgraha-vastūni* = *bsdu-baḥi-dṅos-po-bźi*, 86.
*cāturdvīpaka lokadhātu* = *gliṅ-bźiḥi-ḥjig-rten-gyi-khams*, 152.
*citta* = *sems*, 134.
*citta-abhisaṁskāra* = *sems-mṅon-par-ḥdu-byed-pa*, 176.
*citta-utpāda* = *sems-bskyed* (= *bodhi-citta-utpāda*), 162.
*citta-caryā* = *sems-kyi-spyod-pa*, 154.
*citta-svabhāva* = *sems-kyi-raṅ-bźin*, 105.
*citta-svabhāva-paramārtha-satya* = *sems-kyi-raṅ-bźin-don-dam-bden-pa*, 187.
*cintāmaṇi* = *yid-bźin-nor-bu*, 148.
*cintāmaṇi-ratna-rāja* (= *yid-bźin-nor-buḥi-rgyal-po*), 251.
*cintāmayī prajñā* = *bsam-pa-las-byuṅ-baḥi-śes-rab*, 112.
*caitta* = *sems-byuṅ*, 97.
*cyuty-upapatti-jñāna-bala* = *ḥchi-ḥpho-daṅ-skye-ba-mkhyen-paḥi-stobs*, 260.
*chanda* = *ḥdun-pa*, 176.
*jarā-maraṇa* = *rga-śi*, 171.
*jāti* = *skye-ba*, 124, 125.
*jāti-saṁkleśa* = *skye-baḥi-kun-nas-ñon-moṅs-pa*, 136.
*jina* = *rgyal-ba*, 116.
*jinātmaja* = *rgyal-sras*, 200.
*jīva* = *srog*, 196.
*jñāna-kāya* (= *ye-śes-kyi-sku*), 109.
*jñāna-dharma-kāya* (= *ye-śes-chos-sku*), 258.
*jñāna-pūrvaṁgama-jñāna-anuparivarti* (*kāya-vāṅ-manas-karma*), 262.
*jñeya-āvaraṇa* = *śes-sgrib* or *śes-byaḥi-sgrib-pa*, 130, 181, 210, 242, 291.
*tathatā* = *de-bźin-ñid*, 104, 111, 157, 168, 178, 183, 228.
*tathāgata* = *de-bźin-gśegs-pa*, 183, 205, 228.
*tathāgata-garbha* = *de-bźin-gśegs-paḥi-sñiṅ-po*, 82, 89, 104, 108, 114.
*tathāgatatvam*, 157, 229.
*tarka* = *rtog-ge*, 133.
*tīrthika* = *mu-stegs-pa*, 106, 163, 173.
*tejo-dhātu* = *meḥi-khams*, 262.
*trimaṇḍala-pariśuddhi* (*viśuddhi*) = *ḥkhor-gsum-yoṅs-su-dag-pa*, 120, 254.
*trisāhasra-mahāsāhasra-lokadhātu* = *stoṅ-gsum-gyi-stoṅ-chen-poḥi-ḥjig-rten-gyi-khams*, 151.
*trīṇi kuśala-mūlāni* = *dge-rtsa-gsum*, 97.
*trīṇi śaraṇāni* = *skyabs-gsum*, 143.
*darśana-mārga* = *mthoṅ-lam*, 135, 141, 202.
*daśa-bala* = *stobs-bcu*, 112, 122.
*daśa vaśitāḥ* = *dbaṅ-bcu*, 116, 143.
*dāna-pāramitā* (= *sbyin-paḥi-pha-rol-tu-phyin-pa*), 291.
*dāna-maya-puṇyakriyā-vastu*, 291.
*divya-cakṣuḥ* = *lhaḥi-mig*, 214.
*duḥkha* (= *sdug-bsṅal*), 132, 171, 173, 184.

*duḥkha-samudaya*, 238.
*dūraṁgamā* (= *riṅ-du-soṅ-ba*), 221.
*dṛḍha-adhyāśaya* = *lhag-paḥi-bsam-pa-brtan-pa*, 199.
*dṛṣṭānta* = *dpe*, 286.
*dṛṣṭi-heya* = *mthoṅ-bas-spaṅs-pa*, 127, 213, 221.
*deśanā-dharma* = *bstan-paḥi-chos*, 145, 227.
*dravya-sat* = *rdsas-yod*, 161.
*dravya-sat-pudgala* = *gaṅ-zag-rdzas-yod-pa* (= *ālaya-vijñāna*), 99.
*dvādaśāṅga-dharma-pravacana* (= *gsuṅ-rab-yan-lag-bcu-gñis*), 145.
*dveṣa* = *że-sdaṅ*, 136, 213, 244.
*dharma* (= *chos*), 87.
*dharma-āyatana* (= *chos-kyi-skye, mched*), 248.
*dharma-kāya* = *chos-sku*, 101 *passim*.
*dharma-kāya-bhūta-koṭi-prabhāvita* = *chos-kyi-sku-yaṅ-dag-paḥi-mthas-rab-tu-phye-ba*, 126.
*dharma-dhātu* (= *chos-kyi-khams*), 248.
*dharma-dhātu* = *chos-kyi-dbyiṅs*, 104, 141, 251.
*dharma-dhātu* = *gotra*, 103.
*dharma-dhātu-viśuddhi* = *chos-dbyiṅs-rnam-par-dag-pa*, 101.
*dharma-dhātu-svabhāvaka* (= *chos-kyi-dbyiṅs-kyi-raṅ-bźin*), 89.
*dharma-nairātmya* = *chos-kyi-bdag-med*, 138, 196.
*dharma-paryāya* = *chos-kyi-rnam-graṅs*, 118.
*dharma-meghā* = *chos-kyi-sprin*, 116, 117, 170, 201, 210, 221.
*dharma-skandha* (= *chos-kyi-phuṅ-po*), 184.
*dharmatā* (= *chos-ñid*), 87, 88, 165.
*dharmeśvara* = *chos-kyi-dbaṅ-phyug*, 255.
*dharmin* = *chos-can* (= *tathatā*), 178.
*dhātu* = *khams*, 82, 89, 96, 111, 230.
*dhātu* = *gotra*, 89.
*dhātu* = *khams* (the 18 comp. elements), 105, 187.
*dhāraṇī* = *gzuṅs*, 121, 210.
*dharaṇī-mukhatā* = *gzuṅs-kyi-sgo*, 210.
*dhīmat* = *blo-ldan*, 116.
*dhyāna* = *bsam-gtan*, 288.
*nānā-adhimukti-jñāna-bala* = *mos-pa-sna-tshogs-mkhyen-paḥi-stobs*, 259.
*nānā-dhātu-jñāna-bala* = *khams-sna-tshogs-mkhyen-paḥi-stobs*, 259.
*nānātva-saṁjñā* = *sna-tshogs-paḥi-ḥdu-śes*, 261.
*nāma-rūpa* = *miṅ-daṅ-gzugs*, 124, 127.
*nāma-rūpa-saṁgṛhīta-janma* = *miṅ-gzugs-kyis-bsdus-paḥi-skye-ba*, 193.
*nitya* = *rtag-pa*, 100, 104, 165.
*nitya-pāramitā* = *rtag-paḥi-pha-rol-tu-phyin-pa*, 166.
*nidāna* = *gleṅ-gźi*, 227.
*nidāna-parivarta* = *gleṅ-gźiḥi-leḥu*, 115.
*nimitta-grāhiṇaḥ* = *mtshan-mar-ḥdzin-pa-can*, 136.
*nirukti* = *ṅes-tshig*, 133.
*nirodha* = *ḥgog-pa*, 98, 111, 131, 132, 147, 173.
*nirodha-satya* = *ḥgog-bden*, 108, 246, 250.
*nirmāṇa-kāya* = *sprul-sku*, 101, 110, 112, 230, 241, 251, 252.
*nirvāṇa* = *tathatā*, 207.
*nirvāṇa-dhātu* = *mya-ṅan-las-ḥdas-paḥi-dbyiṅs*, 114.
*nirvikalpaka* = *rnam-par-mi-rtog-pa*, 150, 209, 210, 226.
= *rnam-par-rtog-pa-med-pa*, 236, 241.
*nirvikalpaka-jñāna* (= *rnam-par-mi-rtog-paḥi-ye-śes*), 225.
*nirvedha-bhāgīya* (= *ṅes-par-ḥbyed-paḥi-cha-daṅ-mthun-pa*), 86.
*niḥśreyasa* = *ṅes-legs*, 148.
*niṣprapañca* = *spros-bral*, 150.
*niṣyanda-phala* = *rgyu-mthun-paḥi-ḥbras-bu*, 123, 226, 295.

niḥsvabhāva (= raṅ-bźin-med-pa), 255.
nītārtha = ṅes-don, 94, 226, 294.
neyārtha = draṅ-don, 94, 226, 294.
nairātmya = bdag-med-pa, 120.
nairyāṇika = ṅes-ḥbyin, 268.
pañca-dvāra-vijñāna = sgo-lṅaḥi-rnam-śes, 101.
paratantra = gźan-dbaṅ, 85, 87, 88.
para-pratyaya-agamya = gźan-gyi-rkyen-gyis-rtogs-min-pa, 124.
para-pratyayair akṛta = rkyen-gźan-gyis-ma-byas-pa, 135.
paramātman = dam-paḥi-bdag, 109, 168.
paramārtha = don-dam-pa, 110, 111, 165.
paramārtha-śūnyatā = don-dam-pa-stoṅ-pa-ñid, 236.
paramārtha-satya = don-dam-bden-pa, 123, 205.
paramārtha-satyena saṁgṛhīta-dhātu = don-dam-paḥi-bden-pas-bsdus-paḥi-khams, 194.
paramārthena saṁgṛhītaṁ buddhatvam, 125.
paraṁparayā = brgyud-nas, 206.
parārtha-saṁpatti = gźan-gyi-don-phun-sum-tshogs-pa, 124.
parāvṛtti = yoṅs-su-gyur-pa, 99, 100, 149, 181, 240, 290.
parikarman = yoṅs-su-sbyoṅ-ba, 119.
parikalpanā = kun-tu-rtog-pa, 197.
parikalpita = kun-tu-brtags-pa, 189.
parikalpita = kun-btags, 85, 87.
parigraha = yoṅs-ḥdzin, 268.
pariniṣpanna = yoṅs-grub, 85, 87, 100.
paripācana = yoṅs-su-smin-pa, 194.
paripuṣṭa-gotra = rgyas-ḥgyur-gyi-rigs, 100, 107, 113, 157.
paripuṣṭa-gotra = samudānīta-gotra, 96.
pāramārthika śaraṇa = don-dam-paḥi-skyabs, 146, 147.
pāramitā (= pha-rol-tu-phyin-pa), 194, 209.
piṭaka = sde-snod, 160.
puṇya-jñāna-saṁbhāra (= bsod-nams-daṅ-ye-śes-kyi-tshogs), 86, 208, 268.
puṇya-saṁbhāra = bsod-nams-kyi-tshogs, 194, 291.
pudgala = gaṅ-zag, 87, 196.
pudgala-nairātmya = gaṅ-zag-gi-bdag-med, 138.
pūrva-nivāsa-anusmṛti-jñāna-bala = sṅon-gyi-gnas-rjes-su-dran-pa-mkhyen-paḥi-stobs, 260.
pūrva-praṇidhana = sṅon-gyi-smon-lam, 126.
pṛthagjana = so-soḥi-skye-bo, 114, 151, 182, 222.
pṛthivī-dhātu = saḥi-khams, 262.
pṛṣṭha-labdha = rjes-su-thob-pa, 211, 240, 241, 242.
prakṛti-parinirvṛtta = raṅ-bźin-gyis-yoṅs-su-mya-ṅan-las-ḥdas-pa, 88, 109.
prakṛtistha-gotra = raṅ-bźin-gnas-rigs, 100, 107, 157, 206, 214, 229.
prajñapti-sat = btags-yod, 161.
prajñā = śes-rab, 164, 292.
prajñā-upāya (= śes-rab-daṅ-thabs), 255.
prajñā-pāramitā (= śes-rab-kyi-pha-rol-tu-phyin-pa), 160, 163, 164, 198, 292.
praṇidhāna = smon-pa, 165, 176.
praṇīta = gya-nom-pa, 212.
pratijñā = dam-bcaḥ, 285.
pratipakṣa = gñen-po, 102, 163.
= gñen-poḥi-phyogs, 131, 132.
pratipatter ādhāraḥ = sgrub-paḥi-rten, 84.
pratibimba = gzugs-brñan, 257.
pratibhāna = spobs-pa, 118.
pratisaṁvid = so-so-yaṅ-dag-par-rig-pa, 117, 292.
pratītya-samutpāda-dharma = rten-ḥbrel-gyi-chos, 144.
pratyaya = rkyen, 149, 155, 170.
pratyavekṣaṇa-jñāna = so-sor-rtog-paḥi-ye-śes, 101.
pratyātma-vedya = so-so-raṅ-gis-rig-par-bya-ba, 112.

*prapañca* = *spros-pa*, 171, 182.
*pramuditā* = *rab-tu-dgaḥ-ba*, 127, 140, 201, 221.
*pravacana* = *gsuṅ-rab*, 111, 292.
*prahāṇa* = *spaṅs-pa*, 181, 243.
*prahāṇa-jñāna-saṁpatti* = *spaṅs-pa-daṅ-ye-śes-phun-sum-tshogs-pa*, 111.
*prātihārya* = *cho-ḥphrul*, 271, 275.
*prādeśika* = *ñi-tshe-ba*, 141, 142, 274.
*prārthanā* = *don-du-gñer-ba*, 176.
*preta* = *yi-dvags*, 278.
*phalāsākṣātkriyātmakam* (*kāritram*), 198.
*bāla* = *byis-pa*, 114.
*bāhya-artha-śūnyatā* (= *phyi-rol-gyi-don-gyi-stoṅ-ñid*), 81.
*bīja* = *sāmarthya*, 95, 98.
*buddha-kṣetra* = *saṅs-rgyas-kyi-źiṅ*, 154.
*buddha-cakṣuḥ* = *saṅs-rgyas-kyi-spyan*, 130, 214.
*buddha-dharmatā* (= *saṅs-rgyas-kyi-chos-ñid*), 208.
*buddha-bhūmi* = *saṅs-rgyas-kyi-sa*, 286.
*buddha-samavadhāna* = *saṅs-rgyas-daṅ-phrad-pa*, 194.
*bodhi* = *byaṅ-chub*, 112.
*bodhi-citta* = *byaṅ-chub-kyi-sems*, 127, 239, 291.
*bodhi-citta-utpāda* = *byaṅ-chub-tu-sems-bskyed*, 84.
*bodhipakṣika-dharma* = *byaṅ-chub-kyi-phyogs-daṅ-mthun-paḥi-chos*, 86.
*bodhi-maṇḍa* = *byaṅ-chub-kyi-sñiṅ-po*, 116.
*bodhisattva-piṭaka* = *byaṅ-chub-sems-dpaḥi-sde-snod*, 227.
*bodhy-aṅga* = *byaṅ-chub-kyi-yan-lag*, 155.
*bhava-ārṇava* = *srid-paḥi-mtsho*, 282.
*bhavāgra* = *srid-rtse*, 286.
*bhājana* = *snod*, 179, 277.
*bhājana-loka* = *snod-kyi-ḥjig-rten*, 169, 186.
*bhāvanā-mārga* = *sgom-lam*, 135.
*bhāvanā-maya-puṇyakriyā-vastu*, 291.
*bhāvanā-heya* (= *sgom-pas-spaṅs-pa*), 213, 221.
*madhya-cakra*(*-pravartana*) = *ḥkhor-lo-tha-ma*, 81.
*madhyama-pratipad* = *dbu-maḥi-lam*, 87.
*mana-āyatana* (= *yid-kyi-skye-mched*), 100.
*manas* = *yid*, 134.
*mano-jalpa* = *yid-kyi-brjod-pa*, 133.
*manomaya-kāya* = *yid-kyi-raṅ-bźin-gyi-lus*, 170, 173, 193, 198, 203, 222.
*mano-vijñāna* = *yid-kyi-rnam-par-śes-pa*, 101.
*mala-śuddhita* (= *dri-mas-dag-pa*), 244.
*mahā-karuṇā* = *thugs-rje-chen-po* and *sñiṅ-rje-chen-po*, 179.
*mātsarya* = *ser-sna*, 209.
*mahā-cakravāla* = *khor-yug-chen-po*, 151.
*mahā-puruṣa-lakṣaṇa* (= *skyes-bu-chen-poḥi-mtshan*), 249.
*mārga* = *lam*, 111, 131, 132, 147.
*muni-ṛṣabha* = *thub-paḥi-khyu-mchog*, 244.
*mūla-kleśa* = *rtsa-baḥi-ñon-moṅs-pa*, 186.
*moha* = *gti-mug*, 136, 213, 244.
*yogin* = *rnal-ḥbyor-ba*, 251.
*ratna-traya* = *dkon-mchog-gsum*, 116.
*ravita* = *ca-co*, 261.
*rāga* = *ḥdod-chags*, 136, 213, 244.
*rūpa* = *gzugs*, 165.
*rūpa-kāya* = *gzugs-sku*, 110, 111, 124.
*rūpa-dhātu* = *gzugs-khams*, 127, 152, 222.
*lokottara* = *ḥjig-rten-las-ḥdas-pa*, 111, 123, 148, 168, 241.
*lokottara-jñāna* = *ḥjig-rten-las-ḥdas-paḥi-ye-śes*, 222.
*lokottara-dharma* = *ḥjig-rten-las-ḥdas-paḥi-chos*, 156.
*laukika* = *ḥjig-rten-pa*, 148, 168, 241.
*laukika-vyavahāra* = *ḥjig-rten-gyi-tha-sñad*, 192.
*vajropamā-samādhi* = *rdo-rje-lta-buḥi-tiṅ-ṅe-ḥdzin*, 223.
*vaśitā-prāpta* = *dbaṅ-thob*, 258.
*vācaka-śabda* = *rjod-byed-kyi-sgra*, 133.
*vāyu-dhātu* = *rluṅ-gi-khams*, 262.

*vāyu-maṇḍala* = *rluṅ-gi-dkyil-ḥkhor*, 189.
*vāsanā* = *bag-chags*, 117, 134, 146, 153, 209, 221, 251, 268.
*vāsanā-anusaṁdhi* = *bag-chags-kyi-mtshams-sbyor*, 173.
*vikalpa* = *rnam-par-rtog-pa*, 109.
*vicāra* (= *dpyod-pa*), 250.
*vijñapti* = *rnam-rig*, 283.
*vijñāna* = *rnam-par-śes-pa*, 134.
*vitarka* (= *rtog-pa*), 250.
*vināśa* = *ḥjig-pa*, 124, 125.
*vipakṣa* = *mi-mthun-phyogs*, 209, 223.
*vipaśyanā* = *lhag-mthoṅ*, 189.
*vipāka* = *rnam-par-smin-pa*, 191, 258.
*viprayukta-saṁskāra* = *ldan-min-ḥdu-byed*, 98.
*vimalā* = *dri-ma-med-pa*, 202.
*vimukti-jñāna-darśana* = *rnam-par-grol-baḥi-ye-śes-mthoṅ-ba*, 212.
*viśeṣa-lakṣaṇa* = *khyad-par-gyi-mtshan-ñid*, 173.
*viṣaya* = *yul*, 113, 133.
*visaṁyoga* = *bral-ba*, 258.
*visaṁyoga-phala* = *bral-baḥi-ḥbras-bu*, 246.
*vaiyavadānika* = *rnam-par-byaṅ-ba*, 88, 132, 185.
*vaiyavahārika* = *tha-sñad-pa*, 113.
*vaiśāradya* = *mi-ḥjigs-pa*, 118, 260.
*vyatireka-alaṁkāra*, 287.
*vyavahāra* = *tha-sñad*, 133.
*vyākaraṇa* = *luṅ-du-bstan-pa*, 149, 227.
*śāśvata-anta* = *rtag-mthaḥ*, 87, 174.
*śāstra* (= *bstan-bcos*), 293.
*śilībhūta* = *bsil-bar-gyur-pa*, 128.
*śīla-maya-puṇyakriyā-vastu*, 291.
*śukla-dharma* = *dkar-poḥi-chos*, 177, 248.
*śuddhi* (*śuci*)-*pāramitā* = *gtsaṅ-baḥi-pha-rol-tu-phyin-pa*, 166.
*śūnya* = *stoṅ-pa*, 235.
*śūnyatā* = *stoṅ-pa-ñid*, 120, 150, 161, 166, 232, 234.
*śūnyatā-karuṇā-garbham* (*bodhicittam*), 199.
*śūnyatā*(-*vimokṣa-mukha*) = *stoṅ-pa-ñid* (-*kyi-rnam-thar-gyi-sgo*), 120, 234.
*śaikṣa* = *slob-pa*, 222.
*śrutimayī prajñā* = *thos-pa-las-byuṅ-baḥi-śes-rab*, 112.
*ṣaḍ-āyatana* = *skye-mched-drug*, 96.
*saṁvṛti* = *kun-rdzob*, 87, 96, 110, 111, 144, 165.
*saṁskāra* = *ḥdu-byed*, 146, 170, 174, 192, 222.
*saṁskṛta* = *ḥdus-byas*, 100, 104, 125, 145, 192.
*saṁskṛta-dharma* (= *ḥdus-byas-kyi-chos*), 174.
*saṁketa* = *brda*, 133.
*saṁjñā* = *ḥdu-śes*, 151.
*satkāya-dṛṣṭi* = *ḥjig-tshogs-la-lta-ba*, 127, 236.
*sattva-loka* = *sems-can-gyi-ḥjig-rten*, 169.
*satpuruṣa* = *skyes-bu-dam-pa*, 177.
*sad-anta* = *yod-mthaḥ*, 87.
*saṁtāna* = *rgyud*, 103, 113, 222.
*samatā-jñāna* = *mñam-ñid-ye-śes*, 101.
*samādhi-ṛṣabha* = *tiṅ-ṅe-ḥdzin-khyu-mchog*, 118.
*samādhi-mukha* = *tiṅ-ṅe-ḥdzin-gyi-sgo*, 160, 179.
*samādhi-mukhatā*, 210.
*samāpatty-āvaraṇa* = *sñoms-ḥjug-gi-sgrib-pa*, 252.
*samāropa* = *sgro-ḥdogs*, 236, 252.
*samāhita-jñāna* = *mñam-bźag-ye-śes*, 211, 240.
*samucchinna-kuśala-mūla* = *dge-baḥi-rtsa-ba-kun-tu-chad-pa*, 98.
*samudaya* = *kun-ḥbyuṅ*, 132, 173.
*samudānīta* (*gotra*) = *yaṅ-dag-par-bsgrub-pa*, 113.
= *yaṅ-dag-par-blaṅs-pa*, 157, 214, 229.
*saṁbhoga-kāya* = *loṅs-spyod-rdzogs-paḥi-sku* = *loṅs-sku*, 101, 110, 112, 229, 241, 251, 252, 267.

sarva-ākāra-vara-upeta-śūnyatā = rnam-pa-thams-cad-kyi-mchog-daṅ-ldan-paḥi-stoṅ-pa-ñid, 208.
sarvagata = kun-tu-soṅ-ba, 151, 157, 184, 228.
sarvatra-gāminī-pratipaj-jñāna-bala = kun-tu-ḥgro-baḥi-lam-mkhyen-paḥi-stobs, 259.
sarva-dharma-śūnyatā (= chos-thams-cad-kyi-stoṅ-ñid), 81.
sarva-dharma-samatā = chos-thams-cad-mñam-pa-ñid, 117.
sarva-dhyāna-vimokṣa-samādhi-samāpatti-saṁkleśa-vyavadāna-vyutthāna-jñāna-bala = bsam-gtan-daṅ-rnam-par-thar-ba-daṅ-tiṅ-ṅe-ḥdzin-daṅ-sñoms-par-ḥjug-paḥi-kun-nas-ñon-moṅs-pa-daṅ-rnam-par-byaṅ-ba-mkhyen-paḥi-stobs, 260.
sarva-prapañca-anta-vinirmukta = spros-paḥi-mthaḥ-thams-cad-daṅ-bral-ba, 123.
sāṁketika-kāya = brdaḥi-sku, 259.
sāṁkleśika = kun-nas-ñon-moṅs-pa, 88, 132, 185.
sādhumatī = legs-paḥi-blo-gros, 116, 170, 210, 221.
sāmānya-lakṣaṇa = spyiḥi-mtshan-ñid, 159, 173, 182.
sāṁbhogika (kāya) = saṁbhoga-kāya, 229.
sāsrava = zag-bcas, 232.
siṁhāsana = seṅ-geḥi-khri, 118.
sukha-pāramitā = bde-baḥi-pha-rol-tu-phyin-pa, 166.
sūtra = mdo-sde, 227.
skandha = phuṅ-po, 105, 161, 171, 187.
skhalita = ḥkhrul-ba, 261.
sthāna-asthāna-jñāna-bāla = gnas-daṅ-gnas-min-mkhyen-paḥi-stobs, 259.
sthiti = gnas-pa, 124, 125.
svatantra-ātman = raṅ-dbaṅ-can-gyi-bdag, 163.
svato'nutpanna = raṅ-ñid-ma-skyes-pa, 135.
svabhāva-kāya = ṅo-bo-ñid-sku, 104, 109, 229, 251, 252.
svabhāva-śuddha = raṅ-bźin-gyis-dag-pa, 135, 244.
svabhāva-hetu = raṅ-bźin-gtan-tshigs, 286.
svayambhū = raṅ-byuṅ (= pratyeka-buddha), 160.
svarga = mtho-ris, 290.
svalakṣaṇa = raṅ-gi-mtshan-ñid, 116, 159.
svastika = gyuṅ-druṅ, 147.
svābhāvika (kāya) = svabhāva-kāya, 252.
svārtha-sampatti = raṅ-gi-don-phun-sum-tshogs-pa, 124.
hetu = gtan-tshigs, 285.
hetu = rgyu, 149, 155, 170.

## Works, Authors, and Schools.

Akṣayamati-nirdeśa-sūtra, 92.
Abhidharma, 97.
Abhidharmakośa (= Mdzod), 96, 98, 171, 246, 262.
Abhidharmakośa-vyākhyā, 98.
Abhidharma-samuccaya (= Mṅon-pa-kun-btus), 83, 94.
Abhidharma-sūtra = Chos-mṅon-paḥi-mdo, 230.
Abhisamayālaṁkāra = Mṅon-rtogs-rgyan, 81, 82, 83, 88, 89, 92, 93, 94, 95, 96, 97, 103, 104, 126, 138, 141, 142, 147, 149, 154, 160, 163, 165, 174, 175, 193, 198, 200, 229, 235, 236, 253, 255, 267.
Abhisamayālaṁkārālokā, 103, 165, 170, 183, 199, 206, 207.
Aṣṭasāhasrikā, 237.
Āgama-anusāriṇo vijñānavādinaḥ = Luṅ-gi-rjes-ḥbraṅs-sems-tsam-pa, 99.
Ārya-Vimuktasena (= Ḥphags-pa Grol-sde), 83.

Āryāsanga i.e. Ārya-Asanga (Ḥphags-pa-Thogs-med), 81, 83, 90, 92, 94, 95, 96, 99, 106, 286, 296.

Uttaratantra = Rgyud-bla-ma, 81, passim.

Uttaratantra-vyakhyā = Thogs-ḥgrel, 90.

Kāla-cakra, 106.

Kāśyapa-paripṛcchā = Ḥod-sruṅs-kyis-źus-paḥi-mdo, 161.

Skabs-brgyad-ka, 97, 98, 101, 102, 104, 105.

Gaganagañja-sūtra = Nam-mkaḥi-mdzod-kyi-mdo, 91, 189.

Guṇabhadra, 91.

Gūḍhārtha = Don-gsaṅ, Commentary on the Mahāyāna-saṁgraha, 100.

Gyal-tshab-dar-ma-rin-chen, Commentary on the Uttaratantra (Dar-ṭik), 90, passim.

Grub-mthaḥ, v. Siddhānta.

Grub-mthaḥ-rtsa-baḥi-tshig-ṭik-śel-dkar-me-loṅ, 92.

Grub-mthaḥ-rin-chen-phreṅ-ba, 130.

Candragomin, 101.

Cārvāka, 161.

Jam-yaṅ-gā-b[a]i-lo-ḍō (Ḥjam-dbyaṅs-dgaḥ-baḥi-blo-gros), Commentary on the Abhisamayālaṁkāra, 82, 84, 85, 88.

Jam-yaṅ-źad-pa (Ḥjam-dbyaṅs-bźad-pa), 84, 92, 97, 103, 104, 110.

Jo-naṅ-pa, 106.

Jñana-āloka-alaṁkāra-sūtra = Ye-śes-snaṅ-ba-rgyan-gyi-mdo, 91, 109, 128, 134, 177, 206, 228, 248, 269, 270, 273—285.

Jñānagarbha (= Ye-śes-sñiṅ-po), 105.

Ḥjigs-med-dbaṅ-po, 130.

Tathāgata-garbha-sūtra = De-bźin-gśegs-paḥi-sñiṅ-poḥi-mdo, 91, 92, 95, 107, 156, 214—220, 231.

Tathāgata-mahā-karuṇā-nirdeśa = Dhāraṇīsvara-rāja-paripṛcchā, q. v., 91.

Dar-ṭik, v. Gyal-tshab-dar-ma-rin-chen.

Daśabhūmaka-Sūtra, 119.

Dignāga (= Phyogs-kyi-glaṅ-po *or* Phyogs-glaṅ), 99.

Dolbopa-śeirab-gyaltshan, 106.

Dharma-dharmatā-vibhanga = Chos-daṅ-chos-ñid-rnam-ḥbyed, 81, 83, 86, 87, 88, 94.

Dharmarakṣa (Ku-fa-hu), 91.

Dhāraṇīśvara-rāja-paripṛcchā = Gzuṅs-kyi-dbaṅ-phyug-rgyal-pos-źus-paḥi-mdo, 91, 115, 116, 119, 150, 153, 154.

Nāgārjuna (= Klu-sgrub), 81, 92.

Nāyāyika, 96.

Nyāya-anusāriṇo vijñānavādinaḥ = Rigs-paḥi-rjes-ḥbraṅs-sems-tsam-pa, 99.

Pañcaviṁśatisāhasrikā, 95, 103.

Parivrājaka = Kun-tu-rgyu, 161.

Prajñā-pāramitā-sūtras, 82, 83, 94, 95, 137.

Phar-phyin-skabs-brgyad-ka, v. Skabs-bryad-ka.

Bu-ton (Bu-ston), History of Buddhism (Chos-ḥbyuṅ), 83, 87, 88, 92, 94, 136, 293.

Bodhicaryāvatāra, 148, 249, 257.

Bodhiruci, 91.

Bodhisattva-bhūmi, 95.

Bodhisattva-bhūmi-vyākhyā, 102.

Blo-bzaṅ-dkon-mchog, 92.

Bhadanta-Vimuktasena (= Btsun-pa Grol-sde), 83.

Madhyānta-vibhanga = Dbus-mthaḥ-rnam-ḥbyed, 81, 83, 86, 87, 94.

Mahāyāna-saṁgraha (= Theg-bsdus), 83, 94, 102.

Mahāparinirvāṇa-sūtra = Yoṅs-su-mya-ṅan-las-ḥdas-pa-chen-poḥi-mdo, 91, 177, 233.

Mahāvyutpatti, 116, 122, 129, 132, 144, 151, 152, 167, 259, 260, 263.

Mādhyamika (= Dbu-ma-pa), 81, 83, 88, 89, 92, 95, 96, 97, 103, 104.

Mādhyamika-Prāsangika = Dbu-ma-thal-ḥgyur-ba, 83, 95, 96, 130, 292.

Mādhyamika-Svātantrika (= Dbu-ma-raṅ-rgyud-pa), 96.
Meghadūta, Uttaramegha, 180.
Maitreya (= Byams-pa), 81, 83, 92, 296.
Tsoṅ-kha-pa, 83, 95, 96, 103, 104, 110.
Yaśomitra, 98.
Yoga, 96.
Yogacaryā-bhūmi, 83, 94.
Yogācāra (= Rnal-ḥbyor-spyod-pa) = Vijñānavāda (= Rnam-par-rig-par-smra-ba) = Citta-mātra-vāda (= Sems-tsam-pa), 81, 84, 85, 86, 87, 89, 92, 94, 95, 96, 97, 99, 100, 101, 103, 107, 235.
Yogācāra-Mādhyamika-Svātantrika = Rnal-ḥbyor-spyod-paḥi-dbu-ma-raṅ-rgyud-pa, 83.
Ratnakūṭa (= Dkon-brtsegs), 104.
Ratna-dārikā-paripṛcchā (= Bu-mo-rin-po-cheḥi-mdo), 91, 265.
Ratna-mati, 91.
Ratnākaraśānti, 103.
Ratnāvalī, 117.
Lalita-vistara, 128.
Luṅ-gi-sñe-ma, 92, 97, 138.
Loṅ-dol (Kloṅ-rdol) Lama, 82.
Vasubandhu (= Dbyig-gñen), 83, 99.
Vasubandu on Sūtrālaṁkāra, 103, 109, 141, 157, 168, 242, 252, 291.
Vācaspatimiśra, 96.
Vātsiputrīya, 102, 161.
Vijñāna-vāda = Yogācāra.
Vinaya, 97.
Vaibhāṣika (= Bye-smra-ba), 96, 97, 98.
Vedānta, 96.
Śatasāhasrikā, 237.
Śuddhimatī (= Dag-ldan), 103.
Śrāvaka-bhūmi, 95, 102.
Śrī-mālā-devī-siṁhanāda-sūtra = Dpal-phreṅ-seṅ-geḥi-sgraḥi-mdo (= Dpal-phreṅ-gi-mdo), 91, 114, 123, 134, 139, 140, 145, 146, 147, 150, 166, 172, 174, 176, 178, 192, 198, 206, 207, 211, 230, 231, 232, 241.
Satya-dvaya-vibhanga (= Bden-gñis), 105.
Saddharma-puṇḍarīka (= Dam-paḥi-chos-kyi-padma-dkar-po), 254.
Saṁdhinirmocana = Dgons-pa-ṅes-par-ḥgrel-pa (*alias* Mdo-sde-dgoṅs-ḥgrel), 84, 86, 92, 94.
Sarva-buddha-viṣaya-avatāra-jñāna-āloka-alaṁkāra-sūtra = Saṅs-rgyas-kyi-yul-thams-cad-la-ḥjug-pa-ye-śes-snaṅ-ba-rgyan-gyi-mdo, v. Jñāna-āloka-alaṁkāra-sūtra.
Sāgaramati-paripṛcchā = Blo-gros-rgya-mtshos-źus-paḥi-mdo, 91, 194, 195, 196.
Sāgaramegha (= Rgya-mtshoḥi-sprin), 102.
Siddhānta = Grub-mthaḥ, 84, 92.
Sūtrālaṁkāra = Mdo-sde-rgyan, 81, 82, 83, 86, 93, 94, 95, 105, 109, 110, 157, 164, 168, 184, 210, 228, 229, 242, 244, 255, 291.
Sautrāntika (= Mdo-sde-ba), 96, 97, 98, 100.
Sthira-adhyāśaya-parivarta (= Lhag-paḥi-bsam-pa-brtan-paḥi-leḥu), 113.
Gser-phreṅ, 95, 96, 97, 98, 100, 102, 103, 104.
Haribhadra (= Seṅ-ge-bzaṅ-po), 83, 103, 104, 165.